The Constitution's Text in Foreign Affairs

The Constitution's Text in Foreign Affairs

Michael D. Ramsey

Harvard University Press

Cambridge, Massachusetts, and London, England | 2007

Library of Congress Cataloging-in-Publication Data

Ramsey, Michael D., 1964–
 The constitution's text in foreign affairs / Michael D. Ramsey.
   p. cm.
 Includes bibliographical references and index.
 ISBN-13: 978-0-674-02490-8 (alk. paper)
 ISBN-10: 0-674-02490-7 (alk. paper)
  1. United States—Foreign relations—Law and legislation.
 2. Constitutional law—United States. 3. Separation of powers—United
States. 4. Constitutional history—United States. I. Title.
 KF4651.R36 2007
 342.73'0412—dc22   2006102566

Contents

Preface   *vii*

Introduction: A Textual Theory of Foreign Affairs Law   *1*

I   **Sources of National Power**

    1   Do Foreign Affairs Powers Come from the Constitution? *Curtiss-Wright* and the Myth of Inherent Powers   *13*

    2   Foreign Affairs and the Articles of Confederation: The Constitution in Context   *29*

II   **Presidential Power in Foreign Affairs**

    3   The *Steel Seizure* Case and Executive Power over Foreign Affairs   *51*

    4   Executive Foreign Affairs Power and the Washington Administration   *74*

    5   *Steel Seizure* Revisited: The Limits of Executive Power   *91*

    6   Executive Power and Its Critics   *115*

III   **Shared Powers of the Senate**

    7   The Executive Senate: Treaties and Appointments   *135*

    8   *Goldwater v. Carter:* Do Treaties Bind the President?   *155*

9 The Non-treaty Power: Executive Agreements and *United States v. Belmont*   *174*

IV Congress's Foreign Affairs Powers

10 Legislative Power in Foreign Affairs: Why NAFTA Is (Sort of) Unconstitutional   *197*

11 The Meanings of Declaring War   *218*

12 Beyond Declaring War: War Powers of Congress and the President   *239*

V States and Foreign Affairs

13 Can States Have Foreign Policies? *Zschernig v. Miller* and the Limits of Framers' Intent   *259*

14 States versus the President: The *Holocaust Insurance* Case   *283*

15 *Missouri v. Holland* and the Seventeenth Amendment   *300*

VI Courts and Foreign Affairs

16 Judging Foreign Affairs: *Goldwater v. Carter* Revisited   *321*

17 *The Paquete Habana:* Is International Law Part of Our Law?   *342*

18 Courts, Presidents, and International Law   *362*

Conclusion: The Textual Structure of Foreign Affairs Law   *377*

Notes   *385*

Index   *485*

Preface

This is a book about the constitutional law of foreign affairs, written at a time of violent conflict against foreign enemies, and of intense domestic debate over the respective roles of the different branches of government in that struggle. It addresses directly neither that conflict nor that debate. In particular, it is not a guide for the constitutional conduct of the "war on terrorism," nor a brief for either side in the accompanying legal and political arguments. Its subjects are the timeless controversies of foreign affairs law that have been with us throughout the Constitution's history, though some perhaps have been made more immediate by current events.

Nor is it a treatment of modern constitutional law, either as that law is or as it should be. The book undertakes instead an exploration of the Constitution's text at the time the Constitution was adopted, to determine (to the best of our imperfect ability, looking across centuries of time) that text's meaning to founding-era Americans. What that meaning should itself mean for modern debates it leaves to others. To the extent it takes examples from modern debates, it does so not to show how those matters must be resolved today, but to make more concrete and immediate the historical meaning of the text. Modern constitutional theory contains a great range of ideas about how we should regard the Constitution's original meaning, from those who would treat it as largely determinative, to those who would use it as an important starting point, to those who would value it little at all. This work does not examine these debates, nor seek to resolve them.

It does, though, engage modern constitutional theory in at least one core respect. It is often said that the Constitution's historical meaning *cannot* be discovered to any satisfactory degree, or that it cannot be applied to resolve later-arising controversies nor provide any useful anchor for modern debates. And this is especially true, it is said, in foreign affairs, where the Constitution's text is considered particularly opaque or incomplete. This work, then, in a sense takes up a challenge, one laid down by some of our greatest foreign affairs scholars: that a framework of foreign affairs law based on the Constitution's original design cannot be described, or cannot be used to resolve actual modern cases and disputes. I hope to show that it can be. Whether it should be is, of course, another matter.

This work owes immense debts to countless people. Foremost are my foundational inspirations: the late John Ely, whose foreign affairs law course first engaged me as a student of this subject; and the great Louis Henkin, whose *Foreign Affairs and the U.S. Constitution* (2d ed. 1996) remains the single incomparable and unrivaled authority in the field, in knowledge and style, in wit and wisdom. My colleague and co-author Saikrishna Prakash has been an invaluable partner in developing ideas of executive power, as has my co-author Brannon Denning in developing ideas of state/federal relations. My colleagues Michael Rappaport, Larry Alexander, and Steven Smith have greatly aided in developing my ideas about constitutional meaning and in encouraging this project. Throughout it I have benefited from the extraordinary academic environment of the University of San Diego Law School, the encouragement of all of my colleagues on its faculty, and the most generous financial and institutional support of Dean Daniel Rodriguez and Dean Kevin Cole.

Today the field of foreign affairs law nationwide may easily be described as among the most dynamic, competitive and yet supportive. I have benefited from the thoughts, suggestions, criticisms and objections—and most of all from the encouragement and example—of so many scholars that to mention some is inevitably to slight others. In particular I thank Roger Alford, Curtis Bradley, Bradford Clark, Sarah Cleveland, William Dodge, Martin Flaherty, Jack Goldsmith, David Golove, Julian Ku, Thomas Lee, John McGinnis, Michael Paulsen, Jefferson Powell, David Sloss, Peter Spiro, Paul Stephan, Edward Swaine, Carlos Vazquez, Mark Weisburd, Ingrid Wuerth, John Yoo, and Ernest Young. I expect each of them to disagree strongly with at least some of what I have written, but it could not have happened without them. And I am especially grateful to Michael Aronson of Harvard University Press for his support of this project.

None of the chapters in this work has been previously published in the current form, but some portions of them are based on thoughts originally sketched in, and in some cases more fully developed by, prior articles, and I thank earlier publishers for permission to borrow from them. In particular: "Toward a Rule of Law in Foreign Affairs," 106 *Columbia Law Review* 1450

(2006); "Torturing Executive Power," 93 *Georgetown Law Journal* 1213 (2005); Saikrishna Prakash and Michael Ramsey, "Foreign Affairs and the Jeffersonian Executive: A Defense," 89 *Minnesota Law Review* 1591 (2005); "Textualism and War Powers," 69 *University of Chicago Law Review* 1543 (2002) and "Text and History in the War Powers Debate: A Reply to Professor Yoo," 69 *University of Chicago Law Review* 1685 (2002); "International Law as Non-preemptive Federal Law," 42 *Virginia Journal of International Law* 555 (2002); Saikrishna Prakash and Michael Ramsey, "The Executive Power over Foreign Affairs," 111 *Yale Law Journal* 231 (2001), by permission of the Yale Law Journal Company and William S. Hein Company; "The Myth of Extraconstitutional Foreign Affairs Power," 42 *William and Mary Law Review* 379 (2000), and Brannon Denning and Michael Ramsey, "American Insurance Association v. Garamendi and Executive Preemption in Foreign Affairs," 46 *William and Mary Law Review* 825 (2004), © 2000 and 2004 by the *William and Mary Law Review;* "Executive Agreements and the (Non)Treaty Power," 77 *North Carolina Law Review* 133 (1999); and "The Power of the States in Foreign Affairs: The Original Understanding of Foreign Policy Federalism," 75 *Notre Dame Law Review* 341 (1999), with permission © by *Notre Dame Law Review,* University of Notre Dame.

Finally, but most emphatically, I thank my family, Lisa P. Ramsey, Harry and Anne Ramsey, and Carolyn Ramsey, for their inspiration and support—and their willingness to listen to seemingly endless discussions of foreign affairs law. I dedicate this work to Christopher Pondrom Ramsey, hoping that he and his generation may find something of value in our history, as I have.

The Constitution's Text in Foreign Affairs

Introduction: A Textual Theory of Foreign Affairs Law

Foreign affairs law is, at its root, constitutional law. How the United States conducts diplomacy, makes international agreements, follows or fails to follow those agreements, and exerts its military and economic power are questions governed in the first instance by the U.S. Constitution. We expect the Constitution to tell us which branch of the federal government—President, Congress, President-plus-Senate—is the appropriate decisionmaker on these matters; to tell us the relationship between the federal government and the states; and to provide a role for the courts. The war against terrorism, expanding economic integration, and the accelerating pace of global events make these timeless questions all the more acute and immediate.

Yet constitutional law—never the most precise of sciences—faces special difficulties in foreign affairs. As many authorities have pointed out, the Constitution's text seems opaque (to say the least) on key foreign affairs matters. Court decisions have been infrequent and contradictory, and commentators seem unable to agree on the most basic framework with which to approach the subject. Depending on the authority one consults, the President has or does not have great independent powers in foreign affairs, courts are playing far too large or far too small a role in foreign affairs controversies, states are wholly excluded from foreign affairs matters or have vital roles to play in them, and so forth.

Modern conventional wisdom holds that the Constitution's text does not go very far toward resolving these and other debates over the control of U.S. actions on the international stage. Louis Henkin, who wrote the seminal and still-definitive study of the field, spoke for most scholars when he called the Constitution in foreign affairs a "strange laconic document," adding that "[a]ttempts to build all the foreign affairs powers of the federal government with the few bricks provided by the Constitution have not been widely accepted."[1] Another of the field's great scholars, Harold Koh, has said that for-

1

eign affairs debates should not rely on "textual exegisis" because "[m]ost often the text simply says nothing about who controls certain domains"; we should, he suggests, instead look to a "normative vision of the foreign policy making process" that "lurks within our constitutional system."[2] These views are reinforced by the perception that founding-era Americans themselves did not seem to agree on the Constitution's fundamental foreign affairs principles. And so foreign affairs controversies seem especially driven by modern policy considerations: as Professor Henkin concludes, "I am disposed to state the question as: How should foreign affairs be run in a republic that has become a democracy?"[3]

The U.S. Supreme Court, in its relatively rare ventures into foreign affairs law, has also said little about the Constitution's text. Indeed, in perhaps its most famous (or infamous) foreign affairs case—*United States v. Curtiss-Wright Export Co.*—the Court said that foreign affairs powers might not be constitutional powers at all, but could arise from inherent rights of sovereignty that would exist even without the Constitution.[4] Though the Court has backed off this claim in more modern cases, its foreign affairs decisions continue to owe little to the Constitution's text.

This book argues that we have too quickly given up on the Constitution's text. The following chapters attempt to outline a textual framework for the constitutional law of foreign affairs. The central contention is that through close attention to the Constitution's language and the historical and linguistic context in which it was written, we can uncover the text's basic foreign affairs structure as it was designed and understood in the founding era. Approached in this manner, we find that the text's foreign affairs provisions are not fundamentally incomplete—and indeed, it would be surprising if they were. The Constitution's drafters and ratifiers had foreign affairs much in their minds: the new nation confronted daunting foreign affairs challenges, and the foreign affairs structure of its prior government under the Articles of Confederation appeared dysfunctional and ill-designed. With foreign affairs concerns occupying such a central role, it seems most unlikely that founding-era Americans simply forgot to provide a foreign affairs framework for their new government. It is more likely that, with passing time, we have lost sight of the foreign affairs structure they created. This book, then, is an attempt at rediscovery.

In selecting this focus, I do not mean to enter into the complex debates over the proper grounding of modern constitutional law. It should be made clear from the outset that this book does not argue that we must be bound today by the founders' foreign affairs text. Whether we are, or should be, so bound is a question of political theory far beyond the scope of this book. Opinions on this matter vary widely. Although there is general consensus in constitutional law (outside of foreign affairs) that the text's historical meaning is an important starting point, there is much debate over the extent to which other considerations, such as practice, precedent, and modern conditions, should influence modern results.

Rather, this book only contends, contrary to the assumptions of much modern debate, that the text's historical meaning does provide a fairly complete basic framework for foreign affairs law. Of course, it does not answer all questions, and the ensuing discussion notes several important matters that seem extraordinarily difficult to resolve from the text. But I do hope to show that the text marks out the boundaries of foreign affairs authority more clearly than commonly supposed, in a way that can be used to resolve key modern yet timeless controversies. We can, that is, recover and apply the basic structure of foreign affairs law that the Constitution's drafters provided for us. Whether and to what extent we want to use that structure are different questions, not addressed here. They are questions not of foreign affairs law but of constitutional theory.[5]

What, then, is the nature of the founders' foreign affairs text? It is obviously difficult to reduce the ensuing chapters to a few words. But if one searches for a central theme, it is this: the text is a compromise. Most famously, of course, it is a compromise at its broadest levels—between small and large states, between nationalists and localists, between north and south. It is also a compromise over normative visions of foreign affairs decisionmaking: between strong and weak versions of the presidency, for example, and of the states and of the courts.

Perhaps because there is no agreed starting point, modern foreign affairs debates tend to the extremes. Those who would give the President almost unbounded control of foreign affairs, for example, contend with those who would concede the President no meaningful independent powers at all. Those who would "legalize" most aspects of foreign affairs, by bringing them under the authority of courts applying treaties and unwritten international law, stand against those who regard almost all of foreign affairs as political, unsuited for legalistic resolution. And so on, as we will see, through the range of core foreign affairs issues. These debates tend to be driven by normative ideas about who should control foreign affairs decisionmaking. They miss the fact that the text, being a compromise, does not adopt any of them in full; it favors each of the branches some of the time.

Indeed, the text's approach might also be summed by saying that there is nothing distinct or unusual about the Constitution's foreign affairs provisions, as compared to its other provisions. In foreign affairs, as elsewhere, the text seeks both effective government and "checks and balances" by allocating powers among various competing entities, with specified procedures setting forth how these powers can be exercised and how the various entities interact. There is no "foreign affairs" clause, nor any single "foreign affairs power" allocated in a single place; there are only discrete powers that bear upon the conduct of foreign affairs, variously allocated. An understanding of how these powers interact cannot be deduced from any general theory of foreign affairs, whether it is supposed to arise from the founders' beliefs or modern needs. The question is not what must be true from the nature of foreign affairs, but how the text treats particular powers and relationships.

Once we give the text its historical meaning, we will see that incompleteness of the Constitution's text in foreign affairs is greatly overstated. It is true that the text explicitly mentions only some of the powers commonly exercised in foreign affairs, and does not mention, in so many words, a blanket "foreign affairs power." Nonetheless, the text does establish a series of default rules that guide us when specific provisions are lacking. Under the Constitution's Tenth Amendment, powers not assigned to the federal government are reserved to the states (or the people). Within the federal government, the text directs that, subject to specific exceptions, executive powers go to the President, legislative powers go to Congress, and judicial powers belong to the courts. These familiar principles may seem trite and unhelpful—truisms, even—but we shall see that they contain a background structure of constitutional foreign affairs law that is neither incomplete nor inaccessible. Much confusion in modern foreign affairs law arises from failure to use these principles as a starting point.

Our first step will be to embrace the proposition that there are no "inherent" foreign affairs powers (Chapters 1–2). The reach for inherent powers is a natural response to the assumption that the Constitution's foreign affairs text is substantially incomplete. And a natural further extension of that view is that these "inherent" powers lodge in a particular branch of government—in particular, it is said, in the President. That, in any event, was the Supreme Court's conclusion in the *Curtiss-Wright* case, which has been a favorite of presidential advocates ever since. Of course, in domestic matters such a claim would stand contrary to our most fundamental constitutional proposition, that the national government is one of limited powers delegated to it by the Constitution, as set forth in the Tenth Amendment. The discussion here will begin by insisting that, in the founders' Constitution, this fundamental proposition has no foreign affairs exception. Any part of the national government that wishes to exercise foreign affairs power must find its authority in the Constitution; correspondingly, any limit upon the states must also find such a source.

The second step is to appreciate that the Constitution begins with a three-way division of federal power as executive, legislative, and judicial, assigned by the opening clauses of Articles I, II, and III. Giving content to these clauses depends upon finding common understandings—at least in general terms—of what these terms encompass. Again, in domestic matters, this is part of our constitutional fundamentals: legislative power means the power to make laws affecting the rights and duties of individuals; executive power means the power to enforce those laws; and judicial power means the power to decide cases and impose remedies. As we will see, these classifications arose from the eighteenth-century idea of separation of powers, as explained by political theorists who influenced the founders' ideas of government.

Applied to foreign affairs, this idea points in a direction that has proved much more controversial. Article II, Section 1 directs that the "executive Power shall be vested" in the President. To modern ears this phrase sounds unrelated to foreign affairs—instead being associated with power to enforce ("execute") laws. But this book also emphasizes that phrases used in the Constitution often had meanings in the eighteenth century that have become obscured in modern speech. Thus "making treaties" and "declaring war" carried meanings that do not necessarily resonate fully with us today, but formed an important part of how the Constitution was understood in its time. That is also the case with "executive" power (Chapters 3–4). The eighteenth-century theorists' descriptions included as "executive" powers the important foreign affairs powers encompassing a nation's relationship with those outside it—principally, diplomatic and military powers. When the Constitution's drafters wrote that the President would have "executive" power, they used a word that conveyed the idea of foreign affairs power; that is, they did not say that the President would have "law execution power and foreign affairs power," but they used a word—"executive"—that (to them) meant the same thing.

Modern Presidents and presidential advocates have seized upon this idea (as they have seized upon *Curtiss-Wright*'s inherent powers) to argue for presidential control of foreign affairs, because (by Article II, Section 1) the

President is "vested" with the nation's "executive Power." Opponents strongly resist it, for they see in it the same dangers of concentrated presidential power suggested by *Curtiss-Wright*. Subsequent chapters argue that presidential advocates are half right. The founders did understand "executive Power" to include important foreign affairs powers, as Thomas Jefferson and Alexander Hamilton (among others) explained. Reading Article II, Section 1 to assign diplomatic and military power to the President resolves much of the mystery arising from the supposedly "missing" foreign affairs powers, such as the power to conduct diplomacy: these are, in fact, "executive" presidential powers. Those who think otherwise are left with no way to account for such obviously necessary powers, and hence they fall back on the implausible claim of incompleteness.

But modern executive power advocates, though correct in their initial claim, go far beyond what the text can support.[6] The founders did not use the grant of "executive Power" to give the President control of U.S. foreign affairs. While the first part of this book establishes a textual grounding for the President's independent foreign affairs power, the remaining parts are chiefly dedicated to showing how the text circumscribed that power—giving the President an important role without concentrating foreign affairs powers, either in the executive branch or elsewhere.

First, as discussed in Chapters 5–6, the President has, not a general power over all matters touching foreign affairs, but only the foreign affairs powers the eighteenth century considered "executive." In particular, the President cannot alter rights and duties within the domestic legal system, even in the pursuit of foreign affairs objectives, because that is a "legislative" (lawmaking) function, not an executive one. Second, the founders thought the executive foreign affairs powers as defined in eighteenth-century writing were far too sweeping to be held by a single person, so they assigned important parts of them—particularly powers over treaties and war—in whole or part to other branches (Chapters 7–12). As explored below, despite efforts by modern presidential advocates to minimize these limits, they were designed precisely to prevent the President's "executive Power" from amounting to foreign affairs preeminence. At the same time, these provisions also do not go to the other extreme, to shift the whole of foreign affairs back to Congress (or the Senate). They mean what they say, and not more: they are important, but specific, exceptions to presidential power. Again, what we see is a set of checks and balances, just as we commonly understand to exist in domestic matters.

The final steps integrate the states (Chapters 13–15) and the courts

(Chapters 16–18) into this framework. Again this may require calling much conventional wisdom substantially into question. It is often said that foreign affairs are necessarily (or "inherently") national, such that state and local governments have little constitutional role. And it is often said that foreign affairs are necessarily "political," so that courts have little constitutional role. As we will see, neither assumption accords with the founders' design. Of course, the founders did want to create a stronger national government in foreign affairs, after frustrations experienced under the Articles of Confederation. But they did so in specific ways, not by a general (unstated) exclusion of the states. Rather, they used the Constitution's Article I, Section 10 to exclude states from a few specified matters, and declared in Article VI that the Constitution, federal laws, and treaties were superior to state law (and thus binding upon the states). This means, though, that so long as states do not act contrary to federal laws or treaties, or particular provisions in the Constitution, they are free to act in matters that affect foreign affairs. We can understand this in part as a necessary (though perhaps unfortunate) compromise, in the face of strong attachments to state sovereignty felt by many at the time; but we can also understand it as part of the founders' foreign affairs checks and balances. At the same time, this conclusion should not be taken to suggest inherent limits on the textual exercise of federal foreign affairs power in defense of unstated rights of the states. As with their allocation between the President and Congress, the drafters wanted their foreign affairs decisionmakers to be strong but not unlimited.

Relatedly, there is no textual principle excluding courts from "judicial" roles in deciding foreign affairs cases. That of course does not mean that courts may undertake foreign affairs policymaking or enforce principles not adopted into the text. It does not put courts in charge of foreign affairs. It does mean, though, that the founders understood the courts as enforcers of the constitutional divisions of power, just as in domestic matters.

In sum, then, the Constitution in foreign affairs, as in domestic affairs, is fundamentally about distributing power across numerous independent yet interrelated branches of government—the President, the Senate, Congress, the courts, and the states. On one hand, that should come as no surprise. The idea of "checks and balances" achieved through a system of separation of powers is elemental to U.S. constitutional law, and is a staple of any American civics course. Yet there is resistance to separating and checking foreign affairs powers, summed up in the common observation that the nation must speak with one voice in foreign affairs (although there is little consensus over whose voice that should be).

The "one voice" invocation is, of course, ultimately a policy prescription. America's relations with other nations can be conducted more effectively (it is said) if the nation presents a single face to the world, so that various parts of the American polity do not undercut each other in the eyes of foreigners. But this is often presented as such an overriding policy concern, given the acute danger of missteps in foreign affairs, that it gains constitutional dimensions, even though (as we shall see) the Constitution's text does not support it. Whatever one thinks of the "one voice" idea as a policy matter, it is fundamentally opposed to the constitutional design. The Constitution's text divides foreign affairs power among multiple independent power centers. And looking behind the text, it is plain that this did not occur by accident. The Constitution deliberately fosters multiple voices in foreign affairs, as it fosters multiple voices in domestic affairs.

A few caveats are needed. First, this book adopts a simple though perhaps underdeveloped methodology. It is a search for what one scholar has called the "meaning that a reasonable listener would place on the words used in the constitutional provision[s] at the time of [their] enactment."[7] It is, then, about the words, not about an "intention of the framers" that rests upon the private thoughts of particular individuals or upon a set of abstract principles some of them (or even all of them) may have held. Ultimately, the Constitution, as a document, is composed of words, not of intentions.

Nonetheless, this is not a claim that the Constitution has a "plain meaning" we can grasp simply by reading it in isolation. A text's historical meaning arises from the context in which it was written. Although the starting point of the inquiry will always be the Constitution's text, complete understanding of its meaning will entail examination of this context. That should not collapse into a search for framers' intent apart from the text, but it does demand inquiry into the eighteenth-century world in which the text was written—and in particular, into the way that world used language. That in turn may lead to frequent reliance upon writers of the time (including but not limited to the Constitution's actual drafters and ratifiers), to see what the text seemed to mean to those closest to it in time and context.[8]

Despite that historical element, though, this is a work of interpretation, not of history. The history of the constitutional period has received close attention from many of the nation's greatest historians. I rely upon them in seeking to understand the Constitution's context, but my project is not to improve upon them or to recount everything they have said. My history is necessarily incomplete; it is given to aid interpretation, not as an account in itself.

Relatedly, I seek the most plausible meaning of the language, but I do not claim that historical interpretations can often be established beyond all reasonable dispute. History may be nuanced, contradictory, or incomplete; often we can only guess at a text's historical meaning. In making interpretive judgments, we only ask: is a proposed interpretation more likely than not, or more likely than alternative explanations? In the interests of style and brevity, I may often say that text and context demonstrate particular meanings, but I mean only that the proposed meaning is the best available, not that it is proven beyond all doubt.

I

Sources of National Power

1

Do Foreign Affairs Powers Come from the Constitution? *Curtiss-Wright* and the Myth of Inherent Powers

In seeking a framework for foreign affairs law in the Constitution's text, we face a challenge on first principles. Perhaps the national government's foreign affairs powers do not arise from the Constitution, but exist outside it. Perhaps, that is, the United States can conduct diplomacy, make international agreements, fight wars and use its international economic power, not because the Constitution says it can, but because that is what it means to be a nation. These powers, we might say, are "inherent" in the "conception of nationality" and do not depend on anything written in the Constitution.

This idea may sound extraordinary, because it runs contrary to our basic understanding of how the U.S. Constitution works. Ordinarily, we suppose, the national government's powers arise from express or implied grants of powers in the Constitution (and limitations on state governments arise from the Constitution's express or implied restrictions). This is what we mean by a Constitution of delegated powers, formed by a union of states. The Constitution's Tenth Amendment says so explicitly: "The powers not delegated to the United States by the Constitution, nor prohibited by it to the States, are reserved to the States respectively, or to the people." One would think, therefore, that the national government's foreign affairs powers must, as the Amendment declares, be "delegated to the United States by the Constitution."

But the suggestion that the national government has inherent, extra-constitutional foreign affairs powers is not as farfetched as it seems. The U.S. Supreme Court embraced the idea in 1936, in *United States v. Curtiss-Wright Export Co*. Justice George Sutherland wrote for the Court in that case that "the powers of external sovereignty"—meaning foreign affairs powers—"if they had never been mentioned in the Constitution, would have vested in the federal government as necessary concomitants of nationality. . . . [They] exist as inherently inseparable from the conception of nationality." And,

13

Sutherland added, these inherent powers are held by the President, who is the nation's "sole organ" of interaction with foreign nations.[1]

Whether *Curtiss-Wright* should be seen as a centerpiece of foreign affairs law is subject to much debate. Much modern commentary sharply questions it,[2] and subsequent Supreme Court decisions have not given it great weight. But courts, legal practitioners, and scholars continue to invoke *Curtiss-Wright* for the proposition that the national government—and more specifically the President—has a special role in foreign affairs (meaning at least something beyond the text, and often something entirely beyond ordinary constitutional law). Not surprisingly, the case is favored by Presidents and presidential advocates, who see it as authority for independent presidential action in foreign affairs without the need for explicit constitutional justification: it has been called "a mainstay in the executive branch lawyer's kit"; and, as Professor Koh relates, "[a]mong government attorneys, Justice Sutherland's lavish description of the President's power is so often quoted that it has come to be known as the 'Curtiss-Wright so I'm right' cite." And the case is at least implicit authority behind the more general proposition that foreign affairs powers cannot be understood simply in terms of the Constitution's text.[3]

We must, therefore, consider *Curtiss-Wright*'s theory before inquiring into the textual basis of foreign affairs powers—for if *Curtiss-Wright* is correct, there *is* no textual basis, and need not be.

Curtiss-Wright and Extra-constitutional Foreign Affairs Power

In 1934, President Franklin Roosevelt imposed an embargo on arms sales to Bolivia and Paraguay, which were then at war over disputed territory. He acted under congressional legislation authorizing the President to impose an embargo if the President believed it would promote peace between the combatants. The U.S. government subsequently prosecuted the Curtiss-Wright Export Co. for violating the embargo. In its defense, the company claimed the embargo was unconstitutional because Congress had given the President too much lawmaking discretion.[4]

On its face, the dispute had nothing to do with inherent powers. Congress has explicit textual power to regulate foreign commerce (Article I, Section 8), and its legislation authorized Roosevelt to do what he did. The defense seemed to have a point in its delegation argument, though, for only a year earlier the Supreme Court had overturned congressional legislation in other areas because it gave the President too much lawmaking discretion,[5] and the embargo legislation seemed similarly open-ended. The Court nonetheless upheld the embargo. Because the President already had broad power in foreign affairs, Sutherland wrote, laws in that field could grant more discretion than in domestic matters—so the company could not rely on the Court's earlier domestic-law decisions.

But here Sutherland faced a substantial obstacle. Nothing in the Constitution seems to say, in so many words, that the President has broad power in foreign affairs, and the powers the text specifically grants to the President do not seem to encompass embargoes. To get around this difficulty, Sutherland invoked his idea of extra-constitutional power in foreign affairs. If foreign affairs powers arose outside the Constitution, the Constitution's failure to mention the President's broad power in foreign affairs did not mean it did not exist. As a result, Sutherland's reasoning relied on inherent powers, though the case itself concerned matters plainly within Congress's constitutional authority.

Sutherland's argument, which incorporated ideas he had advanced before joining the Court,[6] ran as follows: Prior to independence, sovereign power over the colonies of course lay with Britain. Upon independence, Sutherland said, sovereignty divided: "internal sovereignty"—control over domestic matters—passed to the individual states; "external sovereignty"—that is, foreign affairs power—passed to the unified entity "the United States." As he put it:

> As a result of the separation from Great Britain by the colonies, acting as a unit, the powers of external sovereignty passed from the Crown not to the colonies severally, but to the colonies in their collective and corporate capacity as the United States of America. . . . Sovereignty is never held in suspense. When, therefore, the external sovereignty of Great Britain in respect of the colonies ceased, it immediately passed to the Union.[7]

Sutherland next claimed that this power of "external sovereignty" passed from the initial informal Union to the formal confederated government under the Articles of Confederation (the governing document of the United States from 1781 to 1789). As a result, when American leaders met in Philadelphia in 1787 to draft a proposed Constitution to supersede the Articles, they had a background assumption of inherent foreign affairs powers: "The Framers' Convention was called and exerted its powers upon the irrefutable postulate that though the states were several their people in respect of foreign affairs were one."[8]

The Constitution's structure of national powers delegated by the states, in this view, simply did not apply (and logically could not apply) to foreign affairs. The states could not delegate what they never had. As Sutherland explained:

> [T]he primary purpose of the Constitution was to carve from the general mass of legislative powers then possessed by the states such portions as it was thought desirable to vest in the federal government, leaving those not included in the enumeration still in the states. That this doctrine applies only to powers which the states had is self-evident. And since the states severally never possessed international powers, such powers could not have been carved from the mass of state powers but obviously were transmitted to the United States from some other source.[9]

As a result, when the Tenth Amendment says the national government has only powers given to it by the states, that statement was (in Sutherland's view) subject to an important caveat: it did not apply to foreign affairs powers. The national government already had those powers, as natural attributes of its status as national sovereign, inherited from Britain by way of the initial informal Union after independence and the formal Union under the Articles of Confederation.

Completing this view, the President is the natural location of the national government's inherent foreign affairs powers, because (Sutherland said) the President is the nation's international representative. This last point (which, it must be said, does not necessarily follow even if one accepts the idea of inherent powers) allowed Sutherland to uphold the discretion given to the President in *Curtiss-Wright*. Because (in his view) the President had inherent foreign affairs powers, the constitutional rule against giving the President too much legislative discretion could not apply with the same force as it did in domestic law.[10]

Curtiss-Wright's result seems uncontroversial—especially because the modern Court allows Congress to give the President much more lawmaking discretion, even in domestic matters, than was the case in the 1930s.[11] But the way Sutherland reached his result, if accepted, would transform all of foreign affairs law into something wholly unlike ordinary constitutional law. Sutherland claimed, moreover, to be applying the Constitution's historical meaning: in his view, founding-era Americans assumed the national government had inherent foreign affairs powers, and premised their entire constitutional system upon this assumption.

Curtiss-Wright and the Constitution's Text

Although Sutherland claimed to be applying the Constitution (or rather, an assumption underlying the Constitution) in deciding *Curtiss-Wright,* he said little about the Constitution's text itself. Most of his arguments were purely historical, focused on the period prior to the Constitution's drafting, or pragmatic, focused on the modern role of the President in foreign affairs. Conventional academic critiques of *Curtiss-Wright* also focus not on the text, but upon Sutherland's historical account of the time immediately surrounding independence or on the practical effects of giving "too much" power to the President. As we shall see, focusing the inquiry upon the meaning of the text allows a more convincing rejection of *Curtiss-Wright*'s theory.

The Tenth Amendment

Nothing in the original Constitution—that is, the document adopted in 1789—explicitly speaks to the question. But the Tenth Amendment, added two years later as part of the package of amendments that included the Bill of Rights, appears categorically to deny the idea of inherent national powers. By its language, powers of government fall into only two categories, reserved and delegated. Powers not delegated by the Constitution are reserved. Delegated powers are national powers; reserved powers are state powers, or powers of the people. There is no third category. The Amendment states in full and without qualification: "The powers not delegated to the United States by the Constitution, nor prohibited by it to the States, are reserved to the States respectively, or to the people."

Historical context confirms that the Tenth Amendment was adopted precisely to counter claims that the national government had powers beyond those delegated. The Constitution's drafters claimed that the Constitution itself established that principle; as drafter James Wilson argued, "every thing which is not given, is reserved."[12] In the subsequent ratification debates, the Constitution's defenders—the "federalists"—pressed this understanding strongly upon its "anti-federalist" opponents, who feared that the new system would permit undue concentration of national power. James Madison argued that "[t]he powers delegated . . . to the federal government are few and defined," and, as he said at Virginia's ratifying convention, echoing Wilson, the principle of the Constitution was that "every thing not granted, is reserved. . . . Can the general government exercise any power not dele-

gated? . . . The reverse of the proposition holds. The delegation alone warrants the exercise of any power."[13]

These arguments did little to reassure anti-federalists. The Constitution
(Article VII) required nine states' approval to take effect, with approval to be
given in state ratifying conventions. As the conventions began meeting, anti-
federalists, in addition to urging outright rejection, called for amendments to
address specific problems with the proposal. At first, states ratified the Constitution quickly enough, despite anti-federalist concerns. But as more-
divided states took up the question, it became doubtful whether nine states
would approve, and anti-federalist objections had to be taken more seriously.
In particular, in the pivotal state of Massachusetts, John Hancock and
Samuel Adams brokered a compromise by which the generally anti-federalist
convention gave its approval, together with a list of proposed amendments.
Other key states—notably Virginia and New York—added their own reluctant approvals, with their own lists of proposed amendments.[14]

Many anti-federalist proposals centered on the Constitution's lack of protection for individual rights (thus leading to the Bill of Rights). But some
were structural, including the concern about delegated powers. Massachusetts, for example, proposed to add language "that all powers not expressly
delegated by the aforesaid Constitution are reserved to the several
states. . . ."—a point echoed in New York and Virginia as well. Samuel
Adams explained that the amendment was needed to confirm that "if any law
made by the federal government shall extend beyond the power granted by
the proposed Constitution," it "will be an error, and adjudged by the courts
of law to be void."[15]

The Constitution got its nine-state approval in 1788, without any changes
being formally made, but when its new government convened in 1789, there
remained a sense that some modifications were needed. Madison, now a
prominent member of the new national Congress, took the lead in drafting
proposed amendments, ten of which were adopted in 1791.[16] He prepared
what became the Tenth Amendment to incorporate proposals on the delegation question.[17] "I find," he explained to Congress, "from looking into the
amendments proposed by the State conventions, that several are particularly
anxious that it should be declared in the Constitution, that the powers not
therein delegated [to the federal government] should be reserved to the several States. . . . [T]here can be no harm in making such a declaration, if gentlemen will allow that the fact is as stated. I am sure I understand it so, and
do therefore propose it."[18]

The Amendment thus at minimum seems firmly to reject the idea of inherent, extra-constitutional federal power. (Other uses of the Tenth Amend-

ment, to support ideas of inherent state sovereignty, are far more controversial but distinct from the point made here.)[19] No one seriously disputes, as a general matter, that the Tenth Amendment meant what Madison said it meant: that "delegation alone warrants the exercise of any power" by the national government. Applied to foreign affairs, though, this reading is exactly contrary to *Curtiss-Wright*'s claim that foreign affairs powers exist outside the framework of delegated powers. We might say, therefore, that Sutherland's inherent powers theory is rejected by the Constitution's plain language, and leave it at that.

But one can only go so far with this argument. As we have seen, Sutherland in effect argued that the Tenth Amendment's language cannot be taken literally, because the Constitution's drafters had a background understanding that foreign affairs powers *could not* be delegated (because the states never possessed them) and *could not* be reserved (for the same reason). Foreign affairs powers therefore cannot be placed in either of the two supposedly comprehensive categories the Amendment establishes.

In Sutherland's favor, the idea of inherent extra-constitutional powers of the national government is not as extraordinary as the Tenth Amendment suggests. Arguments based on inherent powers date to the very beginnings of constitutional history. In 1781, for example, the Continental Congress chartered a national bank, although nothing in the Articles of Confederation (then the nation's governing document) gave it such a power. James Wilson, who later played a leading role in debating the Constitution's structure of delegated powers, defended the charter as an inherent power. "To many purposes," he argued, "the United States are to be considered as one undivided, independent nation; and as possessed of all the rights, and powers, and properties, by the law of nations incident to such. Whenever an object occurs, to the direction of which no particular state is competent, the management of it must, of necessity, belong to the United States."[20] And Wilson, among others (including future Chief Justice John Marshall), sometimes qualified discussions of the proposed Constitution's delegated powers in ways that seemed to leave open the idea of inherent powers. The federal government, Wilson told the Pennsylvania ratifying convention, is one whose "powers are particularly enumerated," and "nothing more is intended to be given, than what is so enumerated, unless it results from the nature of the government itself."[21]

As a result, one's initial reaction—that *Curtiss-Wright* upended the usual thinking about delegated power—must be somewhat modified: in at least some areas, inherent power arguments have been and continue to be advanced. Using similar arguments, nineteenth-century Supreme Court decisions directly embraced inherent national powers in areas such as immigration and Indian law, despite the Tenth Amendment.[22] And in the specific context of foreign affairs, there is a further structural point in Sutherland's favor (although Sutherland himself did not make it). One of the daunting challenges of foreign affairs law is the apparent "lacunae" (Louis Henkin's word) in the Constitution's grants of foreign affairs power. Of course, the Constitution allocates a number of key foreign affairs powers, including declaring war, sending and receiving ambassadors, and making treaties. But other key foreign affairs powers seem to be missing: at least as conventionally read, the Constitution's text does not seem to provide a complete framework in foreign affairs.[23]

Later chapters dispute this claim, but it is powerfully ingrained in constitutional thought. And if true, it could be used to support the idea of inherent powers. If foreign affairs powers must be delegated to the national government, it would be hard to explain why the Constitution's text did not cover them completely. If they are inherent, though, it may be understandable that the text covered only the most important ones. Henkin's "lacunae" may be not just puzzling, but affirmative indications that the Constitution's drafters shared Sutherland's view.

For these reasons, it may not be sufficient simply to stand upon the Tenth Amendment. The Amendment remains crucial for the discussion, though, because it establishes (at minimum) a presumption to overcome. In the ordinary case, national powers are those the text delegated to the national government. To depart from that basic rule, decreed by the Tenth Amendment, we need powerful evidence of a background understanding that the Tenth Amendment would not apply to foreign affairs.

Other Parts of the Constitution

We can also look to other parts of the constitutional text (as Sutherland did not) for evidence of the background understanding Sutherland thought he had identified. Specifically, we may ask whether the Constitution's text as a whole suggests that foreign affairs powers are somehow outside its ambit.

Several core aspects of the text are hard to square with Sutherland's theory. First, many of its provisions assign specific foreign affairs powers to the national government. By Article I, Section 8, Congress has power to regulate foreign commerce; declare war; grant letters of marque; punish piracies, felonies on the high seas, and offenses against the law of nations; and regulate the armed forces. By Article II, Sections 2 and 3, the President receives ambassadors and commands the military, and the President and Senate together make treaties and appoint ambassadors. The text contains at least ten separate assignments of core foreign affairs powers.

These clauses look like *grants* of foreign affairs powers to the national government. If the Constitution presumed that the national government had all foreign affairs powers inherently, it did not need to specify the national government's foreign affairs powers. But, Sutherland might respond, the point of these clauses was perhaps not to grant foreign affairs powers to the national government (which already had them inherently), but to allocate these powers within the national government. Thus, on *Curtiss-Wright*'s theory, the declare-war clause (for example) is not superfluous, for even though the national government inherently had that power it would not be clear, absent the clause, whether Congress or the President had it.

A bigger problem for Sutherland is that the Constitution also prohibits states from exercising specific foreign affairs powers. By Article I, Section 10, states cannot make treaties or grant letters of marque; they cannot, without Congress's consent, tax imports or exports, keep troops or ships of war in peacetime, enter into agreements with foreign powers, or engage in war unless invaded. For advocates of inherent powers, these provisions are hard to explain. If states never had "external sovereignty," the Constitution would not need to bar them from exercising specific foreign affairs powers.

The rejoinder must be that these clauses were indeed superfluous, but were intended as insurance. Even if the Constitution's drafters believed that states necessarily lacked foreign affairs powers, perhaps they thought state exercises of these powers were so dangerous that they should make doubly sure by including specific textual prohibitions. These clauses had no immediate operative purpose, the argument runs, but they ensure that even if the national government's inherent exclusive external sovereignty were later abandoned or forgotten, states still could not claim key foreign affairs powers.

The Constitution no doubt contains redundancies, but we should read it to avoid them where possible—especially ones of this magnitude. And this explanation of Article I, Section 10 seems unsatisfactory on several additional grounds. To begin, it does not seem the most natural reading of the text. If the Constitution meant to declare a preexisting limitation, it should have begun with a general statement—that states are excluded from foreign affairs—and then listed specific examples of powers denied to the states. Specific limitations, without the general statement, imply that the only limitations are those listed. Because specific limitations undercut the idea of a general restriction, anyone who valued the general restriction should have hesitated to list specifics, at least without further explanation.

Indeed, the Constitution's drafters struggled with this problem in other areas. It is familiar history, for example, that one chief anti-federalist objection raised against the Constitution was its lack of a Bill of Rights, and that one principal federalist response was that one could not hope to name all individual rights in one list and the inclusion of some would imply the nonexistence of others. As Wilson observed, "if we attempt an enumeration, everything that is not enumerated is presumed given."[24] Surely Article I, Section 10 posed the same danger, were it merely declaratory: states would claim that they impliedly retained foreign affairs powers not listed; yet no one seemed concerned about it.[25]

The structure of Article I, Section 10 also stands against the idea of inherent foreign affairs powers, for it includes in the same clauses both international and domestic powers denied to the states. Its first sentence, for example, reads:

> No State shall enter into any Treaty, Alliance, or Confederation; grant Letters of Marque and Reprisal; coin Money, emit Bills of Credit; make any Thing but gold and silver Coin a Tender in Payment of Debts; pass any Bill of Attainder, ex post facto Law, or Law impairing the Obligation of Contracts, or grant any Title of Nobility.

By *Curtiss-Wright's* theory, the first two of these powers are inherently national and would not be state powers even without constitutional prohibitions. But other listed powers were widely exercised by states after 1776; plainly they were not beyond states' sovereign authority. No one doubted, for example, that states in 1787 had power to coin money and print paper money, and would continue to do so unless the Constitution prevented them (as Madison himself described).[26] In *Curtiss-Wright's* terminology, these were powers of "internal sovereignty" held, as an initial matter, by the states; they formed part of the Constitution's textual delegation of powers to the national government and denial of powers to the states. Article I, Section 10's equivalent treatment of treatymaking and printing money suggests they are similar powers: things that states might otherwise do, but should be prevented from doing on policy grounds. The contrary view makes Article I, Section 10 an odd tangle of substantive prohibitions against powers states would otherwise have and declaratory statements of powers states never had.

Sutherland might still object, though, that this reads the text in a vacuum, without considering background assumptions. True, the text's best reading in isolation might see foreign affairs powers as delegable powers, but it also may be possible (though awkward) to explain its foreign affairs provisions by the need to allocate foreign affairs powers among branches of the national government and the desire to be especially careful in limiting the states' worst practices.[27] True also, the document itself does not appear to contain affirmative evidence of the supposed background assumption (nor did Sutherland claim it did). But background assumptions are necessarily hard to discern from the text itself. To identify them, Sutherland would argue, we must look beyond the text, to its historical context.

Curtiss-Wright and Founding-Era Commentary

Another place to look for evidence of Sutherland's supposed background assumption is contemporaneous commentary upon the text. There is an enormous amount of this commentary. The Constitution's anti-federalist opponents worked hard for its defeat, generating an extended debate over the proposal conducted through and around the ratifying conventions of the individual states. This debate produced an outpouring of commentary upon the draft, by supporters and opponents, much of it mature and thoughtful—and much of it shallow, alarmist, incoherent, and illogical. The foreign affairs provisions received some attention, but perhaps less than their fair share. In any event, the ratification debates provide an array of materials indicating the various ways the constitutional generation read the Convention's product.

Obviously one must be cautious in using this commentary for interpretive purposes. Our records are incomplete. Much of what we do have was advocacy for one side or the other, and, as lawyers know too well, not all advocacy is genuinely felt. Much of it—especially but not exclusively comments made orally—was not well thought out. And most importantly, many people, with a broad range of views and motivations, participated. To pick out what any one individual said may prove little more than what that individual thought (if it even proves that much). How much weight can be placed on the commentary necessarily depends upon what proposition one is trying to establish.

Here, our specific question is whether there is evidence of a background assumption that foreign affairs powers were not delegated powers (and thus not included in the Tenth Amendment). Sutherland himself did not claim that there was much evidence; he looked instead at experiences preceding the Constitution, which are addressed in the next chapter. And it is true that, so far as surviving records reflect, the specific question did not come up directly. As discussed, the question of delegated power did arise in force, with federalists asserting that the Constitution's structure required national power to be delegated (as the Tenth Amendment ultimately confirmed) and antifederalists arguing that nothing in the text said so in so many words. Also as discussed, it is true that even some federalists (including Wilson and Marshall) seemed to believe that *some* national power could arise from the nature of government, despite what they said about the general rule of delegated power. But none of these comments or debates directly addressed foreign affairs (nor is it clear whether Marshall and Wilson represented common thinking, or whether even they thought their interpretation survived the Tenth Amendment or applied to foreign affairs).

This lack of evidence should in itself be somewhat troubling to *Curtiss-Wright*'s supporters. *Curtiss-Wright* depends on using background assumptions to override the Tenth Amendment's text. Its evidence of background assumptions, then, should be quite strong. Yet in the whole intense ratification debate, there is no evidence Sutherland thought worth citing.[28]

It is also true that there is not much direct evidence refuting Sutherland's claim. But there is substantial indirect evidence. When leading commentary such as *The Federalist* discussed foreign affairs, it did so in terms of delegated powers, not inherent powers.

The Federalist—the famous series of essays defending the Constitution written by drafters Madison and Alexander Hamilton, along with the Confederation's Foreign Affairs Secretary John Jay—was a piece of advocacy, and, like other ratification-era sources, must be used with caution. Its authors wrote with a specific goal—ratification—in mind, and may have understated or overstated constitutional principles in pursuit of it; their discussion is, moreover, sometimes opaque and occasionally flatly wrong.[29] But it is also the most extensive and systematic examination of the Constitution's text made in the text's own language and historical setting, by and for people with that period's common understandings. It is surely not definitive, but, used properly, can be highly instructive.[30]

It is especially revealing here because it did not directly take a position on delegated versus inherent powers, nor even seem to recognize the importance of the matter. Rather, its authors *assumed* a delegated power structure in foreign affairs. In Federalist Nos. 41–46, for example, Madison presented an overview of the national government's powers. Federalist No. 41, opening this series, is titled "General View of the Powers Proposed to Be Vested in the Union." It begins:

The Constitution proposed by the convention may be considered under two general points of view. The FIRST relates to the sum or quantity of power which *it vests* in the government. . . .

Under the first view of the subject, two important questions arise: 1. Whether any part of the powers *transferred* to the general government be unnecessary or improper? 2. Whether the entire mass of them be dangerous to the portion of jurisdiction left in the several States?[31]

Madison's language leaves no doubt that he is discussing powers *granted to* the national government. His subject is powers "transferred to" or "vested in" the national government by the Constitution. This language would not be appropriate for inherent powers.

Many of the specific powers Madison then described as "transferred to" (or, later, "conferred on") the national government are foreign affairs powers. They included, in general, "[s]ecurity against foreign danger," meaning specifically powers over war, letters of marque, and armies and fleets. Madison's central point was that the national government would be too weak internationally without these powers, so it was appropriate for the Constitution to grant them.

Federalist No. 42 then addressed powers "which regulate intercourse with foreign nations." Again, Madison described these powers as "lodged in the general government" by the Constitution. Under this heading, he discussed additional foreign affairs powers: treaties, ambassadors, regulation of foreign commerce, and punishment of piracy, crimes on the high seas and law-of-nations violations. Again, he assumed that if the Constitution did not grant these powers, the national government would not have them. Speaking of the very power at issue in *Curtiss-Wright,* Madison said that "[t]he regulation of foreign commerce . . . has been too fully discussed to need additional proofs here of its being properly submitted to the federal administration." He concluded "that no one of the powers transferred to the federal government is unnecessary or improper. . . ."[32]

This language makes no sense if everyone understood that the national government had inherent foreign affairs powers and that the Constitution's foreign affairs clauses served only to allocate those powers between the President and Congress. Madison's statements assumed the opposite—that unless the Constitution granted a particular foreign affairs power, the national government would not have it. All of his foreign affairs discussions described the Constitution as "vesting" power in, "conferring" power on, or "transferring" power to the national government.

The same is true of Madison's co-author, Hamilton. As he explained in Federalist No. 23:

> Whether there ought to be a federal government intrusted with the care of the common defense is a question in the first instance open to discussion; but the moment it is decided in the affirmative, it will follow that that government ought to be clothed with all the powers requisite to complete execution of its trust.[33]

In Federalist No. 24, Hamilton then discussed "the powers proposed to be conferred upon the federal government, in respect to the creation and direction of the national forces. . . ." His argument tracked Madison's in Federalist No. 41: the Constitution appropriately gave the national government the powers of national defense, rather than leaving them to the states.[34] Again, this way of framing the discussion makes no sense if the national government had inherent foreign affairs powers, which would surely include powers of national defense.

The Constitution's affirmative grants of various foreign affairs powers, coupled with the insistence by the Constitution's defenders that these clauses were necessary to vest the national government with foreign affairs powers, greatly undermine the purported background understanding that foreign affairs powers were seen as extra-constitutional. That might be countered by a contrary line of thinking, treating foreign affairs powers as inherent. However, this contrary idea cannot be found in any surviving founding-era discussions of foreign affairs powers. That may not be conclusive—perhaps such commentary has been lost—but it surely suggests that Hamilton and Madison reflect a conventional founding-era view that the federal government depended on the Constitution's text for its foreign affairs powers.

Similarly, *The Federalist* explained prohibitions on state foreign affairs powers as operative, not declaratory. Madison, summarizing Article I, Section 10, wrote: "A *fifth* class of provisions in favor of the federal authority consists of the following restrictions on the authority of the several States." "The prohibition against treaties, alliances, and confederations," he added, "makes a part of the existing articles of Union; and for reasons which need no explanation, is copied into the new Constitution." With respect to letters of marque and reprisal, he continued:

> The prohibition of letters of marque is another part of the old system, but is somewhat extended in the new. According to the former, letters of marque could be granted by the States after a declaration of war; according to the latter, these licenses must be obtained, as well during war

as previous to its declaration, from the government of the United States. This alteration is fully justified by the advantage of uniformity in all points which relate to foreign powers, and of immediate responsibility to the nation in all those for whose conduct the nation itself is to be responsible.[35]

Plainly Madison saw Article I, Section 10 as an operative provision *creating* a "restriction" upon "the authority" states would otherwise have, not as a provision restating an inherent preexisting lack of state power. Further, Madison discussed Article I, Section 10's foreign affairs restrictions in the same way, and in the same essay, as its restrictions on the states that were indisputably *not* declaratory of inherent limitations on state sovereignty, such as limitations on printing money and interfering with the obligation of contracts. And in each case, Madison did not say states inherently lacked foreign affairs powers; rather, he gave policy reasons for restricting the states, implying that without the restrictions, the evils of state involvement in these matters would likely occur.

These discussions again show an understanding that foreign affairs powers had to be granted to the national government and denied to the states by the Constitution in the same manner as ordinary domestic powers. True, the text and commentary show that founding-era Americans generally thought foreign affairs powers were *more appropriately* exercised by the national government—but they also show that founding-era Americans thought this was a structural choice needing to be established by the nation's governing document rather than one arising automatically from some abstract theory of sovereignty.

The Federalist is of course not the last word on constitutional meaning. But, on the whole, these discussions (and similar ones in other contemporaneous commentary) are important evidence. In these passages, Madison and Hamilton were not trying to convince anyone that foreign affairs powers were or were not delegated powers. These parts of *The Federalist* were advocacy, but they were not advocacy on this issue (and, indeed, do not even mention it directly). Rather, they suggest an important background assumption—but not the background assumption that Sutherland posited. Instead, they show a background assumption that foreign affairs powers *did* have to be delegated to the national government and denied to the states: the language of *The Federalist* simply does not make sense without that assumption. And this, in turn, tends to confirm that the Tenth Amendment means what it says, including with respect to foreign affairs.

Again, though, this may not be enough to settle the argument. Sutherland and those who defend him rest most of their case on the period before the

Constitution. In their view, the eleven years from 1776 to 1787 entrenched a background assumption about the relationship of the states and the national government in foreign affairs that was so strong it necessarily affected founding-era thinking about the Constitution, even if there is no evidence from the drafting and ratifying period that it did so.

It is true, of course, that the Constitution's text cannot be understood in isolation, or even solely in the context of its drafting and ratification; we must also consider what went before it. The next chapter turns to that history. But in doing so, we must bear in mind that the text, and contemporaneous commentary upon it, point away from inherent foreign affairs powers. The burden on Sutherland, to show that the text *cannot* have meant what it appears to mean, remains substantial.

2

Foreign Affairs and the Articles of Confederation: The Constitution in Context

To read the Constitution's text as founding-era Americans did, we must know something of what came before it. *Curtiss-Wright*'s core contention, as we have seen, is historical, focusing on (supposed) common understandings of sovereignty in the period between the Declaration of Independence and the Constitution (1776–1787). According to Justice Sutherland, in this period everyone thought foreign affairs powers were inherently national, not possessed by the states, and so when it came time to draft the Constitution, there was no need to write that proposition into the text. Even if unexpressed in text and commentary, this background understanding must (it is said) be honored in reading the text (specifically the Tenth Amendment), else we would not truly be giving it the meaning it had to informed readers of the time.

Unstated background assumptions may exist, and should be taken into account. If everyone at the time shared common understandings about the sources of foreign affairs powers, those assumptions might not show up in the text itself, nor—perhaps—even in contemporaneous commentary upon the text. Yet they surely would affect how the text was read at the time; if that is what we are trying to discover, then we must be faithful to background assumptions as well as to the text itself.

The challenge for Sutherland and *Curtiss-Wright* is to establish that this particular background assumption actually existed. Claims of decisive background assumptions must be backed up with powerful evidence when they ask us to disregard what appear to be clear textual commands. And as discussed below, the early years after independence remain somewhat ambiguous, but there seems little doubt that under the Articles of Confederation (1781–1788), the common assumption was the exact opposite of what Sutherland contended: foreign affairs powers were understood to lie with the states, not the national government, unless the governing document said otherwise. Indeed, the central criticism of the Articles, then and now, was and is that it left *too much* foreign affairs power to the states and did not give *enough* to the national government. This chapter reviews some of that history, to provide further reason to reject *Curtiss-Wright* and to lay some background for later discussions.

The Early Years of Union

In Sutherland's version of history, as we have seen, the states were never fully sovereign: they never possessed "external sovereignty"—foreign affairs power—which passed directly from Britain to the Union at the moment of independence in 1776. To many *Curtiss-Wright* critics, this is Sutherland's key misstep. In their view, at independence the states individually became sovereign and then formed a Union by delegation from complete sovereignty. If that was so, the national government could not "inherit" foreign affairs power directly from Britain, as Sutherland claimed. Rather, the *states* would have started with foreign affairs powers (and all other powers), some of which they then gave to the national government. And if so, then Sutherland's non-literal reading of the Tenth Amendment is untenable.[1]

The "state sovereignty" position claims substantial support, and historians such as Charles Lofgren have made a powerful case for it. But historians are divided: Richard Morris forcefully argues to the contrary that "[t]he federal Union not only preceded the States in time, but initiated their formation," and so Sutherland's "historical analysis of the inherent foreign affairs powers of the national government would not have seemed alien to the thinking of many, if not all, of the Founding Fathers." Jack Rakove, another leading modern historian, concludes that Morris has the better of the argument. A third prominent historian, Gordon Wood, sums the matter: "The authority of the Continental Congress and the Continental Army was in fact so great during the critical years of Independence and the war as to provoke a continuing if fruitless debate . . . over the priority of the Union or the states."[2]

The difficulty is that Americans did not adopt a charter of government at the moment of independence (nor, indeed, for another five years afterward). Prior to the 1770s, the American colonies had no common domestic authority; each colony had its own government, unrelated to one another and answerable directly to the British King and Parliament. As disputes with Britain accelerated in the 1770s, the colonies sought a collective approach through two successive Continental Congresses—gatherings of delegates appointed by each of the colonies separately, which sought to develop a unified front against Britain. The Second Continental Congress assumed control of the revolution once fighting began (1775) and declared independence (1776).[3]

These events hid a substantial theoretical question: did the "Congress" act on behalf of a collective entity, "the United States," or on behalf of thirteen separate entities, the colonies (now reconceived as individual independent "states")? The answer is complex and perhaps unascertainable—but the practical result was to introduce a location-of-powers question that had no analogue in British theory or practice: how would power be allocated between the national Congress and the individual colonies-turned-states? That, of course, was not a question limited to foreign affairs, but as applied to foreign affairs it became a central concern of the nation's first decade. On the other hand, the emergence of the Congress pushed to one side—at least initially— the issue of allocating powers at the national level. As the Congress became first the *de facto* and then the *de jure* national government, it took over all functions entrusted to the national government: there were no "branches" of government, and hence there was no need to allocate powers within the national government.

From the outset, the Congress assumed broad powers over foreign affairs, which principally meant directing the war effort (to 1781) and conducting diplomacy—first in securing an alliance with France (1778) and then in negotiating peace with Britain (1781–1783). Prior to 1781, the Congress had no documentary mandate for its foreign affairs powers, but it had a practical one: no great insight was needed to see that the colonies could hope to prevail against Britain only through united action. As a result, the Congress, in the exigency of revolution, exercised powers needed as a practical matter to achieve independence. The initial concern was winning the war, not establishing theoretical grounding for powers it necessarily claimed.

The issue of precedence arose almost as soon as the shooting stopped, but on a distinct matter: the question whether the *states* had inherent rights as "sovereigns." In the view of states' rights proponents, "the idea that the states preceded and created the Union proved that they retained certain inherent powers that the Union could never supersede."[4] The debate periodically recurred with vehemence: during the crisis preceding the Civil War, for example, southern states asserted a right to secede based on inherent sovereignty, which Lincoln disputed by arguing that the states had never been fully sovereign.[5] In short, views of the precedence of the states or the Union tended, from the beginning, to be shaped by views of inherent state rights and immunities *against* the federal government—a question tangential at best to the issue in *Curtiss-Wright* and one where consensus has proved impossible. In this manner, much of the leading academic discussion of *Curtiss-Wright* has been drawn into difficult historical and metaphysical questions about the nature of sovereignty. By focusing on the early period, the debate becomes inseparable from one of the most basic and intractable debates of federalism: as historian Rakove puts it, "Which came first, the Union or the states?"[6]

None of this proves Sutherland right, and for defenders of strong versions of federalism it may be enough to show that he was wrong. But it will leave many readers—who are *not* defenders of strong versions of federalism—without clear reason to reject Sutherland's claims.

Fortunately, we need not go back to the Declaration and revisit Professor Rakove's "which came first" question, nor take a position on larger issues of federalism and state sovereignty. The lack of a clear allocation of powers between the Congress and the states troubled American leaders almost immediately, and efforts soon began to draft a charter addressing the issue. The result was the Articles of Confederation (approved by the Congress in 1777, ratified by the states in 1781). The Articles provide a textual yardstick to measure the assumptions of the period preceding the Constitution. Thus we may assume that the "nationalist" account of the early years of independence may be largely correct—that is, that the national government emerged prior to (or at least simultaneously with) the states, and the national government, not the states, primarily exercised foreign affairs power during this time. A better starting point is 1781, when Maryland's ratification of the Articles brought that document into force as the first formal charter of the United States.[7] Focusing on this period, and focusing specifically on foreign affairs, may allow us to reach stronger conclusions than can be found on broader questions of state sovereignty.

The Articles of Confederation

Prior to 1781, government at the national level was necessarily *ad hoc* and informal. Formal ideas of delegated and inherent powers could not easily develop, as there was no formal constituting act. Theories of sovereignty were, as one might imagine, vague, amorphous, and unsettled.[8] The period after 1781 saw the first formal constitutional government at the national level. If there had been background ideas of inherent foreign affairs powers existing outside the "constitutional" framework of delegated powers, we would expect to see evidence of such thinking in the formalities or the practice under the Articles.

This is a critical test of *Curtiss-Wright*'s theory. The reason (to Sutherland's mind) that foreign affairs powers had to be inherent was that they *could not* be delegated by the states, because the states never had them. That view is essential to any theory of inherent power consistent with the Constitution's text, for it is the only way to avoid the apparently categorical language of the Tenth Amendment. If Sutherland were right, examination of the Articles should show an assumed national power over foreign affairs and an assumed lack of foreign affairs power in the states.

The reality, though, seems quite the opposite. As we shall see, the Articles' text and 1780s practice show an understanding of foreign affairs powers as delegated powers and an assumption that foreign affairs powers not delegated to the national government remained with the states. Indeed, a fundamental problem of the Articles was failure to delegate *enough* foreign affairs power to the Congress to make it a credible international actor. The national government's weakness in foreign affairs bedeviled its conduct of international relations, played a central part in contemporary criticism of the Articles, and became a leading argument for replacing the Articles with the Constitution.[9] Though this failing is widely remarked, few have noted how completely it undermines *Curtiss-Wright*'s idea of inherent powers.

The Text of the Articles

The Articles' text, like the Constitution's text, does not on its face suggest inherent foreign affairs power. Like the Constitution, the Articles listed key foreign affairs powers of the national government, including powers to determine on war and peace, make treaties, and send and receive ambassadors.[10] As with the Constitution, this enumeration suggests that there was no background idea of inherent foreign affairs power—else why list these powers in specific terms? Moreover, the rejoinder to this argument under the Constitution—that specification was necessary to show which branch of government had the power in question—is unavailable under the Articles. The Articles established only a single branch of national government, the Congress. The main reason for mentioning powers in the Articles had to be to give them to the national government.[11]

The Articles, again like the Constitution, also had specific limitations upon state activity in foreign affairs. Most of the Congress's enumerated foreign affairs powers were "sole and exclusive." States could enter into treaties, make war, or issue letters of marque only with the Congress's consent, and could not send or receive ambassadors.[12] And a number of other provisions imply a preexisting state role in matters affecting foreign affairs. Under Article 6, states could not tax imports in a way "which may interfere with any stipulations in treaties." Under Article 9, the Congress could not enter into commercial treaties requiring states to impose lower duties on foreigners than upon their own citizens or preventing states from "prohibiting the exportation or importation of any species of goods or commodities whatsoever." These provisions appear to recognize that (at minimum) states started from a position of complete control over imports and exports and then gave up some of that power. Further, although the Articles' restrictions on state foreign affairs power are substantial, they are not comprehensive. States could not, for example, issue letters of marque, or keep ships of war, *in peacetime*. This does not read like a *grant* of power to the states to take these actions in wartime—rather, it recognizes and limits preexisting powers of the states.

In sum, the Congress had most (but not all) diplomatic, war, and military powers by express grants; the Articles said almost nothing about the Congress's ability to make or enforce law in support of foreign affairs objectives. Limitations on the states similarly related to diplomatic and military powers, and where states could exercise these powers, it was usually with the permission of the Congress or in times of emergency. On the other hand, the Articles said little about the states' ability to enact laws and regulations relating to foreign affairs.

The Articles also explicitly limited the national government's power to matters delegated to it in the document. Its initial draft, prepared by John Dickinson shortly after independence, had no clear framework of delegated powers. Instead, it loosely indicated that internal matters would be left to the states and that the Congress would take care of matters affecting the entire Confederation—followed by a list of some specific powers. One could easily read this language to embrace "national" powers beyond those specifically listed. To guard against this possibility, the Congress—at the behest of North Carolina delegate Thomas Burke—amended Dickinson's draft to remove the general reference to exercising power over matters affecting the entire confederation, and added what became Article 2.[13] According to that Article: "Each state retains its sovereignty, freedom, and independence, and every Power, Jurisdiction, and right which is not by this confederation, expressly delegated to the United States, in Congress assembled." Like the Constitution's Tenth Amendment, this provision appears to say that powers not mentioned belong to the states and not to the national government. As Madison later observed, "[the state] constitutions invest the State legislatures with absolute sovereignty in all cases not excepted by the existing Articles of Confederation."[14] The Articles' text thus seems to reject the idea of inherent foreign affairs powers. Otherwise, we would have to view its foreign affairs provisions as surplusage, and dismiss Article 2 (and Madison's description of it) as inapplicable to foreign affairs.

This textual argument may not yet be entirely decisive, however. Advocates of inherent powers can still argue from background understandings. We are assuming that the Congress before the Articles had something like inherent foreign affairs powers (at least in the sense of exercising foreign affairs powers without formal authorization), and that the historical record is at least ambiguous as to whether the states ever had full sovereignty in some external matters. Under this view, the Articles themselves may have been drafted against a background of assumed inherent foreign affairs power. One could then argue that Article 2 did not apply to foreign affairs: by its terms, Article 2 (like the Tenth Amendment) only confirmed *existing* state sovereignty—and, by this reasoning, foreign affairs might not have been part of the states' existing sovereignty.[15] We will, therefore, need to examine the actual conduct of government under the Articles to reach firm conclusions.

Government under the Articles

Curtiss-Wright's idea of inherent powers must claim that under the Articles, Americans understood the national government (and not the states) to have all foreign affairs powers as a natural attribute of national sovereignty, whatever the Articles themselves had to say about it. Yet in practice, the exercise of foreign affairs powers under the Articles closely followed its textual allocations. The Congress exercised the foreign affairs powers granted to it in the document—principally war, diplomacy, and treatymaking.[16] The states, for the most part, did not exercise these powers, and when they did, they were charged with violating the Articles.[17] More significantly, where the Articles neither granted foreign affairs powers to the Congress nor denied them to the states, the powers in question were exercised by the states and not the Congress. These powers principally related to making laws with foreign affairs implications and enforcing foreign policy objectives the Congress articulated. As discussed in more detail below, essentially all foreign-affairs-related legislation and enforcement occurred at the state level.[18]

This system worked well enough early on. The Congress managed to keep an army in the field, and maintained cordial relations with allies France and the Netherlands while negotiating a favorable peace with Britain. True, this may have been due more to the individual talents of its appointees than any special competence of the Congress. But nonetheless, the Congress succeeded in its two overriding foreign affairs goals: winning the war and securing peace.

After 1783, though, structural troubles began in earnest. With the peace treaty signed, the Congress turned to the problem of governing the new nation in peacetime. This promptly pointed up a striking feature of the Articles' Congress. Today we associate "Congress" with lawmaking, because that is the principal power of the modern U.S. Congress. But the Articles' Congress had little lawmaking power. Its great powers lay in foreign affairs—war and diplomacy. Indeed, it is important to see that the term "Congress," in the 1770s and 1780s, carried no implication of lawmaking authority. A "congress" was a meeting of diplomats; lawmaking bodies were called "parliaments," "assemblies," "legislatures," and the like.[19] (The former use survived, for example, in the "Congress of Vienna"—the peace conference of European powers after the defeat of Napoleon, which was an assembly of diplomats, not a lawmaking institution; no state lawmaking body of the time was called a "congress.") The Continental Congress was formed not to make national laws, but to manage diplomatic and military relations with foreign nations.

In terms of domestic governance, this was not an overriding problem in most respects. State legislatures had lawmaking power, and at that time most domestic issues were sufficiently local that states could handle them without national action. Paradoxically, the place the new nation ran into substantial trouble was in foreign affairs, supposedly the Congress's reason for being. As in other areas, the Congress did not have lawmaking power in foreign affairs—that is, it did not have the power to make national laws in support of foreign affairs objectives; and that, it soon appeared, was a critical oversight.

American leaders quickly concluded, for example, that they needed to enact national regulations of foreign commerce. Partly this was financial necessity: the Congress had substantial debts and no reliable source of income, and tariffs or "imposts" (taxes on imports) normally formed a nation's prime source of revenue in those days. Further, foreign nations (especially Britain) discriminated against or flatly prohibited American imports. Many of the colonies, pre-independence, had been substantial trading economies. The Congress needed to negotiate to gain favorable treatment for U.S. exports— but to do that (it was thought), the Congress needed credible threats against the imports of foreign nations. That is, it needed to say to (for example)

Britain that unless Britain allowed American exports to Britain, America would ban British exports to America.[20]

Nothing in the Articles said anything about taxing or regulating foreign commerce. Without those powers, the Congress had no way to enhance its revenue, and no way to achieve reciprocal trade deals. As these difficulties mounted, American leaders in and out of the Congress began campaigns to amend the Articles to provide the missing powers. But amending the Articles required unanimous approval of the states. And although at any given time ten to twelve states favored amendment, for various reasons unanimity proved elusive. No amendment ever passed, and the Congress never did anything with respect to tariffs or foreign commercial regulation.[21]

If action could not be had at the national level, the only remedy seemed to lie with the states. States did tax and regulate foreign commerce during the 1780s, but coordinated action proved impossible, and therefore no effective support of foreign affairs policies could be developed. In particular, states could bring no useful leverage against foreign nations to promote reciprocal trade agreements. Substantial campaigns were mounted to this effect. Some states tried to pressure foreign nations on their own, by enacting discriminatory tariffs and regulations. But no individual state was large enough to gain leverage; no coordinated policy could be achieved, and the targeted commerce simply flowed into the ports of neighboring states.[22]

The Congress's inability to enact national laws to support foreign policy goals produced at least two other systemic problems. While the Congress had initial success in making agreements with foreign nations, it could not make the changes in domestic (state) law these agreements contemplated. And, to the extent foreign nations expected the United States to conform to a customary "law of nations" (see Chapter 17)—or, for that matter, simply to treat foreign interests within the United States fairly—the Congress had no means to assure this would be done.

The greatest difficulties here arose from the 1783 Treaty of Peace with Britain. On the whole, the treaty favored the United States, not only recognizing its independence unconditionally, but also accepting U.S. claims to lands as far west as the Mississippi River, far beyond the settled parts of the colonies.[23] But a few particular provisions troubled the states. For one, a number of states passed laws during the Revolution confiscating or discharging debts owed by their citizens to British creditors. Britain insisted that these acts be repealed, and the Congress, in the treaty, agreed that "no lawful impediment" should prevent British debtors from collecting pre-war debts. The treaty also provided that loyalists (those who supported Britain in the Revolution) should have the ability to return to the United States without punishment or discrimination.

In the broader context of the treaty, these concessions appeared minor; in the domestic politics of some states they proved unacceptable. Several states flatly refused to comply. Britain argued, threatened, and refused to surrender military posts in U.S. territory whose evacuation had been promised, causing great unease to the national government. The Congress took Britain's side, requesting that states obey the treaty. The states continued to refuse. In particular, the issue assumed enormous proportions in Virginia (which had the largest stock of confiscated debts) and in Pennsylvania and New York (where returning loyalists and their property were a serious matter). Ultimately the Congress had no recourse, for it had no way to override state legislation. This in turn had debilitating consequences for the Congress's continuing diplomatic efforts. Once Britain (and other nations) saw that the Congress could not implement its promises, further agreements were impossible. In effect, the Congress could not really speak for the nation in its diplomacy, at least as to matters that required domestic legal implementation.[24] As Hamilton described it: "The treaties of the United States under the present Constitution [i.e., the Articles] are liable to the infractions of thirteen different legislatures. . . . The faith, the reputation, the peace of the whole are thus continually at the mercy of the prejudices, the passions, and the interests of every member of which it is composed."[25]

A similar theme developed with respect to foreign interests protected by the law of nations (what today we would call customary international law). During the 1780s, foreign countries appealed to the Congress, as the Union's diplomatic representative, to protect rights under the law of nations. The Congress saw some of these protests as serious matters, but could do little beyond referring them to the relevant state government. In the best-known incident, in 1784 a French citizen, Charles de Longchamps, assaulted France's Consul General Marbois in Philadelphia. France demanded that the Congress surrender the assailant to French authorities. The Congress, believing it lacked power in the matter, suggested that France apply instead to the Pennsylvania government (which France angrily did); the Congress merely recommended that states pass laws "punishing the infractions of the laws of nations, and more especially for securing the privileges and immunities of public Ministers from foreign powers."[26] Similar events arose from unlawful seizures of foreign ships in Massachusetts (1783) and South Carolina (1784); in both cases the foreign nation appealed to the Congress, which referred the matter to the relevant state.[27] In general, the states acted fairly responsibly—Pennsylvania did punish de Longchamps, although it refused to extradite him[28]—but the Congress's lack of authority made it look weak and ineffectual to foreign powers, and leaving matters in the hands of individual states seemed dangerous in an era when nations went speedily to war over real and imagined violations of their rights.[29]

Historians debate the extent to which these and related foreign affairs problems led to the 1787 Convention in Philadelphia that drafted the Constitution. To some, the Articles' foreign affairs dysfunctions were an essential factor. Others object that domestic matters, such as the state governments' failure to protect property rights, played decisive roles. But there is general agreement that foreign affairs difficulties were a root—if not the root—of the drive to replace the Articles.[30]

That can be seen from the commentary of the time, which highlighted the Articles' foreign affairs problems. Madison's memorandum *Vices of the Political System of Government in the United States* (1787) pointed to, among other things, the Congress's lack of power over tariffs and regulation of foreign trade and its inability to legislate in support of treaty obligations and the law of nations.[31] These complaints were also prominent at the Philadelphia Convention itself. Virginia governor Edmund Randolph opened the Convention's substantive debate by listing the Articles' difficulties, including the foreign affairs problems outlined by Madison.[32] And once the Convention proposed a new system of government, its proponents continued that critique in publications such as *The Federalist,* which emphasized the dangerous foreign affairs weaknesses of the Articles.[33]

The Problems of the Articles and Attempts at Reform

In sum, a core problem of the Articles was that separating the Congress from the legislative machinery of foreign affairs made realization of national foreign affairs goals difficult. The remedy proposed was always to amend the Articles to add the missing powers, and energetic though unsuccessful campaigns were launched to this effect. No one argued that the Congress could exercise missing foreign affairs powers inherently; the common thought was that exercise of these powers depended upon *the states* adding to the Congress's textual grants. Conversely, in the absence of amendment, the only alternative appeared to be coordinated action at the state level—and no one seemed to doubt that the states had power to act (though, in practice, they lacked the ability to act effectively). When both amendment and state coordination proved impossible, the ultimate remedy was the 1787 Convention, called in large part to give the national government *more* textual foreign affairs powers.

These general observations are illustrated by the leading foreign affairs issues of the 1780s: regulation of foreign commerce, tariffs, embargoes, and enforcement of treaties and the law of nations. In each case, despite crippling gaps in the Congress's textual foreign affairs powers, the common assumption was that missing powers lay with the states unless they could be given to the Congress by amendment of the Articles.

FOREIGN COMMERCE. As discussed, a central foreign affairs challenge under the Articles was that European nations—especially Britain—refused to allow American products and shipping to land at their ports, while aggressively promoting exports to the United States. American commercial interests, especially in New England, wanted something done about this. The obvious strategy was to threaten retaliation against foreign products and shipping—but this proved difficult given the Articles' structure of government.

At the national level, confederation diplomats, at the Congress's direction, sought commercial treaties with Britain and the European powers with little success: foreign nations had little incentive for cooperation. A congressional committee reported: "Already has Great Britain adopted regulations destructive of our commerce. . . . It would be the duty of Congress, as it is their wish, to meet the attempts of Great Britain with similar restrictions on her commerce; but their powers on this hand are not explicit. . . ." As a result, the Congress concluded, "Unless the United States in Congress assembled shall be vested with powers competent to the protection of commerce, they can never command reciprocal advantages in trade; and without these, our foreign commerce must decline, and eventually be annihilated." The problem, plainly, was that no one thought the Congress had power to bar British (or other foreign) imports. The Congress then proposed a surprisingly narrow remedy—not that it be given power over foreign commerce generally, but rather:

> That it be, and hereby is, recommended to the legislatures of the several states, to vest the United States in Congress assembled, for the term of fifteen years, with power to prohibit any goods, wares or merchandize from being imported into or exported from any of the states in vessels belonging to or navigated by the subjects of any power with whom these states shall not have formed treaties of Commerce . . . [and]

That it be recommended to the legislatures of the several states, to vest the United States in Congress assembled, for the term of fifteen years, with the power of prohibiting the subjects of any foreign state, kingdom or empire, unless authorized by treaty, from importing into the United States, any goods, wares or merchandise which are not the produce or manufacture of the dominions of the sovereign whose subjects they are.[34]

Supporters of commercial interests, such as Massachusetts governor James Bowdoin, pushed hard for the proposed amendments, contending in similar terms that the states must give the Congress additional powers. Bowdoin argued:

[Britain and the European powers] have an undoubted right to regulate their trade with us, and to admit into their ports on their own terms, the vessels and cargoes that go from the United States, or to refuse all admittance. . . . The United States have the same right, and can and ought to regulate their foreign trade on the same principles. But it is a misfortune that the Congress have not yet been authorized for that purpose by all the States.

As a result, he continued,

It is of great importance . . . that Congress should be vested with all the powers necessary to preserve the Union, to manage the general concerns of it, and secure and promote its common interest. That interest, so far as it is dependent on a commercial intercourse with foreign nations, the confederation does not sufficiently provide; and this state, and the United States in general, are now experiencing by the oppression of their trade with some of these nations, particularly Great Britain, the want of such provision. This deficiency of power may be the result of a just principle, a caution to preserve to each state all the powers not necessary to be delegated; with respect to which, as there was room for a variety of opinions concerning them, they could not all be certainly known at the time of forming the confederation. Experience, however, has shown the necessity of delegating to Congress further powers.[35]

Bowdoin's language shows that he (like the Congress itself) saw the matter as one of the states giving the Congress additional foreign affairs powers—a view he shared with other key leaders in the debate[36] and with the state legislatures themselves, which passed acts that in explicit terms "empowered" the Congress with, or "vested in Congress," limited power to regulate foreign commerce.[37] But not everyone trusted the national government: some who later became anti-federalists argued against national power over foreign trade. New York's Abraham Yates wrote that he was "rather Suspitious that the advocates for augmenting the powers of Congress will try to effect their Scheme under the Cloak of investing Congress with power to make Commercial Regulations." Virginia's George Mason, opposing the proposed amendments, wrote that "Congress should not even have the appearance of such a power."[38] In the end, Bowdoin and his allies carried most states, but the Articles required unanimity, which could never be achieved.[39]

While pushing for national legislation, Bowdoin also campaigned at the state level. State regulation of foreign commerce dated to the earliest times, and, not surprisingly, during the war states targeted British interests for punishment. But much of this regulation was relaxed after the war, and in any event it was not directed at the specific problem of reciprocal trade. At Bowdoin's urging, Massachusetts enacted a new array of regulations designed to deal with the unequal trading regimes, including bans on imports of certain goods, bans on exports in British and other foreign ships, and limits on places foreign ships could unload. Many restrictions applied only to foreign nations that refused to give the United States reciprocal trading rights.[40]

Recognizing that Massachusetts acting alone would only shift imports to neighboring states, Bowdoin and others tried to organize a nationwide campaign at the state level; they did persuade a few neighboring states to enact coordinated regulatory regimes. But outside New England, interests were too divergent to permit a unified front: Bowdoin's proposals attracted little interest; other states pursued unrelated attempts to deal with similar problems, and some (especially Connecticut) actively undercut them. As a result, the states could gain no international leverage.[41] The impasse continued until 1787, when the new Constitution explicitly gave the new Congress power to regulate foreign trade.

TARIFFS. Parallel events occurred with respect to tariffs and related duties on imports. As with foreign commerce, the Articles gave the Congress no power to tax imports. It soon became apparent that the Congress needed that power, both for domestic reasons (principally revenue) and as an additional lever to negotiate reciprocal trading rights. Again, the common assumption was that the Articles needed to be amended to give the Congress a power it otherwise lacked. Proponents urged amendments specifically couched in terms of states *granting to* the Congress additional powers; others countered that the states should not give up any additional power.

Despite widespread agreement on the need for amendment, a unanimous vote of the states could never be delivered. The result was, again, an impasse that critics of the Articles widely cited in the years leading up to the 1787 Convention.[42]

On the other hand, by common assumption the states retained the power to tax imports, and most did so. Indeed, many did so in a discriminatory fashion, often to achieve specific foreign policy goals.[43] This produced its own set of problems, including that imports destined for one state ended up being taxed in a different state where they were first landed, provoking substantial inter-state hostility. But no one thought the states *lacked* the power to tax imports as a matter of sovereignty—only that they should not have it. And at the Convention, the delegates again dealt with the problem textually by including taxation of foreign commerce as one of the powers Article I, Section 10 denied to the states.

EMBARGOES.   Although lacking the high profile of foreign commerce and tariffs, discussions of embargo power (the power actually at issue in *Curtiss-Wright*) reinforce the pattern discussed above. During the Revolution, states embargoed exports of particular products and prohibited trade with Britain in general.[44] As in other areas, lack of national coordination rendered these measures largely ineffectual. In 1781, a committee of the Congress met to consider changes to the Articles and recommended seven amendments, including one granting the Congress power to impose embargoes in wartime. As with other foreign commercial powers, no one argued that this was an inherent power. Rather, the committee recommended to the Congress additional powers to solicit *from the states*.[45]

The Congress never acted on the committee's recommendation, and as a result it was thought to lack embargo power, beyond mere recommendations. The decline in *de facto* hostilities after 1781 saw renewed trade with Britain, still nominally an enemy, between 1781 and 1783; because the Congress lacked power to suppress this trade, it had to rely upon the uneven efforts of the states.[46] Similarly, when the Confederation encountered hostilities from Algerian pirates in the mid-1780s, Foreign Secretary Jay recommended among other things embargoes upon countries friendly to Algiers. The Congress took no action on the matter, presumably because it assumed it lacked direct power over the matter, and coordination of embargoes at the state level had proved futile.[47]

ENFORCEMENT OF THE LAW OF NATIONS.   Another troublesome issue, law-of-nations enforcement, was likewise understood to arise from a lack of delegated power. As Madison described it: "These articles contain no provision for the case of offenses against the law of nations; and consequently leave it in the power of any indiscreet member to embroil the Confederacy with foreign nations."[48] That view is consistent with practice under the Articles, as reflected in episodes such as the de Longchamps incident, in which the states and not the Congress dealt with foreign powers in matters concerning the law of nations. In that case, after finding it lacked power to deal with French demands, the Congress directed Foreign Secretary Jay to

> explain to [the French representative] the difficulties that may arise on this head from the nature of a federal union in which each State retains a distinct and absolute sovereignty in all matters not expressly delegated to Congress leaving to them [i.e., the Congress] only that of advising in many of those cases in which other governments decree.[49]

Although this was thought a dysfunctional system, it seemed inevitable (as Madison indicated) given the limited grants of foreign relations power in the Articles. Indeed, the Congress apparently thought it lacked power to punish even violations of its own passports and safe conducts, and requested the states to provide appropriate punishments.[50]

ENFORCEMENT OF TREATIES. The same theme runs through the critical problems of state enforcement (or non-enforcement) of U.S. treaty obligations, particularly the clauses of the 1783 treaty with Britain relating to debt confiscation and treatment of loyalists. State violations undermined the new nation's credibility and nearly provoked renewed war. Yet most people thought that under the Articles, the Congress lacked recourse against the states.[51] True, some prominent figures, including Hamilton and Jay, argued that states had no authority to violate national treaties. They appealed not to inherent distributions of foreign affairs power, but to the Articles' text, in terms that made clear their understanding that the Congress's powers were those given to the Congress by the states in the Articles. Hamilton asked:

> Does not the act of confederation place the exclusive right of war and peace in the United States in Congress? Have they not the sole power of making treaties with foreign nations? Are not these among the first rights of sovereignty, and does not the delegation of them to the general confederacy, so far abridge the sovereignty of each particular state?[52]

Similarly Jay argued that the states "by express delegation of power, formed and vested in Congress perfect though limited sovereignty" including powers of war and peace, and this "express delegation" implied agreement to be bound by congressional treaties.[53] In short, arguments about state power in this area turned on the extent of delegation in the Articles, not upon inherent power.

The Experience under the Articles—Implications

These events make it difficult to claim a widespread understanding of inherent national foreign affairs powers under the Articles. It is essentially incontestable that everyone during the relevant period thought that (a) the national government lacked power over foreign commerce and navigation, embargoes, tariffs, and enforcement of treaties and the law of nations; (b) state governments had power over these matters; (c) this was a problem arising from the limited grants of foreign affairs power to the national government in the Articles' text; and (d) the problem could only be fixed by including these powers in further grants of authority to the national government, ultimately in Article I, Section 8 of the Constitution.[54]

Crucially, many key issues on which states acted (and the Congress did not) were overtly matters of influencing foreign nations. Of course, states often did legislate for domestic goals in ways that happened to have international implications. But in many cases, the international element was paramount. Most obviously, the central issue in the campaign for broader powers over foreign commerce was the need to gain leverage against foreign nations to pursue access to foreign markets. While the Congress unsuccessfully sought such powers, many states enacted legislation specifically designed to pressure foreign nations—particularly Britain—to lower trade barriers. The elaborate Massachusetts trade regulations of 1785, for example, enhanced duties and curtailed the navigation rights of countries with trade barriers against U.S. commerce, singling out Britain in particular.[55] Other states, notably Virginia and Pennsylvania, targeted nations that did not give access to U.S. commerce and granted special privileges to nations favoring the United States.[56] Virginia conditioned repeal of its anti-British debt legislation upon Britain's surrender of the western military posts in accordance with the 1783 peace treaty.[57] As reflected in the de Longchamps incident, states handled extradition requests from foreign nations. And the very power at issue in *Curtiss-Wright*—embargo—was understood as a state rather than national power under the Articles. In short, even in matters in which the United States directly sought to affect foreign nations, the legislative and enforcement initiatives lay with the states rather than the Congress.[58]

It is equally striking that the Congress—bitterly frustrated by its anemic foreign affairs showing—never reached for inherent power to break the impasse (as James Wilson did with the national bank). Though the Congress was not primarily a lawmaking body, it did exercise legislative and enforcement powers in areas encompassed by the Articles' text. The Congress promulgated military regulations, passed laws with respect to the territories (most notably the 1787 Northwest Ordinance), and regulated the mail.[59] If the Congress thought it had general foreign affairs powers (as it did believe it had power over the national army, the territories, and the mail), these instances of congressional power would have been models for foreign-affairs-related ordinances. Instead, advocates of national power in foreign affairs argued that the states should *delegate* more foreign affairs powers to the Congress. This was the theme of the Congress's own resolutions, of Bowdoin's campaign, of Madison's *Vices*, and ultimately of the 1787 Convention.

Conclusion: *Curtiss-Wright* Revisited

The structure of the Articles, of course, does not necessarily determine the proper view of the Constitution. In adopting the Constitution, the drafters and ratifiers did not merely build upon the Articles; created a new system to correct the Articles' failings. It is possible, as Louis Henkin suggests, that even if the Articles' Congress did not have inherent power in foreign affairs, the new government might.[60] That is, we might suppose that the federal government under the Constitution was the first truly national government (whereas the "national" government under the Articles more closely approximated a system of alliances among independent states);[61] thus the government under the Articles, not being a true national government, lacked inherent external sovereignty, but once the Constitution established a true national government, that government gained the inherent rights of national sovereignty (including foreign affairs powers).

But this argument faces substantial difficulties. First, it is surely true that the drafters and ratifiers of the Constitution thought the Articles failed by not establishing a truly national system of foreign affairs and by leaving too much control over foreign affairs to the states. But they solved that problem by taking the basic template of the Articles and expanding the delegations to the national government while increasing limitations on the states. Many of the Articles' foreign affairs provisions were adapted with detailed modifications into the new Constitution. For example, the treaty power was carried over but modified so that states were not able to violate treaty obligations.

Provisions against states entering into international agreements were strengthened. Under the Articles, states could issue letters of marque only during wartime; under the Constitution they could not issue them at all. The congressional foreign affairs powers most strikingly lacking under the Articles—tariffs, commercial regulations, and enforcement of treaties and the law of nations—were added as specific congressional powers.

Further, in *The Federalist,* Madison and Hamilton's discussions of the new Constitution's foreign affairs provisions show that they (and presumably their audience) were working squarely within the Articles' framework of delegated foreign affairs powers. As we have seen, Hamilton and Madison emphasized the continuity between the Articles and the Constitution, explicitly describing their project as carrying over the foreign affairs powers and restrictions of the Articles into the new document, with modifications to remedy the Articles' defects (see Chapter 1).[62] They had no idea of an inherent division of powers into "external sovereignty" and "internal sovereignty" that automatically governed which powers would be held by the national government and which by the states; they were groping for the right balance in a very practical manner—carrying over allocations from the Articles to the Constitution where they seemed to work and making adjustments where problems had arisen.

In any event, Henkin's "nationalist" suggestion flatly contradicts the Tenth Amendment's direction that all powers not delegated to the national government are reserved to the states. As discussed, there might be grounds for not reading this direction literally, if some powers could be neither delegated nor reserved because the states never held them. Whatever the merits of such a claim as a general matter, though, the Articles' experience was that foreign affairs powers *were* held by the states (if not granted to the Congress). The Tenth Amendment therefore confirms that, as to foreign affairs matters, powers are either delegated or reserved (not inherent).

We may now appear to have come full circle. Once again, the rejoinder is that while no one seriously challenges the idea of delegated powers as the Constitution's basic framework, there may be particular exceptions to it, based on the idea of national sovereignty. And because of the obvious national characteristics of foreign affairs, it is likely (it is said) that foreign affairs power was one of the exceptions. Now, though, it should be clear (as it was not before) that there is insufficient evidence that anyone in the founding era treated foreign affairs powers differently from ordinary powers. Perhaps background assumptions can supplement or even overturn seemingly clear constitutional text, but background assumptions must be proven, not merely hypothesized. History is crucial to Sutherland's idea of inherent power, and without evidence of a historical background understanding, inherent power is left without foundation.

As we have seen, Sutherland relied upon a (claimed) background understanding at the moment of independence. But however one reads the events of 1776, our exploration of government under the Articles shows that after 1781, what Sutherland thought he had found (if it ever existed) was supplanted by a background understanding of delegated powers in foreign affairs. The Articles' Congress did not exercise inherent foreign affairs powers. Where the Articles did not give a particular foreign affairs power to the Congress, the Congress thought it lacked that power, and did not exercise it even when action by the Congress seemed the only effective approach. When the Articles did not deny a power to the states, the states thought they had it, and frequently exercised it, even when its exercise seemed unwise. This pattern recurred with respect to tariffs, navigation acts and other restraints of international trade, extradition, embargoes, and enforcement of the law of nations and treaties—the major foreign affairs powers unmentioned by the Articles. As a result, readers of the new Constitution in 1787 would not have assumed inherent foreign affairs powers—quite the contrary. And if that is the case, there seems little justification for reading the Tenth Amendment not to apply to foreign affairs. Thus in foreign affairs, as in domestic affairs, national powers are those delegated by the Constitution.[63]

This, of course, is not the end of the story—only the beginning. The central challenge of *Curtiss-Wright* remains: if foreign affairs powers are not inherent powers, but must arise from constitutional delegations, how are we to make sense of an apparently incomplete foreign affairs text? Professor Henkin writes: "Students of the Constitution may have to accept Sutherland's theory, with all its difficulties, or leave constitutional deficiencies unrepaired."[64] In abandoning *Curtiss-Wright*, do we also abandon hope of a textual framework for foreign affairs law? Ensuing chapters take up that challenge.

II

Presidential Power in Foreign Affairs

3

The *Steel Seizure* Case and Executive Power over Foreign Affairs

In addition to *Curtiss-Wright,* the Supreme Court's other great structural foreign affairs decision is *Youngstown Sheet & Tube Co. v. Sawyer* (1952), sometimes called the *Steel Seizure* case.[1] Unfortunately, the two cases seem to point in entirely opposite directions. As we have seen (Chapter 1), the Court in *Curtiss-Wright* said that the national government, and more particularly the President, had broad powers in foreign affairs that arise, not from any grant of power in the Constitution, but inherently from the idea of nationhood. In the *Steel Seizure* case fifteen years later, Justice Hugo Black, writing for the Court, said approximately the opposite: presidential actions must be based on statutory law or a specific grant of power in the Constitution.

Black's claim sounds reasonable enough until one examines it closely. The problem is not that it contradicts *Curtiss-Wright* (though it does), but that it cannot account for many of the President's ordinary foreign affairs activities. It does not, for example, explain the President's role as the chief instrument of U.S. diplomacy. Professor Henkin rightly says: "That the President is the sole organ of official communication by and to the United States has not been questioned and has not been a source of significant controversy."[2] Similarly, the President instructs, controls, and recalls U.S. ambassadors and other diplomatic personnel. And, only slightly more controversially, the President formulates the United States' views on international questions. That is, the President not only makes communications but also decides their substance. Will the United States urge other countries to respect human rights, to lower trade barriers, to fight communism, terrorism, or drugs? On these and other matters, the President decides what goals to proclaim, to whom, and with what priorities.

Yet if the President has no inherent foreign affairs powers (as we decided in previous chapters, and as Justice Black said in *Youngstown*), what is the source of these diplomatic powers? They are not found in any statute. The

President's specific foreign affairs powers, listed in Article II, Sections 2 and 3, are (only) to receive foreign ambassadors and act as commander-in-chief of the military, plus shared power, with the Senate, to make treaties and diplomatic appointments. Surely none of these powers singly or together could encompass the complete power over U.S. diplomacy the President seems to possess—nor has anyone materially argued that they do.[3]

If we are to take Justice Black's statement seriously, then, we must find the textual source of these powers. That has proved sufficiently difficult that neither the Court (in *Youngstown* or otherwise) nor conventional legal scholarship has made satisfactory arguments. The solution is usually thought to lie beyond the Constitution's text, in an array of implications and inferences from structure, convenience, practice, and necessity.[4]

This chapter suggests a textual basis for the President's commonly assumed foreign affairs powers. By Article II, Section 1, the President has the "executive Power" of the United States. Although in today's language we might not associate this power with foreign affairs, we will see that it *was* associated with foreign affairs in eighteenth-century uses of the term. Thus, as part of the Constitution's historical meaning, it may provide the beginning of a textual explanation for presidential foreign affairs powers.[5]

The Supreme Court and the *Steel Seizure* Case

The *Steel Seizure* case arose during the Korean War, when an impending strike at leading U.S. steel mills threatened the flow of supplies needed for the war effort. President Harry Truman ordered a government takeover of the mills. No law authorized his action. Instead, Truman claimed to be acting under his own constitutional authority as President. The Court, per Justice Black, disagreed. Black argued—in fine disregard of *Curtiss-Wright*—that all presidential power had to come from an act of Congress or from the Constitution. Because Congress had not authorized the takeover and Truman could not point to any specific provision in the Constitution granting him authority, the seizure was (Black said) unconstitutional.[6]

Black's argument may seem plausible if one only considers seizing steel mills. But measured against the President's diplomatic power, it faces worrisome objections. If the President has only the powers in the Constitution (as Black claimed), and if the powers listed in Article II, Sections 2 and 3 are not sufficient to include, for example, the President's powers of international communication, then the President cannot be the sole diplomatic voice of the nation, as assumed throughout constitutional history. Unless we are prepared to abandon the President's diplomatic power, it seems that the President must have *some* foreign affairs powers beyond those specifically mentioned in the Constitution. Yet if the President does have these powers, where do they come from, and how is one to say that seizing steel mills in support of foreign wars is not another of those powers? Justice Black's simple syllogism collapses in the face of this challenge.

This objection was sufficiently serious that several other Justices wrote separately to suggest that Black had oversimplified matters. Justice Robert Jackson, in the best-known of these concurrences, relied on the fact that Congress had (he said) *disapproved* of the seizure, and when Congress disapproves, the President's power is at its "lowest ebb"—effectively preventing presidential action unless it rests upon strong affirmative textual authorization. Jackson added that if Congress had not spoken, the President would act in a "zone of twilight" where constitutional powers would be unclear, but (he implied) presidential authority might often be found.[7] The latter is not a particularly helpful formulation, and it owes little to the Constitution's text, but it allowed Jackson to finesse the problem that the President seems frequently to act in foreign affairs without specific congressional or constitutional approval.

Another of the Court's intellectual heavyweights, Felix Frankfurter, argued that long-standing practice might provide a "gloss" upon the Constitution's foreign affairs provisions and (implicitly) that this might help to explain the President's possession of seemingly extra-textual powers. Thus the President could exercise diplomatic powers, even if they were not mentioned in the Constitution, on the basis of long-standing practice; but the President could not seize steel mills, because practice did not support that power.[8]

Neither Jackson nor Frankfurter (nor others who wrote separately) grappled with how the Constitution's text *originally* allocated foreign affairs power. Like much modern scholarship, they assumed that the Constitution was incomplete on key foreign affairs matters, and that gaps would be filled in other ways: Jackson through a practical sense of whether the branches of government were, at least implicitly, working together; Frankfurter by examining how the branches had over time agreed, at least implicitly, to share power. As Jackson said directly, the historical understanding, if it ever actually existed, was too remote for modern judges to decipher: "Just what our forefathers did envision, or would have envisioned had they foreseen modern conditions, must be divined from materials almost as enigmatic as the dreams Joseph was called upon to interpret for Pharaoh. A century and a half of partisan debate and scholarly speculation yields no net result but only supplies more or less apt quotations from respected sources on each side of any question."[9]

Of course *Curtiss-Wright* would have solved the Justices' problem by providing a basis for presidential powers such as diplomatic communication outside the Constitution's text. But the Justices naturally hesitated to reach for this power (only Jackson cited the case, indirectly): once invoked it would prove difficult to limit. If *Curtiss-Wright* explained the President's diplomatic power, it could also support the President's power to seize steel mills.

For similar reasons, the Justices avoided the idea that the President's Article II, Section 1 "executive Power" could solve their dilemma. Truman invoked that clause (among others) as a basis for his power, as did Chief Justice Fred Vinson in dissent.[10] Anyone who used the executive power clause to explain the President's diplomatic powers needed to explain why the clause did not also authorize the seizure—and the Justices apparently could not.

Closer examination suggests that the Justices should have considered the executive power clause more fully, for careful study of its eighteenth-century meaning indicates that it can do much to resolve their dilemma. Specifically, it helps explain the constitutional basis for the President's ordinary diplomatic activity while also explaining why Truman's action in *Steel Seizure* was (as the Court said) unconstitutional.

Presidential Powers and the Constitution's Text

We, like Justice Black, start from the proposition that the President's powers in foreign affairs—like all national powers in foreign affairs—must arise from the Constitution. That is a necessary consequence of rejecting *Curtiss-Wright*'s inherent power (Chapters 1–2). But the Constitution's text is, at first inspection, unpromising. The President's specific powers are listed in Article II, Sections 2 and 3. As they relate to foreign affairs, they are:

> The President shall be Commander in Chief of the Army and Navy of the United States, and of the Militia of the several States. . . .
>
> He shall have Power, by and with the Advice and Consent of the Senate, to make Treaties, provided two-thirds of the Senators present concur; and he shall nominate, and by and with the Advice and Consent of the Senate, shall appoint Ambassadors, other public Ministers and Consuls. . . .
>
> [H]e shall receive Ambassadors and other public Ministers; he shall take Care that the Laws be faithfully executed, and shall Commission all the Officers of the United States.

No one seriously argues that these provisions cover everything the President does in foreign affairs, nor in particular that they cover the diplomatic examples mentioned above.[11] Some presidential communications will be about treaties, ambassadors, or the military, but many will not be, and no one has ever thought that the President needs to tie diplomatic efforts to particular clauses in Article II, Sections 2 and 3. Expressing concerns about foreign nations' human rights records, for example, would not seem to fit within any of these categories.

Justice Black's view in *Steel Seizure* appears to mean that in matters outside the powers listed in Article II, Sections 2 and 3, the President would depend upon authorization from Congress. Yet not only has the Constitution never worked this way in practice (including at its outset; see Chapter 4), that view faces its own formidable textual barriers. Congress too has only delegated powers, principally located in the Constitution's Article I, Section 8. These include many foreign affairs powers: declaring war, issuing letters of marque, regulating foreign commerce, and enforcing the law of nations. They do not, however, seem to add up to a general power over foreign affairs. In particular, there is no general power of communication with foreign nations. Even if Congress has implied power to communicate about matters within its enumerated powers, this (like the Article II, Section 2 and 3 powers) is a finite set. Expressing concern about a human rights record, to continue that example, may not fall within it.[12]

In short, it seems hard to stretch the specifically enumerated powers of *any* branch of the national government to cover all the diplomatic activities (and other foreign affairs activities) the national government undertakes. The Constitution appears to lack a default rule, or catchall category: once all the specific foreign affairs powers it mentions are allocated, explained, and defined, what is to be done with the remaining, unmentioned ones? The specific congressional powers in Article I, Section 8 are no more helpful on this point than the specific presidential powers in Article II, Sections 2 and 3.

The President has one further potential source of textual power: by Article II, Section 1, the "executive Power shall be vested in a President of the United States of America." True, at first glance this "vesting clause" also does not seem promising. "Executive" power, in modern terms, is associated with law enforcement. To "execute" a law is to enforce it, to carry it into effect (that is, put it into execution). Executive power seems to be a derivative power—it presupposes laws *to be executed*.[13] With respect to foreign affairs activities such as diplomatic power, there is no law behind what the President does—indeed, that is the whole difficulty. It is hard to speak of the President, in exercising many foreign affairs powers, as enforcing ("executing") laws. If the vesting clause refers only to law execution, it does not resolve the dilemma of unallocated foreign affairs powers.[14]

Perhaps, though, "executive Power" meant something more in the 1780s. Obviously, language changes meaning. The way we understand "executive power" today, at the beginning of the twenty-first century, may differ from the way eighteenth-century speakers understood it. Words do not have intrinsic meaning—only meanings given to them in the context and at the time they are used. To reconstruct what a text meant *at the time it was written,* we must look to see what its relevant words and phrases meant at that time, not in our time.

With this in mind, we quickly encounter evidence of a broader meaning of "executive Power." Thomas Jefferson, in a legal opinion he wrote as Secretary of State in 1790, included diplomatic power as part of Article II, Section 1's "executive" power. Jefferson first observed (quoting the vesting clause) that " 'the Executive powers shall be vested in the President,' submitting only special articles of it to a negative by the senate." He continued: "The transaction of business with foreign nations is Executive altogether; it belongs, then, to the head of that department, except as to such portions of it as are specially submitted to the senate." Matters "specially submitted to the senate" were treatymaking and appointments mentioned in Article II, Section 2; beyond these, Jefferson said, Article II, Section 1 gave diplomatic power to the President.[15]

Perhaps, then, Article II, Section 1 is a way out of the *Curtiss-Wright/Steel Seizure* dilemma. If "executive Power" includes foreign affairs power, the clause could be read to grant ("vest") general diplomatic power to the President. That would (as Jefferson said) not override specific grants of particular foreign affairs powers to the Senate (or, it should be added, to Congress); but it would serve as a catchall allocation of "executive" foreign affairs powers not otherwise specifically mentioned. And this would provide a textual basis for the President's diplomatic power, avoiding the need to rely on *Curtiss-Wright*'s inherent power and allowing Justice Black to make his bold statement in *Steel Seizure.*

Hamilton, another key member of President Washington's administration, expressed a similar view in 1793. In that year, Washington announced, on his own initiative, that the United States would remain neutral in hostilities between Britain and France. Some contemporaries charged that Washington exceeded his constitutional powers by acting without consulting Congress. Hamilton, under the pseudonym "Pacificus," wrote a series of essays in Washington's defense, basing his constitutional argument squarely upon the foreign affairs powers granted by Article II, Section 1. Hamilton (like Jefferson) argued that "executive" power traditionally included foreign affairs power. The power to decide upon neutrality fell within the ordinary scope of "executive power," he said, because the executive was the "*organ* of intercourse between the Nation and foreign Nations." The Constitution gave the President "executive Power," but also gave aspects of the traditional executive foreign affairs power, including war and treatymaking, to other branches. Thus, Hamilton explained, "[t]he general doctrine then of our constitution is, that the EXECUTIVE POWER of the Nation is vested in the President, subject only to the exceptions and qualifications which are expressed in the instrument." And since the power to decide upon neutrality was an executive power and not part of the powers allocated elsewhere, it remained with the executive/President.[16]

Despite these statements by prominent founding-era Americans, modern commentary has not embraced the Jefferson/Hamilton use of "executive" foreign affairs power, and the *Steel Seizure* Justices carefully avoided it—likely for two reasons. First, unless kept within manageable limits, it could give the President uncomfortably broad and ill-defined power. True, Hamilton and Jefferson acknowledged that constitutional provisions such as the treatymaking and declare-war clauses limited the grant of executive power, but these, they said, should be read narrowly; in any event, much that happens in foreign affairs falls outside them. Truman, for example, relied on the executive power clause in *Youngstown,* and if we agree that the clause can be a source of *some* "unenumerated" foreign affairs powers, it may be hard to say why it does not include seizing steel mills to support a war effort (and other things as well).[17]

Second, there may be reason to doubt that Hamilton's Pacificus is a reliable indicator of eighteenth-century meaning. Hamilton was an outlier among his generation in many ways, including on presidential power.[18] Jefferson himself thought Pacificus overreached in some respects and urged his friend Madison—perhaps the preeminent constitutional theorist of his generation—to write a response. Madison published a series of essays under the pseudonym "Helvidius," disagreeing with Pacificus on key points. In particular, Helvidius denied that the vesting clause granted power beyond law execution: "The natural province of the executive magistrate is to execute laws, as that of the legislature is to make laws. All his acts, therefore, properly executive, must pre-suppose the existence of the laws to be executed."[19]

Faced with divergent framers, we may hesitate to claim one as the authoritative voice. Justice Jackson in *Youngstown* made this point, complaining that Madison and Hamilton largely cancel each other, leaving little insight to be gleaned from the views of the founding era.[20] Yet Jackson may have given up too quickly. The question is not whether Madison or Hamilton (or Jefferson) is more authoritative (surely an unanswerable question), but whether one of them echoed common understandings of terms used in the Constitution's text. To decide this matter, it is not sufficient merely to note that they had inconsistent views, for both spoke as advocates of partisan positions. We must, instead, look at the common usage before these positions arose.

Executive Power in Eighteenth-Century Political Writing

An inquiry into the eighteenth-century meaning of "executive power" should, naturally, begin with its dictionary definition. The leading dictionary of the time, Samuel Johnson's, gives something quite close to the intuitive modern meaning: although "executive power" as a phrase is not defined, the word "executive" means, it says, the body that "puts in act the laws"—without mention of foreign affairs.[21] The question, then, is whether we should stop there, with a dictionary-based rejection of the Jefferson/Hamilton usage.

There are reasons to think we should not. Of course Jefferson and Hamilton (as cabinet secretaries) had institutional interests in promoting presidential powers, and Hamilton (though not Jefferson) was a long-time believer in a powerful presidency. But Jefferson and Hamilton must have gotten their definition from somewhere; it is unlikely that they simply made it up, and (as Chapter 4 explores) in general their arguments on this point were well-received at the time. Further inquiry seems appropriate.

This leads to an important point about language and meaning. Particularly in the eighteenth century, when dictionary writing was somewhat new and unsystematic, it may be helpful to look also at the way words and phrases were actually used by influential writers. They can provide supplementary evidence of meaning, especially with respect to phrases that may have become terms of art in their fields.

A good place to start, therefore, is with the political writings that most influenced founding-era Americans. Eighteenth-century Americans were, among other things, products of the intellectual movement known as the Enlightenment, which believed that human problems could be solved by rational inquiry. One focus of Enlightenment scholarship was what Madison later called the "science of politics": Enlightenment writers believed that rational study of human experience and the nature of humankind could allow conclusions about the best governmental structure. That was obviously of interest to eighteenth-century Americans, as they set about designing their own systems of government.[22]

The Theory of Separation of Powers

Our inquiry begins, therefore, with the seventeenth- and eighteenth-century political theory known as separation of powers. Writers in this tradition included an array of famous names who became important influences in America, especially John Locke, Baron de Montesquieu, and William Blackstone.[23] Although, as we shall see, Americans modified the political theorists' ideas in unique ways, the concept of separation of powers remained a cornerstone in their constitutional thought.

The core idea of separation of powers—that governments should be formed by multiple independent branches with distinct constituencies—is of course much older. It formed the basis of the Roman Republic, made up of the consuls, the senate, and the popular assembly,[24] and carried over to describe the English system of king, lords, and commons. But the older form, sometimes called "mixed government," focused more on what the branches represented (monarch, aristocracy, people) than on what they did. What came to the forefront in the seventeenth century and after was the idea that particular functions should be given to particular entities—that is, for effective and nontyrannical government, powers should be separated not just by who exercised them, but by the type of activities they involved.

As scholars who study this period have explained, this approach had at least two key components, one descriptive (or definitional) and the other prescriptive (normative). The descriptive element sought to classify or categorize the different powers or "functions" of government. The prescriptive or normative element outlined how these functions should be allocated among the various institutions of government. These two projects were related, for it was an axiom of separation-of-powers theory that the functions of government should be "separated"—meaning that they should, at least to some extent, be exercised by separate institutions.

As a descriptive matter, the project ultimately settled on a now-familiar trinity of functions: executive, legislative, and judicial. This descriptive division was not obvious; it was uncommon before the end of the seventeenth century (when writers tended to speak only of legislative and executive powers), and later modern versions propose a fourth "administrative" power.[25] But the mid-eighteenth century stood fairly firmly in favor of the three-part division. As John Adams put it in 1775: "A legislative, an executive and a judicial power comprehend the whole of what is meant and understood by government."[26]

This categorization of powers did not turn on what type of institution exercised the power in question. Modern American discourse often speaks in terms of "branches," calling everything the President does "executive," everything Congress does "legislative," and everything courts do "judicial." But eighteenth-century theory held that *every* government exercised the three types of power, even if they were all exercised by a single person (as in a dictatorship). The "legislative" function, for example, consisted of establishing the rights and duties of members of the community through general laws.[27] Acting in this way was exercising "legislative" power, regardless of what body did it—it could be done, for example, by a prince (ruling by decree), by an oligarchy (like the Roman senate), or by a popular assembly.[28] Classification depended on what was done, not on what type of entity did it.

Using the classifications of governmental functions, political theory then sought to allocate these functions among different institutions, in order to produce the best structure for securing rights and maintaining effective government. This was its normative aspect. Here again, by mid-century there was a fair degree of consensus, at least at the broadest level, that there should be three branches of government tracking, at least roughly, the three categories of functions. Lawmaking, for example, should be done by an assembly, which could represent the people and deliberate; law execution should be handled by a single magistrate, who could act swiftly, decisively, and consistently; and dispute resolution should be done by independent courts.

These two aspects of eighteenth-century thought are captured succinctly by the great separation-of-powers scholar M. J. C. Vile:

> The second element in the doctrine [of separation of powers] is the assertion that there are three specific "functions" of government. Unlike the first element, which *recommends* that there should be three branches of government, this second part of the doctrine asserts a sociological truth or "law," that there are in all governmental situations three necessary functions to be performed, whether or not they are in fact all performed by one person or group, or whether there is a division among two or more agencies of government. *All* governmental acts, it is claimed, can be classified as an exercise of the legislative, executive, or judicial functions.[29]

As Professor Vile says elsewhere, separation-of-powers theory "depended heavily upon an abstract formulation of the powers of government *and* the allocation of these functions."[30]

The system's central feature was identifying a lawmaking or "legislative" function and a distinct law-implementation or "executive" function. In an absolute monarchy, one might not see this distinction nor assign it importance: the monarch controlled governmental functions without differentiation, issuing decrees and enforcing them. But England was not an absolute monarchy in the seventeenth and (especially) the eighteenth centuries, because it had developed a distinct power center in Parliament. The revolutionary struggles of the seventeenth century involved attempts to define the relationship between the monarchy and Parliament, and separation-of-powers doctrine evolved in the mid-1600s in large part to give this relationship a theoretical framework. As a general matter, it held, the "legislative" functions of government should be exercised by Parliament, while the "executive" functions should be reserved for the monarch.[31]

Some people, especially in the seventeenth century, argued for a precise identity between the *type* of powers exercised and the *branch* that should exercise them. In this version of what Professor Vile calls "pure" separation of powers, well-functioning and just governments should have an executive branch that exercised only executive powers and a legislative branch that exercised only legislative powers: that is, "each branch of the government must be confined to the exercise of its own function."[32] But this "pure" view of separation of powers never prevailed, in part for practical reasons. The principal institutions of English government—king, lords, and commons—did not map precisely onto the three functions of government, particularly because the veto gave the king (in theory, anyway) a role in legislation. This suggested a different prescriptive version, in which each branch generally exercised its respective functions, but with some overlap to assure what came to be called "checks and balances."[33] As we will see, the combination of separation of powers and checks and balances proved highly influential on founding-era Americans, who embraced some mixing of different types of power in the same branch and some distribution of types of power across several branches.[34]

Separation of Powers and Foreign Affairs

Foreign affairs did not materially figure in this system until John Locke's *Second Treatise of Government* (1690). Locke conventionally (for his time) described executive power as concerned with enforcing the laws within society, combining the modern categories of law enforcement and judicial power. But closely allied to this power, he said, was another he called the "federative power": the power over "War and Peace, Leagues and Alliances, and all the Transactions, with all Persons and Communities" outside of the nation.[35]

Locke thought executive and federative powers were related but distinct. Law execution depended upon existing law; federative power required discretion. As Locke put it, federative power could not depend upon "antecedent, standing, positive Laws" because actions taken with respect to foreigners "depend[ed] much upon their actions, and the variation of designs and interests," and thus could not be delineated in advance. For Locke, then, federative power was not "executive" in the sense of carrying out pre-existing law. Locke thought, though, that federative and executive powers should be held by the same branch of government. They "are hardly to be separated, and placed . . . in the hands of distinct Persons" because both require command of the "force of the Society"; to vest them in separate hands would cause "disorder and ruine" because the "Force of the Publick" would be divided. Indeed, Locke himself sometimes used the terms interchangeably (despite earlier insisting on their distinctness). At one point he said that the executive power decides "how far Injuries from without [society] are to be vindicated," though plainly here he meant federative power, not law execution power.[36] In short, while Locke described two distinct powers, he identified a close relationship between them, and so laid the groundwork for eighteenth-century writers to unite them in a single category.

Montesquieu's *The Spirit of Laws* (1748) took that key step. Like Locke—but even more strongly—Montesquieu emphasized that liberty depended upon separating lawmaking and law execution. But unlike Locke, Montesquieu classified foreign affairs and law execution functions as two types of "executive" power, and abandoned the label "federative." "In every government," he wrote, "there are three sorts of power: the legislative; the executive, in respect to things dependent on the law of nations; and the executive, in regard to things that depend on the civil law." He specifically listed as "executive" the principal foreign affairs powers: making war and peace, sending or receiving embassies, establishing public security, and protecting against invasions.[37] Indeed, as a leading modern scholar concludes, "Montesquieu, like most writers of his time, was inclined to think of the executive branch of government as being concerned nearly entirely with foreign affairs." Or, as

M. J. C. Vile puts it, in Montesquieu's work "for Locke's 'federative power' read 'executive power.' "[38]

Montesquieu's definitions carry over into a second crucial work of the mid-eighteenth century: Blackstone's *Commentaries.* William Blackstone, an Oxford law professor, published his four-volume *Commentaries on the Laws of England* between 1760 and 1765. Like many law professors' commentary, it was a mix of what the law was and what the law should be, and so must be used cautiously. Blackstone wrote about the whole range of English law, much of which had nothing to do with separation of powers, and he ignored important constitutional developments of his own time, such as the emergence of the ministerial system of government that came to dominate in the next century.[39] But importantly for our purposes, Blackstone gave an influential account of English constitutional structure, including in foreign affairs. He borrowed heavily from Montesquieu, frequently without attribution; in turn, he heavily influenced eighteenth-century Americans, who regarded his work (perhaps too generously) as a definitive description of the English legal system.

Like Montesquieu, Blackstone described foreign affairs authority as part of "executive" power. He began by noting that "[t]he supreme executive power of these kingdoms is vested by our laws in a single person, the king or queen." In describing the powers "the exertion whereof consists the executive part of government," Blackstone emphasized "foreign concerns." Under the executive authority, he said, the monarch "has the sole power of sending embassadors to foreign states, and receiving embassadors at home"; may "make treaties, leagues, and alliances with foreign states and princes"; has "the sole prerogative of making war and peace"; and has "the power of issuing letters of marque and reprisal when his subjects have suffered some depredation at the hands of a foreign country and have not received satisfaction." According to Blackstone, the executive monarch "is the delegate or representative of his people" who transacts "the affairs of that state" with "another community."[40]

Contemporaries of Blackstone and Montesquieu shared this terminology. Thomas Rutherforth, a leading eighteenth-century English commentator on international law, wrote that the primary function of the executive was law enforcement, but in conventional descriptions

> [t]he second branch of executive power, which is called external executive power . . . is the power of acting with the common strength or joynt force of the society to guard against such injuries, as threaten it

from without; to obtain amends for the damages arising from such injuries; or to inflict punishment upon the authors and abettors of them.[41]

Similarly, Jean de Lolme's *The Constitution of England* (1771)—an influential if idealized treatment of English government—described the monarch's "executive" power to include serving as "the representative and depository of all the power and collective majesty of the nation; he sends and receives ambassadors; he contracts alliances; and has the prerogative of declaring war, and of making peace."[42]

At the time of the Constitution's drafting and ratification, then, key English and European political writers called law execution power and foreign affairs power collectively "executive" powers. The Constitution's drafters and ratifiers surely knew this, for Blackstone and Montesquieu, in particular, were the leading authorities to whom founding-era Americans turned for guidance in structuring their new government. Blackstone was Americans' "standard authorit[y]" on matters of English law, and Montesquieu was their most revered writer on separation of powers: as one historian writes, Americans "could recite the central points of Montesquieu's doctrine as if it had been a catechism."[43] Madison described Blackstone's *Commentaries* as "a book which is in every man's hand" and Montesquieu as "the oracle who is always consulted and cited" on separation of powers.[44] De Lolme and Rutherforth also appear among writers familiar to eighteenth-century Americans.[45]

It is also true, as some modern presidential advocates emphasize, that Montesquieu, Blackstone, and others believed that "executive" foreign affairs powers should be concentrated in a single magistrate (the king) to achieve the best structure of government. But this is not the main lesson of the political writers; rather, it is something of a distraction. As with separation-of-powers theory more generally, Montesquieu's approach to foreign affairs had a definitional element and a prescriptive element. The definitional element defined foreign affairs powers as "executive" powers. The prescriptive element *recommended* that these powers be placed in a single magistrate. As we will see, the Constitution's drafters did not embrace the recommendation, at least not completely: they added important elements of checks and balances by distributing key "executive" powers away from the President. The important point is not how Montesquieu, Blackstone, and other political writers thought "executive" power *should* be allocated, but rather how they used language. Anyone versed in the eighteenth-century political writers would have understood that they used the phrase "executive power" to mean law execution *and* conduct of foreign affairs, regardless of how those powers were allocated in particular countries.[46] When Jefferson and Hamilton later used "executive power" in this way, they followed a common usage of eighteenth-century political writing familiar to educated Americans.[47]

Executive Power and Foreign Affairs in the Early Years of Independence

We should next look for evidence that eighteenth-century Americans adopted the vocabulary of political writers such as Montesquieu and Blackstone in the years leading up to the Constitutional Convention. As discussed (Chapter 2), the Continental Congress assumed broad foreign affairs functions, either *ad hoc* (in the earliest years) or (after 1781) under the express provisions of the Articles of Confederation. Although its foreign affairs powers were far from comprehensive, they included most of the basic components of international diplomatic and military interaction. Indeed, it would not exaggerate to say that managing foreign affairs was the Congress's primary mission, particularly after the conclusion of the domestic war effort; the Articles left internal affairs principally to state governments.

It is especially notable, therefore, that both contemporaneous and modern writing describes the Continental Congress as an *executive* body. Theophilus Parsons's influential pamphlet called the *Essex Result,* drafted during the debate over the Massachusetts state constitution (1778), adopted Montesquieu's terms (and foreshadowed Jefferson and Hamilton) in observing that

> [t]he executive power is sometimes divided into the external executive, and internal executive. The former comprehends war, peace, the sending and receiving ambassadors, and whatever concerns the transactions of the state with any other independent state.

"The confederation of the United States of America," the *Result* continued, "hath lopped off this branch of the executive, and placed it in Congress."[48]

Similarly, in 1785 Madison wrote that the state governors were of lesser importance because "all of the great powers which are properly executive [were] transferd to the Federal Government" by the Articles. By this, historian Jack Rakove confirms, Madison meant "the matters of war and diplomacy which were prerogatives of the British Crown."[49] Madison necessarily meant foreign affairs powers, because the Articles did not vest the Congress with much law execution power, which mainly remained with state governors. Rakove further records that Americans called the Congress a "deliberating Executive assembly," the "Supreme Executive," or the "Supreme Executive Council"; he adds that "[t]he idea that Congress was essentially an executive body persisted because its principal functions, war and diplomacy, were traditionally associated with the crown, whose executive, political prerogatives b[ore] a very striking resemblance to the powers of Congress."[50] During the ratification debates, such leading figures as James Wilson and Edmund Randolph described the Congress as principally an executive institution, as Jefferson and others did later.[51] Indeed, modern historians commonly refer to the Congress as an "executive" body.[52]

As the comments of Madison, Parsons, and others indicate, the Congress could be called "executive" because it principally exercised foreign affairs powers.[53] For the most part, the Congress did not have law execution power, because there was little federal law. The Congress had isolated pockets of lawmaking power in particular areas committed to it, such as the western territories, the Army, and the mail, and in these areas the Congress also had law execution power. But this was not the bulk of the Congress's business—foreign affairs was. And with respect to foreign affairs, as we saw in Chapter 2, the Congress for the most part did not have lawmaking power: it could not enact tariffs, regulate foreign commerce, or implement treaties or international law. But it did have authority over *non-legislative* aspects of foreign affairs: war and peace, ambassadors, foreign policy, and international communications. These were precisely the foreign affairs powers that Montesquieu and Blackstone called "executive," so it is no wonder that Americans thought the Congress principally had executive powers. As historian Rakove puts it, the Congress "had the appearance of a legislature but responsibilities customarily associated with the Crown."[54]

This explains, too, why the Articles' drafters paid little attention to separation of powers at the national level, even though separation of powers became near-orthodoxy in state constitutions of the time.[55] The Congress above all was a foreign affairs executive, and the great political theorists said that foreign affairs power should be unified. Nonetheless, Americans had bad experiences with executive power in the hands of the English monarchs and royal governors. Rather than creating a powerful, single executive, they created a deliberative, heavily constrained, plural executive—the Continental Congress. But because the Congress's business was principally executive, there was no need for multiple branches of government separating power at the national level.

Yet Americans quickly began to see that a deliberative body made a poor executive. Foreign affairs required secrecy, speed, and consistency, which

their plural, fluctuating executive Congress lacked. The Congress tried to respond, in 1781, by creating the Department of Foreign Affairs, headed by a
Secretary. This did little to mitigate the problems, because the Secretary had
no independent authority and depended on the Congress's direction;[56] soon,
some of the sharpest criticism came from the most prominent Secretary,
John Jay. Jay described the Congress's inability to exercise executive (foreign
affairs) power, urging the adoption of a new framework. To Washington, Jay
wrote that "[t]he executive business of sovereignty depending on so many
wills" in the Congress "will in general be but feebly done," and to Jefferson
he wrote that "[t]o vest legislative, judicial and executive powers in one and
the same body of men, and that too in a body daily changing its members,
can never be wise. In my opinion those three great departments of sovereignty should be forever separated, and distributed as to serve as checks on
each other."[57]

The Congress's shortcomings helped motivate the Philadelphia Convention to create a single executive who would provide confidentiality, speed,
and stability.[58] Indeed, as we will see, the initial impulse was simply to shift
the Congress's executive powers in a block to a new executive entity. But because the new executive was to be one person (or, at least, not a deliberative
body) that raised the difficulty of unchecked power. This produced, in the
final document, a result the political theorists would not have countenanced:
dispersion of executive foreign affairs authority across multiple bodies.

Executive Power, Foreign Affairs, and the Philadelphia Convention

The Philadelphia Convention began in 1787 with two leading foreign affairs
objectives: to give the national government additional powers missing under
the Articles, and to reallocate the power it did have so that foreign affairs
could be conducted effectively. Virginia's Governor Randolph opened the
debate by highlighting the Articles' deficiencies, particularly in foreign affairs. He then introduced what has become known as the "Virginia plan," an
outline of government prepared by the Virginia delegation that became the
starting point for discussions in the Convention. The Virginia plan envisioned separate executive, legislative, and judicial branches, with the executive branch having both aspects of the executive power as understood by
Montesquieu and Blackstone. As the plan put it, "besides a general authority
to execute the National laws" the executive "ought to enjoy the Executive
rights vested in Congress by the Confederation."[59]

When Randolph's plan referred to "Executive rights vested in Congress by the Confederation," it must have meant executive foreign affairs powers. The plan already gave the executive branch law execution power (and in any event the Articles' Congress had little of that). The Congress's executive "rights" were mainly foreign affairs powers (as Madison and Parsons indicated earlier), and Randolph's plan did not otherwise allocate foreign affairs power. The terminology (and the recognition of two categories of executive power) directly tracks Montesquieu and the *Essex Result*.

Other delegates recognized what the plan might mean, and it met a barrage of criticism. Charles Pinckney opposed the grant of the "Executive powers of (the existing) Congress" to the new executive, because such powers "might extend to peace & war &c which would render the Executive a Monarchy." John Rutledge opposed vesting the "power of war and peace" in the executive. James Wilson "did not consider the Prerogatives of the British Monarch as a proper guide in defining the Executive powers. Some of those prerogatives were of a Legislative nature. Among others that of war & peace &c." Madison agreed: "[E]xecutive powers ex vi termini do not include the rights of war & peace &c." Madison then moved to strike the plan's list of executive powers and say instead that the executive would implement national laws, appoint officers, and "execute such other powers as may from time to time be delegated by the legislature." The substance of Madison's motion passed, eliminating reference to the executive powers of the old Congress.[60]

These criticisms of the Virginia plan, and the plan's subsequent modification, show that delegates understood "executive rights" to include foreign affairs powers. This explains why Pinckney and Rutledge objected to Randolph's plan on the ground that it gave too many foreign affairs powers to the new executive (even though the plan did not mentioned any foreign affairs powers by name). True, some delegates (principally Wilson and Madison) argued that some of the old Congress's "executive" powers were really legislative and that the true scope of executive power extended only to law execution. Yet these same delegates recognized that common understandings of "executive" power included foreign affairs powers—hence their objection to the proposal and their support for Madison's substitute that omitted this phrasing. The debate over the Virginia plan thus confirms that delegates understood the Montesquieu-ian vocabulary that called foreign affairs powers "executive," while at the same time they rejected Montesquieu's prescription that all executive powers should be held by the same person.[61]

No further sustained consideration of foreign affairs occurred for some time, until the Committee of Detail began the process of finalizing the Constitution's text. As the Committee's initial draftsman, Randolph (displaying new sensitivity to concerns about concentration of foreign affairs authority) specifically allocated the key foreign affairs powers: in an early draft, Congress would "make war," "enact articles of war," send ambassadors, punish offenses against the law of nations, and declare the law of piracy and captures; either Congress or the Senate alone would make treaties. At this stage, the draft did not assign "executive" power by name, and the President's only apparent foreign affairs power was to receive ambassadors. But there was also no catchall category of foreign affairs powers, to allocate powers not specifically listed (such as foreign policy and diplomacy).[62]

Wilson, who earlier spoke against granting the old Congress's "executive rights" to the President, drafted the Committee's final report, which partially restored the wording dropped from the Virginia plan. Congress had "legislative power" along with specific foreign affairs authorities: making war, regulating captures, punishing piracy and law-of-nations offenses, raising armies, and building fleets. The Senate would make treaties and appoint ambassadors. And, in Wilson's version, the President had the "executive Power of the United States."[63] This would not give the President the broad external executive power of the Virginia plan, because key powers such as war and treaties had now been assigned to other branches, according to the wishes delegates expressed in the initial debate over the Virginia plan. But it did seem restore to the President a residual category of foreign affairs powers not granted elsewhere—because (as the debate over the Virginia plan showed) delegates understood "executive" powers to include foreign affairs powers.

The Committee's proposed allocation apparently generated little opposition. Delegates could now accept the assignment of "executive" power to the President, because its new incarnation was much more limited than what the Virginia plan proposed. Their earlier objections had run principally to the President's possession of war and treaty powers, and Wilson's new proposal ensured that the President would not have these powers.

Once the Convention accepted the Committee's language, delegates seemed to assume a significant presidential role in foreign affairs. Pinckney (who had opposed the "executive" power portion of the Virginia plan) and Gouverneur Morris proposed a "Council of State" with a Secretary of Foreign Affairs, serving at the President's "pleasure," to "correspond with all foreign Ministers, prepare plans of Treaties, & consider such as may be transmitted from abroad; and generally to attend to the interests of the U- S- in their connection to foreign powers." The Council idea was subsequently abandoned (in part, we may suppose, because delegates thought the President would appoint subordinates), but it assumed substantial presidential responsibility for key diplomatic functions, and no one objected to it on those grounds. Crucially, at this point the *only* foreign affairs functions the draft gave the President were receiving ambassadors and the general "executive power"; only later did the delegates modify the draft to give the President a role in treatymaking and ambassadorial appointments.[64]

We should be careful not to draw too many conclusions from the Convention, whose records are incomplete and were not published until long after the Constitution was ratified. But several points seem well established. The delegates understood the common association of "executive" power with foreign affairs power. Some delegates did not want the new President to have key foreign affairs powers, such as power over war and peace, and thus objected to Randolph's initial grant of the old Congress's "Executive rights" to the new executive. The Convention initially responded by limiting the President to law execution and by allocating key foreign affairs powers to the Senate and Congress. When the delegates restored the President's general "executive" power in the Committee of Detail, they likely understood this as reviving the earlier idea of executive foreign affairs powers, but subject to important exceptions created by the specific allocations to Congress and the Senate. Delegates had objected to the President having "executive" power because that would include foreign affairs powers they thought should not be concentrated, such as war and treatymaking; but once the draft allocated those powers elsewhere, the delegates became comfortable with the President having "executive" power. Yet they could not have thought that "executive power" no longer included foreign affairs power in general—it simply no longer included the particular foreign affairs powers to which they had earlier objected. In short, the process of creating a catchall executive power in foreign affairs, subject to the allocation of particular foreign affairs powers to other branches, is manifest in the drafting process.[65]

Executive Power and the Ratifying Debates

To confirm this reading of the drafting process, we would ordinarily turn to the ratification debates. These debates, though, at first glance seem somewhat inconclusive. The President's foreign affairs powers were not a major issue in the debates, and when they were discussed, speakers tended to focus on specific powers such as war and treatymaking. Perhaps this was because ratifiers assumed the President would not have unspecified diplomatic powers,[66] but that would seem to leave a substantial block of power unallocated, and there is no record of anyone finding the Constitution incomplete in this respect. It seems more likely that the ratifiers—using the familiar association of "executive" powers and foreign affairs powers—recognized that the Constitution assigned the President general diplomatic powers, but found this unremarkable (because the key powers of declaring war and making treaties were allocated elsewhere).[67]

The common association of "executive" power with foreign affairs power is, though, confirmed by a distinct debate. Much commentary said that the Senate would exercise "executive" powers. The Senate's role in appointments gave the Senate an element of executive power, but speakers also insisted that the Senate's role in treatymaking shifted "executive" power from the President to the Senate. As one leading anti-federalist put it: "The senate . . . is also part of the executive, having a negative in the making of all treaties. . . ."[68] This arrangement became a target of anti-federalist objections, especially in Pennsylvania: it violated the supposed maxim that governmental powers should be strictly separated. Anti-federalist John Smilie said that Senators had "an alarming share of the executive," given their treatymaking role. Pennsylvania's *Dissent of the Minority* agreed that the Senate had "various and great executive powers, viz: in concurrence with the President general, they form treaties with foreign nations."[69]

Federalists generally agreed that treatymaking was executive, but they defended the Constitution's sharing of executive power as an element of checks and balances. Virginia's "Cassius," for example, wrote that "the power of making treaties [has] always been considered, as part of the executive" and that the Senate's participation would be a check on a power that had been "safely exercised in other countries, by the executive authority alone." John Pringle in South Carolina argued that "The making of treaties . . . properly belongs to the executive part of government" because only that branch could act with secrecy and dispatch. William Maclaine in North Carolina observed that when the President made treaties, he acted "in his executive capacity."[70]

Although not directly concerned with the President's general foreign affairs powers, debates over the Senate's treatymaking role confirm that in ordinary language "executive" power included foreign affairs powers. Many ratifiers said that treatymaking was executive in nature. (This view carried over into the post-ratification period: the Senate's 1789 records state that, when considering treaties, the Senate "entered on Executive business.")[71] But treatymaking is not a law execution power. Those who thought that treatymaking was "executive" must have thought that "executive power" meant more than law execution—and, specifically, that it included foreign affairs power (as Blackstone and Montesquieu said it did).[72] This did not mean that they thought, necessarily, that foreign affairs powers always had to be allocated to the President: except to a few uncompromising advocates of "pure" separation of powers, how a power was classified did not dictate who was to exercise it. It does tend to confirm, though, that when the Constitution said the President had "executive" powers, the ratifiers read that to include foreign affairs power (except where the text said otherwise).

The ratifying debates are also important for what was not said. No one complained that the Constitution produced an incomplete allocation of foreign affairs power. To modern commentators, the Constitution's supposed gaps in foreign affairs are self-evident. Yet despite an intense if somewhat disorganized scrutiny in the ratification process, apparently no one noticed what modern commentators now think is obvious. The most likely explanation, of course, is that the ratifiers gave the text a different meaning. As students of Montesquieu and Blackstone, and participants in the debates over the foreign affairs powers of the Continental Congress, they associated executive power with foreign affairs power (as well as law execution power); thus they recognized that foreign affairs powers not specifically mentioned were not omissions but would fall within the "executive Power" of the President.

Further, the debates do not suggest that Congress under the Constitution would be the primary decisionmaker in foreign affairs (as the Continental Congress was under the Articles). If anything, Congress's foreign affairs role went somewhat understated. This is crucial, because one might think (as Madison later argued)[73] that executive power presupposes an act of Congress—that is, that "executive" means only law execution. If so, Congress needs a general power over foreign affairs, and the President would act in this field only at Congress's direction. Yet the ratification debates did not foresee a major foreign affairs role for Congress.

As with the Convention records, it is important not to read too much into the ratifying debates. Our records are similarly incomplete, and foreign affairs was not the main focus of the debate. Further, many views about the Constitution were expressed, some of them ill considered or downright silly. And in any event, we are seeking the best objective reading of the Constitution's text, not assembling the ratifiers' collective consensus upon each specific point (even assuming such a thing were possible). But the debates are useful in identifying common understandings of constitutional language. The ratifiers were much closer to that language and its context than we are, and although they frequently disagreed, they often had common linguistic starting points which, though well ingrained in their day, may have become obscured in ours.

This seems to be true of the phrase "executive Power." As in earlier periods, the ratifiers seem to have understood executive power, as a general term, to include foreign affairs power. Thus it is plausible to identify a common understanding of the use of "executive Power" in the Constitution's Article II, Section 1 to include foreign affairs power (subject, of course, to specific allocations of foreign affairs power elsewhere).[74]

Although important and powerful, there may remain some question whether this evidence is decisive. As we shall see, there are substantial scholarly objections, explored in Chapter 6. Among other things, some definitions of executive power sought to limit it to law execution (as Madison, for one, did in his Helvidius essays). At this point, we may not be able to say more than that *one* meaning of "executive Power" included foreign affairs power. More exploration is needed. The next chapter takes up another important piece of the puzzle: the understanding of "executive Power" in the years immediately following the Constitution's ratification. While the next chapter will emphasize the pitfalls of using this sort of evidence, it will also suggest that in this case, post-ratification practice provides important clues to the Constitution's meaning.

4

Executive Foreign Affairs Power and the Washington Administration

We can now see an eighteenth-century meaning of the phrase "executive power" that had, as the *Essex Result* outlined, internal and external components. "Internal" executive power was the law execution power we commonly associate with the executive branch. "External" executive power included foreign affairs powers. The Constitution divided the previously unified executive foreign affairs powers by giving some of them to Congress, and some to the Senate. But the Constitution's final version also gave "executive Power" generally to the President. This presumably included law execution power,[1] but we can also read it to include the "executive" foreign affairs powers not given to other branches—such as diplomatic communication, controlling ambassadors, and formulating foreign policy. Doing so fills what would otherwise be a substantial gap in the text, which does not seem otherwise to address these powers.

Events after ratification tend to confirm this reading. President Washington, taking office in 1789, immediately took control of diplomatic affairs, without congressional authorization and without sustained objection. And when key leaders explained why he had control over these matters, they relied on the President's executive power, "vested" by Article II, Section 1.[2]

Of course, using this "post-ratification" evidence carries its own caveats and dangers. Once the Constitution was ratified and its government began operating, American leaders developed personal, political, and institutional commitments to views not necessarily founded upon anything in the Constitution's text. Many issues of constitutional law were closely debated from the outset, and (as Justice Jackson said) merely citing one side of these debates lacks much probative value. Nonetheless, post-ratification evidence can be useful in at least two important respects. It can be evidence of background assumptions, if it shows broad consensus upon particular principles. And it

74

can show how founding-era Americans used language—and that in turn can suggest what words in the Constitution's text meant at the time they were written.[3]

In each case, the value of post-ratification evidence diminishes the farther one looks beyond ratification. Although later chapters will (cautiously) look beyond Washington's administration, this chapter focuses on *immediate* post-ratification experiences of 1789–1797.

Executive Power under the Constitution: Early Practice

The President's Control over Diplomacy

Washington promptly established himself as, in the words of two distinguished historians, "the sole channel of official intercourse with foreign governments" and the "foreign-policy-maker-in-chief."[4] When he took office in early 1789, the old Congress's Department of Foreign Affairs, headed by John Jay, remained in place. Washington took control of the Department, treating Jay as his subordinate and using terms such as "order" and "direct." Jay, of course, had been appointed by and answered to the old Congress. But Jay now repeatedly wrote that he acted "in obedience to" or "in pursuance of" the "orders" of the President, whereas he previously had customarily described himself as acting "in obedience to the commands of Congress." Both men saw that something in the Constitution fundamentally shifted foreign affairs authority.[5]

Washington also took control of foreign communications. Previously, the Articles' Congress had received and directed diplomatic correspondence. Writing to the Emperor of Morocco in 1789, Washington explained that since he was now "the supreme executive Authority," the Emperor's letter to the Congress had been delivered to him, and he had authority to answer it. Also in 1789, Washington wrote to France's Louis XVI that "by the change which has taken place in the national government of the United States," he had the "honor of receiving and answering" the king's earlier letter to the Congress. Washington did not consult the new Congress on these matters, even though under the old system, the Articles' Congress controlled diplomatic communication.[6]

The new Congress, rather than objecting to this revolution in diplomatic authority, confirmed it in its July 1789 Act creating a new "Executive department," initially called the Department of Foreign Affairs (later changed to the Department of State), headed by a Secretary. Unlike under the Articles, whose Secretary of Foreign Affairs answered to the Congress, the new Secretary had authority over diplomatic communications and other matters respecting foreign affairs "in such manner as the President of the United States shall from time to time order or instruct."[7] Neither the Secretary nor the Department owed duties to Congress; instead, the Secretary was, as one congressman described, "as much an instrument in the hands of the President, as the pen is the instrument of the Secretary in corresponding with foreign courts." Although the Act envisioned the President delegating foreign affairs authority to the Secretary, neither it nor any other statute gave the President foreign affairs authority in the first place. Congress must have assumed the President had this authority from some other source, presumably the Constitution. As another representative explained, "all the duties detailed in the bill are, by the Constitution, pertaining to the department of the Executive Magistrate."[8]

As initially proposed, the Act would have stated that the President could remove the Secretary. Unlike its other provisions, this ignited substantial constitutional debate: some members objected that Congress or the Senate should have removal authority, or that removal could only be done through impeachment. The House (urged by Madison) ultimately modified the bill to make clear that the President's removal authority came from the Constitution:[9] rather than conveying removal authority, the Act's final version stated that the Department's chief clerk would take charge of its records if the Secretary "shall be removed from office by the President."[10] Because the statute assumed rather than conveyed removal authority, it (as Madison intended) indicated that the President had removal authority as a result of the President's constitutional control over foreign affairs. The final version passed comfortably in the House, but in the Senate needed the tie-breaking vote of Vice President Adams. Notably, no one seems to have doubted that the President would control the Secretary; the question was whether control extended to removal.[11]

Washington next asked Congress for funds so that "intercourse with other nations should be facilitated, by such provisions as will enable me to fulfill my duty in that respect"—confirming his belief that he had *constitutional* power over diplomatic affairs, since no statute assigned him any such "duty." In response, again after substantial debate, Congress provided an annual diplomatic budget, set maximum salaries for U.S. ministers, and made the President responsible for establishing pay grades and disbursing funds.[12]

Some members, led by Virginia's Richard Bland Lee, wanted to provide for the Senate's concurrence in setting the ranks and salaries of particular diplomats. Washington thought this infringed his constitutional powers, and after extended debate Congress appeared to agree—the House rejected Lee's motion, and Congress provided only a general diplomatic budget, leaving substantial presidential discretion on how it should be allocated.[13]

With the new structure in place, Washington continued to control U.S. diplomacy. Jefferson, the new Secretary of State, like Jay operated under Washington's complete direction. Washington also treated the U.S. diplomatic corps as a whole as his subordinates, issuing orders directly or approving instructions drafted by Jefferson, without input from Congress.[14] Most significantly, Washington unilaterally removed U.S. diplomatic agents, again without any statutory authority. In 1793, at France's request, he recalled the U.S. ambassador, Gouverneur Morris. In 1796, on his own initiative, he recalled Morris's successor, James Monroe; Monroe, an enthusiastic supporter of revolutionary France, became increasingly at odds with Washington as the latter worked (unilaterally) toward a diplomatic breakthrough with Britain. Neither Congress nor the Senate had involvement in (or, apparently, even prior knowledge of) either recall. Under the Articles, in contrast, the Congress had recalled John Adams as minister to Britain as recently as 1788.[15]

Conversely, the new Congress (unlike the old) did not claim diplomatic authority. Congress did not communicate directly with other countries (as the old Congress had), nor direct the President to do so. Instead, Congress sometimes *asked* the President to convey messages, in terms styled as requests to an independent body, not as commands.[16] As Jefferson wrote in 1791, "Congress can only correspond through the Executive."[17]

The importance of these events is underscored if we remember the old Congress's complete control over diplomatic matters. A 1782 congressional resolution directed, for example: "All letters to sovereign power, letters of credence, plans of treaties, conventions, manifestoes, instructions, passports, safe conducts and other acts of Congress relative to the department of foreign affairs, when the substance thereof shall have been previously agreed to in Congress, shall be reduced to form in the office of foreign affairs, and submitted to the approval of Congress, and when passed, signed and attended to, sent to the office of foreign affairs to be countersigned and forwarded." The Articles' Secretary of Foreign Affairs was, one diplomatic historian relates, "regarded as little more than a congressional clerk."[18] The events of 1789–1790 worked a revolution in U.S. diplomatic practice, shifting diplomatic powers from the old Congress to the new President; everyone involved seemed to agree, and to attribute the shift to the Constitution.

The President and Foreign Diplomatic Agents

Washington also took full control over dealings with foreign emissaries, best reflected in the activities of the troublesome French ambassador Edouard Genet in 1793.[19] Genet's very arrival raised difficulties, for he was the first emissary from post-revolution republican France. The United States had to decide whether to recognize the French Republic, thus repudiating Louis XVI. In April 1793, Washington asked his cabinet thirteen questions regarding relations with France, the second being whether to receive the republican ambassador. The cabinet agreed that Washington should receive Genet, and Washington did—without consultation with or direction from Congress.[20]

Of course, "receiv[ing]" foreign ambassadors is an explicit presidential power in Article II, Section 3; perhaps this power encompasses recognizing (and de-recognizing) foreign regimes. But Washington also exercised authority over foreign consuls (lower-grade diplomatic postings), not mentioned in Article II, Sections 2 or 3. By international practice, foreign consuls required an "exequatur"—a document from the host country permitting the consul to undertake consular functions.[21] The Articles' Congress had formally recognized consuls but left exequaturs to the state where the consul would be located.[22] Washington, without congressional authorization, began issuing exequaturs himself, insisting upon total formal control over the process. When post-revolution France began establishing consulates in 1793, it addressed its consuls' commissions to Congress. At Washington's direction, Jefferson explained that commissions should be addressed to the President.[23] When Genet objected that Congress was the proper authority, Jefferson replied:

> [The President] being the only channel of communication between this country and foreign nations, it is from him alone that foreign nations or their agents are to learn what is or has been the will of the nation; and whatever he communicates as such, they have a right, and are bound to consider as the expression of the nation, and no foreign agent can be allowed to question it, to interpose between him and any other branch of Government, under the pretext of either's transgressing their functions, nor to make himself the umpire and final judge between them.[24]

Jefferson, on Washington's orders, returned two French commissions addressed to Congress and told Genet that Washington would not issue exequaturs unless the underlying commissions were addressed to Washington.

As Jefferson further explained, after Genet again objected, under the Articles commissions were addressed either to the United States or to Congress, the latter "being then the executive as well as legislative," but under the Constitution, commissions must be addressed to the President (or to the United States generally).[25]

Washington also unilaterally directed recalls of foreign diplomats. In 1788, the Congress (through Jay) requested that France recall its minister Count de Moustier.[26] But in 1793, when French vice consul Antoine Duplaine interfered with a U.S. marshal's seizure of a ship, Washington unilaterally revoked Duplaine's exequatur.[27] Soon afterward, Washington asked France to recall the obstructive Ambassador Genet.[28] No one suggested that these decisions needed to be approved by (or even explained to) Congress.

The President's Control over Foreign Policy

Washington also determined the *content* of U.S. foreign policy, again as highlighted by events in 1793. The news of war between Britain and France—coinciding with Genet's arrival—forced the United States to decide its policy toward the belligerents: strict neutrality favoring neither side, "benevolent" neutrality that as a practical matter favored France, or open support of France. This decision was complicated because the revolutionary-era Treaty of Alliance (signed in 1778) remained in force and might be read to require assistance to France.[29]

Following his cabinet's advice, Washington did not recall Congress (which was then in recess). Instead he decided unilaterally to adopt strict neutrality between Britain and France. With full cabinet support, Washington issued what has become known as the neutrality proclamation, declaring that the United States would "with sincerity and good faith adopt and pursue a conduct friendly and impartial toward the belligerent Powers."[30] The policy's substance, as developed by Washington in ensuing months, was that France would receive no U.S. assistance in the conflict.[31]

Given U.S. military weakness, there was little prospect of joining the actual fighting. The French knew this and never sought U.S. entry into the war. But France did expect the United States to render nonmilitary assistance (and deny assistance to Britain). Specifically, France sought to use U.S. territory to equip and commission privateers, repair ships, condemn prizes, and enlist soldiers and sailors.[32] The question was whether the United States would permit it.

This was a decision of considerable magnitude, and neither law nor policy dictated an obvious answer. Nothing in U.S. treaties or laws, or international law or practice, required neutrality as Washington defined it. Although international theorists wrote inconclusively on neutrals' obligations, and U.S. diplomats later claimed that international law required neutrality, in fact there was ample precedent for what France wanted. European nations frequently followed "benevolent neutrality" favoring one side without engaging in actual hostilities.[33]

Of course, helping France risked war with Britain, but many Americans sympathized with republican France, and in any event refusing assistance might cause France to take what it wanted by force. Local decisionmakers initially adopted policies approaching benevolent neutrality. South Carolina Governor William Moultrie, for example, received Genet when the latter landed at Charleston; Moultrie encouraged Genet to arm privateers and organize expeditions against Spanish Florida.[34] France's sympathizers urged this course nationally, and the United States might well have followed Moultrie's lead—favoring France without actually entering the war. Even after the proclamation, the United States might have gone some way in this direction, given the proclamation's generality. The core of Washington's policy, however, was not just the proclamation, but also strict interpretation of its requirements; for example, the President declared that French privateers should not be outfitted and asked governors such as Moultrie to stop cooperating in such endeavors.

In short, this was a serious policy matter with enormous implications that might easily have been decided differently (as Jefferson, perhaps, preferred).[35] In resolving it, Washington and his cabinet believed the President could act unilaterally, as they decided against reconvening Congress, and Congress, once back in session, congratulated Washington on his actions without raising constitutional concerns.[36]

In sum, Washington exercised independent foreign affairs powers from the beginning of his administration. He took control of the Department of Foreign Affairs (later the State Department). He took control of communications with foreign nations and determined the content of those communications. He instructed, communicated with, and removed U.S. ambassadors. He decided whether to recognize foreign governments and whether to accept their ambassadors and consuls; if those ambassadors or consuls offended him, he directed their recall. And he decided the policy positions of the United States, especially during the most serious foreign policy crisis of the early 1790s. In sum, as one scholar puts it, "[t]here is . . . no real basis for factual disagreement with the assertion that Washington's administration took an active and indeed leading role in the formulation and implementation of United States foreign policy during the first years of government under the Constitution."[37]

Washington acted with little or no basis in the specific constitutional powers of his office,[38] and with little or no congressional authorization.[39] Yet he also acted with little or no congressional objection. With few exceptions, everyone seemed to recognize that Washington was exercising the powers of his office granted by the Constitution. This is difficult to square with the view that the President requires Congress's authorization to act in foreign affairs outside of specifically enumerated powers, or that the Constitution has crippling gaps in its allocation of foreign affairs powers.

If Washington had merely taken over the duties of a prior office under the Articles, one might understand him uncontroversially exercising power without clear authorization. But under the Articles, the Congress exercised most of these powers, and although there were important differences between the Articles' Congress and the Constitution's Congress, there were also important parallels (including, of course, the name). The obvious default position was that "Congress" would continue to exercise powers it had exercised in the past. Yet it did not: everyone seemed to understand that something in the Constitution changed the rules.

"Executive Power" as an Explanation for the President's Diplomatic Power

Jefferson, Washington, and Jay

Throughout these events, American leaders relied on the President's "executive Power" to explain the President's control over diplomatic matters. In his 1789 letter to the Emperor of Morocco, for example, Washington attributed his diplomatic power to his constitutional possession of "the supreme executive Authority." Also in 1789, Jay wrote to an American diplomatic agent: "[Y]ou will observe that the President of the United States appointed under this Constitution is vested with powers and prerogatives of far greater magnitude and importance than any that were confided to the former Presidents of Congress" because the new President possessed "the great executive powers" previously "held and exercised by the Congress itself."[40]

During the 1790 funding debate, Washington asked for advice on his view that setting diplomatic rank and destination were presidential powers that could not be given to the Senate. In response, Jefferson gave the legal opinion described in Chapter 3, directly relying on the "executive Power" clause to grant presidential foreign affairs power. Jefferson began by quoting Article II, Section 1: "The constitution . . . has declared that 'the Executive powers shall be vested in the President,' submitting only special articles of it to a negative by the senate"; he continued:

> The transaction of business with foreign nations is Executive altogether; it belongs, then, to the head of that department, *except* as to such portions of it as are specially submitted to the Senate. *Exceptions* are to be construed strictly; the Constitution itself indeed has taken care to circumscribe this one within very strict limits: for it gives the *nomination* of the foreign Agent to the President, the *appointment* to him and the Senate jointly, and the *commissioning* to the President.

Jefferson thus saw the Senate's role in appointing ambassadors as a specific exception to the general executive/presidential power over transactions with foreign nations. Jefferson explained that although the Constitution specifically grants the powers of appointment, nomination, and commissioning, the powers of setting destination and grade *are not part* of these "specifically enumerated" powers. As Jefferson put it:

> To *nominate* must be to propose: *appointment* seems that act of the will which constitutes or makes the Agent: and the *commission* is the public evidence of it. But there are still other acts previous to these not specifically enumerated in the Constitution; to wit: 1. the destination of a mission to the particular country where the public service calls for it, and 2. the character or grade to be employed in it. The natural order of all these is 1. destination. 2. grade. 3. nomination. 4. appointment. 5. commission. If *appointment* does not comprehend the neighboring acts of *nomination* or *commission*, (and the constitution says it shall not, by giving them exclusively to the President) still less can it pretend to comprehend those previous and more remote of *destination* and *grade*.[41]

And Jefferson repeated in conclusion: "The Constitution, analyzing the three last [i.e., nomination, appointment, and commissioning], shews that they do not comprehend the two first [i.e., setting destination and grade]." As a result, "[a]ll this is left to the President."[42]

Jefferson's reliance on executive foreign affairs power could not be clearer. He wrote that the Constitution vests the President with executive powers (quoting Article II, Section 1); that the transaction of business with foreign nations is "executive," except as has been conveyed elsewhere; that the powers to set grade and destination are not part of the specific powers of nomination, appointment, and commissioning; and that therefore they are part of the President's general executive power.[43]

Washington also sought the views of Jay (newly appointed Chief Justice of the U.S. Supreme Court) and Madison (then a congressional leader) on the matter. Washington noted that Madison's "opinion coincides with Mr. Jay's and Mr. Jefferson's—to wit—that they [i.e., the Senate] have no Constitutional right to interfere with either, . . . their powers extending no farther than to an approbation or disapprobation of the person nominated by the President, all the rest being Executive and vested in the President by the Constitution."[44] Apparently, then, Madison and Jay, like Jefferson (and Washington himself), relied on Article II, Section 1: it is the only textual reason for thinking that "executive" foreign affairs powers not listed elsewhere in the Constitution belong to the President.

Madison and the Removal Debates

The 1789 debates over removal power also illuminate the meaning of executive power. As discussed, a key question was whether the President had constitutional power to remove the Secretary of Foreign Affairs. In arguing that he did, Madison emphasized the executive power clause as granting general power, subject to specific exceptions (as Jefferson did a year later):

> The Constitution affirms, that the Executive power shall be vested in the President. Are there exceptions to this proposition? Yes, there are. The Constitution says, that in appointing to office, the Senate shall be associated with the President. . . . Have we [Congress] a right to extend this exception? I believe not. If the Constitution has invested all executive power in the President, I venture to assert that the Legislature has no right to diminish or modify his executive authority.[45]

Madison then argued that removal was an executive function:

> The question now resolves itself into this, Is the power of displacing, an Executive power. I conceive that if any power whatsoever is in its nature Executive, it is the power of appointing, overseeing and controlling those who execute the laws. If the Constitution had not qualified the power of the President in appointing to office, by associating the Senate with him in that business, would it not be clear that he would have the

right, by virtue of his Executive power to make such appointment? Should we be authorized, in defiance of that clause in the Constitution, "The executive power shall be vested in a President," to unite the Senate with the President in the appointment to office? I conceive not. If it is admitted that we should not be authorized to do this, I think it may be disputed whether we have a right to associate them in removing persons from office, the one power being as much of an Executive nature as the other.[46]

Or, as former Convention delegate George Clymer said more directly: "The power of removal was an Executive power, and as such belonged to the President alone, by the express words of the Constitution: 'the Executive power shall be vested in a President of the United States of America.' "[47] Oliver Ellsworth, another former Convention delegate who had served on the Committee of Detail that drafted the executive power clause, said in the Senate: "There is an explicit grant to the President which contains the power of removal. The executive power is granted; not the executive powers hereinafter enumerated and explained."[48] On this basis Madison and his allies urged revision of the proposed Act to indicate a constitutional removal authority in the President—language Congress ultimately adopted.

Two important qualifications may make this a less-than-definitive endorsement of executive foreign affairs power. First, Madison and others did not say, directly, that foreign affairs was an "executive" function; instead they tended to associate removal with law-execution power. But the Secretary of Foreign Affairs did not "execute" any laws; rather, he exercised diplomatic functions delegated to him *by the President* (not by Congress). As historian Charles Thach points out: "The recognition that the President is the sole constitutional representative of the Union in its foreign relations is made even plainer by the terms of the foreign department bill. . . . The sole purpose of that organization was to carry out, not legislative orders . . . but the will of the executive."[49] To say that the President had "executive" authority over the Secretary was to view foreign affairs as "executive"—and to say that it was "executive" was, as Madison, Ellsworth, and Clymer explained, to say that Article II, Section 1 vested it in the President, unless something else in the Constitution said otherwise.

Second, Madison's view was far from unanimous. Although Congress amended the bill to use language he favored, it passed by a less-than-overwhelming margin in the House and by the narrowest of margins in the Senate. It is not even clear that everyone voting for the Act endorsed

Madison's constitutional vision, and some opponents strongly disputed it.[50] Professor Thach boldly concludes that the "removal debate at least tended to establish . . . that the executive is not limited to the enumerated powers, and that the vesting clause is a grant of power" including powers necessary for "the management of foreign affairs": since they are not enumerated, they are the President's as of constitutional right, being of an executive character." "[T]his line of reasoning," he writes, ". . . was undoubtedly something of the sort that the men who made the Constitution had in mind when they spoke of the executive power."[51] This may overstate what can be concluded from the episode viewed in isolation. Nonetheless, the removal debate does, at minimum, establish that important constitutional thinkers such as Madison read the executive power clause to convey to the President powers believed to be "executive" in nature and not otherwise allocated in the Constitution, and that these presidential powers included the power to control and remove the nation's chief foreign affairs officer.

Hamilton's Pacificus and Madison's Helvidius

The strongest statement identifying "executive" power with foreign affairs power came from Alexander Hamilton in 1793, in his Pacificus essays defending Washington's neutrality proclamation. Hamilton wrote: "The second Article of the Constitution of the UStates, section first, establishes this general proposition, That 'the EXECUTIVE POWER shall be vested in a President of the United States of America.'" The executive power, Hamilton continued, traditionally included acting as "the organ of intercourse between the United States and foreign powers." He acknowledged that the Constitution assigned some executive powers elsewhere—namely war, appointments, and treatymaking—but these were "*exceptions* and *qualifications*" to the "more comprehensive grant contained in the general clause" and "[w]ith these exceptions, the EXECUTIVE POWER of the Union is completely lodged in the President." Establishing foreign policy, as Washington had done in the neutrality proclamation, was an executive foreign affairs power not assigned to another branch, so Hamilton concluded that it was rightfully exercised by the President.[52]

It is important to see Pacificus's argument not as part of Hamilton's sometimes-idiosyncratic political views, but as existing squarely within conventional late-eighteenth century discourse. Hamilton's identification of foreign affairs power with executive power comes directly from Montesquieu and Blackstone, the most widely read theorists of governmental structure in

America. It followed a long line of common usage, running from the Articles' Congress, through the Philadelphia Convention's debate over the Virginia plan, to the ratification conventions' debates over the treatymaking role of the Senate. Most importantly, it fit exactly with, and in many respects merely echoed and refined, common thinking immediately after 1789, as reflected in Madison's views on removal, Washington and Jay's view of diplomatic powers, and the diplomatic practice of the early Washington administration. And it precisely tracks Jefferson's 1790 opinion in the funding debate.

We must consider Madison's Helvidius in this context. Although Jefferson inspired Helvidius, he did not dispute the idea of executive foreign affairs power (and indeed had said three years earlier that the Constitution's executive power clause assigned diplomatic functions to the President). Instead, he thought Washington's proclamation infringed Congress's war power, since deciding *against* war (which declaring neutrality arguably did) should by that clause be a question for Congress. In particular, he thought (contrary to Pacificus's implication) that the proclamation could not bind Congress's later consideration of the matter. Although Jefferson urged Madison to dispute Pacificus, he did not seem to claim the proclamation itself was unconstitutional; he wrote to Madison, somewhat ambiguously: "Upon the whole, my objections to the competence of the Executive to declare neutrality . . . were supposed to be got over by avoiding the use of that term. The declaration of the disposition of the US hardly can be called illegal, tho', it was certainly officious and improper."[53] Jefferson's principal concern was that Congress retain flexibility to aid France when it reconvened.

Helvidius's main points echoed Jefferson's concern about congressional war powers. Pacificus had overreached, especially in claiming that the proclamation was intended to "*make known* to the powers at *war* . . . that [the United States] is . . . under no obligations of Treaty, to become an *associate in the war* with either," although the proclamation said no such thing.[54] In response, Madison adopted Jefferson's argument that this involved Congress's war power. Here he did not quarrel with Hamilton on first principles, for Hamilton agreed that Congress had exclusive war power. The debate was over what its war powers encompassed.[55]

Hamilton argued, among other things, that because war power was an executive power that the Constitution gave to Congress, the grant should be construed strictly. This claim, though tangential to the main dispute, drew Madison into a broader discussion of executive power. In his view, war powers (and treatymaking powers) were not truly executive but were only treated so, incorrectly, by English practice and political theorists. Thus, the Constitution put war power where it belonged, in the legislature (points consistent with Madison's arguments at the Convention); and so, he said, Congress's power should be construed broadly, not strictly.[56]

None of these points is inconsistent with executive foreign affairs power. Madison and Hamilton (and Jefferson) agreed that warmaking and treaty-making were called "executive" in English practice and by Blackstone and Montesquieu, but that the Convention thought assigning them to the President would give too much power to one person, and so the Constitution limited them or conveyed them elsewhere. And according to Madison, to the extent there was a question whether the United States was bound to go to war, that matter was textually assigned to Congress in the declare-war clause. In short, the core Pacificus/Helvidius dispute concerned the scope of Congress's war power.[57]

In the heat of argument, though, Madison made a broader and less-careful claim. He wanted to show that war power was not naturally an executive power. Among other arguments, Madison attempted to define executive power comprehensively, and here he wrote: "The natural province of the executive magistrate is to execute laws, as that of the legislature is to make laws. All his acts, therefore, properly executive, must pre-suppose the existence of the laws to be executed."[58] Madison's main point was that war (and treaty-making) should not be seen as "executive"—but taken at face value, his claim squarely rejects all executive foreign affairs authority, since it would read Article II, Section 1 to convey only law-enforcement power.

Like Justice Black's view in *Steel Seizure*, Madison's position, taken to its logical conclusion, demanded a frontal assault upon the President's diplomatic functions, which had been exercised since 1789 without congressional authorization. And like Black, Madison did not grapple with this problem. Further, he did not see that many of the powers he would deny the President would be difficult to locate in Congress. Madison said, for example, that refusing to receive ambassadors should be decided by Congress, not the President, without explaining how Article I gave Congress that power.[59]

Of course, Madison himself, in less partisan moments, had acknowledged that the President had powers beyond law enforcement, including the power to control diplomatic officers, as part of the executive power. In particular, in the removal debate Madison said the President had power to remove the Secretary of State by Article II, Section 1; in the funding debate he agreed with Jefferson, Washington, and Jay that setting the rank and destination of diplomatic officers was an executive power. And prior to the Convention, as discussed in Chapter 3, Madison used "executive power" in a way that seemed to encompass foreign affairs power. Moreover, as Helvidius he never directly disputed the President's diplomatic power, or even the President's power to formulate substantive foreign policy not connected to war. He (again like Justice Black) was not thinking systematically about the whole of foreign affairs power. His immediate point—that the President cannot make binding decisions on war by interpreting treaties—was distinct from his attack on executive foreign affairs power. His wider claim that the President can only act pursuant to statutes or as enumerated in Article II, Section 2 or 3, was wrong in practice and incoherent in theory, as shown by the President's diplomatic powers.

For even if Madison did believe what he said, it was not the ordinary view. No one raised sustained objections to Washington's control of diplomacy.[60] Helvidius's narrow view of executive power was rejected, not in 1793, but in 1789, when Washington assumed executive foreign affairs powers and began conducting diplomacy without legislative authorization. Essentially everyone at the time accepted the idea that the President had power over communications with foreign governments and control of U.S. diplomats. No one (including Madison) suggested in the years prior to 1793 that the President needed statutory authorization for his diplomatic activity.[61]

Nor did views shift in Helvidius's aftermath. Only a few years later, Oliver Ellsworth—Madison's removal debate ally and former member of the committee that drafted the executive power clause—spoke in familiar terms, saying that under the Constitution communication with foreign powers "is positively placed in the hands of the Executive." And in 1800, John Marshall's well-known statement to Congress that "the President is the sole organ of the nation in its external relations, and its sole representative with foreign nations" rested on the proposition, as Marshall said immediately afterward, that the President "possesses the whole executive power. He holds and directs the force of the nation. Of consequence any act to be performed by the force of the nation, is to be performed by him." Or, as Marshall added, the "executive" is "[t]he department . . . entrusted with the whole foreign intercourse of the nation. . . ."[62]

As a result, Justice Jackson (in *Steel Seizure*) erred in suggesting that Pacificus and Helvidius cancel each other, leaving no meaningful way to discern the eighteenth-century understanding of executive power. Reading them in context (as Jackson did not) shows Helvidius on this point to be a less-reliable indicator of constitutional meaning. Helvidius's vision of executive power ran contrary to that term's use in writings of the great political theorists, in the old government under the Articles, in the Philadelphia Convention and the ratifying debates, and in practice under the new Constitution. These all recognized what Helvidius denied: that executive power had a foreign affairs component not dependent on antecedent law. Pacificus, in contrast, expressed a common understanding of executive power reflected elsewhere and had a coherent vision of the practical and theoretical exercise of foreign affairs powers. Hamilton's work is not the *basis* for executive foreign affairs powers—rather, it confirms (as much other evidence confirms) that this was a common understanding. Madison, who (as Helvidius—but not otherwise) was an outlier on this subject, is not a reason to think differently.

Conclusion: Washington's Executive Power

The proposed reading of "executive Power," then, arises from the following propositions. First, the great eighteenth-century political writers, whom founding-era Americans studied and exalted, said that executive power included foreign affairs powers. In doing so, they followed a model also familiar to founding-era Americans: the English system, which concentrated foreign affairs powers in a chief executive, the monarch. Second, founding-era Americans adopted that terminology, as seen under the Articles and in drafting and ratifying the Constitution. In particular, founding-era Americans described the Articles' Congress as having executive powers, primarily because it had foreign affairs powers. At the Convention, although the Virginia Plan was proposed to shift executive foreign affairs powers in a block to the new executive branch, this was too much concentration of power for most delegates to accept; instead, they made specific allocations that placed key foreign affairs powers in the hands, in whole or part, of other branches. But they also vested a general "executive Power" with the President.

Third, Washington quickly claimed complete diplomatic authority, without statutory authorization. This broad claim of power went largely uncontested in Congress, which might be expected to object if a serious constitutional usurpation had occurred, or even in a case of substantial ambiguity. Acquiescence in Washington's conduct suggests consensus that the Constitution assigned the President diplomatic powers. Even absent further evidence, it would be fair to assume that this consensus rested upon the grant of executive power in Article II, Section 1, given that phrase's common meaning.

But, fourth, we need not assume, because key American leaders explicitly grounded the President's diplomatic powers upon the executive power clause. Among others, Washington, Jay, Madison, Jefferson, Hamilton, Marshall, and Ellsworth identified presidential diplomatic powers with "executive" power. Added together, this evidence provides strong support for the proposition that the phrase "executive Power" in Article II, Section 1 includes foreign affairs powers not otherwise allocated by the Constitution's text.

5

Steel Seizure Revisited: The Limits of Executive Power

The idea that the President's "executive Power" contains independent foreign affairs authority has been around for many years and, as we have seen, has strong roots in eighteenth-century language. It provides a way to begin reading the Constitution as a complete document in foreign affairs, rather than as one that inexplicably fails to mention many key foreign affairs powers. Yet it has not been enthusiastically embraced, by courts or commentators. The most important factor counseling hesitation is, no doubt, a structural one: reading Article II, Section 1 to grant foreign affairs authority would (it is said) give the President too much unchecked and unilateral power.

The framers' commitment to checks and balances among the branches of government is legendary, and scholars who have studied the founding period see no reason to think that this commitment did not extend to foreign affairs. Harold Koh writes: "[T]he Founding Fathers framed the constitutional provisions on foreign affairs with two goals in mind—to fashion a stronger national government while holding each branch of that government accountable to the others through a strong system of checks and balances." Louis Henkin says that "the Framers were hardly ready to replace the representative inefficiency of many with an efficient monarchy, and unhappy memories of royal prerogative, fear of tyranny, and reluctance to repose trust in any one person kept the Framers from giving the new President too much head."[1] We have seen in the drafting and ratifying debates, and in the provisions of the Constitution itself, ample confirmation of these observations.

Yet from these reasonable observations about the framers' concerns, academic commentators have drawn what appear to be too sweeping conclusions about the limits of presidential power. Many of them would reject most independent presidential foreign affairs powers beyond basic diplomacy, and in particular would reject the idea that Article II, Section 1 conveys any substantive authority. For them, *Curtiss-Wright* is anathema, not necessarily because it appeals to extra-constitutional power (although that is part of the problem), but because it locates so much power in the President. And the "executive Power" outlined in Chapters 3–4 is no better, being (in this view) little more than a restatement of *Curtiss-Wright,* albeit hooked to a (debatable) textual provision rather than conjured from inherent powers. By the same token, the *Steel Seizure* case, whatever its difficulties, seems the appropriate structural model, because it provides powerful checks upon the President.

Worries about overreaching executive power have been reinforced by extravagant claims by Presidents and their attorneys and academic supporters. President Theodore Roosevelt wrote in his autobiography:

> The most important factor in getting the right spirit in my Administration, next to the insistence upon courage, honesty, and a genuine democracy of desire to serve the plain people, was my insistence upon the theory that the executive power was limited only by specific restrictions and prohibitions appearing in the Constitution or imposed by Congress under its constitutional powers. . . . I declined to adopt [the] view that what was imperatively necessary for the nation could not be done by the President unless he could find some specific authorization to do it. My belief was that is was not only his right but his duty to do anything that the needs of the nation demanded unless such action was forbidden by the Constitution or by the laws.[2]

As ex-President and future Chief Justice William Howard Taft wrote specifically in response, "the view of . . . Mr. Roosevelt, ascribing an undefined residuum of power to the President, is an unsafe doctrine" that "might lead under emergencies to results of an arbitrary character, doing irremediable injustice to private rights. . . . The wide field of action that this would give to the Executive one can hardly limit."[3]

The purpose of this chapter, and several successive ones, is to show that embracing executive foreign affairs powers, as suggested in Chapters 3–4, does not upset constitutional checks and balances nor provide the President with ill-defined or unlimited authority. That is true in part because the Constitution specifically allocates important foreign affairs authorities away from the President. Subsequent chapters explore these allocations, particularly the declare-war, appointments, and treatymaking clauses.

But even aside from these allocations, it is important to see that the executive power clause itself is not an unlimited or open-ended grant of foreign affairs authority. Giving the clause its historical meaning subjects executive foreign affairs power to at least two key limitations. First, executive foreign affairs power—unlike *Curtiss-Wright*'s inherent presidential power—contains its own limits. It does not grant the President general authority over all matters relating to foreign affairs; it grants a *particular set of powers* identified as "executive" in eighteenth-century political writing. Of course, it will not always be easy to say whether a contested power was or was not part of historical "executive" foreign affairs powers. But often it will be. For example, as explained below, seizing domestic private property to support a foreign war effort—the power at issue in *Steel Seizure*—was not part of the executive powers as they were known in England or described by eighteenth-century writers.

A second limitation—not at issue in the *Steel Seizure* case but important in other contexts—is that executive foreign affairs power does not imply any obligation upon other branches to assist the President. If the executive/President needs other branches' support to achieve foreign affairs objectives, the decision whether to render assistance is entirely in the discretion of the other branches. Again, this is part of the historical meaning of executive power, as practiced in England and explained by political theorists. Above all, it underlies the conclusion that Congress has the final say over spending and lawmaking, and need not provide money or legislation to support presidential initiatives.

The President's Inability to Act beyond Traditional Executive Powers

Under the constitutional reading we have been examining, the President's claim to unilateral foreign affairs authority is tied to a particular constitutional provision, the "executive Power" clause of Article II, Section 1. Although the clause itself does not mention foreign affairs in so many words, we found in Chapters 3–4 that common eighteenth-century understandings of the phrase included foreign affairs powers. More specifically, eighteenth-century understandings defined *some* foreign affairs powers as executive powers. On this basis, the President may say that foreign affairs powers historically called "executive" fall within Article II, Section 1's grant of power. But the President cannot claim that because *some* foreign affairs powers fall within Article II, Section 1, other foreign affairs powers that were *not* traditional executive powers somehow end up within Article II, Section 1 as well. More broadly, the President cannot claim (as Roosevelt did) that the executive power is an open-ended grant of authority for the President to do anything not prohibited by law, or anything required by foreign affairs necessities.

To illustrate, consider two powers sometimes claimed to be within the President's foreign affairs authority: the power to prevent export of military supplies when the United States is at peace; and the power to seize private property within the United States to aid the nation's foreign war effort. President Truman, of course, claimed the latter power in *Steel Seizure;* the Court attributed the former (implicitly, and perhaps not completely) to the President in *Curtiss-Wright.*

As described below, although Article II, Section 1 gives the President some unilateral authority, read correctly it does not give the President either of these powers. More generally, it does not give the President anything amounting to lawmaking authority in foreign affairs. That is, it does not (with minor exceptions) give the President authority to alter domestic rights and duties within the U.S. legal system. The powers claimed in *Curtiss-Wright* and *Steel Seizure* would do this: in one case, preventing the exporter from carrying out previously legal commercial transactions and, in the other, depriving the mill owners of the previously legal use of their property. As Justice Black said in *Steel Seizure,* rejecting what he saw as presidential lawmaking, "the Constitution limits [the President's] functions in the lawmaking process to the recommending of laws he thinks wise and the vetoing of laws he thinks bad."[4]

How can we be sure? After all, in *Steel Seizure* and *Curtiss-Wright* the powers in question were vital to achieving U.S. foreign policy goals announced by the President in pursuance of his executive power. Black in *Steel Seizure* did not explain *why* the President lacked lawmaking authority in foreign affairs. True, the President ordinarily lacks lawmaking power in domestic affairs; but foreign affairs may be different, for there (unlike in domestic affairs) the President has an independent grant of authority in Article II, Section 1. Might that provision also grant some lawmaking authority relating to foreign affairs?[5]

As we have seen, this was Justice Black's dilemma in *Steel Seizure.* He tried to escape it by (implicitly) denying a substantive component to executive power, but this strategy runs up against the problem of the President's undisputed but (to Black) inexplicable diplomatic powers. Our discussion shows a solution. To repeat, the executive power clause is not an open-ended grant of foreign affairs power, but a specific (though generally worded) grant of a *particular set of powers* that the eighteenth century called "executive." The key is to assess whether that set of powers included the particular power the President claims in a given case. As discussed, most diplomatic powers fell within it; lawmaking power in foreign affairs, we will see, did not.

Political Theory and Practice—In General

We should first consider general principles. The core tenet of eighteenth-century separation-of-powers theory was the separation of lawmaking and law execution. Montesquieu laid great stress on this point, in a passage that in many ways came to epitomize his work and was widely quoted in America: "When the legislative and executive powers are united in the same person, or in the same body of magistrates, there can be no liberty; because apprehensions may arise, lest the same monarch or senate should enact tyrannical laws, to execute them in a tyrannical manner."[6]

Blackstone made similar points, equally strongly. "In all tyrannical governments, the supreme magistry, or the right both of making and of enforcing the laws, is vested in one and the same man, or one and the same body of men. . . . With us . . . this supreme power is divided into two branches: the one legislative, to wit, the parliament . . . the other executive, consisting of the king alone."[7] Speaking of royal (executive) proclamations, Blackstone emphasized that "[t]hese proclamations have then a binding force, when . . . they are grounded upon and enforce the laws of the realm. . . . [They] are binding upon the subject, where they do not either contradict the old laws, or tend to establish new ones; but only enforce the execution of such laws as are already in being, in such manner as the king shall judge necessary." He then gave an example based on an existing law prohibiting arms to Catholics:

> A proclamation for disarming papists is also binding, being only in execution of what the legislature has first ordained: but a proclamation for allowing arms to papists, or for disarming any protestant subjects, will not bind; because the first would be to assume a dispensing power, the latter a legislative one; to the vesting of either in any single person the laws of England are absolute strangers.[8]

"Indeed," Blackstone continued, "by the statute 31 Hen. VIII c.8 it was enacted, that the king's proclamations should have the force of acts of parliament: a statute, which was calculated to introduce the most despotic tyranny; and which must have proved fatal to the liberties of this kingdom, had it not been luckily repealed . . . about five years later." As he repeated later, "in England no royal power can introduce a new law, or suspend the execution of the old."[9]

This was the fundamental idea of *separation* of powers, distinguishing eighteenth-century England from absolute monarchies: the English executive/monarch had law-execution power, but this power (usually) depended upon prior statutory authority enacted by Parliament. The monarch could not, as a general matter, unilaterally issue orders to private parties by decree.[10]

For the English, this was not merely abstract theory. Much of the seventeenth-century dispute between the Stuart kings and Parliament was couched in terms of separating lawmaking power (Parliament) and law-execution power (the monarch). According to seventeenth-century English revolutionaries, the Stuart kings overstepped their constitutional role by claiming lawmaking power—for example, Charles I had claimed power to rule by decree when Parliament was not in session, so long as his decrees did not violate existing law, and in some cases kings claimed power to "dispense" with existing law.[11] The subsequent revolution of the 1640s heavily invoked this issue, though once Charles was ousted Oliver Cromwell claimed similar powers to rule by decree. As separation-of-powers theory became more refined in the late seventeenth century, its expositors focused on this point, emphasizing the fundamental tenet that lawmaking and law execution should be separated, in express reaction to the overreaching of prior monarchs and of Cromwell's dictatorship. The constitutional resolution of the struggle, embodied in the Glorious Revolution (1688), the Bill of Rights (1689), and the Act of Settlement (1702), confirmed this fundamental division of power. Though the extent of "executive" and "legislative" powers remained hazy at the margins, these developments underlined the basic point that the executive monarch was not a lawmaker. Montesquieu and Blackstone, writing a half-century later, addressed an audience well versed in this history.[12]

So the general theory was clear enough, and by the eighteenth century it more or less conformed to practice, again as a general matter. To be sure, isolated pockets of what looked like kingly lawmaking remained as holdovers from ancient practice.[13] But in the ordinary case, the events of the mid- to late-seventeenth century settled the matter: actions claiming the force of law depended upon acts of Parliament.[14]

The English System in Foreign Affairs

These broad discussions, though, said little about foreign affairs. The central focus of seventeenth- and eighteenth-century separation-of-powers theory was domestic governance. Many writers did not mention foreign affairs at all, while others did only in passing. Those that did discuss it—especially Blackstone and Montesquieu—emphasized its executive elements and did not discuss how executive foreign affairs powers interacted with lawmaking power. No one doubted that *in general* executive power did not include lawmaking power, but did that also mean that executive power did not include power to make law to support foreign affairs objectives?

Although the leading political writers did not address the question directly, we can gain some insight from English practice. In general, founding-era Americans associated executive power with the powers of the English monarch. This statement must be hedged with caveats: the English monarch held some powers that were explicitly not "executive" (such as the veto), or that arguably were not; and in any event most Americans thought the English monarch had too much power. But in general, they viewed the monarch as the executive branch of English government (Parliament being the legislative branch). This is not to say, it must be emphasized, that the powers of the English monarch can define the President's constitutional powers: though the framers seemed to take the allocations of the English system as a baseline, they did not hesitate to alter them as they thought appropriate. Rather, the point here is that the English monarch's foreign affairs powers provide a likely *maximum* limit—a ceiling—upon what the Constitution meant by "executive Power."[15] It is not likely that Americans thought powers the English king lacked were executive powers, at least unless specific evidence can be found to the contrary.[16]

Seventeenth-century English monarchs did claim lawmaking authority in support of foreign affairs goals—a position reflected, for example, in *Bates' Case* (1606), which found royal taxing power to support of foreign objectives. But such claims (like royal lawmaking more generally) seem fully to have been abandoned by the eighteenth century, in the wake of the post-revolutionary settlement of the 1680s.[17]

It is true, of course, that eighteenth-century theory and practice recognized executive foreign affairs powers not dependent upon prior law (Chapter 3). But the powers in this category (mostly) did not involve alteration of domestic rights. They were, as Blackstone described, aspects of managing affairs with other nations: principally, diplomacy and military affairs. As Locke said, they were their own category, neither lawmaking nor law execution—and they encompassed managing affairs with foreigners outside the domestic legal system.[18]

That division shows up most decisively in the English law of treaties. As discussed (Chapter 3), in eighteenth-century theory and practice treaty-making was an "executive" power of the Crown; treaties were negotiated, signed, and ratified under the monarch's direction. Monarchs often sought parliamentary input, and there may have been some particular classes of treaties for which parliamentary approval was at least theoretically required. But the ordinary rule was that the Crown made treaties, which, Blackstone said, were "binding on the whole community."[19]

English treaties nonetheless were (and continue to be) only international obligations, not domestic legal rules. According to the great English legal historian William Holdsworth, "though . . . Blackstone assigned no limitation to the treaty-making power of the Crown, two very definite limitations were recognized in the eighteenth century, and are still recognized. The Crown can make a treaty; but if the terms of that treaty involve the imposition of any charge [tax] upon the subjects, or an alteration in the rule of English law, they cannot take effect without the sanction of Parliament."[20]

This requirement was a direct consequence of the broader rule against royal/executive lawmaking. As Holdsworth further explains:

> These two limitations are the result of the constitutional settlement effected by the Great Rebellion and the Revolution. If that constitutional settlement had been otherwise, if the king and not the Parliament had prevailed, it is probable that no such limitations on the treaty-making power of the Crown could have been recognized. The reasoning used by the judges in *Bate's Case* would have been followed. According to that reasoning, the power of the Crown over foreign affairs was absolute; and, though the Crown could not impose a tax without the consent of parliament, an exercise of its absolute power over foreign affairs, which incidentally involved a charge on the subject, was valid, because that was merely an incidental effect of the exercise of an undoubted prerogative. It is clear that the same reasoning could easily have been applied to an exercise of this absolute power which incidentally involved a change in the law.[21]

As it was, though, eighteenth-century monarchs sought parliamentary implementation of key treaties (including the 1783 treaty ending the American Revolution); eighteenth-century legal opinion confirmed the necessity of doing so, and Parliament had at least once famously refused to implement a treaty.[22]

Although not reflected in Blackstone, and somewhat obscured in the ratification debates,[23] this relationship seems to have been sufficiently understood in America at the drafting Convention and afterward. Wilson said at the Convention that "all treaties which contravene a law of England or require a law to give them operation or effect are inconclusive till agreed to by the legislature of Great Britain"; Connecticut delegate William Samuel Johnson, putting the matter more precisely, explained that the king made treaties but "if the Parliament should fail to provide the necessary means of execution the treaty would be violated."[24]

Similarly James Iredell (then a Supreme Court Justice) wrote in 1796: "I believe it is an invariable practice in [Britain] when the King makes any stipulation of a legislative nature, that it is carried into effect by an act of Parliament. The Parliament is considered bound, upon a principle of moral obligation, to preserve the public faith, pledged by the treaty, by passing such laws as its obligations require; but until such laws are passed, the system of law, entitled to actual obedience, remains de facto, as before." Speaking of a treaty relating to tariffs, he declared that "no man living will say that a bare proclamation of the King, upon the ground of the treaty, would be authority for the levying of any duties whatever; but it must be done in the constitutional mode, by act of parliament, which afford an additional proof, that where anything of a legislative nature is in contemplation, . . . it can alone be effected by the medium of the legislative authority."[25]

Plainly this limitation would apply equally to decrees based merely on executive foreign policy (as in *Bates' Case*), as well as to decrees based upon treaties. Eighteenth-century English treaty practice confirms a broader principle that the Crown made arrangements with foreign powers, without needing support in antecedent law, but could not make arrangements with respect to domestic legal matters, even where they had international repercussions.

The Articles and the Constitution

The identification of executive power with diplomatic and military matters, but not domestic lawmaking, can also be seen from the Articles of Confederation. We saw in Chapter 3 that the Articles' Congress was often called an executive body, mainly because it had the principal "executive" foreign affairs powers, as defined by the leading theorists: war, military affairs, treaties, and diplomacy. The Congress was not so different from the English monarch in its foreign affairs powers (although of course very different in structure, and thus in effectiveness).

As we also saw, however, the Congress lacked textual power to implement its foreign policy domestically. This was reflected in a number of important categories—enforcing treaties, regulating trade, enforcing the law of nations—and led to all sorts of trouble. No one thought the Congress had some sort of inherent foreign affairs power that overcame its lack of textual power. And few people thought any sort of domestic implementation power flowed from the Congress's executive ability to establish U.S. foreign policy goals. For example, in the de Longchamps incident, discussed in Chapter 2, the Congress's policy was to enforce the law of nations and punish de Longchamps for assaulting the French minister (lest France resort to retaliatory measures). Even though it stated this policy to France and urged it on Pennsylvania, no one thought the Congress itself had domestic implementation power based on its authority to speak for the nation internationally: legislative implementation was up to the state.

The Articles did not give the Congress "executive power" in so many words. The Congress had power (Article 9) to appoint officers to "manage the affairs" of the United States, and in context this assuredly meant, at least in large part, to manage the *foreign* affairs of the United States. That (taken with specific grants of war and treaty power) amounts to what theorists called executive power; it was so described by Americans at the time, who called the Congress an "executive" body. If there had been a conventional understanding of executive foreign affairs powers that included domestic lawmaking and enforcement to effectuate foreign affairs goals, the Congress might have claimed such power under its general authority to "manage the affairs" of the United States. The absence of such arguments confirms that Americans did not think foreign affairs power implied domestic lawmaking power: the "executive" Congress could establish foreign policy goals, but it was up to the legislative authorities—under the Articles, the states—to make law in support.

This understanding is also confirmed by events in the drafting and ratification process. First, there is no recorded discussion of presidential lawmaking power connected to foreign affairs. Further, as explored more fully below (see especially Chapters 8 and 14), significant controversy focused on the Constitution's Article VI, which stated that treaties would be the "supreme Law of the Land." If that meant what it appeared to say, anti-federalists argued, it would depart from English treatymaking practice and render the President (with the Senate) a lawmaker. A manifest assumption behind this argument was that ordinarily the President would not be a lawmaker, even in matters likely to be covered by treaty.

The Washington Administration

We may also measure our reading of executive power against post-ratification practice. Although President Washington took control of U.S. foreign affairs in 1789, few incidents during his tenure look anything like attempts at *do-*

mestic implementation of foreign policy objectives by unilateral presidential decree. The most important exception to this pattern involves the neutrality proclamation, discussed in Chapter 4; it confirms that executive power did not extend very far toward domestic lawmaking.

Recall that in early 1793 the United States risked involvement in war between Britain and France. In particular, the United States had treaties with France that under some interpretations might obligate it to assist France against Britain. Washington, after consulting his cabinet but without consulting Congress, issued the neutrality proclamation, stating that the United States would remain neutral in the conflict. Madison and Hamilton, as Helvidius and Pacificus, debated the proclamation's constitutionality; as we saw in Chapter 4, the best view is that it fell within Washington's executive foreign affairs power.

Washington, though, soon found neutrality easier to announce than enforce. Historians note in strong terms his enforcement problems, primarily arising because the proclamation had no statutory law behind it.[26] Because Washington did not recall Congress, it did not meet until December 1793, giving Washington many months to struggle with carrying his proclamation into effect. These struggles reveal important limits on the executive power to implement foreign policy goals.

Washington probably thought that the proclamation's goals largely could be achieved by diplomatic appeals to the French ambassador, Genet, and the diplomatic agents acting at his direction. If Genet stopped arming privateers and recruiting U.S. citizens to fight for France, many potential difficulties with Britain could be avoided. Diplomatic pressure on Genet, though, proved largely unavailing. Matters came to a head in July 1793, when Genet oversaw the refitting of a captured British ship, the *Little Sarah*, in Philadelphia harbor. Despite direct requests from the administration that the *Little Sarah* not leave port, Genet authorized the ship (renamed the *Petite Democrate*) to sail as a privateer. In response, Washington began the process of requesting Genet's recall; he directly threatened to revoke (and in at least one case actually did revoke) the authority of French consuls who did not abide by the President's neutrality directives.[27]

Washington also appealed to state governors to suppress non-neutral activity in their states. Again, this was a diplomatic rather than a legal measure. His communications do not suggest that Washington thought he could order governors to do anything. But as with Genet, Washington thought presidential requests would be honored—and in many respects they were. Some state governors (such as South Carolina's Moultrie) had been giving support and encouragement to France, but at Washington's request they issued their own proclamations against non-neutral activity; some governors took affirmative actions to suppress that activity.[28] For various reasons, however, state enforcement also proved insufficient.[29]

As state governors proved unable or unwilling to protect neutrality, Washington sought to engage federal officers in preventative measures. Although they did not debate the constitutional issues systematically, Washington's cabinet evidently believed that the President could use military force against foreign military vessels violating the proclamation. In the *Little Sarah* incident in July 1793, the cabinet (in Washington's absence) considered using military force to stop the refitted privateer from leaving port. Concerned over provoking war with France, the cabinet could not reach a decision before the *Little Sarah* sailed, but those who considered the matter (including Jefferson and Hamilton) did not seem to doubt that the President had constitutional authority to use force against the French vessel. (Washington was on vacation at the time, but it seems likely he would have shared this assessment).[30] Following the *Little Sarah* debacle, Washington turned to federal collectors of customs, the principal federal officers in the port cities, to prevent refitting privateers and related activities. In August, Washington, with the advice of his cabinet, issued a set of directives, called "deductions from the laws of neutrality," embodying his neutrality policy, and transmitted them to the state governors and to the customs officers. The idea was that the collectors, who had broad statutory discretion to admit and clear ships, would be able to detain or refuse entry to ships violating Washington's policies.[31]

Finally, and crucial for our discussion, the administration prosecuted U.S. citizens who violated neutrality. The best-known case involved Gideon Henfield, who enlisted on a French privateer (an act contrary to the proclamation).[32] But doubts about the President's constitutional authority plagued the Henfield prosecution and others like it. Ultimately, the prosecutions floundered until 1794, when Congress prohibited non-neutral behavior by statute. These events confirm the view that presidential foreign policy decrees, standing alone, lacked the force of law.[33]

Despite serious doubts about the legal basis of Henfield's prosecution, neither the administration nor the courts claimed the proclamation itself as a source of law (which would have been the obvious move if anyone thought the President could issue lawmaking decrees in foreign affairs). The proclamation itself did not appear to claim legal force: Washington said that he would "cause prosecutions to be instituted against all persons, who shall, within the cognizance of the courts of the United States, violate the law of nations." Jefferson's official direction to the U.S. Attorney in Philadelphia did not mention the proclamation, stating only that "certain citizens of the United States, have engaged in committing depredations on the property and commerce of some of the nations at peace with the United States" and directing him to "take such measures for apprehending and prosecuting them as shall be according to law." Washington also requested Attorney General Edmund Randolph's opinion regarding the authority to prosecute violators of neutrality. Like Jefferson, Randolph did not say the proclamation was law or that citizens could be prosecuted for violating it; he relied on treaties and the common law of disturbing the peace.[34] And Hamilton, writing as Pacificus on behalf of the administration at about the same time, said: "The Proclamation has been represented [by the opposition] as enacting some new law. This view of it is entirely erroneous."[35]

In the court proceedings against Henfield, prosecutors pointed to treaties, the law of nations, and common law—but not the proclamation—as laws that Henfield violated. The court's jury instructions also did not rely upon the proclamation but invoked the law of nations, as part of the common law, and U.S. treaties (made the supreme law of the land through the Constitution's Article VI).[36] Failure to mention the proclamation is especially remarkable because the sources that were used had serious difficulties as foundations for the prosecution. Though Henfield might have caused the United States to breach treaty provisions, nothing in the treaties created or even implied individual criminal liability for violations. Other than the law of nations, the common law had little precedent for the offence, and even the law of nations was unclear (at best) whether an individual who violated neutrality could be subjected to criminal prosecution. Moreover, the very idea of common law crimes (that is, crimes depending only on judicial decision, without support in statutory law) stood on shaky foundations; some years later the Supreme Court ruled that federal courts lacked power try such crimes, and even in 1793 there must have been some doubt.[37] Yet Henfield's prosecutors thought these arguments, with all their difficulties, stronger than reliance on a unilateral executive pronouncement such as the proclamation.

Henfield's supporters, on the other hand, directly argued that the prosecution effectively rested on the proclamation alone, and they opposed it as an attempt to give legal force to an executive act. As John Marshall later recounted, "it was universally asked . . . were the American people already prepared to give to a proclamation the force of a legislative act, and to subject themselves to the will of the executive?"[38]

Despite overwhelming evidence, Henfield's jury refused to convict. A key element seems to have been the view that although Henfield had violated the proclamation, no law made his conduct criminal.[39] The result, Marshall wrote, "exposed [the executive department] to the obloquy of having attempted a measure which the laws would not justify."[40] Washington in response considered and rejected calling Congress into session to pass neutrality laws, but once Congress reconvened he requested an act "to extend the legal code and the jurisdiction of the Courts of the United States to many cases which, although dependent on principles already recognised, demand some further provisions." Congress passed what has become known as the Neutrality Act, endorsing the administration's positions[41]—and neutrality prosecutions became straightforward.[42]

These events suggest that few people in 1793 thought the President could create legal obligations through his constitutional foreign affairs powers. Despite the proclamation's prominence, in enforcing neutrality Washington and his subordinates always claimed to be enforcing something else—common law, treaties, the law of nations—not the proclamation itself. These claims were not very convincing, and the objection laid against the prosecutions was that no law forbade the activities in question. Washington, opponents said, sought to give the proclamation the force of law, a position thought self-evidently indefensible.

The reason the proclamation lacked legal authority was not widely discussed, for the administration did not claim that authority and its critics thought it obviously lacking. The general view of it is consistent, though, with the textual derivation of presidential foreign affairs powers described above. If the President's foreign affairs powers are "inherent" or derivative of some extra-constitutional principle, it is not obvious that they encompass only policy and not lawmaking. If, however, they arise from the textual grant of the "executive Power," the limitation assumed in the 1790s is understandable: The traditional executive foreign affairs powers did not include lawmaking-by-proclamation to support foreign affairs objectives.

Implications of the President's Inability to Act beyond the Traditional Executive Power

Curtiss-Wright and the Steel Seizure Case

Let us now reexamine Steel Seizure and Curtiss-Wright, with this limit upon executive foreign affairs powers in mind. We can see that, as a textual matter, Justice Black was right to say in Steel Seizure that the President can only exercise powers based upon the Constitution or an Act of Congress. But this statement comes with the substantial caveat (which Black did not acknowledge) that the President's power under the Constitution includes executive foreign affairs power. This, as we have seen, is the historical eighteenth-century executive foreign affairs power, less powers the Constitution grants elsewhere.

Adding this caveat does not undermine Black's result. President Truman defended seizing the mills as, among other things, an exercise of executive power. Since he was not implementing pre-existing law, Truman must have been relying on "external" executive foreign affairs power. Now that we see where that power originates, we can see Truman claimed more than it supported. What Truman did was in effect lawmaking by executive order. His order changed the legal status of the mill owners, by taking their property (at least temporarily) for government use.[43] Prior to the order, federal authorities had no legal right to occupy the mills, nor did the mill owners have the obligation to allow them to do so. After his executive order, Truman asserted, federal authorities had the legal authorization they needed. Thus Truman saw his order as a legally determinative step, changing the mill owners' rights and obligations under domestic law. And he claimed an "executive" right to do so (from Article II, Section 1), because seizing the mills was necessary to achieve executive foreign affairs goals.

But eighteenth-century executive foreign affairs power generally did not extend to altering legal rights and duties domestically, even to support foreign affairs goals. Founding-era Americans seemed to share the idea that the President was not authorized to go very far (without legislative support) in enforcing foreign policy domestically—shown most dramatically in Henfield's case. As a result, Article II, Section 1 did not grant the power Truman claimed.

The advantage of this reading is that it preserves Black's result in *Steel Seizure,* imposing an important limit on presidential foreign affairs power, and yet explains many well-accepted things the President does in foreign affairs without specific authorization. Black hesitated to give content to Article II, Section 1 because he did not know how to limit it; if he allowed "executive Power" to explain the President's diplomatic powers, perhaps it could also be used (as Truman sought to use it) to give the President power to seize the mills. Attention to executive power's historical meaning, however, provides a way to give Article II, Section 1 some foreign affairs content and yet to limit it. The difference between the President's diplomatic powers and Truman's asserted power to seize the mills is that one was part of historical executive foreign affairs power and the other was not.

Now let us again reconsider *Curtiss-Wright*. It should be clear that much of what *Curtiss-Wright* claimed for the President as "inherent" in sovereignty is actually contained in the textual executive foreign affairs power. Thus *Curtiss-Wright* correctly emphasized, for example, that the President controls communication with foreign countries, even without explicit constitutional or congressional grants of that power. The explanation comes, though, from a proper reading of Article II, Section 1. As a result, though we rejected *Curtiss-Wright*'s reasoning in Chapters 1–2, we accepted many of its implications in Chapters 3–4.

But the difference between *Curtiss-Wright*'s approach and the textual approach should also now be apparent. Because *Curtiss-Wright* did not ground itself in constitutional text, it had no way to limit itself. The range of powers that are "necessary concomitants of nationality" seems unmanageably open-ended. In particular, it is difficult to say whether domestic implementation of executive foreign policy goals, through measures that change domestic rights and obligations, is an "inherent" power. Justice Sutherland apparently thought so, at least to the extent of believing that his inherent power theory was somehow relevant to the embargo power, but he never explained why (other than to say that the embargo related to foreign affairs, or, as he put it, "external sovereignty").

The idea of "executive" foreign affairs power, in contrast, contains identifiable limits—specifically, that it cannot reach matters not part of eighteenth-century executive power. As with the power Truman claimed in *Steel Seizure,* the specific power *Curtiss-Wright* attributed to the President (embargo, at least in peacetime) was not part of historical executive foreign affairs powers, and so not part of the "executive Power" of Article II, Section 1.[44]

In short, we may conclude that both *Curtiss-Wright* and *Steel Seizure* had basically sound intuitions. They seem so far apart because they failed to recognize executive foreign affairs power. *Curtiss-Wright* was correct (as a textual matter) in its intuition that unallocated foreign affairs power lay with the President, although the Court did not understand why this was true nor how that power could be limited. *Steel Seizure* was correct that presidential foreign affairs power depends upon the Constitution and that seizure of the mills (and lawmaking power generally) lie beyond the President's constitutional powers even when done to support foreign policy goals. The Court did not explain, though, how these statements could be reconciled with the President's diplomatic powers or why those diplomatic powers might not also imply implementation powers. The answers are supplied by the eighteenth-century meaning of the "executive Power."

Further Implications—Executive Detentions and Trials

More broadly, then, we should be extraordinarily suspicious of independent presidential action amounting to lawmaking—that is, altering individuals' legal rights and duties in the domestic legal system—even if done to further foreign policy or national security objectives. This does not mean the President never has such powers, but they must be justified by reference to traditional definitions and practices, recognizing a general rule pointing in the opposite direction.

In the Civil War's early stages, for example, President Abraham Lincoln asserted independent presidential power to suspend the writ of habeas corpus, and thus to detain U.S. citizens without criminal charges, in response to domestic rebellion. Lincoln noted that the Constitution (Article I, Section 9) allows suspension "when in cases of Rebellion or Invasion the public Safety may require it" but does not, in so many words, say which branch should decide the matter:

> It was decided [by the executive branch] that we have a case of rebellion, and that the public safety does require the qualified suspension of the privilege of the writ which was authorized to be made. Now it is insisted that Congress, and not the Executive, is vested with this power. But the Constitution itself, is silent as to . . . who, is to exercise the power; and as the provision was plainly made for a dangerous emergency, it cannot be believed the framers of the instrument intended, that in every case, the danger should run its course, until Congress could be called together. . . . [45]

A leading counterargument is that because the suspension clause is in Article I (rather than Article II), suspension is a congressional power.[46] That seems reasonable, but this chapter gives stronger reasons for thinking Lincoln was wrong. Lincoln relied on his executive powers, as his language suggests.[47] But suspending the writ changes individuals' domestic legal rights and duties. Presumptively, then, suspension is not an "executive" power. The mere fact that it is connected to foreign affairs or, in this case, national emergency is not enough to make it "executive," nor is Lincoln's entirely reasonable policy argument about the need for swift action.

Under this approach, Lincoln's argument seems to fail (as a matter of historical meaning), because there is little history of executive suspension of the writ, either in English practice or political theory. To the contrary, when the writ was suspended in response to domestic insurrection, Parliament suspended it; and Blackstone specifically confirmed that suspension was a parliamentary power: "But the happiness of our constitution is, that it is not left to the executive power to determine when the danger of the state is so great, as to render this measure [detention] expedient. For the parliament only, or legislative power, whenever it sees proper, can authorize the crown, by suspending the *habeas corpus* act for a short and limited time, to imprison suspected persons without giving any reason for so doing."[48] There is no reason to think founding-era Americans had in mind a definition of "executive Power" that included authority to suspend the writ.

To take another example, during World War II, President Franklin Roosevelt claimed power to establish a military tribunal to try German saboteurs (one of whom supposedly was a U.S. citizen) captured in the United States in civilian clothes. The Supreme Court (*In re Quirin*, 1942) strained to find congressional authorization for the tribunal. In somewhat parallel circumstances, after the 2001 terrorist attacks in the United States, President George W. Bush asserted power to detain and try individuals thought complicit in the attacks or otherwise connected to terrorists—partly on the basis of congressional authorization, but also on the basis of independent executive power.[49] On the question of independent executive power, both claims seem to sweep too broadly. Roosevelt and Bush both appear to claim powers that, on initial inspection, seem legislative (or judicial). Under the framework we have been developing, they would need to show that, notwithstanding the apparently nonexecutive features, these matters were ones that traditionally fell within the historical definition of executive power. At least with respect to U.S. citizens not in an area of active hostilities, it seems unlikely that such a showing could be made. As Blackstone's account of *habeas* suspension indicates, subjects within the realm were protected from purely "executive" actions taken on foreign affairs or national security grounds. On the other hand, Presidents would seem on much stronger ground in claiming such powers against noncitizens not within the country.

The President's Inability to Command Support from Other Branches

Although the executive power includes independent foreign affairs authority, there are two crucial things the executive power, under its historical definition, does not contain. The first we saw in previous sections of this chapter: executive foreign affairs power does not include power to implement foreign affairs goals within the domestic legal system. The second is that executive power does not extend to making independent decisions about spending money. The Constitution, carrying over a key aspect of English constitutionalism, states the latter point clearly in Article I, Section 9: "No money shall be drawn from the Treasury, but in Consequence of Appropriations made by Law."

As in England, American federalists saw this as a key constitutional check on executive power. In Madison's view: "The House of Representatives can not only refuse, but they alone can propose the supplies requisite for the support of government. They, in a word, hold the purse. . . . This power of the purse may, in fact, be regarded as the most complete and effectual weapon with which any constitution can arm the immediate representatives of the people." In controlling executive power, federalist James Iredell emphasized, "the authority over money will do everything."[50]

Applied to foreign affairs, though, the importance of these limits turns on whether Congress, in making laws and appropriating money, has any constitutional obligation to support the President's foreign affairs activities. One might argue that the Constitution's grant of executive power implies a congressional obligation to provide funds (and perhaps laws) to enable the executive power to function. Without this obligation, the President may not be able to exercise all of the constitutionally granted executive foreign affairs powers. For example, sending diplomatic agents is an executive power, but if Congress provides no money for diplomatic agents, they cannot be sent—and thus the President appears to be denied a constitutional power, as surely as if Congress prohibited it directly. And if Congress funds some missions (and not others), Congress (not the President) is managing diplomatic relations.

Presidents and their supporters have, at various times, made such arguments, or something approaching them. Indeed, these arguments lie behind most presidential claims of "inherent" power that Congress cannot limit. To take one example, in the 1980s, in the once-famous "Iran-Contra" episode, President Ronald Reagan's administration sought to assist the "contras" (the opposition side in the ongoing Nicaraguan civil war). Congress provided some of the requested funding, but several later laws attempted to limit how the money was spent (laws which the Reagan administration arguably ignored). In the ensuing controversy, the administration and its supporters argued that at least some such limits were unconstitutional (a claim Congress strongly resisted).[51]

Administration defenders began with the proposition that "it is beyond question that Congress did not have the constitutional power to prohibit the

President from sharing information, asking other governments to contribute to the Nicaraguan resistance, or entering into secret negotiations with Iran." Read narrowly, that is likely correct, though it is perhaps more a function of Congress's lack of enumerated powers (see Chapter 10). But the pro-executive position continued, more extravagantly, that Congress could not limit *funding* for presidential activities "that fall within the constitutionally protected rubric of information-sharing and diplomatic communication." Further, "Congress does not have to create a State Department or an intelligence agency," but "[o]nce such departments are created, however, the Congress may not prevent the President from using his executive branch employees from serving as the country's 'eyes and ears' in foreign policy." As a result, "Congress may not use its control over appropriations, including salaries, to prevent the executive . . . from fulfilling Constitutionally mandated obligations" and, even more broadly, "Congressional actions [that] interfere with core presidential foreign policy functions . . . should be struck down" as unconstitutional. In sum, although not put in so many words, Congress (it was argued) has an obligation to fund some presidential foreign affairs activities with which it disagrees.[52]

This argument (for which little textual support was advanced), conflates two very different propositions: (1) that Congress cannot tell the President what to do (or not to do) in foreign affairs, and (2) that Congress must support the President financially. The first seems tolerably supported by the text, which gives the President and not Congress executive power. To make a textual argument for the latter, though, the President would need to claim that Article II, Section 1's "executive Power" implies a duty of support (at least to the extent of funding) on Congress's part. Since the Constitution does not say this in so many words, the argument depends on background understandings of executive power containing such a duty.

Unfortunately for the President, eighteenth-century observers of the English system on whom founding-era Americans relied emphasized Parliament's ability to check the king's executive foreign affairs power. In England, Parliament approved a military budget annually. Montesquieu described this practice as an important protection of liberty: "If the legislative power was to settle the subsidies, not from year to year, but for ever, it would run the risk of losing its liberty, because the executive power would no longer be dependent."[53] More colorfully, de Lolme wrote:

> The king of England . . . has the prerogative of commanding armies, and equipping fleets; but without the concurrence of his parliament he

cannot maintain them. He can bestow places and employments; but without his parliament he cannot pay the salaries attending on them. He can declare war; but without his parliament it is impossible for him to carry it on. In a word, the royal prerogative, destitute as it is of the power of imposing taxes, is like a vast body, which cannot of itself accomplish its motions; or, if you please, it is like a ship completely equipped, but from which the parliament can at pleasure draw off the water, and leave it a-ground—and also set it afloat again, by granting subsidies.[54]

Not only did this checking power exist in theory, but, as historian William Holdsworth confirms, Parliament's "exclusive control over finance enabled it to criticize all the acts of the executive government, to stop projects of which it disapproved, to force the executive to adopt policies of which it approved, and to supervise the methods adopted to carry them out."[55] Parliament commonly refused (or at least threatened to refuse) funds for a war or alliance contemplated by the king; as recounted, in some cases Parliament refused to fund or enact obligations already undertaken by the king in treaties.[56] And some of Parliament's involvement occurred at a level of considerable detail.[57] Parliament's assertion of these rights produced sharp conflicts with the seventeenth-century monarchs, playing a role in the mid-century civil war and the Glorious Revolution in 1688. By the eighteenth century, a fairly stable system emerged, with the monarchy (through its ministers) maintaining formal control over foreign affairs, but Parliament as a whole exercising a checking power through control over spending.

As a result, eighteenth-century Americans, who were familiar with this system and commentary upon it,[58] would not have thought the traditional executive power implied any obligation for supporting funds or legislation. Of course, they might have decided that this was a bad idea. Under the Articles, a common complaint was that the Congress chronically lacked money. It had no direct taxing power, but (in theory) it made "requisitions" upon the states as its source of revenue. In practice, the states frequently paid late or refused to pay on various pretexts, and the Congress often lacked funds to support foreign affairs activities.[59] Yet the Constitution's text did not make any special provision for funding executive activities. It solved the problem of an underfunded national government by giving the new Congress direct taxing power, and also sole appropriations power, while assigning executive foreign affairs powers to the President. This replicated the corresponding parts of the English system, and in that system the monarch's executive power carried no implicit obligation upon Parliament to supply funding. So Americans would not have understood the new President's executive power to carry such an obligation unless the text said so directly—which it did not. Despite the Articles experience, Americans seem to have embraced the system of checking-through-appropriations. As indicated, when the drafters and ratifiers spoke of the appropriations system, they saw it as checking the President's power, without noting exceptions for foreign affairs power. And in the 1790 debate over funding diplomatic posts (discussed in Chapter 4), South Carolina's Representative Smith said of ambassadors: "To be sure, if [Congress] were of opinion that all intercourse with foreign nations should be cut off, they might decline to make provision for them." No one argued to the contrary; President Washington's position was not that Congress had to fund diplomatic missions, but that Congress could not give another body (the Senate) an "executive" role in administering them.[60]

It is important to see that most modern presidential claims to "inherent" power lying beyond Congress's regulatory reach depend on claims to obligatory funding (and thus are textually difficult to support). Returning to the Iran-Contra debate, one administration claim was, for example, that Congress could not limit the President's ability to "enter into secret negotiations with Iran." That may be true, so long as the President personally is negotiating (and is not spending any money to do so). But as soon as the President paid emissaries, or otherwise spent money, Congress's funding involvement became necessary—and Congress can presumably pass laws clarifying what its appropriations cover and do not cover (and punishing misuse). Thus, if Congress directs that no money be spent on negotiations for a particular purpose or with a particular country, that should be an end to it. Without entering an exhaustive review of particular controversies of this nature, this principle would seem capable of resolving most of them. Though Congress might have difficulty limiting what the President can say (and cannot oblige the President to say anything), it should generally be able to limit what the President, through the executive branch, can do.[61]

We should, however, also note a corresponding check on Congress. Although Congress can restrict the President's conduct of foreign affairs, it cannot accomplish much affirmatively without the President's cooperation. Congress faces the constraint that it must rely on the President, and presidential subordinates, to carry out any foreign affairs activities that it funds: it cannot carry out executive powers itself, nor create executive power centers outside the presidency (the latter being the true lesson of the 1790 funding debate). Further, as a practical matter, Congress will likely take its funding decisions at a relatively general level (as it in fact did in 1790), because of the relative difficulty of obtaining information and specifying contingencies in advance.[62] As a result, the President is likely to have (though is not constitutionally entitled to) a large stock of discretionary funding for "executive" activities. Thus the constitutional system carries a cooperative imperative, but with a bias toward presidential initiative and congressional checks.[63]

Conclusion

In sum, the traditional idea of executive power, derived from theorists like Montesquieu and from the experience of the English system, is neither ill-defined nor unlimited. Once we see that Article II, Section 1 gives the President foreign affairs power by incorporating the traditional definition of executive power, we also see that substantial limits are built into the constitutional system. We will see in later chapters that the founding-era Americans (unlike the theorists of the English system) thought these checks upon executive power were not sufficient, so they designed additional checks in the Constitution. But that does not mean that they abandoned or minimized the traditional limitations of executive power. To the contrary, their incorporation of the traditional system in Article II, Section 1 shows that they used it as a baseline.

In practice, this means that if the President claims power from Article II, Section 1, the President must show as a threshold matter that this power was part of the traditional executive power of foreign affairs. That showing does not automatically entitle the President to exercise the power, but it is a necessary step. This is where the President's argument failed in *Steel Seizure* (though the Court did not put it this way): the power Truman claimed was not part of the traditional definition of executive power. It is similarly where Lincoln's argument in the suspension cases and Roosevelt's argument in *Quirin* deserved to fail. And it is also where a President would fail with any argument that Congress must support foreign affairs goals with funding or legislation. The President may exercise the executive foreign affairs powers *to the extent of the laws and money available* but cannot demand that more laws or money be made available.[64]

Measured against actual modern practice, there is nothing radical in any of the above statements. To be sure, there have been debates at the margins, as with Truman's claim in *Steel Seizure* or Reagan's claim in the Nicaraguan controversy. But as a general matter, everyone understands that Congress, not the President, holds lawmaking and funding power. As a distinguished authority on presidential power observes, if an "implied law-making authority [in foreign affairs] can inhere in the general grants of executive power" then "the fundamental premises of the constitutional order are overturned."[65] We see here how the Constitution's text makes this clear—and in particular makes clear that this common understanding is not relaxed in foreign affairs, despite the President's executive foreign affairs powers.

6

Executive Power and Its Critics

The idea of "executive" foreign affairs power is so central to a textual theory of foreign affairs that objections to it must be considered carefully. Two main textual objections stand out. First, perhaps Article II, Section 1 has no substantive content: it might mean only that there shall be a single executive (rather than an executive council), called the President (rather than "Governor" or similar title), who will exercise the powers listed in subsequent sections (Article II, Sections 2 and 3). Alternatively, perhaps "executive Power" gives some substantive authority to the President, principally the power to execute laws, but does not grant foreign affairs powers. As we shall see, each position has its advantages, but each also has serious flaws.

Overshadowing this debate about text, though, is a deeply held structural intuition. The Constitution's drafters knew about and distrusted strong executives, both from the practical example of the English monarchy and from broader fears stoked by the history of republics falling into dictatorship. After the Revolution, Americans constituted their state governments with extraordinarily weak executives. Surely—whatever the nuances of Article II, Section 1—they did not re-create the English monarchy in the U.S. President. This intuition may counsel hesitation to give "executive Power" broad substantive meaning, whatever other arguments might be advanced.[1]

These points may also combine with a complementary observation about the drafting and ratifying debates. Leaving aside the initial debate over the Virginia plan, very little was said about the President's diplomatic power, or about the clause vesting executive power in the President. From the Committee of Detail's introduction of the clause, in its near-final form, until after ratification, it provoked essentially no recorded discussion.[2] Of course, our records are incomplete—perhaps it was debated—and surely the Constitution's text meant what it meant, whether or not the debates fully explored that meaning. But, one might say, it is at least curious that, at a time when executive power was viewed with suspicion, the provision excited so little interest.

Executive Power in Early America

Let us begin with the intuition—that no matter what the text may appear to say, it is implausible that the founding generation intended to give generalized "executive" foreign affairs power to the President. It is implausible, we might think, not because it leads to irrational or bizarre results—a strong foreign affairs executive is not irrational, though many people find it undesirable—but because we cannot imagine that anyone at the particular time would have found such a result acceptable.

Though they do not depend on text (and indeed may contradict it), arguments of this type cannot automatically be discounted. It is true that, in some times and places, the currents of thought are so unanimously in one direction that contrary results are simply unimaginable. Even if clever lawyers could argue that the Constitution somehow left open the possibility of monarchy, we would have a hard time believing that this is the way the founding generation read the text. Perhaps some Americans did favor monarchy (Hamilton wanted something resembling it), but they were so overwhelmingly outnumbered that the subject was not seriously open for discussion—as Hamilton himself recognized.[3] Any purported reading of the text permitting monarchy would face insurmountable problems of historical plausibility: whatever the text seems to mean today, it could not have had that meaning when drafted and ratified.

Nonetheless, arguments from historical implausibility are hard to sustain. It is obviously insufficient to show that *some* founding-era Americans had beliefs that seem to contradict the text. It is similarly insufficient to show that all (or most) of them held a set of abstract beliefs in common and to reason from there that they must also have shared ideas about specific implications of those beliefs. There is much loose talk about the "intent of the framers"— we must be careful lest we are drawn too far along by it.

Fear of the Executive

Americans' views of executive power were shaped in the first instance by the man whom they (figuratively) fought in the Revolution: George III. Historians debate how much of the oppression felt by the colonists can be traced to King George himself, as opposed to his ministers or Parliament. But Americans saw the monarchy as part of the problem, if not the whole problem:

"The colonial period ended with the belief prevalent that the 'executive magistracy' was the natural enemy, the legislative assembly the natural friend of liberty, a sentiment strengthened by the contemporary spectacle of George III's domination of Parliament."[4] They were also fascinated by the historical experience of republics, which all too often collapsed into executive dictatorship. We will see more of their views of Rome in particular in later chapters, but for now it is sufficient to say that the Roman republic was closely studied by Americans, who attributed its end to executive overreaching.

These general impulses found concrete expression in the early forms of government after the Revolution. In every state government formed in the Revolution's immediate aftermath, executive authority was heavily constrained. The states' chief magistrates (called "Governors" or "Presidents") were appointed by state legislatures, often for very short terms and sometimes without ability to stand for reelection. None had veto power. Many had executive councils that they had to consult, and from which some had to gain approval for important actions. State governors were, as Madison put it, "little more than Cyphers."[5]

At the national level, as Chapter 2 outlines, initially there was no chief executive magistrate. The "President" of the Articles' Congress was an empty title (so much so that hardly anyone today remembers who held that post). Executive powers were exercised by the Congress as a whole—a body so cumbersome that surely the remotest fear was that it might seize dictatorial powers. And if its structure were not enough, the Congress's exercise of the most important executive foreign affairs powers—war and treatymaking—required supermajority approval.

In sum, then, Americans feared executive power, and the governmental structures they created after the Revolution ensured that no single person would accumulate any meaningful amount of it. Deliberative assemblies—state legislatures, the states' executive councils, the Congress—controlled its exercise. In this climate, a Constitution that gave broad unspecified executive powers to one person, outside the direct control of a deliberative assembly, was surely unthinkable; had it been proposed, it would have been buried as completely as Hamilton's plan for a quasi-monarchy. Or so it is argued.

The Embrace of Executive Power

As is often the case when history seems too one-sided, the foregoing discussion oversimplifies. It may accurately describe where matters stood in 1776, but much happened in the ensuing eleven years to change perceptions of executive power.

First, many Americans judged the legislative-supremacy model of early state constitutions—and the deliberating executive assembly of the Continental Congress—to be structural failures. Whether they actually were failures is another question, and much debated; the key point is that they were perceived this way at the time. Under the Articles, the Congress had many structural problems, some of which—lack of legislative and enforcement powers, for example—we have already examined (Chapter 2). Another overriding problem, though, was its sheer inability to get anything done. This in turn had various causes, including that its delegates often failed even to attend.[6] But one important commonly perceived problem was that the Congress lacked a single person with executive authority to manage the operation of government. Anything the Congress did had to be approved by a vote of the delegates—meaning that effectively nothing could be done when the Congress was out of session or lacked a quorum, or when delegates deadlocked or became bogged down in minor matters (as they frequently did). Foreign Secretary Jay complained of "unseasonable delays and successive obstacles in obtaining the decision and sentiments of Congress" and concluded that "the executive business of sovereignty, depending on so many wills," could not adequately be performed.[7] The project of bringing energy and focus to the national executive thus became central to the campaign for reform.[8]

A parallel reawakening of executive power occurred in the states. Soon after the Revolution, voices began to be heard in favor of strengthening state governors. Historians record a shift from the early state constitutions (such as Pennsylvania in 1776), which gave almost complete control to legislatures and councils, to gradually more powerful governors. In 1777, New York adopted a constitution with a somewhat stronger governor; in 1778, Massachusetts (pressed by Parsons's *Essex Result*) rejected a proposed constitution, partly because its governor was not strong enough; Massachusetts then adopted a constitution influenced by New York's model in 1780, but added, for the first time, an executive veto. Although state governors on the whole remained weak, constitution writers began to show some interest the chief magistrate's independent powers.[9]

Partly these developments reflected desire for an executive branch with "energy"—that is, one that could accomplish things. They were also driven by new appreciations of legislatures' excesses. Americans began to believe that the structures adopted in early state constitutions were defective forms of separation of powers, because (at least in practice) most power accrued to the legislatures. In this way, Americans began thinking about what we now call "checks and balances": that each of the different branches had to have a store of *independent* power to restrain the power of the others. This thinking, for example, explicitly underlay the revival of the veto, a feature of royal government avoided in early state constitutions because it was thought to concentrate too much power in the governor.[10] By 1787, "the delegates' chief concern was thus to secure an executive strong enough, not one weak enough."[11]

Even within the Philadelphia Convention, the shift is noticeable. Most delegates seemed to assume that the chief magistrate should have a longer term in office than the state Governors and have a veto. But in early drafts Congress appointed the President, and it was not even clear that executive powers would be held by a single person (Randolph, among others, thought they should not).[12] Only after much debate did delegates reconcile themselves to a single, independent chief magistrate. As they did so, a single magistrate's energy and effectiveness became a central argument.[13]

It is, therefore, incomplete to say that Americans feared unified executive power. They did; but they also embraced unified executive power, as a means to get things done and to resist legislative excesses. The Constitution's provisions on presidential power—both in their drafting history and in their final product—reflect an interplay between these two competing goals. No doubt most, though perhaps not all, founding-era Americans had their own share of this tension; in the country as a whole, made up of people who balanced these goals in different ways, there were surely multitudes of opinions.

Implications for Foreign Affairs

What, then, does this mean for the Constitution's foreign affairs provisions? Standing alone, nothing. Various scholars and advocates have claimed, explicitly or implicitly, that the "currents of history" (as one puts it)[14] led to inevitable results at the Convention, and that the new structure of government necessarily chosen by the delegates can be deduced from events that preceded it. But the currents of history do not all run in the same direction, particularly those underlying the constitutional law of foreign affairs. Americans both admired and deplored the structure of English government; they celebrated, yet departed from, the separation of powers theories of Locke, Blackstone, and Montesquieu; they saw that their national government needed more power (especially in foreign affairs) than it had under the Articles, yet they mistrusted centralization of power; they longed for, yet feared, the leadership of a strong chief executive.

Particularly with respect to the President's role in foreign affairs, then, one must read the text without preconceived intuitions of the "framers' intent" derived from imprecise generalizations about prevailing views of executive power. The prevailing views were nothing more than a mix of concerns about having enough—but not too much—power vested in a chief magistrate.[15] How these concerns were resolved in their specific applications can be found only by examining the final product.

These observations, of course, apply equally to arguments *in favor of* the historical inevitability of executive foreign affairs powers. Just as one might argue that the framers' experiences with executive power made it implausible that they would establish a strong independent foreign affairs executive, one might argue that these experiences made it inevitable. After all, the framers' main historical experience was a system that united executive powers in a single monarch. Key political writers they admired—especially Locke, Montesquieu, and Blackstone—argued strongly for unified foreign affairs power (see Chapter 3); Locke said any other system would lead to "ruine." Separation-of-powers theory, in its purest form, insisted upon absolute identity between the type of power exercised and the type of institution exercising it: that is, only Parliament should exercise legislative power and only the king should exercise executive power.[16] Perhaps (one might argue) the framers, reading these authorities and reviewing their own history, thought foreign affairs powers necessarily had to be vested in one chief magistrate— from an inherent meaning of "executive"; because political theory said it had to be done that way; or because it had always been done that way.[17]

As with "inevitability" arguments against executive power, these claims should be unpersuasive.[18] They radically oversimplify the framers' experience with executive power, and with political commentary upon it. The framers (and the political commentators) knew that executive foreign affairs power could be vested in any of a number of ways. Montesquieu in particular emphasized that Roman practice split executive foreign affairs power across three branches—consuls, senate, and popular assembly. He thought this was a mistake for policy reasons, but the framers knew from their own education in Roman history that it had worked well enough for hundreds of years. Even Locke recognized that foreign affairs powers *could* be vested other than in a chief magistrate, and he gave little evidence supporting his claim that this would be dangerous folly. The English king's concentration of foreign affairs power, celebrated by Blackstone, was (as the framers knew) as much the product of historical accident as high political theory (and, in any event, by the framers' time was exercised through a ministry that more resembled an executive council). The "pure" version of separation of powers, if it ever held much sway, had given way, in the framers' thought, to the more complex idea of checks and balances, which promoted some intermingling of powers among branches. And the Articles' Congress—which held foreign affairs power in a deliberating assembly—had, for all its problems, not been a complete failure: it managed the war effort, formed key alliances, and negotiated a successful peace. The Constitution's text itself shows that the framers rejected the idea of unified foreign affairs power, at least with respect to declaring war, treatymaking, and diplomatic appointments (Chapters 7–12). The framers were surely not compelled by their background to adopt any particular allocation of foreign affairs powers.

It is important to distinguish (as some critics do not) the textual view of executive foreign affairs power from claims of historical and logical inevitability. The textual view says that the phrase "executive power," in eighteenth-century writing, as a definitional matter included foreign affairs powers. This does *not* claim it was inevitable (or even likely) that the framers would vest executive foreign affairs power in an independent magistrate. All it says is that *if* the framers chose to use the phrase "executive power," as they did, the phrase should be given its ordinary meaning at the time. The framers might have given "executive power" to a different branch (such as the Senate). They might have avoided the phrase "executive power" altogether and tried to allocate each component of executive power individually (an approach the Convention pursued for a while).[19] To decide what was done, we must read the text—and reading the text, in light of its ordinary meaning at the time, suggests that the framers pursued an intermediate course, allocating "executive Power" generally to the President but directing that key parts of it be given to or shared with other branches.

Is There Power in "Executive Power"?

Let us now consider textual objections. The most serious challenge relies on the structure of Article II as a whole; it runs as follows: The proposed reading, it is said, places undue weight on what is basically a preface to Article II; Section 1's general grant of "the executive Power" likely lacks substance, because an enumeration of specific powers follows in Sections 2 and 3. As Representative White said in 1789, arguing against executive removal power, "the Executive Powers so vested, are those enumerated in the Constitution"; or, as a modern commentary contends, Article II, Section 1 "says who has the executive power; not what that power is."[20] The clause's insertion by the Committee of Detail apparently provoked little discussion, which makes sense if it is prefatory but is puzzling if it is substantive. And later prominent explications of the President's power (including Hamilton's Federalist No. 75) wholly omit any mention of powers arising from Article II, Section 1.[21]

The matter deeply divides the academic commentary,[22] but for our purposes we should be able to explore it fairly summarily.[23] The "prefatory" argument depends on an implicit claim that the phrase "executive Power" lacked a common substantive meaning in the eighteenth century—that is, that there was not a set of governmental functions that people of the time commonly called "executive." Rather, "executive powers" would be powers a chief magistrate exercised, whatever those powers were (just as "legislative powers" would be whatever was done by an assembly). Thus Article II, Section 1 simply says that the "President" is the executive, and Sections 2 and 3 list what the President's executive powers will be.

Using "executive power" in this way has some resonance in modern language, as we tend to associate the phrase "executive power" with whatever the President does. But that is not how eighteenth-century separation-of-powers writing used the phrase. "Executive power" referred to a set of governmental functions that might be exercised by different bodies in different political systems: this is why founding-era Americans (and the theoretical writers who inspired them) could complain about undue concentration of "executive" and "legislative" powers in one entity (which could be a unitary magistrate or an assembly).[24] One simply cannot say (as eighteenth-century writers repeatedly did) that, for example, an assembly has too much executive power without some substantive definition of what "executive power" is, independent of what body exercises it. Separation of powers discourse saw itself as addressing, among other things, what part of government should exercise executive powers; that discussion assumes an identifiable set of powers called "executive."[25]

Further, it seems clear that at least *some* specific substantive powers were routinely called "executive" (just as others were called "legislative" or "judicial") without regard to what entity exercised them. Plainly almost everyone at the time associated "executive power" with power to enforce the law. When, for example, Montesquieu famously said that executive power and legislative power should always be separated, everyone understood this to mean that (at least) power to enforce law should be separated from power to make law. This was so because "executive power" *meant* "power to enforce the law" (as "legislative power" meant "power to make law"). These were, in fact, the dictionary definitions.[26]

As a result, it seems hard to deny that Article II, Section 1's literal meaning is a substantive grant of power. To "vest" something meant—as it means today—to give or grant it: by Johnson's 1755 dictionary definition, to "invest with" or "place in possession."[27] If "executive power" meant power to enforce the law, Article II, Section 1 simply says that the power to enforce the law shall be given to the President. The only way around this reading would be to say that "executive power" did *not* mean power to enforce the law, which is flatly contrary to the way eighteenth-century writers used the phrase.

This reading is confirmed by the parallel structure of Article III, Section 1, establishing the judicial branch. It says that the "judicial Power" of the United States is "vested" in the Supreme Court and in lower federal courts Congress may establish (followed in Section 2 by a list of the *types of cases* to which "the judicial power shall extend"). Aside from its reference to "judicial Power," nothing in Article III gives the judiciary its substantive powers (principally, to decide cases, plus associated powers such as authority to establish court procedures and issue orders).[28] These are sometimes called "inherent" powers of the judiciary, but surely it makes sense to read them as arising from Article III, Section 1: to eighteenth-century readers, "judicial power" *meant* the power to decide cases, *etc.*, so the Article's opening sentence means that these powers are given to ("vested in") the federal courts (and Section 2 then lists the types of cases in which federal courts can exercise them).[29] And if Article III, Section 1 grants a substantive set of powers, rather than being merely prefatory, it is natural to read Article II, Section 1 in the same way.[30]

The counterargument, of course, relies on the presence of Article II, Sections 2 and 3. If Article II, Section 1 grants the President all "executive" powers, what is the point of the subsequent sections? Does it not make more sense to read the subsequent sections to completely list the President's powers?[31]

It is far from clear, however, that this is a necessary implication. Madison in a different context wrote in *The Federalist* that "[n]othing is more natural or common than first to use a general phrase, and then to explain and qualify it by a recitation of particulars."[32] In the 1789 removal debates, Oliver Ellsworth—formerly a member of the Committee of Detail that drafted the executive power clause—emphasized: "The executive power is granted; not the executive powers hereinafter enumerated and explained."[33] And Hamilton directly focused on this point in his Pacificus essay, explaining that it would be inconsistent "with the rules of sound construction, to consider [Article II's] enumeration of particulars as derogating from the more comprehensive grant contained in the general clause. . . . [T]he difficulty of a complete and perfect specification of all the cases of Executive authority would naturally dictate the use of general terms—and would render it improbable that a specification of certain particulars was designed as a substitute for those terms, when antecedently used."[34] Madison's Helvidius, arguing against Hamilton, did not dispute this proposition; in the 1789 removal debate, Madison (like Ellsworth) agreed that Article II, Section 1 gave the President law execution power.[35]

It is especially problematic for the "prefatory" view of Section 1 that nothing in Sections 2 and 3 gives the President explicit law-enforcement power. True, Section 3 directs that the President "shall take Care that the Laws be faithfully executed." But the take-care clause, like some other clauses in Section 3, is phrased as a duty, not a power; it does not give the President authority to enforce the law but only imposes the obligation to use other presidential powers to that end. In particular, it presumably arises from a discredited feature of English law, that the Crown could "suspend" operation of Parliament's acts; the President's take-care duty assures that, whatever one thought of the "suspensive" power, the President had no such authority.[36] Reading the take-care clause as the *source* of the President's law-execution power would make an extraordinary puzzle of its placement almost at the end of Article II, after such trivial matters as the obligation to report to Congress on the state of the Union, and sandwiched between the minor activities of receiving foreign ambassadors and commissioning officers of the United States. To the contrary, the most natural reading is also the literal one: Article II, Section 1 gives the President power to execute the laws, and Article II, Section 3 assures that the President cannot suspend the laws.[37]

Ultimately, then, the argument against a substantive reading of Article II, Section 1 rests on the claim that the specific list of substantive presidential powers in Sections 2 and 3 would be redundant if Section 1 has substantive meaning. Addressed only to law execution, though, there is not much force to this argument. Most powers set forth in Sections 2 and 3 are either not obviously law-execution powers (such as powers to convene Congress or make recess appointments) or are duties rather than powers (the take-care clause or commissioning officers). Those that relate directly to law execution are necessary clarifications: for example, the pardon clause clarifies that the President has pardoning power (with respect to federal law only, and not for impeachments), despite Section 3's take-care obligation, and despite the fact that some might claim pardoning (like vetoing) is really making law.[38]

More importantly, though, the redundancy argument, addressed to law execution, is incoherent on its own terms. If Article II, Section 1 does not convey law execution power, then either the take-care clause must be stretched to convey it, or the President lacks it. The latter view seems unsustainable in the face of countless founding-era commentaries affirming that the President has this power;[39] the former would create all the same supposed redundancies.

In sum, the most natural reading is that at minimum Section 1 grants ("vests") power to enforce the laws ("executive power"), and Sections 2 and 3 clarify specific instances of that power or add additional powers and duties not obviously encompassed by it. That reading is consistent with dictionary definitions and ordinary meaning, with the corresponding provisions of Articles I and III, and with common understandings expressed by the drafters and ratifiers. Contrary arguments strain to add phrases the text does not contain and to deny historical meanings.

Of course, concluding that Article II, Section 1 vests law execution power does not, on its face, go very far toward establishing that it vests foreign affairs powers. But it does take the first step, rejecting claims that the clause is merely prefatory. If we accept that the clause vests law execution power, we must accept the more general proposition that it vests the President with (at least some) powers that were by eighteenth-century definition called "executive."

Is There Foreign Affairs Power in "Executive Power"?

Even if Article II, Section 1 vests law execution power, it might not vest foreign affairs powers. We might think that law execution easily falls within the ordinary meaning of "executive" power, but including foreign affairs power is a linguistic stretch. Even if some authorities defined it this way, perhaps that was not the consensus view: drafter Roger Sherman said at the Convention, for example, that "he considered the Executive magistry as nothing more than an institution for carrying the will of the Legislature into effect."[40] Moreover, the redundancy arguments mentioned above have particular force in foreign affairs, since many of the specific powers granted by Article II, Sections 2 and 3 relate to foreign affairs.

With respect to history, too, there may be particular concern about what was not said. Unlike law execution, the drafting and ratification records contain few direct indications that the President would have "executive" foreign affairs power. Almost all the evidence is indirect: comments that the President would have (some) foreign affairs powers, comments that (some) foreign affairs powers such as treatymaking were called "executive." The direct associations of executive power and foreign affairs power belong mostly to the post-ratification period, when perhaps those who spoke had institutional reasons for doing so. Relatedly, the executive power clause went almost undiscussed, from its introduction at the Convention and throughout the intense examination of the Constitution during the ratification period.[41] That does not mean it lacked all substance: if everyone agreed that the President should have law execution power, there might be little objection to a clause vesting law execution power. But foreign affairs power was different: the delegates opened the Convention with a rousing rejection of presidential power over war and treaties, and when founding-era Americans spoke of the dangers of monarchical power, they often had foreign affairs activities in mind. Could it be that foreign affairs power might nonetheless slip almost unnoticed into to the President's hands, by virtue of a clause added to the draft without recorded debate and hardly addressed in the ratification?

Textual Objections

To begin, the textual objection again appeals to an intuitive modern sense of what executive power means, which cannot overcome historical evidence of what executive power actually meant. As discussed (Chapters 3–4), leading writers used "executive power" to include foreign affairs powers; no matter how odd that may sound to modern ears, counterarguments have made little headway in disputing that claim.[42] It is quite likely that founding-era Americans lacked agreement on a definitive set of "executive powers," but it seems hard to escape the conclusion that, in the writings they studied and in their own discussions, they generally (though not universally) associated "executive" power and foreign affairs powers.

The principal force of the counterargument must come from its appeal to supposed redundancies created by Article II, Sections 2 and 3. At first glance, the objection seems formidable: these sections contain an array of foreign affairs powers that writers such as Montesquieu and Blackstone called "executive" (and thus, one would suppose, would already be included in Article II, Section 1). But closer examination shows that the supposed foreign affairs redundancies are not so problematic as they appear. The leading foreign affairs powers mentioned in Sections 2 and 3—treatymaking and diplomatic appointments—are *limits* on the President's executive power, creating a Senate role in what would otherwise be purely presidential powers (see

Chapter 7). The commander-in-chief clause is a necessary clarification: because the Constitution grants Congress substantial military powers in Article I, Section 8—in particular, to make "rules for the Government and Regulation of the land and naval Forces"—absent the commander-in-chief clause, one might think the Constitution entirely divested the President of previously "executive" military powers. Among other things, the clause assures that Congress cannot create a commander-in-chief independent of the President, and allows the President to direct the military in ways not dependent on antecedent laws (Chapter 12).

Receiving ambassadors, however, would seem part of the President's "executive Power" without the express reference in Article II, Section 3 and thus appears damagingly redundant. But several explanations are possible. One is that the specific clause establishes a duty (in addition to a power): its phrasing (that the President "shall receive" rather than "shall have power to receive") tracks other clauses that plainly impose duties and is distinct from those that only grant powers.[43] Perhaps, then, most foreign affairs powers are discretionary, but the President, as ceremonial head of state, *must* receive ambassadors (in the formal sense).

The clause may also emphasize an *exclusive* power. The Articles' Congress received ambassadors, and perhaps otherwise the new Congress might continue to claim that ceremonial right. And absent the clause, it would be less clear that states lacked power to receive ambassadors. States of course could not receive ambassadors on behalf of the United States (that being an aspect of the executive power of the United States), but states might otherwise think they could receive ambassadors on their own behalf—and might be particularly tempted to do so (or even feel under an obligation to do so) when ambassadors were physically present in the state.[44] The exclusive duty reading is also supported by the clause's omission of consuls, even though the Constitution, everywhere else it refers to ambassadors, mentions consuls as well.[45] The President naturally would not be *obliged* to receive minor officials like consuls (though of course he could), and it would be appropriate for states to interact with them.

The clause might also have resulted from oversight. During much of the Convention, the draft did not give the President general executive power (as recounted above, it was added by the Committee of Detail). The Committee's first draft gave the President the power/duty to receive ambassadors, and gave other specific foreign affairs powers to Congress; in subsequent drafts, it added the general executive power.[46] The ambassadors clause thus was not redundant when written, and the Committee may simply have neglected to delete it after adding the general power. It is quite possible (indeed, likely) that the Constitution includes minor redundancies of this type.[47] We should read the text to avoid them where possible, but single-minded desire to avoid redundancy should not drive us to accept distortions in other directions. In particular, small redundancies should not defeat an otherwise-persuasive reading in the absence of a satisfactory alternative.

And here is the core textual counter-consideration: whatever textual problems are created by foreign affairs redundancies, the difficulties of any alternative solution may be even greater. The foreign affairs reading of Article II, Section 1 has particular structural advantages in its fit with the rest of the Constitution, because it appears to be the only way to find complete allocation of foreign affairs powers in the text. The difficulty for its opponents is that they have no plausible competing theory. An alternative solution must identify an alternative source of unspecified foreign affairs authorities (which no one has yet been able to do), claim (implausibly) that the few specific grants can be stretched to cover all of foreign affairs, or assert (oddly) that the Constitution does not grant key foreign affairs authorities such as power over diplomacy.[48]

Although the latter claim is made (often implicitly) by commentary and can be attributed to some Justices in *Steel Seizure,* the historical case for it seems quite problematic. Of course, the Constitution likely does contain errors and omissions, but we may doubt that this particular one is plausible. The Constitution was drafted in large part to remedy the Articles' foreign affairs failings (see Chapter 2). Diplomacy is, of course, an integral part of well-managed foreign affairs. One key complaint about the Articles was that the Congress had not managed diplomacy well—Secretary Jay, as discussed, was continually frustrated by its difficulty in coming to decisions. That does not mean the framers inevitably gave the President control of diplomacy in the new system: they might have decided that, on balance, deliberative diplomacy was worth its inefficiency. But it seems most unlikely that they *forgot* to allocate diplomatic power—to the contrary, its allocation likely was an important concern.

That being so, one would like to see significant historical evidence for a reading producing radically incomplete allocations of foreign affairs powers. Yet so far as anyone has been able to determine, *no one* during the drafting or ratifying debates, nor during the Washington administration, pointed out that the Constitution failed to allocate diplomatic power, or any other foreign affairs power. The modern assumption that the Constitution does not fully allocate foreign affairs power arises from a quick reading of the text, not from historical evidence of founding-era understandings. The Constitution's "gaps" in foreign affairs are an artifact of modern commentary: no one at the time seemed to notice them.

The Precedent of State Constitutions

A related textual objection is that pre-1787 state constitutions did not contemplate grants of "unenumerated" power (or at least not foreign affairs power) arising solely from the definition of "executive power," and therefore we should hesitate to read the federal Constitution in this way.[49] It is true, of course, that the way prior state constitutions used language can offer important clues as to the way the federal Constitution used similar language.[50] In this case, though, state precedents tend to confirm rather than undermine a substantive reading of "executive power."

Most tellingly, Delaware, Maryland, and North Carolina stated that their governors would have several specific powers (such as pardons and embargoes) "and may exercise all the other executive powers of government," without further definition or explanation. This phrasing is obviously inconsistent with the idea that "executive power" is only prefatory, to be given specific substantive content later in the document. Rather, the early constitution-writers must have been appealing to a set of powers commonly defined as "executive." And these states did not give their governors explicit law-execution or diplomatic powers—because (one may presume) they thought these were among the "other executive powers" granted by the general clause.[51]

Four other states—Georgia, New Jersey, South Carolina, and Virginia—granted their chief magistrates "the executive power" (or similar phrasing) followed by a short list of specific powers. Of course, it is possible that they meant their governors to exercise *only* these specific powers, but that seems unlikely. Virginia's 1776 constitution, for example, stated that the governor "shall, with the Advice of a Council of State, exercise the executive power of government, according to the laws of this Commonwealth." It went on to say that the governor "shall not, under any pretense, exercise any power or prerogative, by virtue of any law, statute or custom of England," but it gave the governor specific power only to grant pardons, embody and direct the militia, and make some appointments; in particular, it did not give the governor specific powers to execute the law or conduct diplomatic correspondence.[52] Virginia's governor and council nonetheless routinely exercised these powers,[53] presumably because they were understood as part of the "executive powers of government" granted by its constitution. Further, South Carolina's constitution explicitly declared that its "president" could exercise specified foreign affairs powers (making "war or peace" or entering into "final" treaties) only in conjunction with the legislature (an odd provision unless one thought the office would otherwise have such powers).[54] In contrast, only four states (Massachusetts, New Hampshire, New York, and Pennsylvania) attempted an extensive list of the specific powers of their executive branches, and only the latter two specifically vested law execution.[55] In sum, at least a majority of state constitutions appeared to grant substantive powers through the phrase "executive power," just as we have concluded that the federal Constitution does.

Historical Objections

Yet it still may seem odd that no one in the drafting or ratifying process appeared to notice (or at least to comment on) the Constitution's allocation of executive foreign affairs power to the President. This may be especially troubling when combined with the structural intuition that worried the Justices in *Steel Seizure:* that the foreign affairs reading concentrates too much authority in the President. One might quickly (though prematurely) dismiss the grant of executive power as a source of foreign affairs power, as Justice Jackson did, simply because such a reading would give the President so much power. When added to the drafters' and ratifiers' lack of objection to (or even comment upon) this power, one might rightly hesitate to read the text in such a way.[56]

It is important, though, not to overstate the Constitution's executive foreign affairs powers (as many critics do). Recognizing Article II, Section 1 as a source of these powers does not yield presidential supremacy in foreign affairs. Although "the executive Power" contains substantial foreign affairs authority, it is checked by two substantial limitations. First, as Chapter 5 explains, executive power is limited by its eighteenth-century definition. As discussed, this limitation sustains the Court's ultimate result in *Steel Seizure* and confirms the broader separation-of-powers principles that exclude the President from lawmaking and funding.

Moreover, the Constitution's limits on executive power go much further. Founding-era Americans rejected the royal dominance over foreign affairs reflected in the English system and in Montesquieu's philosophy. That is consistent with the idea of executive foreign affairs powers—in fact, the two ideas are complementary. The Constitution's executive foreign affairs power comes into play only for powers the Constitution does not otherwise allocate—and the most important powers are specifically allocated. Despite the President's executive power, for example, only Congress has power to declare war, and the President cannot make treaties or diplomatic appointments without the Senate's approval. As we have seen (Chapter 3), allocating these key foreign affairs powers away from the President allowed delegates to accept the language that became Article II, Section 1, after previously rejecting corresponding language in the Virginia plan. The next chapters examine the foreign affairs powers of other branches, which operate as a check upon the President's executive power to produce a system of shared control over foreign affairs.

As a result, the fact that no one discussed or objected to the President's executive foreign affairs power in the drafting and ratifying process is less problematic than it initially appears. It seems plausible that commentators of the time were comfortable with the broad outlines of foreign affairs power sketched here. We cannot suppose that the constitutional generation had thought through all the potential implications of giving the President "executive" foreign affairs power, but the basic points surely could be easily appreciated. The President would not be a lawmaker or make funding decisions (since that was beyond the meaning of executive power). The President would not control the most important foreign affairs powers—treatymaking, declaring war, appointments, regulating the military—because the text gave these, in whole or part, to other branches. The President would control lesser aspects of foreign affairs, such as diplomacy—bringing focus and energy where the Articles had lacked it. Once the system is described in this way, it is quite possible to suppose that it excited no great comment.

III

Shared Powers of the Senate

7

The Executive Senate:
Treaties and Appointments

As previous chapters suggest, if Article II, Section 1 had stood alone, it likely would have vested the President with the executive foreign affairs power wielded by the English monarch. That would not have given the President "unchecked" foreign affairs power, any more than the king had unchecked power; as Americans knew, kings and Parliaments had used their distinct powers to struggle for control of English foreign policy, and the President would face further checks in the need to stand for re-election and in exposure to impeachment. It was not unthinkable that the Convention might have adopted such as system, and as we have seen, Randolph's "Virginia plan" effectively proposed it. But as the response to the Virginia plan showed, delegates were unwilling to vest so much power in one branch—especially because most of them (although not Randolph himself) favored a single chief magistrate in place of the Articles' divided, plural executive.

One important result was the second paragraph of Article II, Section 2. Here the Constitution showed decisively its break with English practice and Montesquieu's theory, by giving the Senate a share of traditional executive powers: requiring its "advice and consent" for diplomatic (and other) appointments and for treatymaking, the latter by a two-thirds vote. These powers were wholly "executive," and assigned to the Crown, under the traditional formulation; Section 2 takes them away (in part) from the principal holder of executive power and gives them to a branch of the legislature. This chapter considers how this innovation came about and what it means.

Political and academic debates tend to over-read or under-read this part of Article II, Section 2, depending on the debater's general preference for presidential power. To presidential advocates, it is an odd exception to a general theme of continuity between English foreign affairs practice and the Constitution's system, deserving to be read narrowly. To opponents, it severs the connection to English practice, introducing the Senate as a lead player in foreign affairs. As we shall see, neither view provides a complete picture.

The debate focuses most forcefully on the Senate's treatymaking role. Is the Senate's role little more than a formality at the end of a process dominated by the President (as presidential advocates would have it), or is the Senate expected to control, or at least participate in, the process from its outset (as many scholars argue)? The text's answer lies in between these extremes; pursuing it allows us to develop a sense of Article II, Section 2's place in the Constitution's overall foreign affairs framework. It reflects, we shall see, two important and to some extent competing themes. It confirms the text's commitment to divided executive powers, foreshadowed by the Convention's early debate on the Virginia plan. Thus it means what it says: it establishes checks on presidential foreign affairs power, contemplating an *independent* role for the Senate. It does not, however, mean more than it says. It is an important—but specific—re-allocation of traditional executive foreign affairs powers. It does not give the Senate general power over diplomats, or treaties.

Appointing Diplomats

Article II, Section 2 provides in relevant part:

> [The President] shall have Power, by and with the Advice and Consent of the Senate, to make Treaties, provided two-thirds of the Senators present concur; and he shall nominate, and by and with the Advice and Consent of the Senate, shall appoint Ambassadors, other public Ministers and Consuls, Judges of the supreme Court, and all other Officers of the United States. . . .

According to its less-controversial appointments clause, diplomatic personnel (like other officers of the United States), though identified ("nominated") by the President, must gain Senate approval. This does not give (and generally is not understood to give) the Senate a general policymaking role in diplomatic affairs: instruction and removal of ambassadors and other foreign affairs officers remain, as seen in Chapters 3–4, presidential powers.[1] Nonetheless, it imposes a constraint upon the President that traditional chief executives did not face (and Presidents sometimes seek to avoid).[2]

The appointments clause shows the drafters' rejection, in some degree, of the traditional unity of executive foreign affairs powers. Ambassadorial appointments were an executive authority in traditional definitions.[3] But in the states' post-independence constitutional systems, appointments were usually shared (or taken from the chief magistrate altogether);[4] despite renewed interest in stronger, unified executives after the early experiences of the states and the Articles (Chapter 6), the framers were not prepared to resurrect fully the traditional appointments system, even in foreign affairs.

The appointments clause also shows, though, that the delegates did not endorse the system—common in many states[5]—of an executive "council" to "assist" the chief magistrate in appointments and other matters. As Hamilton's Federalist No. 70 explained, the councils had been unsatisfactory, because they lacked transparency and accountability and because they reduced the "energy" in the executive branch (that is, its ability to get things done).[6] Rather than create a council, the Constitution gave one piece of the executive diplomatic power to the Senate. Anti-federalists objected during the ratification debates, both on the ground that it departed from the states' example and on the ground that it was "mixing" executive and legislative power contrary to Montesquieu's prescription (points the federalists conceded, but discounted).[7] The goal was to achieve checks, without sacrificing effectiveness—that is, to get the best of the royal system without its excesses.[8]

It is worth revisiting here Jefferson's careful textual exploration of the appointments clause, discussed in Chapter 4.[9] According to Jefferson, creating diplomatic posts had five components: (1) selecting a destination; (2) establishing the rank of the person being sent there; (3) nominating a person; (4) approving that person; and (5) issuing the formal commission. He emphasized that the text provided for Senate participation only in the fourth step, and that it specifically listed the third and fifth steps as presidential powers.[10] Thus, he said, steps one and two necessarily were presidential powers as well ("vested" in the President by Article II, Section 1).

This analysis seems exactly right, and it confirms a broader point: the appointments clause does not give the Senate general power over diplomats (or diplomatic communications). Jefferson might have added that instructing, directing, and removing diplomats are powers that come logically *after* appointment and commissioning. They too are not part of the Senate's appointments power—and so remain with the President. To reiterate Jefferson's conclusion, diplomatic powers are presidential powers, except where *specifically* shared with the Senate. This, of course, is how Washington conducted diplomacy from the outset, without material objection (Chapter 4), and how the constitutional structure is viewed today.

Treatymaking and the Text

The treatymaking clause, in contrast, is sharply disputed at its foundations. In particular, most scholarly commentary reads it to give the Senate a far greater role than modern practice and modern Presidents admit.[11]

In modern treatymaking, the President (or, more usually, the President's diplomats) will negotiate treaties, and the President (or the diplomats) will sign them, without formal consultation—often with little input at all—from the Senate. Under international practice, treaties are not binding on the United States until "ratified," meaning that the President officially confirms the nation's intent to undertake the treaty's obligations. Before ratification occurs, the President submits the treaty to the Senate, which then votes approval or disapproval. Or, the Senate may vote only partial approval—for example, approving the treaty subject to deleting one provision. If the treaty receives the required two-thirds vote, the President may (but does not have to) "ratify" the treaty (that is, declare that the nation undertakes its obligations); if Senate approval is conditional, the President's ratification must also be conditional (and other treaty parties could reject it, because it is now not what they agreed to), and if the Senate fails to approve, the President lacks power to ratify, so the United States cannot undertake the treaty's obligations.[12]

Measured solely against the Constitution's text, this system might seem appropriate. The President's executive power includes control over diplomats and foreign communications, so we would expect the President to control treaty negotiations. From the U.S. perspective, treaties are not "made" (that is, completed) until ratified. Everything the President does prior to ratification—including signature—is preliminary, part of the communicative function. Because ratification "makes" the treaty, Article II, Section 2 demands that Senate "advice and consent" occur prior to that point. But the clause does not seem, on its face, to require the President to seek Senate advice and consent at any particular time (other than before the treaty is finally made) or continuously throughout the process. Indeed, linking "advice" with "consent" in a single phrase, modified by "provided two-thirds of the Senators present concur," suggests that they are (or at least may be) unified actions taken together, in a single sitting. "Consent," at least, must be taken at the end of the process: to measure the number "present" one must speak of one moment in time, and if Senators are to "concur" to the making of *the* treaty (not to some treaty in the abstract, but a particular treaty), concurrence is best done after signing—the signing does not "make" (complete) the treaty, but it sets the terms to which concurrence is sought. Nothing in the clause seems to say directly that "advice" could not be sought at the same time (as, for example, through conditional approvals, or suggestions for re-negotiation).

The Meaning of "Advice"

We may object, though—as many commentators have—that this reading does not give enough content to "advice." Consent, to be sure, can be given at the end of the process, but might not the use of both words (instead of *only* "consent") mean that the Senate's "advice" must be taken throughout the treatymaking process, or at least sometime before the terms are fixed, thereby converting the Senate into something like an equal partner in the endeavor? As one leading authority argues: " 'Advice' and 'consent' are not synonyms. . . . [T]hey stand for two quite different things—indeed, two quite different stages in what may be a continuing process . . . The word 'advice,' if given any defensible meaning, signifies with great precision the task of deciding upon the policy to be pursued in treaty negotiation. . . ."[13]

This view, though, fails to account for eighteenth-century meaning in several respects. First, that is *not* what "advice and consent" means in the appointments clause: the President selects a nominee and the Senate gives the nominee—that is, the President's final product—a yes-or-no vote, called its "advice and consent." As Hamilton said, the Senate "can only ratify or reject the choice he [the President] may have made."[14] True, the appointments clause is specific on this point in a way that the treatymaking clause is not: the President alone may "nominate" and with the Senate's "advice and consent" may appoint. Nonetheless, in the appointments clause "advice" means a single review of the President's fully formed proposal, not "advice" in a continuous process. The appointments clause's distinct structure makes clear that this is the *only* way appointments can work; but the use of "advice and consent" in the appointments clause to mean a yes-or-no vote at one sitting seems on its face to reject the idea that the phrase necessarily implies continuing consultative processes. The treatymaking clause is less precise, but "advice and consent" there seems capable of bearing the same meaning: an after-the-fact review of the President's proposal, coupled with "advice" that the President proceed as proposed or adopt an alternate course.[15]

Moreover, this appears to be the way the Senate used the phrase in the immediate post-ratification period. Entries from its 1789 proceedings report that the Senate "advised and consented" to a list of Washington's nominees; apparently Senators did not see anything odd about using the phrase to mean an after-the-fact review of a presidential proposal. In the Senate's first action under the treatymaking clause, it used "advice" in the way suggested by the appointments clause. The Articles' Congress had negotiated, but not ratified, a consular convention with France in 1788, before the Constitution came into effect. In 1789 the Senate approved the Convention; as it told Washington: "the Senate do consent to the said convention, and advise the President of the United States to ratify the same." Of course, given the timing, the Senate could not have given earlier "advice," but crucially the Senate apparently thought it normal to use "advice" and "consent" together to refer to a single after-the-fact review.[16]

Important evidence also comes from state constitutional practice. "Advice and consent" was a common phrase at the time. The formal preface to English statutory enactments was (and still is) that an act is done by the monarch "by and with the advice and consent" of Parliament.[17] Many state constitutions carried over this phrasing after independence when they created executive councils to oversee their chief executives, directing that the governor act with the council's "advice and consent" (or sometimes only its "advice") in specified matters.[18] Although the Constitution abandoned the executive councils, they were surely the source of the "advice and consent" language. As a result, the key question is not what "advice and consent" seems to mean to us today, but what it actually meant in pre-1787 state practice. *If* the common meaning of "advice" in the state constitutions necessarily encompassed *continuing,* not merely after-the-fact, "advice," it likely should be read the same way in the Constitution (and the appointments clause would present a textual puzzle). Historical arguments for the Senate rely heavily upon this point.[19] But the evidence that "advice" was read in only this way is, at best, weak; rather, the contrary appears to be true.

In Virginia, for example, the executive "governor" acted with the "advice" of the council, although the reality more resembled the "advice and consent" formulation of some other states: the governor rarely (if ever) acted contrary to the council's "advice." The council held regular meetings, at which it discussed policy and formally voted approval of particular plans of action, sometimes with recorded dissents. Crucially, though, there was no understanding that the council had to be involved in the governor's policy *formulation.* Sometimes the governor brought particular problems to the council's attention, requesting assistance in formulating responses. But sometimes the governor presented the council with fully formed plans of action and asked for approval. The council did not seem to think this infringed its constitutional authority of "advice"; it formally recorded its "advice" with respect to the governor's fully formed plan without complaint.[20] Thus the constitutional "advice" function apparently *could be* fulfilled by a single session rendering written approval of the governor's proposed action (although the council often did not proceed in this way).

Returning to the Constitution's text, we can see that the eighteenth-century practice of "advice" strengthens the case for modern practice. If the state constitutions' "advice" requirement could be satisfied by post-formulation review of governors' proposed policies (as Virginia's experience suggests), that is presumably true also of the U.S. Constitution's "advice" requirements—as the appointments clause indicates. Indeed, as noted, the appointments clause *requires* that "advice" be given with respect to a fully formed proposal (a nomination); the treatymaking clause's different language does not appear to require it, but it also does not seem to forbid it. Again, the key is that nothing is finally decided with respect to treaties until ratification, so only then is Senate involvement prerequisite (since only then are treaties "made").[21] In sum, the Senate's textual treatymaking role parallels the state councils: it can be consulted *either* during policy formulation *or* upon a fully formed proposal.

Alternative Visions: Presidential or Senate Supremacy?

Once we examine context, though, we may doubt that we are reading the text correctly. This system looks odd compared to eighteenth-century theory and practice. Treatymaking, in England and in political theory, was done by the executive/monarch alone—as was obviously also true in absolute monarchies such as Spain and France.[22] Eighteenth-century kings rarely negotiated or signed treaties in person (as sometimes occurred in earlier times); they sent representatives (ambassadors) who typically operated under fairly precise instructions from the monarch. However, because the monarch, not the ambassador, spoke for the nation, treaties could not bind the nation without the monarch's personal approval. This was the role of what eighteenth-century international law called "ratification": the ambassadors returned with the signed treaty, and the respective monarchs signified, by ratification, that the ambassador had spoken for the monarch in making the treaty.[23]

Given this backdrop, one might wonder whether the drafters could have intended modern U.S. treaty making practice, even though it seems to conform to the text. First, it splits the executive foreign affairs power, and as we have seen (Chapter 3), Montesquieu and Blackstone (and, before them,

Locke) urged that executive foreign affairs powers remain in one hand. Second, modern practice transforms the relationship between signature and ratification. In the eighteenth century, at least in theory, signature was the critical moment. Ambassadors were not expected to agree to treaties without appropriate instructions, and kings were not expected to refuse ratification unless the ambassador exceeded those instructions.[24] Although technically not "made" until ratification, treaties were effectively "made" by signature. The modern U.S. system reverses the importance of the two: Senate "consent" comes after signature but without apparent constraints related to instructions, prior policy, or even prior knowledge. Third, the system seems open to serious practical objections. Either the President may seem to promise more than can be delivered, if other nations fail to understand the Senate's role, or—if they do—negotiations may have difficulty proceeding because U.S. negotiators actually lack authority to agree to anything.[25]

As a result, though modern practice seems consistent with the text read in isolation, it may be questioned on the basis of context. Critics of the present system make this point forcefully but divide on the conclusion. The apparent problem could be solved by insisting upon greater Senate participation throughout the process. If the Senate approved ambassadors' instructions, so that ambassadors (and, for that matter, the President) amounted to negotiating arms of the Senate, the Senate's post-signature concurrence would look more like the traditional post-signature concurrence: confirmation that the ambassador (or President) had not exceeded instructions.[26]

But one might also solve the problem by insisting on much *less* substantive Senate participation, with the Senate's "consent" function analogous to the monarch's post-signature concurrence in the traditional system. The Senate's role could not be limited to comparing the final result with the ambassador's instructions (since, in this version, the Senate would not draft instructions); but perhaps the Senate's role is only to ensure that the President did not exceed the Constitution's mandate—that is, that the President did not promise unconstitutional acts or use treaties for personal advancement. This would give the Senate's role some substance, but would not give the Senate policy-making power over treaties.

Again, this second view rests upon the practical observations that it may be difficult for the United States to function diplomatically with divided treaty-making power and that systems most familiar to the framers had unified treatymaking power. As Woodrow Wilson wrote, while a professor: "The President . . . need disclose no step of negotiation until it is complete, and when in any critical matter it is completed the government is virtually committed. Whatever its disinclination, the Senate may feel itself committed also."[27] True, Wilson as President found the Senate less deferential than he hoped, leading to substantial breakdown of U.S. foreign policy in 1919–1920, when the Senate rejected the Versailles Treaty and the League of Nations on which Wilson staked much of his own and the nation's prestige.[28] That does not show Wilson was wrong as a constitutional matter, though, and we might say (as Wilson did) that the Senate acted unwisely and outside its constitutional role.

Neither version seems mandated by the text read literally, but again we may face claims that, read in context, it means something more (or less) than it appears to say. And we have seen that such arguments cannot be dismissed out of hand: depending upon the strength of the background evidence, they can be more or less persuasive. An eighteenth-century idea of inherent foreign affairs power, if proved, would affect our reading of the Tenth Amendment (Chapter 1), and eighteenth-century definitions of executive power do affect our reading of Article II, Section 1 (Chapter 3).

Precedents for Divided Treaty Power: The Roman Republic

Further review of the Constitution's background, though, tends to confirm that the text means what it says in establishing divided treatymaking power. The structure of the treatymaking power, and its division between President and Senate, may indeed appear odd if one considers only eighteenth-century theory and practice. Without denying the importance of these influences, we should not overlook others. One of these is classical history, especially the Roman republic. As historian Bernard Bailyn confirms: "Most conspicuous in the writings of the Revolutionary period was the heritage of classical antiquity. Knowledge of classical authors was universal among colonists with any degree of education, and references to them and their works abound in the literature."[29]

Americans looked to the classical period, especially the Roman republic, because of the dearth of republican practice in their own time. The leading eighteenth-century nations were monarchies, a system Americans rejected. Although many Americans admired the English system, or at least an idealized form of it, monarchical England could not be a complete model. The few contemporary republics had met only fleeting success. The Roman republic, though, endured for centuries, achieving great diplomatic, economic, and military successes. Rome's governmental structure incorporated elements of separation of powers;[30] and, at least in conventional wisdom, it succumbed to dictatorship (a fate Americans feared for their own republic) when its constitution broke down in the face of Julius Caesar, the civil wars, and the rise of Augustus.[31]

We should, therefore, consider not just Americans' contemporary influences, but also those of classical history, especially the Roman republic. In Montesquieu's account, the Roman senate held most "executive" powers, including treatymaking power: it instructed and sent ambassadors to foreign nations, received and negotiated with foreign ambassadors, and approved or disapproved treaties negotiated by its ambassadors.[32] The reality was more complex. As Americans surely knew from Roman sources, the senate did not always control treaties' negotiation and signature, but instead reviewed "preliminary" treaties prepared by the consuls. The consuls—not to be confused with the modern diplomatic officers of that name—were chosen annually by the senate to serve as chief executive magistrates. They had limited power within Rome itself, but had broad power while serving (as they often did) as military leaders in overseas provinces. Among other matters, they often negotiated and signed treaties with foreign powers. But these treaties were not binding until formally approved in Rome by the senate, and, at least in some cases, by the popular assembly (effectively the Roman lower house) as well. As Roman sources reflect, the consuls' treaties were closely debated and sometimes rejected.[33]

Roman historian Polybius, for example, recounted that the 263 B.C. peace treaty with Syracuse was negotiated and signed by the Roman consul in the field; "the terms of the treaty were referred to Rome" and "the people . . . accepted and ratified this agreement."[34] In 241 B.C. consul Lutatius Catulus negotiated and signed a treaty with Carthage, Rome's great North African rival, but that agreement, Polybius said, was rejected in Rome and had to be renegotiated. Subsequently, as historian Livy described, Rome "denied that [it was] bound by the treaty which Gaius Lutatius, the consul, originally entered into with [Carthage], because it had been made without the senate's sanction or the people's command."[35] The pattern repeated with new rounds of hostilities and negotiations with Syracuse in 214–211 B.C.[36] and Carthage in 203–202 B.C.[37] In the campaign leading to Syracuse's defeat in 212 S.C., Roman consul Marcellus negotiated a series of treaties in the field, but they "could not claim permanent validity until the senate in Rome officially approved them."[38] At the end of the war with Carthage in 202 B.C., Roman consul Scipio Africanus negotiated a comprehensive settlement without instructions from the senate, but after signature referred it to Rome, where (Livy recorded) it was aggressively debated though finally approved.[39]

In sum, it would have been clear to anyone reading historians Livy and Polybius that treatymaking could be a more divided process than the eighteenth-century idea of executive power suggested, and in particular that in a republican system treaties might be negotiated and signed by single executive magistrates, subject to after-the-fact review by deliberative assemblies.[40]

Treaties (and Ambassadors) in the Drafting Process

We may now revisit some of the drafting process, with treatymaking power specifically in mind, to see if (as some commentators maintain) it suggests any necessary conclusions about the delegates' understandings. As discussed (Chapter 3), Governor Randolph opened the Philadelphia Convention by proposing the Virginia plan, which assigned the old Congress's "Executive rights" to the new executive branch. This provoked heavy criticism: delegates recognized that it would likely include treatymaking power (among others), as that was part of the old Congress's "executive" foreign affairs power—and on Madison's motion the delegates deleted the provision.[41]

Thinking only of English precedents, we might wonder why delegates would believe the executive branch should not have treatymaking power—after all, it was a power exercised by the English monarch, in the system Blackstone and Montesquieu exalted. Of course, in the Convention's final product, one compelling reason might be identified: treaties would of their own force be "supreme Law of the Land" (see Chapter 8) and therefore—as Hamilton and others later said—seemed under the new system to be as much legislative as executive.[42] But this provision was not part of the Virginia plan, and delegates still rejected presidential control of treatymaking. It seems plausible that they also had Roman precedents in mind—precedents that suggested a deliberative check upon executive treatymaking in a republican system.[43]

The Committee of Detail, charged among many other matters with sorting out foreign affairs authority, tentatively honored the delegates' apparent wishes by giving Congress treatymaking power. It may have had doubts, though, about the whole Congress's ability to handle negotiations (such doubts were expressed at several later points). In any event, the Committee's final draft shifted treatymaking and ambassadorial appointments to the Senate, and (as discussed in Chapter 3) gave the President "executive power" (along with power to receive foreign ambassadors).[44]

In the Convention's debate on the Committee report, as Randolph noted, "almost every speaker . . . made objections to the clause as it stood." Madison, who had earlier denied that treatymaking was an executive power, now "observed that the Senate represented the States alone, and for that and other obvious reasons it was proper that the President should be an agent in Treaties." Gouverneur Morris unsuccessfully proposed restoring a role for Congress; the delegates then referred the clause to a new committee.[45] And indeed the Committee of Detail's vision of the diplomatic process is anything but clear. Who spoke for the nation through its ambassadors—the Senate, who appointed them and "made" treaties, or the President, holder of the "executive power"? What of negotiations with foreign ambassadors, whom the President would "receive": would the President's communications to them conflict with communications of the Senate's ambassadors overseas? Would foreign ambassadors have to go to the Senate if they wanted to negotiate treaties (despite the reception clause), allowing the President to talk to them only about non-treaty matters? Or could the President conduct treaty negotiations with them as well (despite the Senate's treatymaking power), meaning that control of negotiations depended upon the fortuity of where the negotiators met? And at least some delegates must have had doubts about the Senate's ability to direct negotiations: although smaller than the whole new Congress, the Senate would be roughly the size of the Articles' Congress, which had a notoriously hard time getting anything done.[46]

In response to the general dissatisfaction, the next Committee (the so-called Committee of Eleven, or Committee of Postponed Parts) completely reworked the draft to produce the language we have now. Instead of "The Senate . . . shall have power to make treaties, and to appoint Ambassadors. . . .", the new draft said the *President* "shall have" those powers, subject to Senate "advice and consent." And the new Committee moved the language from its previous location in what was then Article IX (listing the Senate's powers), adding it to what had been the Committee of Detail's Article X (listing the President's powers, the precursor of the final Article II). After apparently brief debate, resulting from renewed attempts to give the House a treatymaking role, delegates accepted the new language.[47]

We may plausibly see these changes as shifting treatymaking initiative to the President (and indeed, it is hard to see them otherwise).[48] First, the Committee made similar changes to the appointments procedure, which clearly produced presidential instead of senatorial initiative. Second, the new draft at minimum seemed to unify diplomatic power in the President: since the Senate's appointment power was now a yes-or-no vote on the President's nominee, it could not include power to direct ambassadors once the appointment had been made (so the President seemed to control communications through U.S. ambassadors, as well as through foreign ambassadors). And third, the new system echoed the state executive councils, which generally were bodies consulted by the governor rather than ones with their own independent initiative.

Nothing in the revisions or the debates speaks conclusively to *when* consultation had to occur (other than before ratification), so it seems plausible that the delegates thought this would be worked out between the President and the Senate, with at least the possibility that the President might negotiate independently and present the Senate with a finished proposal.[49] True, this might result in the Senate rejecting what the President had agreed to. But the delegates knew from Roman history that the proposed constitutional model resembled Roman practice, in which consuls in the field sometimes negotiated and signed treaties on their own initiative and then sent them back to Rome for approval or disapproval. Moreover, the new model solved two important problems. On one hand, delegates did not endorse the Blackstone-Montesquieu idea of vesting treatymaking power in a single magistrate, but preferred the Roman model of deliberative approval of treaties (and thus initially thought of putting the power in Congress). On the other, they likely recognized the difficulties a deliberative body would have in negotiating treaties (seen first-hand under the Articles). They first tried to fix the latter problem by shifting treatymaking power from Congress to the Senate, but they surely realized that the Senate (like the Articles' Congress) would have similar problems. The system they ultimately produced took advantage of the "energy" of the new single executive (derived from the English model), while subjecting that power to (at least) an after-the-fact check (derived from the Roman model)—as in appointments.

At this point, though, one might ask whether the intent was to shift almost all treatymaking power back to the President, with Senate approval largely a formality. Here it is important to consider the supermajority rule, which first appeared in the Committee of Eleven's report. Obviously it did not come from English law, nor from Rome. It is tempting to see it as an unreflective carryover from the Articles, which required a supermajority (of states) to approve treaties. But the explanation is not so simple, for treaties were not unique in the Articles—its Article 9 subjected many major foreign policy decisions to the nine-states rule. The Constitution required a supermajority for only one—treatymaking. The delegates must have thought treatymaking in particular justified heightened protection.

We can readily see why. The delegates had sharp memories of the Articles' most bitter treaty controversy, concerning navigation of the Mississippi River. The Articles' Congress had wanted a treaty with Spain. Spain controlled the Mississippi at New Orleans, so it could close the river to U.S. trade. Western interests in the United States wanted to force Spain to concede rights of free navigation, which they thought vital to developing the western territories. In 1786, the Congress sent John Jay to negotiate with Spain, with instructions to insist on free navigation of the Mississippi. Jay quickly saw this would produce no agreement and suggested modifying his instructions to defer the Mississippi issue for twenty years in return for a favorable agreement with Spain on other issues.

Under the Articles, a majority of states could modify instructions, and the northeastern states—more interested in trade than in the Mississippi—agreed to do so, despite intense opposition from states with western interests. The opposing five states indicated that they would nonetheless block the nine-state approval. This obviously would not be because Jay failed to follow instructions; it was manifestly a political and strategic decision. Jay ultimately gave up on the project, and the lesson learned (especially by states in the minority) was that without supermajority protection, their Mississippi claims would have been conceded.[50]

The Articles' Mississippi experience was much in the delegates' minds at the Convention.[51] The lesson many drew from it was that treaties were dangerous, because they frequently would give up one matter of international concern to achieve breakthroughs on others. International concerns seemed likely to affect different regions of the nation differently: as with the Mississippi, one region might be vitally affected by matters in which other regions had little interest. This made negotiation by a national entity difficult, because bargains benefiting the nation as a whole might be exceptionally bad for one region. Or, of even greater concern, a national entity controlled by a bare majority might trade off a point of vital interest to one region to achieve something only incidentally benefiting the majority. At least in the south and west, that is how the Mississippi deal was perceived. As a result, the treaty-making supermajority would ensure that treaties reflected the interests of the whole country and not bare regional majorities.[52] That in turn, indicates that the Senate's power was meant as a serious check and not a formality.

We should now pause to consider the impact of the foregoing evidence. It is important to see what it does and does not prove. One might say that Roman influence, the experience of the Mississippi negotiations, and the evidence of the Convention records show that the drafters envisioned the Senate as a material after-the-fact check upon the President's treatymaking. Perhaps so, but we must remember that the basic idea of our inquiry is to develop a framework of foreign affairs power from the Constitution's text, not from the private thoughts of particular framers. Thus it is important to restate the argument to this point.

We began with the proposition that the text itself suggests a system of presidential treatymaking, with a senatorial after-the-fact check. The President's control over U.S. ambassadors and reception of foreign ambassadors appears to put the President in charge of negotiations. The Senate's power is only "advice and consent" before a treaty is *made* (as the Senate's power is "advice and consent" before a nominee is appointed). A treaty is not made until completed by ratification, so nothing seems to require senatorial participation at any particular prior point (although nothing prevents it). But the Senate's "advice and consent" also is not qualified. There is no reason (on text alone) to think the Senate should not exercise independent judgment. The text establishes at least a preliminary case for modern practice.

Counterarguments rely upon supposed background understandings: that foreign affairs power should not be divided, that the framers envisioned a greater role for the Senate, or that post-signature review of treaties should be limited. The evidence of influences on the drafters, and of the evolution of their thinking, shows that these background understandings were not strong enough to establish a rule the text does not contain. Rather, it is perfectly plausible that the drafters meant what they said in the treatymaking clause— that is, that they adopted a system that would (or at least could) replicate the Roman system.

The Senate as Dominant Partner? Treaties in the Ratifying Process

The foregoing account seems satisfactory until we examine the ratifying debates. These debates confirm the Senate's role as a substantial check on the President's treatymaking authority. But many participants went far in the other direction, describing the Senate as having much more influence over the process than the text seems to justify. This again forces us to reexamine our conclusions.

Although some commentary emphasized presidential leadership, none indicated that the President would have effectively unchecked treatymaking power or that the Senate would ordinarily defer to the President's treaty preferences. To the contrary, Hamilton's Federalist No. 75 celebrated divided treatymaking, because it would not be "wise" for a nation "to commit interests of so delicate and momentous a kind, as those which concern its intercourse with the rest of the world" to the President alone. James Wilson agreed that "[n]either the President nor the Senate, solely can complete a treaty; they are checks upon each other, and are so balanced, as to produce security to the people."[53]

But many commentators went further. Hamilton at the New York convention, perhaps speaking more loosely than in *The Federalist,* said that the President and the Senate together would manage the nation's foreign concerns. He also said, in Federalist No. 66, that the Senate might impeach the President for failure to adhere to treaty negotiation instructions. A leading anti-federalist observed that the Senate would have a "negative" on presidential treatymaking "and in managing foreign affairs." Chancellor Livingston in New York said that the Senate would "transact all foreign business."[54]

These statements, and others like them,[55] suggest that some ratifiers envisioned the Senate as (at least) an equal partner in treaty negotiations, rather than merely exercising an after-the-fact veto. To this we can add the potential difficulties of the after-the-fact veto (that the President could promise more than the Senate would deliver) and the fact that division of executive treatymaking power departs radically from the English system. If the Senate controlled negotiation, the problem of overpromising would be reduced, and treatymaking power would not be so much divided as spread across a multimember body (which was the Articles' system).[56]

The "Senate dominance" argument, when based on the ratifying debates, has two serious drawbacks, however. First, there is no obvious tie to constitutional language. In fact, the ratifiers who seemed to envision it did *not* tie it to any particular phrase; perhaps they simply assumed this is how treatymaking would work in practice. After all, Presidents facing the ultimate need to obtain two-thirds approval might prudently seek Senate participation, even if not required to do so, and the Senate might use its ultimate right of approval as leverage to gain earlier participation. It has not worked that way in practice, but one can imagine such a supposition, especially because the state executive councils often (though not always) operated this way.

Further, emphasizing these ratification statements tells only part of the story. Other ratifiers, directly or implicitly, described treatymaking as primarily a presidential power, with Senate approval or disapproval at the end. Iredell in North Carolina said the President would "regulate all intercourse with foreign powers"; even in treatymaking, he said, the President was the "primary agent," with Senate approval to "validate proper, or restrain improper, conduct." Hamilton's Federalist No. 84 said that the "management of foreign negotiations will naturally devolve" upon the President "according to general principles concerted with the Senate, and subject to their final concurrence."[57] Drafter Charles Cotesworth Pinckney related that "it was agreed [at the Convention] to give the President a power of proposing treaties . . . and to vest the Senate . . . with a power of agreeing or disagreeing to the terms proposed."[58]

To draw anything conclusive from the ratifying debates, we must show more than merely that some ratifiers thought—for unspecified reasons—the Senate would have a substantial ongoing role throughout the treatymaking process. The question is not what some (or even most) members of the constitutional generation *thought* would happen under the Constitution, but what the ordinary meaning of its text requires.

Post-ratification Treatymaking

The final and decisive evidence comes from post-1789 events. Early practice is often thought to favor a greater Senate role. In the conventional telling, Washington began by seeking a significant Senate role in negotiations, but finding that approach inconvenient and constraining, shifted to something resembling the modern system; the Senate eventually acquiesced despite the departure from constitutional requirements.[59] As we shall see, part of this account is correct—though it errs in finding constitutional dimensions to these developments. More importantly, it undervalues key evidence from a slightly later time: the debates over the Jay Treaty in 1795–1796.

The treatymaking clause's first full implementation came in the first year of President Washington's administration. Washington hoped to make treaties with the tribes in the southern United States and went in person to the Senate to seek advice on how to handle the matter. The meeting did not go well. Apparently Senators were reluctant to speak in Washington's presence; ultimately nothing was decided or even materially discussed (although the Senate provided advice several days later). The next year Washington tried a different approach, asking in writing for advice on how to handle ongoing negotiations with Britain over the Canadian boundary; in 1792, he asked for (and received) Senate approval of the general outlines of a deal he proposed to negotiate with Algiers.[60]

Washington soon shifted, however, to the modern practice of negotiating and signing treaties first, and then submitting them to the Senate. In particular, he followed this course with the nation's most important treaty of the 1790s, the so-called Jay Treaty with Britain, which his emissary John Jay negotiated secretly without Senate input.[61] Jay's result was reasonably satisfactory, all things considered, but it gave Britain substantial concessions and proved extremely controversial. When Washington submitted the completed treaty to the Senate in 1795, he encountered major constitutional and policy-based objections; the Senate ultimately approved it by the narrowest two-thirds vote, after rejecting one article (thus requiring Washington to get British agreement to an amended treaty).[62]

These events surely stand against any suggestion that the Senate must defer to the President in treaty approvals. Although Washington was greatly respected (so much so that his physical presence seemed to overawe the Senate), his treaties received no deference. The Jay Treaty in particular was energetically debated, sharply criticized, and nearly defeated. Although constitutional arguments were made against it, the anti-treaty forces' leading objection was that it gave too much to Britain, as a policy matter. Further, one article—concerning trade with the West Indies—was specifically rejected; Senators objected that it gave the British too favorable terms—again, a matter of pure policy.[63] The Senate plainly evaluated the treaty on its merits, with no policy deference, and did not hesitate to reject the deal struck by the President.

Practice of the 1790s is also (though less obviously) damaging to the "equal partner" theory of senatorial participation. It is true that Washington's first approach to treatymaking approximated the route prescribed by "equal partner" advocates. Washington went to the Senate, not with fully formed treaty proposals, but with only general ideas of reaching accommodations with the southern tribes: he expected the Senate to give him advice on the deal to seek. Washington later shifted to what has become the modern practice of after-the-fact approval. Advocates of an ongoing Senate role in negotiations see Washington's shift as usurpation. In their account, Washington first tried to take the constitutional approach, and when this seemed impractical, he seized upon an unconstitutional procedure that the Senate then reluctantly accepted.[64]

But this may read too much into 1790s practice. Washington did attempt pre-negotiations consultation with the Senate, but it is not clear he felt constitutionally compelled to do so. He knew the Senate had the ultimate right of disapproval, on a supermajority vote. He may simply have thought it prudent to consult the Senate in advance, to see what sort of treaty might be approved, before undertaking negotiations in an unproductive direction; later, he may have decided that proposing a finished product was more practical. There is no necessary constitutional dimension in that choice. Secretary of State Jefferson, for example, plainly saw it as a practical, not a constitutional, consideration. In advising Washington over the 1792 negotiations with Algiers, he observed: "The subsequent approbation of the Senate being necessary to validate a treaty, they expect to be consulted beforehand, if the case admits." And since the Algiers deal also involved money, "[s]o the subsequent act of the Representatives being necessary where money is given, why should not they expect to be consulted in like manner, when the case admits." That is, Jefferson saw pre-signature consultation with the Senate in parallel terms as pre-signature consultation with the House, which assuredly was not constitutionally required. Jefferson therefore said, obviously on policy grounds, that he was "against hazarding this transaction [the treaty with Algiers] without the sanction of both Houses."[65]

Better evidence comes not from what Washington did initially (which might have been driven by practicalities rather than his reading of the Constitution), but from what happened when he shifted policies. Here the Jay Treaty controversy is surely the most telling. This was arguably the 1790s' greatest foreign affairs debate: to proponents like Hamilton, the treaty was essential to avoid devastating war with Britain; to opponents like Madison and Jefferson, it represented a precipitous break with republican France, threatening renewed British domination. It is no exaggeration that Americans debated the treaty as if their very independence were at stake.

The debate came, moreover, as political divisions were hardening into a system of rival parties, pitting the Federalists, led by Hamilton and Vice-President John Adams, against Madison and Jefferson, who joined with prominent former anti-federalists in the new Republican party. As a result, we must be especially cautious in drawing conclusions from the Jay Treaty debates. Constitutional arguments were often deployed in support of positions adopted for other reasons, and what any one person argued might have been driven only by political affiliation. Given the level of discord, though, we may gain some insight by focusing on what appeared to be areas of agreement.

Once Jay returned with the signed treaty, Republicans began an energetic campaign to defeat it—first in the Senate and, after narrow Senate consent, in the House, where funding for implementation needed approval. Republicans raised a barrage of constitutional arguments against the treaty (some of which are examined in later chapters). Among other things, it was said to interfere with Congress's powers (because it regulated commerce) and states' prerogatives (because it regulated such local matters as treatment of aliens); and it supposedly interfered with various individual rights as well. One constitutional argument that was *not* made in any sustained way, however, was that Washington failed to consult the Senate before signing the treaty—even though the Senate was not told of the course of negotiations or the content of the agreement until the moment Washington presented the Senate with Jay's final product.[66]

It is hard to imagine that, had even a substantial minority at the time read the text to require advance Senate involvement, this objection would not have been pressed along with all the others (some of which seem far less plausible as a textual matter, and many of which were simply abandoned in the face of Hamilton's energetic defense). Of course, we do not know everything said in the Senate (its proceedings were not recorded) or outside it; but we can be confident that, at least, this was not a major objection. And that seems to undermine to any suggestion that, only seven years earlier, the common reading of the treatymaking clause was that it *required* ongoing Senate participation in pre-signature policy formulation.

In sum, Senate "advice and consent" represents a check on executive foreign affairs power and a major structural innovation (or rather, a recurrence to Rome's republican system) compared with English monarchical practice. It was one of several specific steps the Constitution took to make its foreign affairs executive less king-like, despite its grant of "executive Power." But it seems difficult to go further, to require continuous Senate participation throughout the treatymaking process. Senate approval requires a cooperative approach to treatymaking, but it appears to leave implementation of that approach to the affected branches, rather than requiring a particular mode of cooperation.

8

Goldwater v. Carter: Do Treaties Bind the President?

Louis Henkin writes that "the Constitution tells us only who may make treaties for the United States; it does not say who can un-make them." Legal scholarship provides an array of inconclusive non-textual arguments on behalf of Congress, the Senate, and the President.[1] In *Goldwater v. Carter,* the principal modern case on the subject, lower courts reached opposite conclusions and the Supreme Court declined to reach the merits. In 2001, President George W. Bush unilaterally terminated the Anti-Ballistic Missile (ABM) Treaty despite constitutional objections, and his Justice Department later caused a stir by claiming that the President could "suspend" the Geneva Conventions on the treatment of prisoners of war.[2]

Closer examination shows that the theory we have been examining can help close this supposed hole in the Constitution's text. Prior chapters develop the idea that the President has executive foreign affairs power from Article II, Section 1 (Chapters 3–6), and that Article II, Section 2's treaty-making clause is a specific exception giving the Senate a share of the executive power over treaties (Chapter 7). A first look at these provisions suggests that the President has treaty termination power, because it is part of the traditional executive power and is not included in the treaty*making* clause. That was the Court of Appeals' view in *Goldwater,*[3] and we will see that it is correct as far as it goes. But important additional considerations arise from the Constitution's Article VI and Article II, Section 3. Together, these provisions give treaties a status similar to laws—and thus make them binding, at least to some degree, on the President.

The ABM Treaty and *Goldwater:* Withdrawing from Treaties

At the outset, we must frame the question carefully. Treaty "termination" may mean two very different things. A nation may terminate treaties according to their express or implied terms, consistent with the international law of treaties.[4] Or a nation may announce, without justification in international law, that it will no longer comply with its obligations under a treaty. Both may be called termination, yet they raise distinct constitutional issues.[5]

The difference arises from the Constitution's Article VI, which says that treaties (like statutes) are the "supreme Law of the Land." Terminating treaties without legal justification may violate the "supreme Law" established by Article VI. Terminating treaties *according to* their express or implied terms does not implicate Article VI, because it does not violate supreme law. Terminating treaties by their terms is perhaps better labeled "withdrawal," while termination in violation of a treaty's terms we may call "abrogation" (or simply violation).

The Modern Practice of Withdrawing from Treaties

In *Goldwater*, the courts considered a challenge to President Carter's withdrawal from the U.S.-Taiwan mutual defense treaty. Under Article X of the treaty, either side could withdraw by one year's notice to the other. In 1978, Carter delivered a withdrawal notice to the Taiwanese government, effective January 1, 1980—that is, in accordance with Article X's one-year notice provision. No one doubted that the United States had power under the treaty and international law to withdraw from the treaty. The only question was *which branch* of the U.S. government had this power.[6]

Carter thought he did. Senator Goldwater, plaintiff in the legal challenge, thought Senate approval was required. According to the district court, the Senate's role in approving treaties implied a reciprocal role in withdrawal. The court of appeals thought the President had unilateral decisionmaking authority, as part of his constitutional role in foreign affairs, specifically the executive power of Article II, Section 1. The Supreme Court declined to resolve the case, although Justice Brennan would have decided for the President.[7]

A similar example is President Bush's 2001 withdrawal from the Anti-Ballistic Missile (ABM) Treaty between the United States and the former Soviet Union. The ABM Treaty also had a (vaguer) termination provision: either party could withdraw "if it decides that extraordinary events related to the subject matter of this treaty have jeopardized its supreme interests." The withdrawing party had to give six months notice and state the extraordinary events leading to withdrawal.[8] Bush gave the requisite notice, stating that the emergence of terrorist groups dedicated to mass murder of American civilians, and the impending proliferation of nuclear weapons to these groups and to governments in sympathy with them, qualified as extraordinary events jeopardizing U.S. supreme interests.

The international law of treaties also allows nations to withdraw from treaties in various circumstances, even if the treaty language does not permit it in so many words.[9] For example, it is generally thought that parties may withdraw from treaties on the basis of fundamentally changed circumstances.[10] The customary law of treaties is a background understanding against which treaties are drafted, so its provisions are in a sense incorporated into treaties' provisions even though not included explicitly. Withdrawal under international treaty law (an implied term) is thus not materially different from withdrawal under an express term (as in *Goldwater*). Changed circumstances might also support withdrawal from the ABM Treaty, since it was a relic of the Cold War, entered into with a nation that no longer existed, under vastly different strategic circumstances.

As a result, termination of the ABM Treaty (whether resulting from "extraordinary events" under the Treaty's Article XV or from "substantially changed circumstances" under international law) raised similar questions to those raised by *Goldwater*. Both are examples of "withdrawal" under the terminology suggested above. In each case, withdrawal was made (or claimed to be made) according to each treaty's express or implied terms, and assuming this was correctly done, neither withdrawal implicated Article VI of the Constitution (or international law). But though *the United States* had (or at least claimed) the legal right to withdraw, that does not answer the constitutional question of *which branch* of the U.S. government could make the decision to withdraw. And the ABM Treaty withdrawal posed the related issue of which branch could decide whether the conditions for withdrawal were met (since they depended on non-obvious factual and geostrategic questions).

The Constitution's Text and Withdrawal from Treaties

The Constitution on its face says nothing about which branch has power to withdraw from treaties. From the framework elaborated in prior chapters, we can now fill this supposed gap. The key language is again Article II, Section 1, which vests the President with the "executive Power" of the United States. To the Constitution's framers, this power had two important components, both relevant to the question of treaty withdrawals. First, the most familiar aspect of executive power is the power to "execute" the laws—that is, to enforce them or carry them into effect (see Chapter 6).[11] Under Article VI, treaties are part of "supreme Law" and so presumably are part of the "laws" that the President executes. One element of "executing" a law (or treaty) is deciding when it does not apply, or no longer applies, under its own terms. When the President decides that a treaty no longer applies, the President is executing the treaty—in the case of the ABM Treaty, for example, the President was executing the Treaty's Article XV, which provided when and how the United States could withdraw.

Even if one views withdrawal as separate from implementation (perhaps because it has a policymaking component), in eighteenth-century terms "executive" power included general power over treaties—including, of course, the decision whether or not to withdraw. As discussed (Chapter 7), the Constitution's drafters thought that unified executive powers gave too much foreign affairs authority to a single branch, so they allocated some executive power to other branches (specifically, for appointments and treatymaking power, to the Senate). But the Constitution's grant of "executive Power" left the President with the traditional executive foreign affairs powers not conveyed elsewhere. As Jefferson wrote, in the opinion examined earlier, "the transaction of business with foreign nations is Executive altogether; it belongs, then, to the head of that department [that is, the President], except as to such portions of it as are specially submitted to the Senate."[12]

The question, then, is whether the Constitution's text assigns the Senate power (or partial power) over the decision to withdraw from treaties. It seems plain that it does not. The text states the Senate's treaty power clearly: it is the power of "advice and consent" to the *making* of treaties. Professor Henkin is right that the *treatymaking clause* does not say anything about the power to "un-make" treaties. This does not mean that the Constitution as a whole says nothing about that power. The treatymaking clause is the basis of the Senate's claim to power over treaties, so his reading shows only that *the Senate* has no "un-making" power. That means, though, that the power stayed with the President as part of the "executive Power" to transact business with foreign nations. The treatymaking clause does not mean more than it says (and hence this discussion's insistence that what is often called the "treaty clause" be called the "treaty*making* clause").[13]

That reading, though, might fail to consider what one scholar calls a "basic rule of legal construction" that "when a power is given to do an act, the power is also given to repeal it."[14] If founding-era Americans generally had this background assumption—which they surely had for statutes[15]—it would suggest that the Senate (presumably by supermajority) would have to approve withdrawal from treaties. And some founding-era Americans did take that view of appointments, especially in the 1789 congressional debates over removal discussed in Chapter 4. As drafter Roger Sherman argued: "It is a general principle in law, as well as reason, that there shall be the same authority to remove as to establish. It is so in legislation, where the several branches whose concurrence is necessary to pass a law, must concur in repealing it. Just so I take it to be in cases of appointment."[16] And if that were true of appointments, it would surely also be true of the near-parallel power over treaties.

But Sherman's appointments position was a substantial minority. Congress rejected his colleague Richard Bland Lee's motion to describe removal as a Senate power.[17] Some representatives thought Congress could vest removal power as it chose (a position inconsistent with Sherman's), while others argued that removal could be done only by impeachment.[18] And, as we have seen in Chapter 4, the most sophisticated constitutional theorists, including Madison in the House and Ellsworth in the Senate, argued that the President had constitutional power over removals as part of Article II's executive power—a position Congress appeared ultimately to adopt. The removal debate, whatever else it shows, seems decisively to show that there was no widely held background assumption of the type Sherman contended for.

In fact, though, it probably shows a bit more. As we have seen, Madison and Ellsworth not only prevailed in the debate, but appear to have had the better of the textual arguments. And their idea of removal points to the correct idea of treaty termination. "I will not by any means suppose," Representative Livermore said in the debates, "that gentlemen mean, when they argue in favor of removal by the President alone, to contemplate the extension of the power to the repeal of treaties."[19] But the arguments are indeed parallel.

Appointing and removing ambassadors and other executive officers is an "executive" function, and ordinarily would fall within the President's executive power. The text, to enhance checks upon the President, establishes the Senate's role in approving appointments. However, it does not mention any Senate role in removing executive officers (except after impeachment). Therefore, that power remained part of the President's "executive Power." Indeed, this is exactly how former Convention delegates Madison, Ellsworth, and George Clymer described the Constitution's allocation of removal power (see Chapter 4). Similarly, power over treaties was a traditional "executive" function. To enhance checks and balances, the text gave the Senate a role in treatymaking. It did not give the Senate a role in treaty withdrawal, so that power remained part of the President's executive power.

As a result, the Senate's textual claim to a role in treaty termination is quite weak. The constitutional treatment of appointments shows that Senate participation in *approving* a presidential executive action did not conventionally imply Senate participation in *undoing* it.[20] And aside from the Senate's role in treatymaking, there is no constitutional language that, even by implication, suggests a Senate role in withdrawal. Much of the intuitive appeal of a Senate role arises from the sense that the Constitution's text does not give *any* branch the power, so some gap-filler must be invented, and for policy reasons the Senate seems a good candidate. But we now see that the Constitution's text itself supplies an answer.[21]

Treaty Withdrawals in Washington's Administration

Confirming the foregoing analysis, key members of Washington's administration saw treaty withdrawals as a presidential power. As discussed (Chapter 4), in early 1793 Washington faced a major foreign policy challenge from the war between Britain and France. Among other matters, attention focused on two 1778 treaties between the United States and France. Several clauses of these treaties could be read to obligate the United States to enter the war on France's side, or at least to take actions risking conflict with Britain. Of greatest concern, the Treaty of Alliance, Article XI, required the United States to guarantee the security of France's Caribbean possessions, which in 1793 lay under threat from Britain.[22]

As we explored in Chapter 4, once news of war arrived, Washington met with his cabinet to discuss the U.S. response. The news arrived after the end of the 1792–1793 congressional term, so Washington first had to decide whether to call Congress back into session. Washington and the cabinet decided not to recall Congress (meaning that the President would deal with the matter under his independent authority). Washington then decided (with cabinet agreement) on a policy of neutrality toward the warring nations.

Deciding on neutrality directly implicated the treaties, since they might not allow it. Washington thus asked the cabinet, "[w]ith a view to forming a general plan of conduct for the Executive," whether "the United States" should "renounce [the French treaties] or hold them suspended."[23] Hamilton argued that "the United States" may "consider the operation of the Treaties as suspended, and will have eventually a right to renounce them"—primarily because the treaties had been made with the monarchy, and the new government was not an appropriate successor. Jefferson objected that international law saw treaties as between nations, not between governments, and even violent succession was not ground for termination (or suspension). He added—correctly, as it happened—that France would not ask the United States to perform the guarantee and that the other provisions of the treaties would not become material issues for U.S. neutrality; as a result he opposed termination or suspension. Washington followed Jefferson and took no action on the treaties.[24]

For present purposes, the key point is that everyone in this discussion assumed Washington had constitutional authority to withdraw from, or suspend, the treaties. Washington had already decided not to reconvene Congress, so in asking whether "the United States" should "renounce" the treaties, as part of the "general plan of conduct for the Executive," he was asking whether *he* alone should renounce the treaties. Similarly, when Hamilton argued that the United States should suspend the treaties, he meant the President should suspend the treaties (since Hamilton opposed recalling Congress).[25] Jefferson, arguing against suspension, might have contested the President's constitutional authority, but did not.[26] Rather, he argued within the framework Washington presented—that is, that the decision was the President's.

Given that eighteenth-century executive power was widely understood to include treaty powers, it is not surprising that Washington, Hamilton, and Jefferson believed the President could decide whether to withdraw from treaties. The House had no direct treaty role and the Senate's role was a check on treaty*making*. Because the Constitution did not qualify or burden the power to withdraw from treaties, it remained part of the President's executive power.[27]

The President's Power to Violate Treaties: The Case of the Geneva Conventions

We can now turn to a distinct question: may the President violate treaties, or withdraw from or suspend them contrary to their express or implied terms? Consider, for example, the debate over the application of the Geneva Conventions, governing the treatment of wartime prisoners, to U.S. actions during the post-2001 war on terrorism. Although President Bush did not publicly say he was authorizing violation or suspension of the Conventions, his lawyers apparently told him that he could. They did not distinguish this situation from *Goldwater* and the ABM Treaty, citing both as precedents. Yet two additional constitutional clauses—Article VI and Article II, Section 3— make the analysis quite distinct.[28]

Article VI: Treaties as Supreme Law

The analysis should begin with the Constitution's Article VI: "This Constitution, and the Laws of the United States which shall be made in Pursuance thereof, and all Treaties made, or which shall be made, under the Authority of the United States, shall be the supreme Law of the Land." This was another of the Constitution's great structural foreign affairs innovations. As discussed (Chapter 5), in England treaties generally were not lawmaking acts: in most cases, at least, they required implementation by Parliament to have effect in domestic law. That was also true, at least as a practical matter, under the Articles, except the Articles had the further difficulty that the Congress lacked legislative power to implement treaties—only the states could, and they often refused. States' intransigence on this point frustrated and worried American leaders of the 1780s, because foreign nations threatened adverse consequences for failure to keep treaty promises and hesitated to have further dealings with a government that could not implement its own treaties (see Chapter 2).

One way the Constitution addressed this problem was by giving the new Congress legislative powers and (through Article VI) authority to displace state law. Calling federal statutes "supreme Law of the Land" would—as everyone at the time understood—make them judicially enforceable and binding on states and individuals.[29] Making this change alone would have largely revived the English system of executive treatymaking and legislative treaty implementation. But the Constitution went further, in Article VI, by making treaties themselves part of the "supreme Law of the Land," in the same language as statutes. That appears to mean, in general terms, that treaties have a similar status to statutory law, of their own force, without needing Congress to enact them by statute (as Parliament did). They are, it is now commonly said, "self-executing" (that is, not requiring "execution"—perhaps it would be better to say "enactment"—by statute). The prime motivation for these provisions, it seems, was to make treaties automatically override state law, which we generally suppose that they do (see Chapter 14) and as the Supreme Court found in one of its earliest cases, *Ware v. Hylton* (1796).[30]

Article VI, though, appears to have consequences beyond its effect on state law. It describes the status of federal statutory law and federal treaties in the same clause, using the same language: both "shall be the supreme Law of the Land." This seems to say not only that treaties displace state law (a point that could be made in less sweeping terms), but also that treaties have *the same status* as federal statutory law. That might have a number of consequences, some of which we can defer to later chapters. For present purposes, the question is how this provision interacts with the President's executive power.

Article II, Section 3: The Take-Care Clause

We have already examined briefly the portion of Article II, Section 3 known as the take-care clause (Chapter 6). By this provision, the President "shall take Care that the Laws be faithfully executed." As discussed, it principally addressed a possible claim that the President's executive power included power to ignore existing law under certain circumstances. Blackstone had specifically said that what he called the "dispensing" power was legislative in nature and not vested in the monarch, but kings of earlier times had claimed it, and the Constitution's drafters likely wanted to be clear that the President would not have it. The President, then, has both the power and duty to see that Congress's laws are enforced.[31]

The key question here is whether the take-care duty also extends to treaties (or, put more precisely, whether the phrase "the Laws" in Article II, Section 3 includes treaty obligations). Absent Article VI, there would be little reason to think so. Treaties were not called "laws" in a domestic sense under the English system (or any other system Americans likely would have studied), and the monarch had no domestic legal obligation—nor even the power—to enforce them except as authorized by domestic law. Blackstone's discussion of the dispensing power, a likely inspiration of the take-care clause, encompassed only statutes, not treaties. The English monarch could violate/suspend/dispense with treaties, because treaties were not laws, and the executive power gave complete control over treaties; Americans surely knew that English monarchs sometimes *did* violate treaties, without constitutional repercussions.

Article VI, though, makes treaties part of the "supreme Law of the Land" (which they previously were not). That phrase had a particular meaning in English law: the foundation of the English system of divided government, going back to Magna Charta in the thirteenth century, was that the monarch was bound by the *legem terrae*—the "law of the land."[32] The English "law of the land" protected individual rights (which could not be transgressed except pursuant to it); and it was judicially enforceable—not against the monarch personally, but against the monarch's agents.[33] Article VI surely uses that phrase, with respect to the Constitution and statutes, to mean that they are binding in domestic law, including upon the President; it is hard to see how it would not carry the same meaning for treaties.[34] Of course, in English law treaties were *not* part of the law of the land in this sense, but Article VI adds them. That is a substantial change, but it seems a necessary consequence of the clause's language, and it is wholly consistent with the frustrations of treaty enforcement under the Articles.

Once one thinks of treaties as a new element added to the "laws of the land" in the English sense, it seems natural that they would form part of the Article II, Section 3 "Laws" that the President must enforce. And that reading seems to preclude presidential power to violate or abrogate treaties. The President's claim to power in this area arises from the executive power, but Article II, Section 1's executive power is expressly qualified by Article II, Section 3.

Practice and Commentary

Presidential treaty violations are not directly discussed in surviving founding-era commentary, nor did early Presidents claim the power. There is indirect evidence, though, that the reading developed above is consistent with the way the founding generation viewed the text.

First, it is surely plausible as a historical matter that the framers wished to bind the President to treaties. American leaders of the 1780s were obsessed with the danger of treaty violations. This concern was, for example, central to Jay's criticisms of the Articles' Congress, to Madison's indictment of the Articles, to Randolph's opening speech at the Convention, and to several numbers of *The Federalist* (see Chapter 2). True, these comments were mostly directed at *state* violations of treaties, which were more common and more dangerous—but similar concerns could easily support a plan to bind the President as well as the states.

Second, founding-era commentary is simply permeated with comments from all sides that equate "treaties" with "laws" in the Constitution's system. To anti-federalists, this was a major point of objection. George Mason complained that "[b]y declaring all Treaties supreme laws of the land, the Executive & the Senate have, in many Cases, an exclusive power of legislation." Other anti-federalist writers objected that "[t]he president and two thirds of the Senate have power to make laws in the form of treaties, independent of the legislature itself"; and that "there is one of the most important duties

[that] may be managed by the Senate and executive alone, and to have all the force of law paramount without the aid or interference of the house of representatives; that is the power of making treaties." Federalists generally did not deny the point, but defended it: Hamilton's Federalist No. 75 embraced "the operation of treaties as laws," and answered anti-federalist objections by pointing out that (unlike in England) part of the legislature was involved in making them. A reply to Mason urged the "necessity of treaties having the force of laws."[35]

The same association occurred before and after ratification. At the Convention, for example, Gouverneur Morris observed that "treaties were to be laws" and thus a provision of the draft giving Congress power to call out the militia to enforce "laws and treaties" was redundant; the Convention agreed and deleted "and treaties" from what became Article I, Section 8, clause 17. In the early 1790s, not only strong nationalists, but also those more skeptical of federal power, such as Madison and Jefferson, equated law and treaties.[36] And Chief Justice Marshall wrote in *The Schooner Peggy* (1801) that "where a treaty is the law of the land . . . [it] is as much to be regarded by the court as an act of congress."[37]

In sum, while the commentary did not go into all of the consequences of equating treaties with laws, the weight of opinion plainly did make that association, and ascribed it to Article VI. If a narrower meaning had been the intended one, both text and commentary could easily have said only that state laws in violation of treaty obligations were void (phrasing used, to a very limited extent, in Article 6 of the Articles); calling them "laws" indicates that they have all attributes of ordinary federal law, not just superiority over state law—which in turn indicates that, at least absent other considerations, the President's duty to "the laws" includes treaties.[38]

Third, there is no early practice of Presidents claiming power to violate treaties or being advised that they had that power. As we saw earlier (Chapter 4), in the 1793 neutrality debates Washington's cabinet assumed that he would not act contrary to the international law of treaties. Hamilton, who wanted the French treaties suspended, argued that their implied terms allowed suspension because of the change of government in France; he did not claim the President could suspend the treaties in violation of international treaty law. Jefferson, in reply, insisted that international treaty law did not allow U.S. suspension.

This is not overwhelming evidence in support, and if the constitutional language were otherwise, it might not be sufficient to carry the day. But the constitutional language is tolerably clear on its face; counterarguments (to which we now turn) largely depend on considerations outside the text, which will ultimately prove unpersuasive.

Congress's Treaty Powers: The Last in Time Rule

To begin, we may object that, as a structural matter, the United States must have power to violate treaty obligations, as a sovereign right. Relatedly, inflexibly requiring the President to adhere to treaties will (it may be said) impede the President's conduct of U.S. foreign affairs: the President, as the "sole organ" of U.S. foreign policy, should have authority to decide when the nation will exercise its ability to violate treaty obligations.

As we are beginning to see, though, the Constitution's text does not establish the President as the sole instrument of U.S. foreign affairs, and contrary arguments owe more to *Curtiss-Wright* than they do to the text. The text does give the President substantial independent powers, but it also subjects them to substantial checks. We have examined several of these already: requiring appointments and treaties to receive approval of an independent body; denying the President lawmaking and law-suspending authority, even in foreign-affairs-related matters; requiring the President to obtain funding from Congress. Imposing treaties as restraints upon the President would not be an anomaly, but only another of these divisions of foreign affairs authority. In the abstract, one cannot say whether the constitutional generation would or would not have embraced this further limit. As a result, it is not a reason to depart from the text's best reading.

The appeal to sovereign rights has only a little more force. True, it might seem odd if the Constitution did not allow the U.S. government to violate treaties (although those with strong attachment to honoring treaty obligations might find this an appropriate system). Of course, in a regime of delegated powers it is always possible that there are powers that (intentionally or not) are not delegated. Contrary to what courts and commentators sometimes claim, it is never the case that *the United States* lacks a nondelegated power; at most, the federal government lacks it. All nondelegated powers are reserved to "the People," so the people always have authority to assert power by constitutional amendment. But in any event, the text appears to give the federal government power to violate most—perhaps all—treaties; it simply does not give the power to the President.

In modern practice, the long-standing rule is that a later federal statute overrides an earlier treaty (and a later treaty overrides an earlier statute).[39] The text does not state this "last in time" rule in so many words, but strongly implies it. Article VI gives treaties their domestic legal force, but it does not do any more than place treaties on the same plane as federal statutes; it does not give treaties a *higher* status than federal statutes. As is true today, eighteenth-century understandings of legislative power in general included power to displace earlier legislative acts. That is, a later law always displaced a conflicting earlier law, and conversely an earlier legislature could not bind later legislatures—background rules the Constitution surely adopted with respect to conflicting statutes. As Blackstone elaborated, it is a "maxim of universal law" that "acts of parliament derogatory of the power of subsequent parliaments bind not." Hamilton explained: "It not uncommonly happens that there are two statutes existing at one time, clashing in whole or in part with each other. . . . The rule which has obtained in the courts for determining their relative validity is that the last in order of time shall be preferred to the first. . . . They thought it reasonable that between the interfering acts of an *equal* authority that which was the last indication of its will should have the preference."[40]

If treaties have the same constitutional status as statutes (as Article VI indicates), we may suppose they should be treated equally for this purpose as well—which is the basis of the modern "last-in-time" rule. It cannot be objected that treaties are the supreme law of the land, because federal statutes are as well: the text does not provide any way to pick between them, other than by the background understanding of the last-in-time rule.[41] And when President Washington raised this precise issue in 1796, Hamilton and Secretary of Treasury Oliver Wolcott resolved it in this way: as Wolcott put it, "Statutes and treaties of the United States are alike the supreme law of the land, and the last act of whichever description, will control the former."[42]

Thus Congress has power to violate treaties (or, more accurately, to override the domestic legal effect of treaties).[43] This may not completely answer the structural objection raised above, because Congress can act only upon enumerated subjects (that is, it can only exercise the powers "herein granted," as Article I, Section 1 declares). Congress does not have an enumerated power to override treaties, so any conflicting legislation must be founded upon some other enumerated power. Sometimes this will be easily satisfied: Congress can, for example, pass legislation displacing commercial treaties under its power to regulate foreign commerce. For some treaties, though, an enumerated power will not so readily be found.

This point is discussed further in Chapter 10; for now we may say that, although Congress does not have a general authority over foreign affairs, it comes close through its power to enact laws "necessary and proper" to support the exercise of other powers granted by the Constitution. To the extent that the President needs authority to violate a treaty in order to exercise another power granted by the Constitution, including the executive foreign affairs power, the "necessary and proper" power should allow Congress to grant that authority.

Foster v. Neilson and the Puzzle of Non-self-executing Treaties

Another way to defend the President's power to violate treaties arises from the idea of "non-self-executing" treaties. According to the Supreme Court, in cases going back at least to *Foster v. Neilson* (1829), some treaties do not have "self-executing" effect in domestic law, whatever Article VI may appear to say; rather, they require legislative implementation to become part of the law of the land. As Chief Justice Marshall explained, when "the treaty addresses itself to the political, not the judicial department . . . the legislature must execute the contract before it can become a rule for the Court."[44] Perhaps, then, the President is not bound by non-self-executing treaties (since they are not of their own force part of the "Laws" the President is bound to enforce). And if one thought most treaties were non-self-executing, treaties would not be a substantial limit on the President.[45]

The problem, of course, is that Article VI says without qualification that "all treaties," not some treaties, are part of supreme law (if made under the authority of the United States). How, then, can some treaties be "non-self-executing"?

UNCONSTITUTIONAL TREATIES. Article VI states that treaties made "under the Authority of the United States" are part of supreme law. As a result, treaties that violate the Constitution are not part of supreme law, because they are not made "under the Authority of the United States"—that is, the United States acts *ultra vires* in making them. This might occur because the treaty seeks to do something the Constitution forbids the United States as a whole to do: "[A] delegated authority cannot rightfully transcend the constituting act," Hamilton said in 1796, and thus "[a] treaty for example cannot transfer the legislative power to the Executive Department" or say "that the Judges and not the President shall command the national forces."[46] It might also occur when the President and the Senate seek to exercise by treaty powers the Constitution vests exclusively in another part of government. For example, Article I, Section 7 states that "all Bills for raising Revenue shall originate in the House of Representatives." If this is read—as it usually is—to give the House an exclusive right to propose taxes, a treaty could not in itself impose taxes. With slightly more of a stretch, Article I, Section 9's direction that "No money shall be drawn from the Treasury, but in Consequence of Appropriations made by Law" is usually read to mean that Congress has an exclusive right of appropriations by statute (so appropriations cannot be done by treaty).[47]

One might say that treaties purporting to exercise an exclusive power of Congress are simply unconstitutional. But another way of looking at them is that, although binding in international law, they require legislative approval to have effect in domestic law—that is, they are not (and cannot be) self-executing. This appears to be the way founding-era Americans viewed treaties requiring appropriations in the immediate post-ratification era. As discussed in Chapter 7, in the 1792 Algiers negotiations, Jefferson and Washington appeared to believe that they (with the Senate's concurrence) could make a treaty with Algiers to pay money for hostages, but that the House's approval would be needed to obtain the necessary funding. The same view was taken on all sides in the Jay Treaty debates: no one argued that the treaty was unconstitutional because it committed the nation to expenditures, but everyone understood that funding would require House (as well as Senate) approval.[48] Presumably founding-era Americans would have understood treaties affecting other exclusive powers of Congress to operate in the same way. And arguably, at least, the President would not be bound by treaty provisions that require, but have not yet received, legislative implementation.

In the Jay Treaty debates, Madison—as leader of the opposition—sought to take this principle one step further, arguing that treaties could not be self-executing if they touched upon *any* congressional power: the Constitution, he said, "left with the PRESIDENT and Senate the power of making treaties, but required at the same time the Legislative sanction and cooperation, in those cases where the Constitution had given express and specific powers to the Legislature."[49] That would seem to require, for example, commercial treaties to be non-self-executing (because foreign commerce is among Congress's "express and specific powers"). In the ratification debates, the anti-federalist "Federal Farmer" had made this point explicitly: "I do not see how any commercial regulations can be made in treaties, that will not infringe upon this power in the legislature; therefore, I infer, that the true construction is, that the president and senate shall make treaties; but all commercial treaties shall be subject to be confirmed by the legislature."[50]

These arguments wrongly assume, though, that two branches of government cannot have *concurrent* authority over the same matter. There is little textual basis for that assumption as a general matter (although the language of specific clauses, such as Article I, Sections 7 and 9, may state or imply it with respect to particular powers). In the case of commercial regulations, for example, Congress's ability to regulate commerce is not negated by the treatymakers' parallel ability to regulate commerce—nor, conversely, is the treatymakers' ability to make commercial treaties, which the framers seemed broadly to assume, negated by Congress's ability to regulate foreign commerce, including—pursuant to the last-in-time rule—in ways that violate treaties. Different grants of power may allow different branches to operate on the same subject in different ways, unless there is a reason to think otherwise, arising from particular text or from widely held background assumptions.

In the case of treatymaking power, there is no text indicating a general reservation for Congress's Article I powers, and the reference to "all" treaties in Article VI stands against an exception that would extend to such a large class.[51] It is true that Madison and others argued for such a construction, but they did not rely on specific text, and their comments seem more like advocacy than reflections of common background assumptions.[52]

Although apparently addressed to the relative powers of Congress and the treatymakers, these arguments affect the relationship between the President and treaties as well. To continue the example of the Geneva Conventions: despite Article VI, the President would not be limited by the Geneva Conventions if (a) they are unconstitutional because they infringe an exclusive power of the President as, for example, commander-in-chief, or (b) they are non-self-executing because they address an exclusive power of Congress—as, for example, regulating the military. We will defer the first argument until we examine war powers in Chapter 12, but we can say that the second argument seems unpersuasive as a textual matter, because Congress's power is concurrent rather than exclusive (as in the analogous case of commerce).

TREATIES ADDRESSED TO THE LEGISLATURE. We now turn to the most difficult part of the topic: treaties which do not involve an exclusive power of Congress, but which themselves explicitly or implicitly indicate that they require congressional implementation. In *Foster*, Marshall read the relevant treaty provision as an agreement that Congress would pass a law confirming land titles. Congress had not passed the law called for, and Marshall held that the treaty itself did not create any domestic obligation, despite Article VI; the treaty, he said, was addressed to the legislature, and required implementation. Although Marshall did not use the phrase, *Foster* is the genesis of the principal modern doctrine of "non-self-executing" treaties: that is, that a treaty's language (or the Senate's approval of it) may indicate that it requires legislative implementation before it becomes part of domestic law.[53]

Although this proposition is well entrenched in modern law, it divides academic commentators, and proves surprisingly hard to resolve on the basis of the Constitution's text. We might say—roughly as Marshall did—that such treaties are analogous to treaties touching an exclusive power of Congress: they create an international obligation but not a domestic obligation. Although they are part of "supreme Law," and thus may place Congress under a duty to execute them, by their own terms they have no further domestic effect until Congress does so. The result is that the treatymakers can replicate, on a treaty-by-treaty basis, the English system that separated a treaty's international effect and its domestic effect.[54]

Alternatively, we might say that this arrangement contradicts the Constitution's text. The text rejects the English system by directly linking treaties' international effect and their domestic effect (presumably because the gap between these two had proved so disruptive under the Articles). The treatymakers can no more alter that decision than they can alter any other structural provision in the Constitution.[55]

Oddly, though, regardless of the correct resolution, the practical effect is likely similar. An unconstitutional treaty has, of course, no effect in domestic law. So unless the non-self-execution provision can be separated from the rest of the treaty, an explicitly non-self-executing treaty probably lacks legal effect in either case: either because it says it lacks legal effect, or because it is unconstitutional. And further, the effect on the President is probably similar: in either event, the President would not be bound to execute a treaty that lacked domestic legal effect.

In sum, treaties are always part of supreme law (under Article VI), unless (i) they are unconstitutional; (ii) they are terminated in accordance with their terms, which is an executive/presidential power; or (iii) they are overridden by statute. However, a treaty may itself disclaim legal effect, either implicitly or explicitly, except as a direction for political branch elaboration—in which case it will have no legal effect aside from the disclaimer. That does not mean it is not part of supreme law—only that, as supreme law, by its own terms it does not provide rules of conduct. In none of these three cases would the treaty bind the President.[56]

It is important to note, however, that courts and commentators sometimes use the phrase "non-self-executing" to mean a different concept: that a treaty may not be judicially enforceable because, for example, it does not provide a private right of action that can be the basis of a suit for damages.[57] We will consider the justiciability of treaty-based claims in Chapter 18. At present, though, it is important to see that this issue does not have any bearing on the binding nature of treaties. Constitutional provisions may be binding even if they are not enforceable in court. Whether or not a treaty can be enforced by private suit does not affect whether the treaty binds the President—it only affects what sort of remedies there are for violation.

We can illustrate this distinction by revisiting the controversy over the Geneva Conventions. Under the analysis developed above, the President cannot constitutionally violate the Geneva Conventions unless they are unconstitutional, non-self-executing, or overridden by Congress. Some courts and commentators have claimed that they are non-self-executing. But by this they typically mean that the Conventions are not enforceable in court by private parties, for various reasons, not that they explicitly or implicitly say they are not part of supreme law. Nothing in the Conventions or their Senate approval explicitly limits self-execution, and many of the Conventions' obligations are very specific, seeming to require no legislative elaboration to provide a rule of conduct. As a result, they are likely self-executing, in that they bind the President though Article VI and Article II Section 3; what remedy may be available for violation is, of course, a different question.[58]

Conclusion

The foregoing discussion shows the importance of distinguishing between withdrawing from a treaty (terminating it in accordance with its express or implied terms) and violating or abrogating it (acting contrary to its express or implied terms). The former is part of the President's executive foreign affairs power, because it is not qualified or assigned to any other branch by the text. President Carter's termination of the Taiwan treaty in *Goldwater* and President Bush's termination of the ABM Treaty were constitutional under the text's historical meaning.

In contrast, the President's power to violate treaties is denied by a combination of Article VI (making treaties part of supreme law) and Article II, Section 3 (requiring the President to enforce "the Laws"). These provisions do not apply to *Goldwater*-type terminations, because there the President does not act contrary to the treaty. But they do show that the President cannot violate (or suspend) treaties without regard to their terms, as the Bush administration in theory claimed.

The last statement is subject to two qualifications. The President may violate treaties when authorized by Congress. Congress's legislative power allows it to displace treaties, as a matter of domestic law, with later statutes—and the President is bound to execute the later statute, not the earlier treaty. Article VI gives treaties the status of statutes, but it does not make treaties superior to statutes. The President also is not bound by non-self-executing treaties—that is, treaties that say, implicitly or explicitly, that they are not part of domestic law until implemented legislatively. Such treaties may be constitutional, despite Article VI—depending on what one thinks of Marshall's decision in *Foster*—but they are likely a small category. In particular, treaties are not non-self-executing (in this sense) just because they act upon a matter also within Congress's power or fail to provide a complete set of private remedies.

9

The Non-treaty Power: Executive Agreements and *United States v. Belmont*

The Constitution's text expressly describes only one way that the United States may make international agreements: Article II, Section 2's treaty-making clause, discussed in Chapter 7. In modern practice, though, there are two others. In some instances, the President negotiates and signs an international agreement, but rather than submitting it to the Senate for supermajority approval, relies upon the approval of a simple majority of each House of Congress (given either before or after the agreement is signed). These so-called congressional-executive agreements, not approved by two-thirds of the Senate, today constitute some of the nation's most important international obligations, especially in the area of international trade. Most prominently, the North American Free Trade Agreement (NAFTA) was approved in 1994 in this way.

The President also sometimes enters into international agreements without approval from the House or the Senate. These "executive agreements" are an important part of modern diplomatic practice, although rarely rising to the level of NAFTA in importance.[1]

This chapter considers the constitutionality of executive agreements (congressional-executive agreements are considered in Chapter 10). Three times in the last century the U.S. Supreme Court upheld agreements made only on the authority of the President, and in 2003 it seemed to assume that their constitutionality lay beyond doubt.[2] Yet none of these decisions explains how the practice could be consistent with the Constitution's command that treaties be approved by two-thirds of the Senate.

At first blush the question may seem an easy one: the treatymaking clause says that the President may make treaties "provided" two-thirds of the Senators present concur. Presumably, then, the President cannot make treaties if two-thirds of the Senators do *not* concur. As we will see, this argument is correct as far as it goes—but it does not go as far as it may appear. Although

174

the President can make *treaties* only through the treatymaking clause, not all international agreements are treaties. As a result, much of the modern practice of executive agreements may be consistent with the Constitution's historical meaning.[3]

The Supreme Court and Executive Agreements

Modern consensus gives the President the independent power, at least in some circumstances, to make international agreements without the approval of Congress or the Senate. Louis Henkin observes:

> The President can . . . make many [international] agreements on his own authority, including, surely, those related to establishing and maintaining diplomatic relations, agreements settling international claims, and military agreements within the Presidential authority as Commander in Chief. There are doubtless many other "sole" agreements within the President's foreign affairs powers, but which they are is hardly agreed.[4]

The modern consensus rests largely upon three Supreme Court cases: *United States v. Belmont* (1937); *United States v. Pink* (1942); and *Dames & Moore v. Regan* (1981). *Belmont* approved an executive agreement with the U.S.S.R., entered into by President Franklin Roosevelt. *Pink* reaffirmed the same agreement against a slightly different constitutional challenge. In *Dames & Moore v. Regan*, the Court upheld President Carter's executive agreement with Iran ending the 1980 Tehran hostage crisis.[5]

Belmont is an appropriate starting point. We should leave *Dames & Moore* aside for the moment, as it relied in part upon powers of Congress we have not yet considered (see Chapter 10), and *Pink* is essentially derivative of *Belmont*.[6]

In 1933, President Franklin Roosevelt gave diplomatic recognition to the Soviet Union, the first time the United States had done so. In connection with recognition, the two governments entered into an agreement resolving several outstanding issues, including claims of the U.S. government and U.S. citizens against the Soviet government and Soviet claims against the United States and U.S. residents. Central to *Belmont*, the latter category included Soviet claims on property in the United States owned by Russian nationals that the U.S.S.R. had purportedly nationalized by post-revolutionary decrees but over which it lacked physical control. In the agreement accompanying recognition (known as the Litvinov Agreement after the principal Soviet negotiator), the United

States waived its claims against the Soviet Union in return for an assignment to the U.S. government of the Soviet claims to property located in the United States. Roosevelt neither asked for nor received authority from either House of Congress.

The U.S. government later identified purportedly nationalized Russian property held by the estate of August Belmont, a New York banker, and sought its recovery. It faced a problem, though: under New York law, nationalization decrees operated only territorially. Property located in New York could not be affected by the Soviet nationalization decree, and title remained with its original owner. Since the Litvinov Agreement gave the United States only the Soviet interest, and since the Soviets, under New York law, had no interest in Belmont's property, it appeared that the United States also had no interest. The United States responded that the Agreement validated the Soviet nationalization, giving the Soviets (and derivatively the United States) title to the property. The lower court held for Belmont, and the case reached the U.S. Supreme Court as *United States v. Belmont.*

Without the Litvinov Agreement, Belmont's argument would have seemed unassailable: a private party purchasing the Soviet Union's interest in the property would have received the interest recognized by applicable (New York) law—namely, nothing. Had the Agreement been a treaty under Article II, Section 2, its terms would have preempted New York law under the Constitution's Article VI (Chapter 14). *Belmont* turned upon (1) whether the Agreement was a constitutional exercise of the President's power, and (2) if so, whether it preempted the New York rule on which Belmont relied. The Court, per Justice Sutherland of *Curtiss-Wright* fame, ruled for the United States on both points.

Sutherland said little about the President's power to make the Agreement. He observed (without citation) that the President's power "may not be doubted," and continued:

> [I]n respect of what was done here, the Executive had authority to speak as the sole organ of [the U.S.] government. The assignment and the agreements in connection therewith did not, as in the case of treaties, as that term is used in the treaty making clause of the Constitution (article II, §2), require the advice and consent of the Senate.[7]

The paragraph contains no explanation for *why* the Senate's advice and consent was not required. Sutherland quickly moved on to explain that state law could not override the executive agreement:

[T]he external powers of the United States are to be exercised without regard to state laws or policies. . . . Within the field of its powers, whatever the United States rightfully undertakes, it necessarily has warrant to consummate. And when judicial authority is invoked in aid of such consummation, State Constitutions, state laws, and state policies are irrelevant to the inquiry and decision. It is inconceivable that any of them can be interposed as an obstacle to the effective operation of a federal constitutional power.[8]

But this discussion misses the central point: surely the Litvinov Agreement, if approved by the Senate, would have displaced New York law. No one denied that making a settlement agreement under Article II, Section 2 would have been a "federal constitutional power" superior to state law. The issue was whether the Agreement, *despite* bypassing Article II, Section 2, was an exercise of "federal constitutional power."

Although Sutherland did not say so in *Belmont,* it is clear enough what he thought of the matter. Sutherland wrote the opinion in *Curtiss-Wright,* decided only a year before *Belmont* (Chapter 1). He referred to *Curtiss-Wright* only once in *Belmont,* but in *Curtiss-Wright* he used the power to make executive agreements as an example of inherent presidential power in foreign affairs.[9] So there was no need for Sutherland to search the Constitution for presidential power to enter into executive agreements: he had already decided that the President's foreign affairs powers could come from outside the Constitution—and that executive agreements were an example of extra-constitutional power.

As a result, the President's power to enter into executive agreements stands upon much weaker constitutional ground than modern writing suggests. Chapter 1 rejected the extra-constitutional theory of *Curtiss-Wright.* *Belmont*'s reasoning can be no stronger than *Curtiss-Wright,* on which it implicitly depends. *United States v. Pink* added nothing to *Belmont*'s reasoning, and *Dames & Moore,* as noted, relied upon powers of Congress. Nonetheless, ensuing sections show that a constitutional case can be made for at least some of what Sutherland claimed.

The Exclusivity of the Treatymaking Clause

We can begin by asking whether the President may make treaties other than through Article II, Section 2. From that clause's plain language alone, it seems clear that the President cannot. The President has power to make treaties, it says, "provided two-thirds of the Senators present concur." If two-thirds do not concur, then, the President does not have the power. "Provided" in this context means "only if."

One might object, on the basis of prior chapters, that although the President does not have independent treatymaking power from Article II, Section 2, it might arise from Article II, Section 1. As discussed, treatymaking was an "executive" function in the eighteenth century. The English executive/monarch had treatymaking power, and theorists such as Montesquieu and Blackstone described treaty power as executive (see Chapter 3). Should not the President's "executive Power" extend to traditional executive powers, including the making of treaties?

But this argument is easily rejected on two grounds. First, it is flatly contrary to the text, which gives the President power to make treaties *provided* two-thirds of the Senators approve. It is difficult to see how the President, acting alone, could have power to make treaties *without* approval of two-thirds of the Senate. This greater power, if given elsewhere in the Constitution, would include the lesser power described in Article II, Section 2: a President who could act on independent authority surely could act with Senate approval—so the enumerated power of Article II, Section 2 would be superfluous. Article II, Section 2 presupposes that the President has no independent avenue for treatymaking; it grants power to the Senate and limits the President's traditional executive power.

In response, presidential advocates might tone down their claims to assert independent treatymaking power over only subjects closely identified with other presidential powers. This seems to be Professor Henkin's thinking, in saying that the President can make executive agreements with respect to recognition of foreign governments (related to receiving ambassadors) and military affairs (related to the commander-in-chief power), and perhaps other matters.[10] Even this more modest claim, though, does not seem to overcome the textual objection. Even if, in the absence of the treatymaking clause, an independent treatymaking ability in military affairs could be implied into the general power granted by the commander-in-chief clause, the specific prohibition in Article II, Section 2 would seem to trump that more general language.

Second, a quick look at founding-era understandings confirms the exclusive reading. As recounted in Chapter 3, the treatymaking power was one of the previously "executive" powers that the drafters objected to including within the President's authority. Post-drafting commentary immediately assumed that the President had no independent treatymaking power, confirming the text's natural reading (see Chapter 7). No one in any of the early discussions suggested that the President might have even a partial independent treaty power over particular subjects: the discussions are categorical in saying that the President cannot make a treaty—any treaty—without the Senate.[11]

Treaties and Other International Agreements

From the foregoing, one might say (as one leading scholar does) that "the specific objective of the treaty clause was to preclude the President, acting alone, from entering into international agreements."[12] That conclusion, though, assumes that "treaty" means "international agreement." The point of the treatymaking clause, we may agree, was to prevent the President, acting alone, from entering into *treaties;* to reach the wider conclusion, one must show that "treaty" encompasses all undertakings between nations. Perhaps, though, in eighteenth-century terms, "treaty" was a subset of "international agreement" rather than a synonym.

The argument here parallels Chapter 3's argument regarding the meaning of "executive power." In modern speech, we may use the term "treaty" to mean any international agreement, just as we may use "executive power" to mean law-enforcement power. But we cannot assume that terms carried the same meaning in the eighteenth century. Executive power meant more than just law-enforcement power; treaties may have included less than all international agreements.

Constitutional Text

The case for a narrower meaning of "treaty" finds immediate support in the Constitution's language. In addition to Article II, Section 2, the word "treaty" appears three times in the Constitution: in Article III, Section 2 (giving federal courts jurisdiction over cases arising under treaties); in Article VI (making treaties supreme law of the land); and in Article I, Section 10. The latter provision says: "No State shall enter into any Treaty, Alliance, or Confederation. . . . No State shall, without the Consent of Congress, . . . enter into any Agreement or Compact with another State, or with a foreign Power. . . ." As several commentators have noted, this language indicates that "treaty" is a subclass of all possible international agreements. By these provisions, state treatymaking was absolutely banned, yet states might (with Congress's consent) enter into "Agreements or Compacts" with foreign nations. That formulation is troublesome if one believes that the word "treaty" encompasses all international agreements.[13]

The Articles of Confederation, Article 6, had a similar distinction:

> No State, without the consent of the United States, in Congress assembled, shall . . . enter into any conference, agreement, alliance, or treaty with any king, prince, or state. . . .

> No two or more states shall enter into any treaty, confederation, or alliance, whatever, between them, without the consent of the United States, in Congress assembled.

In other words, treaties and agreements between a state and a foreign nation required the Congress's consent, but among the U.S. states treaties *but not agreements* required such consent.

In keeping with the Constitution's design to strengthen the national government, Article I, Section 10 went beyond the Articles to preclude state treaties altogether and require congressional consent for all state/foreign and interstate agreements. Yet it also incorporated the Articles' differential treatment of state "treaties" and state "agreements," suggesting that the differential was not accidental, but reflected a deliberate understanding that treaties did not encompass the entire field of international agreements.[14]

Treaties and International Agreements before the Constitution

Tracing the origins of this distinction requires us to take up another category of influences upon founding era-Americans. Ordinary eighteenth-century English speech—and eighteenth-century English theory and practice—did not distinguish among different types of international agreements, and related dictionary definitions are unhelpful.[15] But another body of works did: the writers on what was then called the law of nations (what today we would call international law). The eighteenth-century vision of international law and its interaction with our Constitution is discussed in Chapter 17; for now, we may say that the seventeenth and (especially) the eighteenth centuries produced an array of works devoted to outlining a set of legal principles that governed the interactions among nations, and that these works were widely studied in founding-era America.[16] Crucially for the present discussion, key law-of-nations writers, including Hugo Grotius, Emmerich de Vattel, and Christian Wolff, used the equivalent of "treaty" to mean a subset of all international agreements, not as a generic term to mean all international agreements.

Distinguishing among classes of international agreements actually dates to Roman times. Roman practice recognized three types of agreements. The *foedus* was a formal undertaking of the Roman state whose conclusion required specified ceremonies and whose violation was said to risk divine retribution. The *sponsio* was the name given to the practice, described in Chapter 7, of Roman commanders in the field signing agreements on their own authority and initiative, subject to ratification or rejection in Rome. A third designation, *alias pactiones,* was apparently a catchall phrase for agreements not included in either of the foregoing categories.[17]

Educated Americans likely knew of this terminology from Roman sources, but in any event Grotius's widely read *De Jure Belli ac Pacis* (On the Laws of War and Peace) (1625) described it clearly. Grotius, writing in Latin, adopted Roman terms to describe international agreements: *foedus, sponsio,* and *alias pactiones.* The conventional English translation of *foedus* was "treaty," and *alias pactiones* meant "other agreements." (*Sponsio* had no obvious translation.) A reader of Grotius would have in mind a hierarchy of international agreements in which "treaty" was only one (albeit the most important) category: the entire class consisted of "treaties, *sponsios,* and other agreements."[18]

Vattel's *Droit des Gens* (The Law of Nations) (1758), written in French, distinguished between *traite* on one hand, and *accords, conventions, pactions* on the other. He equated the Latin *foedus* with the French *traite* (the English "treaty"). *Accords, conventions, pactions* would conventionally translate as "agreements, conventions, arrangements [or compacts]." So Vattel too did not use "treaty" (or its equivalent) as a comprehensive term but as a subset of the larger class of international understandings, composed of treaties and other agreements.[19]

In European law-of-nations scholarship, a key intermediary between Grotius and Vattel was Christian Wolff. A German writer in Grotius's intellectual tradition, Wolff also wrote his principal work in Latin; Vattel's 1758 treatise was, in a sense, a popularized version of Wolff in French.[20] Wolff titled one chapter "Of treaties and other agreements of nations"; like Grotius, he outlined three categories of agreements: the *foedus,* the *sponsio,* and a third he called *pactiones.* As Wolff emphasized, "nations and their rulers can enter into stipulations [*pactiones*] which are distinguishable from treaties."[21] Vattel's French rendition of Wolff retained the distinction between *foedus* (French *traite*) and *pactiones* (French *paction* [arrangement or compact] and its French synonyms *accords* and *conventions*). Thus Vattel was repeating the Roman terminology, passed through Grotius and Wolff.[22]

For Romans, the categories mattered because different types of agreements required the authority of different actors within the Roman polity. By the eighteenth century these practical effects had largely disappeared, since most monarchs held all diplomatic power, and not all international writers maintained the distinction. But the historical terminology remained available through Grotius, Wolff, and Vattel for those, such as the drafters of the Articles and the Constitution, who wanted to distribute diplomatic power among various entities.

This in turn is crucial because law-of-nations writers such as Grotius and Vattel, and to a lesser extent Wolff, were well-known and widely consulted by the constitutional generation in America. As one might expect in the context of the creation of a new nation from revolution and the guidance of that nation in its difficult diplomacy with the established powers, international questions often stood in the forefront of debate; the authorities frequently cited on these occasions were the European treatise writers, in particular Vattel:

> In ascertaining principles of the law of nations, lawyers and judges of [the eighteenth century] relied heavily on continental treatise writers, Vattel being the most often consulted by Americans. An essential part of a sound legal education consisted of reading Vattel, Grotius, Pufendorf, and Burlamaqui, among others. Quotations from these sources appeared not only in briefs and opinions, but also in discussions of critical foreign policy matters by the President's Cabinet and in the popular press.[23]

Wolff, though less canonical, was also cited in founding-era materials.[24]

It is of central importance, then, that Vattel, Grotius, and Wolff described treaties as a subset of all international agreements. Their use of "treaty" as a restricted term would have been familiar to the drafters of Article 6 of the Articles and Article I, Section 10 of the Constitution, so it is reasonable to suppose that those documents employed the international law terminology to differentiate the states' power over the various kinds of international agreements—and thus that the word "treaty" in Article II, Section 2 was also understood, following Vattel, Wolff, and Grotius, to mean only a subset of international agreements.

Post-ratification Commentary

This seems to be strong evidence, but it might be overthrown (or at least called into question) by founding-era commentary to the contrary. Advocates of a comprehensive definition of "treaty" claim support from this commentary, but in fact there is little if any material discussion in support of either side.[25] It is true that, especially in the 1975–1976 Jay Treaty debates, advocates of treaty power emphasized its broad scope: as Hamilton said, treaties are "competent to all the stipulations, which the exigencies of National Affairs might require—competent to the making of Treaties of Alliance, Treaties of Commerce, Treaties of Peace and every other species of Convention usual among nations. . . ."[26] But Hamilton and related commentary addressed a different argument: that treaties could not reach certain subjects, because those were reserved to Congress or to the states. Hamilton's point was that all (or, accounting for rhetorical overstatement, most) matters between nations could be handled by treaty; he was not considering whether all such matters *had to* be handled by treaty, or whether some lesser instrument would suffice.[27] Given the context, Hamilton's statement is not a good indicator of his view of executive agreement power.

Non-treaty Agreements in Practice

Opponents of non-treaty agreements rely on founding-era commentary (without much foundation, as we have seen); defenders rely on practice. Courts and commentators refer to a "longstanding practice of settlement of [international] claims by executive agreement" and affirm that "[f]rom the nation's earliest days, the President has been understood to have inherent power to make limited types of agreements with foreign nations. . . ."[28]

If that were true, it should be enough to seal the argument. Unfortunately, although such statements contain some truth, they vastly overstate the relevant historical record. To an inquiry into historical meaning, the post-ratification record is only indirect evidence; the further removed from the constitutional period, the less suggestive it will be. What interpreters in, say, 1910 thought of non-treaty agreements may (depending upon one's interpretive theory) be relevant to the proper rule today, but its remoteness from the constitutional period renders it poor evidence of the historical meaning. If we use post-ratification practice as an indicator of what the text meant in 1789, we must focus upon immediate post-ratification practice and strongly devalue historical evidence removed from that period.

Once recast in this fashion, the historical evidence becomes less overwhelming than commonly suggested. President Washington, who (as seen in Chapter 4) aggressively asserted executive diplomatic power, did not make any executive agreements. John Adams made only one. For the first fifty years of post-ratification history (through 1839), compilations of U.S. international agreements contain at most twelve agreements resting upon the President's independent authority. They are: (1) Adams's 1799 claims settlement with the Netherlands involving the ship *Wilmington Packet;* (2) an agreement with Britain relating to exchange of prisoners during the War of 1812; (3) the 1817 Rush-Bagot Agreement demilitarizing the Great Lakes; (4)—(5) agreements settling claims with Russia and Colombia in 1825; (6)—(7) commercial agreements with Hawaii and Tahiti in 1826; (8)—(11) claims settlements with Brazil and Colombia in 1829, Portugal in 1832, and the Netherlands in 1839; and (12) a commercial agreement with Samoa in 1839.[29]

Moreover, many of these are subject to substantial difficulties as precedent for non-treaty agreements. The Rush-Bagot Agreement, sometimes cited as an early non-treaty agreement, received belated Senate approval under Article II, Section 2.[30] The commercial agreements with Hawaii, Tahiti, and Samoa do not appear actually to be undertakings of the United States; they were made by naval captains operating without specific instructions, and there is no record of any U.S. President embracing them as international acts of the United States.[31] Two settlement agreements are also problematic. They involved undertakings by the foreign government to pay money to resolve U.S. citizens' claims arising from the detention or seizure of U.S. merchant ships, which the United States accepted in final settlement of the claim.[32] Where the claim was paid in full (as it apparently was by Colombia in 1829 and Portugal in 1832), the "settlement" involved only a one-sided obligation to pay; the United States and the private claimant effectively surrendered no asserted right, and thus these "agreements" may not be said to involve undertakings on the part of the United States.[33]

That leaves one military agreement and five settlements—not an impressive record for fifty years of practice. Further, the bulk of these agreements occurred near the end of the period. The first twenty-four years of post-constitutional practice saw one executive agreement; in the first thirty-six years there were only two. One cannot say that executive agreements were a common feature of early constitutional practice.

Nonetheless, history cannot be wholly discounted: early U.S. Presidents did sometimes make international promises on their own authority. President Madison's 1813 agreement with Britain, for example, outlined where prisoners of war would be housed, how they would be treated, upon what terms they would be exchanged, details of their conditions of parole, and how costs of exchanges would be allocated.[34] If we understand (as founding-era Americans appeared to) that the President lacked unilateral power to enter into treaties and if we think that the term "treaty" encompasses all international agreements, Madison's agreement seems contrary to the text. But there is no record that anyone at the time raised such an objection.

Further, in five settlement agreements during this period Presidents did make promises to foreign nations on behalf of the United States. For example, in the 1825 settlement with Russia, the U.S. government (on the authority of President John Quincy Adams) agreed that if Russia would pay a reduced amount, it would not press the claims further. In the 1839 agreement with the Netherlands, the U.S. government accepted a compromised payment and also assumed responsibility for any further claims against the Dutch government (including claims by non-U.S. parties) arising out of the relevant incident.[35] Although these agreements are not the commanding historical record modern authorities suggest, there is some historical evidence that, in the early nineteenth century, Americans did recognize some species of international agreement in addition to treaties.[36]

Accordingly, post-ratification practice may provide some limited support for the idea that "treaty" was not understood to encompass every international agreement. But it also seems clear that the Court and sympathetic commentators have overstated it. Non-treaty agreements were not used at all in Washington's administration; they were used once under Adams and once under Madison, but did not become routine until James Buchanan's administration almost seventy years after ratification. Without a powerful textual basis, this practice could not carry the weight modern commentary would place upon it.

But as we have seen, non-treaty agreements have powerful textual support. Textual evidence shows that, at least with regard to state practice, some kinds of international agreements were treated differently from "treaties," and the pre-1789 law-of-nations terminology distinguishes between "treaties" and other international agreements. The evidence of historical practice should be seen for what it is: weak confirmation of a reading soundly based in the text and the eighteenth-century meaning of its relevant phrases.

Who Holds the Non-treaty Power?

If Article II, Section 2's reference to "treaties" includes only some international agreements, there appears to be a gap in the Constitution's allocation of agreement-making powers. This is one example Professor Henkin cites in noting the Constitution's supposed incompleteness in foreign affairs.[37] We will quickly see, though, that the textual framework discussed in Chapter 3 provides a solution.

The basic principle is that the President's "executive Power" (Article II, Section 1) includes unallocated "executive" foreign affairs authority. That is, traditional executive foreign affairs powers, if not given elsewhere by the Constitution's text, are presidential powers. Applied to international agreements, the implication is clear. The traditional system in England, and in the writings of authorities such as Montesquieu and Blackstone, called all power over international agreements "executive" power. Article II, Section 2 divides the most important part of that power—treatymaking—between the President and Senate. It leaves unmentioned the "non-treaty" power—that is, the power to make international agreements that are not treaties—which therefore remains a presidential (executive) power. So Justice Sutherland was correct, in *Curtiss-Wright* and *Belmont,* to conclude that the President has non-treaty power—except that it comes not from some extra-constitutional source, but from Article II, Section 1.

What Are "Non-treaty" Agreements?

So far, we have found that the Constitution's text indicates a class of international agreements that are not "treaties" and are within the President's unilateral executive power under Article II, Section 1. (Another way to put the matter is that the President can conduct diplomacy through agreements, among other ways, so long as the agreements are not treaties). The next step is to identify the difference between treaties and non-treaty agreements. So far we have proceeded with some confidence in our conclusions, but here we may find resolution more problematic.

Textual and Structural Considerations

The Constitution's text, standing alone, says nothing definitive on this matter, but it does offer some clues. At the national level, treaties require the Senate's supermajority approval; non-treaty agreements (we have decided) are a power of the President alone. At the state level, states cannot make treaties but can make non-treaty agreements with Congress's consent. Both differences suggest that the drafters were substantially more worried about treaties (as compared to other agreements).

Founding-era Americans of course worried about ill-advised treaties, in part from the after-effects of Jay's 1786 Mississippi negotiations described in

Chapter 7. But treaties were a special worry not merely because they establish U.S. policy on important matters: that also can be done by statute, or by presidential announcement (as in the neutrality proclamation). Treaties raise special concerns because they establish U.S. foreign policy *and* commit the nation to that policy for the future, as a matter of international law; they are the nation's legal commitment to a foreign power (in those days, often a more powerful foreign power). That does not make the policy irrevocable (treaty obligations can be changed or ignored); but it does impose costs upon changing policy that would not exist if the policy were only a presidential announcement (or even a statute). If one President makes a treaty, the next President cannot easily take it back; state treaties are dangerous because once they become binding commitments, Congress cannot overturn them without repercussions.[38]

We may ask why the drafters did not think the same considerations applied to non-treaty agreements. They could easily have said "treaties and other international agreements" instead of just "treaties" in Article II, Section 2 and treated treaties and other agreements in parallel in Article I, Section 10. The text does not tell us why there is a difference, but any explanation should be consistent with the textual suggestion that non-treaty agreements require fewer checks than treaties.

Nonbinding Agreements

To eighteenth-century international authorities, a treaty's central feature was that it created legally binding obligations. The imperative of honoring treaty obligations, reflected in the maxim *pacta sunt servanda,* echoes Roman law, which (in theory) made treaties sacred undertakings whose violation was punishable by divine retribution.

Modern diplomatic practice, though, encompasses interchanges that, although "agreements" in some sense, do not invoke legal obligations. Just as business relations frequently proceed on the basis of informal understandings that do not claim the protection of contract law, the President may reach understandings on diplomatic matters that are convenient but do not claim the protection of treaty law. Day-to-day low-level understandings about how diplomacy is conducted form one category. Some agreements, while more formal in nature, expressly disclaim the imperatives of treaty law: the signers of the Helsinki Accords of the 1970s, for example, recited that the Accords were not binding and were not governed by the law of treaties. Some Presidents—notably Theodore Roosevelt—operated through "gentlemen's agreements," which Roosevelt saw as binding on himself as a matter of honor but not binding upon the United States, nor upon subsequent administrations, under international law. Justice Sutherland, author of *Curtiss-Wright* and *Belmont,* in other writings described "protocols" that, unlike treaties, "constitute only a moral obligation."[39]

Surely nonbinding agreements differ from "treaties" in the Article II, Section 2 sense. They fall within the President's Article II, Section 1 authority, for they are plainly part of "executive" diplomatic power, and are not affected by Article II, Section 2. This allocation makes structural sense, in light of the likely concerns motivating the treatymaking clause. Nonbinding agreements are much closer to presidential announcements of policy than to treaties. Unlike treaties, they do not impose material costs upon changes in policy. They do not commit the nation to particular policies for the future, legally or practically. As a result, it makes sense that they are treated like policy announcements rather than like treaties.

But this conclusion does not wholly solve the puzzle of non-treaty agreements. We might say that the fundamental distinction between executive agreements and treaties is that the latter are binding in international law and the former are not.[40] But that categorical view runs afoul of eighteenth-century terminology. Vattel, Wolff, and Grotius—the writers who distinguished between "treaties" and "other agreements"—did not do so on the basis of binding effect. Rather, each thought all international agreements were binding. In Vattel's view, for example:

> The public compacts called conventions, agreements, etc., when they are made between sovereigns, differ from treaties only in the subjects with which they deal. All that we have said of the validity of treaties, of their execution, their dissolution, their obligation, and the rights they give rise to, etc., is applicable to the various conventions which sovereigns may conclude with one another. Treaties, conventions, agreements, are all public contracts and are . . . governed by the same law and the same principles.[41]

Thus, if the framers had Vattel's terminology in mind (as seems likely), they would not have thought of non-treaty agreements only as nonbinding ones.

Similarly, post-ratification practice does not support the proposition that non-treaty agreements were necessarily nonbinding, since those agreements often contained binding language. The 1813 prisoner-of-war agreement states, for example:

This cartel is to be submitted for ratification to the secretary of State for and in behalf of the government of the United States and to the Right Honourable the Lords Commissioners of the Admiralty for and in behalf of the Government of Great Britain. . . . [I]t is further agreed that after the mutual ratification of this cartel, either of the parties on six months notice to the other may declare and render the same null and no longer binding.[42]

No non-treaty agreement in this period contains language disclaiming binding effect, and several employ the same form and contractual formalities as would a treaty. Nor does there appear to be any record in early U.S. diplomacy of an assertion that the terms of an international understanding were not obligatory. The common use of nonbinding arrangements as instruments of policy seems a more recent development.

Consequently, although it is likely correct that Article II, Section 2 would not preclude the President alone from making nonbinding arrangements, that does not explain the Constitution's distinction between treaties and non-treaty agreements. Some non-treaty agreements likely are not binding, but it appears that the founding-era understanding also encompassed some non-treaty agreements that were.

Temporary and Fully Executed Agreements

We have seen that in Vattel's view non-treaty agreements are legal obligations that "differ from treaties only in the subject with which they deal." This suggests that Vattel and his contemporaries made a substantive distinction between treaties and non-treaty agreements. Further examination bears this out. According to Wolff:

A treaty [*foedus*] is defined as a stipulation entered into reciprocally by supreme powers for the public good, to last for ever or at least for a considerable time. But stipulations, which contain temporary promises or those not to be repeated, retain the name of compacts [*pactiones*].

For example, if two nations reciprocally agree to furnish troops to each other in time of war, this stipulation is called a treaty [*foedus*]; but if one nation permits another, on account of the high price of grain, to purchase in its territory, this will be a compact [*paction*]. A compact [*paction*] of that sort, also, is the truce made after a battle for the purpose of burying the dead.[43]

Vattel made a similar distinction:

> A treaty, in Latin, *foedus,* is a compact entered into by sovereigns . . . either in perpetuity, or for a considerable length of time.
>
> Compacts which have for their object matters of temporary interest are called agreements, conventions, arrangements [*accords, conventions, pactions*]. They are fulfilled by one single act, and not by a continuous performance of acts. When the act in question is performed these compacts are executed once for all; whereas treaties are executory in character and the acts called for must continue as long as the treaty lasts.[44]

Although these definitions do not conform exactly, a common element is temporal: long-term agreements are treaties; short-term agreements are not.[45]

Broadly speaking, this conforms to our structural intuitions. As discussed, the special danger of treaties (compared to presidential policy statements) is that they are more difficult to reverse. Put another way, a policy is just policy for the moment; a treaty constrains future behavior. Nonbinding agreements are like policy because they do not materially constrain behavior. Similarly, binding short-term agreements are (somewhat) like policy, because they do not constrain behavior over a long period of time. For example, Madison's prisoner-of-war agreement with Britain (an executive agreement) seems to fit within Wolff's idea of a temporary agreement. It covered only matters during the war (which was not expected to last long) and had much in common with the wartime truce, which Wolff identified as a non-treaty agreement. In contrast, it is difficult to identify any agreement submitted to the Senate in the early period that had only short-term implications.

On the other hand, the Rush-Bagot Agreement (President James Monroe's agreement demilitarizing the Great Lakes) shows why long-term agreements require the Article II, Section 2 process. Monroe originally made the Agreement, calling for withdrawal of U.S. and British military forces, on his own authority. He may have reasoned as follows: as President, he surely could withdraw U.S. ships from the Lakes; equally, combining his diplomatic and military power, he could announce that he would withdraw U.S. ships so long as Britain withdrew its ships. Therefore, he might fairly ask, why did he not have power to make an agreement for reciprocal withdrawal?

The answer, using Vattel's definitions, is that Monroe probably did have power to make an agreement for reciprocal withdrawal. But Monroe's actual agreement went further: it stipulated that ships would be withdrawn *and* that the Lakes would *remain* demilitarized for the future.[46] In Vattel's definition, the latter provision turned the agreement into a treaty, for it became a long-term obligation. And in constitutional terms, the long-term obligation triggered the requirement for Senate approval. Monroe had unilateral power to announce a *policy* of demilitarization (just as he had power to announce the policy of the Monroe doctrine),[47] and he had unilateral power to commit *himself* to following that policy; but he did not have unilateral power to commit future Presidents to his policy as a matter of international law.

The settlement agreements require further explanation. As discussed, most early executive agreements were settlement agreements—that is, the United States agreed, on behalf of a private claimant, to accept a payment, and promised not to pursue the claim further.[48] For example, in the *Wilmington Packet* agreement, President Adams (on his own authority) agreed to accept Dutch payment in full satisfaction of U.S. claims against the Netherlands.[49] Yet at first inspection, this seems like a continuing, long-term commitment, which should be a treaty in Vattel's terminology: Adams agreed for himself and for later administrations not to make further complaints on behalf of the *Wilmington Packet*.

There may be an answer, though, in closer examination of Vattel's terminology. Vattel said that non-treaty agreements "are accomplished by one single act, and not by repeated acts. These compacts are executed once for all." Similarly, Wolff said that non-treaty agreements are "stipulations which contain temporary promises *or those not to be repeated*." It seems that these writers were trying to capture something resembling the English law distinction between executory contracts and fully executed contracts. That is, a fully executed contract is a simultaneous exchange of, say, money for property; an executory contract involves continuing obligations, so that an exchange of property for future payment is executory as to the party making the payment.

If this is correct, it may be that Americans thought of settlement agreements as fully executed agreements—resembling an exchange of property for money. Thus they may have thought of settlements such as the *Wilmington Packet* as one-time exchanges which fell outside the Vattel/Wolff idea of a treaty.

This supposition is confirmed by the way early administrations treated another type of settlement agreement. The *Wilmington Packet* settlement involved payment of an agreed sum. But often nations could not agree on an amount, even where they could agree that one nation had wronged the other. In these circumstances, it became common to establish an arbitration panel of neutral parties to examine the claims and make awards (which the nations then agreed to pay). Almost all of the fixed-sum settlements were done as executive agreements; arbitration settlements were done by treaty.[50] This shows that early practitioners did not think settlement agreements as a class fell outside the treaty requirements. Rather, they thought that the fixed-sum settlements (but not the others) did. The likely explanation, in Vattel's terminology, is that arbitration agreements involved continuing (executory) obligations—among others, to fund the arbitration and to pay the future award.

Informal Agreements

A final suggestion might be that executive agreements and treaties differ in their level of formality: that is, that the same subject matter can be addressed, with the same level of legal commitment, in either type of agreement, with a difference only in form.

This idea cannot be squared with constitutional text and commentary. If the President had that power, it would render the treatymaking clause essentially meaningless, for the President could evade the clause simply by a change in form—a matter over which the Senate would have little control and in which the foreign party would ordinarily have little interest. Had that been the understanding, statements in the ratifying conventions and elsewhere that treatymaking power had been purposefully denied the President—because of the dangers of placing such power in a single person—become nonsensical: if the President could accomplish the same result in another way, the protection applauded by the founding generation would be entirely illusory.

Moreover, the anti-federalist attack on Article II, Section 2 contended that approval of treaties was too easy: somewhat fancifully, the Constitution's opponents argued that because Article II, Section 2 required only two-thirds of the Senators present to approve, and because a majority constituted a quorum, treaties could be approved by only two-thirds of half the Senators, which in practice meant only ten Senators representing five states.[51] Not one anti-federalist discussion mentioned the danger that the President alone might accomplish what they feared the President plus ten Senators could do. Yet if presidential "agreements" differ from treaties only in formality, that would be the result. Had this been an available interpretation, assuredly the anti-federalists—who strained to produce the contorted fear of betrayal by ten Senators—would have mentioned it.

The "formality" argument also ignores Article I, Section 10. If "treaties" are distinguished only by form, then states may (with congressional approval) enter into any understandings with foreign governments so long as those understandings remain informal. But there is no reason to think that the drafters would have employed the elaborate scheme of Article I, Section 10 (no state treaties; state agreements only with congressional approval) merely to force states to adopt informal, rather than formal, diplomacy.

Finally, post-ratification practice does not support a distinction based on form. Whereas some of the early non-treaty agreements, such as the *Wilmington Packet* settlement, are informal exchanges of diplomatic notes, others—such as the Prisoner-of-War agreement—have the physical appearance of a treaty, with ceremonial recitations, contractual forms, and dual signatures. Some agreements submitted to the Senate, such as the Rush-Bagot Agreement, have an informal appearance. As a result, making the constitutional distinction turn on the form of the agreement is not supported by constitutional text, constitutional structure, international law usage, or post-ratification practice.

Conclusion: The President's *Belmont* Powers

Let us now return to the *Belmont* case to consider the implications of the points discussed above. We can now see that Justice Sutherland was correct that there are some kinds of agreements the President can make without the Senate (although the proof is more complex than he suggested). And it seems likely that the agreement in *Belmont* fell within that category.

Under that agreement, the United States undertook two obligations: extending diplomatic recognition to the Soviet Union and exchanging some of its claims against the Soviet Union. The first does not require a treaty, for it carries no prospective obligations (Roosevelt did not commit to *maintaining* diplomatic relations). The exchange of claims is more substantive, but as an assignment of property it resembles what the eighteenth century called a fully executed agreement—it was a one-time property settlement, like many of the agreements made in early constitutional history, including the 1799 *Wilmington Packet* agreement.

In sum, the United States did not undertake material continuing obligations to the Soviet Union, so Senate approval was not required. This does not mean, though, that Sutherland decided *Belmont* correctly. *Belmont* asked two questions: whether the President acted constitutionally in concluding the agreement and whether the agreement overrode New York law on the ownership of Russian property. So far, we have addressed only the first question (for the second, see Chapter 14). But on that point, at least, it appears that Sutherland decided in accordance with the Constitution's historical meaning.

IV

Congress's Foreign Affairs Powers

10

Legislative Power in Foreign Affairs: Why NAFTA Is (Sort of) Unconstitutional

We now turn our attention to the legislative powers of Congress. One way to frame an inquiry into Congress's foreign affairs powers is to consider a leading modern controversy mentioned briefly in Chapter 9: the question of congressional-executive agreements.

The North American Free Trade Agreement (NAFTA) is an important, but not unusual, example of an international obligation undertaken on the authority of the President plus Congress, but without the supermajority of the Senate described in Article II, Section 2. We have seen in Chapter 9 that the President alone has some power to undertake international obligations on behalf of the United States. We have also seen that this power does not extend to material long-term agreements, which NAFTA surely is. And no President has ever claimed authority to make agreements like NAFTA unilaterally. Rather, Presidents rely, in NAFTA and similar free trade agreements, on Congress's approval.

This raises the question of the extent of Congress's foreign affairs powers: can Congress authorize the President's agreement-making? Article II, Section 2 gives treatymaking power to the President-plus-Senate, as Chapter 7 explored. Congress, though, has power to "regulate Commerce with foreign Nations," plus power to "make all Laws which shall be necessary and proper" to effectuate its enumerated powers (Article I, Section 8). Does this mean that Congress may, if it finds it necessary and proper for the regulation of foreign commerce, make treaties (or equivalent international agreements) relating to foreign commerce, or authorize the President to do so?

The modern reality is that Congress claims this power, in the form of so-called congressional-executive agreements, such as NAFTA, that are treaties in all but name; but the issue deeply divides commentators.[1] One might suppose that it turns on Article II, Section 2's treatymaking clause—the question being whether that clause excludes all other ways of making treaties.

That is how many commentators approach it, but as indicated, little consensus has been achieved. This chapter suggests that viewing the matter as a question of Congress's legislative powers may provide clearer resolution. As set forth below, Congress has power to enact the substantive regulations embodied in NAFTA but lacks power to undertake international obligations (or authorize the President to do so), because that is not a legislative power.

The Debate over Congressional-Executive Agreements: An Initial Assessment

We can begin by dismissing the "easy" answers on both sides of the question. First, it might be said that NAFTA (and agreements like it) are not "treaties." Article II, Section 2 only addresses how "treaties" are made. Because "agreements" are not "treaties," the argument might run, the treaty-making clause poses no obstacle to Congress, rather than two-thirds of the Senate, authorizing them.

But this argument seems unsatisfactory, as a matter of historical meaning, for three reasons. First, it should be clear that NAFTA, and agreements like it, *are* "treaties" in that term's eighteenth-century meaning. To eighteenth-century writers, it did not matter whether an agreement's caption was "treaty" or some other word; the characterization of an agreement as a treaty depended upon whether it created important long-term obligations (see Chapter 9). NAFTA plainly does.

Second, the argument proves too much, because if NAFTA is not a treaty, it would be within the President's independent power. As Chapter 9 also shows, the "non-treaty" power is an "executive" power and thus within the President's Article II, Section 1 power unless otherwise excluded. Article II, Section 2 qualifies the President's *treaty* power. If NAFTA is not a treaty (in the constitutional sense), power to make it remains with the President. Proponents of congressional-executive agreements, though, would require Congress's approval. Calling these agreements something other than treaties does not explain where this requirement comes from.

Third, and most important, the argument does not explain where Congress gets power to approve NAFTA. Even if it is true that Article II, Section 2 does not *prevent* Congress from approving NAFTA, Congress must have an affirmative basis for acting, and simply saying that NAFTA is not a treaty is not sufficient.

On the other hand, the "easy" argument in the other direction also seems unsatisfactory. That argument assumes (correctly) that NAFTA is a treaty in the constitutional sense and insists that treaties can only be made through Article II, Section 2. We have seen that this proposition is quite strong with respect to the President. Since the text gives the President the power to make treaties *with* the Senate's supermajority consent, surely the President cannot make treaties *without* the Senate's supermajority consent (else the Senate's consent would be superfluous). But the argument seems less compelling once Congress is involved. If Article I, Section 8 gives Congress power to make treaties, it is not obvious that Article II, Section 2 limits it. Perhaps there is concurrent power to make treaties: through the President-plus-Senate, under Article II, Section 2; and through Congress, under Article I, Section 8. This does not make the treatymaking clause superfluous, for it means that either a supermajority of one House or a majority of both is needed—a perfectly reasonable set of alternatives.

Although neither side can claim victory on the basis of these initial arguments, they show that a key issue is whether (entirely aside from Article II, Section 2) the Constitution grants Congress power over international agreements. If it does, we face the difficult task of deciding whether Article II, Section 2 then removes that power by negative implication. But if the Constitution does not give Congress the power in the first place, there is no need to struggle with Article II, Section 2. This suggests the need to develop a broader understanding of Congress's foreign affairs powers.

Legislative Power in Foreign Affairs: Textual versus Inherent Powers

Article I, Section 1 of the Constitution begins: "All legislative Powers herein granted shall be vested in the Congress of the United States." Although the phrase "Congress of the United States" echoed the old Congress of the Articles of Confederation, the new body had little in common with the old, as Article I's first sentence made clear. The Articles' Congress was, with a few exceptions, not a legislative body. As we have seen, that was particularly true in foreign affairs. The Articles' Congress had few legislative powers in foreign affairs; instead, it had the executive foreign affairs powers of diplomacy and war (see Chapter 2).

Article I, Section 1 signaled that the new Congress would be like the English Parliament and the post-independence state legislatures, which were primarily legislative bodies. That had enormous importance in foreign affairs, for a central indictment of the Articles' foreign affairs system was the lack of national legislative powers. It also signaled that the new Congress would not principally wield executive powers (an allocation confirmed by Article II, Section 1). In this respect, the model for the new Congress was surely Parliament; rather than executive powers, it had legislative foreign affairs powers unified in a national body.

Subject-Matter Limitations on Congress: The Text

Unlike Article II, Section 1, the text's grant of "legislative Powers" in Article I, Section 1 is limited by subject matter. The President has "the executive Power"; Congress has only the "legislative Powers herein granted." As a result, to exercise a power, Congress must show not only that the power is legislative, but also that it falls within a grant of power occurring later in Article I (or elsewhere in the text). Most of these grants occurred in Article I, Section 8, the list of Congress's powers. (Sections 2–7 deal with the structure of the House and Senate, elections, rules of procedure, rights and duties of Members, and the way in which bills are passed and submitted to the President for signature or veto.) The principal foreign-affairs-related powers of Article I, Section 8 are clause 1 (to "lay and collect Taxes, Duties, Imposts and Excises"), clause 3 (to "regulate Commerce with foreign Nations"), clause 4 ("to establish an uniform Rule of Naturalization"), clause 10 (to "define and punish Piracies and Felonies committed on the high Seas, and Offenses against the Law of Nations"), and clauses 11–16 (the war and military powers to be discussed in Chapters 11–12).

Congress also has important powers common to domestic and foreign affairs. Most notably, it has spending power "to pay the Debts and provide for the common Defense and general Welfare of the United States"; and, by clause 18, it has power "to make all Laws which shall be necessary and proper for carrying into execution the foregoing powers [i.e., those listed in clauses 1–17], and all other Powers vested by this Constitution in the Government of the United States."

Gaps in the Enumerated Powers?

Notably, this enumeration does not list a general foreign affairs power. The Virginia plan—in effect, the Philadelphia Convention's first draft of the Constitution—generally gave Congress power to legislate in matters concerning the Union as a whole (presumably including foreign affairs). But during the Convention the delegates dropped that language and substituted the specific list of powers in Article I, Section 8.[2]

Limiting Congress to enumerated powers leads to familiar concerns. As Louis Henkin, among others, points out, Congress's specific powers do not seem to encompass everything Congress does in foreign affairs (just as the President's specific powers in Article II, Sections 2 and 3 do not seem to encompass everything the President does in foreign affairs).[3] Sometimes Congress's actions are clearly within an enumerated subject matter: NAFTA's subject matter obviously falls within Article I, Section 8, clause 3's "Power . . . To regulate Commerce with foreign Nations. . . ." But often it is not so easy.

Professor Henkin lists various matters which, he says, seem outside Congress's enumerated powers yet are commonly assumed to be powers of Congress: among others, "statutes governing the conduct of U.S. nationals abroad"; immigration laws; "legislation regulating and protecting foreign diplomatic activities in the United States, providing for cooperation with foreign governments . . . or imposing restrictions on foreign governments, e.g., by freezing their assets"; and laws relating to the loss of U.S. citizenship.[4] We may quibble with some of these—protection of diplomatic activities seems to be an aspect of the law of nations, committed to Congress by Article I, Section 8, clause 10, for example—but the ultimate conclusion is difficult to dispute.

For the President, there is a textual way around gaps in the enumerated powers, described in Chapter 3. Because the President has "executive Power," which includes foreign affairs power, specific executive foreign affairs powers do not need to be listed to be presidential powers. Article II, Section 1 takes care of unmentioned powers, so long as they are "executive." Congress does not have this recourse, because Article I, Section 1 is not a grant of general legislative powers, in foreign affairs or otherwise. Congress, unlike the President, must identify a specific grant of power, and so the possibility of "gaps" in the legislative power of foreign affairs is quite real.

Inherent Powers Revisited: The Chinese Exclusion Case

Professor Henkin insists that to fill these gaps we must resort to extra-textual legislative powers in foreign affairs (much like the extra-textual executive power in foreign affairs posited by the *Curtiss-Wright* case). In his view, "Congress derives additional legislative authority from the powers of the United States inherent in its sovereignty and nationhood"—what he calls the "Foreign Affairs Power." This claim is important to congressional-executive agreements, for although NAFTA falls comfortably within an enumerated subject matter (foreign commerce), other agreements might not, and, as Henkin says, "[i]t is presumably under [the inherent Foreign Affairs Power] that Congress has authorized or approved international agreements on matters that may not be within its enumerated powers."[5]

This view has some support in Supreme Court decisions. Long before *Curtiss-Wright* claimed to identify inherent presidential powers in foreign affairs, the Court found inherent congressional powers in the context of immigration. Congress had passed laws largely excluding from the United States Chinese immigrants, which were challenged as beyond Congress's enumerated powers. In the so-called *Chinese Exclusion Case*, the Court said:

> Jurisdiction over its own territory to that extent [i.e., of determining who is admitted] is an incident of every independent nation. It is part of its independence. . . . [T]he United States, in their relation to foreign countries and their subjects or citizens are one nation, invested with powers which belong to independent nations, the exercise of which can be invoked for the maintenance of its absolute independence and security throughout its entire territory.[6]

The Court did not identify any basis for this power, and it is probably correct to conclude—as Professor Henkin does—that the Court thought it arose outside the Constitution's text.[7]

Thus, although *Chinese Exclusion* lacks the elaborate (and, as we have seen, faulty) historical grounding of *Curtiss-Wright*, it has much in common with that case. Its reasoning is not so much historical as logical: independent nations have these powers; the United States is an independent nation; therefore it must have these powers. But, as with *Curtiss-Wright*, there is little textual basis for *Chinese Exclusion*–type inherent powers or historical basis for thinking that they would have been assumed in the founding era. In particular, there is little basis for inherent national *legislative* powers. Under the Articles, the legislative foreign affairs powers were, with minor exceptions, lodged in the states: states set tariffs, regulated foreign commerce, regulated with respect to the law of nations, etc. (Chapter 2). Of course, Article I, Section 8's specific provisions shifted many of these powers to the national Congress. But those not shifted surely would have been understood to remain with the states (as the Tenth Amendment indicates, again as discussed in Chapters 1–2).

Article I, Section 8 itself confirms the point. Although Congress has no general textual power over foreign affairs, it has many specific textual powers that are purely foreign affairs matters. For example, Professor Henkin argues that Congress must have an inherent, non-textual power to regulate conduct abroad. Article I, Section 8, however, textually gives Congress power to regulate piracies, felonies on the high seas, and offenses against the law of nations. Any entity with inherent power to regulate conduct abroad would have inherent power to do all of these things (especially to regulate felonies on the high seas). Henkin's view makes much of Article I, Section 8, clause 10 superfluous.

The same might be said of immigration. By Article I, Section 8, clause 4, Congress has power "To establish a uniform rule of Naturalization"—that is, to decide when aliens may become citizens. Unless that clause is superfluous, we must conclude that Congress lacks inherent power to decide when aliens become citizens. Yet if that is so, it seems difficult to conclude that Congress has inherent power over other aspects of the regulation of aliens (or, as Professor Henkin suggests, other aspects of gaining and losing U.S. citizenship).

Moreover, both immigration and regulating conduct abroad show the fallacy of the Supreme Court's *Chinese Exclusion* logic. According to the Court, the United States has the powers all independent nations necessarily have. Surely this is true; but the Court's error was to suppose that the *national government* of the United States must have the powers that independent nations necessarily have. Powers not possessed by the national government remain with the states or the people, under the Tenth Amendment. The *United States* still has these powers—they just have not been granted to its national government. Perhaps this formulation would not work for powers that were not and could never be exercised by the states (if such powers exist), but immigration and conduct abroad were regulated by the states in the founding era.[8]

Put another way, presumably the Constitution could have denied the national government (and states, for that matter) power to regulate immigration. This would not have made the United States any less an independent nation under international law (or whatever authority the *Chinese Exclusion* Court thought it was appealing to); it would simply mean that the people— the ultimate sovereign, as founding-era Americans saw it—retained that power for themselves and did not give it to any of their governments. Whatever international law or the concept of nationhood might say about the total powers possessed by a sovereign people, they have nothing to say about how those powers are allocated within a domestic legal system.

We may be tempted to see *Curtiss-Wright* and the *Chinese Exclusion Case* as reflecting similar thinking, with the latter being a natural elaboration of the former.[9] In result, this may be true. But their reasoning is in sharp, though subtle, conflict. As Chapter 2 describes, whatever the situation after the Constitution was ratified, under the Articles the legislative powers of foreign affairs lay with the states. If, as the Court said in *Chinese Exclusion,* the United States could not be an independent nation without legislative foreign affairs powers at the national level, then it was not truly a nation prior to 1789. But if that is the case, prior to 1789 it must have been merely an association of sovereign states. This turns *Curtiss-Wright* on its head, paradoxically reaffirming the strongest version of states-rights history. In other words, the Supreme Court has said that between 1776 and 1789 the states were both fully sovereign and not sovereign at all.

The contorted reasoning of *Curtiss-Wright* and *Chinese Exclusion* suggests that neither has it right and that the true answer is the one indicated by the text itself. The national government has foreign affairs powers delegated to it by the Constitution. Other foreign affairs powers remain with the states, or with the people (who possess ultimate residual sovereignty). To the extent Congress exercises legislative foreign affairs powers, it must find its power in the Constitution, usually in Article I, Section 8. Otherwise, legislative foreign affairs powers would be exercised by the states (as under the Articles), unless they are denied to the states by the Constitution (a matter explored in Chapters 13–14). The problem arises not from any incompleteness of the text, but from extra-textual attempts to deduce specific outcomes from abstract concepts like sovereignty.

Congress's "Necessary and Proper" Power

This conclusion stills leaves the problem Professor Henkin identifies, namely that Congress does not seem to have enough enumerated powers to justify its foreign affairs activities. We could simply say that Congress has overstepped and that the text leaves these matters to the states. But this would create tension with much modern practice and raise charges of a dysfunctional foreign affairs system. Moreover, we have not fully explored Congress's constitutional powers.

By clause 18 of Article I, Section 8, Congress has power "[t]o make all Laws which shall be necessary and proper for carrying into Execution the foregoing power, and all other powers vested by this Constitution in the Government of the United States. . . ." The first part of this clause was the subject of the pivotal domestic law case, *McCulloch v. Maryland* (1819).[10] *McCulloch* addressed the constitutionality of the National Bank of the United States, chartered by Congress in 1791. Article I, Section 8 contains no enumerated power to charter a bank (in fact, the Convention delegates had decided against including it). But, argued Chief Justice Marshall in *McCulloch*, Congress has enumerated powers that would be more easily exercised if a bank existed. Thus, chartering the bank was "necessary and proper" to "carry[] into Execution" Congress's enumerated powers. True, the bank was not "necessary" in the sense of being "indispensable"—but, said Marshall, "necessary" could also mean "needful" or "conducive to."[11]

Of course, *McCulloch*'s result was controversial in its time and in the immediate post-ratification period (when Madison and Hamilton debated the Bank's constitutionality). Its rejection of the "indispensable" reading of "necessary" should be less so. As Marshall pointed out (adopting arguments Hamilton made earlier), "necessary" in ordinary speech at the time meant a range of things, of varying strictness. When the text meant "indispensably necessary," it said so (in Article I, Section 10: no state shall place any tax on imports or exports, "except what may be absolutely necessary for executing its inspection Laws"). Whatever one thought of the Bank, Congress uncontroversially passed many laws in its earliest years that related to its enumerated powers but were not strictly within them nor indispensable to their exercise. Marshall did not establish a wholly open-ended test, as both critics and admirers have later implied: he said that the means Congress adopted must be "plainly adapted" to ends within its enumerated powers and must not be a "pretext . . . for the accomplishment of objects not entrusted to the government." That echoes *The Federalist*'s discussions of the clause (Hamilton's and Madison's), and—as both said—a stricter reading would cripple the national government beyond what the Constitution seemed to contemplate.[12]

This formulation may help extend Congress's powers to cover some of the supposedly missing foreign affairs powers. One of Henkin's examples is Congress's establishment of "an extensive criminal code . . . for dependants of U.S. service personnel and for civilian employees of the military forces living abroad."[13] Congress has enumerated power to regulate the military; regulating civilians associated with the military seems "necessary and proper" to "carrying into Execution" its power to regulate the military itself, at least in the sense accepted by *McCulloch*. Similarly, it may be that the power to establish uniform rules of naturalization (Article I, Section 8, clause 4) supports federal control over admitting aliens, because eligibility for naturalization often turns on the length of an alien's residency in the United States.

"Necessary and proper" arguments based upon Congress's need to support its own powers—as in *McCulloch*—are quite common. The second part of clause 18 is less frequently examined. Congress can legislate as necessary and proper to carry into execution "the foregoing Powers" (i.e., those already granted in Article I, Section 8) and also "all other Powers vested by this Constitution in the Government of the United States. . . ." The second part of the clause is not principally directed to effectuating congressional powers, which are mostly covered by the phrase "the foregoing Powers." And if it meant only congressional powers, it would have said "all other Powers vested by this Constitution in Congress," not ". . . vested by this Constitution in the Government of the United States. . . ." The principal point of this part of the clause is that Congress can legislate to carry into effect the powers of other branches of the national government—most obviously (in foreign affairs), the President.

As we have seen, the President has broad executive foreign affairs powers (Chapters 3–4) but lacks power to support those executive powers through lawmaking (Chapter 5). If the President's executive foreign affairs powers need to be carried into effect in the domestic legal system, the President needs help from Congress. Yet a Congress limited to the powers listed in Article I, Section 8's first seventeen clauses might not always be able to give legislative backing to executive foreign affairs power. Clause 18 assures that this will not be a problem. Congress can "make all Laws which shall be necessary and proper for carrying into Execution" the executive foreign affairs powers Article II, Section 1 vests in the President.

To see how this works, consider the example of passports. The eighteenth-century passport served no domestic legal purposes. A passport was, rather, a communication from the U.S. government addressed to foreign powers, identifying its holder as a U.S. citizen and requesting appropriate treatment.[14] It was a diplomatic instrument, and thus part of the "executive" functions of government. In keeping with this view, the Articles' Congress—the executive power—issued passports. Once the Constitution came into effect, President Washington took over the power of issuing passports. Although no act of Congress granted this power, no one seemed to think Washington acted inappropriately, and his successors continued the practice.[15] As everyone presumably recognized, issuing passports was part of Washington's Article II, Section 1 powers; the practice further confirms Chapter 3's reading of executive power.

Passports also required legislative support, though—for example, to prevent forgeries, or to exclude other entities (such as states) from issuing them. In keeping with prior discussions, the President did not claim independent lawmaking power here; Washington went to Congress for assistance, and Congress passed the first U.S. passport–related legislation in 1790. Congress did not grant the President power to issue passports, presumably because everyone thought the President had that power under the Constitution itself. It criminalized misuse, suggesting that everyone thought Congress, not the President, had this power.[16] In sum, early passport practice exactly replicates the division of powers described in Chapters 3–5.

Where did Congress get subject-matter authority to enact passport legislation? It does not seem necessary (even in *McCulloch*'s sense) to any of Congress's enumerated powers. It is closely associated, though, with the President's executive power to issue passports, and indeed seems "necessary" to the satisfactory execution of the President's passport power, in an even stronger sense than *McCulloch*.

Although Congress did not explicitly rely on this power for its passport legislation, there is at least some historical evidence that founding-era Americans understood Congress's power in this way. During the late-1790s hostilities between the United States and France, a private U.S. citizen, George Logan, on his own initiative went to France to try to negotiate a reconciliation. Prompted by Logan's disruptions, Congress (at President Adams's request) in 1799 enacted a law (which became known as the Logan Act) prohibiting U.S. citizens from corresponding with foreign governments to influence them or to defeat measures of the U.S. government.[17]

Like passport legislation, the Logan Act is difficult to place within Congress's specific enumerated powers. No one suggested that Congress might lack power to enact it, though, and the reason seems evident. The law protects U.S. diplomacy, an executive power of the President. When Congress prohibited correspondence aimed at defeating measures "of the U.S. government," it meant measures of the executive, which was the branch conducting diplomacy. In introducing the legislation, Representative Griswold said that it "punish[ed] a crime which goes to the destruction of the Executive power of the Government."[18]

Another likely illustration of this way of thinking is the 1794 Neutrality Act. As discussed (Chapter 5), though Washington declared neutrality in the war between France and Britain in 1793, he had trouble enforcing that policy, culminating in the debacle of the Henfield prosecution. When Congress reconvened in December 1793, Washington asked for measures supporting the neutrality prosecutions, which Congress provided in early 1794.[19] The ensuing Act is sometimes explained as part of Congress's power to define and punish offenses against the law of nations.[20] But its provisions seem to go beyond anything the law of nations required at the time. Instead, the Act is better understood as carrying into effect the President's power to set foreign policy (in this case, to declare neutrality). The context makes it likely that Congress viewed the Act in this way: Washington declared his policy but had difficulty enforcing it, and so he asked Congress to legislate in support.

Many of the supposed gaps in Congress's foreign affairs powers may be explained in this way. For example, Congress's power to pass laws relating to foreign governments seems supportive of the President's power to conduct relations with foreign governments, as is much of Congress's power to regulate the conduct of U.S. citizens abroad and foreign diplomats within the United States. This approach may also explain Congress's immigration power (if one is not satisfied with the naturalization clause). The traditional eighteenth-century executive—notably the English monarch—had the power to decide when to admit aliens to the realm as part of the executive power of foreign affairs.[21] If that remained an executive power under the Constitution, Congress would have the authority to create administrative and legal machinery to support it, under clause 18.

In sum, Congress does not have general foreign affairs power, but its powers are nonetheless broad and fall into three categories. First, Congress has the powers listed in Article I, Section 8, clauses 1–17 (plus a few others scattered through the document). These include the core legislative foreign affairs powers whose lack was so keenly felt by the Articles' Congress: imposing tariffs, regulating foreign commerce, and enforcing the law of nations. Second, Congress has the associated power to pass laws "necessary and proper" to support its enumerated powers, as recognized in *McCulloch*. Third, and often overlooked, Congress has derivative power to pass laws "necessary and proper" to support other branches' powers. Most important for our purposes, that includes power to legislate to support the executive foreign affairs power, which opens to Congress a spectrum of foreign-affairs-related subjects that do not seem otherwise to fall within its enumerated powers. It is important to emphasize that because these powers are derivative of the executive power, they (unlike Congress's other powers) must be exercised in coordination with (and not as a restraint upon) the President. But with this qualification, we can now see that Congress has a broad legislative mandate in foreign affairs, without needing to reach for inherent powers.

Non-legislative Powers of Congress?

We have now come a long way, but without making much apparent progress on the question of NAFTA. From the foregoing discussion, it should be clear that Congress does not—contrary to Professor Henkin's suggestion—have textual power to authorize or approve international agreements in areas outside the subject matters enumerated in Article I, Section 8. But NAFTA is squarely within an enumerated subject matter. So we are back to the question posed at the outset: does Congress's enumerated power over foreign commerce give it power to make international agreements (or authorize the President to make international agreements) concerning foreign commerce?

It should also now be clear that, to the extent the President has constitutional power to make agreements under the executive power (Chapter 9), Congress can pass legislation incorporating those agreements into U.S. law. Indeed, this would be true even if the President's agreement concerned a matter not part of Congress's enumerated subject matter (such as passports or diplomacy), for Congress would have power to support the President's agreement through Article I, Section 8, clause 18.[22] But this also does not help with respect to NAFTA, because we have already concluded that the President lacks independent power to make agreements such as NAFTA (and even today no one seriously contends that the President alone has this power). The question, again, is whether Congress can *create* that power.

To begin, consider the difference between an ordinary statute regulating international trade and an international agreement such as NAFTA. Any trade regulation contained in NAFTA's text could be enacted as an ordinary statute obviously within Congress's Article I, Section 8 powers. This may suggest that there is little substance to the dispute. Imagine a NAFTA-like statute, enacted by Congress as ordinary legislation, containing all the changes to U.S. trade barriers contained in NAFTA and making those changes depend upon Mexico and Canada adopting and maintaining similar legislation. This hypothetical statute seems easily within Congress's power to regulate foreign commerce. Indeed, Congress has long passed reciprocal trade legislation, granting benefits to the imports of nations that do not discriminate against U.S. exports.[23]

If Congress can enact these measures by statute, why should it not be able to create them in another manner—namely, by approving an international agreement? The answer lies in an important difference between NAFTA itself and the hypothetical NAFTA-like statute. NAFTA entails a continuing obligation, under international law, not to increase tariffs. The NAFTA-like statute does not. As a result, exiting the NAFTA regime has more practical and legal costs than repealing the NAFTA-like statute. Exit under NAFTA would require following the withdrawal process specified in NAFTA or abrogating the agreement contrary to international law. In contrast, eliminating the NAFTA-like statute would only require the vote of a majority of Congress (and the President's signature) to repeal it.

The only constitutionally problematic piece of NAFTA and similar congressional-executive agreements, then, is the creation of U.S. obligations under international law. This piece is, of course, the one that seems to conflict most directly with the power of the treatymakers under Article II, Section 2. But it is not necessary to find a negative implication of the treaty-making clause to reject congressional power here, for Congress does not have this power in the first place.

The limitation arises not from subject matter, but because Congress, by Article I, Section 1, has "legislative Powers." In eighteenth-century terms, legislative power signified (as it does today) making laws within the U.S. domestic legal system (see Chapter 5).[24] NAFTA goes beyond this, to create by agreement (not by domestic law) an international obligation outside of the U.S. domestic legal system. In eighteenth-century terms, creating international obligations was an executive, not legislative, function.

To give a less-controversial example, it has been assumed throughout constitutional history that Congress lacks power to make diplomatic communications. That is, the President has diplomatic power (from the executive power clause), and the President's power is exclusive. The President is (as Marshall said in 1800) the "sole organ" of diplomatic communication; as Jefferson wrote in 1791, Congress can make no communication except through the President.[25] Exclusivity, though, may not obviously follow from the executive power clause: just because the President has communicative power does not mean Congress does not.

Instead, the "sole organ" conclusion arises from a combination of the executive power clause and the limits on Congress's Article I powers. For Congress to assert power to communicate with foreign nations, it must find a grant of power in support (since we have now decided that Congress, like the President, lacks inherent foreign affairs powers). Aside from declaring war (Chapter 11), Congress's specifically enumerated powers do not relate to foreign communications. Congress also can invoke its "necessary and proper" power, but that power is only to "make laws" in support of other powers. Communicating with foreign nations is only executive: it does not involve making laws (altering rights and duties in domestic law).

This, then, explains Congress's inability to make diplomatic communications (and, for that matter, Congress's wider inability to formulate and announce U.S. foreign policy). These are executive powers, given to the President by Article II, Section 1, and—as important—*not* given to Congress by anything in Article I. The text thus sets up an important division of foreign affairs powers: the President can communicate and announce policy but must rely on Congress to implement policy legislatively. Congress cannot communicate or announce policies but can pass domestic laws with foreign affairs implications. In the area of its enumerated powers, Congress can take the legislative initiative, without depending on prior presidential policies. In areas outside its enumerated powers, Congress cannot take the initiative but can legislate in support of foreign affairs goals established by the President.

Now we can apply these principles to congressional-executive agreements. In eighteenth-century terms, making international agreements was an "executive" power. Montesquieu referred to the "executive [power] in respect to things dependent on the law of nations," under which he included the power to make international agreements. Blackstone confirmed that the English monarch, exercising the executive power, had the sole authority to make agreements with foreign nations. In theory and practice, the legislative power has nothing to do with making international agreements. Parliament was responsible for implementing treaties, in the sense of passing legislation to give them domestic legal effect, but the decision whether or not to undertake international commitments in the first place was taken only by the executive monarch.[26]

Of course, founding-era Americans did not embrace the English system in this regard and instead gave the Senate shared treatymaking power. But they typically continued to describe this power as an "executive" power—albeit one the President had to share with the Senate. (As discussed in Chapter 3, the ratification debates repeatedly referred to the Senate's treatymaking power as an "executive" function.) Hamilton saw in Federalist No. 75 that the Constitution's invention of the self-executing treaty rendered the agreement-making power under the American system partially "legislative" (in that it created domestic legal obligations), a point echoed in other founding-era commentary. Yet even Hamilton thought that agreement-making was only partially legislative. No one—Hamilton included—called the international component (as opposed to the domestic component) of treaties "legislative," and there would have been no basis for doing so.[27]

This means that, as with diplomatic communications, Congress lacks power to create international obligations, because that is not a legislative power. Congress has power to pass laws implementing international obligations constitutionally created by the President, just as Congress has power to pass laws supporting and protecting diplomatic endeavors of the President. But just as Congress cannot communicate or negotiate, it also cannot agree.

And if Congress itself lacks this power, surely it cannot convey the power upon another branch.

It may be objected that, in NAFTA and like cases, Congress is not itself making a treaty but rather authorizing the President to do so. Superficially, then, its action may look like other instances of "delegation" to the President—for example, legislation authorizing the President to impose an embargo if he thought appropriate. Such delegations were common enough in the early period,[28] and while modern commentators debate their constitutionality, quite a number of scholars think they (or at least some of them) are permissible exercises of Congress's necessary-and-proper power to effectuate its own authority.[29]

Without entering the complex debate over delegation, once we conclude that Congress itself lacks power to make international agreements, we can see that it also lacks associated power to delegate. Because neither Congress nor the President has power to make an agreement like NAFTA, laws purporting to authorize the President to make such agreements do not carry into effect any constitutional power (of either the President or Congress); they create a new one. Whatever one thinks of delegation, Congress cannot use its necessary-and-proper power to give the President something neither it nor the President possesses. Analogously, Congress could not give Article III judicial power to the President. That would not be delegating but simply rewriting the structural Constitution, something surely not "proper" for Congress to do.[30]

This reading of the text is solidly confirmed by the drafting and ratifying debates and subsequent events. So far as our records reflect, *no one* in the debates or subsequent practice asserted that Congress had Article I power to make international agreements or that it could convey such a power to the President without two-thirds of the Senate. Again, the Constitution means what it says, whether anyone at the time specifically recited that meaning in debates or practice, and drawing conclusions from silence, especially given incomplete records, carries significant dangers. But meanings not expressed by at least some contemporary readers must begin with some presumption against them being "ordinary" meanings of the time, particularly in an area that was widely debated.

Context makes it especially unlikely that congressional power in this area was assumed and accepted without comment. As discussed (Chapters 7–9), the Constitution's opponents focused on Article II, Section 2's treatymaking power, because (among other things) they thought treaties could be made too easily and would be used to surrender important rights such as the Mississippi navigation. In particular, the central lesson of the 1786 Mississippi navigation controversy and its lingering aftermath, as anti-federalists and many southern federalists understood it, was the threat that a narrow sectional majority of the country might make treaties deeply unacceptable to other parts. Federalists argued that Article II, Section 2's supermajority approval offered sufficient protection; anti-federalists replied that a greater supermajority was needed—two-thirds of all Senators (not just those present) or three-fourths of all Senators.[31]

Especially in Virginia, the threat from treatymaking and from sectional majorities was sharply felt and extensively (one might say exhaustively) considered. "[T]he Mississippi," historian Lance Banning relates, "was the issue that transfixed contemporary minds"—particularly with ratification potentially turning on the votes of Kentucky delegates, who held a vital interest in the matter. As Patrick Henry pointed out, "the majority of Congress is to the north" in both population and number of states; in other matters Virginia anti-federalists feared, as William Grayson said, "that this government will operate as a faction of seven states to oppress the rest of the union." And Henry highlighted the infamous attempt by a majority of the Confederation to relinquish the Mississippi. But Virginians did not put the two concerns together, to worry about a sectional majority in Congress making unfavorable treaties; they worried only about the treatymaking power of the Senate.[32]

If there had been any possible reading of Article I giving a bare majority of Congress power to make treaties (including a treaty surrendering navigation of the Mississippi), the lack of objections seems almost inconceivable. True, a bare majority of Congress is not necessarily easier to obtain than a Senate supermajority (although the modern impetus toward agreements such as NAFTA suggests that often it is). Nonetheless, the particular concern at the time was not just bad treatymaking in general, but bad treatymaking by sectional majorities. An Article I treatymaking process would offer no protection whatever against this threat, something that surely would not have passed in silence. A far more plausible explanation is that no one thought Congress had treatymaking power. And the most likely reason is that everyone understood Congress to have only "legislative" power, whose ordinary definition did not include making international agreements.

Relatedly, at the Philadelphia Convention delegates initially did give treatymaking power to Congress, then shifted it first to the Senate and then to the ultimate Article II, Section 2 arrangement. Several drafters tried to maintain the House role and were outvoted, with delegates explicitly arguing that Congress should not participate in treatymaking (see Chapter 8). Perhaps the delegates nonetheless saw that Congress could make treaties through Article I, with Article II, Section 2 as just an alternative avenue—but again it seems likely that, if so, someone would have mentioned it. To the contrary, the drafting discussions, like the ratification debates, seem to assume that Article II, Section 2 is the only source of treatymaking power.[33]

These observations would be cast into doubt if, after ratification, Congress claimed general treatymaking power. But again, so far as our records reflect, no one made such a claim. The only action Congress took in this direction in the early years was its 1792 authorization of postal agreements to be made by the executive branch governing international mail.[34] These, though, may not have been considered international agreements in a legal sense (they are not included in even the most comprehensive compilations of U.S. international agreements), and we may hesitate to place much weight upon them. No agreement that plainly had treaty-like status was even suggested to fall within Congress's power during the early period. And whenever the issue came up, key figures denied that Congress had any treatymaking power: Hamilton and Washington expressly said so in the 1795–1796 Jay Treaty debates (Washington pointing to the rejection of a House role at the Convention), and Madison, leading the opposition, agreed: he said only that Congress had a role in implementing treaties already made.[35] These comments do not directly address the possibility of an Article I treaty power—they were made in the context of denying a House role in approving an Article II, Section 2 treaty—but they seem to assume the absence of one.[36]

Dames & Moore and Congress's Power of Implicit Approval

The Supreme Court has assumed the constitutionality of congressional-executive agreements in several cases and came closest to endorsing them (albeit in a backhanded way) in *Dames & Moore v. Regan* (1981).[37] *Dames* involved a challenge to presidential implementation of the Algiers Declarations ending the 1979–1980 Iran hostage crisis. In the Declarations, Iran agreed to obtain release of American hostages held in Tehran; the United States agreed (among other things) to refer claims then pending in U.S. court against Iran to an international tribunal and to release Iranian funds frozen in the United States, partly to Iran and partly to fund the tribunal. President Carter and later President Reagan issued executive orders terminating claims against Iran pending in U.S. court.[38]

Dames & Moore, a U.S. construction company with claims against Iran, objected to the President's termination of its suit. The President claimed authority to implement the Declarations, placing their constitutionality derivatively at issue. In terms of independent executive power, the President's position seems textually problematic. Although Chapter 9 accepted a limited executive agreement power, that conclusion depends upon the agreement not meeting the eighteenth-century definition of a treaty. Even the part of the Declarations at issue in *Dames* involved substantial future commitments relating to the arbitration, which would seem to make them a "treaty" in constitutional terms (a point confirmed by the fact that nineteenth-century agreements to arbitrate typically were structured as treaties approved by the Senate rather than as executive settlement agreements). And the Declarations as a whole posed even greater difficulties—for example, the United States purported to agree not to interfere in Iran's internal affairs, an obligation that in eighteenth-century terms plainly entailed a treaty.[39]

Would the President's position be stronger if Congress approved the Declarations? The Supreme Court thought so, for in rejecting Dames's claim it emphasized that Congress had acquiesced in a long historical practice of executive claims settlements. Relying on Justice Jackson's celebrated concurrence in *Steel Seizure* (see Chapter 3), it noted that the President had greatest authority in foreign affairs when acting with congressional assent. As commentators have noted, that conclusion is problematic on several grounds: Congress had not done anything to approve the Declarations themselves, or even to approve settlements in general; the *Dames* settlement was unlike many historical ones, especially in that it established a complex arbitration process and undertook other material obligations not directly related to the claims.[40]

Even if Congress had approved the settlement, constitutional problems would remain. First, if Congress did so informally or by implication (as the Court seemed to allow), it would circumvent the lawmaking process of Article I, Section 7. It is likely true that Congress could have enacted a statute terminating claims against Iran using its power to regulate foreign commerce, leaving Dames no better off than in the actual case. But a statute would require the formal process; presumably no court would allow Congress to terminate claims, or take other action affecting legal rights, by informal action.[41] Second, even if Congress acted formally, the Declarations would still amount to no more than a congressional-executive agreement; that would not solve the problem of Article II, Section 2. And unlike the tariff-reduction parts of NAFTA, at least part of the Declarations would seem difficult to accomplish by reciprocal legislation.

Mysteriously, the Supreme Court treated *Dames & Moore* as presenting a potential intrusion of the President upon the powers of Congress (and therefore gave weight to Congress's implicit approval). But it was really an intrusion of the President upon the powers of the Senate, as reflected in the treatymaking clause. Correctly framed, the question was whether the agreement was a treaty (requiring Senate approval) or not a treaty (where the President could act on his own).

Dames's reliance on the Jackson concurrence was, therefore, as a textual matter entirely misplaced. Jackson contended that when Congress approves presidential action, the President's "authority is at its maximum, for it includes all that he possesses in his own right plus all that Congress can delegate. In these circumstances, and in these only, may he be said (for what it may be worth), to personify the federal sovereignty. If his act is held unconstitutional under these circumstances, it usually means that the Federal Government as an undivided whole lacks power."[42] Again, this shows the dangers of generalizing about foreign affairs law without close reference to the text. Jackson's statement may generally be true, but it is not true where Congress has not followed constitutional procedures, and it is not true for international agreements, where the President and a majority of Congress do not possess the full power of the federal government.

Conclusion: Why NAFTA Is Almost Constitutional

Examination of NAFTA and Congress's foreign affairs powers reveals two distinct limitations on what Congress may do. First, as goes without saying in domestic matters, in foreign affairs Congress must act within its enumerated powers. Congress (like the President) has no inherent foreign affairs powers. As with the President, the Tenth Amendment demands that Congress look to the powers granted. These powers may be somewhat broader than conventionally understood, however, because Congress can act to support the President's foreign affairs powers (which are themselves quite broad) in addition to acting in support of its own powers.

Second, Congress can only act legislatively, except in the few specific cases where the Constitution explicitly invests it with what was formerly called an executive power. Even with respect to enumerated powers, Congress ordinarily can act upon the subject matter only through legislation—that is, by passing laws affecting domestic rights and duties. In particular, Congress cannot exercise executive power—and thus, for example, it cannot communicate with foreign nations (even with respect to, say, foreign commerce).

In the case of NAFTA, the first limitation is plainly satisfied, because the subject is international commerce. Only the second is problematic. To the extent Congress has acted legislatively in approving NAFTA, there is no constitutional objection. This is why no court case could successfully challenge NAFTA's implementing statute, which modifies U.S. domestic law to implement the undertakings reached in NAFTA. With or without the NAFTA agreement, modifying U.S. laws regulating international trade is obviously within Congress's power.

But when Congress approves international agreements, it exercises an executive power it is not given by the Constitution's text—and thus violates the second limitation. (The same would be true if Congress engaged in diplomacy, issued passports, etc.). What is wrong with NAFTA, then, is not that Congress lowered trade barriers (which it can always do), or even that it lowered trade barriers conditional upon Mexico and Canada lowering their own trade barriers. Rather, it is that Congress agreed (or authorized the President to agree), on behalf of the United States, not to raise trade barriers in the future. This places a constraint on future Congresses that is beyond the legislative power of a current Congress. (True, a later Congress could still raise trade barriers, but only by violating the international agreement—and thus the later Congress faces a constraint it otherwise would not face.)

This in turn suggests two things about the modern practice of congressional-executive agreements, especially in the free-trade context. First, those who object to agreements such as NAFTA typically object to the immediate lowering of trade barriers, not to the future commitment not to raise them. As a result, they object to the (constitutional) legislative part of Congress's act, not to the (unconstitutional) executive part. These challenges accordingly deserve to fail (as they have).[43] Second, because NAFTA's unconstitutionality arises from the degree to which it constrains future action, our practical concerns may be lessened; NAFTA (like most modern trade agreements) permits withdrawal upon short notice (six months, in the case of NAFTA). That does not, of course, cure the constitutional objection, but it greatly mitigates it.[44]

As a result, so long as congressional-executive agreements remain within the enumerated subject-matter powers of Congress, and so long as the United States retains the ability to withdraw from them upon short notice, they are not enormous departures from the text's historical meaning. Agreements such as NAFTA are not far removed from trade legislation passed on condition of reciprocity, which is surely within Congress's textual power. The greater danger is that, if we accept congressional-executive trade agreements like NAFTA with equanimity, we will forget *why* they do not raise enormous constitutional concerns and end up with the conclusion advanced by some scholars that congressional-executive agreements are in all cases acceptable alternatives to treaties under the Constitution's text.

11

The Meanings of Declaring War

Few topics in foreign affairs have been as exhaustively studied, analyzed, and debated as the question of war powers. Academic and political writing on this topic may exceed in volume the body of foreign affairs scholarship on all other matters combined. Yet we have made little progress on the most fundamental question: who has constitutional power to commit the nation to war?[1]

This is all the more remarkable because the Constitution's text devotes as much space to war and military power as it does to any other foreign affairs subject. The drafters were closely concerned with the matter, as war (and desire to avoid war) occupied a central place in their vision of international relations; and unlike many underexamined foreign affairs subjects, it held an important place in their debates.

Unfortunately, it has proved surprisingly difficult in modern times to coax a definitive meaning out of the record they left, despite its volume and the intensity of effort expended upon it. The persistently vexing problem is that the text and the framers' intent appear to point in opposite directions. In the post-ratification period, when leading Americans spoke of initiating war, they almost always spoke of it as a congressional power. On this point Madison and Hamilton, despite their other differences, agreed. Madison wrote: "The Constitution supposes, what the History of all Govts. demonstrates, that the Ex. is the branch of power most interested in war, and most prone to it. It has accordingly with studied care, vested the question of war in the Legisl."[2] Hamilton agreed: "It is the province and duty of the Executive to preserve to the Nation the blessings of peace. The Legislature alone can interrupt those blessings by placing the nation in a state of War."[3] And Chief Justice Marshall later said that "[t]he whole powers of war" were "by the Constitution of the United States vested in Congress."[4]

The Constitution's text, though, seems on first inspection to fall short of such clear statements, despite the "studied care" Madison claimed went into it. And we now know much of it was Madison's fault. An early draft of the Constitution gave Congress power "to make war"—a clear enough allocation. But the Convention, on a motion from Madison and Elbridge Gerry, substituted "declare" for "make," so that the final text (Article I, Section 8) gives Congress power "to declare War."[5] Later statements (including Hamilton's and Madison's) seem to read the Constitution to say that Congress has power to "begin" war. But the text does not say "begin"—it says "declare," and there lies the trouble.

The most obvious meaning of "to declare war" is, of course, to issue a formal proclamation announcing a state of war. That was true in the eighteenth century as it is today: when we say (and they said) a conflict began "without declaration of war," that means it began without formal pronouncement. But no one, then or now, could claim that wars begin *only* with formal pronouncements. So if Congress only has power over formal announcement, it is hard to see how Congress gets full power over war initiation.

And if Congress's power over war initiation is incomplete, that in turns points to war as a presidential power. The President is the "Commander in Chief" of the armed forces, by Article II, Section 2, and the President holds the "executive Power" of Article II, Section 1. As we have seen (Chapter 3), the eighteenth-century concept of "executive" power included non-legislative foreign affairs powers. Chief among these was war: every major writer on the subject called war an "executive" power, and English monarchs exercised war-initiation power as an executive power in both theory and practice. This adds up to a powerful textual claim for the President's war-initiation power.[6]

The result is an interpretive impasse between the President and Congress, with neither side able to square the Constitution's text with what its drafters said about it.[7] We may be able to make some progress, however, by applying the framework developed in preceding chapters. Previous chapters show that advocates of presidential war power are right to emphasize the President's executive foreign affairs power, which would include war-initiation power (along with diplomacy, treaty termination, executive agreements, and other executive foreign affairs powers not mentioned directly in the Constitution), unless some other clause shifts war-initiation power to Congress. That clause could only be the declare-war clause.

We will see, though, that the presidential side goes astray in insisting upon too narrow a meaning of the phrase "to declare war." True, its most common

meaning was to issue a formal proclamation. But eighteenth-century terminology also recognized that war could be "declared" by conduct. That is,
a nation could "declare" its intention to go to war simply by launching
an open attack. Once this broader meaning is appreciated, we can make sense
of founding-era statements about war-initiation power as a congressional
power.

War and Executive Power

The inquiry should begin, not with the declare-war clause, but with Article
II. As discussed in Chapter 3, Article II, Section 1 vests the President with
the "executive Power"—meaning not just law execution power, but also the
foreign affairs powers labeled "executive" functions in eighteenth-century
theory and practice. There can be no doubt that, at the time the Constitution was drafted and ratified, the idea of "executive" foreign affairs power included war and military powers. Montesquieu, the period's principal theorist
of separation of powers, identified war power as one of the leading categories
of executive power. In this respect he followed John Locke, who (as discussed
in Chapter 3) labeled foreign affairs power a distinct category called "federative power," which (Locke said) was almost always held by the executive
branch. War power was a central element of Locke's federative power; Montesquieu, who re-labeled Locke's federative power as the "external" executive power, carried over Locke's identification of war power with other foreign affairs powers. Jean de Lolme, who followed Montesquieu in describing
the English system, similarly saw war power as a core element of the king's
executive power, as did Blackstone's treatise on English law.[8] And as a practical matter, that is how the system worked: English monarchs decided where
and when to go to war, subject to Parliament's funding and impeachment
checks. Founding-era Americans were, of course, intimately familiar with this
system.[9]

In America, the Continental Congress controlled war-related matters from
the outset, and the Articles of Confederation confirmed that allocation (Article 9) by granting the Congress "sole and exclusive right and power of determining on war and peace." We might think this allocation undermined
war's traditional "executive" associations. But of course it did not: as we have
seen, the Articles' Congress was—particularly in foreign affairs—primarily an
executive body, as its contemporaries recognized. And, as described in
Chapter 3, when the Virginia plan, at the Convention's outset, proposed to

give "the Executive rights vested in Congress by the Confederation" to the new executive branch, a number of delegates objected that this would likely include war powers.[10]

The question, though, is whether war-initiation power is part of the "executive Power" Article II, Section 1 ultimately vested in the President. As we have seen, the Constitution's drafters rejected the traditional idea that all executive power should be unified in a single branch. So they voted down the Virginia plan's proposal to shift the whole of the old Congress's executive power to the new executive, and they distributed key executive powers to other branches. In particular, as Chapter 7 illustrates, they assigned the previously executive treatymaking and appointments powers to the Senate—at first in whole, and then, in the final draft, as a shared arrangement with the President in Article II, Section 2.

This brings us to the question of declaring war. Like treatymaking and appointments, war initiation was another traditional executive power that at least some delegates thought should not be unified in the Constitution's chief magistrate.[11] Article I, Section 8's declare-war clause is the text's response to that concern: "Congress shall have power . . . [t]o declare War, to issue Letters of Marque and Reprisal, and to make Rules concerning Captures on Land and Water."

This clause plainly gives *some* previously "executive" war power to Congress. Issuing letters of marque and reprisal was, under the traditional system, an executive power. In eighteenth-century law-of-nations terminology, seizing ships and property on the high seas, other than in wartime, generally constituted piracy. But if a nation's government officially approved the seizure, as a response to a perceived violation of that nation's (or its subjects') rights, then the perpetrators were not pirates but official agents of the sovereign, with the same protections as soldiers in wartime. This eighteenth-century version of limited conflict, in which nations seized each other's property as a means of redress without invoking full-scale hostilities, was called reprisal; and the official approval distinguishing it from piracy was the "letter of marque and reprisal."[12] Prior to the Constitution, issuing these letters was called an executive function, part of the executive war power exercised by English monarchs and the executive Congress under the Articles.[13]

Further, the act of "declaring" war, whatever its full definition, is also obviously a traditional executive power. The English monarch (not Parliament) issued formal declarations of war in the eighteenth century, and under any definition of the phrase it was part of what Montesquieu, Blackstone, and others labeled "executive" war powers. So there is not much doubt that the

Constitution's text gives *some* previously "executive" war-related power to Congress. The question is how much.

The parallel with treatymaking power is useful. As shown in Chapters 7–9, the treatymaking clause of Article II, Section 2 is a major re-allocation of the eighteenth-century executive power over international agreements. But the President retains the general executive power of Article II, Section 1, so powers not included within the power-shifting clause remain with the President. As a result, for example, the President shares treatymaking power with the Senate but retains power to terminate treaties (Chapter 8) and make non-treaty agreements (Chapter 9), because neither is included within the power-shifting text of Article II, Section 2. Similarly, Congress has the executive war-making power encompassed by the phrase "to declare war" (plus letters of marque and reprisal), and the President has the executive war-making power *not* so encompassed. The challenge, then, is to figure out what "declare war" means.

The Meanings of Declaring War

Declaring by Formal Proclamation

The most obvious meaning of the Constitution's phrase "declare war" encompasses the eighteenth-century practice of issuing a formal proclamation, styled a "declaration of war," which announced the existence of a state of hostilities. Emmerich de Vattel, one of the law-of-nations authorities widely read in eighteenth-century America (see Chapter 9), wrote:

> [W]e owe it to mankind, and above all to the lives and happiness of our subjects, to give notice to that unjust nation, or to its ruler, that we are now going to have recourse to the final remedy and make use of open force, in order to bring him to reason. This is what is called a *declaration of war*.[14]

Matthew Hale, an English treatise-writer studied by founding-era Americans, referred to *"bellum solemniter denunciatum"* (war solemnly denounced), which he described as "when war is solemnly declared or proclaimed by our king against another prince or state."[15] In practice, this happened frequently between warring European nations: in eighteenth-century England, for example, the king issued proclamations titled "declarations of war" against France, Spain, the Netherlands, and others.[16]

Our first reaction, therefore, should be that the Constitution's text refers to this practice and assigns it to Congress. But that does not advance the argument much, for we still must work out what the power of issuing such procla-mations encompasses.

One possibility is that the drafters thought declarations of war, in this sense, were prerequisite to using armed force under the law of nations. At least three leading eighteenth-century law-of-nations writers—Vattel, Wolff, and Jean Burlamaqui—explicitly said it was. Burlamaqui wrote:

> [I]f after having used all our endeavors to terminate differences in an amicable manner, there remains no further hope, and we are absolutely constrained to undertake a war, we ought first to declare it in form. . . . [P]rudence and natural equity equally require, that, before we take up arms against any state, we should try all amicable methods to avoid coming to such an extremity. We ought then to summon him, who has injured us, to make a speedy satisfaction, that we may see whether he will not have regard to himself, and not put us to the hard necessity of pursuing our right by force of arms.[17]

The declaration, that is, was a way to make sure that war—which these writers regarded as a last resort—was truly the only alternative. Wolff elaborated:

> [W]e must not resort to this remedy [i.e., war], which is especially to be avoided, because it draws after it a great mass of evils for each of the bel-ligerent parties, as long as there is even the least hope that without it we can acquire what we are striving to acquire by force of arms; it is there-fore necessary that we should indicate that we are going to bring war upon another, in order that, before there may be a resort to arms, he can offer fair conditions for peace, and thus war may be avoided.[18]

Perhaps, then, founding-era Americans thought that the United States could not begin a war without a formal declaration. If that was so, then giving Congress control over the formal declaration amounted to giving Congress control over the decision to go to war (since one presupposed the other). This conclusion, though, seems unlikely for at least two reasons, and few scholars—even those most supportive of congressional power—rely upon it.

First, leading law-of-nations writers did not agree on the necessity of a formal declaration. Wolff, Burlamaqui, and Vattel thought declarations nec-essary (as did Grotius and Samuel Pufendorf in the seventeenth century), but others did not. The great Dutch authority Cornelius van Bynkershoek dis-missed the idea as a throwback to medieval chivalry, as did England's leading commentator, Thomas Rutherforth.[19] Second, the law-of-nations writers were entirely out of step with common practice. Eighteenth-century nations did sometimes issue formal declarations, but rarely before hostilities commenced—and often not at all. Matthew Hale wrote: "A war that is *non solemniter denunciatum* [not solemnly declared] is, when two nations slip suddenly into war without any solemnity; and this ordinarily happeneth among us."[20] The wars most immediately familiar to founding-era Americans—the Seven Years War and the conflict between Britain and France accompanying the American Revolution—began without formal declarations. Hamilton stated the obvious when he said, in Federalist No. 25, that "the ceremony of a formal denunciation of war has of late fallen into disuse."[21] In short, there could be no common background understanding among founding-era Americans that a formal declaration had to precede war; perhaps some drafters thought there should be such a requirement, but it does not exist in the text and cannot be read in as an assumption. For this reason, few advocates of congressional war power rely on this idea; they want to say, not that Congress must issue a formal proclamation before war begins, but that Congress must give some sort of approval (perhaps just implicit approval) before it begins. At this point, though, we have no justification for reading the text in this way.

Presidential advocates—most notably Professor John Yoo—suggest a different idea of the formal declaration. Yoo, relying heavily on Grotius, has argued that the formal declaration was prerequisite to a *legal* state of war. That is, nations might begin hostilities with or without formal declarations, but they needed to make a formal declaration before the international laws of war would apply. That in turn was crucial, because the laws of war protected nations' armed forces from charges of murder and piracy. Soldiers who killed during wartime did their duty; soldiers who killed in peacetime were murderers. According to Yoo, the declaration's "primary function was to trigger the international laws of war, which would clothe in legitimacy certain actions taken against one's own and enemy citizens."[22]

There is surely something to be said for this reading. It gives Congress the legislative aspect of war—deciding whether to trigger the laws of war—while the President retains "executive" authority to use military force (without the protection of the laws of war). It also parallels the marque-and-reprisal clause, which uncontroversially gives Congress power to decide whether to give similar legal protection to privateers. And this view has strong foundations in Grotius's writing: according to Grotius, in "solemn" (that is, formally declared) war, a person who "doth thus injure his Enemy, though he be apprehended in another Prince's Dominion," cannot "be proceeded against as an Homicide, or as a Thief" for "[b]y the Law of Arms all things are lawfull." The effect of "just and solemn war"—by which Grotius meant formally declared war—is a "license and impunity" to injure the enemy in ways that would be criminal in peacetime. Or, as Grotius quoted a Roman source: "They are enemies . . . against whom we publickly denounce War, or who do the like against us; the rest are but Pyrats and Robbers."[23]

This suggestion, though, suffers the same problem as attempts to invoke the Wolff/Burlamaqui/Vattel interpretation. Despite what Grotius said, a formal declaration was *not* prerequisite to a legal state of war in the seventeenth century (when Grotius wrote) or in the eighteenth. Matthew Hale, writing in the 1670s, said that "in very deed there was a state of war between the crowns of England and Spain, and the Spaniards were actual enemies, especially after the attempt of invasion in [15]88 by the Spanish Armada, and yet there was no war declared or proclaimed between the two crowns." That showed, he continued, "that a state of war may be between two kingdoms without any proclamation or indication thereof or other matter of record to prove it." Rutherforth, commenting on Grotius a century later, confirmed that Grotius's "license and impunity" "may be produced . . . without a declaration of war. For in the less solemn kinds of war, what the members do, who act under the particular direction and authority of their nation, is by the law of nations no personal crime in them: they cannot therefore be punished consistently with this law for any act, in which it considers them only as the instruments, and the nation as the agent."[24]

As a matter of practice, Hale and Rutherforth had it right. The difference, in eighteenth-century law, between lawful violence and unlawful pillage and piracy was sovereign authorization. That authorization could be shown by the formal declaration, which, as Blackstone said, created a "perfect" war in which all acts of violence were authorized. But it did not have to be. Eighteenth-century conflicts, if authorized by sovereigns, were governed by the laws of war, whether formally declared or not (and many were not). Bynkershoek wrote: "[I]f two sovereigns are engaged in hostilities without having declared war, can we have any doubt that war is being waged according to the will of both? In that case there can be no need of a declaration, since it is being waged publicly and needs no proof."[25] Or as an English court put it in *The Maria Magdalena* (1779), applying the laws of war to an undeclared conflict:

Where is the difference, whether a war is proclaimed by a Herald at the Royal Exchange, with his trumpets, and on the Pont Neuf at Paris, and by reading and affixing a printed paper on public buildings; or whether war is announced by royal ships, and whole fleets, at the mouths of cannon? . . . If learned authorities are to be quoted, Bynkershoek has a whole chapter to prove, from the history of Europe, that a lawful and perfect state of war may exist without proclamation.[26]

Thus it is true that *some* law-of-nations writers thought a formal declaration was required prior to commencing hostilities, and *some* law-of-nations writers thought a declaration was needed to trigger a legal state of war. But anyone familiar with the full sweep of law-of-nations scholarship and with eighteenth-century practice would have realized that these were not consensus positions but rather disputed views running sharply counter to actual practice. As a result, we must be extraordinarily hesitant to incorporate them into the constitutional text.

What, then, was the general view of the formal declaration in the eighteenth century? The best answer seems to be that the declaration was exactly what it appeared to be, and no more: it was an official announcement. Making an official announcement had multiple advantages. In a time of slow and uncertain communication, when wars developed at sea or in remote areas, it was an official source of news. It let people know that war had broken out, so they could arrange their affairs accordingly. It was frequently a sort of primitive press release on behalf of the warring nation, describing the reasons for the war. And, as Hale indicated, it could be evidence in court that a war had in fact begun.[27]

The key is that all these uses were optional. The formal declaration, as actually used, was an official *but not mandatory* source of news, of justification for war, and of evidence in court. It had its advantages, but they were practical rather than legal, and thus it could be dispensed with, if strategic conditions warranted. That is why eighteenth-century wars were rarely declared formally in advance, and sometimes not formally declared at all—and why there was no legal consequence in failing to formally declare them.[28]

We should, though, now be quite worried about our reading of the Constitution's declare-war clause. Under this meaning of declaring war, the clause appears to give Congress power to make an optional official announcement of war, while leaving the President all of the substantive decisions about whether and when to begin hostilities. That seems enormously problematic, because it is hard to see any reason to adopt such an odd system. As we saw in Chapter 3, ordinarily the President is the only channel of communications with other nations about U.S. foreign policy. Here would be an exception to that rule, yet in an area in which the President otherwise retained full discretion. The President would be able to start a war but would have to rely on Congress to explain why.

Of course, just because a result seems odd today is not enough to overcome the plain meaning of the Constitution's text where no other reading is available. But this oddity does suggest a need to revisit the common assumption that "declare war" refers only to issuing formal declarations.

Declaration by Action

Most modern discussions of war powers have been content, without much analysis, to equate the constitutional phrase "declare war" with the eighteenth-century practice of issuing a formal proclamation announcing the war. This approach misses an important alternate use of the phrase that makes more constitutional sense. Closer review makes clear that a nation might "declare" war, not only by formal announcement, but also by an act of hostility. As John Locke wrote, one may declare "by Word or Action."[29]

First, the dictionary definition: Samuel Johnson's 1755 dictionary does not define "declare war" as a phrase, but its individual definitions are consistent with the idea that "declaring war" could be done by pronouncement or hostile act. Johnson defined war as "the exercise of violence under sovereign command against withstanders." This reflects the common seventeenth- and eighteenth-century view that sovereign authorization ("sovereign command") distinguished war from ordinary violence.[30]

For "declare," Johnson listed as relevant definitions: "to make known; to tell evidently and openly"; "to publish; to proclaim"; "to shew in open view." Since sovereign command was the distinguishing characteristic of war (as opposed to other violence), presumably this element was what the sovereign needed to "make known."[31] A formal proclamation would, of course, accomplish the task, so issuing a proclamation obviously came within the definition of "declaring" war, as everyone at the time understood. But it seems difficult to say (as Grotius did) that this was the only way of making the sovereign command known. As Burlamaqui objected: "are we more assured, that the war is made by public authority, when a herald for instance comes to declare it with certain ceremonies, than we should be, when we see an army upon our frontiers, commanded by a principal person of the state, and ready to enter our country?"[32] In short, public use of armed force will "shew in open view" a sovereign's determination to go to war as surely as a proclamation.[33]

That reading of the dictionary definition is confirmed by the way prominent authorities actually used the word "declare" in conjunction with a state of war. Locke wrote:

The *State of War* is a State of Enmity and Destruction; And therefore declaring by Word or Action, not a passionate and hasty, but a sedate se-tled Design, upon another Mans Life, *puts him in a State of War* with him against whom he has declared such an Intention.[34]

This passage highlights three key points. First, Locke gave "declaring" a broad meaning that included physical acts, as well as spoken or written an-nouncements ("by Word or Action"), manifesting one's intent ("setled De-sign"). Second, Locke directly linked this use of "declaring" to creating a state of war: "declaring by Word or Action . . . puts him [the declarer] in a State of War." Finally, the "Action" Locke presumably had in mind was at-tack. Launching an attack is the action most evidently manifesting a "setled Design upon another Man's Life." For Locke, then, an attack declared the intention to enter a state of war.[35]

Similarly, Blackstone's discussion of piracy uses "declare war" in a way that can only mean announce through hostilities:

[T]he crime of *piracy,* or robbery and depredation upon the high seas, is an offence against the universal law of society. . . . As therefore [a pirate] has renounced all the benefits of society and government, and has re-duced himself afresh to the savage state of nature, by declaring war against all mankind, all mankind must declare war against him.[36]

Plainly Blackstone means declaring war by conduct, for communications with pirates were normally made by action and not through embassies. This use is further echoed by the English court quoted earlier: asked to find that no war existed because there had been no formal announcement, the court found instead that a state of war could be "announced . . . at the mouths of cannon"—that is, declared by hostile act.[37]

Among the important continental writers, Vattel wrote: "from the mo-ment a Nation takes up arms against another, it declares itself the enemy to all the individual citizens of the latter, and justifies them in treating it in turn as such."[38] Again, this passage uses "declare" to mean an act (taking up arms) that itself makes a statement. It is no casual use, but specifically addresses the way a state of war is created. In the section where this passage appears, Vattel discusses the right of subjects of nations involved in hostilities to attack op-posing nations' subjects. This right, Vattel said, is given by the laws of war; in the passage quoted, he added that by taking up arms the aggressor nation in-vokes the laws of war, because this act "declares" a state of enmity. Vattel also wrote that when enemies "take up arms against me," war "is declared by their own conduct," and in giving an example from Roman history, he recounted that "[t]he Galatians, by furnishing troops for an offensive war against the Romans, had declared themselves enemies to Rome."[39] Similarly Wolff, speaking of alliances during war, wrote: "he who allies himself to my enemy, as by sending troops or subsidies, or by assisting him in any other way, declares by that very fact that he wishes to be a participant in the war carried on against me."[40]

In sum, in initiating eighteenth-century war, actions spoke at least as loudly as words. There would have been nothing remarkable in using "declare war" to mean initiating a state of war by sovereign act, as well as by proclamation. "Declare" meant, among other things, to make known or show in open view. The eighteenth-century military (unlike in some earlier times) was obviously a sovereign instrument in most European nations. Use of military force showed in open view the sovereign's approval of hostilities as surely as did a proclamation. Hostilities under sovereign command created a state of war. Thus hostilities under sovereign command *declared* the war, for they made known the sovereign's determination to settle a dispute by force.

This discussion is surely not the end of the matter, for the fact that Locke, Blackstone, Vattel, and Wolff, among others, sometimes used "declare" in this way does not prove that this is how it should be read in the Constitution's text. It is, though, sufficient to overthrow the common assumption that the only possible meaning of the declare-war clause is declaration by formal proclamation. It establishes an ambiguity, for surely "declare war" was also sometimes used—including by some of the same writers, as well as by some framers[41]—to mean only the formal proclamation. This requires us to consider which eighteenth-century meaning fits best with the Constitution's text and structure as a whole.

The Constitutional Meaning of Declaring War

We have now established that the eighteenth-century phrase "declare war" had two common meanings. First, used narrowly it referred to formal proclamations announcing the existence of a state of war. Second, used broadly it referred to acts creating a state of war, done by "word or action"—that is, announcement or attack. The question, therefore, is which meaning is the best reading of the Constitution. As discussed below, the narrow meaning is less consistent with the Constitution's text and structure, and with contemporaneous and near-contemporaneous readings of it; giving "declare war" its broader meaning provides a better harmonization with each.

Text and Structure

As Chapter 3 concluded, Article II, Section I gave the President the traditional "executive" foreign affairs powers, except for "executive" powers expressly given to other branches. So, for example, when the Constitution gave marque-and-reprisal power—a traditional executive power—to Congress, it also transferred that power away from the President. The declare-war clause presumably works the same way, transferring the declare-war power from the President to Congress; as discussed below, that is how every contemporaneous account read it. The question is how broadly to read that power—or, as framed above, which of that clause's two ordinary eighteenth-century meanings to adopt.

Under the broad meaning, "declaring" war amounts to placing the nation in a state of war, so despite the President's executive power over diplomatic and military affairs, the President would not have the independent ability to proclaim a state of war (declaring by word) nor to signal the beginning of war by ordering an armed attack (declaring by action). Although the President has general power to command the military (under the commander-in-chief power of Article II, Section 2), in this view the President would lack the more specific power to command the military in a way that signals the start of a war; similarly, although the President has general power to communicate on behalf of the nation, the President lacks the more specific power to communicate on behalf of the nation in a way that signals the beginning of a state of war. As for Congress's power, Congress can easily issue a formal proclamation itself; there is a practical limit on its ability to declare war by action, because Congress does not command an army, although Congress could (in this view) direct the President, as commander-in-chief, to use the military to begin a state of war. In either event Congress would surely have practical difficulty forcing war on an unwilling commander-in-chief, so Congress's war power is necessarily a cooperative authority that gives Congress a role—but not a sole voice—in war-initiation. Congress's role therefore somewhat resembles the Senate's role in treatymaking (another instance in which the Constitution departed from the traditional understanding of unified executive power in foreign affairs).

This allocation makes structural sense and is plausible as a policy matter. Given the deliberative policymaking elements of the decision to initiate war, and war's potentially calamitous consequences, one might well believe that such a momentous decision should not be made by one person. True, there are opposing policy considerations as well, but it is surely not an unreasonable allocation of power.

The broad meaning of "declaring war" also makes the clause fit with its immediate neighbor, the marque-and-reprisal clause. As discussed, "marque and reprisal" referred specifically to seizing foreign property to remedy injuries committed by foreign nations. The power was, in short, a specific form of limited hostilities—and it was an "executive" power of the monarch. The Constitution moves this power to Congress, another instance of the text rejecting unified executive power in foreign affairs. Apparently, therefore, founding-era Americans thought the decision to engage in this limited form of offensive hostility was properly a congressional, rather than a presidential, responsibility. Given this outlook, it seems quite plausible that founding-era Americans also thought the decision to enter into wider forms of hostility— war—should also involve Congress. Read this way, both clauses were efforts to shift decisionmaking about offensive war from the executive magistrate (where traditionally it had resided) to Congress. It particularly makes sense to shift the two powers together, because reprisals were often a prelude to open war.

To be clear, all we can claim so far is that the broader meaning of declaring war is a plausible reading of the declare-war clause, given its textual and structural context.[42] The drafters may have wanted to divide power in this way, but we cannot, on this basis alone, be sure that they did so. It remains to evaluate the alternative reading.

In the narrow view of "declaring" war, the declare-war clause encompasses only the power to make official announcements about the existence of a state of war. Why, though, would the Constitution single out this particular executive power—of all the many "executive" war powers—to shift to Congress? The President is the communicative organ of the nation in foreign affairs on all other international subjects (see Chapter 3). Why would the President also not be the best communicator regarding war, particularly if wars can start by presidential initiative? It is hard to see any separation-of-powers value served by this allocation. If the declare-war clause, given its narrow reading, moved substantive power away from the President (for example, if formal declarations were prerequisite to engaging in hostilities or invoking the legal state of war), one might understand the shift; but, as explained above, formal declarations were not generally understood in this way. As a result, the clause, given its narrow interpretation, ends up meaning that the President can start a war but cannot officially say anything about it. This seems both inexplicable and counterproductive.

It is true, of course, that this narrow vision of the declare-war clause would mean that the President could not begin war by proclamation. The President would, however, be able to begin war by attack. It is hard to see why the President should have one power but not the other. Presumably all the reasons against the President having power to begin war by proclamation would also apply to the power to begin war by attack.[43]

Nor does there seem any good reason to give Congress a purely communicative power. The legislative branch is the nation's deliberative policymaker. One would expect that, to the extent that the Constitution shifted formerly executive powers to the legislative branch, they would be deliberative functions. The other executive powers transferred in whole or part by the Constitution *are* deliberative: for example, treatymaking, appointments, and marque and reprisal. It is, therefore, difficult to find any structural role for the declare-war clause, if given its narrow meaning.

The narrow meaning of the declare-war clause also fits poorly with the marque-and-reprisal clause. As discussed, that clause shifts to Congress policymaking power over a limited form of offensive hostilities. This shift makes sense if policymaking power over wider hostilities is also shifted. There is no satisfactory explanation for why the President should have comprehensive powers to initiate hostilities, including war, but not initiate reprisals. Rather, belief that the lesser power should be shifted implies belief that the greater power should also be shifted. One would expect *more* deliberation with respect to exercise of the greater power, not less. Further, that the two shifts of power occur in the same clause of Article I, Section 8 suggests that they are directed to similar goals. Finally, shifting marque-and-reprisal power without shifting war-initiation power is likely to be ineffective in practice. Presumably Presidents denied congressional authority to make reprisals could simply start a war (by attack) and direct property seizures as wartime measures. In sum, the narrow meaning of declaring war does not provide a satisfactory account of the text and the structural role of the declare-war clause.

Context and Background: The Roman Precedent

Advocates of presidential power have argued as a historical matter that the drafters probably did not mean to give Congress war-initiation power because that would run contrary to the drafters' experiences, especially under the English system of executive war power.[44] It does run counter to their experiences, but there are reasons to think they made an intentional break. First, it is clear that at least a substantial number of prominent Americans wished to give Congress war-initiation power, and the Convention draft at one point did so in unmistakable terms.[45] At minimum, congressional control over war-initiation was very much in the drafters' contemplation. And we know that the drafters went against their English background in shifting treatymaking and diplomatic appointments in part away from their chief magistrate; it is plausible that they would have done so with war initiation as well. Further, as Chapter 7 discusses, in allocating treatymaking power, the drafters used the Roman republican model rather than the English one. Giving Congress war-initiation power similarly adopts something like Roman republican practice instead of English royal practice.

Although Roman war-making practice (like Roman treatymaking practice) remains somewhat unclear, in general the senate and the popular assembly made the decision, not the consuls (who were the "executive" military commanders).[46] That allocation of power was surely known to founding-era Americans from their own knowledge of Roman sources (see Chapter 7) and from eighteenth-century English accounts of Roman government.[47] Grotius likewise mentioned the Roman people's role in approving war, as did Montesquieu (although the latter was quite critical of it); John Adams noted in his comprehensive survey of ancient constitutions that in Rome the people "determine concerning peace and war."[48] Elbridge Gerry may have had this in mind when he said at the Convention (in response to Pierce Butler's suggestion) that he "never expected to hear in a republic a motion to empower the Executive alone to declare war."[49]

Ratification

We should now turn to supporting evidence in the ratification debates. Aside from one statement from James Wilson, the scope of the declare-war power was not discussed directly, but indirect evidence suggests that the ratifiers had in mind the broader meaning. Federalists invoked the clause as an example of how the Constitution limited the power of the executive/President, responding to anti-federalist complaints that the office was too powerful. Although anti-federalists remained concerned about presidential power, they did not dispute federalist claims that the declare-war clause materially distinguished the President from the English monarch.

Hamilton, for example, argued in Federalist No. 69 that under the Constitution the President's power was less than the monarch's power because, among other things, the power of "the British king extends to the *declaring* of war . . . which, by the Constitution under consideration, would appertain to the legislature."[50] Of course, this observation does not in so many words equate declaring war with control over commencing hostilities. But it is nonetheless inconsistent with the narrow reading of "declare war." Hamilton's comment confirms the general view that allocations of traditional executive foreign affairs power to Congress were understood as exclusive—that is, the declare-war clause gives power to Congress and denies it to the President. Further, it is only consistent with a reading of "declare war" that imposes a material reduction in executive war power (else it would be pointless to emphasize it as a limitation). As discussed above, the narrow reading of "declare war" does not impose any such material reduction, since the President could still initiate war by armed attack and there was no difference between war begun by proclamation and one begun by armed attack. If the declare-war clause is read narrowly to refer only to issuing formal proclamations, Hamilton would have had no basis to conclude that the President's power was materially less than the English monarch's power due to the President's inability to declare war. On the other hand, if the clause is read broadly to encompass declaring war by word or action, Hamilton's argument is perfectly understandable, for the clause would create a substantial difference between the monarch's war power and the President's war power.

Similarly, James Iredell, a leading member of the North Carolina convention, said that "[t]he President has not the power of declaring war by his own authority" but rather this and other powers "are vested in other hands." Iredell, like Hamilton, was describing the Constitution's limits on presidential power. His comment (like Hamilton's) is coherent only if the clause produces material constraints on the President. Likewise, Charles Pinckney told the South Carolina convention that "the President's powers did not permit him to declare war," in the context of describing limits on presidential power. Again, if the declare-war clause only prevented the President from issuing formal proclamations (but not from launching armed attacks), this would hardly seem worth mentioning. Only if the clause is read to include declaring war by word or action can we make sense of Iredell's and Pinckney's (and Hamilton's) emphasis on its role in reducing the President's executive power.[51]

This context confirms the importance of James Wilson's often-cited remark at the Pennsylvania convention: "It will not be in the power of a single man" to involve the nation in war, "for the important power of declaring war is vested in the legislature at large."[52] We would not want to place undue weight on this quotation standing alone, for Wilson was not representative of his generation on some key issues; he did appear to be overstating in some respects, and he did not explain what he mean by "declaring war." But the preceding quotations show that on this point, at least, Wilson was not obscure or an outlier, for he used "declare war" in the same sense as Iredell, Pinckney, and Hamilton.

In a different context, Madison in Federalist No. 41 wrote: "Is the power of declaring war necessary? No man will answer this question in the negative."[53] Again, this observation does not directly prove the extent of Congress's war initiation power. However, it is only consistent with the broad meaning of "declare war." If "declare war" is read narrowly to mean only the power to issue a formal proclamation, it could hardly be thought so essential to government that "no man" would think it unnecessary. Because a state of war could be created by an armed attack without any formal proclamation, the formal proclamation was indeed regarded by some eighteenth-century writers as an outdated and superfluous ceremony.[54] But if "declare war" is taken in its broader sense to mean declaring war by word or action, Madison's comment makes sense, for in the eighteenth century it is likely that almost everyone thought nations must have the right to initiate war to insist on their rights.

Post-ratification Commentary and Practice

The centerpiece of pro-Congress war powers scholarship is an array of post-ratification quotations and events apparently showing that U.S. leaders of the 1790s thought Congress had very substantial control over the decision to go to war. But this scholarship has been rightly criticized for invoking post-ratification authorities without any satisfactory tie to the Constitution's text. Without a textual explanation of *why* anyone might have thought Congress had sole war-initiation powers, the post-ratification evidence is more puzzling than persuasive.

Our earlier discussion shows the problem to be the mistaken equation of the declare-war clause with formal proclamations. Once we see that "declare war" could broadly mean "initiate a state of war" as well as narrowly mean "issue a formal proclamation," the post-ratification evidence becomes both understandable and valuable.

To pick one example, Hamilton said in his 1793 Pacificus essays that "[t]he Legislature alone" can "plac[e]" the Nation in a state of War."[55] If "declare war" means only issuing a formal proclamation, there is a considerable skip in Hamilton's reasoning. He was surely familiar with the long-standing English view that a state of war would be triggered by open hostilities, and he had said earlier, in Federalist No. 25, that the formal proclamation had fallen into disuse. He surely did not think formal declarations were the only way to place the nation in a state of war. Viewed in this way, Hamilton's statement seems simply incoherent.

Once the textual inquiry is framed properly, however, Hamilton's statement becomes much more useful. If Hamilton thought war could be declared by word or action, then he of course would associate "declar[ing] war" with "placing the Nation in a state of War." Hamilton simply used "plac[e] the Nation in a state of War" (Pacificus's term for Congress's war power) as a synonym for "declare war" (the Constitution's term). This is precisely consistent with the broad meaning of "declare War" identifiable in the works of earlier treatise writers. Recovering the broad meaning of "declare War" allows us to understand Hamilton's statement.

This in turn renders Hamilton's statement important evidence of the historical meaning of the declare-war clause. The question, of course, is not ultimately what Hamilton himself thought, but what the declare-war clause meant to ordinary readers. Hamilton's view is highly probative, though. He vigorously advocated presidential powers in general, so his concession that the war-initiation power lay with Congress seems substantial. In the Pacificus essays, for example, he argued that the President controlled most foreign affairs powers other than war-initiation and treatymaking. Hamilton wrote the essays, moreover, defending Washington's 1793 proclamation against charges that it interfered with Congress's war power. If there were a plausible reading of the Constitution that would preserve some war-initiation power with the President, we would not expect Hamilton to concede the point. We must conclude that Hamilton thought reading the declare-war clause narrowly to refer only to formal declarations, and thereby preserving substantial independent presidential power to initiate war, was not tenable in light of the clause's common understanding.

Similar observations apply to other leading post-ratification commentary. We need not review all the evidence here, as it has been thoroughly canvassed by prior scholars. However, the inability of prior accounts to tie the commentary to an ordinary meaning of "declare war" has greatly undermined their persuasiveness. Viewed in the light of the textual argument made here, additional weight must be given to the argument favoring a broad view of "declare war" over a narrow one. Although a proper interpretation of the constitutional text need not accord with every post-ratification statement, the explanatory power of the broad reading of "declare war" must count in its favor, especially compared with the difficulties of competing versions.[56]

A second important point about the post-ratification period is that practice conformed to the broad meaning of "declare war." Again, scholars have emphasized that early Presidents generally deferred to Congress on the question of war initiation, and early presidential advisors generally counseled such deference.[57] But without a textual explanation for this deference, we cannot know whether it should be counted as evidence of constitutional meaning, or merely evidence that early Presidents hesitated, for non-constitutional reasons, to use force unilaterally. Surely U.S. military weakness in the early years did contribute to presidential circumspection. It is also somewhat significant, though, that the United States faced questions of war at least five times between 1789 and 1800, and in each case the President looked to Congress to decide whether war should be pursued. This practice standing alone might not establish the text's meaning, but taken with other evidence, it further indicates that the broad rather than the narrow meaning of "declare war" should be preferred.[58]

A third key fact about the post-ratification period is that it provides no evidence supporting the narrow meaning of "declare war." So far as surviving records reflect, no one in the 1790s took the view that the President alone could initiate war. That would not in itself be decisive were the text clear, but once the interpretive project is recast as choosing between two possible meanings, the fact that one meaning was commonly ascribed to the constitutional text in the post-ratification period, and the other was never advanced, becomes an important factor. Taken with other evidence, we may now venture a definitive conclusion.

Conclusion

In sum, the central point about "declaring war" is that the phrase was used in two ways in the eighteenth century: narrowly, to refer to formal proclamations that announced the existence of war; and broadly, to refer to proclamations *or actions* that created a state of war. In isolation, we might read the text to adopt either meaning. But structural evidence, ratification commentary, post-ratification understandings, and post-ratification practice all point to the broader meaning. Perhaps none of these alone would be sufficient, but taken together they strongly indicate that founding-era Americans understood the clause to carry the broader meaning: Congress, not the President, has power to place the nation in a state of war through words (issuing formal proclamations) or action (directing armed attacks).

This conclusion, though, may not vindicate congressional war power to the extent claimed by Congress and many scholars. Like the Senate's treaty-making power, Congress's war power is not general authority over war, but a specific exception to the traditional executive foreign affairs powers vested in the President. Thus, just as the Senate's treaty power extends only to *making* treaties (not to other aspects of treaties), Congress's declare-war power extends only to *declaring* war (that is, initiating a state of war by word or action) and not to other aspects of using military force. The next chapter explores the implications of this conclusion.

12

Beyond Declaring War: War Powers of Congress and the President

Although the meaning of "declar[ing] War" receives the greatest attention in war power debates, it is not the only (nor, perhaps, even the most important) war-related matter to resolve. This chapter considers three related issues. First, once we recognize the declare-war power as covering both declaring-by-proclamation and declaring-by-action, what independent war powers remain with the President? Second, to what extent can Congress give war-initiation power to the President? And third, to what extent can Congress limit the President's war powers? Each question poses substantial difficulties, but as we will see, what seems to emerge from the text is a complex picture in which the President has significant powers, but Congress has substantial powers to limit them.

The President's Power to Fight Defensive Wars

Almost everyone agrees that the President has some independent power to fight defensive wars without Congress's authorization. There is little agreement, though, on the scope of "defensive" war. In particular, it is not clear whether the President's power includes responding to "imminent" threats, as well as actual attacks; nor is it clear whether the allowed response only includes fending off attack or also includes taking the offensive against attackers.[1]

The Source of the President's Power

To begin answering these questions, it is important first to explain *why* the President has power to fight defensive wars. Modern war-powers scholars accept that the President must have power to "repel sudden attacks"; not only would it be absurd not to give the President this power, but Madison specif-

239

ically said at the Philadelphia Convention that his substitution of "declare" for "make" in the draft Constitution would "leav[e] to the Executive the power to repel sudden attack."[2] Its textual basis, though, may not be immediately apparent. Madison's statement is often treated almost as if it were part of the text, rather than a statement in a private meeting whose records were not published until long after ratification.[3] Getting this first step right is important in approaching correctly the more difficult and disputed questions outlined above.

The answer flows from the framework we have developed earlier. Congress's declare-war power is the power to initiate a state of war; war powers distinct from war-initiation remain part of the President's executive power (unless affected by some other provision). Crucially, defending against attacks did not, in eighteenth-century terms, *create* a state of war. As a result, although the declare-war clause gives Congress all the nation's power to create a state of war, it does not cover situations where a state of war is created *by the opposing party*.

Eighteenth-century law-of-nations writers agreed that formal proclamations were unnecessary in defensive wars, even though some writers would have required them for offensive wars. Defensive wars, they said, presupposed an enemy's declaration, either formally or by hostile act. The prior declaration created a state of war; no reciprocal manifestation of intent was needed, because nations under attack necessarily would defend themselves. Vattel wrote: "He who is attacked and only wages defensive war need make no declaration of it, for the declaration on the part of the opposing sovereign, or his open hostilities, are sufficient to set up a state of war." Christian Wolff explained that declaration "is superfluous for the party waging the defensive war" because "the supreme power owes defense to its citizens, who have united into a state for the purpose of defending themselves against the forces of outsiders" and "therefore, since the supreme power necessarily wages defensive war as part of its duty, it certainly seems incongruous to announce to another that we intend to do what we cannot omit without neglect of duty, nor without injury to our citizens." Thus, "by nature a defensive war is not to be declared."[4]

These writers of course overstated the formal proclamation's role, for it rarely preceded even offensive war in eighteenth-century practice (see Chapter 11). According to writers describing that practice, an attack also triggered the state of war; but again, they focused on the attack—not the response to attack—as the trigger. The English admiralty court, for example, said that the state of war could be "announced by royal ships, and whole fleets, at the mouths of cannon"—indicating that the initial attack created the state of war.[5] (This is consistent with Vattel's observation noted above that "the state of war" can be created by the enemy's "open hostilities.")

Applied to the Constitution, this explains the President's ability to wage defensive war without Congress's authorization. The nation can be placed in a state of war in three ways: by formal U.S. declaration, by U.S. declaration through hostilities, or by a foreign power's declaration (formal or by hostilities). The first two require Congress's approval, under the declare-war clause. But the President, using the executive power, can wage war once the state of war exists. If another nation creates the state of war (which it can do unilaterally, by proclamation or act), the U.S. response is not a declaration because there is nothing to "declare"—the state of war already exists. Any "declaration" by Congress is superfluous to the war's existence, and the President can use the executive power to fight the war created by the other side. The President, then, has power to "repel sudden attacks"—not because Madison privately said so, but because that is part of the President's executive power not conveyed to Congress in the declare-war clause.[6]

Reading the "executive" power to include power to respond to attacks appears consistent with founding-era interpretations. First, it tracks the approach to executive power reflected in Jefferson's funding opinion and Hamilton's Pacificus essay, outlined in Chapter 4: that is, the President has the traditional "executive" powers, subject to specific derogations in the text.[7] Second, it is consistent with founding-era descriptions of Congress's war power as specifically the power to *create* a state of war and with the substantial post-ratification consensus that the President had defensive war powers.[8] And third, it is exactly the way important American leaders resolved the question of defensive force (although the key quotations come a little later in constitutional history and thus must be appropriately discounted). Albert Gallatin, a close Jefferson ally, argued in 1801 that "the exve cannot put us in a state of war, but if we be put into that state either by the decree of Congress or of the other nation, the command and direction of the public force then belongs to the exve." Former Convention delegate William Paterson, as a circuit justice in 1806, agreed:

> If indeed a foreign nation should invade the territories of the United States, it would I apprehend, be not only lawful for the president to resist such an invasion, but also to carry hostilities into the enemy's county; and for this plain reason, that a state of complete and absolute war actually exists between the two nations. In the case of invasive hos-

tilities, there cannot be war on one side and peace on the other. . . . There is a manifest distinction between our going to war with a nation at peace, and a war being made against us by an actual invasion, or a formal declaration.

Madison wrote in 1827, referring to events during Jefferson's presidency: "The only case in which the Executive can enter on a war, undeclared by Congress, is when a state of war has been actually produced by the conduct of another power." The common thread in these statements is that after an attack on the United States, there is no need for a declaration to create the state of war with the attacker—and hence Congress's declare-war power is not implicated by the President's response.[9]

The Scope of the President's Power to Fight a Defensive War

Although almost everyone concedes the President some power to fight defensive wars, debate persists on the scope of this power. The debate has two dimensions: what counts as defensive war, and what measures are permitted. Without textual grounding of the President's power, it may be quite difficult to assess these matters. The textual framework suggested above—namely, describing Congress's power as authority to create a state of war—provides grounds for rejecting the more extravagant claims on behalf of both the President and Congress.

WHAT COUNTS AS A DEFENSIVE WAR? Presidential advocates might define "defensive" broadly to encompass attacks on or threats to allies, or threats to U.S. national interests, loosely described. We begin, though, with the textural understanding that the President has independent power to fight wars only where the state of war has already been created ("declared") by the enemy. A "defensive" war in this sense encompasses a narrower eighteenth-century meaning than Presidents might like to claim. In eighteenth-century writing, "defensive" war arose when a nation was actually attacked or war was formally declared against it. Wars undertaken to defend national interests, such as trading rights, treatment of citizens or ambassadors by foreign powers, etc., were "offensive" (though justified), not defensive. Jean Jacques Burlamaqui, who wrote most extensively on the point, emphasized that the distinction between offensive and defensive war should not be confused with the distinction between just and unjust war. As he emphasized, in a passage Hamilton later quoted at length in his Pacificus essays, "defensive" simply meant responding to attack (whether or not justified); "offensive" meant initiating attack (which could be done with or without good reason).[10]

Thus acts declaring war—that is, actually creating a state of war—should not be confused with acts giving rise to just causes of war. Many acts might constitute causes of war (including, for example, wrongfully seizing private property by reprisal). But war did not necessarily result. Causes of war might or might not be acted upon, depending upon the circumstances, and therefore one could not say that a state of war automatically arose from them. The cause of war did not create war. Instead, the response to the cause of war (whether by formal declaration or armed attack) created the war, and if no response was made in spite of just cause—a reasonable result under some circumstances—then no state of war occurred.[11]

Further, the state of war was said to exist, not in the abstract, but between contending nations; non-contending nations were neutrals. If a previously uninvolved nation joined one side of the fighting, that nation "declared" that it was no longer a neutral, but a belligerent. Thus assisting an ally militarily, even in its defense, amounted to a declaration.[12] In constitutional terms, if the United States were to give military assistance to an ally under attack, this would create war between the United States and the ally's attacker where none previously existed—and would, in eighteenth-century terms, be a U.S. declaration of war.

A "defensive" war for these purposes, then, responds to an attack (or declaration) that has *already* created a state of war—much less than some presidential advocates have claimed. For example, prior to the 1991 Persian Gulf War, the executive branch suggested that no congressional action was needed to authorize using force against Iraq—either because Iraq's 1990 invasion of Kuwait threatened U.S. strategic interests or because the United States would be acting defensively to support its ally Kuwait, pursuant to a U.N. Security Council resolution.[13] Our review of eighteenth-century terminology indicates that these claims exceed textual presidential powers. Although in eighteenth-century terms the U.S. war against Iraq may have been "justified," it was not "defensive."[14] Before the U.S. attack on Iraqi forces, no state of war existed between the United States and Iraq (although one did exist between Iraq and Kuwait). The U.S. attack amounted to a declaration, creating a U.S.-Iraq state of war where none previously existed.[15]

Relatedly, this suggests—contrary to substantial commentary[16]—that the President alone generally cannot launch preemptive or preventative attacks against developing threats, even if the threats are "imminent." Unless a threat constitutes an act of war (and most mere threats did not, in eighteenth-century terms), a preemptive move would itself initiate a state of war—which is a textual power of Congress. We may debate the policy wisdom in this, but there is not much founding-era support for a contrary conclusion.[17]

TAKING THE OFFENSE AGAINST ATTACKERS. The next question is how far the President may go in waging defensive war without congressional approval. Here the textual analysis seems to favor the President. From the reasoning described above, the President cannot take military action that "declares" war (initiates a state of war). Once war begins, the declare-war clause no longer limits the President's military options against the enemy, because nothing the President does "declares" (initiates) war. Conducting the war is an executive power, including not just fending off attacks, but also taking the offensive against an attacker.

Eighteenth-century law-of-nations writing tends to confirm this analysis. An attack justified not only purely defensive measures to fend it off, but also counterattacks—including against the attacker's home territory—to gain ultimate victory in the war. As English treatise-writer Richard Lee explained in 1760: "whoever declares himself my enemy, gives me a liberty to use violence against him in infinitum, or as far as I please; and that, not only till I have repulsed the danger which threatened me." Changing from the tactical defensive to the tactical offensive was not called "declaring" war by any major law-of-nations writer, and doing so would not have made sense on their terms: as described above, they understood that war had already been "declared" by the attack, and no further declaration was needed.[18]

Post-ratification evidence is somewhat less conclusive on this point. Some evidence indicates that Washington thought his authority extended only to purely defensive measures, and President Adams sought congressional approval before responding to French attacks on U.S. shipping in the 1790s' naval war.[19] On the other hand, President Jefferson's engagement with Tripoli in 1801, while somewhat ambiguous, seems to point in the opposite direction.

Tripoli, one of the "Barbary" powers on Africa's north coast, began attacking U.S. merchant ships and eventually issued a formal declaration of war. Jefferson sent the U.S. Navy to the Mediterranean without consulting Congress. From the President's authority to repel attacks, most everyone agreed that the Navy could defend itself. The more difficult question was whether it could initiate attacks on Tripoli's ships.[20]

When a battle actually occurred, Jefferson's report to Congress empha-sized the defensive nature of the fight and went so far as to say that offensive actions required Congress's assent. This drew a sharp response from Hamilton, who made the textual argument outlined above: "[W]hen a for-eign nation declares, or openly and avowedly makes war upon the United States, they are then by the very fact, already at war, and any declaration on the part of Congress is nugatory; it is at least unnecessary. It is self-evident, that a declaration by one nation against another produces at once a complete state of war between both; and that no declaration on the one side can at all vary their relative situation; and in practice it is well known, that nothing is more common, than when war is declared by one party, to prosecute mutual hostilities, without a declaration by the other." As a result, Hamilton said, Tripoli's declaration allowed the President to take offensive as well as defen-sive measures.[21]

This, in fact, was what Jefferson's cabinet had advised and what Jefferson's orders to the fleet contemplated (unbeknownst to Hamilton).[22] As quoted above, Gallatin—advising Jefferson—and Madison, commenting on the episode later, argued in general terms that the President could fight wars begun by the other side, without limitation. And a few years later, as we have seen, framer Paterson's circuit court opinion agreed, saying that when a state of war exists due to an enemy attack, the President would have power not only to defend "but also to carry hostilities into the enemy's county." Al-though some modern commentary claims the Tripoli episode as evidence of limited presidential power in defensive war, in fact the weight of practice and opinion at that time seems to favor the opposite view.[23]

The President's Power to Act Short of War

The foregoing discussion underlines a broader principle: the declare-war clause gives Congress an exclusive but specific power over the decision to ini-tiate war (plus authority over letters of marque and reprisal, a specific form of non-war hostilities), but not an exclusive general power over the use of the military. Uses of force and other matters not included in declaring war or is-suing letters of marque are "executive" presidential powers. Again we may note the parallel with treaties: Congress has power to initiate war (Chapter 11), as the Senate has power to approve treaties (Chapter 7); but the Presi-dent has independent power over non-treaties (executive agreements, Chapter 9) and non-wars.

This conclusion might lead Presidents to suppose that only some conflicts amount to "war" (in the constitutional sense), and thus that Congress's power embraces much less than the full range of hostilities. Perhaps the term "war" applies only to conflicts where war is formally declared, or to those the United States officially calls a war (so that if the conflict in, say, Korea in the 1950s was called a "police action,"[24] congressional approval might be unneeded). Or, more plausibly, perhaps "war" means only broad conflicts in which each nation fully engages the other (so that, for example, the limited U.S. bombing campaign against Yugoslavia in 1999, or the planned 1994 intervention in Haiti, might not rise to the level of war).[25]

A key inquiry, then, is the eighteenth-century definition of "war." Whether Congress's power to initiate war amounts to near-complete control over the use of military force depends in large part upon the scope of that term. Contrary to some presidential claims, eighteenth-century sources show that "war" had a broad meaning, encompassing most sovereign uses of force against another sovereign or quasi-sovereign entity. According to Johnson's 1755 dictionary, "war may be defined as the exercise of violence under sovereign command."[26] Thomas Rutherforth similarly wrote in 1754: "War is a contention by force." In treatise-writer Richard Lee's words (1760), "war is the state or situation of those . . . who dispute by force of arms." European writers also spoke broadly. Bynkershoek defined war as "a contest of independent persons carried on by force or fraud for the sake of asserting their rights." For Vattel, "[W]ar is that state in which we prosecute our rights by force. . . . Public war is that which takes place between Nations or sovereigns, which is carried on in the name of the public authority, and by its order." Burlamaqui called war "the state of those, who try to determine their differences by the ways of force," and Wolff said it is war "if one enters into violent contest with another." Thus by "war" eighteenth-century writers apparently meant any violent conflict, with the usual connotation of sovereign approval.[27]

Moreover, eighteenth-century writers explicitly recognized the idea of limited war. Burlamaqui said that "we may also distinguish [wars] into *perfect* and *imperfect*. A perfect war is that, which entirely interrupts the tranquillity of the state, and lays a foundation for all possible acts of hostility. An imperfect war, on the contrary, is that, which does not entirely interrupt the peace, but only in certain particulars, the public tranquillity being in other respects undisturbed."[28] In this case the theorists reflected eighteenth-century reality. Limited conflicts and conflicts begun without formal declaration were common, yet both were called wars.[29] The core idea was a sovereign resolving its disputes by force. That the force was not formally announced, was limited in scope, or was given some other name by the sovereign would not alter that description. This definition is also consistent with post-ratification writing, which called the late-1790s limited naval conflict with France a "war," albeit often an "undeclared" or "imperfect" war.[30] As a result, there is little historical basis for claims that small conflicts are not really wars within the meaning of the declare-war clause.

Nonetheless, the historical definition leaves the President considerable independent power. Without attempting to list all ways the President might act in the shadow of the war power short of exercising power constitutionally conveyed to Congress, the range may be suggested by considering a few prominent categories and examples.

The President surely may direct the movements of the military in ways that do not attack another sovereign's territory or armed forces. This leaves many controversial deployments within the President's power. A peacekeeping mission approved by the relevant territorial sovereign or sovereigns, for example, would not be a declaration of war against anyone.[31] Further, military incursions, even without the territorial sovereign's consent, do not declare war (in the eighteenth-century sense) if they are not targeted against the territorial sovereign and the territorial sovereign does not oppose them.[32] Relatedly, the President's commonly asserted power to rescue U.S. citizens abroad (at least where the menace does not come from the foreign sovereign) does not involve use of force directed at a foreign sovereign and thus does not declare war. And military deployments that appear hostile or threatening to another sovereign also do not declare war; eighteenth-century writers were clear that mere threats do not begin wars (indeed, some writers argued that threats were not even just causes of war).[33]

The latter conclusion seems to leave the President with substantial ability to provoke war. In a well-known example, President James Polk dispatched U.S. troops into territory disputed between the United States and Mexico in 1846, leading to a Mexican attack on those troops and Polk's claim that Mexico had declared war. Some U.S. congressmen objected on constitutional grounds; the House—with the support of then-congressman Abraham Lincoln—later described the war as "unconstitutionally begun."[34]

Although we need not resolve the specific question here, our framework makes the war's constitutionality somewhat more manageable. The question is whether Polk's actions declared war. If not, Polk was on firm ground in claiming executive power to direct military deployment.

Ordinarily, military deployments—even threatening ones—would not create a state of war. Thus if Polk had deployed U.S. forces in a threatening manner along the Mexican border in unambiguously American territory, that would have been within Polk's constitutional power. If Polk had ordered an invasion of Mexico, that would have been an unconstitutional presidential declaration of war. The difficulty arises because the case lies in the middle—Polk directed occupation of disputed territory. The right question, therefore, is not whether the deployment was provocative (surely it was, but that does not matter), or even whether it violated international law, but whether it counted as a declaration of war.

From these examples, we may conclude that the President has considerable latitude to provoke war. Many acts may cause another nation to go to war against the United States, including insults, threats, and incursions short of war. Eighteenth-century writers distinguished between acts giving just cause for war and acts creating the state of war. The declare-war clause assigns only the latter to Congress. To the extent the others are executive powers, the President may undertake them (even if the likely result is a declaration of war by the other side, which in turn entitles the President independently to fight unlimited "defensive" war).

It is important to keep in mind, though, that the declare-war clause is not the only constitutional protection (and perhaps not even the primary constitutional protection) against presidential military excesses. In particular, as early Americans knew from English experience (see Chapter 5), appropriations power is a powerful check on executive war ambitions, for wars cannot be fought without money. Had Congress wished, for example, to limit Polk to defensive operations against Mexico, it could have made appropriations limited to that purpose. Instead, Congress voted money for two major offensive expeditions, with the result that all material fighting after the initial battles occurred in Mexican territory, fully funded by Congress. The problem for the war's opponents was that Congress generally supported the war, not that checks were lacking.[35]

The President's Use of Force in War

Once Congress declares war, the President's strategic and tactical control of war-making is an obvious consequence of the textual framework we have been developing. Although it has been called "an implied power,"[36] textually it arises from the President's executive power, as delegate Rufus King said at the Convention.[37] Military command was a traditional executive function,[38] and is not part of the declare-war power (which is only about *beginning* hostilities); once hostilities begin, the President can exercise executive powers without the need for further congressional authorization. In this sense Congress's declaration of war (or an opposing nation's declaration) does not so much authorize the President's wartime power as remove a barrier to its exercise: that the President's military power cannot be used to initiate war.

Nonetheless, we must be careful lest this power be stretched too far. In Chapter 5 we concluded that the President's executive power to conduct war does not extend to seizing steel mills within the United States to supply the war effort. Similarly, in *Brown v. United States* (1814), Chief Justice Marshall concluded that the President could not seize an enemy alien's property in the United States without Congress's authorization, even in support of a formally declared war.[39] How can these conclusions be reconciled with the broad statement that the President has executive power to "conduct" war? Answering this question requires careful phrasing of presidential authority: the President has authority to conduct war *to the extent of the executive power.* The President cannot take *every* action that furthers the war effort; the President can exercise any *executive* power to further the war effort (unless the text gives it to another branch). Truman lacked textual authority to seize the mills, although that was part of conducting the war, because domestic wartime seizure was not an "executive" act in eighteenth-century terms. By parallel reasoning, the President cannot unilaterally make treaties, attack neutral countries, or rule by decree—even when these acts support the war effort—either because they are not traditional executive acts or because the text assigns them to other branches. The President must show, not merely that an action is taken in the course of war, but that it is part of the "executive Power" described in Chapters 3–5.

As those chapters indicate, in England the executive/monarch alone usually could not make domestic law (that is, alter rights and duties within the English legal system) but depended on Parliament. The English monarch had substantial independent authority to act internationally, and political writers described "executive" foreign affairs power as power to conduct the nation with respect to foreigners outside the nation. War did not materially alter this division of power. Of course, the existence of war in itself might make some acts illegal that had previously been legal (such as trading with the enemy), and the executive power could enforce those new rules once war began. But war did not invest the executive power with domestic lawmaking power.

Marshall's decision in *Brown* rested substantially on this proposition. As Justice Story's dissent pointed out, there was not much doubt that the President had executive power to seize enemy property outside the nation during wartime. But the existence of war would not allow the President to seize citizens' property in the United States (as the Court later concluded in *Steel Seizure*). *Brown* was more difficult because it involved enemy alien property located in U.S. territory. Marshall argued that the war's outbreak did not *automatically* cause enemy aliens to forfeit their property in the United States (a proposition Story disputed). If Marshall was right on this point, the rest of his conclusion seemed to follow from the historical idea of executive power: seizing the property—especially, as occurred in *Brown*, through the forfeiture procedures of domestic law—needed to rest on legislative authorization beyond approval of the war; otherwise it would amount to executive lawmaking.[40]

Congress's War Powers

Delegating War Powers

Having marked out categories of presidential war-related powers, we may now examine how Congress may augment or limit them. Congress can, of course, initiate a state of war ("declare war") (Chapter 11), and doing so in general terms opens the way for the President's wartime executive powers described above, allowing the President to use military force against nations with which the United States was previously at peace. Under this (somewhat oversimplified) model, Congress decides for or against war, and the President "executes" that decision by fighting the war.[41] This division reflects themes that were surely present in founding-era thought: that war's deliberative elements should be allocated to Congress and its active elements to the President.

In practice, though, it is often not so simple. Modern Congresses, rather than declaring war themselves, have authorized the President to commence hostilities. This happened explicitly with respect to Iraq in 2002, Afghanistan in 2001, and Iraq in 1991. More controversially, Congress appeared to authorize the 1999 bombing of Yugoslavia by approving funding for it and to authorize the Vietnam War by the open-ended Gulf of Tonkin resolution in 1964.[42] Most modern commentators accept these authorizations, with some dispute over how specific and how formal they must be.[43]

Textually this practice requires more explanation than is usually given for it. Congress's authorizations typically allow but do not require military action, in the President's discretion. They are not, then, declarations of war, because they do not create a state of war (for example, Congress authorized the President to use force against Iraq in October 2002, but no state of war existed until the following March, when the President acted upon this authorization, and it would never have existed if the President had not acted). Although often not discussed in these terms, what actually happens in these circumstances is that Congress delegates to the President its power to declare war, authorizing the President (rather than Congress) to make the final decision for or against war.[44]

Are these delegations constitutionally permissible? In domestic constitutional law, Congress's power to delegate its authority to the President is widely debated, with no consensus on the correct textual or historical answer.[45] As we have seen (Chapter 1), the Supreme Court earlier took a restrictive view of Congress's power in domestic matters, which it relaxed in foreign affairs—for dubious reasons—in the *Curtiss-Wright* case. (*Curtiss-Wright*'s delegation of embargo power, it may be noted, parallels Congress's typical "authorization" of war-declaring power, as seen for example in the 2002 Iraq resolution). The modern Court has substantially limited its earlier cases, so that even in domestic law it says it will uphold delegations that provide an "intelligible principle" guiding the President's decision (which most modern war-declaration delegations would satisfy).

The question of war-declaration delegations is sufficiently complex and bound up with broader questions of domestic law that we may be excused for not reaching a definitive conclusion. But two points can be highlighted. The first is that where Congress has authorized the President to begin war at the President's discretion, the question is properly seen as a delegation question, not one of war powers *per se*. The second is that this is by no means a new question. Delegations of war power (and objections to them) date to the early post-ratification period. One representative argued in 1798 that delegating war-declaration authority to the President "would at once appear so outrageous, that it would meet with immediate opposition"; yet the series of statutes Congress passed in 1798 approving the naval war with France broadly authorized but did not require the President to take military action.[46] In subsequent cases, the Supreme Court saw no constitutional problem with any of them. Marshall's comment in *Talbot v. Seeman* (1801), discussed in Chapter 11, that Congress had the "whole powers of war" was made in reference to one of these authorizing statutes.[47] In 1815, facing renewed tensions with the "Barbary" powers, President Madison asked Congress to formally declare war against Algiers, and Congress instead authorized

Madison to use force as he thought appropriate.[48] While some objections to delegations were made, including in the foreign affairs field, the weight of opinion and practice in the early period seems to favor permitting these (fairly specific) delegations.[49]

Congressional Limits on Presidential Wartime Powers

We now come to the most contested part of the picture. Often Congress may not want to exercise a simple binary choice for or against war (or delegate it to the President) but instead may wish to control where and how war is fought. Presidents may regard this as an infringement of their constitutional powers. One scholar writes that the President has "the Commander-in-Chief power to conduct war: the power to 'execute,' as it were, any authorized war; the power to decide whether, when, and how to employ the Nation's armed force in carrying out Congress' authorization to use such force; and the power to decide when to cease such use of force. . . . Congress does not possess any of these executive war powers."[50] Or as Bush administration lawyers contended, even more pointedly, in 2002:

> Any effort by Congress to regulate the interrogation of battlefield combatants would violate the Constitution's sole vesting of the Commander-in-Chief authority in the President. . . . Just as statutes that order the President to conduct warfare in a certain manner or for specific goals would be unconstitutional, so too are laws that seek to prevent the President from gaining the intelligence he believes necessary to prevent attacks upon the United States.[51]

These conclusions seem to ignore important textual powers of Congress. To begin, the President depends on Congress to fund executive wartime activity, under Article I, Section 9's commitment of appropriations power to Congress. As discussed in Chapter 5, Congress has no constitutional obligation to fund executive activities, and may fund them selectively. There seems little reason to think military activities are any different than, say, diplomatic activities in this regard. Thus military appropriations limited to, say, certain "specific goals," or which in effect "decide when to cease [the] use of force" (to take two examples posited above), seem well within Congress's powers. As with diplomatic power, nothing in the text says that Congress cannot restrict, in fairly specific terms, how its money is spent. And presumably Congress's necessary-and-proper power allows it to make regulations that enforce limits it makes upon its appropriations. It is true, of course, that Congress cannot make affirmative directions through appropriations—it can only prevent things from happening—but for the most part that is what is at stake in these debates. It is true also that appropriations limits may not be able to prevent the President *personally* from taking certain actions (as we saw with respect to diplomatic activities); but especially in military matters, personal action seems most unlikely. Battlefield interrogations, for example, will be done by the President's military, and that military depends for its existence on funds from Congress; there seems no textual basis for preventing Congress from directing that no money is to be spent on certain types of interrogations (or, for that matter, that no money is to be spent on interrogations of any sort). Of course, Congress often does make its military appropriations in very broad terms, for sound strategic reasons, but that does not mean it cannot act more specifically.

Further, by Article I, Section 8 Congress has power "[t]o make Rules for the Government and Regulation of the land and naval Forces" (as well as the power to raise and support armies and make rules regarding captures). As a result, Congress has, if anything, *greater* textual power to regulate military personnel directly than it does for other executive branch personnel. It seems quite difficult to see how a general regulation that (for example) military personnel must refrain from certain interrogation tactics is not a "Rule for the . . . Regulation" of the armed forces.

Although executive branch arguments in this area appear surprisingly underdeveloped (especially given the stakes), their thrust seems to be that Congress cannot regulate contrary to the President's wishes without infringing the President's position as commander-in-chief. (The executive power clause—covering, as discussed, only matters not allocated elsewhere—could not give the President powers conflicting with those textually assigned to Congress.) It is far from clear, though, that the President's position as commander-in-chief amounts to an immunity from military regulation that overrides the government-and-regulation clause. It is true that the commander-in-chief clause likely gives the President concurrent power over military regulation. Without it, the government-and-regulation clause might appear to deny the President any lawmaking power over the military that would otherwise arise from Article II, Section 1. Article II, Section 2 clarifies that the President may direct the military *in the absence of* congressional regulation (as the nineteenth-century Supreme Court rightly held).[52]

Further, the commander-in-chief clause shows that Congress cannot assign ultimate command responsibilities to someone other than the President, either as part of the government-and-regulation power or as part of an appropriation. As we found in Chapter 5, Congress need not fund diplomatic activities, but to the extent it does, they must be carried out by (or under the direction of) the President (since all "executive Power shall be vested" in the President). Similarly, Congress need not fund an army, but if it does, the commander-in-chief clause ensures that it must be commanded by the President and not someone else. This aspect of the clause responds to troubles in the Revolutionary War, when it was often unclear who was the supreme military commander, with different generals—Washington, Henry Lee, Horatio Gates—operating independently or in competition, and when the Congress sent committees to oversee Washington's military operations.[53] As Hamilton wrote in *The Federalist,* the conduct of war demands a single commander, a point he thought "so evident in itself and . . . at the same time so consonant to the precedence of the State constitutions in general, that little need be said" to defend it.[54] But that is different from saying that the military should be immune from congressional regulation.

A third likely consequence, accepted even by many commentators not sympathetic to presidential claims in this area, is that Congress cannot take tactical command of military operations. Congress's "regulations" (it is said) must be generalized standards of conduct, not tactical directions addressed to specific command situations. Such a division of command reconciles the government-and-regulation power with the President's status as commander-in-chief—but leaves regulation of military conduct during war a concurrent congressional and presidential authority.

These meanings demonstrate important roles for the commander-in-chief clause. It seems doubtful that it could be read much more broadly without rendering the government-and-regulation clause largely superfluous: if Congress cannot regulate the military contrary to the President's wishes, what would be the point of the clause (given that the President can regulate in the absence of congressional action)? In addition, it seems likely that the Constitution's chief remedy for congressional overreaching against the President is the President's veto. Hamilton in Federalist No. 73 defended the veto as a "shield for the executive" against the "propensity of the legislative department to intrude upon the rights, and to absorb the powers, of the other departments. . . ."[55] We can easily imagine that the drafters expected the veto to prevent Congress from taking control of the military through too-intrusive regulation.

In any event, presidential advocates would need much more than text alone to convince us that the text goes further in establishing presidential immunity from regulation in this area. There is little else in their favor, though, and post-ratification evidence points in the opposite direction. Early Congresses did often regulate the military, beginning with re-enactment of the Confederation's Articles of War in 1790.[56] During the naval war with France, Congress authorized President Adams to conduct hostilities through a series of highly specific statutes approving particular limited offensive actions.[57] The law at issue in *Little v. Barreme* (1801), for example, bizarrely authorized the President to seize ships bound *to* (but not from) French ports. Adams sensibly told his navy to seize ships coming *from* French ports as well (since one could not easily tell where ships were going *to* until they arrived). *Little* was a challenge to Adams's order, and Chief Justice Marshall, reading the statute literally, found a "from" seizure directed by Adams to be illegal. Leaving aside the question whether the President could order such seizures without authorization, Marshall found that the statute allowing "to" seizures implicitly prohibited "from" seizures. He seemed unconcerned that this might infringe the President's commander-in-chief power.[58] We might say, perhaps, that these events are too far from ratification to be conclusive, but it seems especially suggestive that presidential advocates have not been able to point to any sustained founding-era arguments contending that Congress could not regulate military operations by statute. Combined with the appropriations power—which had been used to give Parliament a role in military decisionmaking far back into English history—there seems little basis for presidential claims of exclusivity.

Conclusion

In sum, Congress has power to initiate a state of war (Chapter 11), but this power does not extend as far as modern advocates of congressional war power would have it. Once eighteenth-century war began by one side's actions or words, a state of war existed and required no declaration by the other side to sustain it. Accordingly, carrying on war begun by another nation is not part of the declare-war power. It therefore remains part of the President's executive power. A portion of this power is commonly recognized in the President's conceded ability to "repel sudden attacks," but the President's textual power is considerably broader, extending to carrying hostilities into the enemy's own country in response to an attack. In addition, taking potentially provocative actions that might incite another nation into war with the United States is not part of the declare-war power. Insults, threats, hostile military deployments, and so forth, might have been just causes of war in eighteenth-century terms, but they were not seen as actions "declaring" war. They are not, then, part of Congress's declare-war power and instead fall to the President under the executive diplomatic and military powers. As a result, although the President cannot strike the first blow, the President has broad power to respond to a blow struck by the other side, and broad power to incite the striking of such a blow.

These presidential powers are, however, limited by important congressional powers. The declare-war clause is not the sole check (or, perhaps, even the most important check) on presidential ambitions, for Congress retains appropriations power (and, in extreme cases, impeachment power). Even a weaker version of these powers allowed eighteenth-century English Parliaments to claim a substantial role in war-making decisions, despite the English monarch's power to declare war. Further, the Constitution gave Congress substantial regulatory powers in military affairs, allowing Congress to govern the general conduct of the military. Yet these powers in turn are balanced by the President's commander-in-chief power, which first restores to the President regulatory authority in the absence of Congress's action and second assures that Congress—despite its regulatory authority—cannot take direct command of the military. In this way, the Constitution's text produces complex layers of checks and balances in war powers, rather than entrusting war wholly to a single branch.

V

States and Foreign Affairs

13

Can States Have Foreign Policies? *Zschernig v. Miller* and the Limits of Framers' Intent

This chapter begins consideration of the role state and local governments play in the foreign affairs of the United States. Specifically, it asks whether the Constitution permits these governments to establish their own foreign policies.

Readers will be forgiven for expecting a short chapter. After all, federalism's core theory is that matters of local concern should be decided at the local level, and the national government should address matters with national implications.[1] Whatever one's views on how this abstract theory should reduce to practice, it is hard not to conclude that foreign affairs—above almost all other matters—are fundamentally national in implication. Perhaps no one felt this as keenly as the Constitution's drafters, who suffered through the dysfunctions of the Articles; a chief complaint was that the Articles gave states too much foreign affairs power, obstructing national unity needed in dealing with other nations (see Chapter 2).

What, then, to make of state and local ventures into foreign policy?[2] Despite federalism's intuitions, they are not as rare as might be supposed. In 1996, for example, Massachusetts adopted a law penalizing companies doing business in Burma (Myanmar), in response to the human rights record of that nation's military regime. Other local jurisdictions have adopted or proposed similar measures targeting the perceived misdeeds of, among others, Indonesia, Pakistan, Switzerland, Nigeria, and, earlier, South Africa, Northern Ireland, and the Soviet Union. Moreover, local laws of general application may raise international issues—intentionally or not—when imposed upon foreign nationals or governments, or when they conflict with a foreign nation's public policies.[3] As we saw in Chapter 2, for example, a key foreign policy problem for the newly independent United States was the way states, especially Virginia, treated foreign citizens (especially British creditors).

Of course, some state ventures into international affairs would manifestly violate the Constitution's text. Article I, Section 10 lists specific foreign affairs powers the states may not exercise; and state actions are generally unconstitutional if they conflict with federal laws and treaties (see Chapters 14–15).[4] This chapter considers state foreign affairs activities neither specifically excluded by the Constitution's text nor directly conflicting with the national government's policies. Addressing precisely this question, the U.S. Supreme Court in *Zschernig v. Miller* (1968) invalidated an Oregon law that, it said, was "an intrusion by the State into the field of foreign affairs which the Constitution entrusts to the President and the Congress," even though Oregon's law did not conflict with Article I, Section 10 or any particular national policy.[5]

The Court did not claim any constitutional text to support its conclusion, nor has any subsequent case or commentary. This chapter concludes that there is none. Nor is it clear that eighteenth-century Americans shared a background understanding in this regard so fundamental that it could establish a constitutional rule in the absence of text. It is true that some key framers declared or implied in general terms the need for national unity in foreign affairs, and these statements have gained interpretive priority almost as if they were written into the text. But they were not—and to an interpretive theory based on text, that should be conclusive.

Zschernig v. Miller and the Case against the States

Zschernig arose because Oregon, and several other states, tried to fight the Cold War. Among other things, Oregon's law denied inheritance rights to citizens of countries where inherited property might be confiscated—in effect, communist countries. This was, at least, a negative comment on the communist system of property rights, and some saw it as a "wartime" measure preventing resources from accruing to the enemy. It was one of several similar state laws, some of which inspired inflammatory rhetoric by state judges against the evils of communism, and communist nations had complained to the U.S. government about them.[6]

Oswald Zschernig, an East German citizen and heir to property in Oregon, challenged Oregon's law. As the U.S. Supreme Court said, the law was surely an "intrusion" by Oregon into Cold War politics. But was it unconstitutional? No federal law applied, and the Justices decided that the only related treaty did not address the matter. Neither Article I, Section 10 nor any other specific constitutional provision excluded Oregon's action, and regulation of inheritance (including to foreign heirs) had long been a matter of state law. The U.S. government acknowledged that the law did not "unduly interfere[ ] with the United States' conduct of foreign relations."[7]

Justice William Douglas, writing for the Court, found Oregon's law unconstitutional, over objections by Justices Harlan and White. He spent most of the opinion arguing that the law materially implicated foreign affairs. Apparently Douglas thought it obvious that once he established this proposition, the law could not stand: "The several States, of course, have traditionally regulated the descent and distribution of estates. But those regulations must give way if they impair the effective exercise of the Nation's foreign policy." He did not say *why* they "must give way," though, nor point to any constitutional provision accomplishing this result.[8]

Although Douglas did not provide much explanation, *Zschernig's* result presumably arises from long-standing structural intuitions about the policy imperatives of federalism. In *Chy Lung v. Freeman* (1875), for example, the Court invalidated a California law that, responding to unwanted Chinese immigration, established a state Commissioner of Immigration who could require a bond to admit supposedly undesirable immigrants (meaning, in effect, Chinese). The statute was arguably invalid under the so-called dormant commerce clause doctrine, discussed later in this chapter, but Justice Samuel Miller, writing for the Court, seemed to have a larger principle in mind:

[A] silly, an obstinate, or a wicked [state] commissioner may bring disgrace upon the whole country, the enmity of a powerful nation, or the loss of an equally powerful friend. . . . [I]f this plaintiff and her twenty companions had been subjects of the Queen of Great Britain, can any one doubt that this matter would have been the subject of international inquiry, if not a direct claim for redress? Upon whom would such a claim be made? Not upon the State of California; for, by our Constitution, she can have no exterior relations with other nations. It would be made upon the government of the United States. If that government should get into a difficulty which would lead to war, or to suspension of intercourse, would California alone suffer, or all the Union? If we should conclude that a pecuniary indemnity was proper as a satisfaction for the injury, would California pay it, or the Federal government? If that government has forbidden the States to hold negotiations with any foreign nations, or to declare war, and has taken the whole subject of these relations upon herself, has the Constitution, which provides for this, done so foolish a thing as to leave it in the power of the States to pass laws whose enforcement renders the general government liable to just reclamations which it must answer, while it does not prohibit to the States the acts for which it is held responsible?

The Constitution of the United States is no such instrument. . . . If it be otherwise, a single State can, at her pleasure, embroil us in disastrous quarrels with other nations.[9]

This is very near to saying that the nature of the U.S. federal system requires that, at least with respect to matters likely to give offense to foreign nations, states lack power to pass laws with international implications. As the Court added a decade later in *Chae Chan Ping v. United States:*

The control of local matters being left to local authorities, and national matters being entrusted to the government of the Union, the problem of free institutions existing over a widely extended country . . . has been happily solved. For local interests the several states of the Union exist, but for national purposes, embracing our relations with foreign nations, we are but one people, one nation, one power.[10]

And it repeated in *Hines v. Davidowitz* (1941), a case *Zschernig* heavily cited:

The federal government . . . is entrusted with full and exclusive responsibility for the conduct of affairs with foreign sovereignties. . . . Our system of government is such that the interests of the cities, counties and states, no less than the interest of the people of the whole nation, imperatively requires that federal power in the field affecting foreign relations be left entirely free from local interference.[11]

None of these opinions invoked specific constitutional text to support their broad generalizations. Rather, they rest upon what one scholar later called "the logic of the federal system."[12] Simply as a matter of common sense, it seems, the federal government, not the states, should conduct foreign relations, because otherwise one state could create international troubles that would affect the whole nation.

It seems clear that this thinking underlay Douglas's *Zschernig* opinion, even if he did not exactly say so. But *Zschernig* was crucially different from its predecessors. It is one thing to say that, as a general matter, foreign policy decisions are best made at the national level; it is another to show how, in a particular case, the Constitution accomplishes that result. In *Hines*, for example, the specific answer was clear: the state law conflicted with a federal statute and so was displaced by the Constitution's Article VI, as Justice Black's opinion for the Court emphasized.[13] In *Zschernig* there was no conflicting statute, but Douglas allowed the structural intuition to carry him to the same result, even though he could not say how the Constitution produced it.[14]

Subsequent events have delivered a mixed verdict on *Zschernig*. The Court has not used it to strike down any state law since 1968, and courts of appeal have stayed fairly well clear of it as well. Academic commentary has criticized its lack of reasoning, and Professor Henkin suggests it might be merely a "relic of the Cold War."[15]

Yet its intuition retains a powerful hold, and something like *Zschernig*'s rule has been defended by a wide array of legal writers.[16] Following Justice Miller in *Chy Lung*, most accounts urge that any system permitting state "intrusions" into foreign affairs would (like the Articles) have unmanageable structural problems. States lack the national government's expertise in foreign affairs. Even where the national government has not yet adopted a policy, states' fragmented voices may convey confusion and weakness, preventing the nation as a whole from taking coherent positions.[17] And policies popular in some states may be injurious to others, or to the nation as a whole, as Miller emphasized in *Chy Lung*. "[C]arrying parochial concerns to the international stage," one commentary argues, "could have repercussions well beyond the localities themselves. No harm is done when Boston's large population of Irish politicians gathers to sing Irish songs on St. Patrick's day; there may be harm done, however, if Boston is allowed to instigate a skirmish with the United Kingdom over Northern Ireland in which the rest of the country is not inclined to participate."[18]

Much of this, to be clear, is based purely on policy: to pursue unified goals and avoid conflicting signals to foreign nations, a federal system *should* concentrate foreign affairs power in the national government. But, it is said, it is a policy implicit within the Constitution's structure. As another commentary emphasizes:

> The constitutional architecture itself evinces a norm of federal exclusivity in foreign affairs, on the one hand granting expansive foreign relations powers to the federal government, on the other denying them to the states. . . . [A]gainst the landscape of foreign relations as they were conducted at the time of the Founding, the allocation seems decisively to have established a principle of federal exclusivity. War, trade, treaties, and the maintenance of diplomatic relations—arguably the foreign relations of the Founding era consisted of nothing else.[19]

Or, as a third puts it: "Exclusive federal authority over the conduct of foreign affairs is well established. The Constitution contains no single clause vesting exclusive authority over this area in the federal government. But the sum of its parts, considered in light of the constitutional structure, leaves little doubt in this regard."[20]

Even some commentators sympathetic to banishing states from foreign policy, though, have worried about the "absence of a more compelling constitutional foundation" for the doctrine.[21] As a result, appeals to the framers' intent play a key supporting role. "The states' cession of authority over foreign affairs to the central government was one of the foundational elements of the Constitution," one writer emphasizes, citing Madison's Federalist No. 42; another begins by noting that "[a] major purpose of the Constitution was to place control of foreign relations in the hands of the national Government."[22] The Articles' problems are of course a central feature here, as are statements by individual framers and the general impulse at the framing to place foreign affairs in the national government's hands.

These "intent" arguments unfortunately have little connection to the Constitution's text. (The closest anyone comes to text is a "norm" "evince[d]" by "constitutional architecture.") Many reduce to not much more than a simple proposition: as shown by the Articles' experience, excluding states from foreign affairs *would be a good idea*. At most, it is claimed to be a good idea that some framers shared—or would have shared had they thought about it. Perhaps so. For a textual interpretation of the Constitution, though, the question is whether and how that good idea made it into the Constitution's text.

States, Foreign Affairs, and the Constitution's Text

A textual evaluation begins with several points established in earlier chapters. First, the Tenth Amendment declares that matters not granted to the national government by the Constitution, nor denied by it to the states, are reserved to the states (or the people); there are no inherent national powers (Chapter 1) nor, conversely, are there inherent limitations on the states. Second, during the Articles period, states exercised considerable power in foreign affairs, including passing laws directly designed to influence the policies of foreign nations (Chapter 2). These powers, then, are "reserved" to the states unless something in the Constitution takes them away: the burden is on those who would deny state power to find something that does.

Relatedly, the Articles' experience shows it is not inconceivable for a federal system to give states considerable foreign affairs power. It may well be a bad idea, but it is the system the nation had prior to 1789. Of course, the nationally minded framers determined to change that system, but it was their starting point, and they had to find votes for change. And though the no-state-activities-in-foreign-affairs rule may be easily agreed upon in the abstract, its implementation is less simple. Despite loose talk to the contrary, there is no bright line between foreign affairs and domestic affairs. " 'Foreign affairs' are not autonomous; they are always 'about' something—trade, tariffs, land, shipping—and these are all things in which states can have considerable interest."[23] In any federal system, some entity will have to decide *which* state activities trench "too much" on foreign affairs. The broader that category is found to be, the more matters are taken from the states that states would like to (and perhaps should) decide.

It should be clear, then, that the Constitution might have modified the Articles in various ways, and to varying degrees, to enhance national authority in foreign affairs. Neither history nor policy provides inevitable results. The only way to see how the drafters changed the prior system is to examine what they actually did.

Article I, Section 10

An obvious way to stop state "intrusions" into foreign affairs is to list specifically things states cannot do. As Chapter 1 briefly examined, the Constitution's Article I, Section 10 prohibits states from entering into treaties and granting letters of marque, and, unless Congress approves, from taxing imports and exports, keeping armies or navies in peacetime, entering into non-treaty agreements with foreign powers, or engaging in war. These limits have some exceptions (states can engage in war if invaded or threatened with invasion), but the general effect is to exclude states from core aspects of foreign affairs: war and military matters, international agreements, and tariffs.

Many of these restrictions carried over directly from the Articles (which also, for example, excluded states from war and treatymaking); in some cases restrictions were tightened a little. The biggest new restriction was tariffs, which states had imposed under the Articles. But the restriction on state tariff laws points up the biggest category *not* included in Article I, Section 10: other state legislation affecting foreign affairs. As we have seen (Chapter 2), under the Articles states used an array of legislative activity to influence foreign affairs, including but not limited to tariffs. Yet tariffs are the only state foreign affairs legislation that Article I, Section 10 prohibits.

Standing alone, Article I, Section 10 surely does not generally bar state foreign affairs activity,[24] nor could it support Douglas's result in *Zschernig*. It also suggests that the Constitution as a whole imposes no general bar. If states are barred from foreign affairs activities by the "logic of the federal system," what is the point of Article I, Section 10? Whatever part of the Constitution kept Oregon from limiting East German inheritances in *Zschernig* should keep Oregon from, say, declaring war on or making treaties with East Germany. Chapter 1 concluded that Article I, Section 10 (and the framers' commentary upon it) argues against extra-constitutional limitations on state foreign affairs power; it stands equally against finding an unstated general limit elsewhere in the Constitution, or in constitutional "architecture."

We have also seen, though, that arguments from redundancy are not entirely conclusive. Perhaps the drafters did write a general prohibition into the Constitution, but added Article I, Section 10 to ensure that the most dangerous state practices would not occur even if future interpreters lost sight of the general rule. Moreover, if the drafters meant to change materially the national-state balance in foreign affairs, as is generally supposed,[25] Article I, Section 10 is not the way they did it: aside from tariffs, it makes no major change from the Articles (as Madison pointed out).[26] While keeping Article I, Section 10 in mind, we must turn to other parts of the Constitution.

Article VI

One might fairly say that, for national-state relations, the Constitution's Article VI is its single most important provision, and the single most important change from the Articles. Later chapters have much more to say about Article VI, but for now we may note that it establishes national supremacy over the states. As seen in Chapter 8, under Article VI federal statutes and treaties (and the Constitution itself) are part of the "supreme Law of the Land" and, as such, superior to state law. In modern terms, we say that federal statutes and treaties "preempt" (that is, override) state law as a result of Article VI.[27]

Article VI must be viewed in tandem with another huge change the Constitution wrought: expansion of federal legislative power. Recall that under the Articles the national government was mostly a diplomatic and military body, not a legislature (see Chapter 2). Hence it was called a "congress," an eighteenth-century word for meetings of diplomats. The new Constitution kept the word, but wholly recast its role: the new Congress was a lawmaking entity, like the British Parliament or the state legislatures (see Chapter 10). True, Article I, Section 8 limited Congress's authority to a designated set of powers, but even reading those powers narrowly the new Congress had immensely more legislative power than the old. Article VI assured that when Congress exercised that power, it displaced inconsistent state law.

To see the revolution Article VI produced in foreign affairs, consider two issues that bedevilled government under the Articles. First, the Articles' Congress could make treaties, but because it had no way to assure state compliance, treaties went unenforced, to the fury of treaty partners such as Britain. Second, the Articles' Congress lacked power to establish commercial policy toward foreign nations, both because it could not enact its own regulations and because it could not do anything about the jumble of conflicting state regulations. After 1789, these matters largely became non-issues. The new national government had power to make and enforce treaties and commercial regulations; Article VI assured that state activities would not conflict with them.[28]

Although Article VI says nothing directly about a general constitutional exclusion of states from foreign affairs, taken with Article I, Section 10 it shows the existence of a plausible alternative. These provisions together offer a solution to the problems of state involvement in foreign affairs without resort to a general constitutional exclusion. Article I, Section 10 excludes outright the most serious state interferences—separate wars, treaties, and tariffs. Under Article VI (combined with powers delegated to the national government in Articles I, II, and III), essentially any other state interference in foreign affairs can be displaced by conflicting federal statutes or treaties—with enforcement assured by federal courts.[29]

Of course, this system might not be *as effective* for foreign policy as a general preclusion. States still might provoke confrontations with foreign nations before Congress or the treatymakers could do anything to stop them. The burden of overcoming legislative or treatymaking inertia would lie with the national government instead of the states, and the system would err on the side of more frequent counterproductive state intrusions into foreign affairs. It would, though, be much more effective than the Articles.

And, as suggested above, there are considerations on the other side as well. Barring state "intrusions" into foreign affairs sounds attractive in theory, but is not easy to administer. Especially today, but even in the framers' time, intrusion into foreign affairs is a matter of degree. All state regulations of the activities of nationals and businesses of foreign countries, for example, likely have *some* potential effect on foreign affairs;[30] to hold foreigners immune from state regulation immensely curtails ordinary state power, and it is hard to believe that eighteenth-century Americans would have accepted such a rule. But if some entity must decide which state regulations are "too much" of an intrusion, that entity (presumably the courts) may also be slow and error-prone, at least as much as Congress.[31]

The point here is not to argue that one or the other system is better, as a practical matter. Rather, it is that a general constitutional exclusion is not the only way to approach the matter. One might choose a system in which states are generally barred unless Congress lets them act; a system in which states are generally empowered unless Congress bars them; or a system combining these two approaches. Any of these systems would be an improvement over the Articles (whose Congress was largely powerless to control the states). The question is which system the drafters chose. Looking at Article I, Section 10 and Article VI, it appears that they chose constitutionally to prohibit states from key areas and let Congress (or the treatymakers) decide elsewhere. Those who would argue otherwise must show some specific text or historical understanding in support—they cannot merely rely (as the Court has) on claims that the general exclusion would work better.

Here it is crucial to emphasize an overriding point, not disputed by even the warmest advocates of a general state preclusion: No provision of the Constitution, other than Article I, Section 10 and Article VI, in plain terms excludes state foreign affairs activity. As we shall see, that is not the end of the analysis, but it must weigh heavily against the general prohibition found in *Zschernig*.

State Power and the Framers' Intent

At this point we should, as in prior analyses, check our textual conclusions against what founding-era Americans said about the Constitution. Defenses of *Zschernig*-like rules strongly invoke the framers' beliefs in support. Closer examination, however, reveals this supposed support to be illusory, and in fact contemporaneous commentary is consistent with the textual analysis described above.

To begin, we may dismiss reliance on the general observation that the constitutional generation sought to replace the Articles with a structure more conducive to unified conduct of foreign affairs. This is undoubtedly true— not only of those who gathered in Philadelphia, but also of those who voted to ratify their product, and even of many anti-federalists. But with or without *Zschernig*, the Constitution far surpasses the Articles in this regard, for reasons discussed above. Any interpretation of the Constitution's text that left the national government not materially stronger in foreign affairs than it was under the Articles *would* be highly dubious, even if it otherwise seemed textually plausible. No such interpretation is proposed, however, and little additional mileage can be gained from the fact that the constitutional generation wanted more foreign affairs power at the national level.

Moreover, the Articles' specific international difficulties stemmed from weaknesses of the Congress, which lacked power to pass trade legislation and to enforce treaties and the law of nations. The national government was not supreme in foreign affairs—states could (and did) establish foreign policies *in competition with* the Congress. The drafters principally had this problem in mind; not surprisingly, the Constitution forcefully responds by enhancing legislative powers over international trade and the law of nations (Article I, Section 8) and making federal laws and treaties supreme over the states (Article VI). It is not obvious, though, that it did anything more. Its drafters were not immediately concerned with whether federal legislative supremacy in foreign affairs would be sufficient—they were concerned with establishing federal legislative supremacy in the first place, since it had not previously existed. Perhaps the framers thought that the preemptive effect of treaties and statutes (an enormous advance over the Articles) would be sufficient to establish an effective national government in foreign affairs; perhaps not. The general outlines of constitutional history do not answer this question. The fallacy of general appeals to the Constitution's "intent" (or "structure") is that federal supremacy—indisputably a constitutional goal—does not require a general constitutional preclusion of the states but can be accomplished through Article VI.

It is important to see that the question is not whether the federal government's foreign affairs powers are superior to those of the states. We assume, for present purposes, that they are (qualifications upon this principle are addressed in Chapters 14–15). The question here is whether states are precluded from foreign affairs where federal policy is *not* in conflict. The issue, in short, is not one of federal supremacy but of federal exclusivity. Observations showing founding-era Americans' general consensus that the national government should be supreme in foreign affairs—that is, fully empowered, as against the states, to conduct foreign policy—are beside the point.

But, it is said, the framers' specific statements show intent to establish national exclusivity in foreign affairs—or at least to establish the strongest national unity in foreign affairs (a goal requiring broad exclusion of the states). This line of argument requires closer attention, because if contemporaneous statements reveal a broad understanding that the national government would *exclusively* control matters touching foreign affairs, we would need to proceed quite cautiously before concluding the opposite. It turns out, though, that proponents of *Zschernig*-like rules simply have not established such an understanding.

Consider some of the supposed leading authorities. First, Madison in Federalist No. 42: "If we are to be one nation in any respect, it clearly ought to be in respect to other nations."[32] Even in isolation, this comment does not necessarily argue for any more than national supremacy in foreign affairs. The key question is *how* Madison thought we should become "one nation . . . in respect to other nations."

In context, Madison sought to justify granting specific foreign affairs powers *to* the federal government (saying nothing about the states). Federalist No. 42—examined in Chapter 1—is part of the series (Nos. 41–46) called "General View of the Powers Proposed to Be Vested in the Union." The purpose, Madison says, is "to review the several powers conferred on the government of the Union," which he groups into five categories. Federalist No. 41 discusses the first category, relating to war and military power. No. 42, containing the key quote, begins:

> The *second* class of powers lodged in the general government consist of those which regulate the intercourse with foreign nations, to wit: to make treaties; to send and receive ambassadors, other public ministers, and consuls; to define and punish piracies and felonies on the high seas, and offenses against the law of nations; to regulate foreign commerce. . . .

> This class of powers forms an obvious and essential branch of the federal administration. If we are to be one nation in any respect, it clearly ought to be in respect to other nations.[33]

The balance of Federalist No. 42 analyzes and defends each particular power described in the first paragraph. So the quotation is part of an argument for granting the national government a particularized list of powers. It does not discuss foreign affairs powers in general, for part of that subject falls under the first category (security) discussed in No. 41. Nor does it even discuss specific limits upon state power; that is Madison's fifth category, in Federalist No. 44. Madison was not saying anything about generalized bars against *Zschernig*-like "intrusions"—and in fact was not saying anything about the states.

Another commonly invoked quotation is from Hamilton's Federalist No. 80: "[T]he peace of the WHOLE ought not to be left at the disposal of a PART. The Union will undoubtedly be answerable to foreign powers for the conduct of its members."[34] Again, even in isolation it seems to do no more than argue for federal foreign affairs supremacy; it does not compel state preclusion. Context confirms that, like Madison in Federalist No. 42, Hamilton had something much different in mind. No. 80 is part of a series, beginning at No. 78, discussing the federal judiciary; it considers the judiciary's five "proper objects":

> 1st, to all those which arise out of the laws of the United States . . . ; 2nd, to all those which concern the execution of the provisions expressly contained in the articles of Union; 3rd, to all those in which the United States are a party; 4th, to all those which involve the PEACE of the CONFEDERACY, whether they relate to the intercourse between the United States and foreign nations or to that between the States themselves; 5th, to all those which originate on the high seas, and are of admiralty or maritime jurisdiction; and lastly, to all those in which the State tribunals cannot be supposed to be impartial and unbiased.

In working through each of these matters, Hamilton comes to the fourth category:

> The fourth point rests upon this plain proposition, that the PEACE of the whole ought not to be left at the disposal of a PART. The Union will undoubtedly be answerable to foreign powers for the conduct of its members. And the responsibility for an injury ought ever to be accompanied with the faculty of preventing it. As the denial or perversion of justice by the sentences of courts, as well as in any other manner, is with reason classed among the just causes of war, it will follow that the federal judiciary ought to have cognizance of all causes in which the citizens of other countries are concerned.[35]

Thus Hamilton was justifying something very specific: federal courts' jurisdiction over cases where one party was a foreign citizen (Article III, Section 2). This has nothing to do with a generalized foreign affairs power; it has nothing to do with *any* limit on the states, as state courts might have concurrent jurisdiction over such cases. Hamilton's only point was that federal courts should have this jurisdiction (even, he emphasized, where the issues were ones of state law) so that if state courts did not give justice to foreigners, federal courts could.

Using these quotes to support *Zschernig*-like limits upon states illustrates a common-enough ploy in legal rhetoric, but one that should not ultimately be at all persuasive. We are asked, in effect, to suppose that because Madison and Hamilton made these statements when thinking about issues unrelated to *Zschernig*-preclusion, they (and their audience) would necessarily have thought such preclusion was appropriate (had they thought about it). But this conclusion is pure speculation—and doubly so because both quotations are simply statements of policy, not interpretations of the Constitution. We have no way of knowing how Madison and Hamilton would have viewed the policy they articulated in an entirely distinct context, where different considerations applied.

The point can be amplified by another quotation from Madison: "It ought therefore to be effectually provided," he told the Convention, "that no part of the nation shall have it in its power to bring them [i.e., disputes with foreign nations] on the whole."[36] At first glance, this appears to support *Zschernig*-like preclusions. In context, though, Madison was defending not a constitutional preclusion, but a general power in Congress to "negative" (invalidate) state laws conflicting with national priorities. Thus Madison saw Congress as the bulwark against state interferences; moreover, the Convention voted his proposal down, preferring to insist that Congress act against state laws only within its enumerated powers, through Article I, Section 8 and Article VI.

A third key quotation is Jefferson's: it is "indispensably necessary that with respect to everything external we be one nation, firmly hooped together."[37] This is particularly problematic evidence, though not (as sometimes argued) because Jefferson was in Paris while the Constitution was drafted and ratified. As an articulate member of the constitutional generation, Jefferson is surely worth studying for evidence of constitutional meaning (as earlier chapters have done). But this statement is not an interpretation of the Constitution's text, or of words that it uses. It comes from a letter written before the Convention and does not use words or concepts later incorporated into the text. It states a structural philosophy at an abstract level, saying nothing about what measures Jefferson thought were required to assure that the nation be "firmly hooped together." Perhaps he thought the textual provisions the Constitution ultimately adopted were enough. And finally, even if we are to suppose from this quote that Jefferson favored a *Zschernig*-like preclusion (a dubious prospect, given Jefferson's subsequent defense of states' rights and distrust of the federal judiciary), there is no evidence, from this quote or otherwise, that Jefferson's views influenced anyone else.

As an argument from framers' intent, these quotes are quite weak. To be clear, these quotes do make it plausible that the constitutional generation *might* have endorsed federal exclusivity—but they are typically asked to do much more. A textual approach to constitutional meaning will embrace statements of the framers, and other founding-era Americans such as Jefferson, to show the meaning of constitutional words and phrases. But that is not what is being done here. It would be a different matter if individual framers such as Madison had said that states would be barred from activities implicating foreign affairs (and, especially, pointed to constitutional provisions in support). But neither Madison nor anyone else said such a thing; rather, we are asked to conclude, from statements generally suggesting the need for strong national control over foreign policy, that the Constitution picked a particular strategy to achieve that end, even though nothing in the Constitution itself *or in the statements of founding-era Americans* says anything about such a choice.

State Power and Negative Implications

A leading academic commentary concludes, in keeping with the foregoing analysis, that "the most natural inference" from the text "is that all foreign relations matters not excluded by Article I, Section 10 fall within the concurrent power of the state and federal governments until preempted by federal statute or treaty."[38] It is tempting to simply end on that note, but at least one important further consideration remains: the question of negative implications.

We have seen in earlier chapters that, even in the absence of explicit preclusions, grants of power to one entity can implicitly limit powers of another entity. For example, Chapter 11 concluded that granting Congress power "to declare War" (Article I, Section 8) implicitly limits the President's executive war power (Article II, Section 1). That is, Congress's declare-war power has the "negative implication" that the President *cannot* declare war, even though the Constitution does not say so in so many words.

In terms of federalism, this suggests that granting power to the national government may, by negative implication, take power from the states, even if state activity is not specifically prohibited by provisions such as Article I, Section 10. Of course, if the national government acts within its power, typically Article VI displaces conflicting state activity; but what if the national government does *not* act? If federal power exists (as a constitutional matter) but is unexercised (or, one might say, "dormant"), are states still excluded (so that no governmental activity occurs) or can states continue to act until the national government acts? Regrettably, the answer appears to be: sometimes one, sometimes the other.

The "Dormant" Commerce Clause

The most famous and contentious example of this conundrum in modern constitutional law is the so-called dormant commerce clause doctrine. Congress of course can regulate interstate and foreign commerce under Article I, Section 8, and federal statutes enacted through this power displace inconsistent state law under Article VI. Suppose, though, a state regulation of interstate commerce does not conflict with federal law but also is not authorized by federal law. Congress could regulate the area but has not. Is the state's law constitutional?

One possible answer is yes, so long as there is no state-federal conflict. Nothing in the Constitution says directly that states cannot regulate interstate commerce (Article VI only says they cannot regulate it inconsistently with Congress). Another answer is no, because the negative implication of giving Congress power to regulate interstate commerce is that states lack this power, even if Congress's power is unexercised (dormant) on the particular subject.

The dormant commerce clause doctrine is the Supreme Court's long and largely unsatisfying attempt to find middle ground between these two answers. In brief, its cases appear to say that states can regulate interstate commerce where Congress is silent, except in two significant circumstances: (1) where state regulation discriminates against out-of-state commerce, and (2) where the regulation's burdens on interstate commerce exceed local benefits.[39] The middle ground has much to recommend it as a practical matter, although perhaps not as a analytic matter, because complete embrace of the negative implication would be an enormous limit upon states' commercial powers, and complete rejection of the negative implication would open the way to all sorts of abusive state protectionism.

Resolving the dormant commerce clause question in terms of text and historical meaning might require its own book-length treatment, and no apologies are made for not attempting it here, even though it has obvious implications for state regulations of foreign commerce as well.[40] The more immediate question for foreign affairs, though, is whether similar arguments can be constructed for "dormant" exclusion of states from all or most foreign affairs matters not covered by the dormant commerce clause—since most of these matters are conveyed in some fashion to the national government.[41] The text, and contemporaneous commentary, does allow us to make some progress in answering this question.

Negative Implications and the Dormant Foreign Affairs Doctrine

To begin, it is clear that founding-era Americans accepted the general idea of negative implications. Hamilton, for example, argued that under the Constitution, "the State governments would clearly retain all the rights of sovereignty which they before had, and which were not by that act, *exclusively* delegated to the United States." Exclusive delegation would arise, he continued, not only from express federal exclusivity or express preclusion of the states, but also where the Constitution "granted an authority to the Union to which a similar authority in the States would be absolutely and totally *contradictory* and *repugnant*."[42] This general view appears to have been widely accepted; although founding-era Americans disagreed over when implied preclusion might arise, they seemed to agree that it could arise.[43]

The idea of implied preclusion underlies the conventional view of foreign policy preclusion, and its association with the dormant commerce clause theory is suggested by the modern use of "dormant foreign affairs power," or something similar, to refer to *Zschernig*-type limits. Of course, unlike the dormant commerce clause, nothing in the specific grants of power to Congress in Article I, Section 8 supports it. Although there are specific grants of particular foreign affairs powers, there is no grant of generalized foreign affairs power (and thus no dormant foreign affairs clause). Instead, as we have seen, national power in foreign affairs arises from an array of provisions, including the President's power under Article II, Sections 1–3, and Congress's power under the necessary-and-proper clause. Is it possible that the aggregation of these powers creates a "dormant" exclusion of the states? This seems to be what Justice Douglas meant in *Zschernig* when he said that the Constitution entrusted all foreign affairs power to the President and Congress— and thus, he implied, denied it to the states.[44]

Substantial evidence from text and contemporaneous interpretations indicates otherwise, however. First, as discussed, the state foreign affairs activities precluded by Article I, Section 10 would also be barred by the implied general exclusion (if one existed): in particular, war, treaties, and tariffs (the main Article I, Section 10 limitations) are surely barred by *Zschernig*. Apparently the drafters did not think that a negative implication against state power from, say, the treatymaking clause was an obvious, or even appropriate, reading of Article II, Section 2. Unless Article I, Section 10 is superfluous, presumably in its absence treatymaking power would be concurrent, with states able to make treaties absent contrary federal treaties or statutes. That is not absolutely conclusive: the drafters of the Constitution might have added the specific clauses of Article I, Section 10 in an excess of caution, to specify extreme cases, while also relying on a general exclusion covering more ordinary cases. Absolutely no commentary supports this view of Article I, Section 10, though; as discussed in Chapter 1, *The Federalist* describes Article I, Section 10 as an active limit on state power. And as also noted in Chapter 1, the foreign affairs powers denied in Article I, Section 10 are intertwined with denials of domestic powers, such as coining money, that plainly are not superfluous.

There is, moreover, evidence that the drafters would have hesitated to use Article I, Section 10 in redundant ways. As shown above, proponents of *Zschernig*-like limits must argue that bars on particular state foreign affairs powers in Article I, Section 10 are precautionary but ultimately superfluous in light of the general negative implication. However, in other contexts the drafters recognized what Hamilton called a "negative pregnant": denying specific state powers would likely confirm state power in related areas not specifically denied.

Hamilton made this point in Federalist No. 32, specifically with respect to Article I, Section 10. That Section denies states power to tax imports and exports. Anti-federalists claimed the Constitution denied states general taxing authority, by negative implication of Article I, Section 8, which gave Congress taxing power. Hamilton pointed out that such a general denial of taxing power would encompass import and export taxes, as well as other forms of taxes, and thus render superfluous Article I, Section 10's specific rule against import and export taxes. Hamilton thought this an untenable interpretation. Rather, he said, the "negative pregnant" of the import-export clause was that *other* state taxes were *not* precluded:

> This restriction [on taxing imports and exports] implies an admission that if it were not inserted the States would possess the power it excludes; and it implies a further admission that as to all other taxes, the authority of the States remains undiminished. In any other view it would be both unnecessary and dangerous; it would be unnecessary, because if the grant to the Union of the power of laying such duties implied the exclusion of the States . . . there could be no need of such a restriction; it would be dangerous, because the introduction of it leads directly to the conclusion which has been mentioned. . . . The restriction in ques-

tion amounts to what lawyers call a NEGATIVE PREGNANT—that is, a *negation* of one thing, and an *affirmance* of another; a negation of the authority of the States to impose taxes on imports and exports, and an affirmance of their authority to impose them on all other articles.[45]

The same argument can be posed against a generalized preclusion of state foreign affairs powers. As Article I, Section 10 denies states specific foreign affairs powers such as war and treatymaking, that implies that states retain other, non-specified foreign affairs powers—just as denying specific taxing powers such as tariffs implies that states retain other non-specified taxing powers. If the drafters thought there was general foreign affairs preclusion, surely they would have understood that including specific foreign affairs preclusions would undermine it, and so they would not have left the general rule to implication.

Federalist No. 32 also offers an approach to negative implications that resolves much of the dilemma they pose. As Hamilton put it, the Constitution should be read to deny power to the states "where it granted a power to the Union to which a similar authority in the States would be absolutely and totally *contradictory* and *repugnant*"—thus acknowledging the viability of argument by negative implication. He continued,

> I use these terms [i.e., "absolutely and totally contradictory and repugnant"] to distinguish this last case from another which might appear to resemble it, but which would, in fact, be essentially different; I mean where the exercise of a concurrent jurisdiction might be productive of occasional interferences in the policy of any branch of the administration but would not imply any direct contradiction or repugnancy in point of constitutional authority.[46]

The statement's context shows its relevance to *Zschernig* and confirms Hamilton's understanding of a high barrier for arguments from negative implication. As noted, Federalist No. 32 is Hamilton's response to antifederalist arguments that the Constitution denied states taxing power and thus would lead to destruction of the states from lack of revenue. Hamilton began with the point that nothing in the Constitution explicitly gave the national government an exclusive right of taxation; thus the issue turned on whether there was "repugnancy between the power of taxation in the States and in the Union." There was no repugnancy, Hamilton argued,

> in that sense which would be requisite to work an exclusion of the States. It is, indeed, possible that a tax might be laid on a particular ar-

ticle by a State which might render it *inexpedient* that a further tax should be laid on the same article by the Union; but it would not imply a constitutional inability to impose a further tax. . . . It is not, however, a mere possibility of inconvenience in the exercise of powers, but an immediate constitutional repugnancy that can by implication alienate and extinguish a pre-existing right of sovereignty.[47]

In sum, mere inconvenience or inexpediency to federal policy is insufficient to deny concurrent state power.

Foreign policy interference is analogous. Like taxation, foreign affairs power (as a general matter) is not specifically granted exclusively to the federal government nor specifically denied to the states. By Hamilton's reasoning, it would be denied to the states only in extreme cases of "repugnancy," not merely by inexpediency or inconvenience. The principal attacks on state foreign affairs power, though, seem based entirely on expediency and convenience. A *Zschernig*-type state law does not *prevent* the national government from establishing U.S. foreign policy; it only makes the job somewhat more difficult—for example, by irritating nations the national government would prefer not to irritate.

In contrast, the declare-war clause's negative implication probably does meet the standard Hamilton articulated. Power to declare war presumably includes power to decide on the declaration's timing, phrasing, and scope, as well as whether to issue one at all. If another entity (such as the President) had concurrent "declaring" power, Congress's power could be preempted by the other entity acting first: wars once declared are hard to un-declare. (And as discussed in Chapter 11, ratification and post-ratification commentary did seem to assume that the grant of declare-war power to Congress denied it to the President.)

As always, one must be cautious in taking Hamilton as representative of common views. Here, though, others took similar approaches to negative implications during the ratification debates. John Marshall told the Virginia convention: "The truth is, that when power is given to the General Legislature, if it was in the State Legislature before, both shall exercise it; unless there be an incompatibility in the exercise by one to that of the other; or negative words precluding the State Governments from it." At the same convention, George Nicholas said even more strongly:

The power of arming [the militia] is concurrent, between the General and State Governments. For the power of arming them rested in the State Governments before, and although the power be given to the

General Government, yet it is not given exclusively. For, in every instance, where the Constitution intends that the General Government shall exercise any power exclusively of the State Governments, words of exclusion are particularly inserted. Consequently in every case where such words of exclusion are not inserted, the power is concurrent to the State Governments and Congress, unless where it is impossible that the power should be exercised by both.[48]

These comments do indicate that there may be foreign affairs preclusions of the states by negative implication, but not the broad preclusion *Zschernig* claimed. It seems unlikely, for example, that states could speak on behalf of the United States (even where the President had not spoken) or send or receive ambassadors on behalf of the United States. By vesting the President with "the executive Power," the Constitution makes the President the nation's spokesperson in foreign affairs (see Chapter 3). It is true that the Constitution does not say, in so many words, that states cannot also speak for the nation. But plainly giving states this power would be, in Hamilton's phrase, "absolutely and totally contradictory and repugnant" to the President's role. Similarly, state reception of foreign ambassadors may be precluded by the President's power to receive (and, correspondingly, to not receive) ambassadors (Article II, Section 3). Because these points are narrow and self-evidently necessary, there likely was general agreement upon them. In contrast, broader "dormant" preclusions could cut deeply into powers states exercised under the Articles, such as regulating aliens. And exercise of these powers would not be totally repugnant to federal foreign affairs power. For example, if states regulated aliens in a way the national government disapproved, the national government could intervene by statute or treaty, and Article VI would assure that the national policy prevailed. State regulations would be at most inconvenient to the exercise of federal foreign policy—which Hamilton said was insufficient.

Drafting and Ratifying Debates

The drafting and ratification debates also tend to reject a broad negative implication in foreign affairs, albeit largely from silence. Particularly due to our incomplete records, we must be cautious about conclusions based upon silence, for it is possible that we are seeing only gaps in the record. Nonetheless, in conjunction with other evidence we have examined, it is suggestive that, so far as we know, no one in the drafting and ratifying debates, or in immediate post-ratification practice, embraced a *Zschernig*-like preclusion of states from foreign affairs.

The Convention records indicate that when delegates thought about state involvement in foreign affairs, they saw Article I, Section 10 and Article VI as the key provisions. Once they worked out the Constitution's basic outlines, including Congress's Article VI preemptive powers, they referred the draft to the Committee of Detail, whose report first introduced the idea of specific constitutional limits on the states: coining money, granting letters of marque, making treaties, and granting titles of nobility. In ensuing weeks, delegates debated whether other powers (including some foreign affairs powers) should be added to the list—including taxing exports, imposing embargoes, and imposing "tonnage duties" (shipping taxes).[49] The discussions reflect a belief that, if states were not denied particular powers in what became Article I, Section 10, the states would retain them unless preempted under Article VI or excluded by some other specific provision. No one suggested that a general constitutional preemption existed.

Madison, for example, proposed prohibiting state embargoes, as he thought states ought not to have this power. Others objected, arguing that states should have it: George Mason thought that reliance upon the states might be useful "as the Genl. Legislature would not sit constantly and there-fore could not interpose at the necessary moments."[50] This discussion was all nonsense if delegates contemplated some generalized constitutional method of restraining state foreign affairs activities, so it seems likely that someone would have pointed this out, particularly as states had previously exercised embargo power (see Chapter 2). Delegates inconclusively discussed whether state embargo power was precluded by Article I, Section 8's commerce power (what today we would call the dormant commerce clause). But no one mentioned foreign policy preclusion as a possible additional ground, de-spite the obvious importance of the point.

Like the Convention proceedings, the ratification debates offer little with respect to constitutional preclusions of state foreign affairs activities. This is remarkable because, as illustrated by the federalists' discussion of taxes men-tioned above, the ratifiers actively considered the issue of negative implica-tions limiting state power. In addition, the national government's preemi-nence in foreign affairs stood at the forefront of the debate, because federalists used the Articles' external weakness and the need for strong ex-ternal policy as reasons for supporting the Constitution. The ratifiers did dis-cuss, at length, the effect of Article VI upon state laws conflicting with na-tional foreign policy (see Chapter 14). However, there is no record of any material discussion of non-Article VI limitations upon state laws affecting foreign affairs, other than with respect to specific clauses such as those involving wars and treaties. True, silence would be natural if founding-era Americans did not contemplate much state foreign affairs activity.[51] This seems unlikely, though, as, among other matters, states regulated activities of foreign citizens within their borders, often creating tension with foreign nations. These laws would be placed at risk by a *Zschernig*-like rule, depending on how broadly it swept. Given the general paranoia anti-federalists displayed concerning ways the states might be swallowed by the national government, it is noteworthy that this one apparently did not occur to them.

Finally, there was no practice in the immediate post-ratification period (or, for the most part, at any time even in the nineteenth century) of finding "dormant" limits on state laws affecting foreign affairs.[52] The focus was on Article VI preemption and, to some extent, on the beginnings of the dormant commerce clause doctrine. For example, as discussed further in Chapter 14, in the continuing debate over state laws prejudicing British creditors and property owners the argument focused on treaty preemption, not on general interference with foreign affairs, although the state laws continued to disrupt relations with Britain. Justice Miller in *Chy Lung* cited nothing in support of his foreign affairs claims—and with good reason: almost ninety years after ratification, there was nothing to cite.[53]

Conclusion

In sum, *Zschernig*-type claims depend on a negative implication that the national government's foreign affairs powers are not merely supreme over the states, but exclusive of the states. Of course, some powers *are* exclusive, because Article I, Section 10 makes them so. And some other powers—the power to speak for the United States in foreign affairs, for example—presumably are exclusive by negative implication. But text and commentary stand against a broad preclusion of state foreign affairs power, particularly with respect to state laws having foreign affairs implications. The text shows that, in general, when the drafters wanted to make a power exclusive, they did so explicitly, and that the chief remedy for state laws interfering with foreign affairs was Article VI preemption; the commentary confirms that negative implications, although a permissible approach to legal interpretation, were reserved to more extreme circumstances.

We may still think, of course, that this is not the best system—that, as Justice Miller said, it is "foolish" to allow states to take actions that may give offense to foreign nations and to depend on Congress to police the states. But the drafters may well have been foolish (or, more charitably, they may have confronted opponents who would have been unlikely to submit to such broad restrictions on the states and such broad empowerment of the federal judiciary).

And one can make policy arguments for the alternative system. "Intrusion" into foreign affairs is a continuum; it is not easy to say when state laws go "too far" in affecting foreign nations. Courts may not be particularly good at making this assessment; perhaps leaving the matter to Congress and to the treatymakers is a better resolution.[54] In any event, it is hard to say that the drafters *could not* have chosen this approach, when the text, commentary, and implementation indicate that they did.

14

States versus the President: The *Holocaust Insurance* Case

The previous chapter shows that the Constitution's text denies states a few specific foreign affairs powers but leaves states much latitude to act in matters touching upon foreign affairs, especially in terms of enacting general legislation. As discussed, the idea was that, beyond the specified areas, the Constitution would empower the federal government's political branches to decide when state laws would need to give way to federal foreign policy (a power the national government lacked under the Articles). This chapter asks how the federal government can exercise its power to displace state laws affecting foreign relations.

To illustrate, consider a Supreme Court case from 2003: *American Insurance Association v. Garamendi,* the "Holocaust Insurance" case.[1] Various European insurance companies had supposedly failed to pay the beneficiaries of policies covering lives and property lost during the Holocaust. Many beneficiaries came to the United States after the war and continued to press for payment. The insurers claimed to lack evidence of who had owned what policies, and the beneficiaries, for obvious reasons, mostly lacked documentation as well. But in the late 1990s evidence began to mount that the companies knew more that they were telling. A number of states with large Holocaust survivor populations enacted statutes to assist claimants. California, whose law became the subject of the *Holocaust Insurance* case, required that, to do business in California, insurers that issued Holocaust-era policies (or their affiliates) had to disclose all information they had in their files about such policies.[2]

Although this disclosure would no doubt have been quite burdensome,[3] there is nothing odd about states requiring burdensome disclosures as a condition of doing business in the state. What made this law suspect from a foreign affairs perspective was that, alongside California's effort, the U.S. executive branch had begun negotiations with various European countries—Germany and Austria, in particular—to provide a comprehensive restitution settlement for Holocaust victims (including insurance claimants). The principal European governments, and the private industries involved, proved generally willing to reach a settlement, but they wanted protection from ongoing litigation and related regulatory action in the United States. In particular, the insurance companies objected to laws like California's.[4]

U.S. executive branch representatives asked California to suspend its law, due to the negative effects it might have on negotiations, but California refused. In the state's view, the executive branch negotiations were not producing settlements satisfactory to the insurance claimants, and additional leverage needed to be directed against the insurers. As the Supreme Court later characterized the matter, with perhaps some overstatement in each direction, the state wanted to use an "iron first" where the federal government preferred "kid gloves."[5]

The question, then, was what the federal government had to do to compel California to give way. We shall assume that California's law would have been constitutional had the federal government not been involved.[6] But the federal government *was* involved, and its involvement raised exactly the problems Americans had experienced under the Articles: before 1789, the national government (the Congress) would not have had any option aside from mere requests, which the states could ignore. We cannot doubt that the framers wanted to give their new national government power to control states' foreign affairs activities, and as we have seen in the previous chapter, they designed the Constitution's Article VI to give that power. What made the *Holocaust Insurance* case difficult was that the federal government did not use Article VI procedures. The question was whether that mattered. A closely divided Supreme Court said it did not, but, we will see, its decision is difficult to defend on textual grounds.

Ware v. Hylton and Article VI as the Arbiter of Federalism

As discussed in the previous chapter, the Constitution's Article VI powerfully enhanced national authority against the states, as compared with the Articles.[7] Most obviously, it allows Congress to pass laws relating to foreign affairs that override ("preempt")[8] state interferences with national policy, because national laws are the "supreme Law of the Land." In the case of Massachusetts's Burma law, also discussed in Chapter 13, the matter was made relatively easy by the fact that Congress had passed a related statute. It would have been easier still if Congress's statute specifically excluded states from penalizing companies doing business in Burma, which Congress surely could have done under its commerce power; but, as the Supreme Court found in *Crosby v. National Foreign Trade Council* (2000), the federal law implicitly excluded states, and that was sufficient to invoke Article VI.[9]

More controversially at the time of the drafting, Article VI also directed that treaties preempt contrary state law by including them (along with statutes) as "supreme Law of the Land" (see Chapter 8). As recounted (Chapter 2), the Articles' Congress had overwhelming trouble with states violating treaties: this was, perhaps, the central foreign affairs difficulty of the Articles period. It could have been solved simply by giving the federal government treatymaking power and then giving Congress power to enforce treaties (as Article I, Section 8's "necessary-and-proper" clause appears to do).[10] But treaty violations had been such a problem that the drafters went one step further and made treaties (or at least some treaties)[11] automatically preemptive, so that there would be no need for Congress to act (and hence no chance for states to block implementation).

In an early case, *Ware v. Hylton* (1796), the Supreme Court emphasized this motivation. *Ware* involved the 1783 peace treaty's direction that British creditors would meet "no lawful impediment" in recovering their pre-war debts. This provision in particular had been one whose enforcement troubled the Articles' Congress, as states refused to open their courts to British creditors. After ratification, British creditors renewed their efforts, claiming that state laws barring recovery were unconstitutional under Article VI; in *Ware* the Court rightly agreed.[12]

So far we have considered Article VI principally as an enhancement of federal power, as it surely was. But it is important to see its other side, as protective of the states. Article VI not only says what shall be supreme law; it also, by negative implication, shows at least some of what is *not* supreme law.[13] It says, for example, that "supreme" status extends to laws "which shall be made in Pursuance" of the Constitution. As a result, laws *not* made in pursuance of the Constitution are not supreme law (unless made so in some other manner, which seems unlikely). That is, to become "supreme," national laws must go through the procedure specified in Article I, Section 7; unenacted laws, laws the President vetoes, laws that do not get a majority in both Houses, etc., are not "made in Pursuance" of the Constitution. Similarly, treaties must be made on the "Authority" of the United States, so that a post-ratification treaty that did not comply with constitutional processes would not be binding on the states.[14] And, although the point may be slightly more controversial, it seems plain also that laws and treaties that are unconstitutional for other reasons—that are contrary to individual rights protections or alter the constitutional structure specified in Articles I through III, for example—are also not part of supreme law. They are not made "in Pursuance" of the Constitution (but rather contrary to it), nor "on the Authority of the United States," as the United States lacks authority to act contrary to the Constitution.

The difference in language between treaty supremacy and law supremacy is worth noting, as it shows the careful crafting of the clause. Laws are described in the future tense: laws "which shall be made." Treaties are both past and future: those "made or which shall be made." As a result, legislative acts of the Articles' Congress, to the extent there were such things, did not carry over into the new system as supreme law, but had to be re-enacted by the new Congress.[15] Treaties did carry over, because pre-1789 treaties had been "made . . . on the Authority of the United States" under the Articles, albeit not "in Pursuance" of the Constitution. Obviously that language was included to make the 1783 peace treaty, in particular, part of supreme law and enforceable against the states, again as the early Court found in *Ware*.

As a result, Article VI specifies what procedures must be followed to make laws and treaties "supreme." That protects states in two ways. First, the processes are cumbersome. Supreme law requires the agreement of a majority of two independent Houses of Congress, plus the (independent) President; or two-thirds of each of two independent Houses of Congress; or two-thirds of the Senate plus the President and another nation. States are protected in part by the sheer difficulty of getting anything done at the federal level: a disputed policy is less likely to survive the process.[16] Second, states in part controlled the process. That was particularly true under the original Constitution, when states controlled appointments to the Senate.[17] Even in the House, members—being from specific geographic districts—were likely to have local interests in mind to some extent. In sum, Article VI assured that state laws would not lightly be displaced by federal policy.[18]

Returning to the *Holocaust Insurance* case, it should be clear that if California's law had conflicted (even implicitly) with a federal law or treaty, adopted through constitutional processes, it would have been invalid. Following the processes Article VI establishes would place the whole weight of the federal government behind the "kid glove" policy, and the iron-fisted state, under its side of the constitutional bargain, would be obliged to step aside; the case then would have been equivalent to *Crosby* or *Ware*. Correspondingly, if Congress had acted in a manner *not* consistent with constitutional processes—for example, through a one-House resolution or a resolution not sent to the President for signature—its act could not oblige the state to step aside; it would not have become part of "supreme Law," because Congress would not have acted to invoke Article VI.[19]

Executive Preemption

In the *Holocaust Insurance* case, only the President, not Congress (or the Senate), had acted. It was, in fact, difficult to say what Congress thought of the matter. Some members agreed with California that the President's negotiated settlement was inadequate and that more pressure should be placed on the insurers.[20] Others thought differently. Most had not expressed any public opinion, and neither body had taken formal action. (The House had held hearings on the matter, where state insurance commissioners outlined specifically what they were doing, so there was institutional knowledge of the issue.)[21] In any event, nothing of an Article VI nature had occurred.

Indeed, initially the dispute was not argued as a preemption claim, but as a "dormant" foreign affairs case under *Zschernig v. Miller* (see Chapter 13). But the case was distinct from *Zschernig* in two important and off-setting ways: first, it did not involve adverse comments on or action against foreign governments;[22] and second, and more important, the U.S. executive branch strongly opposed the state's action.[23] As the case developed and the executive branch became more deeply involved, it increasingly took on the character of a state-versus-President battle.[24]

At first glance, this did not look promising for the President. In two prior cases, the Court had indicated that mere executive policy could not displace otherwise constitutional state laws. In *Barclays Bank v. Franchise Tax Board* (1994), California (again) had a controversial law—concerning allocation of corporate taxes, in that case—that upset foreign multinational corporations; foreign governments and the U.S. President agreed that California was treating the multinationals unfairly. The Court, however, refused to overturn California's law, pointing out that Congress had not spoken on the matter, even though the President had asked Congress to pass preemptive legislation. As the Court emphasized: "Executive Branch communications that . . . express federal policy but lack the force of law cannot render unconstitutional California's otherwise valid, congressionally condoned, [tax laws]."[25] In *Breard v. Greene* (1998), Virginia planned to execute a foreign national (Breard) who apparently had not received all the procedural protections to which he was entitled under international law. His government protested, and the U.S. President confirmed that the nation's foreign policy interest favored staying Breard's execution; nonetheless, the Court and the President agreed that neither of them could simply order Virginia to grant a stay. The President could, the Court said, only *ask* the state to grant a stay—which the President did, without success. As the Court put it: "Last night the [U.S.] Secretary of State sent a letter to the Governor of Virginia requesting that he stay Breard's execution. If the Governor wishes [to do so] . . . that is his prerogative. But nothing in our existing case law allows us to make that choice for him."[26] In both cases, the absence of an Article VI preemptive act appeared decisive in the state's favor, despite federal executive branch policy expressly to the contrary.

At the same time, there seemed something intuitively odd about California claiming, in the *Holocaust Insurance* case, a foreign-policy-making authority superior to the President. As the President emphasized, he—not the California insurance commissioner—was the nation's constitutional representative in foreign affairs, including in negotiating a Holocaust settlement. In effect the President claimed a preemptive power akin to Congress's Article VI power: even if California's law was otherwise constitutional, it should be displaced when it conflicted with federal policy established by the President, because otherwise the President could not carry out his constitutional duties.

A closely divided Supreme Court agreed. Justice David Souter, writing for the majority, tried to align the case with *Crosby,* the Massachusetts Burma case decided three years earlier. But, as discussed above, *Crosby* involved statutory preemption under Article VI; the question in the *Holocaust Insurance* case was whether preemption could occur *outside of* Article VI. In deciding that it could, Souter had in his favor only the President's foreign affairs power, and ultimately that was what he relied on, calling the case one of "preemption by executive conduct in foreign affairs."[27]

Constitutional Text

As we have seen in Chapter 3, Souter started from the right place. The President's executive power does include independent power to act in foreign affairs, even in the absence of statutory authority. The fact that Congress had done nothing (formally) with respect to settling Holocaust claims did not prevent the President from pursuing a settlement. But Souter set himself up for later error by failing to identify a clear source for the President's power. (Among other things, he cited the extra-constitutional *Curtiss-Wright* case, discussed in Chapter 1—an early sign of trouble.) If Souter did not know where the President's power came from (or if he thought it came from a source as shadowy as *Curtiss-Wright*), one could anticipate that he would not see its limits. And if one thinks of the President's foreign affairs power as an ill-defined, open-ended authority, it may indeed be hard to see how a state could successfully set itself in opposition.

The approach suggested earlier (Chapters 3–5) indicates the correct textual answer. The source of the President's foreign affairs power—that is, in this case, the power to establish and pursue U.S. policy with respect to Holocaust claims—is Article II, Section 1.[28] The Court and the President were right that the President did not need congressional authority to use diplomatic power to encourage the Europeans to establish compensatory funds for Holocaust victims. Even though one usually thinks of "executive power" as power to implement pre-existing law, we have seen that in foreign affairs, its eighteenth-century meaning included, as Jefferson said, "transaction of business" with foreign nations even in the absence of authorizing law.

Once we see the textual source of the President's power in such matters, though, we also see its limitations. The President's power is executive, which means, above all else, that it is not legislative. The President does not need authorization to pursue *policies* with respect to Holocaust compensation, but cannot *make law* in support of those policies. As explored in Chapter 5, the English monarch/executive could not make decrees within the domestic legal system in support of foreign policy, or indeed even incorporate agreements with foreign nations (including treaties) into domestic law, without parliamentary support.

It is important to see that giving the President preemptive power is in effect granting executive lawmaking power. Before the President adopted his policy, the insurers had a legal duty under California law to disclose their Holocaust-era records or cease doing business in the state. The President sought to change their legal duty, to allow them to continue doing business without complying with California law. Or, put another way, the claimants had a right under California law to obtain Holocaust-era records from any insurer doing business in the state; the President sought to overturn that right.

In this respect the case parallels the *Steel Seizure* case, which we found (Chapter 5) to be an unconstitutional example of presidential lawmaking. In *Steel Seizure,* the mill owners had a right under state property law to possession of their mills. President Truman sought, by executive order, to deprive them of that legal right. In effect, then, he sought to displace (preempt) state property law by executive decree. To do so, though, would give the executive decree the force of supreme law, and, as Justice Black recognized, that would give the President lawmaking power.[29]

As we have also seen, Justice Black overstated the matter somewhat, because he said that the President could only implement policies developed by Congress. Black should have said that the President cannot make policies *into domestic law* without Congress's support. But even stated in this more modest way, *Steel Seizure* points to the correct resolution of the *Holocaust Insurance* case: presidential policy alone cannot displace state law, because the "executive Power" does not allow the President to change domestic rights and obligations.

This reading of executive power fits with Article VI; the view of the Court and the executive branch in the *Holocaust Insurance* case creates substantial tension in several respects. First, it should be clear that Congress cannot, merely by adopting a policy—even on something squarely within its enumerated powers, such as interstate commerce—preempt state law. Article VI requires that Congress make law "in Pursuance" of the Constitution (i.e., through Article I, Section 7), not that it merely adopt policies. The Court's result gives the President a greater preemptive power than Congress has— surely an odd result.

Second, Article VI makes clear that only treaties approved by the Senate (that is, made "on the Authority" of the United States, which requires Senate approval) are part of supreme law. Further, by mentioning treaties expressly, Article VI heavily implies that treaties would not be part of supreme law if they were not listed in Article VI. Treaties are, however, necessarily expressions of presidential foreign policy (otherwise the President would not negotiate them). If Presidents could preempt state law merely by establishing policies, then (a) even unapproved treaties—that is, ones endorsed by the President but not yet approved by the Senate—should be preemptive; and (b) including treaties in Article VI would be superfluous, because treaties would displace state law by the preemptive force of the executive power to establish foreign policy. In sum, even on its face, Article VI's negative implication is powerful: it shows how preemption arises, and it shows the *only* way preemption arises.

Confirming History

This view is confirmed by the way founding-era Americans discussed Article VI. In the ratification debates and in the key 1796 decision in *Ware,* speakers understood treaties to overturn state law *as a result of* Article VI. In the debates, for example, we have seen (Chapter 9) that the anti-federalists implausibly argued that the President might act strategically to undermine the

Senate's check on the treaty power: for example, by calling a session when only a bare quorum would be present and then conspiring with two-thirds of the quorum (since Article II, Section 2 requires approval by only two-thirds of the "Senators present"). In this way, the anti-federalists claimed, the President could make law with the approval of less than half of the total number of Senators.

That was particularly problematic, anti-federalists insisted, because Article VI would make treaties, once approved, supreme over state law: "The President and two-thirds of the Senate will be empowered to make treaties indefinitely, and when these treaties shall be made, they will also abolish all laws and state constitutions incompatible with them." As one key anti-federalist wrote, because treaties were included in Article VI, "[t]he most important article in any [state] constitution may therefore be repealed, even without a legislative act."[30]

Apparently it did not occur to anti-federalists that Presidents could displace state constitutions and laws merely by announcing foreign policy, without approval from *any* Senators. If it had, they surely would have focused on this even-greater threat to the states. After all, Article VI only overrode state acts where the President plus two-thirds of the Senate made formal agreements with foreign nations. Executive preemption would surely cover those situations, plus it would allow preemption *without* the Senate (in which the states had an important role).[31] Such a reading must have appeared even less plausible than the far-fetched scenarios the anti-federalists invented.

The opinions in *Ware* show the affirmative side of the same sort of thinking. The Virginia debt confiscation laws challenged in *Ware* had plagued U.S. foreign affairs since 1783. Almost the whole point of Article VI's contorted phrasing ("Treaties made, or which shall be made") was to include the 1783 peace treaty in Article VI's supreme law. When the Court faced the issue in *Ware*, the Justices rested their opinions squarely on Article VI.[32] Further, the principal counterargument in *Ware* was that Virginia's laws, for various technical reasons, did not violate the treaty. This claim convinced Justice Iredell, who may have been the most careful legal analyst on the Court. Although Iredell acknowledged the legal status of treaties under Article VI, making plain that nothing contrary to the treaty could stand, he thought that because Virginia's law did not contravene the treaty, it was not preempted. The other Justices agreed that conflict with the treaty was the essence of the case. Justice Chase, for example, said that the Virginia law would be binding on the Court absent the treaty, and Justice Cushing put the matter most directly: "A State may make what rules it pleases; and those rules must necessarily have place within itself. But here is a treaty, the supreme law, which overrules all State laws upon the subject, to all intents and purposes; and that makes the difference."[33]

The Court's analysis confirms that no one thought mere presidential policy could override state laws. The national government's policy had always been to allow recovery of the debts. President Washington and his emissary John Jay had just concluded a further treaty with Britain (the 1794 Jay Treaty) establishing additional procedures to facilitate recovery of the debts. No one could doubt that Washington's policy favored the creditors. Yet the Justices not mention this as a possible basis for invalidating the Virginia law, nor, so far as our records reflect, did the creditors' attorneys (including future Chief Justice Marshall). That was especially striking in the Supreme Court arguments, because the lower court had held that the treaty did not conflict with Virginia's law; in short, the creditors' attorneys knew before the Supreme Court argument that their treaty-based claim was not ironclad (they were appealing a decision rejecting it), and yet they *still* did not make the secondary argument that national foreign policy, reflected in the Jay Treaty negotiations and an array of diplomatic correspondence dating to the 1780s, was enough to override state law.[34]

In sum, to the extent of our records, no one in the ratification debates or in the arguments and opinions in *Ware* believed (or even suggested) that presidential foreign policy could displace state law, even though in both instances, one side had powerful incentives to make that argument. The best explanation is surely that the argument did not appear plausible, even to advocates whose cause it would have helped. As with much post-ratification evidence, that is not necessarily conclusive. But it is powerful confirmation of what already appears the most natural reading of the text: Article VI is the textual provision that subordinates states' actions to federal actions; states must give way to federal acts listed in Article VI, but not otherwise.

Again, we might hesitate if there were post-ratification evidence pointing in the opposite direction; but there is not. It is not clear that anyone even made the argument that unenacted federal foreign policy displaced state law until far into the nineteenth century, and apparently no court decision accepted it until midway through the twentieth.[35] Even by the time of the *Holocaust Insurance* case, the claim remained so unsupported that Justice Souter's opinion principally relied on *Crosby* (a statutory preemption case) and Justice Harlan's concurrence in *Zschernig* (which did not endorse executive preemption).[36]

Structural Explanations

We may yet feel, though, that the idea of states frustrating presidential foreign policy is so structurally unsound that the framers could not have intended it, whatever the text may appear to say. Perhaps there is a negative implication from Article II, Section 1 that states cannot interfere with the President's executive power to set foreign policy; that interference thus is contrary to Article II, and hence Article VI applies it as a constitutional prohibition.

It may well be true that in exceptional circumstances the President's Article II power displaces state law of its own force. In *Boyle v. United Technologies Corp.* (1987), the Court found that Virginia could not regulate the design standards of military contractors contrary to specifications the President established.[37] Although the Court did not put it exactly this way, one might read *Boyle* as finding that the President's commander-in-chief power gave exclusive authority to set military design standards and "preempted" (if one wanted to use that word) contrary state policies, even though the President's policies did not arise from a statute or treaty. Allowing the state regulation would in effect deny the President military command regarding the type of combat equipment to use; it would require him to seek Congress's assistance to uphold a power that, by the Constitution, should be an independent one. In Hamilton's terms (see Chapter 13), the state law would be "totally repugnant" to the President's power because it would convert an independent power into a shared one.

Even if this reading of *Boyle* is correct, though, it does not support a broader preemptive reading of Article II, Section 1. The commander-in-chief clause is unusual in giving the President something like lawmaking power over the military. Article II, Section 1, in contrast, only gives the President power to establish U.S. policy internationally; it does not give the President power to incorporate policy into domestic law (a legislative, not executive, power). True, states cannot prohibit the President from establishing foreign policy: that would of course be unconstitutional under Article II, Section 1. But California's law did not prevent the President from establishing policy internationally; it only obstructed the President in incorporating his policy into domestic law, which is not part of the President's "executive" power. It may have been inconvenient to the President's policy, but as Hamilton's Federalist No. 32 emphasized, that is not sufficient to show a negative implication.[38]

Second, there are sound structural reasons for insisting that foreign policy preemption be done only through Article VI. As discussed at the outset of this chapter, Article VI protects the states, by requiring that preemptive actions follow channels in which the states retain material power.[39] Allowing executive preemption bypasses these protections, permitting preemption to come from the branch with greatest national focus and the least responsiveness to local concerns.

Of course, we might think that states' Article VI protections are important in domestic matters (and hence few would advocate executive preemption in purely domestic affairs) and yet believe that foreign affairs are different, because states have such diminished interests. This claim, though, depends on sharply distinguishing foreign and domestic affairs, such that one can readily tell when states have legitimately local interests. In practice, this will rarely be easy. The *Holocaust Insurance* case is one example; another, discussed above, is the 1998 *Breard* case, in which Virginia's application of the death penalty, for the murder of a Virginia citizen in Virginia, had substantial international repercussions. Inevitably, some entity must make difficult calls in balancing states' local interests against harm to national foreign policy. Establishing Article VI as the sole method of preemption places that decision with Congress, or the treatymakers—which in turn gives greater protection to the states. Allowing executive preemption gives the decision to the President, with correspondingly less protection for the states. We may, as a policy matter, prefer one or the other; but it is difficult to say, simply as a matter of logic or historical inevitability, that the drafters must have favored the more nationalist solution. In fact, their need to accommodate the states, and the radical change from the Articles that even Article VI standing alone had wrought, suggests that they retained some protections for the states.

There is a further reason to prefer the exclusive reading of Article VI in foreign affairs, arising not from federalism but from national separation of powers. Article VI is not just an allocation of power between the states and the federal government. It also allocates power among the branches of the federal government. This is especially true in foreign affairs, where the Constitution gives the President substantial independent power. We have seen how the framers were conflicted on creating this power: they believed that effective management of foreign affairs required a single, independent chief executive; yet they feared that such an executive, Caeser-like, would threaten liberties and upset the balance of power within the government. As a result, they concluded, the independent executive foreign affairs power requires offsetting checks and balances.

One way executive power can be checked, as the framers recognized, is to deny it associated lawmaking power. As the *Holocaust Insurance* case shows, establishing the states as independent power centers in foreign affairs limits the President's foreign affairs power and enhances Congress's role. As recounted above, the case arose from a substantial policy dispute over how best to achieve compensation for insurance claimants and how best to balance that goal with other foreign policy objectives. The claimants thought (with some justification) that the President's policy would prove ineffective.[40] In the absence of executive preemption, the President would have been required to approach Congress (or the Senate) to obtain legislative (or treaty-making) support for his policy, and the claimants would have had opportunities to object. Once the Court endorsed executive preemption, the burden lay with the claimants to convince a supermajority of Congress to intervene against the President.

Again, for policy reasons we might argue for either result. The crucial point, however, is that either way makes some sense as a policy matter, depending on how much one wishes to limit presidential foreign affairs power. We cannot say that the framers must have chosen one or the other. Indeed, given the framers' concerns about presidential power, and their concerns about mixing executive and legislative power in one person, it is quite plausible that they would have required the President to seek legislative cooperation to overcome state barriers to foreign policy. Doing so would force more cooperative approaches among the federal branches in implementing policy (while leaving the President substantial power to initiate policy in the first place).

In short, the text again seems to point toward a divided foreign affairs power, composed of multiple independent power centers. From what we have seen already, we should not be surprised that the Constitution establishes such a system.

Preemption and Executive Agreements: *Pink* and *Belmont* Revisited

Dissenting in the *Holocaust Insurance* case, Justice Ruth Bader Ginsburg suggested an intermediate position: perhaps the problem was that the President's policy was insufficiently formalized. In particular, if the policy had been reflected in executive agreements with the interested European nations, that likely would have been sufficient for her to find it preemptive; but executive preemption should not (she thought) arise from informal letters of intermediate-level federal officials, or from briefs filed in pending litigation. (There were executive agreements involved in the case indirectly, which the Court's majority used as evidence of the President's policy, but they did not directly conflict with California's law, or at least not with all applications of it).[41]

Several things may be said for Ginsburg's position. As we have seen in Chapter 9, the Constitution's text does appear to envision a (limited) presidential power to enter into "executive agreements"—agreements with foreign nations that would not have been called "treaties" in the eighteenth century. Although not technically treaties, these agreements are official commitments of the United States, intended as binding promises in international law. To allow the President to make these commitments, and yet not make them binding on the states as a matter of constitutional law, would threaten to revive the Articles' problem with treaties: states frustrating the national government's international promises.

As Chapter 9 also explored, when the question of executive agreements reached the Supreme Court, in the *Pink* and *Belmont* cases, the Court upheld them, although its textual grounding was (to put it mildly) unclear. Those cases also considered whether executive agreements could preempt state law. Recall that President Franklin Roosevelt's agreement with the Soviet Union, at issue in *Pink* and *Belmont,* acknowledged Soviet confiscations of Russian property in the United States and transferred title of that property to the U.S. government. When the United States sued to gain possession of the property, it encountered a New York state law that refused to accept the confiscations and left title to the property with its original owner. Thus even if the executive agreement itself was constitutional (as found in Chapter 9), the question remained whether the agreement overturned the state law.[42]

Justice Sutherland in *Belmont* held that it did, as an almost self-evident conclusion. "It is inconceivable," he wrote, that a state law "can be imposed as an obstacle to the effective operation of a federal constitutional power." It is not clear what part of the Constitution Sutherland was relying on—or even if he was relying on the Constitution; Sutherland was, of course, the author of the *Curtiss-Wright* opinion finding extra-constitutional foreign affairs powers. In at least a gesture to Article VI, though, he noted that treaties were preemptive, and executive agreements should be taken as having the same effect.[43] If true, that would support Justice Ginsburg's position in the *Holocaust Insurance* case: the President's policy could be preemptive if sufficiently formalized (and, one might add, requiring some degree of formality would itself check the President by promoting visibility and thus accountability).

This reasonable-enough position is unfortunately difficult to tether to the Constitution's text. There are two possible strategies: perhaps executive agreements are implicitly included in Article VI (as Sutherland seemed to imply); or perhaps their preemptive effect arises from Article II, Section 1, the constitutional source of the executive agreement power. Neither, though, leads to a promising textual argument.

The problem with the Article VI argument is that executive agreements necessarily are not treaties. As we have seen in Chapter 9, Article II, Section 2 says the President can make treaties *provided* two-thirds of the Senate approves; that provision carries the inescapable implication that the President *cannot* make treaties if two-thirds of the Senate does *not* approve. The President can claim textual power to make executive agreements without Senate approval only by saying that they are not treaties. We have seen that this argument has plausible historical and textual support: eighteenth-century sources and the Constitution's Article I, Section 10 appear to say that not all international agreements are treaties.

But if executive agreements, to be constitutional, must by definition not be treaties, they appear categorically excluded from Article VI, which includes only treaties. The President cannot have it both ways: a narrow definition of "treaties" in Article II (necessary to make executive agreements permissible without Senate approval) requires a narrow definition in Article VI (excluding executive agreements from supreme law). The only escape is to say that "treaties" in Article VI means something different from "treaties" in Article II. That would be a difficult position to take even with substantial historical support;[44] here, there is no evidence at all that founding-era Americans adopted such a reading. Although executive agreements have some (limited) support in post-ratification practice, no executive agreement in even the first fifty years of practice claimed the ability to displace conflicting state law, and no commentary suggests that they could. To the contrary, the only executive agreements during this period involved matters beyond the reach of state law—mostly military affairs or claims against foreign sovereigns for injuries occurring outside the United States.[45]

The argument fares little better if we try to derive preemptive effect from Article II, Section 1. All the foregoing arguments about the exclusivity of Article VI preemption apply. There is no textual reason to single out executive agreements, as opposed to all other possible executive foreign affairs actions, as ones that should be preemptive. Nor does distinguishing between formal and informal policies, as Justice Ginsburg suggested, help matters. If any formal executive policy could preempt, then the President could bypass Article VI simply by acting formally, which would be counter to the role Article VI played in the framers' constitutional structure and assumptions, as discussed above. Yet it is not clear, in textual terms, why one would distinguish between executive agreements and other formal executive policies: both are powers the President has by virtue of the broad language of Article II, Section 1. And again, the argument would proceed without any historical support. As discussed, no founding-era practice or commentary suggests that the President alone would have power to displace state law, whether by executive agreement or other formal executive action.

The argument for preemptive executive agreements, instead, must fall back on policy imperatives. This is, in effect, where Justice Sutherland placed it in *Belmont,* when he found any other result "inconceivable." But Sutherland and those who would follow him miss the link between federalism and national separation of powers. What Sutherland actually said was that it was "inconceivable" that states could interfere with policies *"of the National Government."* That is, ordinarily, true. But the policy in *Belmont* (and the *Holocaust Insurance* case), even if reflected in an executive agreement, was a policy not *of the national government* but only of the President. The core issue in these cases is not whether states may resist the federal government, but *which branch* of the federal government can decide that the states must give way. Surely it is not "inconceivable" that the answer is Congress, not the President, just as Article VI suggests.

With respect to executive agreements, there is a particular structural reason to require congressional participation before they can become part of domestic law and thus displace state law. Although the executive agreement power has relatively firm textual foundations, it has particularly opaque textual scope. Article I, Section 10, the textual basis for separating "treaties" and "other agreements," says nothing about the difference. As explored in Chapter 9, pre-ratification law-of-nations writing had some elaboration of the difference, based mainly on temporary versus long-term agreements. Structural considerations and post-constitutional practice also suggest limits, but they are not fully consistent with prior writings or with each other. One might fairly conclude (as Louis Henkin has) that the difference between the two lacks textual determination.[46]

In the hands of an aggressive President, this opacity might be exploited to wrongfully augment executive power. If the President asserts wide-ranging executive agreement powers, it is not clear what the Senate (at whose detriment the expansion would come) could do about it, aside from merely complaining. Even if someone could get the matter into court, in the absence of clear constitutional language courts might be reluctant to take a strong stand.

Denying domestic legal effect to executive agreements goes some way toward mitigating this threat. Presidents will find executive agreements less-attractive avenues to wrongfully expand executive power if the agreements lack legal effect in the United States. As in *Belmont* and the *Holocaust Insurance* case, they would be more subject to checking by the states, forcing the President to seek the cooperation of other federal branches. That would tend to confine them to managing the executive branch's overseas diplomatic and military affairs, which is likely the role they were intended to serve, rather than becoming a tool by which the President can bypass the domestic lawmaking procedures of Article VI. Presidential infringement of the Senate's treaty power would carry a price: the President's acts would lack domestic legal effect.

It is important to stress that this policy explanation would not be sufficient, in itself, to claim a textual basis for the rule proposed. It is, however, reason to think that the text's most natural reading—that executive agreements are excluded from "supreme" (preemptive) law by Article VI—is not only not "inconceivable," but is a perfectly appropriate outcome.

Conclusion: Article VI and the Constitution

In sum, it is crucial to recognize the central role Article VI plays in the Constitution's structure. It accomplishes three things. First, and most obviously, it is the source of the states' constitutional subordination to the national government. It responds to the Articles' problems that states did not feel bound to the Congress's directives and that the Congress could not set and enforce unified national policies. Second, and less obviously, it gives constitutional protection to the states, by assuring that federal acts displacing state law must be made through procedures in which the states have representation. In particular, in foreign affairs this assures that the difficult trade-off between local and national interests is made in fora with local and national representation. Third, and even less commonly remarked, Article VI allocates power at the federal level. It confirms that only particular parts of the federal entity can displace state law—in particular, that displacement cannot be done by the President alone, because the President has no power to make "supreme Law." This is particularly important in foreign affairs, where the President has substantial independent power. That independent power is checked in part by the need to secure other branches' cooperation to make it effective against the states. By the complex interactions of power set forth in Article VI, checks and balances at the federal level reinforce federalism by giving political protections to the states, and federalism reinforces checks and balances at the federal level by limiting how much the President can achieve independently.

15

Missouri v. Holland and the Seventeenth Amendment

This chapter considers whether the Constitution imposes federalism limits on otherwise-valid exercises of federal foreign affairs power. Prior chapters indicate that the allocation of foreign affairs power between the state and federal governments is chiefly governed by Article VI. The central theme has been that, except in particular areas where the Constitution directly excludes state activities, state and federal power is concurrent: states may act until the federal government, acting under Article VI, displaces them. The discussion has so far assumed, though, that when the federal government acts by statute or treaty in foreign affairs, as specified in Article VI, it prevails: the Constitution makes federal power supreme in foreign affairs, although it does not, in general, make it exclusive.

It is now time to examine that assumption closely—that is, to ask whether the Constitution's text limits the federal government's ability to displace state laws by statute or treaty in pursuance of national foreign policy. Of course, the scope of federal statutes is limited by the scope of Congress's delegated powers, chiefly in Article I, Section 8, together with the Tenth Amendment's direction that the national government can exercise only delegated power. But there is no obvious corresponding subject-matter limit on the scope of the treatymaking power, in Article II, Section 2 or elsewhere. Does this mean that treaties may cover any topic (and, derivatively, that if Congress has power to implement treaties, in effect there is also no limit on the scope of Congress's power)?

In *Missouri v. Holland* (1920), the Supreme Court, in rejecting a challenge to a treaty whose scope seemed beyond the subject matter of Article I, Section 8, came close to saying there are no constitutional limits on treaties' subject matter.[1] That conclusion, though, has worried advocates of a meaningful federal system, both before and after *Holland*. It seems to strike at the very idea of limited national powers—that, as Madison said, the national government's powers are "few and defined."[2] If the national government can make treaties on any topic, and those treaties become part of domestic law either automatically (under Article VI) or by congressional implementation (through the "necessary and proper" power), then, contrary to Madison, national power seems unlimited. As one commentary puts it, after *Holland* "the entire federal structure . . . is a President and two-thirds of a quorum of senators (and perhaps a bona fide demand from a foreign government) away from destruction."[3]

Missouri v. Holland, Migratory Birds, and Alien Land Rights

Holland involved protection of birds that migrated between the United States and Canada. Under the 1920s interpretation of Article I, Section 8, Congress lacked power to regulate treatment of the birds, because the birds themselves were not articles of commerce. The United States and Britain concluded a treaty protecting the birds, and Congress enacted a criminal statute to implement it. Missouri, a state the birds visited, objected that this subject lay beyond federal power; Ray Holland was the federal official in charge of enforcing the law.

Justice Oliver Wendell Holmes, writing for the U.S. Supreme Court, denied that the Constitution limited federal treatymaking power by subject matter in any way comparable to its limits on Congress's lawmaking power. Though his opinion (like many Holmes opinions) was long on aphorisms and short on constitutional analysis, in a sense he based his conclusion squarely on the Constitution's text: "The treaty in question does not contravene any prohibitory words to be found in the Constitution. The only question is whether it is forbidden by some invisible radiation from the general terms of the Tenth Amendment." With the question framed in that way, Holmes easily found that Missouri had no "reserved" power in birds "that yesterday had not arrived, tomorrow may be in another State and in a week a thousand miles away."[4]

Holland arguably leaves open arguments that some other, greater state interests might be protected under an "invisible radiation from the general terms of the Tenth Amendment." But Holmes's phrasing seems uninviting to future challenges (especially textual ones), and modern analyses tend to see the opinion as opening the way to effectively unbounded treaty power.

As we shall see, the debate in and over *Holland* echoes arguments that date to the founding era. To use an eighteenth-century example, can the United States make treaties affecting the ability of non-citizens to own land within the states? This was, in at least some understandings, beyond Congress's Article I, Section 8 power at the time, yet formed part of several early treaties—and was strongly resisted on this ground. Robert Livingston argued in 1795 that such a provision

> appears to infringe the constitutional independence of the respective states—Congress alone have the power to naturalize; but neither congress, nor any member of the federal government, appear to me to have any right to declare the tenure by which lands shall be holden in the territories of the individual states, without naturalization. This is an act of sovereignty which is confined to the state legislatures, and which they have not ceded to congress, about which, therefore, I am led to doubt the right of the president and senate to treat. . . . Is this right of the states abridged by the power of the president and senate to make treaties? Are not their powers to treat confined to such objects as the constitution entrusts to the federal government?[5]

Livingston thus summed what modern writers have called the "implementational" view of treatymaking power: treaties can implement federal powers granted elsewhere in the document, but the treatymaking clause does not independently grant authority the federal government would otherwise lack.[6] That view would call *Holland* into serious doubt. As discussed below, however, it is difficult to derive from the Constitution's text.

The Constitution's Text and the Scope of Treatymaking Power

At the outset, we confront an undeniable difference between Congress's law-making power and the treatymaking power. The combination of Article I, Section 1 (giving Congress legislative powers "herein granted") and Article I, Section 8 (listing subject matter over which Congress "shall have power") explicitly limits the scope of Congress's authority. (True, some courts and commentators have ventured that Congress has inherent "Foreign Affairs Power" rendering the textual limitation inapplicable to international matters, but we have seen in Chapter 10 that this claim lacks textual foundation and flatly contradicts the Tenth Amendment.) The power to make treaties, though, is given in general terms, without subject-matter restriction, in Article II, Section 2. Simply comparing these provisions suggests trouble for the states and seems to form the textual basis of Holmes's *Holland* opinion.

Article VI does indicate some limits on treaty power. As we have seen (Chapter 14), it elevates to supreme law statutes "which shall be made in

Pursuance" of the Constitution—thus unconstitutional statutes (including those beyond Article I, Section 8 powers) are not part of supreme law. Article VI also includes in supreme law treaties "made, or which shall be made, under the Authority of the United States." Although it has not appeared so to some commentators, this provision seems similarly to say that unconstitutional treaties are not supreme law. It does not use the "in pursuance" language, because its drafters wanted to include treaties made earlier, especially the 1783 peace treaty with Britain. Article VI needed to use phrasing that encompassed treaties made in pursuance of *either* the Articles or the Constitution (or the Congress's unwritten implicit authority prior to the Articles' ratification in 1781). "Authority of the United States" seems calculated to achieve this meaning: the inquiry, if a treaty is challenged, should be whether the United States had "Authority" under its then-effective constitutional document to conclude it. This is, moreover, the way founding-era commentators, including Hamilton, read Article VI. As Hamilton explained, "a delegated authority cannot rightfully transcend the constituting act"; as a result, "[a] treaty for example cannot transfer the legislative power to the Executive Department" or say "that the Judges and not the President shall command the national forces."[7] And presumably treaties cannot alter the Constitution, as indicated by Article V's much more rigorous amendment process; that is, they cannot create an "Authority" where none previously existed.

We can therefore comfortably identify three—but only three—limitations on treatymaking power. First, treaties cannot alter the constitutional structure set forth in the text or contravene limitations (such as, principally, individual rights limitations) on federal power as a whole. So treaties, for example, cannot grant titles of nobility or eliminate the citizenship requirement for presidential eligibility. They cannot exercise powers given exclusively (by plain language or negative implication) to another branch.[8] Nor can they override individual rights, such as the right to jury trial, as the Supreme Court rightly said in *Reid v. Covert* (1957).[9] None of these actions could be taken on "the Authority of the United States," because the Constitution denies the federal government generally, or the treatymakers specifically, power ("authority") to take them.

Second, more germane to our present topic, treaties cannot overturn protections of state sovereignty that arise from the Constitution's text, implications, or structure as a whole. For example, the Eleventh Amendment declares that judicial power "shall not extend" to suits between a state and citizens of another state. Obviously a treaty cannot change that command. The Supreme Court has further said that the Amendment indicated broader pre-existing constitutional prohibitions on most suits against states without their consent.[10] And the Court has found other core attributes of state sovereignty implicitly protected by the Constitution's structure, in cases such as *Printz v. United States* (1997) and *New York v. United States* (1992). Whatever one thinks of these particular cases, most people would likely agree (and most eighteenth-century readers would likely have agreed) that the federal government cannot, for example, order states to change the location of their capitals or to accept governors appointed by the President in place of elected ones.[11]

Of course, if these limitations arise from Article I, Section 8, they would not appear to constrain treatymaking power. But to the extent they arise elsewhere, it seems that they would. It has been suggested, for example, that the Constitution's use of the word "state" in a number of provisions indicates founding-era Americans' understanding that the "states" would retain at least a core of sovereignty, since "state" in eighteenth-century law-of-nations terminology meant an entity with some sovereign attributes.[12] Other scholars and cases indicate (perhaps less plausibly) that protections for core state sovereignty arise from the Tenth Amendment or from non-textual constitutional structure. In either event, to the extent protections (whatever they may be) arise not from Article I, Section 8 but from federalism-protecting provisions applicable to the federal government as a whole, they should apply to the treatymaking power as clearly as limitations included in the first category.[13]

Third, it seems inescapable that powers claimed under the treatymaking clause must in fact be exercised through something that really is a "treaty," in the eighteenth-century meaning of the word. "Treaty" meant an agreement among nations on matters of mutual interest.[14] As a result, exercises of treatymaking power must actually involve an agreement, an international matter, and interest on the part of both nations. The Constitution thus would reject sham treaties, where the President and the Senate combined to end-run the legislative process for purely domestic reasons, convincing a foreign nation to sign the resulting document to achieve the look of a treaty without any of a treaty's substance.[15]

But even given their broadest reading, none of these categories would amount to limitations on treatymaking power remotely approaching the subject-matter limitations on Congress's lawmaking, nor cast doubt upon *Holland*. The migratory bird agreement, for example, was plainly made on a subject of mutual interest and not a sham; it did not contravene any structural or individual rights provisions applicable against the federal government as a whole; and even if one gives more credit than Holmes did to the "invisible radiations of the Tenth Amendment," or some more state-friendly formulation of inviolable core state sovereignty, the treaty would not seem to exceed them.[16] To find something to contest *Holland,* it is necessary to look beyond the face of the text.

Structural Objections: Can the Treatymaking Power Destroy the States?

The central case against *Holland* arises from a combination of framers' intent and manifestly implausible outcome. It simply cannot be the case (it is said) that the framers, who created and described a limited federal government, would have allowed their entire edifice to be undermined by effectively unlimited treatymaking power. As a result, we must revisit our reading of the text: "The argument is irresistible," according to one commentator, "that if the whole scheme and genius of the Constitution was to save the ungranted powers of the States from interference by the Federal Government, that the framers of the Constitution would not have secured these against the ravages of all departments of the Government, and then quietly bestowed upon one of its branches, the treaty-power, the power to absorb them all."[17]

The argument here is (as we have often seen elsewhere) that we cannot give the text what appears to be its ordinary reading, because that would produce a result so fundamentally at odds with the framers' core values that we cannot believe they would have accepted it. In prior chapters, we have seen that these arguments are difficult to sustain. Sometimes what the advocate takes as *the* core values of the framers often prove, on closer inspection, to be only *some* core values of the framers; others point in the opposite direction. In other cases, there may be little dispute on paramount values, but there is doubt on how the framers carried them into constitutional execution.

Both problems are present here. No one reading the constitutional debates can doubt that the Constitution's drafters and ratifiers had strong attachments to state sovereignty. This is not, of course, true of all individual framers, especially the more nationalistic members of the Philadelphia Convention itself, who might have been happy to abolish the states if they could. They could not, though, because the population generally, and especially the intellectual and political leadership, was attached to the idea of state government and distrusted the creation of a powerful superior federal entity.[18] At the same time, though, the framers wanted strong treatymaking powers—

specifically, stronger ones than they had experienced under the Articles, in which inability to make and enforce treaties hampered confederation diplomacy. The question was how to reconcile and implement those values.

Article I's central protection for the states was the restricted subject matter on which Congress could operate. Article III, Section 2 employs a parallel strategy, giving federal courts limited jurisdiction to ensure that state courts would retain a wide field of operation. Article II, the third great grant of federal power, lacks these explicit subject-matter limitations.

As treaty-power opponents urge, it is not plausible that Article II, unlike the other core articles, had no effective limit on federal power. Indeed, most of it *is* obviously limited, although in distinct ways. The basic Article II power—to execute laws—depends upon laws created within Article I limits. Most Article II powers *not* dependent on Article I—principally, the President's foreign affairs powers (Chapter 3)—do not operate within the domestic legal system, and thus should not threaten the states. Central to this latter point is the principle that the President cannot make law, even in pursuit of foreign affairs objectives (Chapter 5); a contrary view would threaten effectively unbounded presidential authority over the states, as suggested by the *Holocaust Insurance* case (Chapter 14). As a result, most Article II powers are limited, either because they must derive from Article I power or because they operate only externally.

The apparent exception, of course, is treatymaking power, since under Article VI treaties make new law, with apparently only modest subject-matter limitations, and operate internally as well as externally. It is true that treaties are limited in a sense by their definition: they must address matters of concern to foreign nations. Nonetheless, even in the eighteenth century that likely was not much of a limitation, since foreign concerns might range broadly and involve matters deeply intrusive on the states. Hence arises the structural intuition that treatymaking power must be limited in some way not readily seen on the face of the text; otherwise it would produce effectively unbounded Article II power (and, derivatively, unbounded Article I power, if Congress has general power to implement treaties).[19]

There is, though, another way of looking at it. One way to limit power is to limit its scope; another is to limit the ability to exercise it. From the Constitution's text, it is plain that its drafters chose (at least) the latter to limit treatymaking power. Most obviously, treaties require approval of two-thirds of the Senate (plus the President), rather than the majority required, for example, by the same section of Article II for appointments. True, the requirement of a supermajority in one branch is partially offset by omitting the second branch, the House, from treatymaking. Nonetheless, it seems safe to conclude that the supermajority rule was designed to render treatymaking difficult except on widely agreed matters—and the modern urge to substitute congressional-executive agreements (see Chapter 10) indicates pressure for an easier route.[20]

More important, though, was the protection arising from the Senate's composition. Under Article I, Section 3, "the Senate of the United States shall be composed of two Senators from each State, chosen by the Legislatures thereof, for six years." As a result, Senators owed their jobs (and future re-election) to entities most directly affected by federal overreaching. The consequence, in turn, was that Senators could be expected to be especially sensitive to the states' sovereignty-based concerns. That is, even if Senators found a proposal's substance beneficial, they might oppose it on the structural ground that it should be handled at the local level.

We often think of the Senate's role (especially in treatymaking) as protecting geographic interests—that is, assuring that populous states and regions will not oppress less-populated ones. That surely was part of the idea, as reflected, for example, in the Mississippi River controversy discussed in Chapter 7. But this motivation does not explain the text's method of choosing Senators. Rather, the selection method was a direct carryover from the Articles (Article 5), where the states chose their delegates to the Congress. That selection method reflected the idea that the Articles' system was an association of quasi-independent states, not a government of the people of the United States; delegates represented not the people of the respective states but the states themselves. Making the new Senate replicate this aspect of the Articles was the drafters' way of pursuing an intermediate path between the Confederation model and a fully nationalist model. As to most functions, the Constitution divided legislative power between an entity representing the old model, founded upon the states, and a new entity, founded upon the people directly.

As with the express limitations on Congress's authority, selection of Senators by state legislatures was not part of the nationalist Virginia plan initially proposed at the Convention; its Senators were selected by the popularly elected federal House. State control of the Senate appeared later, at the insistence of delegates more focused on state sovereignty. As George Mason said, supporting John Dickinson's motion to that effect: "The State Legislatures also ought to have some means of defending themselves agst. Encroachments of the Natl. Govt. . . . And what better means can we provide than giving them some share in, or rather to make them a constituent part of, the Natl Establishment?"[21] Once this feature was added, even nationalists began to see its advantages, particularly in defending the Constitution against anti-federalist claims of uncontrolled federal power: Wilson emphasized at the Pennsylvania convention that "in the making of treaties, the states are immediately represented," and Hamilton in New York said that Senators would have "uniform attachment to the interests of their several states."[22]

Giving treatymaking power to a supermajority of only one part of this system, then, assumes considerable importance. Treaty approvals would be less acts of the people-plus-the-states (as with ordinary legislation) and more acts of the states only—with a supermajority vote, something required for only three other constitutional acts (overriding vetoes, amending the Constitution, and removing federal officers after impeachment). In sum, treatymaking under the Constitution ended up looking much like treatymaking under the Articles, requiring, in effect, a supermajority of the states (as did the Articles' Article 9). The difference, of course, was that once treaties were made, Article VI legally obligated states to follow them (which nationalists claimed should have been true under the Articles as well). But states' control over treatymaking (as opposed to treaty enforcement) remained similar in the two documents.[23] As one scholar puts it, "the Senate, fortified by a minority veto, was charged with the special *political* task of refusing its consent to any treaty that trenched too far on the interests of the States. . . . This political safeguard goes a long way in explaining why the Founders felt content with a system that delegated the whole treaty power to the national government."[24]

Modern debates may overlook the structural centrality of the state-controlled Senate because the Seventeenth Amendment (1913) eliminated this part of Article I, Section 3 and provided for direct election of Senators by the people of the respective states. Various theories have been advanced for the change, but whatever its motivation, its implications for treatymaking power do not appear to have been generally understood.[25] (No mention was made, for example, in *Holland,* decided only seven years later.) The implications, though, are substantial. Once Senators ceased to owe their offices to state legislatures, they ceased to have personal interests in protecting the state legislatures' prerogatives. Indeed, the Seventeenth Amendment turned Senators from extensions of the state legislatures into potential competitors.

In assessing the Constitution's historical limits on treatymaking power, it is important to see Senators in their original unamended role as the representatives of state legislatures. Once viewed this way, the treatymaking power's threat to the states seems less formidable. Article II, Section 2 could dispense with Article I's subject-matter limitations, because it had a different limit: two-thirds of the representatives *of the states* would have to agree to restrictions on state power effected through the treatymaking clause.

Of course, this does not prove that Article II, Section 2 did not also incorporate implicit subject-matter limitations. It does, though, undermine the claim that Article II, Section 2 *must* incorporate implicit subject-matter limitations or contravene fundamental framing principles. To the contrary, it seems plausible that the drafters relied on an enhanced structural check, rather than a subject-matter check, upon the treatymaking power's threat to the states.[26] That in turn is crucial, because—as even opponents of treaty power concede—a broad subject-matter restriction is not the text's most natural reading but depends on the supposed necessity of avoiding unbounded treaty power.

Treatymaking Power and the Founding Debates

Historical comments and assumptions lie at the center of most attacks upon *Holland;* Justice Holmes did not make matters any easier on himself by observing that "[t]he case must be considered in the light of our whole experience and not merely in that of what was said a hundred years ago" and that "[w]e must consider what this country has become in deciding what [the tenth] amendment reserved."[27] Despite Holmes's half-concession, though, the Constitution's historical context as a whole tends to confirm rather than undermine his result.

It must be said at the outset that some founding-era materials do advocate material non-textual subject-matter limits on the treatymaking power. In particular, in 1795–1796, a central challenge to the constitutionality of the Jay Treaty relied upon this proposition. The argument of Robert Livingston, quoted at the beginning of this chapter, arises from that debate, and modern efforts to limit treatymaking power rest in part upon it and similar statements from that period. For a complete picture, though, we need to begin at an early time.

The Articles of Confederation and the Treatymaking Power

Our first step should be the Articles, which was Americans' first formal attempt at balancing treatymaking power and state interests.[28] On its face, the Articles granted treatymaking power to the Congress in similar terms as the

Constitution: it said, simply, that "[t]he United States, in Congress assembled, shall have . . . power of . . . entering into treaties and alliances." It also made that power exclusive—a provision replicated by the Constitution's Article I, Section 10—and required nine states' consent to approve treaties, a provision approximated by the supermajority requirement of the Constitution's Article II, Section 2.

The Articles (Article 9) also had an explicit, but narrow, subject-matter limitation on treaties: "no treaty of commerce shall be made, whereby the legislative power of the respective states shall be restrained from imposing such imposts and duties on foreigners as their own people are subjected to, or from prohibiting the exportation or importation of any species of goods or commodities whatsoever."[29] And the Articles had a provision (Article 2) resembling the Tenth Amendment, in somewhat stronger terms: "Each state retains its sovereignty, freedom and independence, and every power, jurisdiction and right, which is not by this confederation expressly delegated to the United States. . . ."

For present purposes, the key point here is that essentially no one thought this grant of treatymaking power confined treaties' subject matter only to subjects granted to the Congress elsewhere in the Articles. In particular, the Articles' Congress made commercial treaties with the Netherlands, Sweden and Prussia, and pursued others.[30] These treaties were not seen as beyond Congress's power; the main complaint was that Congress was unable, for practical reasons, to make more of them. Indeed the Articles assumed the Congress had power to make commercial treaties, by placing limits upon that power in Article 9, as set forth above. But the Congress had no express legislative power over commercial regulation; Article 2 insisted that the Congress's power had to be given expressly and, as we saw in Chapter 2, everyone assumed that the Congress did not have power to regulate foreign commerce. The Congress's (assumed) power to make commercial treaties could only have come from the treatymaking clause itself, which granted power only in general terms. In short, the "implementational" view of treatymaking power, argued later by Livingston, had no basis in the Articles.

Subject-matter objections were made to particular provisions in the Congress's treaties. The 1783 peace treaty, for example, affected state contract law (by permitting recovery of pre-war debts) and state property law (by requiring restoration of loyalist property). The commercial treaties guaranteed that foreign nations' citizens could inherit and own property in the United States, contrary to some state laws, and granted various rights to foreign citizens residing in the states.[31] Some of these provisions ran into opposition, as encroaching too heavily upon state sovereignty. Madison, then a Virginia delegate to the Congress, raised early doubts about the commercial treaties. Various state legislators, particularly in New York and Virginia, maintained that the peace treaty overreached on the matter of debts and loyalist property as one of their arguments for not complying with it.[32]

It was not always clear what provision of the Articles these treaties supposedly infringed, or even if the objections were legal, as opposed to political, in nature. The key, though, is that there was no *general* conclusion that the treaties exceeded the Congress's power. Often states did not comply, but this was set as much on the ground that implementation of the treaties was a matter for the states as on the ground that the treaties themselves exceeded the Congress's power. To the contrary, the Congress (whose delegates were, after all, appointed by the state legislatures) approved the treaties by the required supermajority, and strongly urged state compliance.[33] Indeed, as we have seen (Chapter 2), the principal treaty-based complaint against the Articles' Congress was not that it exceeded its power in forming treaties, but that it inappropriately lacked power to enforce the treaties it did make.

In sum, it is difficult to squeeze out of the Articles an implicit subject-matter limit on treatymaking power. The Articles' text indicates that its grant of treatymaking power was not limited by subject matter, except for limitations made explicitly. The Articles protected the states against treatymaking excesses in two main ways: by requiring supermajority approval by delegates appointed by the states themselves and by giving the states, rather than the Congress, enforcement power. No one thought the Congress's treatymaking power was limited to subject matter granted to the Congress elsewhere in the document; although some people at the state level objected to particular clauses in the Congress's treaties as infringing state authority, the Congress systematically pursued treaties on subjects over which otherwise it lacked power and which affected internal affairs of the states. There is little doubt that the Congress saw its treaty power as an independent and general grant of power, as did a substantial proportion of Americans who considered the matter. Even Jefferson, who later advocated the "implementational" view in the Jay Treaty debates, wrote in 1785: "Congress, by the Confederation have no original and inherent power over the commerce of the states. But by the 9th Article they are authorized to enter into treaties of commerce. . . . Congress may by treaty establish any system of commerce they please. But, as I before observed, it is by treaty alone they can do it. Tho' they may exercise their other powers by resolution or ordinance, those over commerce can only be exercised by forming a treaty."[34] It is worth repeating, in light of this quote, that the Articles' Article 9 did not specifically authorize the Congress to enter into treaties of commerce—only treaties in general.

The Drafting Convention

The Philadelphia Convention, then, would not have started with a background assumption of an "implementational" treatymaking power. Rather, the delegates would have understood a grant of treatymaking power to be general, unless textually limited, just as in the Articles. The drafters' focus, moreover, was on *reducing* protections for the states. They broadly agreed that treaty implementation power should be shifted from the states to the federal government, in the face of complaints that states had not upheld treaty commitments.[35] Further, the Convention's initial impulses were to replace the Articles' state-appointed delegates with representatives elected by the people and to eliminate the supermajority requirement for treaty approval.[36]

If these changes had survived, the new treatymaking power would have been a material threat to the states. The latter two, of course, did not. The restoration of state-appointed representatives in one branch of Congress is crucial, because the delegates who proposed it—such as Dickinson and Mason—saw it expressly as protecting the states, and discussed it in those terms. In contrast, the delegates did not discuss subject-matter limitations on the treatymaking power, and they did not even carry over the Articles' express limits.[37]

Yet many, perhaps all, Convention delegates surely understood the Articles' treatymaking clause as granting substantive power to the Congress, without material subject-matter limitations beyond those expressly stated in the text; and in any event all of them knew that broad subject-matter limits were not generally accepted (and had been rejected by the Congress itself). If they had thought the new treatymaking system should have broad subject-matter limits, they surely would not have let the point pass in silence, because the most likely inference from silence was that no such limits were intended. And delegates surely saw the connection between the Articles' treatymaking power and the Constitution's treatymaking power, which were granted in parallel terms. Madison said later, defending the Constitution's treatymaking power, that the Constitution's "power[] to make treaties" was "comprised in the Articles of Confederation, with this difference only, that [it] is disembarrassed by the plan of the convention, of an exception under which treaties might be substantially frustrated by regulations of the States."[38]

Ratification

The new treatymaking power inspired substantial criticism during the ratification debates. As anti-federalists rightly saw, the key was Article VI, which took away states' power to resist treaties made by the national government. That made restrictions on the national government's treatymaking ability a central focus. But their focus was on the supermajority rule, not upon subject-matter limitations. According to federalists, that rule, coupled with the states' representation in the Senate, would protect against encroaching treaties. Not so, anti-federalists responded, because the "two-thirds of the Senators present" language allowed the President and only a handful of Senators (two-thirds of a quorum) to approve.[39] Accordingly, the core anti-federalist demand was to increase this protection, by requiring either three-fourths of Senators present or two-thirds of all Senators.[40] As Mason said, "We wish not to refuse, but to guard, this power . . ."[41]

For the most part, federalists did not deny the treatymaking power's scope but insisted that the Constitution's procedural safeguards were sufficient. That was the theme, for example, of Hamilton's Federalist Nos. 69 and 75. The only material discussion of subject-matter limitations on treaties comes from the Virginia ratifying convention, where treatymaking power was roundly attacked, in particular by Patrick Henry and William Grayson, for being effectively unlimited. (As Henry said, ever-colorfully, "if any thing should be left us, it would be because the President and senators were pleased to admit it.")[42] Federalists gave an array of responses, some more persuasive than others. They asserted, for example, that treaties could not violate the law of nations, and that this should reassure anti-federalist concerns on specific points.[43] There was really only one major comment—by federalist George Nicholas—that seemed to endorse subject-matter limitations, and even this was somewhat ambiguous.[44] Hamilton's later description of the ratification debates seems generally correct: the proposed Constitution, he said gave treatymaking power

> the most ample latitude to render it competent to all the stipulations, which the exigencies of National Affairs might require. . . .
>
> Its great extent and importance . . . were mutually taken for granted— and upon this basis, it was insisted by way of objection—that there were not adequate guards for the safe exercise of so vast a power. . . . The reply to these objections, acknowledging the delicacy and magnitude of the power, was directed to shew that its organization was a proper one and that it was sufficiently guarded.[45]

Of course, if the ratifiers had a background assumption of subject-matter limitations, failure to mention them, though a bit odd, would not be decisive. But the history of the Articles and the drafting suggests that there was no such general background assumption. The ratification debates do not provide support for one either. As Hamilton said, anti-federalists pointed out—and federalists generally did not deny—that treaties had largely unlimited scope; the debate concerned whether the method of approving them afforded the states enough protection.

The Jay Treaty Debates

Most founding-era support for subject-matter limitations on treaties arises from the Jay Treaty debates of 1795–1796, and Jefferson's subsequent comments. To assess the persuasiveness of this evidence, context is important. As outlined (Chapter 7), the Jay Treaty highlighted the political fault lines between the generally pro-French Republican party and the Federalist party, which inclined toward Britain.[46] The treaty favored Britain in key respects, and many Americans saw it as tantamount to alliance with Britain in its ongoing war against revolutionary France. The war, as discussed, motivated Washington's 1793 neutrality proclamation, which itself provoked opposition among some pro-French Americans, although more responsible leaders such as Jefferson and Madison had accepted neutrality. The Jay Treaty, though, united pro-France sentiments in the United States under the banner of the emerging Republican party, with Jefferson and Madison leading the opposition.[47]

The treaty faced two hurdles, and thus two rounds of debate. First, there was approval in the Senate, where it prevailed by a bare two-thirds vote in 1795. The year 1796 then saw renewed debate in the House, whose action was needed to appropriate funds to implement parts of the treaty.[48] The House ultimately went along as well, confirming the nation's re-orientation toward Britain and setting the course for the "quasi-war" with France in the late 1790s.[49]

During the first round, Republicans raised constitutional objections to numerous provisions. Specifically on federalism grounds, they objected to the treaty's Article 9, which allowed British citizens to own land in the United States; this provision drew Livingston's attack quoted above. Other prominent Republicans similarly targeted it as unconstitutionally infringing on state sovereignty.[50]

The question is whether these arguments should be persuasive readings of the text. There are at least four reasons why they should not. First, they are only half of an intensely partisan debate; the treaty's supporters, including Hamilton, strongly defended its constitutionality.[51] Second, they are only weakly linked to any plausible reading of the text. Livingston's textual authority was the Tenth Amendment, but the Amendment on its face does not require anything like he was proposing. It says only that matters not delegated are reserved to the states (i.e., no inherent federal powers); but treatymaking power *is* delegated. As Hamilton argued: "It was impossible for words more comprehensive to be used than those which grant to the power to make treaties. They are such as would naturally be employed to confer a *plenipotentiary* authority. A power 'to make Treaties' granted in these indefinite terms, extends to all kinds of treaties and with all the latitude such a power under any form of Government can possess."[52] Livingston wanted to find a limit on the *delegated* treatymaking power. Holmes in *Holland* referred sarcastically to "invisible radiations from the Tenth Amendment"; the problem for Livingston is that this is essentially what he relied on. Of course, the idea is not as preposterous as Holmes made it sound: there *might* be background assumptions underlying the Tenth Amendment that a textual interpretation would need to take into account. But Livingston simply failed to demonstrate them, and there really was no evidence in his favor; in particular, as discussed above, the experience under the Articles was heavily against him. That he asserted such an understanding in the midst of partisan debate is surely not evidence it existed.

A third problem for Republicans was that they seriously overplayed their hand in raising constitutional objections to the treaty. They also claimed, for example, that treaties could not address matters entrusted to Congress (that is, that the grant of, say, commerce power to Congress in Article I, Section 8 created a negative implication that treaties could not regulate commerce).[53] As Hamilton surely enjoyed pointing out,[54] this was just a bad argument. Everyone at the drafting convention and in the ratifying debates had assumed that treaties would deal with commerce; commercial treaties were a major part of the Congress's diplomacy under the Articles; and indeed commercial treaties formed a major portion of all treaties negotiated at the time. Worse, putting their arguments together, Republicans ended up claiming that treaties could address neither matters committed to Congress *nor* matters left to the states—which would almost wholly disable the treaty power.[55] Even at the time, it must have been hard to escape the feeling that political opposition to the treaty was driving a hunt for constitutional arguments.

And fourth, the Republicans' arguments were not persuasive at the time. Of course they were not persuasive in the sense that the treaty was ultimately approved (and upheld by the Supreme Court many years later, for what that is worth).[56] But they were unpersuasive in a deeper sense. Hamilton and former Philadelphia Convention delegate Rufus King wrote a long series of essays in response, making many of the arguments laid out above. After the Federalist-controlled Senate approved the treaty, debate moved to the Republican-controlled House. By this time, though, Republicans largely abandoned their constitutional objections (especially those based on subject-matter limitations) in the face of Hamilton's defense, and they retreated to more-tenable middle ground. In particular, Madison, the Republican leader in the House, generally avoided Livingston's constitutional arguments. Republicans now principally claimed the right to consider the treaty on the merits before funding it (arguably the treaty, as a "Law of the Land" once ratified, commanded their acceptance; but the Republicans denied this, not without some basis).[57] Ultimately, even on the merits, enough Republicans acquiesced that the treaty got its funding anyway. The key, though, is that after suffering through Hamilton's blistering counterattack, Republicans largely decided not to fight on constitutional grounds. This cannot say much in favor of the persuasiveness of their claims.

In the aftermath of the treaty debate, Jefferson published a manual on Senate practice, in which he made comments that form the centerpiece of at least one important modern attack on *Holland*.[58] According to Jefferson, the Constitution "must have meant to except out of [the treatymaking power] the rights reserved to the states; for surely the President and Senate cannot do by treaty what the whole government is interdicted from doing in any way."[59] By this he meant, as he said in a private letter, that the Constitution "specifies and delineates the operations permitted to the federal government, and gives all powers necessary to carry these into execution. Whatever of these enumerated objects is proper for a law, Congress may make the law; whatever is proper to be executed by way of a treaty, the president and senate may enter into the treaty. . . ."[60]

This analysis, though, merely repeated Republican arguments that had proved unpersuasive earlier, and it is subject to the same objections. Crucially, Jefferson again relied not on constitutional text but on structural imperative— as he put it, if "the treaty making power [is] boundless" then "we have no Constitution."[61] As discussed above, that is simply incorrect. The Constitution limited treatymaking power in several key ways, most notably by requiring that it be exercised by a supermajority of a body controlled by the states.[62]

Conclusion

In sum, to the extent unbounded treatymaking power is a problem in modern constitutionalism, it is not the fault of *Missouri v. Holland* nor a misreading of the 1789 Constitution. The Constitution's text grants treatymaking power in general terms, just as the Articles did, without the subject-matter limitations placed on other federal powers in Articles I and III. It is true that, to be constitutional, treaties must not be shams nor contravene other constitutional restrictions (including protections of the states). But the text's principal protection against overreaching treaties was procedural. Treaties required approval of two-thirds of the Senate, a body then controlled by the state legislatures.

Modern commentators worry because they doubt the Senate's effectiveness as a protector of the states—perhaps with good reason. The principal culprit here, though, is the Seventeenth Amendment, which took away state legislatures' control over the Senate and handed it to a body—the electorate at large—that may be less sympathetic to, or understanding of, state sovereignty. There may be good reasons for making this change, but it is this change, not the original Constitution or the *Holland* case, that creates modern worries. From 1789 to 1913, it is hard to identify treaties that materially interfered with state sovereignty; there is no reason to think the Senate's check did not work or that it was so weak that we must read into the Constitution something its text does not contain.

VI

Courts and Foreign Affairs

16

Judging Foreign Affairs: *Goldwater v. Carter* Revisited

In *Marbury v. Madison* (1803), perhaps the most famous case in all constitutional law, John Marshall declared that it is "emphatically the province and duty of the judicial department to say what the law is." Or, as Justice Antonin Scalia said for the Supreme Court in a modern foreign affairs case, *W. S. Kirkpatrick & Co. v. Environmental Tectonics Corp.* (1990): "Courts in the United States have the power, *and ordinarily the obligation,* to decide cases and controversies properly presented to them."[1] Judicial involvement in foreign affairs controversies nonetheless carries a hint of inappropriateness, driven by an intuition that it is inexpedient and indeed dangerous for courts to undermine or second-guess foreign policy decisions of the President and Congress. An array of judicial "doctrines" stand as barriers to adjudication of modern foreign affairs cases, the most sweeping being the so-called political question doctrine. The idea behind it is that many—perhaps most—foreign affairs decisions should be left to the "political" branches (i.e., the President and Congress), and courts should abstain from (refrain from deciding) cases where such issues are raised.[2]

A plurality of the Supreme Court took this view, for example, in *Goldwater v. Carter,* the case challenging the President's treaty-termination power discussed in Chapter 8. As then-Justice William Rehnquist wrote, "the basic question presented . . . is 'political' and therefore nonjusticiable because it involves the authority of the President in the conduct of our country's foreign relations and the extent to which the Senate or the Congress is authorized to negate the action of the President." Similarly, Justice Jackson (of *Steel Seizure* fame) earlier observed: "It would be intolerable that courts, without the relevant information, should review and perhaps nullify actions of the Executive taken on information properly held secret. . . . But even if courts could require full disclosure, the very nature of executive decision as to foreign policy is political, not judicial. Such decisions are wholly confided by our Constitution to the political departments of the government, Executive and

321

Legislative. They are delicate, complex, and involve large elements of prophecy . . . and have long been held to belong in the domain of political power not subject to judicial intrusion or inquiry."[3]

Although the modern Supreme Court has not often invoked the doctrine, dismissals on this basis are legion among lower courts. During the Vietnam War, for example, the courts of appeal turned aside cases challenging the war's legality as "political questions," as have modern courts asked to consider more recent conflicts.[4] Nonetheless, other decisions insist that "it is error to suppose that every case or controversy which touches foreign relations lies beyond judicial cognizance," and on several occasions the Court has decided foreign affairs cases without much hesitation.[5] Academic commentators (as usual) run the full range of positions, although they generally unite in believing that courts have done a poor job of explaining the basis or scope of foreign affairs abstention.[6]

This chapter begins to consider what the Constitution's text has to say on the matter. It concludes that the sweeping version of the political question doctrine suggested by *Goldwater* is not required and indeed not permitted by the Constitution—but that discrete doctrines of restraint (or abstention) are constitutional and in some cases required. In particular, it argues that the nature of the claim advanced makes a great deal of difference—and that political-question dismissals in constitutional cases are especially hard to defend.

Sources and Limits of Federal Courts' Power

We should begin with some constitutional basics not unique to foreign affairs. First, the source of federal courts' power to decide cases (and to do related things courts must do to carry on their business) is the Constitution's Article III, Section 1. Paralleling the legislative and executive power clauses of Articles I and II, it declares that "the judicial Power of the United States, shall be vested in one supreme Court, and in such inferior Courts as the Congress may from time to time ordain and establish."

As discussed (Chapter 6), this provision—like its Article II counterpart—is a substantive grant of power. Just as the constitutional generation had an abstract category of powers in mind that they called "executive," so also they had a category they called "judicial." The main "judicial" power, of course, is to hear and decide cases; but the category no doubt also included powers traditionally exercised by eighteenth-century courts to carry out the function of deciding cases—establishing rules of procedure, issuing orders and contempts, and so forth. (These matters are sometimes called "inherent" powers of federal courts, but properly understood they are no more "inherent" than the President's foreign affairs power discussed in Chapter 3: they are granted—"vested"—by the Constitution's explicit, though general, words.)[7]

We have also seen in Chapter 6 that as a textual matter this is necessarily so, because nothing else in Article III (or elsewhere in the Constitution) gives federal courts substantive powers. Most of the rest of Article III describes federal courts' jurisdiction (that is, types of cases they can hear). So, just as Congress is (for the most part) limited to exercising its legislative power on the subject matter listed in Article I, Section 8, the federal courts are limited to exercising their judicial power in the disputes listed in Article III, Section 2. Nothing in this section says what sort of power the courts can exercise in these disputes, though. And although much of federal courts' procedural power today is authorized by statute, Article III assumes that the Supreme Court (though not lower federal courts) exists as an independent constitutional entity not dependent upon Congress for its powers. Its independent powers can only come from "the judicial Power."[8]

Article III, Section 1, thus gives federal courts power to decide cases; standing alone, though, it conveys no duty to act. That duty is imposed by the third paragraph of Article VI: state and federal officials, including "all . . . judicial Officers, both of the United States and of the several States, shall be bound by Oath or Affirmation, to support this Constitution." This obligation parallels the President's duty under the take-care clause (and the same clause of Article VI, which also applies to the President): the President has both the power and the duty to use the executive power to uphold the Constitution; the federal courts have both the power and the duty to use the judicial power to the same end.[9]

Any refusal of federal courts to act (including in foreign affairs cases) must be justified in the face of these provisions. At the same time, the combination of these two provisions suggests two important limits on the courts' powers and duties. First, just as the President cannot act beyond the executive power—by seizing steel mills, for example (Chapter 5)—federal courts cannot act beyond the judicial power. Obviously, they cannot command the army to enforce their judgments; that is not within the judicial power even if it would otherwise serve to support the Constitution. Federal courts also cannot make judgments about things not within the judicial power to judge. Courts' obligations—like the President's obligations—extend only as far as their power. Second, the courts' constitutional obligation is only to support the Constitution (and, it seems to follow, law established by constitutional procedures). Cases not involving questions of constitutional power do not invoke Article VI's duty.

Jurisdiction and Standing

There are, of course, many circumstances under which courts must refuse to hear constitutional claims, despite their Article VI duty. Most obviously, of course, federal courts cannot hear claims if they lack jurisdiction—that is, when the claim does not fall into one of the categories listed in Article III, Section 2.[10] Article III, Section 2 also extends their jurisdiction only to "cases" and "controversies." That has rightly been understood to mean that they cannot answer hypothetical questions, give advisory opinions,[11] or otherwise act outside the type of disputes traditionally thought suitable for judicial resolution. As Marshall (speaking as a member of Congress in 1800) explained, saying that courts could decide cases was not the same as saying that every *question* arising under the Constitution could be heard in court:

> A case . . . was a term well understood, and of limited signification. It was a controversy between parties that had taken shape for judicial decision. If the judicial power extended to every *question* under the Constitution it would involve almost every subject proper for legislative discussion and decision. If to every *question* under the laws and treaties of the United States, it would involve almost every subject on which the executive could act. The division of power could exist no longer, and the other departments would be swallowed up by the judiciary.[12]

The Supreme Court has elaborated this understanding to impose the requirement now known as "standing": a claim must involve an actual or imminent tangible injury to the plaintiff, causally connected to the defendant's conduct and redressable by the court.[13] Assuming this is a fair interpretation of the historical meaning of the "judicial Power" as limited by the "case or controversy" requirement,[14] it establishes a constitutionally required area in which courts cannot act, arising (as Marshall said) from the scope of "the judicial Power" and forming a key element of the Constitution's separation of powers.

Standing and related doctrines apply generally but often have particular force in foreign affairs. It is worth mentioning a few cases to show how these doctrines are (or should be) applied, consistent with the Constitution's text, because often they would resolve cases (mis)described as "political questions." Consider, for example, the constitutional challenge to the North American Free Trade Agreement (NAFTA) (see Chapter 10).[15] As discussed, it claimed that NAFTA was unconstitutional because it was a treaty not approved by two-thirds of the Senate. The court of appeals dismissed the claim as a "political question," but we should now see that this is, at minimum, dubious under Article VI, since the court had a duty to support the Constitution, which should include using its "judicial Power" in cases challenging supposedly unconstitutional actions. A far better ground is standing. No one disputed that Congress had power to pass the regulations of commerce needed to implement NAFTA, which were the only laws directly affecting the plaintiffs. The international obligation to pass those laws may well have been created unconstitutionally (Chapter 10 argues that it was), but that could not make the laws themselves unconstitutional. And the existence of the international obligation had no immediate impact upon the plaintiffs. Put another way, even if the court found NAFTA's international obligations unconstitutional, that would not help the plaintiffs, because they really objected to the (constitutional) implementing statutes. There was thus no "case," in the constitutional sense.

This resolution is wholly consistent with the courts' Article VI obligation. Courts are obliged to use their judicial power to uphold the Constitution, but not obliged (nor allowed) to act outside their judicial power to uphold the Constitution. To the extent that standing requirements are constitutional limitations on judicial power, courts must respect them, and doing so creates no tension with Article VI. Declaring NAFTA's international obligations unconstitutional would not have been consistent with the judicial power—it would have been in effect an advisory opinion—and the courts properly refused to do it.

Particularly in foreign affairs, standing requirements may create situations in which no one can bring a judicial challenge—as is likely true with NAFTA. There is nothing constitutionally odd about that conclusion—it only means that other branches, not the courts, have responsibility to uphold the constitutional limitation. These matters thus become "political" questions, not through some legal doctrine of that name, but because the political branches are the only ones with power to answer them.

These points are also illustrated by Justice Lewis Powell's opinion in *Goldwater*. Powell provided the fifth vote for dismissal (with Rehnquist's "political question" plurality).[16] Although Powell thought the matter did not present a political question, he found it not "ripe for judicial review" because "we do not know whether there ever will be an actual confrontation between the Legislative and Executive branches. . . . If the Congress chooses not to confront the President, it is not our task to do so." If by this Powell meant that Senator Goldwater lacked standing, he likely had a point. It is hard to see what tangible injury Goldwater suffered from the treaty's termination, beyond his belief that the treaty was, strategically, a good idea.[17]

Further, to allow branches of the U.S. government (or members of those branches) to sue each other would make judicial questions out of what are, literally, political questions. It seems doubtful at best that the eighteenth-century understanding of judicial power included authority to resolve abstract constitutional disputes between the President and members of Congress. Goldwater's complaint was fundamentally political—that he had been bypassed in his political decisionmaking capacity; the response also should have been political, by enlisting the Senate to respond using its political powers.

But Powell seemed to have something else in mind, because he said "[p]rudential considerations persuade me" that the case should not be reviewed "until and unless each branch has taken action asserting its constitutional authority." Put this way, his position seems troubling. Appealing to "prudential considerations" is little more than saying he thought it best not to hear the case for policy reasons. If Senator Goldwater had actually suffered constitutional injury, though, Powell's view might still have required Goldwater to get the Senate behind him before Powell would be willing to vindicate that injury. Assuming Goldwater's injury did not depend on the Senate recognizing it, Powell in effect simply refused to right a (potential) constitutional wrong. In terms of our present discussion, he stands on the same ground as Rehnquist's plurality: needing (and not supplying) an explanation of how that course is consistent with the duty imposed by Article VI.[18] The core issue in *Goldwater,* then, is better grasped by imagining a private citizen with tangible interests in rights secured by a treaty, challenging a presidential termination: all of Rehnquist's (and perhaps some of Powell's) purported justifications would remain, but the constitutional tension would be much more troublesome.

Factual and Policy Determinations

Two other related justifications for political question dismissals seem constitutionally sound, but they operate more narrowly than is sometimes suggested (and are not much help in *Goldwater*). First, it is surely true that, especially in international matters, courts sometimes lack access to factual information needed to resolve cases. As Justice Jackson suggested, in the case quoted above, the President may be a far better international fact finder than the courts, and courts should often hesitate to believe that they are acting on complete information. One might suppose that dismissals on this ground could as easily be called decisions on the merits—that is, that the claim had not been proved—but however described, there seems no constitutional barrier to such a conclusion.

Second, as Marshall recognized in *Marbury* itself, the judicial power would not include review of executive policy decisions in foreign affairs. As he put it: "The province of the Court is solely to decide the rights of individuals, not to inquire how the executive, or executive officers, perform duties in which they have a discretion. Questions in their nature political, or which are, by the Constitution and law, submitted to the executive, can never be made in this court."[19] The full scope of what Marshall meant by this is explored later (Chapter 18), but its most obvious applications can hardly be denied. Consider, for example, a claim raised in *Ware*, the British debts litigation, in 1796. Recall that the plaintiffs claimed the 1783 Treaty of Peace overrode Virginia's law preventing recovery by British creditors. One argument in response was that the treaty should not be honored, because Britain had violated it. Under customary treaty practice of the time, it was true that one party's breach made a treaty voidable by the other party. As Justice Iredell pointed out, though, the non-breaching party could also disregard the breach and treat the agreement as remaining in place. That was a policy decision vested with the President under the executive power (see Chapter 8); it was not something courts could decide, because it depended on considerations beyond law. Again, one could call this a "political question"—or simply call it (as Iredell did) something outside the judicial power to address.[20]

Neither point comes close to justifying judicial abstention in *Goldwater*. *Goldwater* did not turn on difficult factual determinations. Nor did it involve an exercise of executive policy discretion, unless one thought interpreting the Constitution was subject to executive discretion. Courts could not judge whether the mutual defense treaty at issue *ought* to be terminated as a policy matter; but (unlike *Ware*) that was not the question asked. Rather, *Goldwater* asked which branch—President or President-plus-Senate—the Constitution required to make that determination; that is simply a question of constitutional interpretation (though, as Rehnquist said, perhaps not an easy one).

Matters Committed to Another Branch

Specific Matters—The Example of Recognition

Justifying the Powell-Rehnquist position in *Goldwater*, then, depends upon finding something *in the Constitution* allowing courts to avoid decisions *on matters of constitutional interpretation*. Courts have a duty to uphold the Constitution, and therefore cannot refuse a claimant's request that they enforce constitutional limitations simply because it might be inconvenient. *Goldwater* itself was likely decided correctly, because Senator Goldwater had no "case" in the constitutional sense (not having suffered a tangible injury). But it is easy to imagine someone tangibly injured by a treaty's termination properly placing the question before the court (in an Article III sense) as Goldwater did not. The question then would be whether the court still could refuse to decide.

A phrase often used is that particular matters are constitutionally committed to other branches.[21] This surely may sometimes be true. To begin, consider a domestic example. The Constitution (Article II, Section 4) provides that federal officers may be removed from office upon impeachment and conviction of "Treason, Bribery, or other high Crimes and Misdemeanors"; Article I, Sections 2 and 3, give impeachment and trial power to the House and Senate respectively. Suppose a federal officer is impeached and convicted but claims some defect in the process—the officer was actually innocent, the act in question was not a high crime or misdemeanor, or there was some procedural irregularity. May the officer now take the claim to federal court? Plainly the court would have Article III, Section 2 jurisdiction and the claimant would have standing. But the Supreme Court has said that federal courts nonetheless cannot decide such cases, because Article I, Section 3 gives the Senate "sole Power to try all Impeachments" and thus prohibits judicial review. If this correctly reads the text, then of course it is perfectly appropriate for courts to refuse to hear the case. And if this is all that is meant by "political questions"—that is, questions the Constitution's text takes away from the courts—then the doctrine is surely consistent with (indeed, required by) the text.[22]

This analysis may have specific applications in foreign affairs. Suppose, for example, that a claim turns upon deciding which is the rightful government of a foreign nation. As Chapter 3 concluded, the Constitution's text gives the President power over recognition and non-recognition of foreign governments, as part of the executive power and the power to receive ambassadors (Chapter 3). A court should not and cannot re-examine which is the rightful government, because in constitutional terms this is a determination given to the President. As Marshall wrote for the Court in *United States v. Palmer* (1818), courts should follow the political branches' determination in deciding whether a revolutionary government in South America was legitimate, because "such questions are generally rather political than legal in their character" and to do otherwise "would transcend the limits prescribed to the judicial department."[23] Whether to accept the Taiwan or Beijing government as the government of China is, then, a question for the President—both because it is a matter of policy and because, to the extent it could be a question of law, it is one committed to the President under the recognition power. The question in *Goldwater*, however, was whether the Constitution allowed the President, acting without the Senate, to terminate a treaty in connection with recognition. This turns on the meaning of the text's "executive Power." A political question dismissal on the grounds outlined above would be appropriate only if the Constitution gave the President power to interpret the phrase "executive Power." But it is hard to identify any language that did so, and the more usual presumption (as in, for example, the *Steel Seizure* case, which broadly raised the same question) is that this is a matter for the courts. Justice Brennan rightly explained in *Goldwater*, "the political-question doctrine restrains courts from reviewing an exercise of foreign policy judgment by the coordinate political branch to which authority to make that judgment has been constitutionally committed. But the doctrine does not pertain when a court is faced with the *antecedent* question whether a particular branch has been constitutionally designated as the repository of political decisionmaking power."[24]

The Vietnam War cases are similar. To the extent they asked whether the war was constitutionally authorized, they turned on interpretation of the Constitution's grants of power to the President and Congress. That interpretation is not committed to the political branches by any specific text. (It would be a different matter if a court were asked to decide whether intervention was "necessary" within the meaning of Congress's authorization of hostilities; this is likely a factual and policy determination given to the President, and thus outside judicial power).[25]

Foreign Affairs in General

Could we argue, however, that all of foreign affairs is "textually committed to the political branches"—specifically, committed to Congress in particular areas by Article I, Section 8 and to the President by Article II? The modern political question doctrine does not claim anything so comprehensive, but the discussion above suggests that this may be the only route to a constitutional defense. And it is a possible reading of Rehnquist's *Goldwater* opinion that, at least where the constitutional text is not plain on its face and the matter concerns foreign affairs, the President should determine the scope of presidential authority.

Answering this question requires a return to broader constitutional principles and attention to the founding-era understanding of the judiciary's role. As a general matter, the text suggests that courts should make independent determinations of constitutionality, by giving federal courts jurisdiction over cases "arising under" the Constitution and giving them the duty to support the Constitution. If courts could not make independent determinations in at least some cases, what would be the point of hearing constitutional cases (which, ordinarily, are challenges to assertions of constitutional authority by some other entity)?

The textual evidence is not wholly conclusive, however, because it is not clear on its face that the "judicial Power" allowed courts to disagree with constitutional claims of other branches of the federal government. (The "arising under" jurisdiction, for example, might only refer to challenges to state actions). English judges traditionally did not have power to overturn acts of Parliament, and their oversight of executive (royal) authority was circumscribed as well (although somewhat less so). One would have to conclude that the constitutional generation envisioned a much-enhanced role for courts in policing the authority of other federal branches.

This role, of course, is what Marshall famously declared in *Marbury*, with respect to the Court's ability to overturn unconstitutional acts of Congress. Commentators have pointed out that Marshall's opinion is not completely airtight, especially from a textual perspective;[26] a complete defense would require its own book-length treatment. We can, however, highlight its key components. The first point is purely textual, as noted above: the Constitution plainly contemplates federal courts deciding constitutional questions; the only issue is whether they should make independent determinations or feel bound by the constitutional determinations of other federal branches.[27] The second point arises from founding-era background understandings that courts would check other federal branches (not just states) by enforcing constitutional boundaries. Such judicial checks are obviously unavailable unless courts make independent constitutional judgments; yet the framers seemed generally to assume they would exist.

A central authority is Hamilton's Federalist No. 78, which sets forth the core ideas of judicial review. Constitutional limitations, Hamilton argued, "can be preserved in practice no other way than through the medium of courts of justice, whose duty it must be to declare all acts contrary to the manifest tenor of the Constitution void." Hamilton went on to reject the idea that courts could not make independent judgments:

> If it be said that the legislative body are themselves the constitutional judges of their own powers and that the construction they put upon them is conclusive upon the other departments it may be answered that this cannot be the natural presumption where it is not to be collected from any particular provisions in the Constitution. It is not otherwise to be supposed that the Constitution could intend to enable the representatives of the people to substitute their *will* to that of their constituents. It is far more rational to suppose that the courts were designed to be an intermediate body between the people and the legislature in order, among other things, to keep the latter within the limits assigned to their authority.[28]

Hamilton's endorsement of judicial review is unmistakable and plainly embraces federal as well as state acts.[29]

The principal response, it seems, is that Hamilton was not representative of common understanding (which is surely true in some cases). And of course it is true that judicial review, in the *Marbury* sense, was not a feature of English law nor widely known in the states prior to the Convention. But Federalist No. 78 echoed the Convention's view of judges as checks upon the constitutional overreaching of other federal branches.[30] As political scientist Keith Whittington explains, founding-era Americans saw the idea of a written Constitution, combined with an independent federal judiciary, as a break with the English system, giving enforceable limits upon their government.[31] That view was widely repeated in the ratifying conventions—James Wilson, for example, told the Pennsylvania convention that "if a law should be made inconsistent with those powers vested by this instrument in Congress, the judges . . . will declare such law to be null and void." As Chapter 1 describes, Samuel Adams made a similar point in urging the adopting of an early version of the Tenth Amendment so that judges could constrain the legislature, and the anti-federalist Brutus agreed that "the judgment of the judiciary, on the constitution, will secure the rule of law to guide the legislature in their construction of their powers."[32] Judicial review was quickly adopted by the federal courts—not just in *Marbury*, but in earlier cases where it was accepted in principle without material hesitation. In 1796

Hamilton wrote of "the appeal to our Courts on the constitutionality of a legislative act" as a right widely understood and embraced.[33]

Even if one accepts judicial review in general, though, that does not establish it in foreign affairs, especially against presidential actions. Rehnquist's claim in *Goldwater* must be that the President's unique role in foreign affairs—and the unique threats to the nation from judicial interference—make judicial review especially inappropriate in foreign affairs even if it is not disputed elsewhere. As a modern academic commentator argues, "[t]he difficulty in deriving judicial standards in foreign affairs controversies is not necessarily due to the complexity or vagueness of the underlying foreign affairs issues, but because the very nature of these foreign affairs powers depend on considerations of 'realpolitik.' "[34]

This is, of course, a plausible position to take as a matter of constitutional policy; the difficulty is that there is essentially no evidence that the framers took it, at least with respect to interpretation of the President's constitutional powers. First, Hamilton's Federalist No. 78 is typical in speaking of judicial review in general terms, without noting a foreign affairs exception (or even a need for courts to be especially cautious in foreign affairs).

Further, this claim seems to misunderstand the historical meaning of executive power and conflate two different types of "foreign affairs" decision-making. As discussed in Chapter 3, "executive" power did include substantial authority to set the nation's policy *with respect to* foreign nations. The extreme difficulty of separating law and policy in this area may indeed support the idea of judicial abstention (or at least deference), as explored in later chapters. *Goldwater* and related cases, though, are not "foreign affairs" cases in this sense. Rather, they concern the *domestic allocation* of foreign affairs authority. *Goldwater* was not about the content of the nation's policy toward China; it was about the allocation of authority between the President and Senate. Nothing in the historical understanding of "executive" power suggests an enhanced role in these sorts of judgments. If anything, the judicial role here seems more consistent with English practice than *Marbury*'s review of legislative authority: English courts were willing to find that acts of the Crown's agents exceeded their constitutional authority.[35]

Third, courts in the early post-ratification years decided *Goldwater*-type cases without any suggestion that they might have an obligation (or even discretion) not to do so. In *Little v. Barreme* (1804), for example, Marshall found that the President exceeded a congressional statute authorizing limited hostilities against France; thus the seizure of the claimant's ship at the President's direction was unlawful as beyond the executive power. In *United States v. Smith* (1806), Justice Paterson, as a circuit judge, found that the

President's executive power did not allow him to violate the federal Neutrality Act by authorizing an attack on a Spanish colony; Paterson flatly declared that "it is the exclusive province of Congress to change a state of peace into a state of war."[36] Earlier, in *Bas v. Tingy* (1800), the claimant asked the Supreme Court to determine whether the United States was at war with France, such that France was an "enemy" within the meaning of a federal statute. The Court (pre-Marshall) delivered an array of opinions, none doubting that the case was appropriately within the Court's power to decide.[37] And in *Brown v. United States* (1814), Marshall found unconstitutional the President's seizure of alien property during wartime because it had not been authorized by Congress—again without any suggestion of "political question" abstention.

As evidence of the Constitution's historical meaning, these cases have obvious difficulties. They took place somewhat after the framing, after the speakers had acquired personal and political interests in the outcomes. In particular, they gave the judiciary power against other branches, and their authors (judges) had institutional reasons for deciding as they did. Nonetheless, they are suggestive. Paterson was an important member of the Philadelphia Convention, and Marshall a strong advocate for ratification in Virginia. Perhaps more important, there is no record that these decisions raised serious constitutional concerns of judicial overreaching.

Further, no judicial opinion of this early period asserted (or even considered) political question abstention of the broader type. It is true that Marshall himself acknowledged "political questions" in foreign affairs beyond the judiciary's cognizance in *Marbury,* and re-affirmed that view in *Palmer.* But, as discussed, Marshall seemed to have in mind the "executive policy" category we have explored (and accepted) earlier, not the sweeping view Rehnquist favored in *Goldwater.* Apparently Marshall did not think *Little,* decided a year after *Marbury,* or *Brown* even arguably posed "political questions" even though they involved constitutional power in wartime. That is presumably because they did not involve the exercise of executive discretion, but rather involved interpretation of legal texts, a power committed to the Court. Again, it is useful to contrast challenges to the content of policies toward foreign nations *(Palmer)* with challenges to authority to formulate policy toward foreign nations *(Little, Smith, Brown). Goldwater* and the NAFTA case fall in the latter category, as do at least some modern war powers cases.

In sum, if one accepts judicial review generally, there is little in the text itself or the founding-era experience suggesting a foreign affairs exception in constitutional cases. If courts are not bound by Congress's constitutional interpretation of congressional powers, presumably they also are not bound by the President's constitutional interpretation of presidential powers. The courts' role in restraining the President within constitutional bounds parallels their role in restraining Congress. To be sure, specific matters (such as recognition) may be exclusively given to the President, just as specific matters (such as impeachment) may be exclusively given to Congress. And where there is a policy determination at stake, which the President makes as a matter of discretion under the executive power, that also is naturally beyond the courts, as Marshall and Iredell said. But these points do not diminish courts' general constitutional duty to decide independently what the Constitution requires, even in foreign affairs. As a result, *Goldwater* seems a poor case for political question abstention: the question addressed the domestic allocation of constitutional powers, which is squarely within the "judicial" power to interpret legal texts, and did not involve executive policy discretion.

Foreign Affairs Abstention in Non-Constitutional Cases

Constitutional cases such as *Goldwater,* NAFTA, and the Vietnam War cases are the most prominent political question decisions, but the doctrine and related principles arise as often in non-constitutional cases. For example, *Kirkpatrick,* mentioned at the outset of the chapter, was a federal statutory case. Although these situations are too varied to give a comprehensive account, we can begin to develop a basic framework for evaluating them.

Claims Not Based on State or Federal Law: *Tel-Oren*

If Article VI is the textual basis of the judiciary's obligation to act, many foreign-affairs-related cases are not implicated by it. Article VI's obligation is appropriately read to include cases arising under federal statutes and treaties, as well as under the Constitution directly; such acts are exercises of constitutional power, and courts fail to support the Constitution if they fail to enforce constitutional exercises of power. Further, as discussed in the next chapter, federal courts appear to have an obligation, in the general case anyway, to apply applicable state law so long as that law is not displaced by Article VI federal lawmaking.

But many cases (especially foreign affairs cases) may not implicate the Constitution even in this indirect way. One court of appeals, for example, was asked to construe provisions of a treaty between Japan and Korea, and declined to do so on political question grounds.[38] Whether or not this was a good result as matter of fairness and practicality, it seems that the Constitution's text has nothing to say in the matter. Assuming that the court had jurisdiction under Article III, Section 2 and that the parties were otherwise properly before it, the court's judicial power might *allow* it to hear the case (and exercise powers traditionally related to hearing it). Declining to hear the case (including on the belief that it might be inconvenient for U.S. foreign affairs) raises no constitutional concerns, though, because Article VI's duty does not apply: the U.S. Constitution is not offended if non-U.S. law is not enforced.

This principle applies broadly to the common situation of claims brought under foreign law. It would also seem true of claims based on the law of nations (international law) (see Chapter 17). In *Tel-Oren v. Libyan Arab Republic,* for example, plaintiffs injured in a terrorist attack in Israel sued the Palestinian Liberation Organization (PLO) and the Libyan government, which allegedly sponsored the terrorists contrary to international law; although the judges disagreed on the appropriate analysis, one (Judge Robb) would have dismissed the case as a political question, because it required courts to make sensitive determinations about the PLO's status and the terrorists' connections to the PLO and Libya.[39] Although, as discussed in the next chapter, courts have statutory and constitutional authority to hear (some) claims based on the law of nations, they have no constitutional obligation to do so, and thus may adopt abstention doctrines to protect the conduct of U.S. foreign affairs, as Judge Robb suggested.[40] And indeed courts commonly apply a range of "abstention" principles to international and foreign law cases, including various considerations grouped under the heading of comity and more specific doctrines of *forum non conveniens* and act of state.[41] So far as the Constitution's text is concerned, this is perfectly acceptable; for the same reasons, political question abstention in this area seems constitutionally defensible.

Conversely, though, all these rules—not just the political question doctrine—are much more problematic applied to claims brought under the Constitution, federal statutes, or treaties (and, perhaps to a lesser extent, state law). It would seem that any abstention rule created solely by a court could not counter the court's constitutionally imposed obligation to uphold constitutionally based law. That does not mean, however, that abstention is never appropriate—only that it must be justified in terms of the Constitution or law based on the Constitution.

Claims Based on Federal Statutes: *Kirkpatrick* and *Japan Whaling*

Claims based on federal statutes may raise foreign affairs difficulties in two ways: statutes may affect the President's foreign affairs power; and private statutory claims may embarrass the conduct of foreign affairs even where no part of the U.S. government is a party, as in *Kirkpatrick*. These require distinct treatment.

Japan Whaling Association v. American Cetacean Society (1986) asked whether federal statutes required the President to certify Japan as violating an international whaling treaty. All nine Justices thought the case justiciable (including Rehnquist, despite *Goldwater*), although they divided 5–4 on the statutes' meaning. The majority concluded: "The political question doctrine excludes from judicial review those controversies which revolve around policy choices and value determinations constitutionally committed for resolution to the halls of Congress or the confines of the Executive Branch. . . . [I]t goes without saying that interpretation of congressional legislation is a recurring and accepted task for the federal courts. It is also evident that the challenge [brought here] . . . presents a purely legal question of statutory interpretation."[42]

This approach is consistent with the discussion above (though hard to reconcile with *Goldwater*), and it seems that we can go further to give the Court an *obligation* to decide. If a statute places a constitutionally authorized limit on the President, the Court's duty to the Constitution includes a duty to the statute. A court could avoid this duty only by finding the statute unconstitutional or finding that the President's construction of the statute bound the court. Of course, the particular statute itself might give the President discretion in certain areas (approximately what the majority found in *Japan Whaling*), and that discretion would not be judicially reviewable[43]—but if it did not, there is no constitutional reason to think that the executive's interpretation of another branch's act should be conclusive. The decision whether the values reflected in the statute are worth its interference with the President's conduct of foreign affairs was already made by Congress in passing the statute; the Court's constitutional duty is to uphold, not revisit, that determination.

Kirkpatrick is more complicated, because it involved a general statute that might cause foreign affairs interference in some situations and not others; such cases typically do not address the executive branch directly, but their resolution might nonetheless "embarrass" the conduct of U.S. foreign relations by, for example, insulting foreign governments or contradicting U.S. foreign policy. In the specific facts of *Kirkpatrick*, one corporation sued another under the federal Foreign Corrupt Practices Act, claiming that the defendant had bribed the Nigerian government and thus secured a contract that should have gone to the plaintiff. The defense argued (unsuccessfully) that deciding the case could embarrass foreign relations by finding the Nigerian government corrupt.

Several approaches are available here, only some of which raise constitutional concerns. As an initial matter, there is a statutory question whether the law should be read to cover the alleged conduct. In making this determination, courts employ a series of presumptions or canons of construction designed to limit unintended interference with foreign policy matters. Courts say, for example, that they will not construe generally worded statutes to have extraterritorial effect, or to violate international law, unless Congress plainly intends to do so.[44] Such presumptions appear to be "sub-constitutional" law, which the text likely neither requires nor forbids. At least now that the presumptions are well established, they seem sensibly incorporated as part of the background understanding against which Congress legislates. And they do not seem in tension with eighteenth-century understandings— at least one, and probably both, of these presumptions can easily be traced to near the founding era.

In addition to rules clearly described as interpretive presumptions, there are several well-established doctrines of restraint whose basis is less certain. Chief among these is the so-called act-of-state doctrine, at issue in *Kirkpatrick,* directing that courts give conclusive effect to the official acts of foreign governments done in their own territory.[45] Another is the related rule of foreign sovereign immunity—now codified in the 1976 Foreign Sovereign Immunities Act, but conceptually troublesome in earlier times.[46] The constitutional interaction of these doctrines and federal law remains poorly understood.

We might say, at least with respect to federal law, that these rules operate as presumptions as well—that is, courts will not assume federal statutes intend to open foreign sovereigns to liability, or allow judgments on foreign acts of state, unless they clearly say so. This appears to be the foundation of the seminal U.S. foreign sovereign immunity case, Marshall's decision in *The Schooner Exchange v. McFadden* (1812).[47] Like presumptions against extraterritoriality and violations of international law, one might see these rules as sub-constitutional law (or, in modern terms, "federal common law") that courts could adopt to aid their interpretation of federal law, but which Congress could overturn generally or in particular statutes.[48] Again, this would not seem precluded (nor required) by constitutional text.

We could also, however, make a stronger case for these doctrines. In *McFadden,* the executive branch argued that courts were obliged to recognize foreign sovereign immunity, because the matter was executive rather than judicial in nature.[49] That is, executive foreign affairs power encompasses relations with foreign sovereigns, such that righting foreign sovereign wrongs is necessarily part of the diplomatic, not the judicial, process. In some early twentieth-century act-of-state cases, the Court seemed to embrace the idea that the constitutional nature of "judicial Power" precluded courts from addressing sovereign wrongs, which were properly matters of negotiation, retaliation, or war.[50] On this view, the foreign sovereign immunity and act-of-state doctrines are required by the constitutional division of foreign affairs authority implicit in the allocation of "executive" and "judicial" power, at least in the absence of contrary direction from the President or Congress. (One might even say they are required *regardless* of congressional or presidential attempts to dispense with them, though this view lacks authority in practice and is emphatically rejected by modern law).

Beyond these specific doctrines and presumptions, one might claim a broader "political question" rule precluding the application of federal statutes in ways that would (as the district court put it in *Kirkpatrick*) "result in embarrassment to the [foreign] sovereign or constitute interference in the conduct of the foreign policy of the United States."[51] This, though, seems hard to sustain as either a presumption or a constitutional command. Unlike the specific doctrines, there is little historical basis for such an approach. Recognizing such a rule is tantamount to giving the President general authority to suspend the operation of federal law by exercising foreign affairs power. It seems unlikely that Congress would intend to grant such a suspensive power if it did not say so directly, and as a constitutional matter it seems in substantial tension with the President's duty to take care that the laws be faithfully executed (Chapter 8). Further, the specific doctrines—to the extent they can be anchored in the founding era—militate against the broader rule. Rather, it seems that the specific doctrines are ways to achieve the general goal of avoiding foreign policy interference, without requiring courts to engage in case-by-case determinations.[52]

In sum, application of federal law can be limited to protect the conduct of foreign policy by specific doctrines and presumptions fairly tied to Congress's intent and background understandings or to constitutional allocations of power. A broad "political question" presumption, though, is difficult to tie to either and thus difficult to find within the powers and duties of federal courts. Ordinarily, as Scalia said in *Kirkpatrick,* a court's obligation is to apply the statute. The "political" evaluation of its effect on foreign affairs is done by Congress in the enactment.

Claims Based on State Law: *Sabbatino*

More difficult questions arise with state laws that interfere with foreign affairs. The Supreme Court in *Banco Nacional de Cuba v. Sabbatino* (1964) applied the act-of-state doctrine to claims brought under state law and appeared to require state courts to do the same. Some federal courts of appeal have gone even further, invoking a supposed "federal common law of foreign relations" to dismiss state-law claims they find potentially embarrassing to the federal conduct of foreign affairs.[53]

The constitutional authority for such judicial power is (at best) unsettled,[54] and as a matter of the text's historical meaning seems problematic. As discussed in Chapters 13, 14, and 17, under the text's historical meaning (and under the 1789 Rules of Decision Act) federal courts have a duty to enforce applicable state law, so long as it is not preempted by federal law under Article VI. If those chapters are correct that state laws interfering with federal foreign policy are not unconstitutional, it would be odd to conclude that federal courts could, as a matter of non-constitutional "common law," ignore them (and especially odd to think that federal courts could on such basis direct state courts not to enforce them).

The best textual argument for this sort of federal common law runs approximately as follows. As a general matter, it is true that federal courts must rely on the Constitution (or statutes or treaties) for authority to create rules binding on the states. Standing alone, it is unlikely that Article III's "judicial Power" conveys this power. Nothing in the history of eighteenth-century courts, or in the founding-era debates, suggests that anyone thought federal courts had free-floating power to displace state law. The anti-federalists' great worry was that federal courts would use expansive readings *of treaties and the Constitution* to displace the states (surely side issues if courts had a general common-law power of displacement). Nonetheless, it is possible that the Constitution elsewhere indicated narrow areas of federal judicial common-law authority.[55]

Article III, Section 2, for example, gives federal courts jurisdiction over disputes between states. What source of law did its drafters think would ordinarily be used to resolve such disputes? Federal statutory law (or constitutional law) would rarely apply; and if state laws conflicted—presumably the usual case in these disputes—federal courts would have no obvious way to pick between them. Perhaps, though, the Constitution implicitly granted federal courts authority to develop rules for resolving state-against-state disputes—rules that necessarily would be binding on the states (and preemptive of their laws). This is, at any rate, what the Supreme Court has long held in cases involving interstate boundary and water disputes.[56]

The *Sabbatino* decision relied heavily on this idea, for obvious reasons. But it is less clear that federal courts must have authority to apply the act-of-state doctrine as preemptive federal common law, in the manner of the law of disputes between states. They had not done so prior to *Sabbatino,* and nothing calamitous had resulted. Nonetheless, an argument might be made, adopting the executive branch's argument in *McFadden:* if executive power encompasses power to redress foreign sovereigns' wrongs, perhaps that displaces federal and state courts from such a role. In other words, if the act-of-state doctrine is constitutionally based, *Sabbatino* is rightly (though confusingly) decided.[57]

Even if *Sabbatino* is correct, though, the modern "federal common law of foreign relations" cases seem too great a stretch to claim support in the text's historical meaning. As discussed, state laws in the early post-ratification period caused foreign policy difficulties, but no one thought that federal courts, on that basis alone, could displace them. If such a power existed, it would make nonsense of the arguments in *Ware,* in which lawyers and Justices debated whether the Treaty of Peace conflicted with the state debt confiscation laws, such that the latter were preempted. In effect, the modern cases seek to establish a *Zschernig*-like (or *Holocaust Insurance*-like) rule through the back door, calling it common law instead of constitutional law. But it suffers from the same absence of textual authority. Article VI—not Article III—is the remedy for state laws threatening the conduct of foreign affairs.[58]

Conclusion

By Article VI, courts have the obligation to use their constitutional powers to support the Constitution. For federal courts, under Article III, those constitutional powers include jurisdiction over and power to decide, among others, cases arising under the Constitution, under federal statutes and treaties, and under state law in some circumstances. These textual provisions combine to convey—in general—an obligation to decide such cases in accordance with the Constitution and constitutionally authorized acts. And the separated-power structure of constitutional government, combined with the evident expectation of the constitutional generation, confirms what Hamilton said in Federalist No. 78 (and Marshall said in *Marbury*): that in exercising this power courts exercise independent judgment.

Cases like *Goldwater* seek a general foreign affairs exception to this judicial role, suggesting that courts may (or must) abstain from this duty in cases affecting the conduct of U.S. foreign relations. There may be specific exceptions to the judicial obligation to decide, created by the text itself (recognition of foreign governments, for example) or by the nature of the judicial power (for, perhaps, the act-of-state doctrine and foreign sovereign immunity). And of course the judicial power does not authorize courts to second-guess discretionary foreign policy decisionmaking, as Marshall said in *Marbury*. But nothing in the text or founding-era history indicates a general foreign affairs exception. It rests instead on policy—a modern view of policy, not one fairly traced to the Constitution's historical meaning or founding-era background assumptions.

17

The Paquete Habana:
Is International Law
Part of Our Law?

"International law is part of our law," Justice Horace Gray wrote for the Supreme Court in 1900, "and must be ascertained and administered by the courts of justice of appropriate jurisdiction as often as questions of right depending upon it are duly presented for their determination." He claimed no text or other constitutional authority in support, and it is not even clear he thought he was interpreting the Constitution. The case itself, *The Paquete Habana,* involved unusual facts—the U.S. Navy's seizure of Spanish fishing boats during the Spanish-American War—and Gray did not elaborate upon his meaning.[1] Yet the case has become pivotal, almost talismanic, in modern debates over the relationship between international law and constitutional law, in part because the Court did not hear another major international law case for 104 years.

If we evaluate the question on what appear to be Gray's literal terms, it takes on an all-or-nothing quality: either international law is part of "our" law—meaning constitutionally incorporated in full into U.S. domestic law—or it is not. This is the tenor of much modern debate, which tends to pose the question as whether international law is or is not "federal" law.[2] As we will see, however, that is not what Gray meant—and more important, not what the Constitution's text provides.

The Eighteenth-Century Law of Nations

The Framers and the Law of Nations

To begin, founding-era Americans recognized a set of international obligations they called the "law of nations." The Constitution's text shows this directly: Article I, Section 8 gives Congress power to "define and punish . . . Offenses against the Law of Nations." The phrase invokes the eighteenth-century conception of a system of rights and duties arising from the nature of the international system, which was binding (at least in some senses) upon the United States and its citizens. As Blackstone wrote:

> [A]s it is impossible for the whole race of mankind to be united in one great society, they must necessarily divide into many; and form separate states, commonwealths and nations; entirely independent of each other, and yet liable to a mutual intercourse. Hence arises a third kind of law to regulate this mutual intercourse, called "the law of nations"; which, as none of these states will acknowledge a superiority in the other, cannot be dictated by either; but depends upon the rules of natural law, or upon mutual compacts, treaties, leagues and agreements between these several communities. . . . [3]

Blackstone echoed the Enlightenment writers encountered in prior chapters—including Vattel, Bynkershoek, Wolff, Burlamaqui, Pufendorf, Grotius, and Rutherforth—who described "legal" relationships among nations and were well known in eighteenth-century America. They called their field the "law of nations," a term often reflected in the very titles of their works: Vattel's *Droit des Gens* (1758); Wolff's *Jus Gentium* (1749). According to Vattel: "The Law of Nations is the science of the rights which exist between Nations or States, and of the obligations corresponding to these rights."[4]

The eighteenth-century law of nations was no mere academic concept. As Americans quickly learned after independence, it could inspire diplomatic protests and threats from nations with which the United States needed good relations. In 1784, for example, as recounted in Chapter 2, Charles de Longchamps assaulted French Consul General Marbois in Philadelphia. France protested strongly, couching its objections as a matter of the law of nations, and demanded that the Congress take action.[5]

Concerns about complying with the law of nations appeared often in the period leading to the Philadelphia Convention and in the ratification debates. The central problem, discussed in Chapter 2, was that the Articles' Congress lacked power to enforce the law of nations. In the de Longchamps incident, it could do little more than refer the matter to the relevant state, Pennsylvania, and hope for the best. Leaders such as Madison, Hamilton, Randolph and Jay thought this problematic, because law-of-nations violations could damage national foreign policy—even lead to war—and needed to be brought under national control.[6]

Early Americans viewed the Articles' law-of-nations problems in tandem with similar problems afflicting treaties. Leading writers called treaties a branch of the law of nations.[7] Like the unwritten law of nations, treaties were international obligations of the national government, but because the Congress lacked enforcement power, it could do little to prevent treaty violations. The national government tried unsuccessfully to encourage compliance; again as discussed in Chapter 2, states' violations, especially of the 1783 peace treaty, soured relations with Britain and frustrated efforts to make additional treaties. As with the unwritten law of nations, treaty enforcement became a key justification for the new Constitution—often the two were combined within a single argument.[8]

As an initial step, then, we may conclude that the constitutional generation in America acknowledged a set of external obligations called "the law of nations" and believed compliance with this law was a national duty and vital to successful foreign policy.

Sources of the Law of Nations

It will also be helpful to sketch briefly eighteenth-century ideas of the law of nations, although any summary is necessarily oversimplified. Modern debate often equates the eighteenth-century "law of nations" with what today we call "customary international law": an unwritten body of law derived from nations' common practices. In the modern positivist account, unwritten international law derives *only* from practice; one could view the system as founded on tacit consent given by national sovereigns.[9]

The eighteenth-century view was more complex, and more openly based on natural law identified by reason. As Vattel put it, "the Law of Nations is in its origin merely the Law of Nature applied to *Nations*."[10] Blackstone, we have seen, said that the law of nations "depends upon the rules of natural law, or upon mutual compacts, treaties, leagues, and agreements between these several communities." Vattel even subtitled his work "Principles of Natural Law Applied to the Conduct and to the Affairs of Nations and of Sovereigns."

The overriding impulse in eighteenth-century law was not positivism but rationalism. Much of the idea, at least, was that principles of international relations could be discovered through reason, from the nature and needs of the international system. Wolff called his 1749 work "The Law of Nations Treated According to a Scientific Method"; as the title indicated, it was methodologically deductive rather than descriptive, deriving rules logically from universally accepted first principles.[11] The law of nations, Vattel explained, is "the law which ought to prevail between Nations or sovereign States"; as he quoted Wolff: "the Law of Nations is certainly connected with the Law of Nature. Hence we call it the natural Law of Nations, by reference to its origins; and by reference to its binding force we call it the *necessary* law of nations. This law is common to all nations, and that nation which does not act according to it violates the common law of all mankind." It was, Vattel said, "founded on the nature of things, and particularly on the nature of man. . . ."[12]

American leaders echoed Vattel's appeal to reason. James Iredell said that "the only way to ascertain the duties which one nation owes another, is to enquire what reason dictates, that attribute which the Almighty has bestowed upon all mankind for the ultimate guide and director of their conduct." James Wilson called the law of nations "the law of nature applied to states and sovereigns." U.S. Supreme Court Justice Joseph Story wrote as late as 1822 that the law of nations "may be fairly deduced by correct reasoning from the rights and duties of nations, and the nature of moral obligation."[13]

Appeals to custom and practice, though, had more actual force than Vattel's theoretical discussions suggested. Vattel himself admitted that his arguments were more persuasive when he could "show[] how the practice of Nations has conformed to principle," and arguments about the usual way of doing things carried significant weight. At another point Vattel described the system in part as resting on "[c]ertain rules and customs, consecrated by long usage, and observed by nations as a sort of law." Blackstone emphasized this hybrid character in describing "a system of rules, deducible by natural reason, and established by universal consent among the civilized inhabitants of the world."[14] And when Americans sought to put the law of nations into practice, reliance on custom became more pronounced. As Jefferson later said, the "principles of the law of nations" were "evidenced by the Declarations, Stipulations and Practice of every civilized Nation."[15] At the risk of some oversimplification, we might say that practice was thought to be evidence of the natural state of nations.

In sum, the eighteenth-century law of nations had complex and not fully articulable foundations. It mixed Enlightenment rationalism with older reliance on tradition and the already-rising ideas that became nineteenth-century positivism. The upshot was that although some principles were well-accepted and understood in considerable detail, others were not. Its substantial foundation on rationalism meant that rules were often not easily agreed. As Blackstone wrote of determining natural law by reason:

> And if our reason were always, as in our first ancestor before his transgression, clear and perfect, unruffled by passions, unclouded by preju-

dice, unimpaired by disease or intemperance, the task would be pleasant and easy; we should need no other guide but this. But every man now finds the contrary in his own experience; that his reason is corrupt, and his understanding full of ignorance and error.[16]

Not surprisingly, authorities frequently disagreed upon the right rule, and equally unsurprisingly, they often appealed to practice (as well as reason) in support. But because the system lacked an internal rank of priorities, it was hard, in such circumstances, to say who was right.[17]

Concern about the law of nations' imprecision showed up, among other places, at the Philadelphia Convention, in drafting Article I, Section 8's define-and-punish clause. Initially, the clause gave Congress power to define and punish offenses on the high seas, and to punish offenses against the law of nations. Gouverneur Morris proposed applying "define and punish" to both high-seas and law-of-nations offenses—"the law of nations," he said, "being often too vague and deficient to be a rule." The Convention adopted his proposal, producing the existing language (over Wilson's objection that purporting to "define" the law of nations for all the world would be presumptuous).[18]

Nonetheless, the vagueness of the eighteenth-century law of nations should not be overstated. Some matters were quite clear—for example, the immunity of ambassadors and the obligation of treaties. As we shall see, some parts were thought suitable for resolution in court, without clarification by enacted law. That was so, in particular, in areas that now seem like part of private transnational law rather than "public" international law but formed part of the eighteenth-century law of nations: matters such as international commercial transactions, admiralty and maritime law, conflicts of law, *etc.*, which governed purely private behavior and regularly appeared in court.[19]

In sum, the eighteenth-century law of nations defies easy description. It arose in part from reason and in part from practice; sovereign consent was sometimes important and sometimes not; it was both accessible and obscure.

The Law of Nations and the Supreme Law of the Land

Incorporation by Statute or Treaty

We can now turn to the question of how the Constitution addressed the law of nations. This was a key issue: although Americans (in theory) thought the law of nations should be followed, they knew from experience it often would not be. Further, while accepting that the law of nations should be followed, they understood that there might be much dispute over what it required, and thus a key question was what entities would make that determination.

The Constitution's text provides two obvious solutions. Article I, Section 8 gives Congress power to make law-of-nations rules part of U.S. law, under its define-and-punish power. Congress could, for example, establish ambassadorial immunities—as it did in 1790.[20] Further, under its many foreign affairs powers, Congress could incorporate law-of-nations provisions. Through its power to provide "Rules for the Government and Regulation of the land and naval Forces," it could require the military to comply with the laws of war (see Chapter 12); and through its foreign commerce power, it could apply law-of-nations standards to commercial transactions.

These powers alone greatly improved the Articles' system. As we have seen, the Articles' Congress mostly lacked legislative authority, outside narrow fields such as the military, other national offices, and the territories. Even absent contrary state law, it frequently could not provide rules enforcing the law of nations, as shown by the de Longchamps incident. The Articles' Congress could only ask states to make law;[21] the new Congress could make law itself.

Further, Article VI assured that any (constitutional) law Congress made was supreme law, for individuals and (most importantly) for the states (Chapter 14). With Article I, Section 8 and Article VI, the new national government would rarely, if ever, be unable to force compliance with the law of nations when it wished, even over state objections (as long, of course, as the law of nations did not require unconstitutional acts). And rules adopted by federal statute became part of federal courts' jurisdiction under Article III, Section 2, so federal courts could insist upon supremacy (though Article VI further emphasized that supreme law also bound state judges). These provisions directly responded to the chief complaint of the Articles' critics, who focused largely upon the Congress's inability to make supreme law.

As we have seen (Chapter 8), Article VI also included treaties, as well as statutes, within supreme law. Congress's Article I powers would likely have allowed it to implement most treaties by statute (Chapter 10), but the drafters had particularly frustrating experiences with state treaty violations and opted to adopt treaties automatically into domestic law (again with a corresponding provision of Article III, Section 2 giving federal courts jurisdiction over "cases . . . arising under . . . Treaties"). With respect to the *written* law of nations, then, Article VI addressed the Articles' structural defects by creating "self-executing" treaties (and of course treatymakers could incorporate unwritten law-of-nations standards into treaties, making them part of supreme law).

In sum, Article I, Section 8 and Article VI provided a solution for the Articles' law-of-nations difficulties. That does not mean it was the *only* solution. The bare fact that Congress and the treatymakers had power to establish law-of-nations rules as supreme law, and to give courts power to enforce them, does not show this power was exclusive. We must ask whether Article VI (or some other provision) went further, making the unwritten law of nations "self-executing" in the sense of entering U.S. "supreme Law" of its own force (as treaties did), with Congress's defining power as a backup and tool for clarification in difficult cases.

The Law of Nations as Supreme Law of Its Own Force

If the Constitution's drafters wanted to make the unwritten law of nations part of supreme law, Article VI would have been the place to do it. Article VI solved the Articles' problems with one part of the law of nations—treaties— and its drafters could have easily included the unwritten law of nations as well (as they did in Article I, Section 8). As discussed in Chapter 14, Article VI defined the basic relationship between state and federal power. Omitting the law of nations from Article VI's catalogue of supreme law suggests it lacks that status, unless one could show a good reason for its omission. And the text shows clearly enough that it was omitted.

Article VI's key clause, again, reads:

> This Constitution, and the Laws of the United States which shall be made in Pursuance thereof; and all Treaties made, or which shall be made, under the Authority of the United States, shall be the supreme Law of the Land; and the judges in every State shall be bound thereby, any Thing in the Constitution or Laws of any State to the Contrary notwithstanding.

Even if the law of nations counts among "the Laws of the United States,"[22] no eighteenth-century writer would have described it as "made in Pursuance" of the U.S. Constitution, as Article VI requires for supreme law. The eighteenth-century law of nations arose outside any single country, partly from rational inquiry into the nature of the international system and partly from long-standing practices.[23] It existed prior to and separate from the United States and U.S. constitutional processes.

Further, Article VI refers to "Laws of the United States" in the future tense: laws "which shall be made," not those already made (mainly indicating that ordinances of the Articles' Congress did not become part of the new system). In contrast, Article VI's treaty supremacy embraces past and future treaties: "Treaties made [past tense], or which shall be made [future tense]" are supreme (unsurprisingly, since the drafters particularly worried about states violating the 1783 peace treaty).[24] As a result, supreme law encompasses treaties made after 1776 but only "laws of the United States" made after 1789.

The law of nations, though, pre-existed the Constitution, in eighteenth-century understandings. There would be no reason to include only *new* parts of the law of nations—the long-established rules, such as ambassadorial immunity, most worried the drafters. Further, the law of nations became applicable to the United States, in eighteenth-century understanding, upon independence in 1776, not after the Constitution's ratification. As John Jay later wrote: "Prior to the date of the Constitution, the United States had, by taking a place among the nations of the earth, become amenable to the law of nations. . . ."[25] Ambassadors' immunities, for example, existed long prior to the Constitution and bound the nation in the Articles period, as shown by the de Longchamps incident; such long-standing rules would not fit within the future-oriented phrasing of Article VI's "Laws of the United States." Of course, excluding the law of nations was not the main point of this language, but if Article VI was supposed to include the law of nations, it would not have been drafted this way.

Context suggests a deliberate omission. The Articles' Congress faced parallel problems with enforcing its own resolutions, treaties, and the law of nations. Key drafters such as Madison and Randolph described treaty enforcement and law-of-nations enforcement as two parts of the same defect. There was no reason to think that the law of nations would somehow become automatically "supreme," absent Article VI, while laws and treaties would not; none had been supreme (at least as a practical matter) under the Articles. And the law of nations—explicitly mentioned in Article I, Section 8—could easily have been explicitly mentioned in Article VI as well. Lack of a parallel reference to the unwritten law of nations in Article VI, despite parallel structural difficulties under the Articles, indicates a conscious decision to treat it differently.

Under this reading, the least-controversial implication is that law-of-nations duties conflicting with otherwise-constitutional federal statutes (or the Constitution itself) do not become duties within the constitutional system and cannot be enforced in U.S. court. Of course they still exist, and individuals or foreign nations can complain about violations. But for constitutional purposes, the law-of-nations duty is subordinate to contrary "supreme Law" under Article VI. Thus Congress could lift ambassadors' immunities, direct naval blockades not recognizing law-of-nations exceptions, or endorse treating wartime prisoners contrary to unwritten laws of war.[26] Article VI directs that, as a constitutional matter, anything within Article VI prevails over anything outside it.[27] For the same reason, statutory "definitions" of the law of nations under Article I, Section 8 bind U.S. courts (even though, as Wilson said at the Convention, these could not be conclusive internationally).

More controversially, state governments and state courts have no constitutional obligation to the law of nations, except as incorporated by statute or treaty. Like the federal government, states could lift ambassadors' law-of-nations immunity (assuming no applicable treaty or statute), and ambassadors would have no recourse in the domestic legal system.[28] That conclusion may seem a troubling echo of the Articles' discredited system, but it follows directly from leaving the law of nations out of Article VI: as Chapter 14 concludes, Article VI is the source of state governments' constitutional duties. Because the law of nations is omitted from Article VI, it is not "federal" law in this sense, at least. State courts and officers are thus (constitutionally) free to disregard it.

So much seems clear from the text itself. But what of federal courts faced with conflicts between state law and the law of nations? Article VI, read literally, only resolves conflicts between supreme law and non-supreme law; the law of nations and state law are two types of non-supreme law. Perhaps federal courts could decline to enforce state laws conflicting with, say, ambassadorial immunity, not because the Constitution required it, but simply because that seemed like good policy.[29] Federal courts could not command states, because they could not appeal to any law superior to state law—but that need not require them to enforce state law.

Here we must rely on background assumptions, which we have seen in prior chapters to be a dangerous enterprise. But here matters seem tolerably clear. To allow federal courts to enforce the law of nations in conflict with state law, we would need to say that Article III, Section 1's "judicial Power" gives federal courts authority to not enforce otherwise-applicable state laws. Previous chapters reject this proposition as a general matter. Article VI, we have concluded, protects not only the federal government but also the states: it assures that state laws are displaced only through processes that incorporate political "safeguards" for state interests.[30] As discussed, the drafting and ratifying debates focused on Article VI as the provision empowering federal courts to refuse enforcement of state laws, a point emphasized by both critics and supporters. To federalists, including treaties in Article VI appeared necessary to allow (not merely compel) courts to override conflicting state laws, such as the Virginia debt statutes.[31] Anti-federalists showed much distrust of (we might say paranoia about) federal courts, but made no sustained objection that federal courts might have an open-ended power to ignore state law, untethered to Article VI. Rather, Article VI and the laws it made supreme were the target of concern. "Brutus," a leading anti-federalist writer, argued that federal courts might use the "reason and spirit of the Constitution" to "effect . . . an entire subversion of the legislative, executive and judicial powers of the individual states." He assumed, though, that courts would need to tie such judgments to the Constitution in some manner; he did not suggest that federal courts could refuse to enforce state laws on the courts' own authority.[32]

Nor is it likely that the law of nations was an exception to this general understanding. If this had been intended, it could easily have been accomplished by including the phrase "law of nations" (already used in Article I, Section 8) in Article VI, instead of leaving matters to implication. Under the Articles, the states decided how their laws interacted with the law of nations and when and whether they should give way. As the Tenth Amendment makes clear, states surrendered sovereignty only to the extent of the Constitution. Federal courts' refusal to enforce state laws derogates from state sovereignty, which courts can only do if authorized by the Constitution. The debates repeatedly assumed that Article VI, not Article III, is the way the Constitution conveys this authority.

Post-ratification events confirm this view, in at least three ways. First, when Congress in 1789 established the federal courts, it directed that "the laws of the several states, except where the constitution, treaties, or statutes of the United States shall otherwise require or provide, shall be regarded as rules of decision in trials at common law in the courts of the United States in cases where they apply."[33] If this so-called Rules of Decisions Act (Section 34 of the Judiciary Act of 1789) simply restated the constitutional rule of Article VI, as seems likely given the absence of debate, that confirms both that Article VI did not include the law of nations and that federal courts lacked power to ignore state law except on the authority of Article VI. Historian Charles Warren concluded of Section 34: "The idea that a Federal Court in a State was to administer any other law than the law of that State . . . or to administer law as an entirely free and independent tribunal, never appears to have entered the mind of anyone."[34]

Second, despite the enormous investment modern commentary has placed in proving international law to be part of our law, it has found no record of federal courts refusing to apply state statutes conflicting with the law of nations (or, generally, on any other non–Article VI ground) in the immediate post-ratification period.[35] (That appears to include, moreover, areas not covered by the Rules of Decisions Act—i.e., matters not "trials at common law.") And the early approach makes much practical sense: because state and federal courts often had concurrent jurisdiction, the opposite rule might result in a state statute being valid or invalid depending on whether the case was in federal or state court.[36]

Third, when this issue confronted the Supreme Court in *Ware v. Hylton* (1796), the Justices who addressed it thought state statutes prevailed over contrary law-of-nations rules. *Ware,* as we have seen, principally held that the 1783 peace treaty overrode Virginia's debt confiscation law; the Justices thought their power to override Virginia's law flowed from Article VI.[37] The British creditors also argued that Virginia's law violated the law of nations, which (supposedly) did not allow seizure of intangible property during wartime. The Justices, though unsympathetic to Virginia and inclined to accept the creditors' view of the law of nations, appeared to think the Virginia legislature's command was definitive unless some constitutionally superior law could be found. As Justice Chase put it:

> It is admitted, that Virginia could not confiscate private debts without a violation of the modern law of nations, yet if in fact, she has so done, the [state] law is obligatory on all the citizens of Virginia, and on her Courts of Justice; and, in my opinion, on all the Courts of the United States. If Virginia by such conduct violated the law of nations, she was answerable to Great Britain, and such injury could only be redressed in the treaty of peace.[38]

Justice Iredell agreed:

> [T]he acts of the Legislature of the State, in regard to the subject in question, so far as they were conformable to the Constitution of the State, and not in violation of any article of the confederation (where that was concerned) were absolutely binding de facto, and that if, in respect to foreign nations, or any individual belonging to them, they were not strictly warranted by the law of nations, which ought to have

been their guide, the acts were not for that reason void, but the State was answerable to the United States, for a violation of the law of nations, which the nation injured might complain of to the sovereignty of the Union.[39]

Iredell went on to say that after ratification, Article VI bound the states; but he (unlike the rest of the Court) thought the treaty did not displace the statute.[40]

Justice Cushing appeared to agree with Iredell and Chase on the effect of the law of nations, similarly focusing on the treaty's Article VI-based status: "A State may make what rules it pleases; and those rules must necessarily have place within itself. But here is a treaty, the supreme law, which overrules all State laws upon the subject, to all intents and purposes; and that makes the difference."[41]

Although not technically a holding (Iredell, who had been on the court below, expressed his views but said he would not vote unless the Court were evenly divided), these opinions indicate that these Justices did not place the law of nations within supreme law nor think federal courts could use the law of nations to disregard conflicting state laws. The early Court did not always reflect constitutional consensus, of course, but its law-of-nations discussion in *Ware* did not seem to provoke contemporaneous objection.[42]

Counterarguments arise mainly not from text but from background understandings and the sheer implausibility of the drafters allowing states to violate the law of nations. Perhaps, it is said, the law of nations' superiority was so broadly assumed that it was not necessary to declare it expressly. The drafters surely thought it bound the nation and did not think its duties could be denied by domestic acts. (When France asserted its ambassador's rights, for example, it would not have been sufficient to point to some domestic act purporting to override them.) In this sense, the law of nations was plainly "superior," in that its duties could not ordinarily be altered by the laws (or even the constitution) of one country.[43] As Louis Henkin suggests, perhaps it became part of supreme law "automatically, tacitly" as "law of extra-constitutional origin."[44]

Relatedly, although the drafters knew that law-of-nations violations did occur and may have believed violations might sometimes be necessary, surely everyone thought such decisions belonged at the national level. States' law-of-nations violations threatened national foreign policy under the Articles, and key framers repeatedly emphasized the need to unify foreign policy—including enforcement of the law of nations. As a result (it is said), even if the text does not strictly accomplish this result, it is compelled by the framers' general design and the logical and practical imperatives of federalism.

Both claims contain some truth but do not compel a different reading of the text. It is indeed unlikely that the drafters wanted to preserve states' authority to violate the law of nations. The question they confronted, though, is *what entity* would decide what the law of nations required. The eighteenth-century law of nations was no clear command: it depended upon reason and deduction from natural principles, which necessarily precluded it being comprehensively and definitively established. As Morris said at the Convention, it was often too vague to form rules of conduct. The drafters thus may have believed that the unwritten law of nations needed congressional definition before it became supreme law; treaty obligations, being written, were more definite and suitable to be supreme law in themselves.

This structural concern becomes stronger if one takes into account competing considerations. States were jealous of their sovereignty. The idea of "self-executing" treaties, a consequence of Article VI, produced firestorms of criticism in the ratifying debates, particularly in Virginia. Some Virginia federalists backpedaled so hard that they almost ended up denying the effect of the provision; they sought to diminish its importance by maintaining—perhaps disingenuously—that Congress as a whole would usually be involved, directly or indirectly, before a treaty became fully effective.[45] Further, key anti-federalists such as Brutus sharply distrusted the federal judiciary, which they thought threatened state sovereignty merely with its power to expound the (written) Constitution. We can easily imagine that constitutionally subjecting states to a "self-executing" but ill-defined law of nations—to be expounded by the distrusted federal judiciary—would have been quite unpopular. Including the law of nations in Article VI would place the "defining" power, in the first instance, in the federal courts, with the states being obliged to seek relief from Congress in the event of judicial overreach. Reversing the procedure—that is, placing the "defining" power only in Congress or the treatymakers—gave the states the "political safeguards of federalism" built into the federal legislative system, and thus presented a more-palatable alternative.[46]

And, even without a "self-executing" law of nations, the Constitution's system was a great improvement upon the Articles. If states created diplomatic troubles by infringing ambassadors' immunities, or otherwise violating the law of nations, Congress could use its Article I, Section 8 define-and-punish power to solve the problem, as it did in the 1790 Crimes Act, and the treatymakers could incorporate law-of-nations obligations into preemptive treaties that federal courts could enforce, as in *Ware*. Merely making these changes was what the Articles' critics called for. Randolph, for example, had argued that *Congress* must be given the power to enforce the law of nations[47]—exactly the effect of Article I, Section 8. It is far from clear that anything more was thought necessary, and material reasons—both structural and practical—counseled against going further. In any event, it is hard to say that the framers *must* have gone further than what the text on its face indicates: Congress and the treatymakers would be responsible for making law-of-nations rules part of supreme law.[48]

The Law of Nations and Judicial Power

If the law of nations is not part of supreme law, as the previous section suggests, and thus not a constitutional obligation of state or federal legislatures, we may be tempted to think that it remains entirely outside U.S. law until particular parts of it are adopted by a constitutionally authorized body. Any judicially cognizable effect would come from acts of domestic lawmakers—at the federal level under Article VI or at the state level through state constitutional processes: in other words, contrary to *Paquete Habana*, international law is *not* part of our law, unless some domestic entity makes it so.[49]

Though this view may seem consistent with the text on its face, post-ratification commentary should cause us to look further. Randolph said as Attorney General in 1792: "The law of nations, although not specially adopted by the constitution or any municipal act, is essentially a part of the law of the land." Hamilton's 1793 Pacificus essays said that "the laws of Nations form a part of the law of the land," as did Madison's Helvidius response, another early Attorney General (Charles Lee), and several key judicial figures (Jay, Wilson, and Iredell).[50] Notably, none of these comments (or others like them) called the law of nations the *supreme* law of the land, so they do not call into question the conclusions of the previous sections. But they do suggest that perhaps the law of nations had some domestic judicial status, and they should provoke further inquiry.

Sosa v. Alvarez-Machain and the Law of Nations as a Rule of Decision

So far, we have examined federal courts' authority when the law of nations conflicts with state or federal law. Perhaps, though, federal courts can use the law of nations to decide cases where no such conflict exists. To illustrate, consider a 2004 Supreme Court case, *Sosa v. Alvarez-Machain*.[51] Alvarez, a Mexican citizen, claimed that Sosa kidnapped and detained him in Mexico at the behest of American authorities, supposedly in violation of international law. He sued for damages in U.S. federal court. Arguably no U.S. law authorized the kidnapping, and no substantive state law had any bearing on the matter. (To simplify, assume a U.S. citizen defendant, so that the court has "diversity" jurisdiction under Article III, Section 2; in the actual case, Sosa's Mexican citizenship raised jurisdictional issues it would be best here to avoid).[52] Can federal courts hear Alvarez's law-of-nations claim?

In mid-nineteenth-century terms, this would be an easy question. Under *Swift v. Tyson* (1842),[53] federal courts in common law cases applied a "general law" not dependent on state common law, but elaborated independently by federal courts. Specifically, in the absence of supreme federal law, federal courts applied state statutes, as discussed above, but in the absence of a state statute, they applied state common law to "local" matters and a "general" common law to non-local matters. The law of nations formed part of this general law and thus could be a rule of decision, unless displaced by statute.[54] Although Justice Gray did not say so, his *Paquete Habana* decision reflected this system (which is why Gray likely did not see it as a constitutional case). No state (or federal) statute had anything to say about the Navy's right to seize ships near Cuba, so (Gray thought) Article VI was not a factor, and he could use "general law"—in that case derived from the law of nations—as a rule of decision. The same, presumably, would be true in *Sosa*.

One cannot place much weight upon nineteenth-century practice here, though, because the Supreme Court famously overruled *Swift* in *Erie R.R. v. Tompkins* (1938), holding that *Swift* adopted an unconstitutional view of federal courts' authority. As *Erie* declared, "the common law so far as it is enforced in a State . . . is not the common law generally but the law of that State existing by the authority of that State"; thus "[e]xcept in matters governed by the Federal Constitution or by acts of Congress, the law to be applied in any case is the law of the state."[55] *Erie* seemingly rejects claims that the law of nations, if not part of state or federal law, could supply rules of decision for federal courts—in effect overruling not only *Swift* but also *Paquete Habana*'s celebrated aphorism.[56] This requires re-examination of constitutional principles, to see if we can reconcile historical practice with *Erie* (and if not, which should prevail).

Judicial Power Revisited

We begin with the proposition that federal courts get their power to act from Article III, Section 1's grant of "the judicial Power" (Chapter 16). *Erie*'s claim that federal courts could not apply "general" common law independent of state law was (implicitly) a claim about Article III, Section 1—as was Gray's observation in *Paquete Habana*. The question thus becomes: did eighteenth-century understandings of "judicial Power" include authority to decide cases according to the law of nations?[57] There are substantial reasons to think it did.

As Blackstone explained in familiar terms, the English "municipal" (domestic) law consisted principally of statutes (passed by Parliament) and common law (unwritten traditional rules developed principally by judges). Together these were the "law of the land," which typically provided the rules of decision for English courts. He also said that the law of nations, although arising externally, was part of English common law, in words later echoed by Randolph: "the law of nations (whenever any question arises which is properly the object of it's jurisdiction) is here adopted in it's full extent by the common law, and is held to be a part of the law of the land."[58] Blackstone elaborated:

> [I]n mercantile questions, such as bills of exchange and the like; in all marine causes, relating to freight, average, demurrage, insurances, bottomry, and others of a similar nature; the law-merchant, which is a branch of the law of nations, is regularly and constantly adhered to. So too in all disputes relating to prizes, to shipwrecks, to hostages, and ransom bills, there is no other rule of decision but this great universal law, collected from history and usage, and such writers of all nations and languages as are generally approved and allowed of.[59]

Thus "in civil transactions and questions of property between the subjects of different states, the law of nations has much scope and extent, as adopted by the law of England. . . ."[60] Blackstone also identified three "offenses against the law of nations" that could be brought before English courts, as criminal matters, without statutory authority: violations of safe conducts, violations of ambassadorial immunity, and piracy.[61]

To some extent, at least, eighteenth-century English practice followed Blackstone's view. In private transnational matters, English courts routinely used law-of-nations rules to decide cases, without seeming to require statutory authorization, as with ordinary common law rules. This also occurred in some cases that we would consider "public law" controversies. In a key opinion, *Triquet v. Bath* (1764), for example, Lord Mansfield decided an ambassadorial immunity claim under the law of nations, stating that "the law of nations, in its full extent was part of the law of England."[62] In early America, some state courts between 1776 and 1789 thought they could decide cases based on the law of nations, which they said (following Blackstone) was part of their common law.[63] Thus founding-era Americans surely understood the law of nations not merely as an abstraction, but as something that could, in appropriate circumstances, be a rule of decision for courts—as Blackstone described it, it (or at least some of it) was part of the common law, which they expected courts to apply.[64]

This background suggests that Article III, Section 1's "judicial Power" might include power to use the law of nations to decide cases, assuming jurisdiction under Article III, Section 2 and no contrary sovereign law. Reading "judicial Power" this way helps explain other parts of Article III. Two of its Section 2 jurisdictional categories mainly involve disputes implicating the law of nations. First, as key drafters recognized, many "cases of admiralty and maritime Jurisdiction" would occur on the high seas beyond state law's normal reach, and so (in the absence of federal law) would depend upon the law of nations.[65] If federal courts could not use the law of nations, this jurisdictional grant would be odd, because federal courts would often lack rules of decision, although having jurisdiction. Second, jurisdiction over "Cases affecting ambassadors" likely assumes law-of-nations authority. As the de Longchamps incident shows, the problem here was that state laws might not afford ambassadors enough substantive protection. Giving federal courts *jurisdiction* did not provide much of a solution if federal courts still depended on state law for rules of decision. Yet the drafters obviously thought this an important matter. It is likely that they thought the Court, when deciding such cases, would (in the absence of statutory law) use the law of nations, which had extensive protections for ambassadors.[66]

This reading is further suggested by the 1789 Judiciary Act, as the modern Supreme Court came close to recognizing in *Sosa*. Section 9 of that Act—now called the Alien Tort Statute (ATS)—gave federal courts jurisdiction over tort claims brought by aliens for violations of treaties or the law of nations. In *Sosa*, the Court struggled to convince itself that the ATS, which it admitted addressed only jurisdiction, nonetheless authorized the law of nations as a rule of decision in such suits. As should be obvious from its language, the ATS does not authorize anything with respect to rules of decision, which are wholly distinct from jurisdiction. The ATS does show, though, the 1789 Congress's understanding that federal courts could use the law of nations as a rule of decision in the absence of contrary sovereign commands. As the Court rightly said in *Sosa*, otherwise the ATS makes no sense—how did Congress think federal courts would decide ATS cases?—but the absence of authorizing language shows that Congress thought courts *already* had that authority. It could only come from Article III, Section 1.[67]

This view of Section 9 accords with Section 34 of the same Act, establishing federal courts' rules of decision, which required federal courts to enforce state laws (unless displaced by Article VI) "in cases where they apply."[68] As discussed, Section 34 confirmed the Constitution's structural implication that federal courts could displace state law only through Article VI's sources of "supreme Law." It also acknowledged that there would be situations where state laws did not "apply"—and assuming no federal law applied either, it left open the ability of courts to draw on other traditional sources as rules of decision (most obviously, the law of nations).

Practice quickly reflected that approach. As a federal district court found in 1792, a court in admiralty cases "determines . . . according to the laws of nations"—a point Supreme Court Justices endorsed without hesitation in *Glass v. The Betsey* (1794) and *Talbot v. Jansen* (1795).[69] Admiralty (especially prize cases) was a natural place for this development, as state law did not extend to disputes about captures on the high seas; but appeal to the law of nations did not arise uniquely in admiralty. Attorney General Randolph's 1792 legal opinion relied on the law of nations to decide ambassadorial immunities not covered by statute, and in this context, Randolph observed that the law of nations "although not specifically adopted by the constitution or any municipal act, is essentially a part of the law of the land."[70] Subsequent Attorney General opinions in 1795 and 1797 similarly looked to the law of nations to provide rules of decision for claims arising from illegal armed attacks on other nations' colonies.[71]

Although they must be treated with caution, statements associated with the neutrality prosecutions of 1793–1794 offer further support. Attempting to maintain neutrality in the war between Britain and France, the Washington administration prosecuted Americans who aided the French war effort (see Chapter 5). Opposition newspapers disputed whether this was constitutional, but most judges considering the matter (including Iredell, Jay, and Wilson) thought the law of nations, of its own force, could be the basis of prosecution in federal court, as did Secretary of State Jefferson and Attorney General Randolph. In this context, these leading figures all said something to the effect that the law of nations was part of the law of the land.[72]

These statements require qualification, because the matter afterward became entangled in bitter partisan disputes over the constitutionality of common law crimes, ignited by the Adams administration's sedition prosecutions. The Supreme Court ultimately decided, in *United States v. Hudson* (1812), that Article III judicial power did not extend to crimes not defined by statute; without much explanation, in *United States v. Coolidge* (1816), it extended that rule to common law crimes based on the law of nations (as in the neutrality prosecutions).[73] These decisions' textual basis was unclear—and they may have been incorrect (Story and apparently Marshall thought they were). But many people supported them, and in the sedition debate Jefferson and Randolph appeared to renounce positions taken earlier in the neutrality cases.[74]

Nonetheless, the argument against the prosecutions was not that the law of nations lay wholly outside courts' cognizance, but that federal courts lacked judicial power over crimes not defined by statute (whether domestic crimes in *Hudson*, or international crimes in *Coolidge*).[75] Despite the common-law-crimes controversy, federal courts continued to derive rules of decision from the law of nations in civil cases.[76]

None of this is inconsistent with *Erie*'s result. *Erie* depends on two propositions we can easily accept. First, federal courts must identify constitutional authority for their decisionmaking. Second, other than through Article VI the Constitution does not give federal courts power to ignore state law, including (and this is *Erie*'s central insight, *contra Swift*) state common law decisions. That is, *Erie* effectively reaffirmed the Chase-Iredell-Cushing view in *Ware*, and extended it to state common law as well as statutes; that in turn seems consistent with Article VI and with the 1789 Rules of Decision Act, which declared that federal courts must follow state law "where it applies."[77]

Neither proposition speaks to situations in which state law, as a substantive matter, does *not* apply—which was true of *Paquete Habana* and *Sosa*.[78] There was no reason to suppose in either case that the outcome implicated by any state law. As a result, the Court's judicial power allowed it to apply rules of decision traditionally employed by courts, including the law of nations.

Erie causes trouble in modern debates because some overbroad language appears to insist that *all* law applied by federal courts must be either state or federal. That proposition, though, was not necessary to decide the case (the actual facts involved conflict with state domestic common law), and to the extent the Court meant it literally, it misread the historical meaning of judicial power. Historically, federal courts had judicial power to use the law of nations to decide cases, so long as it did not conflict with state or federal sovereign commands, even though it came from an external source.

Conclusion

So *Paquete Habana* is correct, if read precisely. The law of nations *is* part of "our" law, in the sense that federal courts can enforce it—but it is not part of Article VI's supreme law (and Justice Gray never claimed otherwise). That means federal courts can use it as a rule of decision, so long as it does not displace otherwise-constitutional state or federal law. This will often be the case for claims arising overseas (as in *Sosa* and *Paquete Habana* itself), and may also be the case for claims that supplement, rather than conflict with, state and federal claims. Modern debates have somehow decided this result is foreclosed by *Erie*, which (supposedly) means that all law applied in federal court must be state or federal law. But that is not how founding-era Americans saw matters. They read federal courts' "judicial Power" to allow law-of-nations claims, which courts had historically adjudicated. These claims could not displace conflicting state or federal law; the law of nations was not included in Article VI, but it could operate in the absence of conflicting state or federal law. That is all Gray claimed in *Paquete Habana*, and the text and founding-era context do not indicate he was wrong.

18

Courts, Presidents, and International Law

The prior chapter defends the most famous statement in *The Paquete Habana*—"international law is part of our law"—provided that statement is read narrowly to mean what Justice Gray meant by it. Gray's next sentence poses even greater difficulties: "For this purpose," he said—that is, when international law "must be ascertained and administered by the courts of justice"—if "there is no treaty, and no controlling executive or legislative act or judicial decision, resort must be had to the customs and usages of civilized nations. . . ."[1]

Paquete Habana involved claims against U.S. naval officers who seized Spanish fishing boats during wartime; the President argued to the Court that no violation of international law had occurred. What did Gray mean by a "controlling executive . . . act"? Because he ruled against the officers, apparently he did not find one, but he did not explain why not.

One approach is suggested by Gray's conjunction with "controlling . . . legislative act." As discussed in the prior chapter, as a constitutional matter Congress has legislative authority to override (or give controlling interpretations of) the law of nations. If Congress had directed seizure of fishing boats, *Paquete Habana* would rightly come out the other way, regardless of the Court's view of what international law required (as Gray seemed to imply) (see Chapter 17). Perhaps Gray meant the same authority should rest with the President. In the actual case, the President had (before the incident) directed generally that the law of nations be followed and said nothing specific about fishing boats. Would the outcome differ if the President had officially directed the boats' capture? Modern courts applying *Paquete Habana* have thought so, interpreting its reference to "controlling executive . . . act" to mean the President (or authorized subordinates) can, like Congress, constitutionally order violations of international law.

Another possibility, of course, is that Gray was simply wrong to refer to controlling executive acts: as in the rest of his opinion, he cited no constitutional authority, and the case for executive superiority vis-à-vis international law is not as obvious as it is for Congress. And a third, intermediate possibility is that the President constitutionally cannot violate international law, but that courts owe the President considerable, if not complete, deference on what it requires. This last option suggests a wider question: when should courts, as a more general matter, follow executive branch determinations of foreign affairs law? This in turn requires us to re-examine some of the questions considered in Chapter 16.

Garcia-Mir v. Meese: Presidential Violations of the Law of Nations

Applying *Paquete Habana,* modern courts of appeal have found that international law does not constitutionally bind the President, if the President (or a subordinate with sufficient authority) establishes an official policy to violate it; the Supreme Court has not directly considered the matter. *Garcia-Mir v. Meese* (1986), for example, dismissed an international law challenge to U.S. detention of illegal aliens, finding that even if the detention violated international law, it was authorized by a "controlling executive . . . act" that courts would not question.[2]

The Constitution's text, though, does not clearly support this proposition. We have concluded, of course, that Article II vests the President with the nation's "executive Power," and this power includes substantial control over foreign affairs (Chapter 3). But Article II, Section 3 also requires that the President "take Care that the Laws be faithfully executed." As discussed (Chapter 8), this means that the President cannot suspend or ignore otherwise-constitutional laws. Of course, it cannot mean the President must faithfully execute *all* laws. Presumably the President need not execute foreign law, or biblical law. It is surely plausible, though, that its "Laws" *might* include the law of nations, for we have seen (Chapter 17) that founding-era Americans recognized a "law of nations" they thought important to obey, and which had some force within the U.S. domestic legal system.

If the law of nations were part of Article VI's "supreme Law," this argument would be much stronger. Presumably the duty to execute "the Laws" includes all "supreme Laws"—else it would be hard to say that those laws were "supreme" or part of the "Law of the Land." As discussed, though, Article VI's text does not include the law of nations. On this basis, one might argue that similarly it is not included in Article II, and so not a presidential obligation.

This argument runs into immediate problems, though, because Article VI and the take-care clause do not have parallel language. In particular, as discussed in Chapter 17, Article VI excludes the law of nations by qualifying its reference to "Laws" with "which shall be made in Pursuance" of the Constitution. The take-care clause does not have this qualifying language. It does not even have the qualifier "Laws of the United States" (which appears in both Article VI and in Article III's grant of federal-question jurisdiction). Perhaps the drafters meant to include these limits implicitly, but that is a large step to take without supporting evidence.[3] Other things being equal, we should hesitate to ignore distinct phrasing in similar textual provisions (just as, in general, we should prefer to give similarly phrased clauses parallel meanings).[4] The non-parallel structure of Article II, Section 3 and Article VI suggests that there are some "Laws" that the President must faithfully execute but are not supreme laws. If so, the law of nations—a body of non-supreme law founding-era Americans thought applicable, in some senses, to the United States—might help explain the different phrasing. Further, once we see that U.S. courts used the law of nations to decide cases within the domestic legal system (Chapter 17), it seems natural to include it within "the Laws"—and so within the literal meaning of the take-care clause.

The text also makes clear that the President holds "executive" power, not legislative power. Thus the President cannot (ordinarily) change laws within the domestic legal system (see Chapter 5). Because the law of nations functioned as law (i.e., a rule of decision) in the domestic legal system, it seems problematic for the President to change that rule of decision. In *The Nereide* (1815), for example, the Supreme Court held that Manuel Pinto, a Spanish passenger on a British ship captured by an American privateer during the War of 1812, was by the law of nations a neutral and thus entitled to keep his property free from condemnation. Suppose, however, that the President affirmatively ordered Pinto's property to be seized (or directed generally that Spanish property on British ships should be seized), contrary to the law of nations. If the Court enforced this order, that would change the law governing Pinto's property rights; the President would be a lawmaker. Chief Justice Marshall perhaps had this in mind when he wrote, in *The Nereide*, that Pinto's law-of-nations rights could be changed only if "an act be passed"— that is, by legislative action.[5]

There is not much founding-era commentary on this precise question, but as Chapter 17 outlines, leading members of the constitutional generation frequently observed that the law of nations was part of "the law of the land." Of course, this seems principally to acknowledge that federal courts could use the law of nations to decide private cases (as Chapter 17 argues). But it is suggestive about presidential power in two ways. In ordinary eighteenth-century speech, it would seem natural to equate "the laws" with "the law of the land"; one would need fairly strong historical arguments to show why the former did not include the latter. Further, the term "law of the land" echoed traditional English phrasing, and in English law, the "law of the land" bound the executive power; the monarch governed according to, not in opposition to, the law of the land (Chapter 8).[6]

Moreover, in a slightly different context, eighteenth-century commentaries did associate the take-care clause with the law of nations. Hamilton's 1793 Pacificus essays stated: "The Executive is charged with the execution of all laws, the laws of Nations as well as the Municipal law" and "The President is the constitutional EXECUTOR of the laws. Our treaties and the laws of nations form a part of the law of the land."[7] Madison, responding as Helvidius, agreed that the President was "bound to the faithful execution" of "external" laws (meaning the law of nations).[8] Both commentaries echoed Montesquieu, who based executive foreign affairs authority upon the idea of powers "executive in respect to things dependant on the law of nations"— implying that the executive power acted pursuant to the law of nations in external matters.[9] Neither Hamilton nor Madison directly addressed the question of violating the law of nations; Hamilton did not say the President was *bound* to execute the law of nations, only empowered to do so. He relied on the take-care clause, though, which is phrased as a duty. It is hard to see how the law of nations could be included in the take-care clause for one purpose but not the other (and it is important to remember that Hamilton wrote within a broader discourse calling the law of nations the "law of the land)."[10]

Somewhat later in constitutional history, several judicial decisions may suggest a presidential duty to the law of nations. As noted, Marshall implied as much in *The Nereide* in 1815; Joseph Story (not a member of the founding generation) made a similar implication in *Brown v. United States* a year earlier. At the beginning of the nineteenth century, several decisions arising from the quasi-war with France also indicated an expectation that the President would fight wars consistent with the law of nations (as had Madison's Helvidius in 1793), although it is not clear this was meant as a constitutional obligation.[11]

This is not much history to build upon (and rather less than some modern commentary suggests), but there is no material evidence in the other direction. In the drafting and ratifying debates, apparently no one claimed that the President should be able to violate the law of nations; in immediate post-ratification practice, apparently no President claimed such an authority. If the law of nations was law applicable in the United States, the most natural reading of "Laws" is to include it: the burden should be on those who would say that Article II, Section 3's "Laws" means something less than all of the laws applicable to the nation. The available evidence does not allow that burden to be carried.

We might object on structural grounds that the President was understood to be the chief foreign affairs actor of the United States, and that subjecting the President to law-of-nations constraints would limit the President's ability to direct U.S. foreign affairs, thus rendering the President a less-effective foreign affairs leader.[12] Although perhaps true as a practical matter, this point tells us little about constitutional meaning. English practice and eighteenth-century political theory indicated that the executive foreign affairs powers should be united in a single chief magistrate, but the Constitution rejected that prescription. As we have seen, its text divides the previously unified executive foreign affairs power, sacrificing some unity and effectiveness to a desire for multiple power centers and divided decisionmaking. This approach appears, for example, in declaring war, making treaties, appointing ambassadors, and regulating the military—all matters where taking power from the foreign affairs executive impairs unity and effectiveness, but where the Constitution did so anyway. And it cannot be doubted that founding-era Americans thought violating the law of nations was a serious step to take. That does not mean they thought it should never be taken, but they might well have thought congressional participation would be appropriate.

A more troubling objection arises from the oddity that, under the proposed reading, the President would lack power to violate the law of nations, absent congressional authorization, but states would have that power unless Congress intervened. This seems to get matters exactly backwards in terms of the best way to manage foreign affairs—and seems strange enough to cause careful reconsideration.

The historical background, though, explains how this oddity might have come about. With respect to the states, the constitutional design was, in the case of the law of nations (as in many other areas), a compromise made necessary by pre-existing state sovereignty and the need to get the Constitution approved. Some members of the founding generation, such as the internationalist Jay and the nationalist Hamilton, probably would have liked to subordinate state law to the law of nations. But the states had not previously faced this restriction under the Articles—and in particular they had not faced it as imposed through the new and distrusted federal judiciary. As discussed in Chapter 17, by establishing Congress or the treatymakers (rather than federal courts) as intermediaries, the Constitution gave political protection to the states. Whatever one thinks of state sovereignty, it was an eighteenth-century value that had to be accommodated, and, as argued above, the omission of the law of nations from supreme law can be understood as just such an accommodation. In contrast, the presidency was a new office, so these concerns did not arise, and compromises did not need to be made. To the extent the drafters embraced a strong presumption in favor of compliance with the law of nations—and all evidence suggests that they did—there is nothing odd about them imposing such a duty on the (new) President, even if political considerations made it impractical to impose it on the (existing) states.

These points may not have been explicit in the drafters' thinking; there is no direct evidence on either side. Nonetheless, the superficially odd allocation of law-of-nations power is consistent with two broad themes in the Constitution's text: first, that states would be protected by having (non-constitutional) supreme law created only through Article VI processes, which they partly controlled; and second, that the powerful new President created by the Constitution would be checked in large part by a lack of lawmaking power.

This discussion does not mean that *Garcia-Mir* and related cases were wrongly decided—only that they wrongly said the President has no constitutional duty to the law of nations. Two points may be made in their favor. First, Congress can violate the law of nations, so presumably it can authorize presidential violations as well—or, more likely, authorize the President, in pursuing a particular policy, to decide whether to violate the law of nations. For example, in 2002 Congress authorized the President to use all force "he determines to be necessary and appropriate" to defend U.S. national security against Iraq.[13] That broad language appears to give the President ultimate decisionmaking authority regarding the war's conduct, including discretion to violate the law of nations where national security requires. Similarly, other congressional acts that give the President broad discretion would seem to include discretion vis-à-vis the law of nations.[14]

Second, although the President must follow the law of nations, it may be difficult to determine what the law of nations requires. A key question, then, is who makes that determination. As the next section shows, it is not obvious that courts, rather than the President, should have this power.

Presidential Interpretation of the Law of Nations

Paquete Habana Revisited

Paquete Habana suggests that Justice Gray thought (some) presidential interpretations of the law of nations would control the courts. His key paragraph—rearranged to make it a bit more comprehensible—says "[i]nternational law . . . must be ascertained and administered by the courts of justice" and "[f]or this purpose" courts would look to the practices of nations and other related sources "where there is no . . . controlling executive . . . act." This statement indicates that where there *is* a presidential act "ascertain[ing] and administer[ing]" the law of nations, courts would look to the executive act, not to the practices of nations and other related sources. That reading is confirmed by Gray's parallel treatment of "controlling" legislative and judicial acts, which would plainly direct the courts' result, as a matter of the Constitution (in the case of Congress) and precedent (in the case of prior courts).[15]

Of course, Gray's views are not good evidence of the text's historical meaning, but this reading of the case suggests an interpretation worth exploring. The vagueness of the law of nations, noted by Gouverneur Morris at the Convention, and its eighteenth-century basis in reason (see Chapter 17) indicate the importance of interpretive power. If the law of nations is often not easily discoverable, the location of final interpretive authority is a critical constitutional matter. It is also one on which the take-care clause gives no direction. Saying the President has a duty to the law of nations does not necessarily mean that federal courts may disagree with the President in interpreting its requirements: the President does not necessarily violate a duty to the law of nations by interpreting it differently from the way a federal court would.

In domestic constitutional and statutory law, we accept the superiority of the courts' interpretations over the President's, not so much from the text, but from the founding generation's commentary and from the traditional role of courts as expositors of the law (as Marshall argued in *Marbury*). As Chapter 16 argues, that should be as true for domestic-law allocations of foreign affairs authority as it is for purely domestic matters. Once we move to international law, however, further substantial powers come into play. The Constitution makes the President the nation's principal voice in external communication, as a result of the executive power (Chapter 3). The law of nations is a material part of these communications, as the U.S. view of its own rights and obligations, and the rights and obligations of other nations, is chiefly conveyed through diplomacy. The President is, therefore, the principal voice of the United States in expounding to the world the U.S. view of international legal obligations. Put another way, the President's foreign affairs role, reflected in the executive power, makes the President an expositor of international law in a way that lacks any domestic counterpart. These considerations may well have stood behind Gray's apparent view that courts would not contradict an authoritative presidential evaluation of the law of nations.

Marshall's Views

We may gain additional insight on the matter by returning to Marshall's idea of "political questions." Marshall said in *Marbury:* "The province of the Court is solely to decide the rights of individuals, not to inquire how the executive, or executive officers, perform duties in which they have a discretion. Questions in their nature political, or which are, by the Constitution and law, submitted to the executive, can never be made in this court."[16] We may be tempted to dismiss the point as obvious, even tautological: of course courts would not decide matters not governed by law. But further exploration indicates Marshall had something more complicated in mind.

As we have briefly examined (Chapter 16), three years before *Marbury,* Marshall (then a Federalist congressman from Virginia) delivered a major speech to Congress defending the foreign policy actions of then-President John Adams.[17] Britain sought the extradition, pursuant to the Jay Treaty, of Jonathan Robbins, who had allegedly led a mutiny on a British ship. The British consul applied to federal Judge Bee in South Carolina, who in turn asked Adams how to proceed; Adams indicated that the extradition should go forward in accordance with the treaty. Republicans in Congress attacked Adams for interfering with the judicial power, and Marshall delivered the principal Federalist response.[18]

Marshall could have said simply that Adams had only "advised," not "directed" Bee (that is how Adams put it).[19] Marshall went much further, though, to insist that this "was a case for executive and not judicial decision" and that "according to the practice, and according to the principles of American government, the question whether the nation has or has not bound itself to deliver up any individual, charged with having committed murder or forgery within the jurisdiction of Britain, is a question the power to decide which, rests alone with the executive department."[20]

In reaching this conclusion, Marshall invoked a concept he called "political law." He acknowledged, as Republicans had argued, that the matter presented "points of law" concerning the correct interpretation of the treaty. He denied, though, that this made the matter "proper for the decision of the courts"; to the contrary, "questions of political law"—as this case was—were "proper to be decided . . . by the executive and not by the courts."[21] As he explained:

> A case in law or equity proper for judicial resolution, may arise under a treaty, where the rights of individuals acquired or secured by a treaty are to be asserted or defended in court. As under the 4th or 6th article of the treaty of peace with Great Britain or under those articles of our late treaties with France, Prussia, and other nations, which secure to the subjects of those nations, their property within the United States. . . . But the judicial power cannot extend to political compacts—as the establishment of the boundary line between the American and British dominions; the case of the late guarantee in our treaty with France; or the case of the delivery of a murderer under the 27th article of our present treaty with Britain.

Summing up later, Marshall explained that "political law" exists where "[t]he question to be decided is whether the particular case proposed be one, in which the nation has bound itself to act"; these, he said, are questions "depending on principles never submitted to courts."[22]

Marshall drew an important parallel with another episode we have studied earlier: Washington's proclamation of neutrality in 1793. Following the proclamation, questions arose in its practical implementation, which Washington purported to decide as matters of deduction from the laws of neutrality (i.e., the law of nations) (see Chapter 5). One of these was what should be done about prizes captured within U.S. waters or captured by privateers equipped in violation of the proclamation. As Marshall explained, these questions of how to implement the law of neutrality also were "questions of political law, proper to be decided . . . by the executive and not by the courts." It was true, he said, that claims raising these questions might be filed in court, and the executive could not interfere directly in these private suits. But, Marshall continued, relying on letters between then-Secretary of State Jefferson and French ambassador Genet, the question "whether a vessel captured within a given distance of the American coast was or was not captured within the jurisdiction of the United States, was a question not to be determined by the courts, but by the executive." Once the President established the legal principle, courts could resolve facts relating to particular captures: "Ultimately it was settled that the fact[s] should be investigated in the courts, but the decision was regulated by the principles established by the executive department."[23]

In sum, Marshall argued that in cases where the interpretation of treaties and the law of nations affected the rights and duties of the United States, the interpretive power lay with the President, as a matter of "political law." And he emphasized that courts would decide according to principles—meaning legal interpretations—set forth by the President in the exercise of the executive power.[24] This meant, Marshall concluded, not only that Adams was right to resolve the question of U.S. extradition obligations under the Jay Treaty, but also that Bee was right to accept Adams's interpretation.[25]

This explanation in turn suggests Marshall's full meaning three years later in *Marbury,* when he said that courts could not investigate the conduct of the executive in "questions in their nature political." In light of the Robbins debate, surely he meant not only matters of pure policy, but also what he called "political law," in which interpretive power lay with the executive and not the judiciary.

Of course, Marshall's speech came more than a decade after ratification, so it is not conclusive of the text's historical meaning; but it is suggestive, especially because Marshall appears to have been persuasive at the time. Republican leader Albert Gallatin, urged to respond, supposedly retorted: "Gentlemen, answer it yourself; for my part, I think it unanswerable."[26] Further, Marshall specifically cast his arguments as an interpretation of the Constitution's text, invoking the President's executive foreign affairs power under Article II, Section 1; it seems clear that he had the constitutional power of judges in mind in saying that the treaty's meaning was not suitable for resolution in court.[27] Although political attacks on Adams's role in the matter continued, Marshall's constitutional analysis was not effectively refuted.

Marshall's view tracks the distinction made in Chapter 16 between cases challenging the domestic allocation of foreign affairs authority (such as *Goldwater*) and cases challenging the content of U.S. policy toward foreign nations. Marshall apparently believed that in the latter cases, courts should follow the lead of the political branches, rather than make independent determinations.

The English Background: Matter of State

Fully understanding Marshall's views requires some further exploration of English law. Seventeenth-century English kings argued for a distinction in legal affairs between "matters of state," to be decided by the Crown, and "matters of law," within the jurisdiction of ordinary courts. The Crown's prerogative to maintain and defend the nation, they argued, encompassed paramount and exclusive control over all matters necessary for such preservation and defense, to the exclusion of the judiciary's ordinary functions. Thus, when the Crown determined that a case implicated what might today be called a matter of national security, courts were said to be unable to interfere with the king's executive power.[28]

As one English historian says: "Of all this much was of course bitterly contested at the time, and all but a little now belongs to the past."[29] After the Glorious Revolution and the Bill of Rights (1688–1689), the courts, and in general the Crown as well, recognized that Crown prerogatives were subject to the "law of the land" and that rights of English citizens under English law were protected by the courts even where national security matters were implicated. *Entick v. Carrington* (1765), for example, involved an illegal search conducted as a result of suspected sedition by the plaintiff; the government suggested that the court defer to the national security aspects of the case and permit redress to be sought only by application to the Crown. That, the court declared, reflected the discredited view of "matter of state": the "necessity of the state could not remove ordinary matters from the jurisdiction of the courts," and "with respect to the argument of state necessity or a distinction that has been arrived at between state offences and others, the common law does not understand that kind of reasoning, nor do our books take notice of any such distinction."[30]

Despite general discrediting of the matter-of-state theory, limitations on courts' authority survived under that name, or the associated "act of state," in foreign affairs. Although the details are anything but clear, the far-reaching seventeenth-century view of "matter of state" as an exception to ordinary jurisdiction seems to have been reformulated as a rule that a "matter *between* States, which, whether it be regulated by international law or not, and whether the acts in question are or are not in accord with international law, is not a subject of municipal jurisdiction."[31] Like Marshall's view of the Robbins case, this idea suggests certain areas of law where the executive authority acts in effect as judge—that is, it has discretion to interpret and apply the law.

In particular, the common thread is that policy toward foreign nations, even if resting to some degree on legal determinations, amounted to matters of state (or, in Marshall's terms, "political law") forming part of the English "executive," not "judicial," power.[32]

Assessment

An initial reaction, then, might be to say that interpretation of international rights and duties, whether treaty-based or unwritten, is textually an executive power. Courts could enforce private claims dependent on such rights and duties—in the case of treaties, because Article VI and Article III, Section 2 said they could; and in the case of the unwritten law of nations, because that had traditionally been part of the judicial power and thus was vested by the general grant of Article III, Section 1 (Chapter 17). But, as Marshall said, in doing so courts would be "regulated by the principles established by the executive department"—that is, legal conclusions (though not necessarily factual judgments) would be made by the President.

Arguments of this type are made in modern practice, though they generally are not based directly on the Constitution's text. Courts may say, for example, that they defer heavily (though not entirely) to executive branch interpretations of treaties—or to executive branch determinations in foreign affairs more broadly.[33] We must be careful, however, not to read Marshall's principle too broadly. First, it cannot resurrect the "political question" idea that Chapter 16 rejects. As that chapter makes clear, there is a difference between determining the *internal* allocation of foreign affairs policymaking authority (as in *Goldwater*) and determining the nation's international policy with respect to foreign countries. Marshall's conception of "political law" encompasses only the latter.

Second, executive interpretation authority does not authorize *violation* of treaties and law-of-nations obligations. That point was not clear in English law, because the monarch had no evident constitutional duty to uphold such obligations, and "matter of state" authority seemed to encompass, at least as a practical matter, discretionary power in both interpretation and enforcement. As we have explored, the U.S. Constitution appears to provide differently, by bringing treaties within the supreme law of the land and providing a presidential duty to see that laws (including treaties and the law of nations) are faithfully executed. Interpretive authority is not violation authority under the Constitution: thus, while defending Adams's executive authority to interpret the Jay Treaty, Marshall also emphasized Adams's constitutional duty, tied explicitly to the take-care clause, to enforce it.[34]

Third, early practice indicates that courts could undertake treaty or law-of-nations interpretation without guidance from the President, at least in cases involving private disputes. As discussed, the law of nations was considered part of English common law, and cases were brought under it; there is little evidence that courts awaited executive determinations—certainly not in private law cases, nor even in "public law" cases such *Triquet v. Bath* (Chapter 17). That continued to be true in America after the Revolution, including in the federal courts immediately after ratification and after Marshall became Chief Justice. Further, early treaty-law cases also did not await executive interpretation. In *Ware v. Hylton,* the British debts case,[35] no one argued that the matter was outside judicial competence, even though it turned in part on obligations in a treaty and a decision adverse to the British creditors would have materially disrupted foreign affairs. Nor did anyone argue that the Court should be bound by presidential interpretation of the treaty, and Justice Iredell would have interpreted the treaty contrary to the way Washington obviously wanted. To the contrary, many founding-era statements indicated that the courts would view treaties substantially as they viewed ordinary law; as Hamilton said, treaties' "true import, as far as respects individuals must, like all other laws, be ascertained by judicial determinations."[36]

Instead, Marshall's "political law" (and the English matter-of-state concept that probably underlay it) meant something less expansive. Disputes that were essentially private matters, affecting the mutual rights of individuals, belonged in court, even if they turned upon international obligations, and even if they had some public component to them. Thus *Triquet* and *Ware* were not "matters of state," or matters of "political law," despite some public law overtones. They did not amount to frontal challenges to executive branch conduct or determinations, nor implicate disputes over the national government's (or a foreign government's) obligations. Although this distinction may sometimes be difficult to make, we could surely say, for example, that treaties and international law primarily directed to private conduct (such as the Warsaw Convention on Aircraft Liability or the Convention on the International Sale of Goods) are fully administrable judicially, but treaties more directed toward conduct of executive policy may not be.[37]

We may object that the Constitution's recasting of treaties as self-executing law (Article VI) and its corresponding inclusion of treaties within the courts' jurisdiction (Article III, Section 2) provide a textual basis for expanded judicial authority vis-à-vis the President. Marshall plainly did not take this view, though, and stated broadly it may overread the purposes of Article VI. The Constitution's drafters wanted treaties to be judicially enforceable against the states; that was Article VI's principal purpose, and whether they also wanted to create judicial supremacy over the President in treaty interpretation is a different matter. Nonetheless, we may legitimately feel that Marshall went too far in the Robbins case, because it was principally about the rights of an individual present in the United States (and, if Robbins were to be believed, a U.S. citizen). Robbins was, moreover, not claiming rights against the President or the United States under a treaty, but seeking to resist the treaty's application as Article VI law to him. In a corresponding situation in England, presumably the executive could not have enforced the treaty against someone in Robbins's position absent a statute and a judicial determination. We might suppose that a President who invoked Article VI to use the treaty as law against Robbins would also have to accept the independent judgment of the courts that accompanies determinations of rights under domestic law.[38] Marshall's arguments seem much stronger in cases where litigants invoke treaties to control presidential action, and especially where that action does not affect citizens or take place within the United States. These examples seem to fit the core of Marshall's idea of "political law," in which independent court decisions would in effect put the courts in charge of foreign policy and thus overstep Article III. Marshall's concerns about interference with executive interpretations also seem particularly forceful in the area of unwritten international obligations. Interpreting the law of nations—whether in an eighteenth-century regime of rational deduction or a positivist regime of custom and practice—is fundamentally an act of foreign relations. As with other diplomatic acts, it establishes the position of the United States on matters of importance for the interaction of nations, in an area where nations may have conflicting and equally authoritative views. "Execution" of the law of nations is done primarily through diplomatic and military interactions, not through courts. It is, therefore, intimately tied to the President's foreign affairs power. If courts claimed general authority to override presidential interpretations of the law of nations, adopted officially as the foreign policy of the United States, they would claim final authority in a central aspect of foreign affairs— one, moreover, that cannot be said to have been ceded to the courts by reducing it to written form or including it in Article VI.[39]

Conclusion

In sum, courts' authority to decide cases may be constitutionally tempered by the President's executive authority to interpret the international rights and duties of the United States and of foreign nations. As Marshall explained in his discussion of the Robbins case and reaffirmed in *Marbury,* simply because matters present questions of law does not mean that they should be resolved in court. In particular, the President's status as the nation's constitutional representative in foreign affairs—a consequence of the textual vesting of executive power—will often mean, in such cases, that the matter is one of "political law" in which the President has interpretive authority. As Marshall further explained, and as the prize adjudications of 1793 reflected, that does not necessarily take the matter entirely away from the judiciary; but the court's judicial power is to evaluate claims (on their factual basis, for example) in accordance with the international legal principles determined by the President.

We should be careful to state this conclusion narrowly. The Constitution requires the President to obey treaties and the law of nations, as part of the presidential duty to take care that the laws be faithfully executed. The President cannot simply disregard international obligations. Presidential interpretations can also be contested politically, through legal debate or by appeal to Congress (which often would have final interpretive authority under its power to "define and punish" law-of-nations offenses and to carry treaties into effect). The Marshallian view of judicial and executive power requires only that, as between official executive branch interpretations and judicial interpretations with respect to the nation's international duties, the former prevail.

Further, embracing executive interpretation power should not resurrect "political question" abstention of the kind suggested in *Goldwater v. Carter* and rejected in Chapter 16. Courts owe the President no deference in constitutional matters, even ones touching foreign affairs, or else the courts' checking function envisioned in Federalist No. 78 would be compromised. And finally, a claim of interpretive authority depends upon the President making an *interpretation* of international obligations. Presidents sometimes ask courts to abstain from deciding cases, not on the basis of interpreting international obligations, but merely because a decision might negatively affect presidential foreign policy. The executive interpretation power suggested in this chapter provides no basis for courts to accede to such requests; and the courts' constitutional duty, outlined in Chapter 16, should often require courts to proceed even if foreign policy interference may result. Again, the constitutional relationship between the President and the courts in foreign affairs is complex, producing neither complete judicial abdication nor complete judicial control.

Conclusion:
The Textual Structure of
Foreign Affairs Law

Scholars and political leaders have long claimed that the Constitution's text is fatally incomplete, or fatally indeterminate, in foreign affairs. The foregoing chapters have sought to show that it is not. To be sure, many specific questions may be difficult, perhaps unanswerable. But the text provides a structural framework, summed in a series of basic principles.

First, there are no inherent foreign affairs powers, nor inherent foreign affairs limitations (Chapters 1–2). The idea that the Constitution is incomplete leads naturally to extra-constitutional appeals: that the President or Congress have inherent powers derived from sovereignty; that the law of nations gives inherent powers or imposes inherent obligations, and so forth. We can only reach these conclusions, though, by ignoring what the Constitution actually says. The Tenth Amendment says there are no inherent powers—or inherent limitations—in our constitutional system, and context shows that (in foreign affairs, anyway) we should take it at its word. *Curtiss-Wright*, the *Chinese Exclusion Case*, and courts and commentators who would embrace all or parts of them err fundamentally in supposing that the Constitution vested full sovereignty (or at least, full foreign affairs sovereignty) in the national government; to the contrary, as the federalists argued—and as the anti-federalists demanded that the Amendment make clear—full sovereignty (in their vision) lay with the people, who by the Constitution delegated some of it to the federal government. True, in foreign affairs they delegated substantial powers, responding to the foreign affairs weaknesses of the Articles of Confederation. But how much they delegated can only be answered by reading the Constitution, not through theoretical speculation about what powers the federal government (and, in particular, the President) "must" have. As Harold Koh rightly argues, under a historical understanding of the Constitution's text, the President has no "secret reservoir of unaccountable power that flows from external sovereignty and not the Constitution."[1]

Second, the opening clauses of the Constitution's first three articles provide the starting points for granting, allocating, and limiting federal foreign affairs power (as they do, uncontroversially, for domestic power). The traditional meaning of "legislative," "executive," and "judicial" power informs the basic nature of the authority exercised by the three branches of government these articles create. In particular, the core organizing principle of the text's foreign affairs law is that the President exercises executive power, which in eighteenth-century language included substantial independent foreign affairs powers (as well as, of course, the conventional power to execute the law) (Chapters 3–4, 6). This principle fills many gaps that prior studies have complained of—the apparent lack of diplomatic power, for example. Yet these grants of power, properly understood, are also limits: the President exercises *only* executive power, which does not include lawmaking power (Chapter 5); Congress exercises legislative power, which does not include the (executive) power to undertake international obligations (Chapter 10). As a result, the President (for example) cannot claim a power simply because it relates to, or has some connection with, foreign affairs; traditional "executive" foreign affairs powers were not those connected to foreign affairs in some abstract sense, but rather were, specifically, a nation's relationships with people and entities outside the domestic polity.[2]

Third, the Constitution makes important, but specific, departures from the traditional allocation of foreign affairs powers—most notably, the assignment of diplomatic appointments and treatymaking, in part, to the Senate and the assignment of the declare-war power to Congress (Chapters 7, 11). These allocations respond to founding-era concerns that the English system unduly concentrated executive foreign affairs power, and they align our separation of powers system in these respects more with that of the Roman republic. They are meant as powerful, independent checks on presidential foreign affairs authority. They allowed founding-era Americans to create the powerful unitary President they thought necessary for "energy," "vigor," and "dispatch" after the debacles of the Articles, without creating a foreign affairs executive in the image of the English monarch. Those who would minimize them overlook the compromise the Constitution wrought in executive power, stemming from the framers' conflicting fear of it (driven by the monarchy) and desire for more of it (driven by the Articles). These provisions do not, however, mean more than they say. They do not convey generalized power over diplomacy, or treaties, or war; they convey only the specific powers to which they actually refer, leaving unspecified executive foreign affairs powers to the executive/President (Chapters 8–9,

12), as Thomas Jefferson said in his key 1790 legal opinion on the matter (Chapter 4).[3]

Fourth, the relationship between the federal government and the states is (with minor exceptions) governed by Article VI, a structural cornerstone of the Constitution as important as—if not more so than—the first three articles. Above all other provisions, Article VI creates a truly national government, particularly in foreign affairs, by giving broad power to displace state law through statute or treaty. But Article VI—and the narrowness of Article I, Section 10's outright prohibitions of state foreign affairs activities— also protects the states. Ordinarily state laws can be displaced *only* by statutes and treaties; enacting statutes and making treaties requires a cumbersome process, giving the states (particularly before the Seventeenth Amendment) substantial power to protect their interests. This preserves the states as independent (though subordinate) power centers. And that in turn promotes cooperative foreign policy at the federal level, for if the President wants to override inconvenient state laws, that cannot be done by executive power alone; it requires assistance from Congress or the treatymakers (Chapters 13–14). At the same time, though, states do not have non-textual protections *beyond* Article VI, from (as Justice Holmes rightly rejected) "some invisible radiation from the general terms of the Tenth Amendment" (Chapter 15).[4]

Fifth, the courts are the arbiters of this system, but they must act within it, as holders of the "judicial Power" bound to uphold the Constitution. Courts lack power to decide that the special needs of foreign affairs demand the invention of special rules, either to enlarge or constrict their role. The judicial power is only the power to decide concrete cases, according to the directions of the Constitution and of other branches, not the power to manage foreign affairs (Chapters 16–18). Courts decide how the different parts of the domestic government relate to each other and to individuals, within the domestic legal system; they do not decide how our government relates to other nations.

As a result, the text, as historically understood, distributes foreign affairs power across multiple independent power centers: the President, the Senate, Congress, the states, and the courts. Each has independent authority that prevents the others from always having their own way.

The most striking feature of this account, perhaps, is how closely it resembles the standard description of constitutional government in domestic affairs. Every one of these core principles is, in domestic matters, a commonplace.

One rarely hears claims of inherent powers in domestic affairs. The three-fold division of executive, legislative, and judicial power appears in every basic civics textbook, and we easily understand that, for example, the President's power of prosecutorial discretion or removal of executive officers arises from Article II, Section 1's "executive Power." We understand checking powers such as the Senate's role in appointing, say, judges and cabinet officers, as meaningful but specific qualifications of the President's executive power: no one thinks the Senate's power to approve the appointment of judges or cabinet officers gives it the power to instruct them. Where the state and federal governments exercise concurrent powers—as they often do, in, for example, commercial regulation—preemption by federal statute or treaty (not presidential decree nor ungrounded judicial directive) is the way state laws are displaced. And courts decide statutory and constitutional matters within their domain without trying to guess whether federal policy might be "embarrassed" as a result, nor whether some "natural" (or otherwise unwritten) principles should be interposed.

Modern foreign affairs law is dominated by the intuition that its different imperatives mean its constitutional law must be different from domestic law in basic structure. Of course, there is little agreement upon what those imperatives might be. But a common thread in modern foreign affairs debates is to reason from the nature of foreign affairs to reach general conclusions about where foreign affairs powers should lie. There is, though, little evidence from the text or founding-era history that this reflects the Constitution's judgment. Rather, the evidence is that founding-era Americans designed foreign affairs law as they designed domestic constitutional law. The text has no generalized foreign affairs exceptions nor generalized treatment of a single unitary "foreign affairs power." Rather, it variously allocates distinct foreign affairs powers (and specifies the procedures for implementing them) among its different branches, just as it allocates various domestic powers.

Our inquiry also contains some implications for reading the text. The first is that simply reading the text closely can go quite a long way in resolving difficult questions, even in an area as supposedly textually incomplete as foreign affairs. The text alone is fairly clear, for example, that the Tenth Amendment provides no inherent federal powers in foreign affairs, that the law of nations is not part of Article VI's supreme law, and that a mere majority of Congress cannot make treaties—regardless of how troublesome these issues have become in modern law. The second, though, is that the text often cannot stand on its own. Without studying the time in which the text was written, we cannot, for example, know what "executive power" or "declaring war" meant nor fully appreciate the relationship between federal courts and state law. In this sense the pre-ratification history is, as we have seen, often more instructive than post-ratification history (though the latter often garners the greater attention). What particular leaders said after ratification about how particular provisions should be read—especially after they had gained a personal or institutional interest, or where they disagreed with other leaders—may be less persuasive than the experiences and ordinary use of language that everyone shared before the Constitution went into operation.

Third, history also cannot stand alone, without the text. We have seen repeated appeals made to what founding-era Americans "must" have believed, cast at a high level of generality and punctuated by selected quotes from particular framers, in efforts to support specific constitutional results. These are rarely satisfactory, because even if one can establish a common general outlook of founding-era Americans, only rarely does that show how they resolved specific constitutional questions. To say, for example, that the framers wanted to obey the law of nations, to protect states from overreaching by the treatymakers, or to create a strong foreign affairs executive, does not say *how* the Constitution accomplished these results.

And there is also the realization that text, or even text plus context, cannot answer everything. True, textual indeterminacy is grossly overstated, especially once we understand that interpretation involves only searching for the best meaning among the available candidates, not searching for a perfect indisputable answer. Textualism is always an enterprise of best guesses. But sometimes even put this way, there is simply not enough evidence, either because sufficient records have not survived or because it never existed in the first place.

Finally, this work has, throughout, insisted that it is only an inquiry into historical meaning and not necessarily a blueprint for modern implementation. It is well to repeat that observation in conclusion. The question of what to do with the text's historical meaning is different from the question of how to find it.

An observation, nonetheless, about the modern world, cannot be resisted. We have seen many cases and situations in which courts, or other constitutional interpreters, have run far astray from the text in foreign affairs matters. At the end of the inquiry, though, we may be struck by how much modern practice has in common with the historical design, despite the courts' atextual moments.[5] Despite *Curtis-Wright,* the national government does not rely heavily on inherent powers to supply authority it would lack under a purely textual reading. While scholars debate the theory of executive power in foreign affairs, the modern President exercises, without much material objection, most of the powers it conveys; and yet ordinarily—despite the *Steel Seizure* case and a few recent instances—the President does not claim domestic lawmaking powers, or other non-executive powers, in support of foreign affairs. Treaty power operates mainly within a textually defensible framework, and "non-treaties" represent less of a departure than one might suppose: most executive agreements do not operate within domestic law (the main textual limit upon them), despite the Court's rulings that they can, and most aspects of most congressional-executive agreements (like the World Trade Organization agreements and the North American Free Trade Agreement) reflect, for domestic purposes, things that Congress could easily do by statute alone. Even with respect to the states in foreign affairs, where the Court's cases seem perhaps most radically disconnected from the text, the reality is less than Supreme Court pronouncements might suggest: in fact, relatively few state foreign-affairs-related laws have been invalidated outside of Article VI, and states continue to play an important though understated role in international matters. The surprise, in sum, is not how much we have departed, but how little.

As a last word, then, this work invites us to consider whether the founders' Constitution in foreign affairs should be binding upon us. We have seen that its basic structures can be found in the text, given its historical understanding. And we have seen that these structures can guide us through modern controversies. That does not mean that they should. We may conclude here, only, that they can.

Notes
Index

Notes

Introduction

1. Louis Henkin, *Foreign Affairs and the U.S. Constitution* 13–14, 15 (2d ed. 1996).
2. Harold Koh, *The National Security Constitution* 68, 67 (1990).
3. Louis Henkin, "Foreign Affairs and the Constitution," 66 *Foreign Affairs* 284, 307 (1987). See also Jefferson Powell, *The President's Authority over Foreign Affairs* 21 (2002) (noting "textual ambiguity which the Constitution displays"); id. at 27 (noting "apparent silence of the text"); Jefferson Powell, "The President's Authority over Foreign Affairs: An Executive Branch Perspective," 67 *Geo. Wash. L. Rev.* 537, 534–35 (1999) (noting "impossibility of resolving many issues involving foreign affairs . . . through textual exegesis" and endorsing arguments based on "claims that a particular principle or practical result is implicit in the structures of government"); Eugene Rostow, "President, Prime Minister, or Constitutional Monarch?" in *Foreign Affairs and the U.S. Constitution* 30–31 (Louis Henkin et al., eds., 1990) ("The international powers of the nation are not to be deduced from the few spare words of the constitutional text, but from their matrix in international law.").
4. 299 U.S. 304, 318–19 (1936).
5. See Keith Whittington, *Constitutional Interpretation* 14–15 (1999) ("[T]he choice of an interpretive method cannot itself be determined through an act of interpretation. The specification of an interpretative method is an important constitutional issue, but it is not a matter of constitutional law. Constitutional law does not specify the terms of its own existence."). For a critical survey of various methods and a defense of historical textual meaning as the cornerstone of modern constitutional law, see id. at 17–46, 110–59; for a range of opinions, see the essays collected in Antonin Scalia, *A Matter of Interpretation* (Amy Gutmann, ed., 1996).

   In the interest of style and brevity, I may refer to what the Constitution "means" without qualifying that as referring to the historical meaning. I do, nonetheless, mean the text's historical meaning and do not mean to imply anything about modern meaning.

6. For example, John Yoo, *The Powers of War and Peace* (2005). See also Michael Ramsey, "Torturing Executive Power," 93 *Georgetown L.J.* 1213 (2005) (discussing the George W. Bush administration's over-reliance on the executive power clause in constitutional argument).

7. Randy Barnett, "An Originalism for Nonoriginalists," 45 *Loyola L. Rev.* 611, 621–22 (1999). See also John McGinnis & Michael Rappaport, "Symmetric Entrenchment: A Constitutional and Normative Theory," 89 *Va. L. Rev.* 385, 391 & n. 14 (2003); Whittington, at 35–36; Scalia, at 37.

8. See Vasan Kesavan & Michael Paulsen, "The Interpretive Force of the Constitution's Secret Drafting History," 91 *Georgetown L.J.* 1113 (2003); John Manning, "Textualism and the Role of The Federalist in Constitutional Adjudication," 66 *G. Wash. L. Rev.* 1332, 1354 (1998); Scalia, at 37–38. On the practical convergence of methodologies of text and intent, see Caleb Nelson, "Originalism and Interpretive Conventions," 70 *U. Chi. L. Rev.* 519 (2003). To be sure, this brief formulation finesses, or at least avoids, substantial academic debate on interpretive approaches. Rather than further describe an abstract interpretive methodology, however, I shall proceed largely by example.

1. Do Foreign Affairs Powers Come from the Constitution?

1. United States v. Curtiss-Wright Export Co., 299 U.S. 304, 318–19 (1936). See Michael Ramsey, "The Myth of Extraconstitutional Foreign Affairs Power," 42 *Wm. & Mary L. Rev.* 379, 387–403, 431–37 (2000), on which parts of the ensuing discussion rely.

2. For example, Michael Glennon, *Constitutional Diplomacy* 18–34 (1990); Harold Koh, *The National Security Constitution* 93–95 (1990). For an intermediate perspective, see Louis Henkin, *Foreign Affairs and the U.S. Constitution* 16–20 (2d ed. 1996).

3. Jefferson Powell, *The President's Authority over Foreign Affairs* 23 (2002); Koh, at 94. For modern Supreme Court invocations, see Pasquantino v. United States, 544 U.S. 349, 369 (2005) (citing *Curtiss-Wright* for the proposition that "the Executive is 'the sole organ of the federal government in the field of international relations'"); United States v. Lara, 541 U.S. 193, 202 (2004) (citing *Curtiss-Wright* for the "Constitution's adoption of preconstitutional powers necessarily inherent in any Federal Government"). For academic endorsement, see Bradford Clark, "Federal Common Law: A Structural Reinterpretation," 144 *U. Pa. L. Rev.* 1245, 1296–97 (1996); Karl Manheim, "State Immigration Laws and Federal Supremacy," 22 *Hastings Const. L.Q.* 939, 940–41 (1995); Richard Morris, "The Forging of the Union Reconsidered: A Historical Refutation of State Sovereignty over Seabeds," 74 *Colum. L. Rev.* 1056, 1060–68 (1974).

4. 299 U.S. at 311–15; Joint Resolution of May 28, 1934, 48 Stat. 811 (President may impose embargo "if the President finds that the prohibition of the sale of arms and munitions of war in the United States to those countries now engaged

in armed conflict in the Chaco may contribute to the reestablishment of peace between those countries").

5. A.L.A. Schechter Poultry Co. v. United States, 295 U.S. 495, 541–42 (1935); Panama Refining Co. v. Ryan, 293 U.S. 388, 418–19 (1935).

6. Glennon, at 21; see George Sutherland, *Constitutional Power and World Affairs* (1919).

7. 299 U.S. at 316–17.

8. Id. at 317.

9. Id. at 316.

10. Id. at 319.

11. Whitman v. American Trucking Association, 531 U.S. 457, 472–76 (2001).

12. 2 *Documentary History of the Ratification of the Constitution* 167–68 (Merrill Jensen et al., eds., 1976–present) (Speech in the State House Yard, Oct. 6, 1787); see also id. at 454–55 (Wilson to Pa. convention) (federal government consists of enumerated powers; failure to enumerate a power leaves it outside the government's authority).

13. Federalist No. 45, in James Madison, Alexander Hamilton, & John Jay, *The Federalist Papers* 296 (Isaac Kramnick, ed., 1987); 10 *Documentary History*, at 1502 (Madison to Va. convention). See also 4 *Debates in the Several State Conventions on the Adoption of the Federal Constitution* 259 (Jonathan Elliot, ed., 1836) (Pinckney to S.C. convention) ("no powers could be executed, or assumed, but such as were expressly delegated"); id. at 249 (Iredell to N.C. convention).

14. For anti-federalist objections, see, for example, 2 *Debates*, at 398–99 (Tredwell to N.Y. convention); "Letters from the Federal Farmer to the Republican," IV, 12 *Documentary History*, at 44–45 (Oct. 12, 1787); Herbert Storing, "What the Anti-Federalists Were For," in *The Complete Anti-Federalist* (Herbert Storing, ed., 1975). For a state-by-state account of ratification, see *Ratifying the Constitution* (Michael Gillespie & Michael Lienesch, eds., 1989); on Massachusetts, see Michael Gillespie, "Massachusetts: Creating Consensus," in id. at 138, 147–58. For a magnificent overview of the Constitution's adoption, see Akhil Amar, *America's Constitution: A Biography* 5–312 (2005).

15. 6 *Documentary History*, at 1469; id. at 1385 (Adams to Mass. convention). Six states recommended such amendments, as did key anti-federalist writers; see "An Additional Number of Letters from the Federal Farmer to the Republican," XVI, 17 *Documentary History*, at 342–43 (May 2, 1788) (describing federal government as "possessing only enumerated power" but proposing early form of Tenth Amendment to quiet anti-federalist fears).

16. See Amar, at 315–32; Stanley Elkins & Eric McKitrick, *The Age of Federalism* 60–61 (1993).

17. On the Amendment's history, see Charles Lofgren, "The Origins of the Tenth Amendment: History, Sovereignty, and the Problem of Constitutional Intention," in *Constitutional Government in America* 331 (Ronald Collins, ed., 1980); Jeremy Telman, "A Truism That Isn't True: The Tenth Amendment and Executive War

Power," 51 *Cath. U. L. Rev.* 135, 140–42 (2001); Raoul Berger, *Federalism: The Founders' Design* 78–81 (1987).

18. 1 *Annals of Congress* 441 (Joseph Gales, ed., 1834) (June 8, 1789). Five years after *Curtiss-Wright,* the Supreme Court, without acknowledging any tension with that case, rightly described the Amendment as intended "to allay fears that the new national government might seek to exercise powers not granted." United States v. Darby, 312 U.S. 100, 124 (1941).

19. See, for example, New York v. United States, 505 U.S. 144, 160 (1992); Printz v. United States, 521 U.S. 898, 918–19 (1997). Rejecting inherent federal powers on the basis of the Tenth Amendment does not necessarily endorse this line of cases.

20. James Wilson, "Considerations on the Bank of North America," 2 *Works of James Wilson* 824, 825, 828–30 (Robert McCloskey, ed., 1967) (1785); see also George Mason to Thomas Jefferson, Sept. 27, 1781, 2 *Papers of George Mason* 697–99 (Robert Rutland, ed., 1970) (objecting to arguments "that the late Revolution has transferred the Sovereignty formerly possessed by Great Britain to the United States, that is to the American Congress"). On inherent and delegated powers during the drafting of the Articles, see especially Merrill Jensen, *The Articles of Confederation* 160–76 (1940).

21. 2 *Documentary History,* at 470; see 10 id. at 1307 (Marshall to Va. convention).

22. Sarah Cleveland, "Powers Inherent in Sovereignty: Indians, Aliens, Territories, and the Nineteenth Century Origins of Plenary Power over Foreign Affairs," 81 *Tex. L. Rev.* 1 (2002).

23. As Henkin, at 14–15, summarizes: "[V]ery much about foreign relations went without or with little saying. . . . Where—for random examples—is the power to recognize other states or governments; to maintain or rupture diplomatic relations; to open consulates in other countries and permit foreign governments to establish consulates in the United States; to acquire or cede territory; to grant or withhold foreign aid; to proclaim a Monroe Doctrine, an Open-Door Policy, or a Reagan Doctrine; indeed to determine all the attitudes and carry out all the details in the myriads of relationships with other nations that are 'the foreign policy' and 'the foreign relations' of the United States? . . . These 'missing' powers, and a host of others, were clearly intended for, and have always been exercised by, the federal government, but where does the Constitution say that it shall be so?"

24. 2 *Documentary History,* at 436; see Jack Rakove, *Original Meanings* 318–38 (1997). This concern gave rise to the Ninth Amendment. See 1 *Annals,* at 439 (June 8, 1789) (Madison describing Ninth Amendment's purpose).

25. See Federalist No. 32, at 221–22 (Hamilton) (arguing that, since Article I, §10 denied states specific powers of taxing imports and exports, they must have general taxing power over items not specifically mentioned).

26. Federalist No. 44, at 286–87 (Madison) ("The right of coining money, which is here taken from the states [in Article I, §10], was left in their hands by the Confederation. . . ."); Amar, at 11 & n.18 ("most state constitutions in place before

1787 had given state legislatures power to issue paper money and emit bills of credit. The federal Constitution abrogated these and other powers. . . ."); Ramsey, at 402 & n.82 (collecting examples). On controversies surrounding states' paper money prior to the Constitution, see Gillespie & Lienesch, at 79–80, 370–75; Allan Nevins, *The American States during and after the Revolution* 478–92, 515–43 (1969 reprint).

27. The threat of states making separate treaties with foreign powers, for example, was particularly worrisome. See Madison to James Monroe, June 21, 1785, 8 *Papers of James Madison* 306–08 & n.2 (William Hutchinson et al., eds., 1962–1991) (discussing report of Georgia sending emissaries to negotiate with Spain).

28. Sutherland's only source from this period was Massachusetts delegate Rufus King's comment at the drafting Convention. 299 U.S. at 317–18. King said, while arguing over inherent state sovereignty, that states were not wholly sovereign under the Articles because only the national government could make war and treaties. 1 *Records of the Federal Convention of 1787*, at 323 (Max Farrand, ed., 1966). Although accurate, this has no bearing on inherent national powers, since the Articles' text (art. 9) explicitly made war and treatymaking exclusive national powers.

29. Madison's Federalist No. 42, at 273–74, for example, misquotes the Constitution as explicitly providing power to receive ambassadors, "other public ministers and consuls," and emphasizes the importance of including consuls; Article II, §3 in fact does *not* explicitly refer to consuls, only "ambassadors and other public ministers."

30. See John Manning, "Textualism and the Role of The Federalist in Constitutional Adjudication," 66 *G. Wash. L. Rev.* 1324, 1332–33 (1998).

31. Federalist No. 41, at 266 (emphases added). These parts responded to antifederalist claims that the Constitution gave the national government too much power.

32. Federalist No. 42, at 273–79; Federalist No. 45, at 292. See also Federalist No. 44, at 292 (question is "whether this amount of power shall be granted or not").

33. Federalist No. 23, at 185.

34. Federalist No. 24, at 188.

35. Federalist No. 44, at 286.

2. Foreign Affairs and the Articles of Confederation

1. David Levitan, "The Foreign Relations Power: An Analysis of Mr. Justice Sutherland's Theory," 55 *Yale L.J.* 467, 478–90 (1946); Charles Lofgren, "United States v. Curtiss-Wright Export Corporation: An Historical Reassessment," 83 *Yale L.J.* 1, 12–20 (1973); Raoul Berger, *Federalism: The Founders' Design* 21–47 (1987). As historian Jack Rakove summarizes, the view is that "the separation from Britain had 'placed the 13 States in a state of nature towards each other,' and that only then had these 'separate sovereignties' formed a federal government for the dual purpose of 'defend[ing] the whole agst. foreign nations' and

'the lesser States agst. the ambition of the larger.'" Jack Rakove, *Original Meanings* 163 (1997) (quoting Luther Martin's statements to the Philadelphia Convention).

2. Lofgren, at 12–32; Richard Morris, "The Forging of the Union Reconsidered: A Historical Refutation of State Sovereignty over Seabeds," 74 *Colum. L. Rev.* 1056, 1057, 1061–62 (1974); Jack Rakove, *The Beginnings of National Politics* 173–74 n.* (1979); Gordon Wood, *The Creation of the American Republic, 1776–1787,* at 355 (2d ed. 1998). As Professor Wood further observes, "the Continental Congress since 1774 exercised an extraordinary degree of political, military, and economic power over the colonists—adopting commercial codes, establishing and maintaining an army, issuing a continental currency, erecting a military code of law, defining crimes against the Union, and negotiating abroad." Id.; see also id. at 356–59 (indicating the difficulty of clear resolutions, given the revolutionaries' own unsettled view of sovereignty); Willi Paul Adams, *The First American Constitutions* 49–51 (1980) (noting complexity and concluding that "the decision for independence and the decision to draft new [state] constitutions occurred simultaneously on several interlocking levels"); Akhil Amar, *America's Constitution: A Biography* 25–28 & nn.51–61(2005) (discussing early ambiguities of sovereignty). For an early statement of the nationalist view, see 1 Joseph Story, *Commentaries on the Constitution of the United States,* §§198–217 (1833).

3. See Jerrilyn Marston, *King and Congress* (1987).

4. Rakove, *Original Meanings,* at 163. See Berger, at 21 ("Whether the States were independent sovereignties before the adoption of the Constitution . . . is fundamental to States' Rights claims. . . ."). See also the exchange between Luther Martin and James Wilson at the Constitutional Convention, recounted in Rakove, *Original Meanings,* at 163, and the related statement of Rufus King, quoted in United States v. Curtiss-Wright Export Co., 299 U.S. 304, 317 (1936). On the political implications of this debate, see Rakove, *Original Meanings,* at 161–202.

5. See Akhil Amar, "Of Sovereignty and Federalism," 96 *Yale L.J.* 1425 (1987). Lincoln argued in terms reminiscent of *Curtiss-Wright:* "The original [states] passed into the Union even before they cast off their British colonial dependence. . . . The Union is older than any of the States, and, in fact, it created them as States." Id. at 1460 n.153 (quoting Lincoln, Message to Congress, July 4, 1861); see also Morris, at 1063–67 (tracing debate from the founding through the nineteenth century).

6. Rakove, *Original Meanings,* at 163; see also Berger, at 21–47 (chapter titled "Nation or Sovereign States: Which Came First?").

7. On drafting the Articles, see Merrill Jensen, *The Articles of Confederation* (1940). Most states approved the Articles promptly, but Maryland held out until 1781 to demand agreement on the western lands, resulting in a four-year delay. See id. at 225–38; 5 *Journals of the Continental Congress* 431 (Worthington Ford et al., eds., 1906–37) (June 11, 1776) (appointing drafting committee); 9 id. at 932–34 (Nov. 17, 1777) (finalizing proposal to the states); 19 id. at 213–23 (March 1, 1781) (Maryland's approval as the thirteenth state and formal promulgation).

8. Jensen, at 107–76; Forrest McDonald, *Novus Ordo Seclorum* 143–52 (1985).

9. On the Articles' difficulties, see especially Rakove, *Beginnings*, at 192–399; Frederick Marks, *Independence on Trial* 3–95 (1973); Richard Morris, *The Forging of the Union, 1781–1789*, at 194–219, 245–66 (1984).

10. Articles of Confederation, art. 9 ("The United States, in Congress assembled, shall have the sole and exclusive right and power" over, among other matters, war and peace, sending and receiving ambassadors, entering into treaties, establishing prize rules, and granting letters of marque and reprisal in peacetime). Article 9 also gave the Congress general power to appoint committees and officers as needed for "managing the general affairs of the United States," under its direction.

11. With respect to war and peace, at least, one could argue that specification was needed, not to grant power, but to show that nine states' consent (not a simple majority) was required. But some foreign affairs powers—such as sending and receiving ambassadors—did not require nine-state approval, yet were specifically listed.

12. Articles, art. 6 (restricting states, without the Congress's consent, from specified activities); id. art. 9 (congressional power over specified foreign affairs activities "sole and exclusive").

13. Jensen, at 126–176; id., app. at 254–64 (Dickinson draft); Adams, at 281–83; Wood, at 358–59.

14. Federalist No. 44, in James Madison, Alexander Hamilton, & John Jay, *The Federalist Papers* 291 (Isaac Kramnick, ed., 1987).

15. Morris, "Forging of the Union Reconsidered," at 1063, expressly reaches this conclusion. This was not Burke's view. See Rakove, *Beginnings*, at 170 (quoting Burke's private description of Article 2 as establishing that "all sovereign power was in the states separately, and that particular acts of it, which should be expressly enumerated, would be exercised in conjunction, and not otherwise; but that in all things else each State would exercise all the rights and power of sovereignty"). But see James Wilson, "Considerations on the Bank of North America," 2 *The Works of James Wilson* 828–30 (Robert McCloskey, ed., 1967) (1785) (arguing that Article 2 did not preclude inherent national powers).

16. When the Congress claimed additional foreign affairs powers, it pointed to specific provisions in the Articles. The Articles, for example, gave the Congress no explicit authority to maintain a navy; during the war, the Congress claimed this authority as part of its powers over war and peace granted in Article 9. After peace with Britain, the question arose whether the Congress could maintain a peacetime navy. It claimed that power, not from inherent sovereignty, but from further extrapolation from the document itself—specifically, as a further implication of Article 9. 25 *Journals*, at 722–24 (Oct. 23, 1783).

17. See James Madison, "Vices of the Political System of the United States," 9 *Papers of James Madison* 348–49 (William Hutchinson et al., eds., 1962–1991) (1787) (criticizing state activities contrary to Article 9); Madison to Monroe, June 21, 1785, 9 id. at 306–8 (Georgia sending emissaries to Spain was a "flagrant

outrage on" the Articles). One might say, as Sutherland did, that states' lack of war and treaty powers under the Articles shows the states had limited external sovereignty. *Curtiss-Wright*, 299 U.S. at 317 (quoting Rufus King's statement in the Philadelphia Convention that states lacked war and treatymaking powers). But lack of these powers is consistent with the idea that the distribution of powers flowed only from the Articles themselves: the Articles had express provisions on the subject. See the Congress's 1782 resolution directing states not to negotiate separately with Britain, and Virginia's resolution accepting that direction because "by the articles of confederation and perpetual union the sole and exclusive right of making peace is vested in the United States in congress assembled. . . ." 11 William Hening, *The Statutes at Large: Being a Collection of All of the Laws of Virginia* 546 (May 24, 1782) (1823).

18. For further elaboration, see Michael Ramsey, "The Myth of Extraconstitutional Foreign Affairs Power," 42 *Wm. & Mary L. Rev.* 379, 404–429 (2000).

19. See Allan Nevins, *The American States during and after the Revolution* (1969).

20. For example, Jefferson to Madison, May 8, 1784, 8 *Papers of Madison*, at 29–30 (discussing need for "arming Congress with powers to frustrate the unfriendly regulations of Great Britain"); Madison to Monroe, Aug. 7, 1785, id. at 333–34 (asking "What is to be done? Must we remain passive victims to foreign politics; or shall we exert the lawful means which our independence has put in our hands, of exhorting redress?"). On foreign nations' trade policies, see Nevins, at 564–65.

21. See especially Rakove, *Beginnings,* at 333–99.

22. Nevins, at 556–64; id. at 601 ("A number of Northern states struck at Great Britain through their tariff laws, which were unfortunately a jumble of incongruities."); see Madison to Jefferson, Mar. 18, 1786, 8 *Papers of Madison*, at 502 ("The States are every day giving proofs that separate regulations are more likely to set them by the ears, than to attain the common object. When Massts. set on foot a retaliation of the policy of G.B. Connecticut declared her ports free. N. Jersey served N. York in the same way. And Delaware I am told had lately followed the example in opposition to the commercial plans of Penna.").

23. Treaty of Peace, Sept. 4, 1783, in 2 *Treaties and Other International Acts of the United States* 151 (Hunter Miller, ed., 1931); see Samuel Bemis, *A Diplomatic History of the United States* 46–64 (4th ed. 1955).

24. 31 *Journals*, at 781–874 (Oct. 13, 1786) (Foreign Secretary Jay's report on state treaty violations); Norman Risjord, *Chesapeake Politics 1781–1800*, at 109–19, 135–38, 150–56 (1978); Robert Brunhouse, *Counterrevolution in Pennsylvania 1776–1790*, at 140–41 (1942); Marks, at 5–15; Nevins, at 268–74 (New York), 336–37 (Virginia), 386–89 (North Carolina; North Carolina did not even acknowledge the treaty until December 1787). For the Congress's efforts to bring states into line, see 24 *Journals* at 373–74 (May 29, 1783); 32 id. at 177–84 (April 13, 1787); David Golove, "Treaty-Making and the Nation: The Historical Foundations of the Nationalist Conception of the Treaty Power," 98 *Mich. L. Rev.* 1075 (2000). See generally Bemis, at 65–84.

25. Federalist No. 22, at 183. Though the peace treaty violations were the most serious, states provoked diplomatic problems by violating other treaties as well. See Van Berkel to Jay, Feb. 20, 1787, and accompanying note by Jay to the Congress, 3 *Diplomatic Correspondence of the United States* 437–42 (U.S. Dept. of State, 1834) (protesting state violations of Netherlands treaty).

26. 1 *Diplomatic Correspondence*, at 89 (Luzern to Continental Congress); 28 *Journals*, at 314–15 (April 27, 1785); 29 id. at 655 (Aug. 24, 1785). For accounts of the episode and its aftermath, see G. S. Rowe & Alexander Knott, "Power, Justice and Foreign Relations in the Confederation Period: The Marbois-Longchamps Affairs, 1784–1786," 104 *Penn. Mag. Hist. & Biog.* 275 (1980); William Casto, "The Federal Courts' Protective Jurisdiction over Torts Committed in Violation of the Law of Nations," 18 *Conn. L. Rev.* 467, 491–94 (1986).

27. 24 *Journals*, at 227–28 (Apr. 4, 1783); 27 id. at 509–12 (June 2, 1784).

28. Respublica v. De Longchamps, 1 U.S. 111 (Pa. 1784).

29. For example, Jefferson to Madison, May 25, 1784, 8 *Papers of Madison*, at 43–45 (discussing dangers of the de Longchamps incident).

30. Compare Marks, at 3–95, giving foreign affairs the central role, with Wood, at 392–429, acknowledging foreign affairs difficulties but emphasizing problems of domestic governance at the state level.

31. 9 *Papers of Madison*, at 349–50. See Rakove, *Original Meanings*, at 42–56.

32. 1 *Records of the Federal Convention of 1787*, at 19 (Max Farrand, ed., 1966) (May 29, 1787).

33. See especially Federalist No. 15, at 146–47 (Hamilton); Federalist No. 22, at 177–84 (Hamilton); Federalist No. 47, at 274 (Madison). In any event, foreign affairs was an immediate trigger for the Convention, whatever other concerns Americans had with the Articles. After a third effort to amend the Articles to give the Congress power over foreign commerce failed, state representatives met in Annapolis, Maryland, in 1786 to discuss a common approach to the issue of commercial regulations. Not enough delegates attended to accomplish anything, but the Annapolis convention's one substantive act was to call a second meeting in Philadelphia, urging all states to send delegates. That convention convened the following year (1787), and from the outset abandoned any idea of amending the Articles. Instead, over the objections of a minority of delegates, it produced a draft of a new government—the document that became the Constitution. Rakove, *Beginnings,* at 368–75.

34. 26 *Journals*, at 321–22 (Apr. 30, 1784).

35. Speech to the Mass. Legislature (May 31, 1785), 1 *Acts and Resolves of the Province of Massachusetts Bay, 1769–1780*, at 706 (1886).

36. For example, Monroe to Madison, July 26, 1785, 8 *Papers of Madison*, at 329 (describing proposal "to invest Congress" with power to regulate trade instead of the states); Madison to Monroe, Aug. 7, 1785, id. at 333 (describing question as whether power "ought to be vested in Congress"); Madison to Jefferson, Aug. 20, 1785, id. at 344 ("The machinations of G.B. with regard to Commerce have produced much distress and noise in the Northern States. . . . [T]he sufferers are

every where calling for such augmentation of the power of Congress as may effect relief.").

37. For example, 1 *Acts of Massachusetts,* at 41 (July 1, 1784) ("An act vesting certain powers in Congress," resolving that "the United States in Congress assembled be, and they hereby are vested with full power" to enact specified regulations of foreign trade); 11 *Laws of Virginia,* at 388 (1784) (An act to invest the United States in congress assembled, with additional powers for a limited time," by which the Congress is "empowered" to prohibit certain foreign commerce); 11 James Mitchell & Henry Flanders, *Statutes at Large of Pennsylvania from 1682 to 1801,* at 391 (Dec. 17, 1784) (1903) ("act to vest Congress with certain powers. . . .").

38. Rakove, *Beginnings,* at 347 (quoting Yates to R.I. delegate David Howell); 2 *Papers of George Mason* 779–82 (Robert Rutland, ed., 1970) (May 30, 1783). On the campaign generally, see Rakove, *Beginnings,* at 346–48; Risjord, at 251–75.

39. Marks, at 85–90. A further proposal, involving broader commercial powers, was suggested by committees in 1785 and 1786 but was never actually proposed to the states. 28 *Journals,* at 201–5 (Mar. 28, 1785).

40. Van Beck Hall, *Politics without Parties: Massachusetts, 1780–1791,* at 122–65 (1972); Nevins, at 564–65. See 1 *Acts of Massachusetts,* at 99, 439 (June 23, 1785) (enacting commercial regulations); id. at 724, 726 (July 2, 1785) (Governor's message on coordination with New Hampshire); id. at 768 (Nov. 14, 1785) (Governor's message on coordination with Rhode Island).

41. Rakove, *Beginnings,* at 342–52 (discussing weakness of national government in addressing foreign commercial threats). On the problems of coordination among the states, see Marks, at 82–83.

42. Rakove, *Beginnings,* at 368–98.

43. See Ramsey, at 409–12; Nevins, at 282, 561, 601.

44. For example, 10 *Laws of Virginia,* at 105 (1779) (authorizing governor to impose embargoes); 11 id. at 101–03 (1782) (limiting trade in British goods); id. at 136–38 (1782) (same, enacted at the Congress' recommendation); 1 *Laws of Massachusetts,* at 1114–15 (Sept. 8, 1779) (embargo on certain items); id. at 51 (Mar. 3, 1781) (limitation on British commerce); 9 *Statutes of Pennsylvania,* at 272 (Sept. 7, 1778) (embargo of specified items); id. at 288 (Sept. 10, 1778) (embargo on British trade); 10 id. at 417 (Apr. 10, 1782) (same); id. at 497 (Sept. 20, 1782) (same).

45. 21 *Journals,* at 894–96. See Rakove, *Beginnings,* at 290; Nevins, at 628–29. In contrast, the same committee proposed giving the Congress explicit power to coerce states to abide by the Articles (chiefly directed at states failing to pay money requested by the Congress). Rakove, *Beginnings,* at 289–90. As to this power, the committee argued that the Congress already had "a general and implied power . . . to enforce and carry into effect all the Articles of the said Confederation against any of the States" but recommended making the power explicit. 20 *Journals,* at 469–70 (Mar. 12, 1781).

46. 25 *Journals,* at 589 (Sept. 19, 1783) (report that the United States had lost ne-

gotiating strength against Britain "by admitting too precipitately English vessels in [American] ports"); see also 11 *Laws of Virginia*, at 101–3 (1782) (act suppressing trade with Britain, conditional upon all other states passing similar laws); id. at 136 (1782) (same); 10 *Statutes of Pennsylvania*, at 497 (1782) (act suppressing trade with Britain).

47. 29 *Journals*, at 842–44 (Oct. 20, 1785).

48. Federalist No. 42, at 274.

49. 28 *Journals*, at 314 (Apr. 27, 1785).

50. 21 id. at 1136 (Nov. 23, 1781).

51. See Ware v. Hylton, 3 U.S. 199, 217, 276–77 (1796) (Iredell) (describing this problem).

52. "Letter from Phocion to the Considerate Citizens of New York," Jan. 1784, 3 *Papers of Alexander Hamilton* 489 (Harold Syrett, ed., 1961–1987). Hamilton further argued that the delegation of the treaty power implied cession by the states of the power to obstruct treaties.

53. 4 *Secret Journals of the Congress of the Confederation* 203–4 (Oct. 13, 1786) (Thomas Wait, ed., 1821). See generally Nevis, at 644–56.

54. See, for example, Hamilton's discussion in Federalist No. 22, at 177, observing that "[t]he want of a power to regulate commerce [on the part of the confederation government] . . . has already operated as a bar to the formation of beneficial treaties with foreign powers" and that "[s]everal states have endeavored by separate prohibitions, restrictions, and exclusions to influence the conduct of [Great Britain] in this particular, but the want of concert, arising from the want of a general authority and from clashing and dissimilar views in the States, has hitherto frustrated every experiment of the kind. . . ." Historians Morris and Rakove, although advocating a "nationalist" interpretation of the revolutionary period, seem to concur with the foregoing picture of the Articles' foreign affairs powers. Morris, *Forging of the Union*, at 130–61, 194–219; Rakove, *Beginnings*, at 331–95.

55. 1 *Laws of Massachusetts*, at 99 (June 23, 1785); see also id. at 439 (Nov. 29, 1785) (continuing discriminatory duties on Britain but ending them against other nations); id. at 726, 768 (1785) (recounting efforts at coordination with New Hampshire and Rhode Island); id. at 36 (1786) (suspending state navigation act due to lack of nationwide cooperation).

56. See 12 *Laws of Virginia*, at 32 (1785) (discriminatory duties on "every ship or vessel trading to this commonwealth, owned wholly or in part by a British subject"); id. at 289–90 (1786) (varying import duties depending upon whether country of origin had a commercial treaty with United States); 11 id. at 494 (1784) (directing that arms purchases be made from France); 10 id. at 202 (1779) (giving commercial privileges to nations recognizing U.S. independence); 11 *Statutes of Pennsylvania*, at 182 (Apr. 2, 1785) (same); 12 id. at 99 (Sept. 20, 1785) (discriminatory duties on countries without commercial treaties with United States); id. at 103 (Sept. 20, 1785) (discriminatory duties on Portugal "to continue for so long as the flour of America is prohibited from being imported into the kingdom and territories [of Portugal]").

57. 12 *Laws of Virginia,* at 528 (1787); see Madison to Monroe, Dec. 24, 1785, 9 *Papers of Madison,* at 456 (reporting that "the general cry [in Virginia] is that the Treaty ought not to be executed here until the posts are surrendered").

58. See Madison to Jefferson, Jan. 9, 1785, 8 *Papers of Madison,* at 227 (Virginia agreeing to make extraditions upon the Congress's request).

59. 27 *Journals,* at 582–85 (July 10, 1784) (describing postal regulations that included fines for individuals interfering with the mail); 32 id. at 334–43 (July 13, 1787) (ordinance providing rules for governing the Northwest Territory); see also Wood, at 355 (commenting on extent of congressional regulatory activity).

60. See Louis Henkin, *Foreign Affairs and the U.S. Constitution* 19 (2d ed. 1996): "Even if it were assumed, contrary to Justice Sutherland, that the states were each independently sovereign up to (and even during) the regime of the Articles of Confederation, the crux of Sutherland's theory might yet stand: the states irrevocably gave up external sovereignty, and the United States became one sovereign nation, upon adopting the Constitution but outside its framework. . . ."

61. See Amar, "Of Sovereignty," at 1446–62 (arguing that the Constitution created a national sovereignty where none had previously existed).

62. As Madison argued in Federalist No. 40, at 262: "The truth is that the great principles of the Constitution . . . may be considered less as absolutely new than as the expansion of principles which are found in the Articles of Confederation."

63. One sees here the interplay of text and history. History illuminates the text, for without the history we have difficulty knowing whether the Tenth Amendment's "reserved" powers apply to foreign affairs; yet the text anchors the history, showing that, even if some framers would have liked a nationalist re-invention of inherent foreign affairs powers in the Constitution, they were not able to achieve it. Sutherland's approach, which postulates an abstract idea of sovereignty and then draws specific nontextual conclusions from it, does not read the text, but reinvents it. As John Yoo explains, "focusing on the text employs history at an effective level of generality. It avoids the dangers of allowing pure intellectual history to scatter our analysis. Although we can use historical works about systems of belief widely held by Americans at the time of the Constitution's framing, such views are relevant only to the extent that they appear in the constitutional text. The Constitution distilled the abstract political theories and beliefs of the time into a workable system of government. . . ." John Yoo, *The Powers of War and Peace* 27 (2005).

64. Henkin, at 20.

3. The *Steel Seizure* Case and Executive Power over Foreign Affairs

1. Youngstown Sheet & Tube Co. v. Sawyer, 343 U.S. 579 (1952).

2. Louis Henkin, *Foreign Affairs and the U.S. Constitution* 31 (2d ed. 1996). Even strongly pro-Congress scholars acknowledge the President's "mastery of our diplomatic communications with the outside world" without explaining its textual basis. Harold Koh, *The National Security Constitution* 95 (1990).

3. See Henkin, at 38–39. As Henkin points out, tying the President's diplomatic power to the shared power over treaties or appointments would seem to require that it be shared with the Senate, which no one seriously proposes.

4. See, for example, Koh, at 67–68.

5. See Saikrishna Prakash & Michael Ramsey, "The Executive Power over Foreign Affairs," 111 *Yale L.J.* 231 (2001) and Saikrishna Prakash & Michael Ramsey, "Foreign Affairs and the Jeffersonian Executive: A Defense," 89 *Minn. L. Rev.* 1591 (2005), on which the ensuing discussion relies. The most comprehensive opposing argument is Curtis Bradley & Martin Flaherty, "Executive Power Essentialism and Foreign Affairs," 102 *Mich. L. Rev.* 545 (2004). For other skeptical views, see Henkin, at 39–41; Jack Rakove, "Solving a Constitutional Puzzle: The Treatymaking Clause as a Case Study," 1 *Persp. in Amer. Hist. (N.S.)* 233 (1984); Koh, at 75. Sources suggesting Article II, §1 to solve the supposed "lacunae" of foreign affairs powers include Charles Thach, *The Creation of the Presidency 1775–1789* (2d ed. 1963); John Yoo, *The Powers of War and Peace* (2005); Gary Lawson & Guy Seidman, "The Jeffersonian Treaty Clause," 2006 *U. Ill. L. Rev.* 1, 22–43; Michael Paulsen, "Youngstown Goes to War," 19 *Const. Comment.* 215 (2002); Robert Turner, *Repealing the War Powers Resolution* 52–80 (1991).

6. 343 U.S. at 585–89.

7. Id. at 635–40 (Jackson, concurring). Unfortunately for Jackson, Congress had not actually done anything (in terms of legislation); Jackson had to arrive at Congress's "view" from Congress's *failure* to act—surely a risky interpretive enterprise. On *Youngstown* and Jackson's concurrence, see Koh, at 105–13; Patricia Bellia, "Executive Power in Youngstown's Shadows," 19 *Const. Comment.* 87 (2002); Paulsen, at 224–37.

8. 343 U.S. at 610–13 (Frankfurter, concurring). More recently, the Court stated, relying in part on Frankfurter, that "the historical gloss on the 'executive Power' vested in Article II of the Constitution has recognized the executive's 'vast share of responsibility for the conduct of our foreign relations.'" Amer. Ins. Ass'n v. Garamendi, 539 U.S. 396, 414 (2003).

9. 343 U.S. at 634–35 & n.1 (Jackson, concurring).

10. Id. at 681–82.

11. The closest anyone has come to sustained argument in this direction is Bradley & Flaherty, "Executive Power Essentialism." Bradley and Flaherty argue that at least during the Washington administration, political leaders relied on specific grants of power to justify presidential actions. Even if this is correct (Chapter 4 argues it is not), Bradley and Flaherty stop well short of making definitive claims about the text, seeming to suggest ultimately that extratextual factors must be consulted. See id. at 627–86, 688 & n.690.

12. Akhil Amar, *America's Constitution: A Biography* 107–8 (2005) suggests that Congress's power over "commerce" with foreign nations included "all forms of intercourse in the affairs of life, whether or not narrowly economic or mediated by explicit markets." But see Randy Barnett, "The Original Meaning of the

Commerce Clause," 68 *U. Chi. L. Rev.* 101 (2001) (arguing that commerce power meant only economic relations).

13. Steven Calabresi & Saikrishna Prakash, "The President's Power to Execute the Laws," 104 *Yale L.J.* 541, 579–81 (1994); Saikrishna Prakash, "The Essential Meaning of Executive Power," 2003 *U. Ill. L. Rev.* 701. This was also the leading eighteenth-century dictionary definition. Samuel Johnson, *Dictionary of the English Language* (1755) (Arno Reprint 1979) (definition of "executive").

14. Some authorities deny that the clause contains *any* substantive powers, but only says that powers subsequently listed (in Article II, §§2 and 3) are exercised by a single person called the President. See Chapter 6.

15. Thomas Jefferson, "Opinion on the Powers of the Senate" (Apr. 24, 1790), 16 *Papers of Thomas Jefferson* 378–79 (Julian Boyd et al., eds., 1950–2005). The context of these statements is discussed in Chapter 4.

16. Pacificus, No. 1 (June 29, 1793), 15 *Papers of Alexander Hamilton* 33, 38–40 (Harold Syrett, ed., 1961–1987).

17. See Michael Paulsen, "The Constitution of Necessity," 79 *N.D. L. Rev.* 1257, 1258 (2004) (arguing for presidential emergency powers as part of the "executive" power).

18. 1 *Records of the Federal Convention of 1787,* at 292 (Max Farrand, ed., 1966) (Hamilton's proposal to the Philadelphia Convention amounting to a quasi-monarchy); see Ron Chernow, *Alexander Hamilton* 219–90 (2004).

19. Helvidius, No. 1 (Aug. 24, 1793), 15 *Papers of James Madison* 66, 69 (William Hutchinson et al., eds., 1962–1991); id. (war and treatymaking are not "executive" because neither "suppose[s] pre-existing laws to be executed"); Jefferson to Madison, June 29, 1793, 26 *Papers of Jefferson,* at 401, 403 (urging Madison to dispute Pacificus). See William Casto, "Pacificus & Helvidius Reconsidered," 28 *N. Ky. L. Rev.* 612, 617–30 (2001).

20. 343 U.S. at 34–35 (Jackson, concurring).

21. Johnson, *Dictionary* (definition of "executive").

22. Federalist No. 47 (Madison), in James Madison, Alexander Hamilton, and John Jay, *The Federalist Papers* 303 (Isaac Kramnick, ed., 1987). On the influence of Enlightenment writers, see Forrest McDonald, *Novus Ordo Seclorum* 54–96 (1985); Bernard Bailyn, *The Ideological Origins of the American Revolution* 25–30 (1967); Donald Lutz, *The Origins of American Constitutionalism* 139–49 (1988).

23. John Locke, *Two Treatises of Government* (1690) (Peter Laslett, ed., 1988); William Blackstone, *Commentaries on the Laws of England* (1765); Baron de Montesquieu, *The Spirit of Laws* (1748) (Prometheus reprint 2002). According to Donald Lutz, the last two were the most cited secular works in American political writing. Lutz, at 136–49. For leading accounts of separation of powers doctrine and its influence in America, see M. J. C. Vile, *Constitutionalism and the Separation of Powers* (2d ed. 1998); W. B. Gwyn, *The Meaning of Separation of Powers* (1965); Francis Wormuth, *The Origins of Modern Constitutionalism* (1949).

24. 3 Polybius, *The Histories,* bk. VI, §§11–18 (W. R. Paton, trans., 1979).

25. Vile, at 23–82, 289–322; Wormuth, at 59–72 (noting early division between legislative and executive).

26. Adams to R. H. Lee, Nov. 15, 1775, 4 *Works of John Adams* 186 (Charles Adams, ed., 1854). See also Federalist No. 48 (Madison), in at 310 (referring to "[a]ll the powers of government, legislative, executive and judiciary"). See Wormuth, at 198–99 (quoting anonymous 1758 English pamphlet applauding that in England "'the fundamental powers of legislation, of judicature, and that of executing the laws, are wisely disjoined from each other'").

27. Locke, at 355–63; 1 Blackstone, at 52; Jean de Lolme, *The Constitution of England* 60–70 (1771) (Gaunt reprint 1998). See Larry Alexander & Saikrishna Prakash, "The Reports of the Delegation Doctrine's Death Are Greatly Exaggerated," 70 *U. Chi. L. Rev.* 1297, 1305–1320 (2003) (concluding that "at the founding, legislative power was understood as the authority to make rules for the government of society"). De Lolme, for example, complained that in continental monarchies the king held legislative power.

28. Of course, theorists did not always agree on how particular powers should be classified—the classifications were, as Professor Vile says, "extremely abstract" and could pose definitional problems in specific application. The discourse was also complicated by tendencies to refer to institutions by the name of the powers they predominantly exercised. Thus, for example, the king was called "the executive" because he principally exercised executive powers (although he also exercised some legislative and judicial powers). This should not obscure the fact that "executive power" referred in the first instance to a set of functions, not to a type of institution. Vile, at 15–18.

29. Id. at 17.

30. Id. at 43 (emphasis added).

31. See de Lolme, at 60–98; Wormuth, at 59–72, 191–206.

32. Vile, at 13–15.

33. As Vile explains, Montesquieu and Blackstone are important parts of this shift. Id. at 83–168.

34. According to Vile, "[b]y the time the Convention met, important sections of opinion among its members had already accepted the two central positions of modern American constitutional thought," namely separation of powers and the idea of checks and balances, which were "considered an essential constitutional weapon to keep all branches of government, and especially the legislature, within bounds." Id. at 168. This was the point of Madison's Federalist Nos. 47–48, defending the Constitution against charges that it violated the doctrine of separation of powers. Madison agreed that "[t]he accumulation of all powers, legislative, executive, and judiciary, in the same hands, whether of one, a few, or many . . . may justly be pronounced the very definition of tyranny." Federalist No. 47, at 303. Thus he accepted the definitional part of separation of powers theory—that "all powers" can be classified, not according to what branch exercises them, but abstractly, as legislative, executive, or judicial. He also accepted part of the prescriptive element—that is, that these functions should not all be exercised by one body.

But Madison rejected the "pure" separation of powers position that there must be absolute identity between branches and powers. Rather, the branches may have "a partial agency" in the functions of the others. Id. at 304. Indeed, "unless these departments be so far connected and blended as to give to each a constitutional control over the others," boundaries between the branches "can never in practice be maintained." Federalist No. 48, at 308. As he pointed out, this view was entirely consistent with the eighteenth-century English constitution, as Montesquieu explained it, and with the post-revolution state constitutions.

35. Locke, at 365–66. See Vile, at 66–67.

36. Locke, at 366, 325. Locke echoed earlier writers like George Lawson, who associated executive and military power without thinking about the matter closely. According to Lawson, in a view that became standard in the eighteenth century: "There is a threefold power civil, or rather three degrees of that power. The first is legislative. The second judicial. The third executive." Executive power included foreign affairs power, because "[o]ne and the same sword must protect from enemies without and unjust subjects within. For the sword of war and justice are but one sword." George Lawson, *An Examination of the Political Part of Mr. Hobbs his Leviathan* 8 (1657), discussed in Vile, at 60–62.

37. Montesquieu, at 151. Montesquieu said, for example, that Rome's senate had most executive powers because it exercised most foreign affairs powers: it "determined on war and peace," "fixed the number of the Roman and allied troops," "received and sent embassies," and "nominated, rewarded, punished and were judges of kings, declared them allies of the Roman people, or stripped them of that title." Id. at 172–73. He added, though, that Roman consuls (magistrates) had some executive power, as they "levied the troops which they were to carry into the field; had command of the forces by sea and by land; disposed of the forces of the allies; were invested with the whole power of the republic in the provinces; gave peace to the vanquished nations, imposed conditions on them, or referred them to the senate." And over time the popular assembly gained more executive power, as it took over nomination of military officers and "decreed that only their own body should have the right of declaring war." Id.

38. Gwyn, at 103; Vile, at 95. Vile comments: "Montesquieu . . . affirms [at the outset of his discussion] that he intends to use the term 'executive power' exclusively to cover the function of the magistrates to make peace or war, send or receive embassies, establish the public security, and provide against invasions. He now seems to wish to confine the term 'executive power' to foreign affairs, for he does not make it at all clear that the power to 'establish the public security' has any internal connotation. . . ." Nonetheless, says Vile, Montesquieu's later usage "clearly include[s] internal as well as external affairs in the executive power. It is this final sense that Montesquieu discusses the relationships between the powers of government. . . ." Id. See also Wormuth, at 195 ("The famous sixth Chapter of Book XI of the *Spirit of the Laws* . . . recognizes . . . the executive power in foreign relations (Locke's federative power)."); Martin Flaherty, "The Most Dangerous Branch," 105 *Yale L.J.* 1725, 1765–66 (1996)

("[A]ccording to Montesquieu, to whom . . . Americans usually turned, . . . executive authority included the power to make peace or war and to establish public security").

39. See J. H. Plumb, *England in the Eighteenth Century* 47–73, 105–15 (1963); 10 William Holdsworth, *A History of English Law* 3–125 (1966 reprint).

40. 1 Blackstone, at 183, 242–50. See Arthur Bestor, "Respective Roles of the Senate and President in the Making and Abrogation of Treaties," 55 *Wash. L. Rev.* 1, 75–77 (1979) (Blackstone described "the conduct of foreign affairs" as an aspect of "the executive part of government"); Martin Flaherty, "History Right?: Historical Scholarship, Original Understanding, and Treaties as 'Supreme Law of the Land,'" 99 *Colum. L. Rev.* 2095, 2106 (1999) ("Blackstone saw foreign affairs authority as quintessentially executive.").

41. Thomas Rutherforth, *Institutes of Natural Law,* bk. II, ch. III, at 54–61 (1754). Rutherforth included as executive powers peace, truce, negotiation, and "the power of adjusting the rights of the society in respect of foreigners" and explained, "when we are speaking of external executive power, we are supposed to include under that head, not only what is properly called military power, but the power likewise of making war or peace, the power of engaging alliances for an encrease of strength, either to carry on war or to secure peace, the power of entering into treaties, and of making leagues to restore peace . . . and the power of adjusting the rights of a nation in respect of navigation, trade, etc. . . ." He added that ambassadors are part of "the rest of that branch of the executive power, which is external," and thus ambassadors are "under the regulation of the executive, as to the degree or extent of their power." Id. While thus describing the by-then conventional view of executive powers, Rutherforth himself then expressed some reservations, including that a good many of these powers might be properly seen as legislative (or, at least, could be supervised by a legislative assembly).

42. De Lolme, at 70–73. As historian Arthur Bestor concludes: "The term 'executive power' . . . was defined in the constitutional traditions of most European countries, in such a way as to include the plenary power to decide, as well as to carry out, the foreign policy of the nation." Bestor, "Respective Roles," at 77. The early nineteenth-century American commentator St. George Tucker observed that the British constitution provides "an hereditary prince, in whom the Supreme Executive Authority, including the power of peace and war, is vested." 1 St. George Tucker, *Blackstone's Commentaries,* app. 51 (1803).

43. McDonald, at 81; Bailyn, at 27; Lutz, at 136–49.

44. 10 *Documentary History of the Ratification of the Constitution* 1382 (Merrill Jensen et al., eds., 1976–present) (Madison to Va. convention); Federalist No. 47, at 303. See Dennis Nolan, "Sir William Blackstone and the New American Republic: A Study of Intellectual Impact," 51 *N.Y.U. L. Rev.* 731 (1976).

45. Bailyn, at 27; Charles Lofgren, "War-Making Under the Constitution: The Original Understanding," 81 *Yale L.J.* 672, 689–90 (1972).

46. For example, Montesquieu, at 172–73, wrote that the Roman senate exercised

"executive" powers in its foreign affairs capacity, although as a prescriptive matter he thought these powers would be better exercised by a single monarch.

47. In their leading critique of executive foreign affairs power, Professors Bradley and Flaherty half-heartedly dispute parts of this description, especially with respect to Blackstone; but as noted, it accords with the leading historical studies of the period and, indeed, with Professor Flaherty's prior work. See Bradley & Flaherty, at 560–71; for specific rejoinders, see Prakash & Ramsey, "Jeffersonian Executive," at 1629–41.

48. "The Essex Result," in 1 *American Political Writing during the Founding Era, 1760–1805,* at 480, 494 (Charles Hyneman & Donald Lutz, eds., 1983). On the significance of the *Result,* see Vile, at 165–66; Willi Paul Adams, *The First American Constitutions* 91 (1980) (calling the *Result* "an essay in political theory and constitutional practice comparable to *The Federalist* in the sophistication of its argument [and in its political outlook]").

49. Madison to Caleb Wallace, Aug. 23, 1785, 8 *Papers of Madison,* at 352; Jack Rakove, *Original Meanings* 253 (1996).

50. Jack Rakove, *The Beginnings of National Politics* 383 (1979) (internal quotation omitted). Again, we should remember that the word "congress" did not, in the 1780s, imply a legislative body.

51. 9 *Documentary History,* at 986 (Randolph to Va. convention); 2 id. at 474 (Wilson to Pa. convention); 6 id. at 1325–26 (Parsons to Mass. convention); Jefferson to Genet, Dec. 9, 1793, 26 *Papers of Jefferson,* at 500–501.

52. See Jerrilyn Marston, *King and Congress* 8, 205 (1987) (describing the Congress as primarily executive); Thach, at 56 (the Congress was a "plural . . . executive body"). See also Flaherty, "History Right," at 2117 (calling the Congress a "plural executive" and noting that historians indicate it had a "jumble" of all three powers of government); Amar, at 57 (calling the Congress an "executive council"); Yoo, at 73.

53. "Congress . . . could work out general policies, but could not enforce them, except against the officers of its own creation." Thach, at 56.

54. Rakove, *Original Meanings,* at 253. This point illustrates how Americans adopted Montesquieu's vocabulary without adopting his prescriptions: contrary to Montesquieu's recommendations, the Articles did not vest foreign affairs power in a single magistrate; but although vested instead in an assembly, it was still called "executive" power (in keeping with Montesquieu's own description of the Roman senate).

55. See Vile, at 131–68.

56. See 22 *Journals of the Continental Congress* 87–92 (Worthington Ford et al., eds., 1906–1937) (Feb. 22, 1782); 19 id. at 43–44 (Jan. 10, 1781).

57. Jay to Washington, Jan. 7, 1787, 3 *Correspondence and Public Papers of John Jay* 227 (Henry Johnston, ed., 1891); Jay to Jefferson, Aug. 18, 1786, id. at 210; see also Jay to Jefferson, Dec. 14, 1786, id. at 222–23 (in the Congress, "so much time is spent in deliberation that the season for action often passes").

58. On the impulse for a more decisive, active executive branch, see, for example,

Jefferson to Edward Carrington, Aug. 14, 1787, 4 *Writings of Thomas Jefferson* 424–25 (Paul Ford, ed., 1894); Hamilton to James Duane, Sept. 3, 1780, 2 *Papers of Hamilton*, at 404–5; Federalist No. 70 (Hamilton), at 402–3. On executive power at the Convention, see Christopher Collier & James Collier, *Decision in Philadelphia* 289–311 (1986).

59. 1 *Records*, at 18–19, 21.

60. Id. at 64–67.

61. Id. In their otherwise excellent and readable account of the Convention, Christopher and James Collier miss this point entirely, writing that the executive rights of the Congress "were few" and thus that the Virginia plan did not give the President power "to run foreign policy." Collier & Collier, at 304–5. This comports neither with contemporaneous descriptions of the Congress nor with the delegates' reaction to the Virginia plan.

62. 2 *Records,* at 143–53. As the discussion indicates, the Committee of "Detail" was a bit of a misnomer, as many important issues remained unresolved at that point. See Thach, at 106.

63. 2 *Records*, at 163–75.

64. Id. at 342–43 (proposed Secretary of Foreign Affairs); id. at 498–99 (shift of treatymaking and appointments).

65. Professor Thach, who, at 165, generally endorses the idea of unenumerated executive power, finds "absolutely no evidence" one way or the other on the intent of the Committee's revisions. Thach, at 118. In terms of direct evidence from debates over the Committee's proposal, that is surely correct—but indirect evidence, taken from the course of the Convention as a whole, is nonetheless quite suggestive. Bradley & Flaherty, at 592–602, reach the opposite conclusion, but they agree that the initial Virginia plan likely conveyed general foreign affairs authority. Id. at 592. They not explain how "executive" rights or powers could have meant one thing in June (when delegates debated the Virginia plan) and another in August (when the Committee of Detail reported). What changed was not the meaning of "executive," but the way the draft allocated the key foreign affairs powers that the delegates did not wish to commit wholly to the President.

66. See Bradley & Flaherty, at 602–26. Bradley and Flaherty also demonstrate at length that the ratifiers debated allocations of power in terms of creating the best structure of government (what they call "functionalist" arguments), generally without reliance upon arguments from the nature or essence of particular powers ("essentialist" arguments). This seems generally correct (and unsurprising), but also irrelevant.

67. Some commentary did assume, without provoking much controversy, a presidential role in foreign affairs beyond specific powers. For example, 4 *Debates in the Several State Conventions on the Adoption of the Federal Constitution* 112–13, 127 (Jonathan Elliot, ed., 1836) (Iredell to N.C. convention) (President could send spies overseas, and would "regulate all intercourse with foreign powers"); Federalist No. 72 (Hamilton), at 412 ("actual conduct of foreign negotiations" is executive in nature and would be controlled by President); Federalist No. 84

(Hamilton), at 519 ("management of foreign negotiations will naturally devolve" upon the President subject to the Senate's general desires and ultimate concurrence in treatymaking). Though they did not tie these powers directly to Article II, §1, it is hard to see what else the speakers could have had in mind. The comments are, though, scattered and somewhat inconclusive. See also Chapter 7 (noting that some commentary assumed the Senate would have a leading role in foreign affairs).

68. "Letters from the Federal Farmer to the Republican," III, Oct. 10, 1787, 12 *Documentary History*, at 42–48.

69. 2 id. at 466 (Smilie), 634 (Dissent); see also Arthur Lee to John Adams, 8 id. at 34 (Constitution vests "legislative, executive & judicial Powers in the Senate"); R. H. Lee to Randolph, Dec. 6, 1787, 14 id. at 367 (Senate exercises "legislative and executive powers" in treatymaking); 6 id. at 1391 (Bowdoin to Mass. convention) (Senate has "not only legislative, but executive powers"); 6 id. at 1326 (Taylor to Mass. convention) (Senate acts "in their executive capacity, in making treaties and conducting negotiations"); 4 *Debates*, at 116 (Spencer to N.C. convention) (Senate possesses "the chief of the executive power" due to treatymaking and appointments roles).

70. Cassius, I, 9 *Documentary History*, at 641, 644–45; 4 *Debates*, at 269 (Pringle); id. at 27–28 (Maclaine). Iredell said that "in the branches of executive government, where [the Senate's] concurrence is required, the President is the primary agent." Id. at 127–28. William Davie likewise remarked that "in all countries and governments" treatymaking was "placed in the executive departments" because of the "secrecy, design, and despatch" needed for negotiations. Id. at 119–20. A response to George Mason's objections about the Senate's role in appointments and treatymaking observed: "Had the convention left the executive power indivisible, I am free to own it would have been better, than giving the senate a share of it." Civis Rusticus, "Reply to Mason's Objections" (Jan. 30, 1788), 1 *The Debate on the Constitution* 358 (Bernard Bailyn, ed., 1993). Wilson referred to "the executive powers of government in which the senate participate," appearing to include treaty power. Id. at 849 (Pa. convention); see also 2 *Documentary History*, at 341 (speech in Philadelphia) (noting Senate's "executive character"). Parsons observed that Senators acted "in their executive capacity in making treaties and conducting the national negotiations." 6 id. at 1326 (Mass. convention).

71. 1 *Annals of Congress* 54–55 (Joseph Gales, ed., 1834).

72. Other commentary described the Senate's treatymaking role as at least partially legislative. Responding to objections that the Senate improperly had executive power, Hamilton's Federalist No. 75, at 424–25, argued that treaties were both international obligations and part of domestic law, and so formed a "distinct department" belonging to neither the executive nor the legislature. Given the writings of Montesquieu and Blackstone (and the numerous complaints voiced during the ratification debates), there is little doubt that treatymaking traditionally was called executive, whatever Hamilton said. Indeed Hamilton acknowl-

edged that "several writers on the subject of government place that power in the class of executive authorities." But the key for Hamilton was that the Constitution made treaties supreme law (Article VI), and that provision (as we shall see) greatly altered the system familiar to Montesquieu and Blackstone. Hamilton did not deny that executive power included foreign affairs power—indeed he made that association himself strongly in later years—but he argued that treaties' (new) status within domestic law, and the importance of treaties generally, justified the Constitution's mixed system. As Hamilton said later, the "cooperation of the Senate" is a "plain[] qualifi[cation] of the general executive power of making treaties." Compare Helvidius [Madison], No. 1, Aug. 24, 1793, 15 *Papers of Madison*, at 69 (treaty "has itself the force of law" and thus is legislative).

73. See Helvidius, No. 1, 15 *Papers of Madison*, at 69.

74. The idea that allocations of formerly "executive" foreign affairs powers to other branches deny such power to the President is explored in more detail in later chapters. This point is crucial, for it explains in large part why the ratification debates did not focus on presidential foreign affairs power: the text stripped the President of the controversial executive foreign affairs powers, principally war and treatymaking. See Chapters 6, 7, and 11.

4. Executive Foreign Affairs Power and the Washington Administration

1. For objections and responses, see Chapter 6.

2. The ensuing discussion is especially indebted to Saikrishna Prakash & Michael Ramsey, "The Executive Power over Foreign Affairs," 111 *Yale L.J.* 231, 295–340 (2001), and Jefferson Powell, *The President's Authority over Foreign Affairs* 34–94 (2002).

3. See Vasan Kesavan & Michael Paulsen, "The Interpretive Force of the Constitution's Secret Drafting History," 91 *Georgetown L.J.* 1113, 1175–83 (2003).

4. James Hart, *American Presidency in Action 1789*, at 79 (1948); Elmer Plischke, *U.S. Department of State: A Reference History* 59 (1999). On Washington's administration generally, see Stanley Elkins & Eric McKitrick, *The Age of Federalism* 31–528 (1993); James Flexner, *George Washington and the New Nation 1783–1793* (1970); Forrest McDonald, *The Presidency of George Washington* (1974); Glenn Phelps, *George Washington and American Constitutionalism* (1993). On foreign affairs aspects in particular, see Abraham Sofaer, *War, Foreign Affairs and Constitutional Power* 61–129 (1984); Powell, at 34–94; Gerhard Casper, "An Essay in Separation of Powers: Some Early Versions and Practices," 30 *Wm. & Mary L. Rev.* 211 (1989).

5. Washington to the Senate, June 11, 1789, 30 *Writings of George Washington* 346–47 (John Fitzpatrick, ed., 1939) (in sending a consular treaty to the Senate, observing that Jay "has my Orders" to communicate to the Senate whatever papers and information it requested); Washington to Knox, Sept. 5, 1789, id. at 394 (reporting that Washington had "seen fit to direct" Jay to send a messenger

to Canada regarding a survey). For Jay's phrasing, see Library of Congress, *George Washington Papers,* Jay to Giuseppe Chiappe, Dec. 1, 1789, available at http://memory.loc.gov/cgi-bin/ampage?collId=mgw2&fileName=gwpage 028.db&rec, image 112, 113 ("[i]n obedience to the orders of the President"); Jay to Guy Carleton, Sept. 4, 1789, id., image 63 ("[i]n pursuance of the President's order"); Jay to Marquis de Lotbiniere, July 15, 1789, id., image 58–59 ("I am ordered [by the President] to inform you" of certain matters, and making further recommendations "[i]n obedience" to the "orders of the President"); Jay to Phineas Bond, Aug. 24, 1789, id., image 53 ("[i]n obedience to his [the President's] orders"). On Jay's prior subservience to the Articles' Congress, see 22 *Journals of the Continental Congress* 87–92 (Feb. 22, 1782) (Worthington Ford et al., eds., 1906–1937); 29 id. at 495 (Jay's correspondence).

6. Washington to Emperor of Morocco, Dec. 1, 1789, 30 *Writings of Washington,* at 474–75; Washington to King of France, Oct. 9, 1789, id. at 431–32 (referring to the King's letter of June 7, 1789).

7. Act of July 27, 1789, §1, 1 Stat. 28–29.

8. 1 *Annals of Congress* 522 (Joseph Gales, ed., 1834) (Sedgwick); id. at 1087 (Benson).

9. Id. at 383–615. On the debate, see especially Saikrishna Prakash, "New Light on the Decision of 1789," 91 *Cornell L. Rev.* 1021 (2006); Hart, at 152–214; David Currie, *The Constitution in Congress: The Federalist Period* 36–41 (1997); Charles Thach, *The Creation of the Presidency 1775–1789,* at 140–65 (2d ed. 1963).

10. Act of July 27, 1789, §2, 1 Stat. 28–29.

11. Hart, at 188; Currie, at 36–41.

12. Act of July 1, 1790, 1 Stat. 128–29; Washington to Congress, Jan. 8, 1790, 30 *Writings of Washington,* at 492. See Jefferson Powell, "The Founders and the President's Authority over Foreign Affairs," 40 *Wm. & Mary L. Rev.* 1471, 1478 (1999) ("It is difficult to read this public address to mean anything other than that it is the President's duty—not Congress's—to direct foreign intercourse.").

13. 1 *Annals,* at 1081 (Lee); id. at 1085 (Sherman) (President and Senate "ought to act together in every transaction which respects the business of negotiation with foreign powers"). For counterarguments, see id. at 1081–92. Lee's motion was defeated on an unrecorded vote, id. at 1092. See Powell, *President's Authority,* at 39–42; Powell, "Founders," at 1478–80.

14. See Prakash & Ramsey, at 307–10. Washington also dispatched emissaries without consulting the Senate: he sent Gouverneur Morris as a "private Agent" to Britain, and similarly sent a "private" representative to Portugal to lay the groundwork for formal diplomatic relations. Washington to Morris, Oct. 13, 1789, 30 *Writings of Washington,* at 439–40; id. at 440–42; Washington to the Senate, February 18, 1791, 31 id. at 219–21; see Plischke, at 58; Flexner, at 220–21.

15. 4 *Secret Journals of the Congress of the Confederation* 399 (Oct. 5, 1787) (Thomas Wait, ed., 1821); Sofaer, at 65n*; Elkins & McKitrick, at 503–4; Flexner, at 218.

President Adams followed this practice by unilaterally removing Secretary of State Timothy Pickering in 1800. Plischke, at 44. On this and other later removal practices, see Steven Calabresi & Christopher Yoo, "The Unitary Executive during the First Half-Century," 47 *Case W. L. Rev.* 1451, 149–95 (1997).

16. 5 *Annals,* at 29; see Prakash & Ramsey, at 318–20 (citing further examples).

17. Jefferson to William Short, March 8, 1791, 19 *Papers of Thomas Jefferson* 425 (Julian Boyd et al., eds., 1950–2005). Congress had passed resolutions praising the new French constitution; Washington thought Congress was "endeavouring to invade the executive." Jefferson advised that Congress acted properly because it had only "resolved to request" the President to communicate its views; "instead of a direct communication," he said, "they should pass their sentiments thro' the President." Memorandum of Consultations with the President, Mar. 12, 1792, id. at 260–61. Ultimately Washington attached the resolutions to his own letter. Washington to Louis XVI, Mar. 14, 1792, id. at 281–82.

18. 22 *Journals,* at 91 (Feb. 22, 1782); Plischke, at 11. See 24 id. at 5–6 (Jan. 3, 1783) (Jay ordered to send letter to French minister); 29 id. at 495–96 (July 2, 1785) (Jay ordered to send letter to Spanish minister). Although the Congress gradually gave Jay more independence, the shift under Washington's administration remains revolutionary. As late as 1787, the Congress was reviewing and approving even the most banal of foreign communications. See 4 *Secret Journals,* at 287 (Feb. 3, 1787) (letters to King of France and to Queen of Portugal).

19. For background, see especially Harry Ammon, *The Genet Mission* (1973).

20. Washington to the Cabinet, April 18, 1793, 25 *Papers of Jefferson,* at 568–69; Washington's Questions on Neutrality, April 19, 1793, 25 id. at 570. The cabinet at this point consisted of Hamilton, Jefferson, Attorney General Randolph, and Secretary of War Henry Knox.

21. Julian Puente, *The Foreign Consul: His Jurisdictional Status in the United States* 20–31 (1926).

22. See 21 *Journals,* at 940–41 (Sept. 7, 1781); 4 *Secret Journals,* at 343 (May 3, 1787).

23. Jefferson to Genet, Oct. 2, 1793, 27 *Papers of Jefferson,* at 175–76 (noting that "no other branch of the government [is] charged with the foreign communication").

24. Jefferson to Genet, Nov. 22, 1793, id. at 414.

25. Jefferson to Genet, Dec. 9, 1793, id. at 500–501. The power to issue and revoke consular exequaturs cannot arise from the power to receive diplomats. The Constitution uses the phrase "Ambassadors, other public Ministers and Consuls" for appointments (Article II, §2) and the Supreme Court's original jurisdiction (Article III). The President's Article II, §3 reception power, however, extends only to "Ambassadors and other public Ministers," not consuls.

26. Ammon, at 23.

27. Washington to Jefferson, Oct. 11, 1793, 33 *Writings of Washington,* at 116; Jefferson to Duplaine, Oct. 3, 1793, 26 *Papers of Jefferson,* at 184–86; Jefferson to Morris, Oct. 3, 1793, id. at 188. Washington also revoked the exequatur of

British Vice-Consul Thomas Moore in 1795. Washington to Pickering, Sept. 28, 1795, 34 *Writings of Washington*, at 318 n.71.

28. Ammon, at 207–9, 256; Jefferson to Genet, Sept. 7, 1793, 27 *Papers of Jefferson*, at 52–53.

29. For leading accounts of the neutrality crisis, see Ammon, at 32–93; Elkins & McKitrick, at 330–73; Charles Thomas, *American Neutrality in 1793* (1931); Charles Hyneman, *The First American Neutrality* 11–53 (1934). The French treaties are reprinted in 2 *Treaties and Other International Acts of the United States* 3, 35 (Hunter Miller, ed., 1931).

30. Thomas, at 26–43; Elkins & McKitrick, at 337–39. The proclamation itself, reprinted in Thomas, at 42–43, did not use the word "neutrality." Washington also refused France's request for advance payment of U.S. debts to France and rejected discussions of a further treaty.

31. See especially Hyneman, at 54–150.

32. On France's outlook, see Ammon, at 21–29, 55–56.

33. Elkins & McKitrick, at 816 n.100 ("[T]hough many authorities on international law . . . had asserted that nations not involved in war ought to observe a strict impartiality in their relation with the belligerents . . . there was little in the international practice of the eighteenth century to indicate general acceptance of such an assumption. It was not regarded as incompatible with neutral status that a nation might give very material assistance to one or more of the belligerents."). See also Hyneman, at 14–19 (same); Emmerich de Vattel, *The Law of Nations* bk. III, §97 (1758) (Charles Fenwick, trans., J. B. Scott, ed., 1964).

34. Ammon, at 45. As to the expedition against Spain, "Moultrie recommended men (including his private secretary, Stephen Drayton) whom Genet might enlist in the enterprise." Id.; see also Elkins & McKitrick, at 335–36.

35. See Ammon, at 51 (Jefferson "anticipated a neutral stance which would permit France all benefits possible while denying them to the British. He wished a benevolent neutrality of the kind then practiced by the European powers."); Hyneman, at 158 ("That Jefferson wished a benevolent neutrality in favor of France can hardly be denied."); but see Elkins & McKitrick, at 338 (disputing this view).

36. 4 *Annals*, at 17–18 (Senate): id. at 138–39 (House). The proclamation and its aftermath did provoke some material objections, which are considered below and in Chapter 5.

37. Powell, *President's Authority*, at 37. See Phelps, at 153; Flexner, at 215.

38. The President's only specific powers are receiving foreign ambassadors and (with the Senate) appointing U.S. diplomats. It would take quite a stretch to derive from these powers general diplomatic authority encompassing all Washington did, including removing U.S. ambassadors, receiving foreign consuls, expelling foreign consuls and ambassadors, undertaking all foreign communications, and formulating foreign policy. In particular, the appointments clause seems a poor candidate, as it would suggest at most a shared power with the Senate, and in any event no one believes that the President has power to instruct or remove federal

judges (who are appointed in the same manner and under the same clause as diplomats). As indicated, the only major work to semi-seriously suggest that the text's specific clauses can support all or most of these powers is Curtis Bradley & Martin Flaherty, "Executive Power Essentialism and Foreign Affairs," 102 *Mich. L. Rev.* 545 (2004), which does so only half-heartedly. See id. at 644 (disclaiming intent to "make conclusive arguments"); id. at 643–44 (using weak wording such as "alludes to," "echoes," and "finds a provenance in" to describe the relationship between specific textual clauses and the powers Washington exercised). The conventional wisdom, rather, is that the text does not grant these powers. See Louis Henkin, *Foreign Affairs and the U.S. Constitution* 15 (2d ed. 1996).

39. Congress's only general foreign affairs legislation during the period was the Act creating the Department of Foreign Affairs. As discussed, it did not grant the President foreign affairs powers but said only that the President could delegate foreign affairs powers to the Secretary.

40. Washington to Emperor of Morocco, Dec. 1, 1789, 30 *Writings of Washington*, at 474–75; Jay to Giuseppe Chiappe, Dec. 1, 1789, http://memory.loc.gov/cgi-bin/ampage?collId=mgw2&fileName=gwpage028.db&rec, image 112, 113. Jay further explained that the diplomatic communications would now go, not to Congress, but to the new President, "who possesses Powers and Prerogatives in many respects similar to those which are enjoyed by the Kings of England." Id., image 114. Chiappe, like other Confederation diplomats, had previously addressed diplomatic communications to the Congress. See Giuseppe Chiappe to President of Congress, July 18, 1789, id., images 106–9.

41. "Opinion on the Powers of the Senate," 16 *Papers of Jefferson*, at 378–79.

42. Id. at 379. Jefferson's opinion also illustrates why some executive foreign affairs powers are listed in Article II, §§2 and 3, despite the grant of residual executive power. Because the Senate's consent is necessary to appoint, one might have argued that this implied a share of the power to nominate, notwithstanding the grant of residual executive power. Article II, §2 makes clear that the Senate's advice-and-consent role in appointments does not include a role in nominations, which remain with the President. As Jefferson said, this phrasing also shows that powers preceding nomination (and, one should add, powers that come after commissioning, such as instructing and recalling) are beyond the Senate's advice-and-consent role. They are, as a result, part of the executive residual, as Jefferson said.

43. See David Mayer, *The Constitutional Thought of Thomas Jefferson* 230–31 (1994) (discussing Jefferson's opinion in similar terms and calling it one of several "broad statements regarding the executive nature of matters involving foreign affairs" made by Jefferson). In particular, Mayer associates Jefferson's later statements to Genet regarding the President's communications monopoly with Jefferson's view of residual executive power. Id. at 231. As Mayer further notes, Jefferson thought (consistent with what is said above) that executive foreign affairs power was limited by the Constitution's specific grants to other branches, especially war and treatymaking powers. Id. at 231–32.

44. 4 *Diaries of George Washington* 122 (April 27, 1790) (John Fitzpatrick, ed.,

1925). Neither Madison's nor Jay's response survives, so they can only be reconstructed from Washington's notes. Of course, there is some risk that Washington put his own interpretation upon them. In Congress, arguing for the position that ultimately prevailed, Representative Egbert Benson similarly urged that "in any business of an Executive nature" Congress had no power to require participation of the Senate where the Constitution itself did not do so. 1 *Annals,* at 1087.

45. 1 *Annals,* at 463 (June 16, 1789).

46. Id. Madison described his argument as being "that the Executive power being in general terms vested in the President, all power of an Executive nature not particularly taken away must belong to that department," and stating that this "opinion has prevailed" in Congress. Madison to Edmund Pendleton, June 21, 1789, 12 *Papers of James Madison* 252 (William Hutchinson et al., eds., 1962–1991); see also Madison to Randolph, June 17, 1789, id. at 229 ("Prsidt . . . is vested with the Executive Power, except so far as it is expressly qualified").

47. 1 *Annals,* at 382 (May 19, 1789); see also id. at 539 (June 18, 1789) (Fisher Ames) ("It is declared that the Executive power shall be vested in the President. Under these terms all the powers properly belonging to the executive branch of Government were given, and such only taken away as are expressly excepted").

48. Thach, at 155–56; 3 *Works of John Adams* 409 (Charles Adams, ed., 1854) (quoting Ellsworth); but see id. at 112 (former delegate William Johnson arguing that "[v]ested in the President would be void for uncertainty. Executive power is uncertain"). See Powell, *President's Authority,* at 39–40.

49. Thach, at 160.

50. Currie, at 36–40. According to Thach, at 158, twelve of the eighteen former members of the Convention who were then in Congress voted with Madison. Others rejected his constitutional analysis, although it is often unclear whether they rejected his reading of Article II, §1, or whether they thought appointments clause conveyed removal power to the Senate. On the meaning of the final vote, see Prakash, "New Light."

51. Thach, at 164–65; compare Currie, at 39 (despite what was said in the removal debates, "it seemed unlikely that the Framers had meant to give the President blanket authority to do everything that could theoretically be termed executive. . . .").

52. Pacificus, No. 1 (June 29, 1793), 15 *Works of Alexander Hamilton* 33, 38–40 (Harold Syrett, ed. 1961–1987). Hamilton pointed to removal power as evidence of Congress's recognition of this reading of executive power. He also argued alternatively that the President's foreign affairs powers arose from the authority to execute treaties and international law. Id. See William Casto, "Pacificus and Helvidius Reconsidered," 28 *N. Ky. L. Rev.* 612, 617–22 (2001).

53. Jefferson to Madison, June 29, 1793, 26 *Papers of Jefferson,* at 401, 403; Jefferson to Madison, July 7, 1793, id. at 443–44. As Jefferson made clear, his concern was over the "right of the *Executive* to declare that *we are not bound to execute the guarantee*"—a question of treaty power. See Casto, at 623–24.

54. 15 *Works of Hamilton,* at 438. This was, in fact, not what Washington intended:

at Jefferson's urging, Washington specifically deferred interpretation of the 1778 Treaty.

55. See Casto, at 623–30.

56. Helvidius, No. 1 (Aug. 24, 1793), 15 *Papers of Madison,* at 66–67.

57. See Casto, at 623–39 (arguing on this basis that Pacificus and Helvidius do not differ on core constitutional principles).

58. Helvidius, No. 1, 15 *Papers of Madison,* at 69.

59. Helvidius, No. 3, id. at 98; see Edward Corwin, *The President's Control of Foreign Relations* 28 (1917) ("the great shortcoming of Madison's argument . . . is its negative character, its failure to suggest either a logical or practicable construction of the Constitution to take the place of the one it combats").

60. As noted, the cabinet approved Washington's actions unanimously, and Congress, when it reconvened, praised Washington's management of the situation without constitutional reservation. "[T]he theory advocated by Madison in 1793 as to appropriate roles of President and Congress had been rejected in practice even before his Helvidius papers saw the light of day." Sofaer, at 115.

61. To be sure, there were substantial debates at the margins: on whether the appointing power implied removal power and whether the Senate's appointments power extended to micromanaging diplomatic rank and pay. None of these, however, went to the core proposition that the President was charged by the Constitution with control over foreign communications.

62. 5 *Annals,* at 32 (Ellsworth) (arguing that the Senate could not tell the President what to communicate); 4 *Papers of John Marshall* 104–5 (Herbert Johnson et al., ed., 1974–2006).

5. *Steel Seizure* Revisited

1. Harold Koh, *The National Security Constitution* 74–75 (1990); Louis Henkin, *Foreign Affairs and the U.S. Constitution* 27–28 (2d ed. 1996).

2. Theodore Roosevelt, *An Autobiography,* 22 *Works of Theodore Roosevelt* 404–5 (1913). Senator Spooner argued even more expansively in 1906: "[S]o far as the conduct of our foreign relations is concerned, excluding only the Senate's participation in the making of treaties, the President has the absolute and uncontrolled and uncontrollable authority." 40 *Congressional Record* 1418 (1906). As discussed in Chapter 3, something of this view appears as well in President Truman's arguments in *Steel Seizure,* and in Chief Justice Vinson's dissent in that case. For a more modest modern version, see Michael Paulsen, "The Constitution of Necessity," 79 *N.D. L. Rev.* 1257 (2004).

3. William Taft, *Our Chief Magistrate and His Powers* 144–45 (1916). Taft was no reflexive opponent of presidential power; his opinion for the Supreme Court in Myers v. United States, 272 U.S. 52 (1926), endorses Madison's view of executive removal power, and he also observed that the President "alone is the representative of our nation in dealing with foreign nations" and "formulate[s] the foreign policy of our government." Taft, at 113.

4. Youngstown Sheet & Tube Co. v. Sawyer, 343 U.S. 579, 587 (1952).

5. Legal scholars, like the Justices, struggle with this question. Professor Henkin says that "[n]o one has suggested that under the President's 'plenary' foreign affairs powers he can, by executive act or order, enact law directly regulating persons or property in the United States." Henkin, at 54. But surely this is exactly what Truman (and Vinson) claimed in *Steel Seizure,* and although the Court found otherwise, its reasoning was not entirely satisfactory. Indeed, Henkin admits that presidential lawmaking sometimes occurs and confesses inability to judge whether these instances represent only "the President's power to make special law in special circumstances, or . . . some broad principle of presidential 'legislative power' in foreign affairs." Id. at 57. Similarly, Henry Monaghan, a distinguished scholar of presidential power, says that "[t]he Constitution contemplates no such law-making prerogative in the President" because otherwise "the congressional role [in foreign affairs] would be substantially limited to that of a checking function. . . ." "The Protective Power of the Presidency," 93 *Colum. L. Rev.* 1, 55 (1993). But he concedes that "virtually every modern commentator acknowledges 'the very delicate, plenary and exclusive power of the President as the sole organ of the federal government in the field of international relations. . . . '" Id. at 48 (quoting *Curtis-Wright*). Why, then, should that not include some lawmaking authority?

6. Baron de Montesquieu, *The Spirit of Laws* 151–52 (1748) (Prometheus reprint 2002). See also id. at 156 (executive power should not have power of "resolving," that is, "ordaining by their own authority").

7. 1 William Blackstone, *Commentaries on the Laws of England* 142–43 (1765).

8. Id. at 261.

9. Id.; 4 id. at 67; see also Jean de Lolme, *The Constitution of England* 82 (1771) (if proclamations, that is, "the will of the king, should have the force of laws . . . the constitution seemed really undone").

10. This separation was subject to the theoretical qualification that in the English system, the monarch could veto legislation and thus seemed also to have a share of legislative power. This worried some writers, though not Montesquieu and Blackstone, for whom the essential point was that the monarch could not make law without Parliament's consent. See Montesquieu, at 159–60.

11. See Randy Beck, "Book Review—Presidential Defiance of Unconstitutional Laws: Reviving the Royal Prerogative," 16 *Const. Comment.* 419, 422–24 (1999); Godden v. Hales, 89 Eng. Rep. 1050, 1051 (1686) (finding that the "King had a power to dispense with any of the laws of Government as he saw necessity for it").

12. See M. J. C. Vile, *Constitutionalism and the Separation of Powers* 23–82 (2d ed. 1998); Francis Wormuth, *The Origins of Modern Constitutionalism* 43–206 (1949). For an early formulation, see Marchamont Needham, *The Excellencie of a Free State* 212–13 (1656) (stressing the "error" of "permitting of the Legislative and Executive Powers of a State, to rest in one and the same hands"). As late as 1690, Locke wrote that the king's prerogative power included "power to act according to discretion, for the publick good, without the prescription of the law

and sometimes even against it." John Locke, *Two Treatises of Government* 382–84 (1690) (Peter Laslett, ed., 1988). By the eighteenth century, though, this power had been abandoned in theory and practice.

13. For example, 1 Blackstone, at 264–67; 10 William Holdsworth, *A History of English Law* 400–403 (1966 reprint).

14. Holdsworth, at 281 (This principle was so well established that, in 1766, ministers who had inadvertently issued a proclamation which contravened the law, were obliged to protect themselves by an Act of Indemnity.").

15. Blackstone, for example, indicated that in England the monarch held all of the executive power. 1 Blackstone, at 142.

16. See Saikrishna Prakash, "The Constitution as Suicide Pact," 79 *N.D. L. Rev.* 1299, 1317 (2004) (using similar reasoning to argue against executive/presidential emergency powers).

17. 11 Holdsworth, at 175–76; Bates' Case, 2 State Trials 371 (1606).

18. There were exceptions, but the exceptions themselves indicate the general rule. Blackstone, for example, noted that in time of national emergency the king could command subjects not to leave the country—or, if they were abroad, command them to return—because their assistance might be needed to defend the nation. This looks like royal lawmaking without parliamentary backing. But Blackstone defended it, not on the basis of a general rule that the king could make law in times of national emergency, but from a special relationship between king and subject allowing the king to call upon the subject's services in wartime. 1 Blackstone, at 256.

19. 1 Blackstone, at 249; de Lolme, at 73. For some qualifications and elaborations of this statement, see Chapter 8.

20. 14 Holdsworth, at 66–67; to be clear, Holdsworth means the treaties' terms "cannot take effect" *in English law,* not that the treaty itself would not be in effect as between nations.

21. Id.

22. Id. at 67–68.

23. In the debates, anti-federalists objected to Article VI's apparent alteration of this principle by making treaties the supreme law of the land of their own force. See Old Whig, III, 7 *Documentary History of the Ratification of the Constitution* 456 (Merrill Jensen et al., eds., 1976–present) ("The law there [in England] is not altered by the treaty itself; but by an act of parliament which confirms the treaty, and alters the law so as to accommodate it to the treaty. The king in council have no such power."). Federalists confusingly responded by trying to deny or obscure the English rule (see Federalist No. 69 (Hamilton), in James Madison, Alexander Hamilton, & John Jay, *The Federalist Papers* 399 (Isaac Kramnick, ed., 1987)), trying to deny or obscure the new constitutional rule (see 2 *Documentary History,* at 562–63 (Wilson to Pa. convention)), or sometimes both (see 10 id. at 1241 (Madison to Va. convention)). See also Chapter 8.

24. See 2 *Records of the Federal Convention of 1787,* at 395 (Max Farrand, ed., 1966) (Wilson); id. at 393 (Johnson). But see Martin Flaherty, "History Right? Histor-

ical Scholarship, Original Understanding, and Treaties as 'Supreme Law of the Land,' " 99 *Colum. L. Rev.* 2095, 2109–12 (1999) (suggesting that some treaties may have had legal status in England, or at least that some framers may have thought they did).

25. *Ware v. Hylton,* 3 U.S. 199, 273–75 (1796).

26. Harry Ammon, *The Genet Mission* 70–71 (1973) (noting "the difficulty of enforcing neutrality without specific statutes imposing punishments"); Forrest McDonald, *The Presidency of George Washington* 128 (1974) (noting "the weakness of the administration's authority" regarding enforcement); Charles Thomas, *American Neutrality in 1793,* at 170 (1931) (noting that Genet's argument "that there was no law of the United States which prevented citizens [from] enlisting . . . gave the cabinet and many attorneys and judges more worry"); Charles Hyneman, *The First American Neutrality* 83 (1934) ("The secretary of state did not explain where he was to find the law which would be relied on to punish the individuals infringing rules laid down by the President and his cabinet.").

27. Ammon, at 65–93; Stanley Elkins & Eric McKitrick, *The Age of Federalism* 341–54 (1993); Hyneman, at 85–86, 118–21. For a legal perspective on the *Little Sarah* incident, see Jefferson Powell, "The Founders and the President's Authority over Foreign Affairs," 40 *Wm. & Mary L. Rev.* 1471, 1489–94 (1999).

28. Washington requested that if assistance to France was occurring, "you will effectively put a stop to it" without specifying how or under what sources of authority. Hyneman, at 77. Washington's letters did not assert that the proclamation placed the governors (or citizens) under any legal duties.

29. On the governors' responses, see id. at 156–57; Powell, "Founders," at 1488–92. In Virginia, Governor Henry Lee tried to use the state militia to suppress outfitting, sending future Chief Justice John Marshall, then a militia commander, to seize a privateer; the expedition failed because Lee hesitated to order the use of actual force. See Jean Smith, *John Marshall: Definer of a Nation* 176 (1996).

30. Cabinet Opinions on the *Little Sarah,* July 8, 1793, 26 *Papers of Thomas Jefferson* 446–52 (Julian Boyd et al., eds., 1950–2005). Hamilton and Secretary of War Knox argued for using force; Jefferson dissented, but not on constitutional grounds. See Powell, "Founders," at 1489–95. "Washington and his advisors clearly believed that the President's authority with respect to foreign affairs carried with it some power to take military action without congressional sanction in order to achieve the executive's goals." Id. at 1495.

31. Hyneman, at 77–78, 156. Washington's phrase "laws of neutrality" presumably referred to the law of nations, as Congress had not yet acted. Washington first asked the Supreme Court for advice in formulating neutrality principles under the law of nations, leading to the Court's refusal to give advisory opinions. David Currie, *The Constitution in the Supreme Court: The First Hundred Years* 11–14 (1985). Again, Washington did not appear to consider the proclamation itself to have legal effect.

32. Henfield's Case, 11 F. Cas. 1099 (C.C. D. Pa. 1793); *State Trials of the United States* 49–89 (Francis Wharton, ed., 1849).

33. On the prosecutions, see especially Hyneman, at 83–84, 128–32.

34. Thomas, at 43; Jefferson to Rawle, May 15, 1793, in *State Trials,* at 51; 1 *American State Papers* 152 (Joseph Gales, ed., 1832–1861) (Randolph). In a private letter, Jefferson discussed various legal theories supporting the prosecutions, without mentioning the proclamation. Jefferson to Monroe, July 14, 1793, 26 *Papers of Jefferson,* at 501–3. Hyneman comments, at 83: "It is hardly likely that the secretary of state was of the opinion that the President's order was in itself sufficient to make illegal the activities complained of; one is all but positive that Randolph, the attorney general, would have vigorously combated any such doctrine."

35. Pacificus, No. 1 (June 29, 1793), 15 *Papers of Alexander Hamilton* 33 (Harold Syrett, ed., 1961–1987).

36. *State Trials,* at 78–83 (prosecution's argument); id. at 84–85 (court's charge). James Wilson, the presiding judge, instructed: "It has been asked by [Henfield's] counsel . . . against what law has he offended? The answer is . . . he was bound to keep the peace in regard to all nations with whom we are at peace. This is the law of nations. . . . There are, also, positive laws, existing previous to the offense committed, and expressly declared to be part of the supreme law of the land [referring to U.S. treaties with Britain and the Netherlands]." Id. at 84. See also id. at 49–54, 59–66 (earlier grand jury charges of Wilson and Jay); Hyneman, at 128–32.

37. United States v. Hudson, 11 U.S. 32 (1812); United States v. Coolidge, 14 U.S. 415 (1816).

38. Thomas, at 172; 5 John Marshall, The Life of George Washington 435 (1807).

39. Ammon, at 71 ("the absence of a statutory prohibition gave the jury (frankly sympathetic to Henfield) convenient grounds for acquittal"); Thomas, at 173 (noting "popular dislike of anything that resembled convicting a man of a crime established only by an executive proclamation").

40. 5 Marshall, at 435.

41. 4 *Annals of Congress* 11 (Washington's address of Dec. 3, 1793) (Joseph Gales, ed., 1834). On the suggestion of a special session, see Thomas, at 175; Washington to the Cabinet, Aug. 3, 1793, 26 *Papers of Jefferson,* at 611 (noting Herfield's acquittal). Jefferson thought Congress should be summoned, among other reasons, because "several legislative prohibitions are wanting to enable the government to steer steadily through the difficulties daily produced by the war of Europe. . . ." "Opinion on Convening Congress," Aug. 4, 1793, id. at 615.

42. See Trial of John Etienne, May 11, 1795, in *State Trials,* at 93.

43. Whether this violated the Fifth Amendment's direction against "taking" private property without compensation is a separate issue not considered by most members of the Court and not addressed here.

44. Of course, *Curtiss-Wright,* in its specifics, was not about the President's unilateral embargo power, but about Congress's power to delegate embargo authority to the President. *Curtiss-Wright* arose in a time of atypical restrictions on delegations, forcing the Court to invent an elaborate theory to justify a fairly modest

delegation. Under modern views, *Curtiss-Wright*'s delegation seems unobjectionable; there is reason to believe this would be true under eighteenth-century views as well. See David Currie, *The Constitution in Congress: The Federalist Period* 146–49, 186–87 (1985) (discussing Congress's early delegations, including with respect to embargoes); 1 Blackstone, at 261 (although the executive lacks lawmaking power, "the manner, time, and circumstances of putting those laws into execution must frequently be left to the discretion of the executive magistrate"); but see Gary Lawson, "Delegation and the Original Meaning," 88 *Va. L. Rev.* 327 (2002) (arguing for narrow view of delegation power under the Constitution's historical meaning).

45. Message to Congress, July 11, 1861, 4 *Collected Works of Abraham Lincoln* 430–31 (Roy Basler, ed., 1953).

46. See Ex parte Merryman, 17 F.Cas. 144 (C.C.D. Md. 1861).

47. See Paulsen, at 1257–58.

48. 1 Blackstone, at 132. See Hamdi v. Rumsfeld, 542 U.S. 507, 543–58 (2004) (Scalia, dissenting) (discussing history).

49. In re Quirin, 317 U.S. 1 (1942); see Hamdi, 542 U.S. at 516; see also Ex parte Milligan, 71 U.S. 2 (1866) (relying on English history to invalidate executive military commission used to try a civilian in the Civil War); Ingrid Wuerth, "The President's Power to Detain 'Enemy Combatants': Modern Lessons from Mr. Madison's Forgotten War," 98 *Nw. U. L. Rev.* 1567 (2004).

50. Federalist No. 58, at 350; 3 *Debates in the Several State Conventions on the Adoption of the Federal Constitution* 129 (Jonathan Elliot, ed., 1836) (Iredell to N.C. convention); William Banks & Peter Raven-Hansen, *National Security Law and the Power of the Purse* 160–63 (1994); Louis Fisher, "The Spending Power," in *The Constitution and the Conduct of American Foreign Policy* 227 (David Adler & Larry George, eds., 1996); Powell, *President's Authority,* at 110.

Some authorities also emphasize impeachment as a weapon wielded by Parliament to control foreign policy decisionmaking. See 1 Blackstone, at 257–58; de Lolme, at 93 & n.(a). The key difference, though, is that impeachment requires an affirmative act (by a two-thirds vote in the Senate, under the Constitution), whereas failure to fund or legislate simply requires Congress to do nothing.

51. See Koh, at 1–37; Fisher, at 232–37.

52. *Report of the Congressional Committees Investigating the Iran-Contra Affair,* S.Rep. No. 100-216, H.Rep. No. 100-433 (1987) (minority report), at 476, 473, 469.

53. Montesquieu, at 160.

54. De Lolme, at 72.

55. 10 Holdsworth, at 585; G. C. Gibbs, "Laying Treaties before Parliament in the Eighteenth Century," in *Studies in Diplomatic History* 119 (Ragnhild Hutton & M. S. Anderson, eds., 1970).

56. See John Brewer, *The Sinews of Power: War, Money, and the English State, 1688–1783* (1989); H. M. Scott, *British Foreign Policy in the Age of the American Rev-*

olution 19–22 (1990); G. C. Gibbs, "Parliament and Foreign Policy in the Age of Stanhope and Walpole," 77 *Eng. Hist. Rev.* 18 (1962).

57. For example, 11 *Cobbett's Parliamentary History of England* 155 (1812) (recording Commons debate in 1739 over details of proposed military expedition).

58. See, for example, Civis Rusticus, "Reply to Mason's Objections," Jan. 30, 1788, in 1 *The Debate on the Constitution* 359 (Bernard Bailyn, ed., 1993) (noting that although the king could declare war or make treaties, "whenever the Commons disapprove of the measures by which these have been brought about, we know the consequences"); Federalist No. 58 (Madison), at 350.

59. See Jack Rakove, *The Beginnings of National Politics* (1979), describing this problem.

60. 1 *Annals*, at 500; Powell, "Founders," at 1478–80. It was later disputed whether Congress had an obligation to fund treaty obligations—a distinct matter from sole executive functions, and one considered in later chapters. See Currie, *Constitution in Congress*, at 211–17.

61. Jefferson Powell argues to the contrary, for example, that Congress could not fund a diplomatic mission subject to the President taking a negotiating position determined by Congress. *President's Authority*, at 143–44. Again, while Congress likely could not tell the President what to say, the textual basis of a broader claim that it could not fund a mission for one purpose but not another is unclear at best. To the extent I have suggested otherwise (see Prakash & Ramsey, at 304 n.310), I withdraw the suggestion.

62. In 1790, Congress appropriated $40,000 for foreign intercourse. Four years later, with greater appreciation of its costs, Congress appropriated $1 million, specifying only that it be used "to defray any expenses which may be incurred, in relation to the intercourse between the United States and foreign nations." Act of March 20, 1794, 1 Stat. 345.

63. As Jefferson Powell, for example, generally argues; despite differing approaches, his result may not diverge greatly from what is suggested here.

64. See Prakash, at 1314.

65. Monaghan, at 55. Professor Monaghan, despite this observation, appears to endorse some independent presidential authority that is difficult to square with the structure presented in the text.

6. Executive Power and Its Critics

1. Among the best accounts incorporating this intuition, at least in part, are Arthur Bestor's classic articles "Separation of Powers in the Domain of Foreign Policy," 5 *Seton H. L. Rev.* 528 (1976) and "Respective Roles of the Senate and President in the Making and Abrogation of Treaties," 55 *Wash. L. Rev.* 1 (1979); and the recent study by Curtis Bradley & Martin Flaherty, "Executive Power Essentialism and Foreign Affairs," 102 *Mich. L. Rev.* 545 (2004).

2. Bestor, "Separation of Powers," at 578–79; Bradley & Flaherty, at 592–626.

3. 1 *Records of the Federal Convention of 1787*, at 282–92 (Max Farrand, ed., 1966).

4. Edward Corwin, *The President: Office and Powers* 5–6 (5th ed. 1984).

5. 2 *Records*, at 35 (Madison). The state constitutions are collected in *The Federal and State Constitutions, Colonial Charters, and Other Organic Laws of the States, Territories, and Colonies Now or Heretofore Forming the United States of America* (Francis Thorpe, ed., 1909). As historian Jack Rakove observes: "The evisceration of executive power was the most conspicuous aspect of the early state constitutions, which deprived the executive of its political independence and nearly every power that smacked of royal prerogative." Jack Rakove, *Original Meanings* 250 (1997). See Allan Nevins, *The American States during and after the Revolution* 166 (1969 reprint) ("The subordination of the executive branch to the legislature [in early constitutions] grew out of the memory of hated British executives, and out of precedents set in the hurried work of retiring troublesome governors and giving their authority to servants of the people. The Americans of 1776 thought that it was easy to keep the legislature a truly popular agency, but they knew of no way of holding a powerful governor responsive to their will."). See also Donald Lutz, *Popular Consent and Popular Control: Whig Political Theory in the Early State Constitutions* (1980); Donald Lutz, *The Origins of American Constitutionalism* 96–110 (1988). For a partial dissenting view, see John Yoo, *The Powers of War and Peace* 60–73 (2005) (emphasizing that restraints on state executives were more procedural than substantive).

6. On the Congress's troubles, see especially Jack Rakove, *The Beginnings of National Politics* 192–359 (1979).

7. Jay to Washington, Jan. 7, 1787, 3 *Correspondence and Public Papers of John Jay* 227 (Henry Johnston, ed., 1891); Jay to Jefferson, Aug. 18, 1786, id. at 210; see also Jay to Jefferson, Dec. 14, 1786, id. at 222–23; Jefferson to Edward Carrington, Aug. 14, 1787, 4 *Writings of Thomas Jefferson* 424–25 (Paul Ford, ed., 1894) (lack of separate executive branch "has been the source of more evil than we have experienced from any other cause"); Hamilton to James Duane, Sept. 3, 1780, 2 *Papers of Alexander Hamilton* 400, 404–5 (Harold Syrett, ed., 1961–1987).

8. Rakove, *Original Meanings*, at 254–55; Charles Thach, *The Creation of the Presidency 1775–1789*, at 25–75 (2d ed. 1963).

9. See Willi Paul Adams, *The First American Constitutions* 271 (1980) ("The conventional wisdom is that the state governments under the first constitutions were characterized by a strong legislature and a weak executive branch; the conventional explanation for this is that in the past the governors, royal or proprietary, had been the enemy and that it was only natural for the republicans of 1776 to free themselves from strong executives. But this observation is only one segment of a larger picture, and, viewed in a comparative and long-range perspective, it is not even the most striking element in the founding situation of the American political system."); id. at 266–72; Gordon Wood, *The Creation of the American Republic, 1776–1787*, at 446–53 (2d ed. 1998); Thach, at 25–54; Lutz, *Popular Consent*, at 93–95.

10. M. J. C. Vile, *Constitutionalism and the Separation of Powers* 131–76 (2d ed. 1998).

11. Thach, at 77.

12. 1 *Records*, at 66.

13. Rakove, *Original Meanings*, at 256–68; Christopher Collier & James Collier, *Decision in Philadelphia* 289–311 (1986); see especially Hamilton's arguments in Federalist No. 70, in James Madison, Alexander Hamilton, & John Jay, *The Federalist Papers* 402–8 (Isaac Kramnick, ed., 1987) (emphasizing need for a "vigorous executive" showing "decision, activity, secrecy, and dispatch"); 8 *Documentary History of the Ratification of the Constitution* 268 (Merrill Jensen et al., eds., 1976–present) (Randoph, public letter, Oct. 10, 1787) (calling for "secrecy, dispatch and vigor" in the executive).

14. John Yoo, "War and the Constitutional Text," 69 *U. Chi. L. Rev.* 1639, 1648 (2002).

15. As even Hamilton emphasized, the "energy" he sought in the executive must be balanced to achieve "safety in the republican sense"—that is, safeguards against executive overreaching. Federalist No. 70, at 403.

16. Vile, at 13–14. As Vile puts it, the view was that "each of these functions [i.e., executive, legislative, and judicial] should be entrusted solely to the appropriate, or 'proper' branch of government." Id. at 46.

17. This is the tone, for example, of some of John Yoo's work on war powers. See Yoo, *Powers of War*; Yoo, "War and the Constitutional Text."

18. A comprehensive refutation is Bradley & Flaherty, "Executive Power Essentialism." As Bradley and Flaherty show, the framers were interested in what structures would work best, and their thinking on this matter shifted over time; as Bradley and Flaherty conclude, the framers surely did not think that all foreign affairs powers "inherently had to be exercised by an executive branch." Id. at 585. See also Bestor, "Respective Roles" (effectively disputing arguments of historical inevitability).

    Bradley and Flaherty go astray, though, in supposing that their demonstration also rejects conclusions based on the historical meaning of the words the framers actually used in Article II, §1. To the contrary, it is entirely plausible, given the history they recount, that the framers decided—for wholly practical reasons—to give independent diplomatic powers to the President, and that they accomplished this allocation by employing phrases—"vesting" of "executive power"—whose ordinary meaning signified granting foreign affairs powers. The latter is not an argument based on inevitability or upon inherent allocations of power.

19. 2 *Records*, at 145 (Randolph's Committee of Detail draft).

20. 1 *Annals of Congress* 466 (Joseph Gales, ed., 1834); Lawrence Lessig & Cass Sunstein, "The President and the Administration," 94 *Colum. L. Rev.* 1, 47–48 (1994).

21. Federalist No. 69, at 396–402; 3 Joseph Story, *Commentaries on the Constitution of the United States*, §§227–474 (1833); James Wilson, "Lectures on Law," 1 *Works of James Wilson* 440 (Robert McCloskey, ed., 1967).

22. The academic case for a substantive reading of Article II, §1 is exhaustively—and to my mind persuasively—laid out in Steven Calabresi & Kevin Rhodes, "The

Structural Constitution: Unitary Executive, Plural Judiciary," 105 *Harv. L. Rev.* 1153 (1992); Steven Calabrasi, "The Vesting Clauses as Power Grants," 88 *Nw. U. L. Rev.* 1377 (1994); Steven Calabresi & Saikrishna Prakash, "The President's Power to Execute the Laws," 104 *Yale L.J.* 541 (1994); and Saikrishna Prakash, "The Essential Meaning of Executive Power," 2003 *U. Ill. L. Rev.* 701; and (if more were needed) it is engagingly reviewed and defended in Gary Lawson & Guy Seidman, "The Jeffersonian Treaty Power," 2006 *U. Ill. L. Rev.* 1, 22–43. For leading counterarguments, see Lessig & Sunstein; Michael Froomkin, "The Imperial President's New Vestments," 88 *Nw. U. L. Rev.* 1346 (1994); Martin Flaherty, "The Most Dangerous Branch," 105 *Yale L.J.* 1725 (1996); Bradley & Flaherty, at 554–58.

23. Some particularly bitter aspects of the controversy, including the extent to which Congress can assign domestic "administrative" functions to independent agencies, see Humphrey's Executor v. United States, 295 U.S. 602 (1935), we can leave aside as not touching directly upon foreign affairs.

24. See especially Marc Kruman, *Between Authority and Liberty: State Constitution-making in Revolutionary America* 113–16 (1997) (complaints that early assemblies had too much executive power, e.g., that "all power, legislative, executive and judicial is lodged in one body"); Wood, at 448–52, 549–50. Theophilus Parsons's "Essex Result" argued that "if the three powers [executive, legislative, and judicial] are united, the government will be absolute, whether these powers are in the hands of one or a large number." 1 *American Political Writing during the Founding Era, 1760–1805*, at 480, 494 (Charles Hyneman & Donald Lutz, eds., 1983). Madison, in Federalist No. 43, at 309, referred to the need for "discriminating, in theory, the several classes of power, as they may in their nature be legislative, executive, or judiciary"; in Federalist No. 48, at 311, he noted problems where "a legislature assumes executive and judicial powers." See also Old Whig, III, 13 *Documentary History,* at 426 (tyranny results where "all power legislative and executive is vested in one man or body of men").

25. As Chapter 3 records, founding-era Americans referred to the Continental Congress, an assembly, as exercising "executive" powers. For example, 8 *Documentary History,* at 267 (Randolph) (under Articles, "legislative and executive are concentrated in the same persons").

26. Samuel Johnson, *Dictionary of the English Language* (1755) (Arno reprint 1979) (defining "executive" as, among other things, "having the power to put in act the laws"); id. (defining "legislative" as "giving laws").

27. Id. (definition of "vest"); Calabresi, at 1380–83. That use can be seen throughout the debates of the period: under the Articles, as we have seen in Chapter 2, it was often said that the Congress needed to be "vested" with additional powers; in the ratifications debates, the core question was framed as how much power should be "vested" in the federal government—for example, in Federalist No. 41 (Madison), at 266.

28. See Robert Pushaw, "The Inherent Power of the Federal Courts and the Structural Constitution," 86 *Iowa L. Rev.* 735 (2001).

29. See Calabresi & Rhodes, at 1176; Calabresi & Prakash, at 570–71. Article III, §1 has long been understood in this way. See Akhil Amar, "A Neo-Federalist View of Article III: Separating the Two Tiers of Federal Jurisdiction," 65 *B.U. L. Rev.* 205, 231–33 (1985). Froomkin, "The Imperial Presidency," argues that courts' powers come from Article III, §2, but the text seems unable to bear that construction: Section 2 says what types of cases the judicial power shall extend to, but does not say anything about what the judicial power is, or who shall exercise it. Calabresi, at 1380–83.

30. It is noteworthy, but not especially decisive, that Article I, §1 (creating the legislative branch) vests Congress with the legislative powers "herein granted." See Pacificus, No. 1, 15 *Papers of Hamilton,* at 39. This phrasing, most everyone agrees, is limiting: it means (consistent with the idea of a national government limited by subject matter) that Congress has legislative power only over the specific subjects listed in the Constitution (although, to be sure, some of those are in themselves quite broad). The phrase "herein granted" was presumably included to confirm that Congress did not have a general legislative power. Although this is sometimes presented as central to the understanding of the vesting clauses, it should not be.

31. For example, Bradley & Flaherty, at 210–11.

32. Federalist No. 41, at 272.

33. Thach, at 155 (Adams's notes).

34. Pacificus, No. 1, 15 *Papers of Hamilton,* at 39. See Akhil Amar, *America's Constitution: A Biography* 185 (2005).

35. Madison's quarrel with Hamilton, as Chapter 4 explains, was not that the clause conveyed power, but that it conveyed more than law-execution power. Helvidius, No. 1, 15 *Papers of James Madison* 66–69 (William Hutchinson et al., eds., 1962–1991).

36. Prakash, at 720–24; Donald Robinson, "Presidential Prerogative and the Spirit of American Constitutionalism," in *The Constitution and the Conduct of American Foreign Policy* 114–16 (David Adler & Larry George, eds., 1996).

37. Calabresi & Rhodes, at 1198; Calabresi & Prakash, at 583–84. The drafting history illuminates this point. At the start of the Convention, in the Virginia plan, the President did have express power to enforce laws; it was the only presidential power than survived the delegates' initial revisions to the Virginia plan. Going into the Committee of Detail, the draft continued to give the President express power to enforce laws, but did not otherwise grant "executive" power to the President. The Committee changed the grant of power to a duty, giving us what is now §3's take-care clause, and added §1's grant of executive power. 2 *Records* at 132, 145–46, 171. It seems likely that the Committee recognized that the President's role in law execution really had two components—a power and a duty—and so they dealt with it in two separate clauses, with the power being "vested" first, as one would expect, in §1, and the duty added as a qualification near the end, in §3. See Calabresi and Prakash, at 616–20.

38. Calabresi & Prakash, at 577–78; Lawson & Seidman, at 29–34. In any event, the

only seriously problematic provision is the opinions clause, which seems hard to explain on any theory other than redundancy. Hamilton said of the opinions clause: "This I consider as a mere redundancy in the plan, as the right for which it provides would result of itself from the office." Federalist No. 74, at 422. As Hamilton recognized, small redundancies may well occur. But see Akhil Amar, "Some Opinions on the Opinions Clause," 82 *Va. L. Rev.* 647 (1996), and Amar, *America's Constitution,* at 187 (giving the clause substantive meaning).

39. Prakash, at 743–800.

40. 1 *Records*, at 65. Madison's Helvidius also seems to take this view, as discussed in Chapter 4.

41. In particular, Hamilton's Federalist discussions of presidential powers, in Nos. 69 and 73–77, do not mention Article II, §1 even though they discuss specific foreign affairs powers at some length.

42. Compare Bradley & Flaherty, at 556–57.

43. For example, the President "shall take Care that the Laws be faithfully executed" (a duty) but "shall have Power" to make treaties (a right, not a duty).

44. Even with the clause, as Chapter 4 discusses, Ambassador Genet maintained that he could interact directly with Congress, and South Carolina Governor Moultrie received him. The exclusity reading is supported by the lack of a clause paralleling the Articles' explicit prohibition on states receiving ambassadors (Article 6)—the drafters may have thought the ambassador-reception clause made it unnecessary.

45. See Article II, §3 (President "shall receive Ambassadors and other public Ministers"); Article II, §2 (President can appoint "Ambassadors, other public Ministers, and Consuls"); Article III, §2 (judicial power extends to cases affecting "Ambassadors, other public Ministers, and Consuls)"; id. (Supreme Court has original jurisdiction over cases concerning "Ambassadors, other public Ministers, and Consuls").

46. 2 *Records*, at 132 (instructions to Committee), 145–46 (Committee draft), 171 (Committee report).

47. Hamilton said this of the opinions clause; see Federalist No. 74, at 422.

48. See Bradley & Flaherty, at 687–88 & n. 690 (disputing the vesting clause theory without affirmatively defending an alternative reading of the text).

49. See especially id., at 571–84.

50. See Rakove, *Original Meanings,* at 31 (states were "great political laboratory" on which framers relied).

51. Del. Const. (1776), art. VII, 1 Thorpe, at 563 (president "may exercise all the other executive powers of government"); Md. Const. (1776), art. XXXIII, 3 id. at 1696 (governor "may alone exercise all the other executive powers of government, where concurrence of the Council is not required"); N.C. Const. (1776), art. XIX, 5 id. at 2791–92 (governor "may exercise all the other executive powers of government").

52. Va. Const. (1776) [unnumbered], 7 id. at 3816–17; N.J. Const., art. VIII, 5 id. at 2596 ("Governor . . . shall have the supreme executive power"); Ga. Const. (1777), art XIX, 2 id. at 781 ("governor shall, with the advice of the executive

council, exercise the executive powers of government"); S.C. Const. (1776), art. XXX, 5 id. at 3247 (directing "that the executive authority be vested in the president").

53. See *Journals of the Council of the State of Virginia* (H. R. McIlwaine et al., eds., 1931–1967) (recording numerous instances of diplomatic activities by the governor and council).

54. S.C. Const. (1776), art. XXVI, 6 Thorpe, at 3247. See Thach, at 29 n.9; Yoo, *Powers of War,* at 60–72. Although a comprehensive historical study remains to be done, it appears that most state governors generally thought they had law execution power and at least some foreign affairs power.

55. Mass. Const. (1780), ch. II, §1, art. 1, 3 Thorpe, at 1899–1903; N.Y. Const., art. XVII & XIX, 5 id. at 2632–33; Pa. Const. (1776), §20, id. at 3087–88; and N.H. Const. (1784), part II, 4 id. at 2463–64. Rhode Island and Connecticut did not adopt new constitutions; Vermont, though not officially a state, adopted a constitution paralleling Pennsylvania's. Most constitutions contained clauses subordinating the executive to the laws of the state (in North Carolina, for example, the governor could "exercise all the other executive powers of government, limited and restrained as by this constitution as mentioned, and according to the laws of the State," 5 id. at 279–92); and governors were heavily constrained in practice by (for the most part) being appointed by the legislature for short terms, being attached to a council, and having limited or no powers of appointment or veto. Their "executive powers" did not make them powerful, but that does not mean the clauses did not have substance.

56. This argument is distinct from, and more subtle and persuasive than, arguments based on historical inevitability. It says, not that the drafters could not have given the President broad foreign affairs powers, but that they would not have given the President such broad powers *without comment.* See especially Bradley & Flaherty, at 592–625.

A related objection is that reading Article II, §1 to grant unspecified foreign affairs powers is in tension with the Constitution's structure of delegated powers, epitomized in Madison's observation that the powers of the federal government are "few and defined." Id. at 558–59, 603; Federalist No. 45 (Madison), at 296. This objection seems to lack force, though. As Chapter 5 explains, "executive" foreign affairs powers are not open-ended; rather, they had well-understood limits. They do not give the President much power in domestic matters. And in any event, essentially no one thinks the diplomatic powers at stake here are not *federal* powers—just that they are perhaps congressional (or senatorial) powers instead of presidential powers.

7. The Executive Senate

1. See Louis Henkin, *Foreign Affairs and the U.S. Constitution* 41–43 (2d ed. 1996).

2. One appointments controversy is whether the President can appoint foreign af-

fairs agents without the Senate's advice and consent, by sending "personal" envoys. Id. at 43–44. Washington did this on several occasions, most notably Gouverneur Morris's 1789 mission to Britain. Washington to Morris, Oct. 13, 1789, 30 *Writings of George Washington* 439 (John Fitzpatrick, ed., 1939). Washington may have thought these "private" missions (as he called them) did not trigger the appointments clause, being neither public ministers nor "other officers of the United States." But despite Washington's description, "private" representatives such as Morris spoke for Washington in his public capacity, as director of U.S. foreign policy, and their discussions concerned U.S. public affairs. See id. at 439–40. It is important here to remember that our inquiry's focus is the Constitution's text. Washington's practice may confirm textual readings or resolve ambiguities; it cannot change the text's meaning. Where practice does not follow what seems the best reading of the text, that should cause us to reexamine the text; it should not cause us to abandon the text if reexamination does not show a different reading. There will be cases—and this may be one of them—where it is impossible to square text with subsequent practice, and in such cases we should not hesitate to say that Washington simply got it wrong.

3. Baron de Montesquieu, *The Spirit of Laws* 151 (1748) (Prometheus reprint 2002); 1 William Blackstone, *Commentaries on the Laws of England* 245 (1765).

4. See *The Federal and State Constitutions, Colonial Charters, and Other Organic Laws of the States, Territories, and Colonies Now or Heretofore Forming the United States of America* (Francis Thorpe, ed., Hein reprint 1993) (collecting eighteenth-century state constitutions); for example, Va. Const. (1776) [unnumbered], 7 id. at 3817–18.

5. See Marc Kruman, *Between Authority and Liberty: State Constitutionmaking in Revolutionary America* 126–30 (1997). In Virginia, for example, the executive council participated not only in appointments, but also in instructing and communicating with diplomatic agents and an array of other governmental functions. Va. Const. (1776) [unnumbered], 7 Thorpe, at 3817–18. See generally *Journals of the Council of the State of Virginia* (H. R. McIlwaine et al., eds., 1931–1967).

6. Federalist No. 70, in James Madison, Alexander Hamilton, & John Jay, *The Federalist Papers* 403–7 (Isaac Kramnick, ed., 1987). See 2 *Records of the Federal Convention of 1787*, at 541–42 (Max Farrand, ed., 1966) (delegates' rejection of George Mason's proposal for a council).

7. Federalist No. 70, at 403–7; Federalist No. 47, at 302–8.

8. See Federalist No. 77, at 435–36 (Hamilton), describing need to attend to "requisites to energy" and "requisites to safety"—meaning sufficient checks—and finding, among other things, that "[i]n the only instances in which the abuse of the executive authority was materially to be feared, the Chief Magistrate of the United States would, by [the Constitution], be subject to the control of a branch of the legislative body."

9. Thomas Jefferson, "Opinion on the Powers of the Senate" (Apr. 24, 1790), 16 *Papers of Thomas Jefferson* 378–79 (Julian Boyd et al., eds., 1950–2005).

10. Article II, §2 gives nominating power; by Article II, §3, the President "shall Commission all the Officers of the United States."

11. Leading works include Arthur Bestor, "Separation of Powers in the Domain of Foreign Policy," 5 *Seton H. L. Rev.* 528 (1976); Arthur Bestor, "Respective Roles of the Senate and President in the Making and Abrogation of Treaties," 55 *Wash. L. Rev.* 1 (1979); Jack Rakove, "Solving a Constitutional Puzzle: The Treaty-making Clause as a Case Study," 1 *Persp. in Amer. H. (N.S.)* 233 (1984); Curtis Bradley & Martin Flaherty, "Executive Power Essentialism and Foreign Affairs," 102 *Mich. L. Rev.* 545, 626–36 (2004); Howard Sklamberg, "The Meaning of Advice and Consent: The Senate's Constitutional Role in Treatymaking," 18 *Mich. J. Int'l L.* 445 (1997).

12. Henkin, at 175–79. In misleading shorthand, it is sometimes said (including by the Supreme Court; see Wilson v. Girard, 354 U.S. 524, 526 (1957)) that the Senate "ratifies" treaties. More precisely, the Senate consents to ratification.

13. Bestor, "Respective Roles," at 112. See also Bestor, "Separation of Powers," at 540 ("If language is used rationally, 'advice' means counsel offered before a decision is reached; 'consent' means acceptance of a proposed course of action after plans have been worked out in detail."); Bradley & Flaherty, at 626 (text "appears to contemplate more than just a veto role for the Senate, since such a role presumably would be encompassed by the word 'consent' ").

14. Federalist No. 66, at 387. This point is disputed in David Strauss & Cass Sunstein, "The Senate, the Constitution, and the Confirmation Process," 101 *Yale L.J.* 1491, 1495 (1992) (arguing that the Senate has "an advisory role before the nomination has occurred and a reviewing function after the fact"). Their view, though, contradicts the text (in which "advice and consent" qualifies "appoint" but not "nominate") and Jefferson's and Hamilton's reading of the clause. It is also contrary to Washington's unchallenged practice from the outset. David Currie, *The Constitution in Congress: The Federalist Period* 25 (1997) ("the President simply submitted the names and the Senate voted yes or no"). See John McGinnis, "The President, the Senate, the Constitution and the Confirmation Process: A Reply to Professors Strauss and Sunstein," 71 *Tex. L. Rev.* 633, 638–46 (1993).

15. Drafter James Wilson in 1791 described the two clauses in parallel: "the observations I have delivered concerning the appointment of officers, apply likewise to treaties; the making of which is another power that the president has, with the advice and consent of the Senate." He did not note any required pre-signing (or pre-nomination) role for the Senate—only that the President act with the Senate's ultimate approval. "Lectures on Law," 2 *Works of James Wilson* 441 (Robert McCloskey, ed., 1967). On this reading "advice" is not redundant: it makes clear that the Senate may give the President outlines of what it would and would not accept, or give conditional approvals, without being accused of unconstitutionally micromanaging negotiations. See Currie, at 209–11 (Senate's conditional approval of the Jay Treaty in 1795). This contrasts with English practice, where arguably Parliament stepped out of its constitutional role in offering advice about what

treaties to make. See Bestor, "Separation of Powers," at 535–36 (recounting 1677 incident in which Charles II objected to Parliament advising him to make a treaty with the Dutch against France). Some authorities have doubted this power, but the text seems to stand against them. See Sen. Comm. on For. Rel., 14th Cong., Feb. 15, 1816 (declining to give advice on negotiation of treaty with Britain, partly on constitutional grounds); Jefferson Powell, *The President's Authority over Foreign Affairs* 134 (2002) (arguing, without clear textual grounds, that "formal Senate involvement in treatymaking beyond its power to veto an agreement is contrary to the underlying goals of the Constitution"). Bestor seems correct, "Respective Roles," at 117, that "nothing . . . precludes the Senate from giving formal advice before the beginning or during the progress of any treaty negotiations"; he errs in suggesting that such ongoing advice is required (or that it would be binding).

16. 1 *Annals of Congress* 54 (1789) (Joseph Gales, ed., 1834) (consular convention); id. at 55–56 (appointments). Later, Washington said he had asked the Senate's "consideration and advice" with respect to the Jay Treaty, by which he meant only that he had asked the Senate to approve the final signed agreement. Message to Congress, Mar. 30, 1796, 35 *Writings of George Washington* 3 (John Fitzpatrick, ed., 1939).

17. Sklamberg, at 448.

18. For example, Va. Const. (1776) [unnumbered], 7 Thorpe, at 3818; Md. Const. (1776), art. XXXIII, 3 id. at 1696; Ga. Const. (1777), art. XIX, 2 id. at 781; see Donald Lutz, *Popular Consent and Popular Control* 93 (1980); Sklamberg, at 449–50; Bestor, "Separation of Powers," at 643–47.

19. See Bestor, "Respective Roles," at 116 (contending that, in state councils, "the phrase signified consultations on policy or appointments between the executive and a small body . . . which gave its advice as an organized entity and in relatively formal terms, and which thereafter had the power to give or refuse final consent to the action that the executive might decide to take"); Arthur Bestor, "Advice from the Very Beginning, Consent when the End Is Achieved," 83 *Amer. J. Int'l L.* 718, 725–26 (1989) ("advice described the close and continuous consultation that was expected to go on, usually face-to-face, between a ruler and a council of state or privy council. . . . In accord with everyday use, advice was something to be given not only at the outset of an enterprise, but also at subsequent steps so long as the process of planning, proposing, negotiating, reviewing and renegotiating went on.").

20. See generally McIlwaine, *Journals;* for example, 4 id. at 37 (Jan. 29, 1787) (correspondence); 3 id. at 16 (Dec. 20, 1781) (war-related proclamations); 3 id. at 118 (correspondence); 3 id. at 307 (Nov. 14, 1783) (correspondence with Indian commissioners); 2 id. at 56 (Jan. 2, 1778) (military instructions); 2 id. at 64 (diplomatic instructions). The Governor also sometimes took action when the council was not meeting, later informing the council and asking for approval. For example, 4 id. at 37 (Jan. 29, 1787) (pardon); 3 id. at 366 (July 20, 1784) (same).

21. This requirement renders problematic, as a textual matter, efforts of modern international law to impose material legal conditions upon treaty parties at the mo-

ment of signature. See Curtis Bradley, "Unratified Treaties, Domestic Politics, and the U.S. Constitution," 48 *Harv. Int'l L.J.* (forthcoming 2007).

22. See Peter Haggenmacher, "Some Hints on the European Origins of Legislative Participation in the Treatymaking Function," 67 *Chi-Kent L. Rev.* 313, 313–15 (1987).

23. Garrett Mattingly, *Renaissance Diplomacy* 36–37 (2d ed. 1988); Emmerich de Vattel, *The Law of Nations*, bk. II, §156 (1758) (Charles Fenwick, trans., J. B. Scott, ed., 1964).

24. For example, Madison to Jefferson, Mar. 16, 1784, 8 *Papers of James Madison* 6 (William Hutchinson et al., eds., 1962–1991) (ratification required absent some "palpable and material default in the minister").

25. Some delegates raised this objection at the Convention. 2 Records, at 392–93 (Gorham) (objecting that "American ministers must go abroad not instructed by the same Authority, which is to ratify their proceedings"); id. (Johnson) ("something of a solecism in saying that the acts of a Minister with plenipotentiary powers from one body would depend for ratification on another body").

26. Bestor, "Respective Roles," at 65, 112.

27. Woodrow Wilson, *Constitutional Government in the United States* 77–78 (1908).

28. George Scott, *The Rise and Fall of the League of Nations* 11–50 (1973).

29. Bernard Bailyn, *The Ideological Origins of the American Revolution* 23–24 (1967).

30. 3 Polybius, *The Histories*, bk. VI, § 11–18 (W. R. Paton, trans., 1979); see Neal Wood, *Cicero's Social and Political Thought* 159 (1988) (discussing influence of Roman structures of government). John Adams, who wrote important commentary upon separation of powers in the early years of independence and influenced the strong separation of powers provisions of the Massachusetts constitution, found Roman practice—particularly as described by Polybius—a key source. 1 John Adams, *Defence of the Constitutions of the United States of America* 169–76 (1778).

31. On these influnces, see Gordon Wood, *The Radicalism of the American Revolution* 100–101 (1991); Forrest McDonald, *Novus Ordo Seclorum* 67–69 (1985).

32. Montesquieu, at 172–73.

33. See Arthur Eckstein, *Senate and General: Individual Decisionmaking and Roman Foreign Relations* (1987); Haggenmacher, at 321–22. Key Roman sources known to founding-era Americans include Polybius's *Histories* and Livy, *History of Rome* (B. O. Foster, trans., 1982).

34. 1 Polybius, bk. 1, §§16–17; see Eckstein, at 115–24.

35. 1 Polybius, bk. 1, §§62–63 (noting that "when these terms were referred to Rome, the people did not accept the treaty. . . ."); Livy, bk. 21, §18; id., §19 (Lutatius's treaty "expressly added that it should be valid only if the people ratified it"). See Eckstein, at 132–33.

36. Livy, bk. 24, §§27–29; id., bk. 25, §40; id., bk. 26, §32 (senate ratification); see Eckstein, at 145, 159, 166.

37. Livy, bk. 30, §16 (negotiation); id., §23 (senate rejection); id., bk. 36, §11 (renegotiation); id., bk. 30, §§42–43 (senate approval after debate); 1 Polybius, bk. 15, §§4, 18; Eckstein, at 247, 256.

38. Eckstein, at 169.

39. Livy, bk. 30, §§42–43.

40. The Syracuse/Carthage experiences, though the most clearly documented, are not isolated cases. See Livy, bk. 9, §34 (senate ratification of treaty with Sparta negotiated by consul in the field); Eckstein, at 276–82 (senate rejection of treaty with Philip of Macedon negotiated by consul in the field). For Rome-inspired European systems which may also have influenced founding-era Americans, see Haggenmacher, at 326–36.

41. 1 *Records*, at 64–67. For an engaging account of treatymaking debates at the Convention, see Rakove, at 236–50. As Rakove concludes, "the remarks of June 1 demonstrate that the framers believed that questions of war and peace—that is, the most critical subjects of foreign policy—were appropriate subjects for legislative determination rather than an inherent prerogative of executive power." Id. at 239.

42. Federalist No. 75 (Hamilton), at 425.

43. Wilson said that writers on the law of nations called treatymaking a legislative power. They did not, at least not directly—but many of those writers relied on Roman practice, and Roman practice suggested a legislative (or at least deliberative) component.

44. 2 *Records*, at 143 (Randolph draft); id. at 169, 171 (committee draft).

45. Id. at 392–94. See Rakove, at 240–42. Rakove also emphasizes some delegates' growing distrust of the Senate, which at that point delegates had agreed would be appointed by the state legislatures, with each state having an equal voice.

46. Consider, for example, the difficulties Confederation diplomats had in negotiating peace with Britain—where agreement probably was reached only because the negotiators violated Congress's instructions. See id., at 268–71; id. at 275 (noting "the dangers of allowing foreign policy to be made exclusively by a Senate that would bear an unfortunate resemblance to the existing Congress").

47. 2 *Records*, at 493–96, 538. This allocation followed part of a plan Hamilton presented earlier. Hamilton's plan had not generated much interest at the time (likely because Hamilton supported what was in effect an elective monarchy), but many of its details reappeared in later drafts—among other things, it envisioned a chief magistrate with "supreme Executive authority" but subject to restrictions including the Senate's advice and consent on treaties and ambassadorial appointments. 1 id. at 292.

48. Bestor in particular argues that the changes merely refined prior proposals; see Bestor, "Respective Roles," at 110–20. But the delegates' prior dissatisfaction with the Committee of Detail draft, plus the substantial changes in language and structure, suggests an entirely new proposal, modeled not on the prior draft but on Hamilton's plan, see 1 *Records* at 292, and on the precedent of the state executive councils.

49. Wilson proposed to require advice and consent of the House, as well as the Senate, saying that treaties "ought to have the sanction of laws also." 2 *Records*, at 538. This appears to equate the Senate's advice and consent with a "sanction" (that is, approval) given through the lawmaking process, seeming to imply an after-the-fact

review. Wilson's proposal was rejected, apparently because the Convention thought the smaller Senate stood a better chance of keeping secrets (a point made both at the Convention and in the ratifying debates). See Federalist No. 75, at 426 (Hamilton); 2 *Debates in the Several State Conventions on the Adoption of the Federal Constitution* 302 (Jonathan Elliot, ed., 1836) (Hamilton to N.Y. convention); Federalist No 64, at 377–78 (Jay). Some commentators rely on this rationale to support a broader Senate role: as Rakove says, "secrecy . . . would not have been the critical point if the role Wilson contemplated for the House was understood to involve ratification alone." Rakove, at 246–47. This reliance may be misplaced, though, because the framers probably contemplated that treaties' terms would often remain secret until after the Senate gave its ultimate post-signature consent—at least, this is how matters worked in the first major post-ratification treaty, the 1794–1796 Jay Treaty discussed below. David Golove, "Treaty-Making and the Nation: The Historical Foundations of the Nationalist Conception of the Treaty Power," 98 *Mich. L. Rev.* 1075, 1161–62 (2000). As a result, the focus on secrecy may not imply anything about the Senate's pre-signature role.

50. See 31 *Journals of the Continental Congress* 510–697 (Worthington Ford et al., eds., 1906–1937) (Aug. 10–Sept. 28, 1786); Charles Warren, "The Mississippi River and the Treaty Clause of the Constitution," 2 *Geo. Wash. L. Rev.* 271, 285–90 (1934); Samuel Bemis, *A Diplomatic History of the United States* 73–81 (4th ed. 1955); Rakove, at 272–74.

51. See Hugh Williamson to Madison, June 2, 1788, 11 *Papers of Madison*, at 71 (noting that "Navigation of the Mississippi after what had already happened in Congress was not to be risqued in the Hands of a meer Majority"); Allan Nevins, *The American States during and after the Revolution* 345–47, 565–68 (1969); Rakove, at 274.

52. Warren, at 287–99; Bemis, at 79–80 (concluding that "the Jay-Gardoqui negotiations were responsible" for the supermajority provision in the Constitution). As Rakove observes, at 275: "Both the two-thirds provision and the requirement of senatorial 'advice and consent' can thus be seen as manifest results of the need to protect the interests of particular states, a need that recent events had vividly legitimated." See also Akhil Amar, *America's Constitution: A Biography* 191 (2005); John McGinnis & Michael Rappaport, Our Supermajoritarian Constitution, 80 *Tex. L. Rev.* 703, 760–63 (2002). A number of proposals suggested setting the supermajority even higher, either at three-quarters of those present or two-thirds of the whole Senate. Warren, at 293–301.

53. Federalist No. 75, at 425–26 (Hamilton) (arguing that "the vast importance of the trust and the operation of treaties as laws plead strongly for the participation of the whole or a portion of the legislative body in the office of making them"); 2 *Documentary History of the Ratification of the Constitution* 563 (Merrill Jensen et al., eds., 1976–present) (Wilson to Pa. convention); see also 1 *Annals*, at 1085 (Sherman to 1st Congress, 1789) ("The establishment of every treaty requires the voice of the Senate. . . . The Constitution contemplates the united wisdom of the President and Senate, in order to make treaties. . . ."); Raoul

Berger, "The Presidential Monopoly of Foreign Relations," 71 *Mich. L. Rev.* 1, 35–42 (1972).

54. 2 *Debates,* at 306 (Hamilton); Federalist No. 66, at 388; "An Additional Number of Letters from the Federal Farmer to the Republican," XI, 16 *Documentary History,* at 303; 2 *Debates,* at 291 (Livingston); see also 2 id. at 291 (Livingston) (Senate would form treaties and negotiate with foreign powers, so Senators should have long terms to gain familiarity with foreign countries and their diplomatic agents "whom, in this capacity, they have to negotiate with").

55. Though Livingston plainly overstated the matter, much more reflective statements gave the Senate a considerable role. For example: Americanus, VII, 2 *The Debate on the Constitution* 61 (Bernard Bailyn, ed., 1993) (Senate was the proper place for management of treaty negotiations); 6 *Documentary History,* at 1326 (Parsons to Mass. convention) (in its "executive capacity," Senate "make[s] treaties and conduct[s] the national negociations"); Federalist No. 62, at 364 (Madison) (Senators would participate "immediately in transactions with foreign nations"); see Bradley & Flaherty, at 630–31.

56. See Bestor, "Respective Roles," at 65.

57. 4 *Debates,* at 127–28 (Iredell); Federalist No. 84, at 580; see also 4 *Works of John Adams* 410 (Charles Adams, ed., 1854) (recording R.H. Lee's 1789 comment that "the greater part of the power of making treaties was in the President").

58. 4 *Debates,* at 265; Pinckney also said that House control over treaties had been rejected because it "would be a very unfit body for negotiation"; it is not clear if he was referring to a sole House role or one joined with the President. Id. at 280–81; see also 4 id., at 120 (Davie to N.C. convention) (Senate has "power of making, or rather ratifying, treaties"); 2 *Documentary History,* at 480 (Wilson to Pa. convention) ("The Senate can make no treaties; they can approve of none, unless the President of the United States lays it before them."). See Charles Thach, *The Creation of the Presidency 1775–1789,* at 162–63 (2d. ed 1963) (discussing competing arguments and concluding that the President's executive power includes "the right to negotiate treaties independently of the Senate").

59. For example, Bradley & Flaherty, at 631–36.

60. Currie, at 24–25; Gerhard Casper, "An Essay in Separation of Powers: Some Early Versions and Practices," 30 *Wm. & Mary L. Rev.* 211, 295–46 (1989).

61. Attorney General Randolph protested strongly at the time that the Senate should have an advisory role earlier in the process, although Randolph apparently went along with Washington's unilateral negotiations with the western tribes a year earlier. See Abraham Sofaer, *War, Foreign Affairs and Constitutional Power* 96 & n. 155 (1976). The Senate approved Jay's appointment, over the constitutional objection that he was simultaneously Chief Justice of the U.S. Supreme Court. Currie, at 209. Washington did not submit Jay's negotiating instructions to the Senate, for approval or otherwise, nor did the Senate demand them.

62. Id. at 209–17; Golove, at 1075.

63. Currie, at 210–11. The Senate was equally non-deferential in diplomatic appointments—very early, for example, contesting Gouverneur Morris's appointment as

ambassador to France. See James Flexner, *George Washington and the New Nation* 355–57 (1970).

64. Currie, at 25 (concluding from these events that "the original understanding seems to have been that, at least with regard to treaties, the Senate would function as a true advisory council, not simply as a check on the arbitrary exercise of power"); Bradley & Flaherty, at 634–36.

65. Memorandum of Conference with the President on Treaty with Algiers, Mar. 11, 1792, 23 *Papers of Jefferson*, at 256; see Casper, at 247–48.

66. Golove, at 1154–93; Camillus [Hamilton], "The Defence," Nos. XXXVI–XXXVIII, Jan. 2–9, 1796, 20 *Papers of Alexander Hamilton*, 3–10, 13–34 (Harold Syrett, ed., 1961–1987) (discussing constitutional objections). See also Sofaer, at 405 n. 155 (noting that Representative Edward Livingston complained about the procedure "timidly and without success").

8. *Goldwater v. Carter*

1. Louis Henkin, *Foreign Affairs and the U.S. Constitution* 211 (2d ed. 1996); see id. at 211–14 (discussing the debate). David Adler, *The Constitution and the Termination of Treaties* (1986), and Arthur Bestor, "Respective Roles of the Senate and President in the Making and Abrogation of Treaties," 55 *Wash. L. Rev.* 1 (1979), are leading arguments for the Senate. Michael Glennon, *Constitutional Diplomacy* 151 (1990), arguing for Congress, says that "[t]he constitutional text does not address the matter" and so "[t]he issue, thus, is which of the political branches is best suited to make the determination that [a treaty] should be terminated, taking into account factors such as the need for swiftness versus deliberation and secrecy versus diverse viewpoints." Jefferson Powell, "The President's Authority over Foreign Affairs: An Executive Branch Perspective," 67 *Geo. Wash. L. Rev.* 527, 562–63 (1999), favors the President for largely non-textual reasons.

2. Goldwater v. Carter, 481 F.Supp. 949 (D.D.C.) (President lacks termination power), *rev'd* 617 F.2d 697 (D.C. Cir.) (President has termination power), *vacated* 444 U.S. 996 (1979) (question is non-justiciable) (see Chapter 16); Kucinich v. Bush, 236 F.Supp. 2d 1 (D.D.C. 2002) (dismissing challenge to termination of ABM treaty); Michael Ramsey, "Torturing Executive Power," 93 *Georgetown L.J.* 1213, 1225–36 (2005) (discussing administration memoranda regarding the Geneva Conventions). In 2005, President Bush also directed, on his own authority, U.S. withdrawal from the Optional Protocol of the Vienna Convention on Consular Relations. Adam Liptak, "U.S. Says It Has Withdrawn from World Judicial Body," *New York Times,* Mar. 10, 2005.

3. 617 F.2d at 703–5.

4. Ian Brownlie, *Principles of Public International Law* 607–39 (6th ed. 2003). See Federalist No. 43 (Madison), in James Madison, Alexander Hamilton, & John Jay, *The Federalist Papers* 285 (Isaac Kramnick, ed., 1987) (noting that under law of nations, breach of a treaty allows the non-breaching party to declare the treaty void).

5. For works emphasizing this distinction, see Ramsey, at 1231–32; Derek Jinks &

David Sloss, "Is the President Bound by the Geneva Conventions?" 90 *Cornell L. Rev.* 97, 154–56 (2004); Akhil Amar, *America's Constitution: A Biography* 562 n.33 (2005). The present discussion treats violation (or suspension) as equivalent to termination for constitutional purposes, although they may raise distinct issues in some circumstances.

6. 617 F.2d at 700; Mutual Defense Treaty, U.S-Taiwan, Dec. 2, 1954, 6 U.S.T. 433, TIAS No. 3178; See Bestor, at 5–9 (recounting historical developments).

7. 481 F.Supp. at 962; 617 F.2d at 704–05; 444 U.S. 996 (1979). See Henkin, at 213–14; David Scheffer, "The Law of Treaty Termination as Applied to United States De-Recognition of the Republic of China," 19 *Harv. Int'l L.J.* 931 (1978); Kenneth Randall, "The Treaty Power," 51 *Ohio St. L.J.* 1089, 1104–8 (1990).

8. Treaty on the Limitation of Anti-Ballistic Missile Systems, May 26, 1972 (U.S.-U.S.S.R.), 23 U.S.T. 3435, art. XV.

9. Brownlie, at 607–39.

10. See Thomas Jefferson, "Opinion on the Treaties with France" (Apr. 28, 1793), 25 *Papers of Thomas Jefferson* 609 (Julian Boyd et al., eds., 1950–2005) (discussing eighteenth-century version of this doctrine, indicating that "circumstances . . . sometimes excuse the non-performance" of treaties).

11. Saikrishna Prakash, "The Essential Meaning of Executive Power," 2003 *U. Ill. L. Rev.* 701.

12. "Opinion on the Powers of the Senate" (Apr. 24, 1790), 16 *Papers of Jefferson*, at 378–79 (emphasis added).

13. See Amar, at 191–92 (adopting this view). This analysis tracks Jefferson's opinion, which said (see Chapter 4) that the appointments clause gave the Senate authority only over approving nominations, and thus that other powers, such as deciding diplomatic ranks and destinations, remained part of the residual executive power of Article II, §1.

14. Adler, at 106; see Bestor, at 17 ("The power to undo an action is obviously a correlative of the power to do it in the first place. The corollary of this is that the two powers normally belong in the same hands."); id. at 20 (relying on Blackstone).

15. 1 William Blackstone, *Commentaries on the Laws of England* 90–91 (1765).

16. 1 *Annals of Congress* 491 (Joseph Gales, ed., 1834); see id. at 373–74 (Lee); id. at 376 (White); id. at 492 (Stone). Hamilton in Federalist No. 77, at 432, said that the Senate would have power over "displacing" officers, without explaining the basis of his view; he apparently changed his mind during the removal debates.

17. 1 *Annals*, at 382.

18. Id. at 372 (Smith); id. at 377 (Lawrence); id. at 477 (Hartley). See David Currie, *The Constitution in Congress: The Federalist Period* 37–41 (1997); Saikrishna Prakash, "New Light on the Decision of 1789," 91 *Cornell L. Rev.* 1021 (2006).

19. 1 *Annals*, at 478.

20. The analogy to statutes, see Bestor, at 29, is misplaced, because (as Blackstone said) suspending statutes was not an "executive" power and thus cannot be part of Article II, §1.

21. The district court in *Goldwater*, reaching a contrary conclusion, went astray at

the first step. According to the court, the Constitution's Article VI required the President not to violate the treaty; but as we have seen, termination of (withdrawal from) a treaty according to its terms does not violate the treaty and thus does not implicate Article VI. See 481 F.Supp. at 962 (claiming that Carter's action "involves a repeal of the law established by the agreement").

22. Stanley Elkins & Eric McKitrick, *The Age of Federalism* 339–40 (1993). The treaties are Treaty of Amity and Commerce, Feb. 6, 1778, and Treaty of Alliance, Feb. 6, 1778, in 2 *Treaties and Other International Acts of the United States* 3–29, 35–41 (Hunter Miller, ed., 1931).

23. Washington to the Cabinet, Apr. 18, 1793, 15 *Papers of Alexander Hamilton* 326–37 (Harold Syrett, ed., 1961–1987).

24. Hamilton and Knox to Washington, May 2, 1793, id. at 372; Jefferson, "Opinion on the Treaties with France," 25 *Papers of Jefferson,* at 608–13. On the episode generally, see Elkins & McKitrick, at 339–40.

25. Hamilton urged Washington to "suspend" the treaties upon receiving French Ambassador Genet, which obviously would not have allowed time to consult Congress. He further suggested, depending upon how events developed, permanently renouncing the treaties, without indicating any need for congressional approval. Hamilton and Knox to Washington, May 2, 1793, 15 *Papers of Hamilton,* at 372–93.

26. "Opinion on the Treaties with France," 25 *Papers of Jefferson,* at 608–13.

27. A subsequent episode relating to the same treaties during the Adams administration is less easy to read. President John Adams asked Congress to terminate the French treaties, and Congress did so, without discussing constitutional matters. It is not clear whether Adams did this for political reasons, if he thought the treaties had been incorporated in part into U.S. law by statute and thus needed congressional repeal, or if he thought Congress had constitutional termination authority. In any event, Adams did not think he needed approval by two-thirds of the Senate. Alexander de Conde, *The Quasi-War* 102–3 (1966).

28. See Ramsey, at 1225–26 (discussing the administration's position). Professor Henkin also appears to combine the two issues, concluding (perhaps prematurely, and without much authority) that "at the end of the twentieth century, it is apparently accepted that the President has authority under the Constitution to denounce or otherwise terminate a treaty, whether such action on behalf of the United States is permissible under international law or would put the United States in violation." Henkin, at 214. See also John Yoo, *The Powers of War and Peace* 190 (2005) (also discussing the matter as a single issue).

29. Caleb Nelson, "Preemption," 86 *Va. L. Rev.* 225, 235–60 (2000).

30. 3 U.S. 199 (1796). Historian Jack Rakove observes that "the framers were virtually of one mind when it came to giving treaties the status of law." "Solving a Constitutional Puzzle: The Treatymaking Clause as a Case Study," 1 *Persp. in Amer. H. (N.S.)* 233, 264 (1984). For an extended scholarly exchange exploring the implications of Article VI's reference to treaties, see John Yoo, "Globalism and the Constitution: Treaties, Non-Self-Execution and the Original Understanding," 99

Colum. L. Rev. 1955 (1999); John Yoo, "Treaties and Public Lawmaking: A Textual and Structural Defense of Non-Self-Execution," 99 *Colum. L. Rev.* 2218 (1999); Carlos Vazquez, "Laughing at Treaties," 99 *Colum. L. Rev.* 2154 (1999); Martin Flaherty, "History Right? Historical Scholarship, Original Understanding, and Treaties as 'Supreme Law of the Land,'" 99 *Colum L. Rev.* 2095 (1999).

31. Prakash, at 724–26; Donald Robinson, "Presidential Prerogative and the Spirit of American Constitutionalism," in *The Constitution and the Conduct of American Foreign Policy* 114–16 (David Adler & Larry George, eds., 1996).

32. 1 Blackstone, at 130–38; Jean de Lolme, *The Constitution of England* 27–29 (1771).

33. See especially Entick v. Carrington, 19 State Trials 1030 (1765).

34. John Yoo argues that Article VI means something different for treaties than it does for statutes and the Constitution. See Yoo, *Powers of War and Peace,* at 232 (claiming that Article VI only gives congress power to enforce treaties if it wishes). He seems to lack any explanation for why, if this is so, the three are treated in parallel. See Michael Ramsey, "Book Review Essay: Toward a Rule of Law in Foreign Affairs, 106 *Colum. L. Rev.* 1450, 1465–66 (2006). For further textual discussion, see Vazquez, at 2169–73.

35. Mason, "Objections to the Constitution," Nov. 22, 1787, 14 *Documentary History of the Ratification of the Constitution* 154 (Merril Jensen et al., eds., 1976–present); Old Whig, III, 13 id. at 426; Cato, IV, 14 id. at 431–32; Federalist No. 75, at 424–25; Civis Rusticus, "Reply to Mason's Objections," Jan. 30, 1788, 1 *The Debate on the Constitution* 359 (Bernard Bailyn, ed., 1993), See also Federalist No. 22, at 182 (Hamilton) (treaties' "true import, as far as respects individuals, must, like other laws, be ascertained by judicial determination"); Federalist No. 64 (Jay), at 378.

36. 2 *Records of the Federal Convention of 1787,* at 389–90 (Max Farrand, ed., 1966); Helvidius, No. 1, Aug. 24, 1793, 15 *Papers of James Madison* 69 (William Hutchinson et al., eds., 1962–1991) (treaties "have the force of law"); Jefferson to Monroe, July 14, 1793, 26 *Papers of Jefferson,* at 501–3 ("Treaties are laws. . . . He who breaks [a treaty], if within our jurisdiction, breaks the laws. . . ."). See also Hamilton to Washington, 20 *Papers of Hamilton,* at 98 ("Treaties therefore in our government of themselves and without any additional sanction have full legal perfection as laws"); id. at 100 (treaty "is conclusive upon ALL and ALL are bound to give it effect"); Hamilton to William Smith, Mar. 16, 1796, id. at 72 (arguing for treaties' binding force because "[i]t is a contradiction to call a thing a law which is not binding").

37. 5 U.S. 103, 109–10 (1801). See also St. George Tucker, *Blackstone's Commentaries,* app. at 440 (1801) (describing treaties as part of the "written law" of Virginia, along with the Constitution and state and federal statutes).

38. John Yoo argues forcefully against this reading, principally on three bases: (1) that in English law treaties were not self-executing; (2) that Article VI is not necessarily addressed to treaties' status as law; and (3) that commentary in the ratification debate indicates the contrary. Yoo, *Powers of War and Peace,* at 131–41, 215–49. The first point is correct (Chapter 5), but not determinative, because Article VI sug-

gests the drafters' desire to alter that aspect of English law. The second point requires an extraordinary stretch of language. Yoo argues that placement of treaties in Article VI might have been merely intended to give Congress power to enforce treaties against the states. But Congress surely has that power from Article I anyway (Chapter 10), and it is an odd reading indeed to say that the reason for including treaties in Article VI is different from the reason for including statutes and the Constitution in the same sentence of the same Article. The third point requires some elaboration. It is true that key anti-federalists objected to the self-executing nature of treaties, and that various federalists tried to respond in ways that were not always clear or helpful. Responding to anti-federalists at the Pennsylvania convention, for example, James Wilson observed: "In England, if the king and his ministers find themselves, during their negotiation, to be embarrassed, because an existing law is not repealed, or a new law is not enacted, they give notice to the legislature of their situation and inform them that it will be necessary, before the treaty can operate, that some law be repealed or some made. And will not the same thing take place here?" 2 *Documentary History*, at 562–63. Madison and others made similar comments in the Virginia convention, where anti-federalist attacks on this point were particularly sharp. But this commentary seems insufficient to undermine the text. First, it is balanced by much commentary equating treaties and laws, tracking the text's apparent meaning. Second, Wilson, Madison, and their allies did not explain how the text accomplished the result they suggested (or even exactly how they understood Congress to have a role in treaty implementation). See 2 *Documentary History*, at 563 (Wilson) (appealing to "prudence," "caution," and "moderation" of "those who negotiate treaties for the United States"). Third, both Wilson and Madison equated treaties and laws shortly after ratification Madison in the Helvidius essays and Wilson in the neutrality prosecutions). And finally, there may be reason to doubt their authority, since both were part of a minority at the Convention that proposed unsuccessfully to give the full Congress a role approving treaties. 2 *Records*, at 538. See Vazquez, *Laughing at Treaties*, at 2163–73; Ramsey, *Toward a Rule of Law*, at 1469–73.

39. Henkin, at 209–11 (finding Congress's power "firmly established"). See Whitney v. Robertson, 124 U.S. 190 (1888).

40. 1 Blackstone, at 89–90 (relying on the maxim *leges posteriores priores contraries abrogant:* later statutes abrogate earlier ones.); Federalist No. 78, at 439. See Henkin, at 485 n.129; Julian Ku, "Treaties as Laws: A Defense of the Last-in-Time Rule for Treaties and Federal Statutes," 80 *Ind. L.J.* 319, 347–85 (2005).

41. This is the essence of the Supreme Court's reasoning in *Whitney:* "By the Constitution a treaty is placed on the same footing, and made of like obligation, with an act of legislation. Both are declared by that instrument to be the supreme law of the land, and no supreme efficacy is given to either over the other." 124 U.S. at 194. Professor Henkin argues that doubt is thrown on the matter because Article VI also makes the Constitution supreme law without differentiating it from statutes and treaties. Henkin, at 210. But Article VI *does* give the Constitution superiority: only statutes made "in pursuance" of the Constitution and only treaties

made "under the Authority of the United States" are supreme law—that is, unconstitutional treaties and statutes do not gain the status of supreme law. (The reason for the differing language is that Article VI makes both pre- and post-ratification treaties part of supreme law—if the former were made "under the authority of the United States" during the Confederation period—but makes only post-ratification statutes part of supreme law, as made "in pursuance" of the Constitution.)

42. Wolcott to Washington, quoted in Ku, at 379–80; Hamilton to Washington, Mar. 29, 1796, 20 *Papers of Hamilton*, at 99; see also Camillus, "The Defence," XXXVI, id. at 16 (arguing under *leges posteriores* principle that a later treaty repeals an earlier statute); Hamilton to King, Mar. 16, 1796, id. at 77. For a detailed defense of the last-in-time rule under the Constitution's historical meaning, see Ku, at 347–85. But see Amar, at 303–7, arguing that treaties cannot override statutes but agreeing that statutes override treaties.

43. To be clear, a conflicting statute "does not affect the validity of the treaty . . . but it compels the United States to be in default." Henkin, at 209–10.

44. *Foster v. Neilson*, 27 U.S. 253, 314 (1829). See Carlos Vazquez, "The Four Doctrines of Self-Executing Treaties," 89 *Am. J. Int'l L.* 695 (1995).

45. Yoo, *Powers of War and Peace*, at 215–49.

46. "The Defense," XXXVI, Jan. 2, 1796, 20 *Papers of Hamilton* at 6–7. See also 10 *Documentary History*, at 1389 (Nicholas to Va. convention) (treaties must be "under the authority of the United States" and so cannot be "repugnant" to the Constitution); Amar, at 300 (United States would have "no authority to enter into a treaty that violated the Constitution"); Reid v. Covert, 354 U.S. 1, 15–18 (1957) (holding that treaties cannot violate the Constitution).

47. That may not be immediately obvious because a treaty is, for at least some purposes, a "law." One might also conclude, though, that the placement of the appropriations clause in Article I implies that it refers to "Laws" passed through the Article I process. See "The Defence," No. XXXVI, 20 *Papers of Hamilton*, at 20–21 (reaching this conclusion). See also Amar, at 592 n.38 (arguing that treaties cannot declare war).

48. Currie, at 211–17. Federalists led by Hamilton argued that the House was obligated to provide funding, since the treaty was a law of the land; Madison and the Republicans, taking the position that has prevailed over time, argued that the House could make an independent judgment on the advisability of the treaty (a view that seems to correspond to Jefferson's 1792 advice).

49. 5 *Annals*, at 493.

50. "An Additional Number of Letters from the Federal Farmer to the Republican," No. XI, 16 *Documentary History*, at 309–10. Building on these and other sources, Professor Yoo argues that all treaties concerning matters within Congress's Article I, §8 powers are non-self-executing. Yoo, *Powers of War and Peace*, at 217–44.

51. For more elaborate textual arguments, see Vazquez, "Laughing at Treaties," at 2169–73 (concluding that the argument for generalized non-self-execution "is simply not an eligible interpretation of [the] text").

52. Madison in particular seems somewhat suspect in this context, because he was leading the House opposition to the Jay Treaty and needed a constitutional explanation for why the House should be involved. Likewise, the "Farmer," who earlier objected to the structure of the treaty power, may have been trying to put an interpretive gloss upon it.

    Professor Amar makes the more-modest claim that treaties, although generally self-executing, cannot overturn existing federal statutes, based upon their respective placement within Article VI. Amar, at 303–7. Article VI does not itself suggest that any hierarchy is intended by the order in which the two are listed, though, and only scattered founding-era authority supports it. If Amar is correct, presumably the President is not bound by a treaty conflicting with a prior statute.

53. Henkin, at 203–4. Much debate in modern law arises from the Senate's common practice of attaching "reservations" to their treaty approvals, stating that the approval is conditioned upon the treaty being non-self-executing. See Curtis Bradley & Jack Goldsmith, "Treaties, Human Rights, and Conditional Consent," 149 *U. Pa. L. Rev.* 349 (2000).

54. Vazquez, "Laughing at Treaties," at 2176–83; Bradley & Goldsmith, at 349. As Justice Chase observed in 1796, "no one can doubt that a treaty may stipulate that certain acts shall be done by the legislature." Ware, 3 U.S. at 244.

55. See Jordan Paust, "Self-Executing Treaties," 82 *Am. J. Int'l L.* 760 (1988); David Sloss, "Non-Self-Executing Treaties: Exposing a Constitutional Fallacy," 36 *U. C. Davis L. Rev.* 1 (2002).

56. Carlos Vazquez, who has made the most sophisticated analysis of the constitutional law of treaties, proposes four categories of non-self-executing treaties that are consistent with the text of Article VI. See Vazquez, "Laughing at Treaties," at 2176–83. The description here roughly captures his first three categories. His final category is treaties that do not provide a private right of action. As he makes clear, he would—consistent with the discussion here—call these latter treaties self-executing but of limited judicial enforceability.

57. Carlos Vazquez, "Treaty-Based Rights and the Remedies of Individuals," 92 *Colum. L. Rev.* 1082 (1992).

58. See Jinks & Sloss, at 154–76 (discussing remedies).

9. The Non-treaty Power

1. Louis Henkin, *Foreign Affairs and the U.S. Constitution* 219–22 (2d ed. 1996).
2. Amer. Ins. Ass'n v. Garamendi, 539 U.S. 396, 415 (2003).
3. This chapter draws upon Michael Ramsey, "Executive Agreements and the (Non)Treaty Power," 77 *N.C. L. Rev.* 133 (1999). See also Joel Paul, "The Geopolitical Constitution: Executive Expediency and Executive Agreements," 86 *Cal. L. Rev.* 671 (1998); Ingrid Wuerth, "The Dangers of Deference: International Claims Settlement by the President," 44 *Harv. Int'l L.J.* 1 (2003).
4. Henkin, at 229; see id. at 222 (executive agreement power's "limits are difficult

to determine and to state"). See also Henry Monaghan, "The Protective Power of the Presidency," 93 *Colum. L. Rev.* 1, 53–55 (1993).

5. Dames & Moore v. Regan, 453 U.S. 654 (1981); United States v. Pink, 315 U.S. 203 (1942); United States v. Belmont, 301 U.S. 324 (1937).

6. On *Belmont*'s historical background, see Stephen Millett, *The Constitutionality of Executive Agreements: An Analysis of United States v. Belmont* 1–57 (1990).

7. 301 U.S. at 330.

8. Id. at 331–32.

9. United States v. Curtiss-Wright Export Co., 299 U.S. 304, 318 (1936).

10. Henkin, at 229.

11. Raoul Berger, "The Presidential Monopoly of Foreign Relations," 71 *Mich. L. Rev.* 1, 35–40 (1972).

12. Id. at 37.

13. See Abraham Weinfeld, "What Did the Framers of the Federal Constitution Mean by 'Agreements or Compacts'?" 3 *U. Chi. L. Rev.* 453, 453–57 (1936); Paul, at 735–36; Laurence Tribe, "Taking Text and Structure Seriously: Reflections on Free-Form Method in Constitutional Interpretation," 108 *Harv. L. Rev.* 1221, 1265–66 (1995).

14. Professor Berger responds, without founding-era support, that "treaty" in Article I does not mean the same thing as "treaty" in Article II. Berger, at 42. David Golove, "Against Free-Form Formalism," 73 *N.Y.U. L. Rev.* 1791, 1909–10 (1998), argues somewhat more plausibly that the second clause of Article I, §10 might be an exception to the first; but Article I, §10 is not written that way (it emphasizes that states cannot "enter into any Treaty"), and in any event Golove's argument does not account for Article VI of the Articles.

15. Nicholas Bailey's 1729 dictionary, relied upon Berger, at 35, defines "treaty" to mean "an agreement between two or more distinct Nations concerning Peace, Commerce, Navigation, etc." Berger concludes from this definition that the term "treaty" is comprehensive. True, Bailey might have meant (as Berger supposes) to define treaties as "[all] agreements between nations [including for example those] concerning Peace, Commerce Navigation, etc." But he also might have meant "[certain kinds of] agreements between nations [such as those] concerning Peace, Commerce, Navigation, etc." Bailey's "etc." is fatally ambiguous; it could include all other agreements, or only those similar (in respects not yet identified) to agreements of peace, commerce, and navigation. Samuel Johnson's 1755 dictionary is even less helpful, defining "treaty" as a "compact of accommodation relating to publick affairs" without indicating whether it includes all agreements (or even all "compacts") between nations. See Weinfeld, at 454.

16. On the historical development of international law during the Enlightenment period, see Arthur Nussbaum, *A Concise History of the Law of Nations* 147–64 (rev. ed. 1962).

17. Peter Haggenmacher, "Some Hints on the European Origins of Legislative Participation in the Treaty-Making Function," 67 *Chi-Kent L. Rev.* 313, 321–22 (1987).

18. Grotius, *De Jure Belli ac Pacis* [On the Laws of War and Peace], bk. II, ch. XV, §II (1625) (William Evats, trans., 1682). See also id., bk. II, ch. XVI, §§III–IV, XIV, XVI.

19. Emmerich de Vattel, *Droit des Gens* [The Law of Nations], bk. II, §§152–53 (1758) (Charles Fenwick, trans., J. B. Scott, ed., 1964).

20. Id. at vii–viii (introduction by Albert de Lapradelle); id. at 6a–10a (author's preface).

21. Christian Wolff, *Jus Gentium Methodo Scientifica Pertractatum*, §§369, 464–65 (1749) ("Gentes enim earumque Rectores pactiones inire possunt, quae foederibus contradistinguuntur.").

22. See Haggenmacher, at 321–25; Weinfeld, at 457–64.

23. Stewart Jay, "The Status of the Law of Nations in Early American Law," 42 *Vand. L. Rev.* 819, 823 (1989). See Vattel, at xxviii–xxx (introduction by Albert de Lapradelle); Nicholas Onuf & Peter Onuf, *Federal Union, Modern World: The Law of Nations in an Age of Revolutions, 1776–1814*, at 11 (1993) (Vattel's work "was unrivaled among such treatises in its influence on the American founders"); David Adler, "The President's Recognition Power," in *The Constitution and the Conduct of American Foreign Policy* 137–38 (David Adler & Larry George, eds., 1990); Paul, at 736 & nn. 328–29; Haggenmacher, at 325–26.

24. See Thomas Jefferson, "Opinion on the Treaties with France" (April 28, 1793), 25 *Papers of Thomas Jefferson* 613–16 (Julian Boyd et al., eds., 1950–2005) (relying heavily on Grotius, Vattel, Wolff, and Pufendorf); Helvidius, No. 1 (Aug. 24, 1793), 15 *Papers of James Madison* 68 (William Hutchinson et al., eds., 1962–1991) (noting international authorities "Wolfius, Burlamaqui and Vattel); Jefferson to Madison, August 5, 1793, id. at 50 (referring to Vattel, Cornelius van Bynkershoek, and Wolff); Ware v. Hylton, 3 U.S. 199, 230 (1796) (Chase) (citing "Baron de Wolfuis").

25. Berger, at 37–40, for example, relies on Wilson's statement that "[n]either the president nor the Senate, solely, can complete a treaty" and Story's later comment that "[i]t is too much to expect that a free people would confide to a single magistrate . . . the sole authority to act conclusively, as well as exclusively, upon the subject of treaties." These observations (and others like them) confirm that the President lacks independent treatymaking authority, but they do not speak to whether there are "non-treaty" agreements.

26. Camillus [Hamilton], "The Defence," XXXVIII, 15 *Papers of Alexander Hamilton* 22 (Harold Syrett, ed., 1961–1987); See also "The Defence," XXXVI, id. at 168.

27. On the scope of treaties and state power, see Chapter 15. On the context of Hamilton's "Defence," see David Golove, "Treaty-Making and the Nation: The Historical Foundations of the Nationalist Conception of the Treaty Power," 98 *Mich. L. Rev.* 1075, 1157–93 (2000).

28. Dames, 453 U.S. at 682 & n.8; Tribe, at 1265. See also Myres McDougal & Asher Lans, "Treaties and Congressional-Executive or Presidential Agreements: Interchangeable Instruments of National Policy," 54 *Yale L.J.* 181 (1945); Wallace McClure, *International Executive Agreements* 3–51 (1941).

29. *Treaties and Other International Acts of the United States* (Hunter Miller, ed., 1931), vols. 2–4; Ramsey, at 174–75.

30. President Monroe initially favored making the agreement on his own authority. He was apparently persuaded otherwise, partly by his advisors and partly by the British, who presumably wanted to avoid controversy over the agreement's binding effect. Monroe submitted the agreement to the Senate with a note asking whether it required Senate approval; the Senate (implicitly answering affirmatively) gave advice and consent, in accordance with Article II, §2. 2 *Treaties*, at 645–48.

31. 3 id., at 249–52, 269–72; 4 id. at 241–44. The Samoa document seems more like a local law than an international agreement: it is titled "Commercial Regulations" and carries the Captain's signature as a "witness" rather than as an agent signing on behalf of the United States. It imposes obligations upon U.S. commercial ships in Samoa (as would be expected from local law) but does not appear to impose international obligations upon the United States as a nation.

32. Nineteenth-century rules of jurisdiction and immunity made private suit against foreign sovereigns essentially impossible; practically, such claims could be vindicated only by negotiation through the U.S. embassy. The private party typically requested State Department assistance, and the U.S. minister in the relevant nation raised the claim with that government and secured what payment could be negotiated.

33. 3 id. at 659–69 (Portugal); 3 id. at 197–99 (Colombia).

34. 2 id. at 557–65.

35. 3 id. at 201–7 (Russia); 4 id. at 179–80 (Netherlands).

36. The experience of the next twenty years—extending the historical period essentially up to the beginning of the Civil War—affords considerably more precedent. Continuing the trend of the 1820s and 1830s, the volume of unilateral executive agreements increased, for a total of around thirty-five agreements between 1840 and 1860. No objections—constitutional or otherwise—are recorded. These agreements had no great significance, but the fact that they occurred without comment suggests that no one saw the practice as inconsistent with earlier assumptions. See Ramsey, at 180–81 & n. 202.

37. Henkin, at 14–15.

38. See John McGinnis & Michael Rappaport, "Our Supermajorititarian Constitution," 80 *Tex. L. Rev.* 703, 763 (linking Article II, § 2's supermajority rule in part to this feature of treaties). Article VI implies that Congress can abrogate treaties by statute, see Chapter 8, but not without violating international law and thus incurring reputational and other sanctions.

39. Edwin Borchard, "Shall the Executive Agreement Replace the Treaty?" 53 *Yale L.J.* 664, 679 & n. 54 (1944); 73 *Dep't of State Bulletin* 204–5, 323 (1975) (Helsinki Accords); George Sutherland, *Constitutional Power and World Affairs* 120 (1919).

40. See Borchard, at 677–80.

41. Vattel, bk. III, §206; see also Grotius, bk. II, ch. XVI; Wolff, §376–78.

42. 2 *Treaties*, at 565.

43. Wolff, §369.

44. Vattel, bk. II, §§152–53.

45. Grotius does not make the point so specifically, but his terminology leads to the same result. As Grotius described Roman practice, the full ceremony of the *foedera* was reserved for elaborately negotiated agreements of great importance; as one moved down through the terminology procedurally, importance lessened as well. Grotius discusses, for example, the truce—which seems characteristic of a temporary, localized agreement lacking long-term significance. Grotius thought the truce was binding, and he thought (as did the Romans) that it could be concluded on behalf of the sovereign by local commanders without the formalities of the *foedus*—it was one of the "alies pactiones." Thus, although not explicit, the Grotian-Roman terminology suggests a substantive hierarchy of international agreements in which the word *foedus* ("treaty") was reserved for the most important. Grotius, bk. II, ch. XV.

46. 2 *Treaties*, at 645–48.

47. See Samuel Bemis, *A Diplomatic History of the United States* 202–8 (4th ed. 1955).

48. Ramsey, at 178–83.

49. *Treaties*, at 1075.

50. See Ramsey, at 200–204 (listing treaties).

51. 10 *Documentary History of the Ratification of the Constitution* 1380 (Merrill Jensen et al., eds., 1976–present) (Mason to Va. convention); id. at 1381 (Henry to Va. convention). Madison, id. at 1381, said it would be "atrocious" for the President to proceed with the support of such few Senators. For further elaboration, see Chapter 14.

10. Legislative Power in Foreign Affairs

1. Bruce Ackerman & David Golove, "Is NAFTA Constitutional?" 108 *Harv. L. Rev.* 801 (1995); Laurence Tribe, "Taking Text and Structure Seriously: Reflections on Free-Form Method in Constitutional Interpretation," 108 *Harv. L. Rev.* 1221 (1995); David Golove, "Against Free-Form Formalism," 73 *N.Y.U. L.* Rev. 1791 (1998); Myres McDougal & Asher Lans, "Treaties and Congressional-Executive or Presidential Agreements: Interchangeable Instruments of National Policy," 54 *Yale L.J.* 181 (1945); Edwin Borchard, "Shall the Executive Agreement Replace the Treaty?" 53 *Yale L.J.* 664 (1945); Edwin Borchard, "Treaties and Executive Agreements—A Reply," 54 *Yale L.J.* 616 (1945). On the older debate, see also Wallace McClure, *International Executive Agreements* (1941); Quincy Wright, "The United States and International Agreements," 38 *Am. J. Int'l. L.* 341 (1944). For intermediate modern approaches, see John Yoo, "The Constitutionality of Congressional-Executive Agreements," 99 *Mich. L. Rev.* 757 (2001); Peter Spiro, "Treaties, Executive Agreements, and Constitutional Method," 79 *Tex. L. Rev.* 961 (2001).

2. 1 *Records of the Federal Convention of 1787*, at 21 (Max Farrand, ed., 1966) (Virginia plan); 2 id. at 181–82 (Committee of Detail report).

3. Louis Henkin, *Foreign Affairs and the U.S. Constitution* 70–72 (2d ed. 1996).

4. Id. at 70–71.

5. Id. at 70.

6. Chae Chan Ping v. United States, 130 U.S. 581, 603–4 (1889).

7. See Sarah Cleveland, "Powers Inherent in Sovereignty: Indians, Aliens, Territories, and the Nineteenth Century Origins of Plenary Power over Foreign Affairs," 81 *Tex. L. Rev.* 1 (2001) (discussing these and related claims of inherent congressional power).

8. For much of early U.S. history, states, not Congress, regulated immigration. Gerald Neuman, "The Lost Century of American Immigration Law (1776–1875)," 93 *Colum. L. Rev.* 1833 (1993).

9. Cleveland, at 81–163; Henkin, at 16–17, 70.

10. 17 U.S. 316 (1819).

11. Id. at 414–19; see David Currie, *The Constitution in the Supreme Court: The First Hundred Years* 160–68 (1985).

12. McCulloch, 17 U.S. at 409–14, 421–23. On the 1791 Bank debate, see Stanley Elkins & Eric McKitrick, *The Age of Federalism* 228–33 (1993); Hamilton to Washington, 8 *Papers of Alexander Hamilton* 63–134 (Harold Syrett, ed., 1961–1987); 1 *Annals of Congress* 1738–48, 1873–94, 1903–14, 1945–54 (Joseph Gales, ed., 1834). For ratification commentary, see especially Federalist No. 33, in James Madison, Alexander Hamilton, & John Jay, *The Federalist Papers* 223–35 (Isaac Kramnick, ed., 1987) (Hamilton); Federalist No. 44, at 288–90 (Madison); Gary Lawson & Patricia Granger, "The 'Proper' Scope of Federal Power: A Jurisdictional Interpretation of the Sweeping Clause," 43 *Duke L.J.* 267 (1993). For the conclusion that Marshall's general principle accorded with founding-era understanding, see Currie, at 162; see also Elkins & McKitrick, at 229–33 (finding Madison's argument against the Bank inconsistent with his arguments in *The Federalist* and generally unpersuasive).

13. Henkin, at 70–71.

14. Gaillard Hunt, *The American Passport: Its History* 4–6 (1898); *The United States Passport: Past, Present, Future* 1–5 (U.S. Dep't of State 1976).

15. *United States Passport*, at 9–26; Hunt, at 36–37. Congress did not enact general passport legislation until 1856. *United States Passport*, at 30–31.

16. Id. at 14.

17. Act of Jan. 30, 1799, 1 Stat. 613; Alexander de Conde, *The Quasi-War* 154–57 (1966); Frederick Tolles, "Unofficial Ambassador: George Logan's Mission to France, 1798," 7 *Wm. & Mary Q.* 4 (1950); Detlev Vagts, "The Logan Act: Paper Tiger or Sleeping Giant?" 60 *Am. J. Int'l L.* 268, 269–72 (1966).

18. 9 *Annals*, at 2488–89 (Dec. 26, 1798); see also id. at 94 (describing bill as punishing actions "usurp[ing] the Executive Authority").

19. Act of June 5, 1794, 1 Stat. 381; David Currie, *The Constitution in Congress: The Federalist Period* 182 (1997).

20. Currie, *Constitution in Congress*, at 182.

21. 1 William Blackstone, *Commentaries on the Laws of England* 251–52 (1765).

22. Nicholas Rosenkranz, "Executing the Treaty Power," 118 *Harv. L. Rev.* 1867 (2005), argues strongly to the contrary on the basis of the historical meaning of the text. In his view, Congress's power to "carry into execution" treaties (and, presumably, executive agreements) means only the power to support their negotiation—for example, through funding—not the power to incorporate them into domestic law. Founding-era terminology, though, appears to refer to enacting a treaty into law as "executing" it. 2 *Records*, at 393 (statements of Wilson and Johnson); Ware v. Hylton, 3 U.S. 199, 277 (Iredell). See also Foster v. Neilson, 27 U.S. 253, 314 (1829) (Marshall, C.J.) (if "the treaty addresses itself to the political, not the judicial department . . . the legislature must execute the contract before it can become a rule for the Court").

23. As Chapter 2 discusses, Americans understood reciprocal trade legislation as a way to get trade concessions as far back as the Confederation (when it was tried unsuccessfully at the state level).

24. See especially Federalist 33 (Hamilton), at 224 ("What is a LEGISLATIVE power but a power of making LAWS?").

25. Jefferson to William Short, Mar. 8, 1791, 19 *Papers of Thomas Jefferson* 425 (Julian Boyd et al., eds., 1950–2005); 4 *Papers of John Marshall* 104–5 (Herbert Johnson, et al., eds., 1974–2006).

26. 1 Blackstone, at 249; Baron de Montesquieu, *The Spirit of Laws* 151 (1748) (Prometheus reprint 2002).

27. Federalist No. 75, at 424–25 (calling treatymaking neither legislative nor executive); compare Pacificus, No. 1, 15 *Papers of Hamilton,* at 33 (calling treatymaking executive). Golove, at 1847, 1871–74, disputes this characterization, arguing that founding-era commentaries often associated treaties with legislative power. They did, but on the basis of treaties' status as law under Article VI. See Thomas Jefferson, *Manual of Parliamentary Practice,* §52 (1801) in *Jefferson's Parliamentary Writings* 420 (Wilbur Howell, ed., 1988) ("Treaties are legislative acts. A treaty is the law of the land.").

28. Act of June 4, 1794, 1 Stat. 372; Act of June 13, 1798, 1 Stat. 565; Act of Feb. 9, 1799, 1 Stat. 613.

29. For discussion of delegations of Congress's declare-war power, see Chapter 12.

30. See Lawson & Granger, at 267. David Golove's sophisticated textual case for congressional-executive agreements relies heavily (at least as a rhetorical matter) on the necessary-and-proper clause. But as Golove recognizes, the clause does not allow Congress to exercise (or give to the President) powers that it lacks, even if it purports to act by statute. Thus Golove ultimately and properly sees the central question to be whether Congress, in creating the authority to make the agreement, is acting legislatively. See Golove, at 1847, 1871–74; see also Ackerman & Golove, at 811.

31. See especially Charles Warren, "The Mississippi River and the Treaty Clause of the Constitution," 2 *Geo. Wash. L. Rev.* 271, 287–99 (1923); Lance Banning,

"Virginia: Sectionalism and the General Good," in *Ratifying the Constitution* 261 (Michael Gillespie & Michael Lienesch, eds., 1989).

32. Banning, at 279–80.

33. As Professor Tribe points out, there are a number of other textual provisions that read awkwardly if Congress has Article I treatymaking power—among other matters, perhaps Congress could (by a veto-proof majority) make treaties without the concurrence of the President, which would in turn require either that Congress compel the President to make a treaty or that Congress appoint its own ambassadors.

34. Act of Feb. 20, 1792, §26, 1 Stat. 236; see McClure, at 38–40.

35. "The Defence," XXXVI, 20 *Papers of Hamilton,* at 8–9; Hamilton to Washington, Mar. 29, 1796, id. at 89–90; Washington to the House, Mar. 30, 1796, 35 *Writings of George Washington* 3 (John Fitzpatrick, ed., 1939) ("the power of making treaties is exclusively vested in the President, by and with the advice and consent of the Senate").

36. See Golove, "Against Free-Form Formalism"; Ackerman & Golove, at 810–11. Ackerman and Golove concede that there was no history or founding-era understanding of congressional treaties, but nonetheless argue that such a thing is possible from the text standing alone. That, though, misses the point of contextual meaning: the question is not what we can possibly make the words mean divorced from their context, but what the words meant in the time and context in which they were written. As a result, the extended debate between Professors Golove and Tribe over the text's meaning in isolation is likewise beside the point for a textual understanding of the Constitution. For a brief but persuasive contextual evaluation, see John McGinnis & Michael Rappaport, "Our Supermajoritarian Constitution," 80 *Tex. L. Rev.* 703, 764–65 & n. 259 (2002).

37. 453 U.S. 654 (1981).

38. See Executive Order No. 12,294, 46 Fed. Reg. 14,111 (1981) (confirming Carter's earlier orders). For the Algiers Declarations, see 20 I.L.M. 224–33 (1981) (agreements of January 19, 1981). Although taking the form of parallel "declarations" by the governments of Algeria, Iran, and the United States, they are clearly intended as binding international agreements. For commentary, see Lee Marks & John Grabow, "The President's Foreign Economic Powers after Dames & Moore v. Regan: Legislation by Acquiescence," 68 *Cornell L. Rev.* 68 (1982).

39. 20 I.L.M. at 224–33. Even if the Accords themselves were constitutional, that would not give the President unilateral authority to make domestic law in their support, as Reagan purported to do. See Chapters 5 and 14.

40. 453 U.S. at 682–83; see Youngstown Sheet & Tube Co. v. Sawyer, 343 U.S. 579, 635–36 (1952); Marks & Grabow, at 68.

41. See Michael Paulsen, "Youngstown Goes to War," 19 *Const. Comment.* 215 (2002); Patricia Bellia, "Executive Power in Youngstown's Shadows," 19 *Const. Comment.* 87 (2002). Compare Immigration & Naturalization Service v. Chadha, 462 U.S. 919 (1983).

42. Youngstown, 343 U.S. at 635–36.

43. Made in the USA Foundation v. United States, 242 F.3d 1300 (11th Cir. 2001). The court of appeals in this case dismissed a constitutional challenge to NAFTA as a non-justiciable "political question," a matter considered in Chapter 16. As discussed below, the analysis here suggests that this was almost right: the more precise answer is that NAFTA's implementing statutes are constitutional, and the plaintiffs lacked standing to challenge NAFTA's international obligations because they were not directly injured by the existence of the international obligations, as opposed to the implementing statutes.

44. As discussed in Chapter 8, future Congresses could override NAFTA as a matter of U.S. domestic law simply by passing an inconsistent statute. But that would violate international law, unless the U.S. gave requisite notice. Congress itself could not give the notice (since it lacks executive communications powers), nor could it order the President to do so. However, Congress could repeal NAFTA, effective six months in the future, and assume that the President would give the appropriate notice under international law.

11. The Meanings of Declaring War

1. For leading modern commentary favoring Congress's power, see Louis Fisher, *Presidential War Power* (2d ed. 2004); William Treanor, "Fame, the Founding and the Power to Declare War," 82 *Cornell L. Rev.* 695 (1997); John Ely, *War and Responsibility* (1993); Michael Glennon, *Constitutional Diplomacy* 71–122 (1990). For commentary endorsing presidential power, see John Yoo, *The Powers of War and Peace* (2005); John Yoo, "The Continuation of Politics by Other Means: The Original Understanding of War Powers," 84 *Cal. L. Rev.* 167 (1996); Robert Turner, *Repealing the War Powers Resolution* 47–107 (1991); William Bradford, "The Duty to Defend Them: A Natural Law Justification for the Bush Doctrine of Preventive War," 79 *N.D. L. Rev.* 1365, 1440–45 (2004). For intermediate positions, see Jefferson Powell, *The President's Authority over Foreign Affairs* 115–22 (2002); Michael Paulsen, "Youngstown Goes to War," 19 *Const. Comment.* 215 (2002). My contributions include Michael Ramsey, "Textualism and War Powers," 69 *U. Chi. L. Rev.* 1543 (2002) and Michael Ramsey, "Presidential Declarations of War," 37 *U.C. Davis L. Rev.* 321 (2003), on which this and the succeeding chapter in part rely. Classics in the field include Francis Wormuth & Edwin Firmage, *To Chain the Dog of War* (2d ed. 1989); Taylor Reveley, *War Powers of the President and Congress* (1981); Raoul Berger, "War-Making by the President," 121 *U. Pa. L. Rev.* 29 (1972); Charles Lofgren, "War-Making under the Constitution," 81 *Yale L.J.* 672 (1972); Henry Monaghan, "Presidential War-making," 50 *B.U. L. Rev.* 19 (1970); William Van Alstyne, "Congress, the President, and the Power to Declare War: A Requiem for Vietnam," 121 *U. Pa. L. Rev.* 1 (1972).

2. Madison to Jefferson, Apr. 2, 1798, 17 *Papers of James Madison* 104 (William

Hutchinson et al., eds., 1962–91). See also Helvidius, No. 1, Aug. 24, 1793, 15 id. at 71 ("Those who are to *conduct a war* cannot in the nature of things, be proper or safe judges of whether *a war ought* to be *commenced*.").

3. Pacificus, No. 1, June 29, 1793, 15 *Papers of Alexander Hamilton* 42 (Harold Syrett, ed., 1961–1987). See also Alexander Hamilton, "The Examination," Dec. 17, 1801, 25 id. at 455 (the "plain meaning" of the Constitution is that "it is the peculiar and exclusive province of Congress, *when the nation is at peace*, to change that state into a state of war; . . . in other words, it belongs to Congress only, *to go to war*").

4. Talbot v. Seeman, 5 U.S. 1, 28 (1801).

5. 2 *Records of the Federal Convention of 1787*, at 318 (Max Farrand, ed., 1966).

6. See especially Yoo, "Continuation of Politics," at 341–56; Turner, at 47–107.

7. For elaboration, see Ramsey, "Textualism," at 1548–69.

8. John Locke, *Two Treatises of Government* 365 (1690) (Peter Laslett, ed., 1988); Baron de Montesquieu, *The Spirit of Laws* 151 (1748) (Prometheus reprint 2002); Jean de Lolme, *The Constitution of England* 73 (1771); 1 William Blackstone, *Commentaries on the Laws of England* 249 (1765).

9. See Yoo, "Continuation of Politics," at 196–217; Yoo, *Powers of War*, at 30–54.

10. 1 *Records*, at 21, 64–70.

11. Id. at 64–70; 2 id. at 318–19. At least eight delegates spoke against presidential war-initiation power.

12. Terminology varied, but the core practice is clear from eighteenth-century international writers. Hugo Grotius, *De Jure Belli ac Pacis*, bk. III, ch. II, §IV (William Evats, trans., 1682); Christian Wolff, *Jus Gentium Methodo Scientifica Pertractatum*, §§589 (1749) (Joseph Drake, trans., J. B. Scott, ed., 1964); Emmerich de Vattel, *The Law of Nations*, bk. II, §§342–43 (1758) (Charles Fenwick, trans., J.B. Scott, ed., 1964); 2 J. J. Burlamaqui, *Principles of Natural and Politic Law* 180 (1727) (Arno reprint 1972).

13. See 1 Blackstone, at 249; 4 id. at 250–51.

14. Vattel, bk. III, §51. See also Wolff, §705 ("A declaration is defined as a public announcement of war made against a nation or its ruler by another nation or its ruler.").

15. 1 Matthew Hale, *History of the Pleas of the Crown* 162–63 (1672). On Hale's influence in America, see Bernard Bailyn, *The Ideological Origins of the American Revolution* 30 & n.11 (1967).

16. J. F. Maurice, *Hostilities without Declaration of War* (1883); Robert Ward, *An Enquiry into the Manner in which the Different Wars in Europe Have Commenced* (1805); Yoo, *Powers of War*, at 51–52.

17. 2 Burlamaqui, at 187.

18. Wolff, §710; Vattel, bk. III, §51.

19. Grotius, bk. III, ch. III, §§5–6; 2 Samuel Pufendorf, *De Jure Naturae et Gentium* 1300 (1680); 2 Cornelius van Bynkershoek, *Quaestionum Juris Publici*, bk. I, ch. II (1737) (Tenney Frank, trans., J. B. Scott, ed., 1964); Thomas Rutherforth, *Institutes of Natural Law* 580 (1754).

20. 1 Hale, at 162–63.
21. Federalist No. 25, in James Madison, Alexander Hamilton, & John Jay, *The Federalist Papers* 194 (Isaac Kramnick, ed., 1987). On eighteenth-century practice, see Yoo, *Powers of War*, at 51–52; Maurice, *Hostilities*; Ward, *Enquiry*; Brien Hallett, *The Lost Art of Declaring War* 61–95 (1998).
22. Yoo, "Continuation of Politics," at 242; id. at 245 ("Americans of the eighteenth century would have understood that the power to declare war dealt with the formal legal relationship between two nations, and not with authorizing real hostilities.").
23. Grotius, bk. III, ch. IV, §§3–4; id., ch. III, §1.
24. 1 Hale, at 162–63; Rutherforth, at 580. See also 2 Bynkershoek, bk. I, ch. II (reviewing European examples and concluding: "Certainly the mutual use of force may begin a war.").
25. 2 Bynkershoek, bk. I, ch. II.
26. The Maria Magdalena, 165 Eng. Rep. 57, 58 (1779).
27. For the argument that televised presidential addresses serve a corresponding modern role, see Ramsey, "Presidential Declarations," at 349–57.
28. See Ramsey, "Textualism," at 1586–87. Professor Yoo's more recent writings seem to agree with this account, although he draws different conclusions from it. See Yoo, *Powers of War*, at 151–53 (adopting the view of declarations as merely announcements, but also tying them to enhanced domestic war-fighting powers).
29. Locke, at 278.
30. Samuel Johnson, *Dictionary of the English Language* (1755) (Arno reprint 1979) (definition of "war").
31. Id. (definition of "declare").
32. 2 Burlamaqui, at 189.
33. That conclusion seems particularly true of the eighteenth century, as compared with earlier times when irregular bands operated with uncertain sovereign authority. Eighteenth-century warfare was principally conducted with regular, uniformed armies, which self-evidently operated as sovereign instruments. See Christopher Duffy, *The Military Experience in the Age of Reason* 14–18 (1987).
34. Locke, at 278.
35. Locke also said at another point that "a Criminal, who . . . hath by the unjust Violence and Slaughter he hath committed upon one, declared War against all Mankind . . ." Id. at 274.
36. 4 Blackstone, at 71.
37. The Maria Magdalena, 165 Eng. Rep. at 58.
38. Vattel, bk. III, §225.
39. Id., bk. II, §102.
40. Wolff, §734.
41. For example, Pacificus [Hamilton], No. 2, July 3, 1793, 15 *Papers of Hamilton*, at 57.

42. Professor Yoo argues that reading "declare" in this way is inconsistent with the text's two other references to war, which do not use the same word: Article I, §10 (states may not "engage" in war); and Article III, §3 (treason consists of "levying" war against the United States). Yoo, *Powers of War*, at 145–47. This argument seems flatly mistaken, although urged with great force. "Engage" and "levy" may mean roughly the same thing, but each is broader than "declare" or "commence"—and purposely so: states could not take part in war (unless authorized), and citizens committed treason by fighting against the United States, in each case regardless of how the war commenced. In neither place could the drafters have written "commence" (or "declare") and preserved the same meaning. See Michael Ramsey, "Book Review Essay: Toward a Rule of Law in Foreign Affairs," 106 *Colum. L. Rev.* 1450, 1463–64 (2006). A better argument is that, had the drafters meant "commence" in Article I, Section 8, they should have simply said so. We can, though, ascribe the awkwardness to Madison's proposing the language from the floor of the Convention, perhaps too hastily. The 1776 South Carolina constitution had apparently used "make war" to mean "commence war," and the Convention initially adopted this language; but delegates realized that "make war" could also include command decisions during war, which they wanted to leave to the President, and in casting around for another word, they unfortunately settled on "declare." See 2 *Records*, at 318–19.

43. Professor Yoo argues that the clause "prevented the president from unilaterally igniting a total war." *Powers of War*, at 104. This claim does not appear to have foundation in text or historical practice, though; the phrase "total war" does not occur in any of the political or international law writing of the time, and it is not clear that it was an eighteenth-century concept. To the extent Yoo is arguing that the President needs authorization to engage in domestic lawmaking in support of war efforts, see id. at 152–53, that is surely true, but that is a result of the scope of executive power, not a result of the declare-war clause.

44. See especially Yoo, *Powers of War*, at 30–54, 88–89.

45. 2 *Records*, at 168 (Committee of Detail draft). At least eight delegates spoke against presidential war-initiation power. 1 id., at 64–65 (Pinckney); id. at 65 (Rutledge); id. at 65–66 (Wilson); id. at 70 (Madison); id. at 292 (Hamilton); 2 id. at 318 (Sherman and Gerry); id. at 319 (Mason). At least two others heavily implied their opposition, id. at 319 (Ellsworth and King).

46. 3 Polybius, *The Histories*, bk. VI, §14 (W. R. Paton, trans., 1960) ("and what is most important of all, they [the popular assembly] deliberate on the question of war and peace"); Wolfgang Kunkel, *An Introduction to Roman Legal and Constitutional History* 9 (2d ed. 1973) ("The body of citizens which gave the state its name [*Populus Romanus*] was also, in the Republic at least, its supreme political organ. In its assembly . . . decisions were taken on war and peace, magistrates were chosen and statutes passed."). Roman historians give at least two prominent examples of the popular assembly debating initiation of war. Livy, *History of Rome*, bk. 31, §§6–8 (B. O. Foster, trans., 1997) (war

against Philip of Macedon); 1 Polybius, bk. I, §11 (204 B.C. war against Syracuse).

47. John Taylor, *A Summary of the Roman Law* 97 (1772) (Lawbook Exch. Repr. 2005) (Roman people "had a right" in "declaring war and peace"); 3 *Encyclopaedia Britannica* 577 (1st ed. 1771) (Roman senate alone could not "decide of war or peace" but was "obliged to consult the people").

48. Grotius, bk. III, ch. III, §10; Montesquieu, at 173–74; 1 John Adams, *A Defence of the Constitutions of the United States of America* 172–73 (1787) (De Capo Repr. 1971). On founding-era Americans' knowledge of and admiration for the Roman republic, see Chapter 7; and especially Federalist No. 34, at 226–27 (Hamilton) (describing structure of Roman government as "well-known" and observing that "the Roman republic attained to the pinnacle of human greatness").

49. 2 *Records,* at 318. The drafting records seem to suggest that the delegates were trying to distinguish between starting war and conducting war or defending against attack. Id. at 318–19. They are probably too fragmented to be much guide, however, and in any event reflect the view of only a few drafters. For an effort to read the drafting records in accord with presidential war power, see Yoo, *Powers of War,* at 97–102.

50. Federalist No. 69, at 398.

51. 4 *Debates in the Several State Conventions on the Adoption of the Federal Constitution* 107–8 (Jonathan Elliot, ed., 1836) (Iredell); id. at 287 (Pinckney).

52. 2 *Documentary History of the Ratification of the Constitution* 528 (Merrill Jensen et al., eds., 1976–present) (Wilson to Pa. convention).

53. Federalist No. 41, at 267.

54. As discussed, this was the view of a number of leading writers, including Hale, Bynkershoek, and Rutherforth. It was also the implicit view of at least two great military leaders, Gustavus Adolphus of Sweden and Frederick the Great of Prussia, who routinely waged wars in the seventeenth and eighteenth centuries without formal proclamations. See Maurice, at 22; 2 Bynkershoek, bk. I, ch. II.

55. Pacificus, No. 1, 15 *Papers of Hamilton,* at 42.

56. See Lofgren, at 678–88, 695 (finding it "plausible" to equate "declare" with "commence," based on the framers' commentary); adding the pre-1787 usage—as Lofgren did not—materially increases the argument's plausibility, as it shows that eighteenth-century usage actually did equate the two words.

57. For example, Fisher, at 17–37.

58. See Abraham Sofaer, *War, Foreign Affairs and Constitutional Power* 100–127 (1976). The five are (1) hostilities with native tribes on the southern and western borders; (2) pirates from Algiers seizing U.S. shipping; (3) the near-war between Britain and Spain arising from the so-called Nootka Sound incident; (4) the 1793 neutrality crisis; and (5) the 1798 naval war with France. On the Algiers matter, see Gerhard Casper, "An Essay in Separation of Powers: Some Early Versions and Practices," 30 *Wm. & Mary L. Rev.* 211, 242–53 (1989), and espe-

cially Jefferson's 1792 report, id. at 245. On the French naval war, see Dean Alfange, "The Quasi-war and Presidential Warmaking," in *The Constitution and the Conduct of American Foreign Policy* 274–90 (David Adler & Larry George, eds., 1996).

12. Beyond Declaring War

1. See Louis Henkin, *Foreign Affairs and the U.S. Constitution* 97–110 (2d ed. 1996); Louis Fisher, *Presidential War Powers* (2d ed. 2004); Abraham Sofaer, *War, Foreign Affairs and Constitution Power* (1976).
2. 2 *Records of the Federal Convention of 1787,* at 318 (Max Farrand, ed., 1966) (Madison). Sofaer, at 213, says this power was "universally held to be granted by the Framers."
3. See Fisher, at 8–.
4. Emmerich de Vattel, *The Law of Nations,* bk. III, §57 (1758) (Charles Fenwick, trans., J. B. Scott, ed., 1964); Christian Wolff, *Jus Gentium Methodo Scientifica Petractatum,* §713 (1749) (Joseph Drake trans., J. B. Scott, ed., 1964); see also 2 Jean Jacques Burlamaqui, *Principles of Natural and Politic Law* 187 (1727) (Arno reprint 1972) ("declaration takes place only in *offensive wars*"); Hugo Grotius, *De Jure Praede Commentarius* 96 (1604) (Gwladys Williams, trans., J. B. Scott, ed., 1964) ("any war undertaken for the necessary repulse of injury, is proclaimed not by a crier nor by a herald but by the voice of Nature herself").
5. The Maria Magdalena, 165 Eng. Rep. 57, 58 (1779); see also 1 Matthew Hale, *History of the Pleas of the Crown* 162 (1672) ("if a foreign prince invades our coasts, or sets upon the king's navy at sea, hereupon a real tho not solemn war may and hath formerly arisen, and therefore to prove a nation to be in enmity to England . . . there is no necessity of showing any war proclaimed").
6. Of course, this does not prevent Congress from issuing formal proclamations in response to attacks, as Congress has sometimes done. See Curtis Bradley & Jack Goldsmith, "Congressional Authorizations and the War on Terrorism," 118 *Harv. L. Rev.* 2047, 2072–78 (2005). Eighteenth-century nations sometimes issued formal proclamations in response to attacks, for rhetorical or informational purposes, and there should be no constitutional objection to this practice. These proclamations may be useful for non-constitutional purposes and may accompany wartime lawmaking measures that have important domestic legal effects. The question, though, is not how to describe Congress's acts, but how to describe the President's. The key is that if the President's military response does not "declare War," it does not require any prior act of Congress under the declare-war clause.
7. Pacificus, No. 1 (June 29, 1793), 15 *Papers of Alexander Hamilton* 38–40 (Harold Syrett, ed., 1961–1987); Thomas Jefferson, "Opinion on the Powers of the Senate" (Apr. 24, 1790), 16 *Papers of Thomas Jefferson* 378–79 (Julian Boyd et al., eds., 1950–2005).

8. Pacificus, No. 1, 15 *Papers of Hamilton*, at 438; Sofaer, at 116–27, 213.

9. Sofaer, at 209 (quoting Gallatin); United States v. Smith, 27 F. Cas. 1192, 1230 (C.C.D. N.Y. 1806) (Paterson); Madison to Monroe, Nov. 16, 1827, 8 *Letters and Other Writings of James Madison* 600 (J. B. Lippincott & Co., 1867).

10. 2 Burlamaqui, at 173–74; See Pacificus, No. 2 (July 3, 1793), 15 *Papers of Hamilton*, at 57; see also Vattel, bk. III, §5 ("He who takes up arms to repel the attack of an enemy, carries on a defensive war. He who is foremost in taking up arms . . . wages offensive war.").

11. 2 Burlamaqui, at 173–74 ("tak[ing] up arms" begins the war; "unjust acts . . . may kindle a war, and yet are not the war"—including "plundering of [another nation's] subjects"); Vattel, bk. III, §5 (offensive war includes punishment for injury, or attack to forestall a threatened danger); id., §97.

12. Wolff, §734; Vattel, bk. III, §§95–102.

13. Fisher, 169–72; Hearings before the Senate Committee on Armed Services, 101st Cong., 2d sess. 701 (1990) (testimony of then-Defense Secretary Richard Cheney).

14. See 2 Burlamaqui, at 173–74 (making this distinction).

15. A similar analysis would reject claims that President Truman had unilateral power to send U.S. troops to defend South Korea.

16. For example, Michael Paulsen, "Youngstown Goes to War," 19 *Const. Comment.* 215, 239 (2002); William Bradford, "The Duty to Defend Them: A Natural Law Justification for the Bush Doctrine of Preventive War," 79 *N.D. L. Rev.* 1365, 1440–46 (2004).

17. Madison, for example, referred only to sudden attacks, not to threats. 2 *Records,* at 318. Presumably the President has as much preemptive power as the states do under Article I, §10: to counter "such imminent danger as will not admit of delay"—but that is true, we may suppose, because the opposing "danger" already amounts to a declaration of war, which would describe only extremely imminent threats, or ones formally declared by the opposing side.

18. Richard Lee, *A Treatise of Captures in War* 47 (1760). See also 2 Burlamaqui, at 173–74; Vattel, bk. III, §§5, 137–39.

19. Sofaer, at 119–24; Fisher, at 17–32; David Currie, *The Constitution in Congress: The Federalist Period* 239–53 (1997); Alexander de Conde, *The Quasi-War* 100–108 (1966).

20. See Sofaer, at 208–24; Gary Schmitt, "Thomas Jefferson and the Presidency," in *Inventing the American Presidency* 326, 336–37 (Thomas Cronin, ed., 1989); Montgomery Kosma, "Our First Real War," 2 *Green Bag* 169 (1999).

21. "The Examination," No. 1, 25 *Papers of Hamilton*, at 455–56.

22. Kosma, at 171 (cabinet meeting advice, over Levi Lincoln's dissent, that "the Captains may be authorized, if war exists, to search for and destroy the enemy's vessels, wherever they can find them"). See Sofaer, at 212–13; Jefferson Powell, *The President's Authority over Foreign Affairs* 91–93 (2002). Jefferson's orders to naval commander Richard Dale directed that if "the Barbary powers have declared war against the United States" he should respond "by sinking, burning,

or destroying their ships and vessels wherever you shall find them." Smith to Dale, May 20, 1801, 2 *American State Papers* 359 (Joseph Gales, ed., 1832–1861).

23. See Sofaer, at 212–13; Powell, at 92–93. Contrary founding-era evidence may be less weighty than at first appears. With respect to Adams, the French attacks were mainly on private shipping and so may not have created a state of war; once Congress acted to authorize limited war in response, that authorization prevented the President from going further. Washington's hesitation in taking the offensive may have arisen as much from U.S. military weakness and statutory and financial limitations as from constitutional concerns.

24. As Truman did. See Louis Fisher, "Truman in Korea," in *The Constitution and the Conduct of American Foreign Policy* 320, 327 (David Adler & Larry George, eds., 1996).

25. See Henkin, at 99–101; Powell, at 122; "Deployment of United States Armed Forces into Haiti," 18 Op. Off. Legal Consel 173 (1994). For a more expansive claim, see John Yoo, *The Powers of War and Peace* 104 (2005) (arguing, without much textual grounding, that the declare-war clause only prevents the President from beginning a "total war").

26. Samuel Johnson, *Dictionary of the English Language* (1755) (Arno reprint 1979) (definition of "war").

27. Thomas Rutherforth, *Institutes of Natural Law* 470 (1754); Lee, at 1; Cornelius van Bynkershoek, *Quaestionum Juris Publici* 15 (1737) (Tenney Frank, trans., J. B. Scott, ed., 1964); Vattel, bk. III, §1–2; 2 Burlamaqui, at 157; Wolff, §180; see also 3 *Encyclopedia Britannica* 933 (1st ed. 1771) (war is "a contest or difference between princes, state, or large bodies of people . . . referred to the decision of the sword").

28. 2 Burlamaqui, at 180.

29. The most obvious example to Americans, of course, was the American Revolution, in which Britain and France spoke of being at war with each other but engaged in limited hostilities and went some time without formal declarations of war. See J. F. Maurice, *Hostilities without Declaration of War* 24–25 (1883).

30. See Bas. v. Tingy, 4 U.S. 37, 43, 45 (1800); 1 Op. Att'y Gen. 85 (1798) (Lee) ("maritime war").

31. For example, President Clinton deployed troops to Bosnia in the mid-1990s, and some members of Congress argued that congressional approval was required. See Lori Damrosch, "The Clinton Administration and War Powers," 63 *L. & Contemp. Prob.* 125, 135–36 (2002). Professor Damrosch, at 135 n.58, says the deployment was constitutional "on the ground that the troops were not expected to become involved in hostilities." As a textual matter, the relevant question was whether the deployment amounted to a declaration of war—which it did not, as it was approved by all contending forces.

32. For example, U.S. General Pershing pursued the revolutionary general Pancho Villa in northern Mexico after Villa's raid on Columbus, New Mexico, in 1916. See Francis Wormuth & Edwin Firmage, *To Chain the Dog of War* 130–31 (2d

ed. 1989). This action was not textually problematic, because it was not a use of force against Mexico; it was a use of force against Villa, but it was "defensive" (in the eighteenth-century sense) because Villa attacked the United States, and thus it did not require congressional approval.

33. See 2 Burlamaqui, at 163, 173–74; Wolff, §§640–41; Vattel, bk. III, §42–46.

34. Fisher, at 29–34; *Congressional Globe*, 30th Cong., 1st Sess. 95 (Jan. 3, 1848); see id. at 779–80; id. app. at 93–95 (Lincoln). The final form of Congress's resolution recognized that "by the act of the Republic of Mexico a state of war exists," Act of May 13, 1846, 9 Stat. 9—a view consistent with Polk's understanding and with eighteenth-century terms.

35. See John Yoo, "The Continuation of Politics by Other Means: The Original Understanding of War Powers," 84 *Cal. L. Rev.* 167, 197–217 (1996). Yoo emphasizes that Congress also has impeachment power. That is, of course, more difficult to employ, and unlike impeachment, funding requires an affirmative act of Congress to continue the war, rather than an affirmative act to stop it.

36. Powell, at 115.

37. As discussed in Chapter 11, the Convention changed an earlier draft giving Congress the power to "make" war to the present "declare war." Massachusetts delegate King explained that the "make war" phrasing might encompass the power to "conduct" war once hostilities began, which, he said, was "an executive function." 2 *Records*, at 318–19. See Paulsen, at 239.

38. 1 William Blackstone, *Commentaries on the Laws of England* 254–55 (1765).

39. 12 U.S. 110 (1814).

40. Id. at 123–24. Debate over U.S. actions in the post-2001 war on terrorism has sometimes lost sight of this distinction. Of course, many of the President's arguments rest on Congress's authorization. See Bradley & Goldsmith, at 2083–2127; Hamdi v. Rumsfeld, 542 U.S. 507 (2004); Hamdan v. Rumsfeld, 126 S.Ct. 2749 (2006). But to the extent President Bush or his advisors claimed independent power to respond to terrorist attacks, we should see that they stand on much stronger textual ground for international acts than for domestic acts. Power to seize and hold prisoners or to establish military commissions in foreign conflicts, for example, seems well supported by the general idea of executive power and by specific eighteenth-century practice and understandings; power to seize and hold prisoners (especially U.S. citizens) within the United States seems textually more difficult to defend. Compare John Yoo, "Transferring Terrorists," 79 *N.D. L. Rev.* 1183 (2004) (President's power to act outside the United States) with Padilla v. Hanft, 423 F. 3d 386 (4th Cir. 2005) (President's power to detain U.S. citizen within the United States).

41. Paulsen, at 239. Although Congress has in the past included, along with its formal declarations, an "authorization" for the President to use force, see Bradley & Goldsmith, at 2072–78, these seem constitutionally unnecessary, at least for "executive" actions outside the United States.

42. Michael Ramsey, "Presidential Declarations of War," 37 *U.C. Davis L. Rev.* 321, 326–35 (2003); John Ely, *War and Responsibility* 15–26 (1993).

43. For leading exceptions, see J. Gregory Sidak, "To Declare War," 41 *Duke L.J.* 27 (1991); Brien Hallett, *The Lost Art of Declaring War* (1998). See also Wormuth & Firmage, at 197–217.

44. For an elaboration of this argument, see Ramsey, "Presidential Declarations," at 335–57. For the Iraq resolution, see 116 Stat. 1498 (2002) ("The President is authorized to use the Armed Forces of the United States as he determines to be necessary and appropriate in order to . . . defend the national security of the United States against the continuing threat posed by Iraq.").

45. For a range of historical views on the nondelegation doctrine generally, see Eric Posner & Adrian Vermeule, "Interring the Nondelegation Doctrine," 69 *U. Chi. L. Rev.* 1721 (2002); Larry Alexander & Saikrishna Prakash, "Reports of the Nondelegation Doctrine's Death Are Greatly Exaggerated," 70 *U. Chi. L. Rev.* 1297 (2003); Gary Lawson, "Delegation and the Original Meaning," 88 *Va. L. Rev.* 327 (2002).

46. 8 *Annals of Congress* 1638 (Joseph Gales, ed., 1834) (Rep. Brent); Dean Alfange, "The Quasi-War and Presidential Warmaking," in Adler & George, eds., at 274, 275–76; Currie, at 239–53; see 1 Stat. 561, 572, 578–80.

47. 5 U.S. 1, 28 (1801); see also Bas v. Tingy, 4 U.S. 37 (1800); Little v. Barreme, 6 U.S. 170 (1804).

48. Louis Fisher, "The Barbary Wars: Legal Precedent for Invading Haiti?" in Adler & George, eds., at 316–17; Act of Mar. 3, 1815, 3 Stat. 230.

49. See Currie, at 239–52; see also Act of June 4, 1794, 1 Stat. 372 (delegating embargo power). Michael Rappaport persuasively argues that under English law some matters (including foreign affairs) were more easily delegable to the monarch, and that this practice supports a corresponding rule in U.S. law. "The Selective Nondelegation Doctrine and the Line Item Veto," 76 *Tul. L. Rev.* 265, 320–40 (2001).

50. Paulsen, at 239.

51. Memorandum from Jay Bybee to Alberto Gonzales, quoted in Michael Ramsey, "Torturing Executive Power," 93 *Georgetown L.J.* 1213, 1239 (2005). The laws in question were the Torture Act and the War Crimes Act, 18 U.S.C. §§2441 *et seq.,* and 18 U.S.C. §§ 2340–2341A. Specifically, the War Crimes Act criminalizes "grave breaches" of the Geneva Conventions, a set of international treaties governing, among other things, treatment of wartime captives; the Torture Act prohibits the use of torture by U.S. persons.

52. United States v. Swaim, 165 U.S. 553, 557–58 (1897); United States v. Eliason, 11 U.S. 291 (1842).

53. See David McCullough, *1776* (2005); Glen Phelps, *George Washington and American Constitutionalism* 142–44 (1993).

54. Federalist No. 74, in James Madison, Alexander Hamilton, & John Jay, *The Federalist Papers* 422 (Isaac Kramnick, ed., 1987).

55. Federalist No. 73, at 418.

56. Act of April 30, 1790, 1 Stat. 119, 121.

57. Currie, at 239–48; De Conde, at 105–8.

58. 6 U.S. 170, 177–79 (1804); see also Bas v. Tingy, 4 U.S. 37 (1800) (acknowledging Congress's ability to regulate a limited war).

13. Can States Have Foreign Policies?

1. Barry Friedman, "Valuing Federalism," 82 *Minn. L. Rev.* 317 (1997). Portions of this chapter draw from Michael Ramsey, "The Power of the States in Foreign Affairs: The Original Understanding of Foreign Policy Federalism," 75 *N.D. L. Rev.* 341 (1999).
2. For convenience, this chapter refers to "state" laws and activities affecting foreign affairs, although meaning also to include activities of local governments.
3. See Ramsey, at 343 & authorities cited nn.4–8.
4. For example, as Chapter 14 discusses, the Supreme Court invalidated Massachusetts's Burma legislation as conflicting with federal law. Crosby v. National Foreign Trade Council, 530 U.S. 363 (2000).
5. 389 U.S. 429, 432 (1968).
6. Id. at 437–38 & nn.7–8.
7. Id. at 435.
8. Id. at 440. Douglas distinguished a similar case, Clark v. Allen, 331 U.S. 503 (1947), where foreign policy effects had not been so evident.
9. 92 U.S. 275, 279–80 (1875).
10. 130 U.S. 581, 605–6 (1889).
11. 312 U.S. 52, 63 (1941).
12. Harold Meier, "Preemption of State Law: A Recommended Analysis," 83 *Am. J. Int'l L.* 832, 835 (1989).
13. Hines, 312 U.S. at 69–75.
14. As Louis Henkin observed: "This was new constitutional doctrine. . . . Here there was no relevant exercise of federal power. . . . The Court told us that the Constitution itself excludes such state intrusions even when the federal branches have not acted." *Foreign Affairs and the U.S. Constitution* 163–64 (2d ed. 1996).
15. Id. at 165 n.**.
16. The "consensus" view, Professor Meier has said, agrees that "the central government alone may directly exercise power in foreign affairs." Maier, at 832–33. For further discussion and a partial defense, see Carlos Vazquez, "W(h)ither Zschernig?" 46 *Vill. L. Rev.* 1259, 1262–66, 1304–24 (2001).
17. See Richard Bilder, "The Role of Cities and States in Foreign Relations," 83 *Am. J. Int'l L.* 821, 827 (1989): "[T]he vital national interest in the effective and efficient achievement of U.S. foreign relations objectives requires that other nations perceive our foreign policy as unified and coherent. . . . Consequently, state and local involvement in international issues, particularly if not in accord with administration policy, may undermine the conduct of U.S. foreign relations and the credibility of our negotiating posture by conveying the appearance of disagreement, confusion, uncertainty and weakness in our Government's stated foreign policy positions."

18. David Schmahmann & James Finch, "The Unconstitutionality of State and Local Enactments in the United States Restricting Business Ties with Burma (Myanmar)," 30 *Vand. J. Trans. L.* 175, 204 (1997).

19. Peter Spiro, "Foreign Relations Federalism," 70 *U. Colo. L. Rev.* 1223, 1228–29 (1999).

20. Bradford Clark, "Federal Common Law: A Structural Reinterpretation," 144 *U. Pa. L. Rev.* 1245, 1295–97 (1996). For a leading contrary view, see Jack Goldsmith, "Federal Courts, Foreign Affairs, and Federalism," 83 *Va. L. Rev.* 1617 (1997).

21. Bilder, at 830.

22. Howard Fenton, "The Fallacy of Federalism in Foreign Affairs," 13 *Nw. J. Int'l L. & Bus.* 563, 588 (1993); Bilder, at 821. See also Clark, at 1297 ("The founders were aware that the states' exercise of concurrent authority over matters touching on 'external sovereignty' would be incompatible with the conduct of foreign affairs," citing Hamilton's Federalist No. 80).

23. M. J. C. Vile, *The Structure of American Federalism* 194–95 (1961). See also Ernest Young, "Dual Federalism, Concurrent Jurisdiction and the Foreign Affairs Exception," 69 *G. Wash. L. Rev.* 139, 188 (2001).

24. Some commentators, notably Spiro, at 1228–29, suggest that because Article I, §10 excludes states from core foreign affairs powers, it implies a comprehensive ban (since it covers everything the framers thought important). Among other things, though, state treatment of foreign citizens was an enormous issue in the eighteenth century and is not implicated by Article I, Section 10 (nor, directly, by anything else in the Constitution's text).

25. See especially Frederick Marks, *Independence on Trial* 142–66 (1973).

26. See Federalist No. 44, in James Madison, Alexander Hamilton, & John Jay, *The Federalist Papers* 286–92 (Isaac Kramnick, ed., 1987).

27. See Caleb Nelson, "Preemption," 86 *Va. L. Rev.* 225, 232–60 (2000). As discussed, this is the basis of many of the Court's state foreign affairs decisions, including *Hines* and *Crosby*.

28. One of the Supreme Court's early cases, Ware v. Hylton (discussed in Chapter 14), addressed the long-running problem of state non-compliance with the 1783 peace treaty with Britain, confirming that the treaty preempted non-complying state laws under Article VI. 3 U.S. 199 (1796).

29. See Goldsmith, at 1644–45.

30. See Barclays Bank v. Franchise Tax Board, 512 U.S. 298, 336–30 (1994) (where a state's method of taxing multinational corporations produced furious diplomatic objections).

31. On this basis, one leading commentator argues that leaving preemption decisions to Congress is the best rule as a matter of policy, as well as the one reflected in the Constitution's text. Goldsmith, at 1690–98.

32. Federalist No. 42, at 273.

33. Federalist No. 41, at 266; Federalist No. 42, at 273.

34. Federalist No. 80, at 446.

35. Id. at 445, 446.

36. 1 *Records of the Federal Convention of 1787*, at 316 (Max Farrand, ed., 1966).

37. Jefferson to Madison, Oct. 8, 1786, 8 *Papers of James Madison* 486 (William Hutchinson et al., eds., 1962–1991). See also Jefferson to Carrington, Aug. 14, 1787, 12 *Papers of Thomas Jefferson* 424 (Julian Boyd et al., eds., 1950–2005) (urging need to "make the states one as to every thing connected with foreign nations").

38. Goldsmith, at 1642.

39. Philadelphia v. New Jersey, 437 U.S. 617 (1978) (facial discrimination); Hunt v. Washington State Apple Advertising Comm'n, 432 U.S. 333 (1977) (discrimination in effect); Pike v. Bruce Church Inc., 397 U.S. 137 (1970) (undue burden). On the doctrine in general see Boris Bittker, *The Regulation of Interstate and Foreign Commerce*, §§6.01–06 (1999 & supp. 2004). On its early history, see David Currie, *The Constitution in the Supreme Court: The First Hundred Years* 222–36 (1985).

40. For some sharp criticisms, see Camps Newfound/Owatonna Inc. v. Harrison, 520 U.S. 564, 610 (1997) (Thomas, dissenting); Tyler Pipe Industries Inc. v. Washington State Dep't of Revenue, 483 U.S. 232, 259–65 (1987) (Scalia, dissenting); Martin Redish & Shane Nugent, "The Dormant Commerce Clause and the Constitutional Balance of Federalism," 1987 *Duke L.J.* 569, 573. For a historical defense, see Brannon Denning, "Confederation-Era Discrimination against Interstate Commerce and the Legitimacy of the Dormant Commerce Clause Doctrine," 94 *Ky. L.J.* 37 (2005).

41. For example, *Zschernig*'s inheritance law likely would not fall under the dormant commerce clause, but presumably the national government had power to make a treaty with East Germany allowing or disallowing inheritances. See Chapter 15.

42. Federalist No. 32, at 220.

43. Hamilton was responding to anti-federalist claims that the Constitution contained broader negative implications. 2 *Debates in the Several State Conventions on the Adoption of the Federal Constitution* 332 (Jonathan Elliot, ed., 1836) (Smith to N.Y. convention); id. at 355 (Hamilton to N.Y. convention).

44. For the argument that the national government's treaty power contains a dormant preclusion similar to the one claimed in *Zschernig*, see Edward Swaine, "Negotiating Federalism: State Bargaining and the Dormant Treaty Power," 49 *Duke L.J.* 1127 (2000).

45. Federalist No. 32, at 221–22. Even worse for *Zschernig*'s proponents, Federalist No. 32 thinks it obvious that Article I, Section 10's restriction on state tariffs is not superfluous, yet tariffs surely seem an "intrusion" into foreign affairs.

46. Id. at 220–21.

47. Id. at 222.

48. 10 *Documentary History of the Ratification of the Constitution* 1307 (Merrill Jensen et al., eds., 1976–present) (Marshall to Va. convention); id. at 1280 (Nicholas to Va. convention).

49. 2 *Records*, at 187 (Committee Report); id. at 358–63 (exports); id. at 440–41 (embargoes); id. at 624–26 (tonnage duties).

50. Id. at 440–41.

51. As suggested in Spiro, at 1228–29.
52. See Goldsmith, at 1649–58 (discussing in particular extradition, immigration, and regulation of aliens); Ramsey, at 418–28 (recounting absence of *Zschernig*-like arguments in key legal disputes of the early nineteenth century).
53. 92 U.S. at 279–80. The strongest claim for anything like a *Zschernig* rule comes from Chief Justice Taney's opinion in Holmes v. Jennison, 39 U.S. 540 (1840). The case involved a state's attempt at extradition, and Taney, writing for four of eight Justices, said the state was constitutionally precluded—in part because extradition involved (he said) an agreement with a foreign nation, barred by Article I, Section 10, but also apparently because he thought states were (for no obvious textual reason) barred from foreign affairs activity in general. One hesitates to claim Taney as a reliable indicator of original meaning, though, and the weight of nineteenth-century opinion and practice is to the contrary.
54. Goldsmith, at 1690–97.

14. States versus the President

1. 539 U.S. 396 (2003). This chapter draws on Brannon Denning & Michael Ramsey, "American Insurance Association v. Garamendi and Executive Preemption in Foreign Affairs," 46 *Wm. & Mary L. Rev.* 825 (2004).
2. Holocaust Victim Insurance Relief Act, Cal. Ins. Code 13800–13807. California enacted several other laws intended to assist claimants, although these were not the focus of the litigation. On the factual background, see Hearing before the House Gov't Reform Subcomm., 107th Cong. (2002).
3. In particular, the law required disclosure of all policies issued in the Holocaust era, not just those issued to Holocaust victims, which likely would have encompassed millions of policies.
4. The negotiations are recounted by one of the chief U.S. negotiators in Stuart Eizenstat, *Imperfect Justice* (2003). See also Ronald Bettauer, "The Role of the United States Government in Recent Holocaust Claims Resolution," 20 *Berkeley J. Int'l L.* 1 (2002).
5. 539 U.S. at 427.
6. The insurers made several other arguments, invoking the dormant preemption principles discussed in Chapter 13, as well as the due process and equal protection clauses of the Fourteenth Amendment. See Gerling Global Reinsurance Corp. v. Low, 296 F.3d 832 (9th Cir. 2002) (rejecting these claims). The Supreme Court addressed only executive preemption.
7. Jack Rakove, *Original Meanings* 171–77 (1997); Caleb Nelson, "Preemption," 86 *Va. L. Rev.* 225, 235–60 (2000).
8. Modern doctrine uses the term "preemption" to describe a federal law or treaty's superiority over conflicting state law. The term was not part of the founding era's legal vocabulary, but it captures the concept Article VI embodies. See Nelson, at 225–32.
9. 530 U.S. 363 (2000). See Jack Goldsmith, "Statutory Foreign Affairs Preemp-

tion," 2000 *Supr. Ct. Rev.* 175. Although some academic commentators found the case difficult, see Denning & Ramsey, at 846 n.75 (citing authorities), their concern arose from the statute's lack of clarity, not Congress's lack of power. But see 530 U.S. at 388–91 (Scalia, concurring) (finding statute clear on its face).

10. As chapter 10 discusses, Congress has power to pass laws to carry into execution powers granted elsewhere in the Constitution. Treatymaking power is granted elsewhere (Article II, Section 2); laws bringing the United States into compliance with its treaties seem "necessary and proper" to "carry into Execution" the treatymaking power, as it would be quite difficult to make treaties if the nation were unable to ensure compliance (a matter pointed up starkly under the Articles). But see Nicholas Rosenkranz, "Executing the Treaty Power," 118 *Harv. L. Rev.* 1867 (2005) (arguing the contrary).

11. As discussed (Chapter 8), the Court recognizes some so-called non-self-executing treaties that do not take automatic effect, despite Article VI; these, of course, are not preemptive.

12. 3 U.S. 199 (1796). *Ware* is a difficult case to read, as there is no opinion of the Court; rather, each of the five Justices delivered a separate opinion. All four in the majority put the matter squarely on Article VI, and Iredell, who dissented, made clear that he thought treaties preempted conflicting state law under Article VI: he merely thought the law and the treaty, for technical reasons, did not conflict. Id. at 235–45 (Chase), 249–55 (Paterson), 271–81 (Iredell), 281 (Wilson), 284 (Cushing).

13. Nelson, at 234 ("As the Supreme Court and virtually all commentators have acknowledged, the Supremacy Clause is the reason that valid federal laws trump state law . . . It requires courts to ignore state law if (but only if) state law contradicts a valid rule established by federal law, so that applying the states law would entail disregarding the valid federal law.").

14. On the clause's exclusion of unconstitutional statutes, see 2 *Documentary History of the Ratification of the Constitution* 416–17 (Merrill Jensen et al., eds., 1976–present) (McKean to Pa. convention) ("The meaning which appears to be plain and well expressed is simply this, that Congress have the power of making laws upon any subject over which the proposed plan gives them a jurisdiction, and that those laws, thus made in pursuance of the Constitution, shall be binding on the states."); Federalist No. 33 (Hamilton), in James Madison, Alexander Hamilton, & John Jay, *The Federalist Papers* 225 (Isaac Kramnick, ed., 1987) ("But it will not follow . . . that acts of the [federal government] which are *not pursuant* to its constitutional powers, but which are invasions of the residuary authorities of the [states], will become the supreme law of the land. These will be merely acts of usurpation, and will deserve to be treated as such."); 4 *Debates in the Several State Conventions on the Adoption of the Federal Constitution* 188 (Jonathan Elliot, ed., 1836) (Johnston to N.C. convention) (explaining that Article VI would only apply to laws made in pursuance of the Constitution, and laws "repugnant" to the Constitution would not be pursuant to it). For academic debate and response, see Bradford Clark, "The Supremacy Clause as a

Constraint on Federal Power," 71 *Geo. Wash. L. Rev.* 91, 115–19 (2003). On the clause's exclusion of unconstitutional treaties, see Chapter 15.

15. Acknowledging this point, the new Congress quickly re-passed key ordinances of the old Congress, including the Articles of War and the Northwest Ordinance (Act of Aug. 7, 1789, 1 Stat. 50–53).

16. See John McGinnis & Michael Rappaport, *Our Supermajoritarian Constitution*, 80 *Tex. L. Rev.* 703 (2002).

17. Under the original Constitution (Article I, § 3) the Senate "shall be composed of two Senators from each state, chosen by the Legislatures thereof." As Chapter 15 discusses, the Seventeenth Amendment (1913) changed this to require popular election of Senators.

18. This analysis leans heavily on Bradford Clark's important article "Separation of Powers as a Safeguard of Federalism," 79 *Tex. L. Rev.* 1321 (2001). See also Clark, "Supremacy Clause," at 105–19; Nelson, at 225–52.

19. See Immigration and Naturalization Service v. Chadha, 462 U.S. 919, 956–58 (1983) ("legislative veto" passed only by the House and not presented to the President lacked legal effect).

20. 2002 Hearing, at 12–18 (statement of Rep. Waxman); Brief of Amici Curiae Rep. Henry Waxman and 51 Other Members of Congress, filed in Garamendi, 539 U.S. 396 (2003).

21. Hearing before the House Comm. on Banking and Fin. Servs., 105th Cong. (1998). Congress passed, in 1998, the U.S. Holocaust Assets Commission Act, 112 Stat. 611, which if anything seemed to endorse the states' position, but it was sufficiently ambiguous that it did not play a central role in the litigation.

22. See Carlos Vazquez, "W(h)ither Zschernig?" 46 *Vill. L. Rev.* 1259, 1316–17 (2001) (suggesting that *Zschernig* should be applied only to state laws singling out foreign governments for adverse comment or treatment).

23. In *Zschernig* the President indicated that the law did not unduly interfere with national foreign policy. For executive branch letters urging California to rethink its position, see Denning & Ramsey, at 842 & n.59.

24. The dispute occurred across two administrations but because their policies did not materially differ, the ensuing discussion refers generically to policies of "the President."

25. 512 U.S. 298, 326–30 (1994). Justice Ruth Bader Ginsburg wrote for the Court that arguments that the law was "unconstitutional because it [was] likely to provoke retaliatory action by foreign governments" were "directed to the wrong forum" and elaborated "that the Executive Branch proposed legislation to outlaw a state taxation practice, but encountered an unreceptive Congress, is not evidence that the practice interfered with the Nation's ability to speak with one voice, but is rather evidence that the preeminent speaker decided to yield the floor to others." Id. at 327–28, 329.

26. 523 U.S. 371 (1998). As the U.S. brief, at 49–51, conceded: "The measures at the United States' disposal under our Constitution may in some cases include only persuasion—such as the Secretary of State's request to the Governor of Vir-

ginia to stay Breard's execution—and not legal compulsion through the judicial system. That is the case here." See "Agora: Breard," 92 *Am. J. Int'l L.* 666, 672 (1998). *Breard* is a complex case, because Breard claimed rights under an apparently self-executing treaty, the Vienna Convention on Consular Relations, but his claim was procedurally defaulted under state and federal law. See id. at 666–73; Curtis Bradley, "Breard, Our Dualist Constitution, and the Internationalist Conception," 51 *Stan. L. Rev.* 529 (1999). The Supreme Court appeared to assume (perhaps wrongly) that the state was under no Article VI duty to give Breard a remedy. See Carlos Vazquez, "Breard and the Federal Power to Require Compliance with ICJ Orders of Provisional Measures," 92 *Amer. J. Int'l L.* 683 (1998).

27. 539 U.S. at 428. On the attempted tie to *Crosby,* see id. at 423 ("The situation created by the California legislation calls to mind the impact of the Massachusetts Burma law. . . .").

28. One who denies a substantive Article II, Section 1 power (see Chapter 6) would seem to face serious problems locating any presidential power to facilitate a Holocaust settlement. The President did not act with congressional authorization, nor in anticipation of making a treaty, nor through his power to receive foreign ambassadors, nor through his shared appointment power.

29. Youngstown Sheet & Tube v. Sawyer, 343 U.S. 579 (1952).

30. "Letters from the Federal Farmer to the Republican," IV, Oct. 12, 1787, 14 *Documentary History,* at 43; Brutus, II, Nov. 1, 1787, 14 id., at 529. See also 4 *Debates,* at 215 (Lancaster to N.C. convention) (Article VI would "repeal the laws of different states" where inconsistent with treaties); 10 *Documentary History,* at 1381–85 (Henry to Va. convention) (opposing Article VI because treaties should not be superior to state laws); Old Whig, III, 13 id., at 426 (similar); Rakove, at 171–77. On the anti-federalist attack on the treaty power, see John Yoo, "Globalism and the Constitution: Treaties, Non-Self-Execution and the Original Understanding," 99 *Colum. L. Rev.* 1955, 2040–2073 (1999).

31. This is all the more remarkable because a separate line of anti-federalist attack was that the President was not subject to enough checks and would become a king. See 9 *Documentary History,* at 963–64 (Henry to Va. convention).

32. 3 U.S. at 236–37 (Chase) (it is "apparent on a view of this 6th Article of the National Constitution . . . that the Constitution, or laws, of any of the States so far as either of them shall be found contrary to that treaty are by force of the said article, prostrated before the treaty"); id. at 282 (Cushing) (treaty had been "sanctioned, in all its parts, by the Constitution of the United States, as the supreme law of the land"); id. at 277 (Iredell) (supremacy clause "extends to subsisting as well as to future treaties. I consider, therefore, that when this constitution was ratified, the case as to the treaty in question stood upon the same footing, as if every act constituting an impediment to a creditor's recovery has been expressly repealed"). Later cases contain similar commentary. United States v. The Schooner Peggy, 5 U.S. 103, 109 (1801) (Marshall) ("The constitution of the United States declares a treaty to be the supreme law of the land. Of consequence its obligation on the courts of the United States must be admitted."); Chirac v.

Chirac, 15 U.S. 259, 270–71 (1817) (Marshall) (1778 treaty with France bound states through Article VI).

33. 3 U.S. at 282.

34. See id. at 207–20 (arguments of counsel); id. at 265–66 (Iredell).

35. See Jack Goldsmith, "Federal Courts, Foreign Affairs, and Federalism," 83 *Va. L. Rev.* 1617, 1649–58 (1997) (recounting history).

36. 539 U.S. at 419–23. Harlan in *Zschernig* argued that "in the absence of a conflicting federal policy or violation of the express mandates of the Constitution the States may legislate in areas of their traditional competence even though their statutes may have an incidental effect on foreign relations." In context, it seems clear that Harlan meant "in the absence of a conflicting federal policy" reflected in a treaty or statute, since all the cases he cited involved statutory or treaty preemption. 389 U.S. at 458–59 & n.25.

37. 487 U.S. 500 (1987). See Bradford Clark, "Federal Common Law: A Structural Reinterpretation," 144 *U. Pa. L. Rev.* 1245, 1368–76 (1996); Ramsey, at 395–96.

38. Federalist No. 32, at 220–21.

39. See especially Clark, "Separation of Powers."

40. In particular, the presidential settlement contained no resolution of the documentation issue, leaving many claimants unable to pursue recovery. Denning & Ramsey, at 903.

41. 539 U.S. at 430–33; Denning & Ramsey, at 899–900. The ensuing discussion draws on Michael Ramsey, "Executive Agreements and the (Non)Treaty Power," 77 *N.C. L. Rev.* 133 (1998). See also David Sloss, "International Agreements and the Political Safeguards of Federalism," 55 *Stan. L. Rev.* 1963 (2003).

42. United States v. Pink, 315 U.S. 203 (1942); United States v. Belmont, 301 U.S. 324 (1937). The Court also appeared to uphold a preemptive executive agreement in Dames & Moore v. Regan, 453 U.S. 654 (1981), although its reasoning invoked implicit congressional authorization, which was not present in *Garamendi* and is difficult to square with Article VI. See Chapter 10.

43. 301 U.S. at 331–32; id. at 330–31.

44. Assuming that the drafters had in mind two categories (treaties and other agreements), as seems likely from Article I, § 10, there appears no reason that they could not have simply written Article VI to say "treaties and other agreements made under the authority of the United States." The failure to do so strongly indicates that the omission was intentional. This view is further confirmed by Article III, §2, which gives federal courts jurisdiction over cases arising under treaties, but not "other agreements." That makes sense if other agreements do not have domestic legal effect. If they do, it presents a puzzle: either the drafters failed to give federal remedies for violations of executive agreements, even though they gave such remedies for treaties, or else they made the same mistake in Article III as they did in Article VI, saying "treaties" when they meant "treaties and other agreements." The reading that makes all of the document's uses of the same word mean the same thing, and gives federal courts jurisdiction

over international agreements to the extent that they form part of supreme law, seems preferable.

45. Ramsey, "Executive Agreements," at 173–83, 229–31.
46. Louis Henkin, *Foreign Affairs and the U.S. Constitution* 222 (2d ed. 1996).

15. *Missouri v. Holland* and the Seventeenth Amendment

1. 252 U.S. 416 (1920).
2. Federalist No. 45, in James Madison, Alexander Hamilton, & John Jay, *The Federalist Papers* 296 (Isaac Kramnick, ed., 1987).
3. Gary Lawson & Guy Seidman, "The Jeffersonian Treaty Clause," 2006 *U. Ill. L. Rev.* 1, 57. See also Curtis Bradley, "The Treaty Power and American Federalism," 97 *Mich. L. Rev.* 391, 417 (1998) ("Without subject matter limitations on the treaty power, the federal government would have essentially unrestricted authority vis-a-vis the states, thereby contradicting one of the core assumptions of the Founders."). The principal critique from *Holland*'s time is Henry Tucker, *Limitations on the Treaty-Making Power* (1915). A distinct but important challenge is Nicholas Rosenkranz, "Executing the Treaty Power," 118 *Harv. L. Rev.* 1867 (2005) (arguing on textual grounds that Congress cannot implement treaties beyond its enumerated powers).

   The most comprehensive historical defense of *Holland*, to which this chapter is much indebted, is David Golove, "Treaty-Making and the Nation: The Historical Foundations of the Nationalist Conception of the Treaty Power," 98 *Mich. L. Rev.* 1075 (2000). For other important defenses, see Martin Flaherty, "Are We to Be a Nation? Federal Power and States Rights in Foreign Affairs," 70 *Colo. L. Rev.* 1277, 1297–1316 (1999); Gerald Neuman, "The Global Dimension of RFRA," 14 *Const. Comment.* 33, 46–49 (1997); Carlos Vazquez, "Breard, Printz, and the Treaty Power," 70 *U. Colo. L. Rev.* 1317, 1337–43 (1999); Louis Henkin, *Foreign Affairs and the U.S. Constitution* 190–93 (2d ed. 1996).
4. 252 U.S. at 433–34.
5. Cato [Robert Livingston], "Observations on Mr. Jay's Treaty," No. XVI, in 3 *The American Remembrancer* 63–64 (Matthew Carey, ed., 1795). Golove, at 1165, calls the Cato essays "among the most influential and most elaborately reasoned" of the time. Jefferson's view tracked Livingston's. Thomas Jefferson, "Manual of Parliamentary Practice," §52 (1801), in *Jefferson's Parliamentary Writings* 353, 420–21 (Wilbur Howell, ed. 1988); Jefferson to Wilson Nicholas, Sept. 7, 1803, 8 *Writings of Thomas Jefferson* 247–48 (Paul Ford, ed., 1894).
6. Lawson & Seidman, at 4–5, 9–16. As Lawson and Seidman emphasize, the claim is not that treatymaking power precisely mirrors congressional lawmaking power; treaties can cover matters within the President's independent power. The key, under this view, is that there must be an affirmative grant over the subject matter somewhere in the Constitution, beyond the treatymaking clause itself.
7. Camillus [Hamilton], "The Defence," XXXVI, Jan. 2, 1796, 20 *Papers of Alexander Hamilton* 6–7 (Harold Syrett, ed., 1961–1987).

8. So, for example, treaties cannot (probably) declare war (Chapter 11). Relatedly, Hamilton argued (and modern commentary tends to assume) that appropriations cannot be done by treaty. Id. at 20–21 ("As to the provision, which restricts the issuing of money from the Treasury to cases of appropriation by law, and which from its intrinsic nature may be considered as applicable to the exercise of every power of the Government, it is in no sort touched by the Treaty. In the constant practice of the Government, the cause of an expense or the contract which incurs it, is a distinct thing from the appropriation for satisfying it. . . . So, the Treaty only stipulates what may be a cause of Expenditure. An appropriation by law will still be requisite for actual payment.").

9. 354 U.S. 1, 15–19 (1957).

10. Seminole Tribe of Florida v. Florida, 517 U.S. 44 (1996).

11. 521 U.S. 898 (1997); 505 U.S. 144 (1992). See also Federalist No. 59, at 353–54 (Hamilton) (finding national government to lack power to regulate state elections); Cato No. XVI, at 64 (treaty could not require New York governor to be a British citizen).

12. Michael Rappaport, "Reconciling Textualism and Federalism: The Proper Textual Basis of the Supreme Court's Tenth and Eleventh Amendment Decisions," 93 *Nw. U. L. Rev.* 819, 821–22 (1999).

13. See Paraguay v. Allen, 134 F.3d 622, 627–29 (4th Cir. 1998) (Eleventh Amendment bars treaty-based claims against states); see also Edward Swaine, "Does Federalism Constrain the Treaty Power?" 103 *Colum. L. Rev.* 403 (2003).

14. Emmerich de Vattel, *The Law of Nations,* bk. II, §152 (1758) (Charles Fenwick, trans. J. B. Scott, ed., 1964); Golove, at 1085–86.

15. Camillus, "The Defence," XXXVI, 20 *Papers of Hamilton,* at 6. See Henkin, at 185 ("there must be an agreement, a bona fide agreement, between [nations], not a 'mock marriage'"); Golove, at 1090 n.41. But see Curtis Bradley, "The Treaty Power and American Federalism, Part II," 99 *Mich. L. Rev.* 98, 107–10 (2000) (rightly questioning the practical significance of this limit).

16. These conclusions also appear true of most human rights treaty provisions that worry some modern commentators; see Bradley, "Treaty Power, Part II," at 108. Although not a matter of mutual concern in the eighteenth century, domestic human rights are matters of mutual concern among nations today; generally these treaties are not contrary to other textual provisions, and even if they take power away from the states in a way Congress likely could not, they again do not strike at the core of state sovereignty as would, for example, the command that a state move its capital.

17. Tucker, at 140. See also Bradley, "Treaty Power," at 417; Lawson & Seidman, at 57–58.

18. See especially Jack Rakove, *Original Meanings* 131–60 (1997); on sentiments during ratification, see *Ratifying the Constitution* (Michael Gillespie & Michael Lienesch, eds., 1989); and especially Lance Banning, "Virginia: Sectionalism and the General Good," in id. at 261. On Hamilton's and others' dislike of the states, and responses, see 1 *Records of the Federal Convention of 1787,* at 322–24 (Max Farrand, ed., 1966).

19. See Bradley, "Treaty Power," at 400–401; Rosenkranz, at 1869.

20. Some key framers, at least, apparently thought treaties would be difficult to conclude and would not be made often. 2 *Records*, at 393 (1966) (Morris); id. at 548 (Madison); see Bradley, "Treaty Power," at 410–11; Henkin, at 442 n.2.

21. 1 *Records*, at 46 (Virginia plan); id. at 150 (Dickinson motion); id. at 155–56 (Mason); id. at 156 (adoption of Dickinson's motion).

22. *Documentary History*, at 507 (Wilson); 2 *Debates*, at 306 (Hamilton); see also Federalist No. 64 (Jay), at 376; Federalist No. 45 (Madison), at 294. See Gordon Wood, *The Creation of the American Republic, 1776–1787*, at 558–59 (2d ed. 1998).

23. One difference, which anti-federalists quickly seized upon, was that the Articles required a supermajority of all states, whereas the Constitution required only a supermajority of a quorum (see Chapter 14).

24. Golove, at 1099.

25. Vikram Amar, "Indirect Effects of Direct Election: A Structural Examination of the Seventeenth Amendment," 49 *Vand. L. Rev.* 1347 (1996); Todd Zywicki, "Senators and Special Interests: A Public Choice Analysis of the Seventeenth Amendment," 73 *Ore. L. Rev.* 1007 (1994).

26. Even after the Seventeenth Amendment, some scholars argue that the "political safeguards of federalism" give sufficient structural protection to the states. See Herbert Wechsler, "The Political Safeguards of Federalism: The Role of the States in the Composition and Selection of the National Government," 54 *Colum. L. Rev.* 543 (1954).

27. 252 U.S. at 383.

28. See Merrill Jensen, *The Articles of Confederation* (1940) (drafting); Jack Rakove, *The Beginnings of National Politics* (1979) (government under the Articles).

29. Article 6 qualified this by prohibiting states from applying "any imposts or duties which may interfere with any stipulations in treaties entered into by the United States, in Congress assembled, with any king, prince, or state, in pursuance of any treaties already proposed by Congress to the court of France or Spain."

30. Samuel Bemis, *A Diplomatic History of the United States* 15–84 (4th ed. 1955); 2 *Treaties and Other International Acts of the United States* 3, 35 (Hunter Miller, ed., 1931) (France); id. at 59, 123, 162 (Netherland, Sweden, Prusia). See 26 *Journals of the Continental Congress* 357–63 (Worthington Ford et al., eds., 1906–1937) (May 7, 1784).

31. See Golove, at 1115–27 (British treaty); id. at 1111–15 (commercial treaties); id. at 1106–7 (French treaty).

32. Id. at 1123–32.

33. The Congress rejected (8–1) Madison's objection, in the form of a report to limit the negotiating instructions of U.S. ministers. 22 *Journals*, at 393–96 (July 17–18, 1782). In New York, Hamilton emerged as a major voice for the first time, defending a broad view of the Congress's treaty power. "Letters of Phocion to the Considerate Citizens of New York," 3 *Papers of Hamilton*, at 489. On the debate broadly, see Golove, at 1123–32. By 1788, Madison had apparently ac-

cepted the general view, observing that under the Articles, "Congress are authorized indefinitely to make treaties" and "the power is precisely in the new Constitution as it is in the Confederation." 10 *Documentary History*, at 1395 (Va. convention). For what it is worth, the Supreme Court affirmed the validity of the debts provision of the 1783 peace treaty in Ware v. Hylton, 3 U.S. 199 (1796).

34. Jefferson to Monroe, June 17, 1785, 8 *Papers of Thomas Jefferson* 230–31 (Julian Boyd, ed., 1950–2005).

35. See 1 *Records*, at 164 (Madison, Pinckney); id. at 316 (Madison); see also 2 *Documentary History*, at 517 (Wilson to Pa. convention).

36. 1 *Records*, at 20–23 (Virginia plan).

37. Bradley, "Treaty Power," at 410–12; Golove, at 1132–37 (noting "surprisingly minimal discussions of the scope of the treaty power").

38. Federalist No. 42, at 273.

39. For anti-federalist appeals to the scope of the treatymaking power, see, for example, Brutus, II, 13 *Documentary History*, at 529 ("I do not find any limitation, or restriction, to the exercise of [treaty] power."); 10 id. at 1211 (Henry to Va. convention) ("The President, and a few Senators, possess [treaty power] in the most unlimited manner."); id. at 1391 (Mason to Va. convention) ("Will any gentlemen say that [the President and Senate] may not make a treaty whereby the subjects of France, England and other powers may buy what lands they please in this country? The President and Senate can make any treaty whatsoever.").

40. 10 id. at 1554 (proposals of Va. convention "that no commercial treaty shall be ratified without the concurrence of two-thirds of the whole number of the members of the Senate" nor treaties relating to territory or navigation without three-quarters of Senators).

41. Id. at 1391.

42. Id. at 1381–82.

43. Id. at 1249 (Madison), 1253–54 (Randolph). On the merits of the arguments, the federalists were likely correct that a treaty that violated the law of nations would be void, because treaty obligations ultimately rested on the law of nations; but their claims as to what the law of nations required of treaties seemed, at best, a stretch.

44. Id. at 1389 (Nicholas) (federal government can "make no treaty which shall be repugnant to the spirit of the Constitution, or inconsistent with delegated powers. The treaties they make must be under the authority of the United States, to be within their province"). Golove, at 1148, argues that the statement should not be read literally. Even read literally, though, it is only one statement, and it is not clear that anyone other than Nicholas accepted it, or what it was based on. Compare Bradley, "Treaty Power," at 413 (relying on other statements from the Virginia convention that seem inconclusive).

45. Camillus, "The Defence," XXXVIII, 20 *Papers of Hamilton*, at 22, 24. Bradley, "Treaty Power," at 410, acknowledges that "the reference to treaties in [the drafting and ratifying] materials principally concern the process by which the federal government would conclude treaties."

46. Treaty of Amity, Commerce and Navigation, Nov. 19, 1794, 2 *Treaties*, at 245.

47. On the treaty and its reception, see Samuel Bemis, *Jay's Treaty: A Study in Commerce and Diplomacy* (rev. ed. 1962); Stanley Elkins & Eric McKitrick, *The Age of Federalism* 406–49 (1993).

48. David Currie, *The Constitution in Congress: The Federalist Period* 212 (1997).

49. See id. at 209–17; Golove, at 1164–86.

50. Cato, XVI, at 63–64; for other examples, see Golove, at 1167–68.

51. See Elkins & McKitrick, at 406–49.

52. Camillus, "The Defence," XXXVI, 20 *Papers of Hamilton*, at 6.

53. Cato, No. XIII, 1 *American Remembrancer*, at 249–50. Livingston raised a host of other unrelated constitutional objections as well, so many that merely listing them would be exhausting.

54. Camillus, "The Defence," XXXVII, 20 *Papers of Hamilton*, at 15–19.

55. Golove, at 1172–73.

56. Fairfax's Devisee v. Hunter's Lessee, 11 U.S. 603, 627–28 (1812).

57. Golove, at 1149–93; on Madison's position, see especially id. at 1179–86. The Republicans' position ended up being that treaties touching Congress's powers required congressional implementation—i.e., they could not be self-executing. See id. at 1183–845; John Yoo, "Globalism and the Constitution: Treaties, Non-Self-Execution and the Original Understanding," 99 *Colum. L. Rev.* 1955, 2080–86 (1999). One Federalist representative said, with little objection, that the treaty's constitutionality "is allowed on all hands." 5 *Annals of Congress* 1204 (Joseph Gales, ed., 1834). On the Republican position, see also Elkins & McKitrick, at 441–45.

58. Lawson & Seidman, at 13–17.

59. Jefferson, *Manual*, §53.

60. Jefferson to Wilson Nicholas, Sept. 7, 1803, 8 *Writings of Jefferson*, at 247–48.

61. Id. at 247. Lawson & Seidman, at 3, while relying on Jefferson's view, acknowledge (with some understatement) that "Jefferson's position was never historically ascendant." They go on to argue that it was, nonetheless, the correct view. Their problem, though, is the same as Jefferson's: they rely almost entirely on a structural imperative that simply does not exist. It is not the case that, without subject-matter limitations, treatymaking power poses manifestly unacceptable threats to the states: one can plausibly believe that the states were adequately protected by Article I, Section 3 and the two-thirds rule.

62. Jefferson also embraced, in the same section, the argument that matters within Congress's authority could not form part of the treaty power. As discussed above, this claim is even less plausible, and combined, they almost eliminate any scope for treatymaking.

16. Judging Foreign Affairs

1. 5 U.S. 137, 177 (1803); W.S. Kirkpatrick & Co. v. Environmental Tectonics Corp., 493 U.S. 400 (1990) (emphasis added).

2. See Louis Henkin, *Foreign Affairs and the U.S. Constitution* 143–48 (2d ed. 1996). Jefferson Powell argues: "The president's constitutional authority to act on the international stage for the United States is the ordinary or default state of constitutional affairs. Disagreements, therefore, must be expressed in terms of policy. . . . Controversies over foreign affairs, under this reading of the Constitution, are intrinsically and almost invariably political disputes. . . ." Jefferson Powell, *The President's Authority over Foreign Affairs* 147 (2002).

3. 444 U.S. 996, 1002 (1979); Chicago & Southern Air Lines Inc. v. Waterman S.S. Corp., 333 U.S. 103, 111 (1948).

4. Henkin, at 146; e.g., DaCosta v. Laird, 471 F.2d 1146 (2nd Cir. 1973); Holtzman v. Schlesinger, 485 F.2d 1307, 1309–11 (2nd Cir. 1973); Sanchez-Espinosa v. Reagan, 770 F.2d 202, 210 (D.C. Cir. 1985); Lowry v. Reagan, 676 F.Supp. 333 (D.D.C. 1987).

5. Baker v. Carr, 369 U.S. 186, 217 (1962); see especially Japan Whaling Ass'n v. American Cetacean Society, 478 U.S. 221 (1986). The modern Court has, cautiously and in the face of considerable criticism, reached the merits of several war-on-terror cases without much discussion of the political question doctrine. See Hamdi v. Rumsfeld, 542 U.S. 507 (2004) (addressing the President's constitutional authority to detain terrorist suspects); Hamdan v. Rumsfeld, 126 S.Ct. 2749 (2006) (addressing the President's statutory authority to establish military commissions).

6. For example, Thomas Franck, *Political Questions/Judicial Answers* (1992); Michael Glennon, "Foreign Affairs and the Political Question Doctrine," 83 *Am. J. Int'l L.* 814 (1989); Louis Henkin, "Is There a Political Question Doctrine?" 85 *Yale L.J.* 597 (1976); Peter Mulhern, "In Defense of the Political Question Doctrine," 137 *U. Pa. L. Rev.* 97 (1988); Rachel Barkow, "More Supreme than Court? The Fall of the Political Question Doctrine and the Rise of Judicial Supremacy," 102 *Colum. L. Rev.* 237 (2002). The classic defense, not addressed specifically to foreign affairs, is Alexander Bickel, "Foreword: The Passive Virtues," 75 *Harv. L. Rev.* 40 (1961); the leading modern foreign affairs defense is Jide Nzelibe, "The Uniqueness of Foreign Affairs," 89 *Iowa L. Rev.* 941 (2004).

7. Robert Pushaw, "The Inherent Power of the Federal Courts and the Structural Constitution," 86 *Iowa L. Rev.* 735 (2001).

8. Steven Calabresi, "The Vesting Clauses as Power Grants," 88 *Nw. U. L. Rev.* 1377, 1380–86 (1994).

9. Although the President's duty might arise from Article VI alone, we have seen in Chapter 8 that the take-care clause was added to counter arguments that the President's executive power included power to suspend laws.

10. Article III lists nine categories of federal jurisdiction. In addition, the Fifth Amendment's due process clause requires courts to have "personal jurisdiction" over defendants, a matter not material to the ensuing discussion.

11. See David Currie, *The Constitution in the Supreme Court: The First Hundred Years* 11–14 (1985) (describing Washington's 1793 attempt to get the Court to answer hypothetical questions about the laws of neutrality and Chief Justice Jay's refusal to answer on the basis of the case-or-controversy requirement).

12. 4 *Papers of John Marshall* 95 (Herbert Johnson et al., ed., 1974–2006). For context, see Chapter 18.

13. Lujan v. Defenders of Wildlife, 504 U.S. 555, 560–61 (1992).

14. See Anthony Bellia, "Article III and the Cause of Action," 89 *Iowa L. Rev.* 777, 817–27 (2004); Steven Winter, "The Metaphor of Standing and the Problem of Self-Governance," 40 *Stan. L. Rev.* 1371 (1987).

15. Made in the USA Foundation v. United States, 242 F.3d 1300 (11th Cir. 2001).

16. 444 U.S. at 996–97. The case was decided summarily. Six Justices voted to dismiss the case (one without explanation); Justice Brennan would have decided on the merits for the President. The other Justices voted to hear further arguments.

17. A subsequent domestic-law decision, Raines v. Byrd, 521 U.S. 811, 826 (1997), suggests that Goldwater would not have standing under modern law, rejecting the claim that "abstract dilution of institutional legislative power" was enough to sustain a "case or controversy" under Article III. See also Campbell v. Clinton, 203 F.3d 19, 20–25 (D.C. Cir. 2000) (congressmen lacked standing to challenge allegedly unconstitutional presidential war-making).

18. 444 U.S. at 534. More elaborate appeals to policy considerations can be found in several Vietnam-era cases, and in Professor Bickel's classic "Foreword." Nonetheless, these remain policy arguments, disconnected from the Constitution's text.

19. Marbury, 5 U.S. at 170.

20. Ware v. Hylton, 3 U.S. 199, 260 (1796) (Iredell) (question involved "considerations of policy . . . entirely incompetent to the examination and decision of a Court of Justice"). See also Moxon v. The Fanny, 17 F.Cas. 942 (D. Pa. 1793) (decision whether to restore prize taken in U.S. waters, when the United States was neutral, depended on U.S. policy and was beyond court's competence).

21. As Herbert Wechsler argued, provoking Bickel's response, "the only proper judgment that may lead to abstention from decision is that the Constitution has committed the determination of the issue to another agency of government than the courts." "Toward Neutral Principles of Constitutional Law," 73 *Harv. L. Rev.* 1, 9 (1959). On the Bickel-Wechsler debate, see Nzelibe, at 948–49.

22. Nixon v. United States, 506 U.S. 224 (1993); Wechsler, at 8; see also Luther v. Borden, 48 U.S. 1, 35 (1849) (enforcement of guarantee (Article IV, §4) clause committed to Congress).

23. 16 U.S. 610, 633–34 (1818).

24. 444 U.S. at 1006–7 (internal quotations and citations omitted). As discussed in Chapter 8, President Carter did have treaty-termination power under the historical meaning of the executive power. That, however, is a resolution of the constitutional question, not a conclusion that courts cannot answer the constitutional question.

25. In the Gulf of Tonkin Resolution, Congress broadly authorized the President to "take all necessary steps including the use of armed force," to aid Southeast Asian nations "requesting assistance in defense of [their] freedom." One might claim that this authorization was constitutionally defective, because it was too general

or because Congress's war power is non-delegable (see Chapter 11), or that the President's actions were not authorized because they were, in fact, not necessary. The latter, but not the former, claim appears to raise a political question, in a sense consistent with the Constitution's text.

26. Currie, at 66–74. See William Van Alstyne, "A Critical Guide to Marbury v. Madison," 1969 *Duke L.J.* 1; Edward Corwin, "Marbury v. Madison and the Doctrine of Judicial Review," 12 *Mich. L. Rev.* 538 (1914).

27. Marshall also relied on Article VI's supremacy clause and judicial oath. See Bradford Clark, "The Supremacy Clause as a Constraint on Federal Power," 71 *Geo. Wash. L. Rev.* 91 (2003) (elaborating argument based on the supremacy clause). But see Currie, at 72–73 (arguing that neither shows that courts may adopt independent views of constitutional meaning).

28. Federalist No. 78, in James Madison, Alexander Hamilton, & John Jay, *The Federalist Papers* 438–39 (Isaac Kramnick, ed., 1987). Note Hamilton's acknowledgment that specific matters might be textually committed to other branches if that implication could be "collected from any particular provisions in the Constitution."

29. Marshall used similar arguments (without citing Federalist No. 78) in *Marbury* itself, arguing that the point of a written Constitution was to limit governmental power, which could be done only if courts exercised independent judgment upon its meaning. 5 U.S. at 176–78.

30. For example, 1 *Records of the Federal Convention of 1787*, at 109 (Max Farrand, ed., 1966) (King) ("the Judges will have the expounding of [the] laws when they come before them; and they will no doubt stop the operation of such as shall appear repugnant to the constitution"); id. at 97 (Gerry) (judges "will have a sufficient check against encroachments on their own department by their exposition of the laws, which involved a power of deciding on their Constitutionality"); see also 2 id. at 73 (Wilson), 76 (Martin), 78 (Mason). For a comprehensive historical and textual defense, see Saikrishna Prakash & John Yoo, "The Origins of Judicial Review," 70 *U. Chi. L. Rev.* 887 (2003). The leading contrary view is Larry Kramer, "Foreword: We the Court," 115 *Harv. L. Rev.* 4 (2001). See also Prakash & Yoo, at 892 n. 24 (listing additional authorities).

31. Keith Whittington, *Constitutional Interpretation* 50–59 (1999). See also Gordon Wood, *The Creation of the American Republic, 1776–1787*, at 461–63 (2d ed. 1998).

32. 2 *Documentary History*, at 517; 6 id. at 1285; 16 id. at 72–75. See Prakash & Yoo at 954–75 (reviewing debates and concluding: "In at least seven state ratifying conventions, leading delegates openly declared that the Constitution authorized judicial review of federal legislation."); Van Alstyne, at 38–45 (collecting additional sources).

33. Hamilton to Washington, Mar. 29, 1796, 20 *Papers of Alexander Hamilton* 97 (Harold Syrett, ed., 1961–1987); see Currie, at 69–70; William Treanor, "Judicial Review Before Marbury," 58 *Stan. L. Rev.* 455 (2005); Prakash & Yoo, at 776–81.

34. Nzelibe, at 983.

35. See Entick v. Carrington, 19 State Trials 1030, 1073 (1765).

36. 6 U.S. 170 (1804); 27 F. Cas. 1192 (1806). On the importance of *Little*, see especially Michael Glennon, *Constitutional Diplomacy* 4–8 (1990).

37. 4 U.S. 37 (1800); 12 U.S. 110 (1814). *Brown* involved the interaction of Congress's power to declare war and the President's power to fight a declared war. It paralleled *Goldwater*, then, in that it concerned not what U.S. policy toward a foreign nation should be, but which branch of government had power to set that policy. Justice Story, dissenting, argued for the President, but not on political question grounds.

38. Hwang Geum Joo v. Japan, 413 F.3d 45 (2005).

39. 726 F.2d 774, 823–27 (D.C. Cir. 1984).

40. See Sosa v. Alvarez-Machain, 542 U.S. 692, 742 n.21 (2004) (suggesting case-specific foreign affairs abstention in law-of-nations cases).

41. Michael Ramsey, "Escaping International Comity," 83 *Iowa L. Rev.* 893 (1998).

42. 478 US. at 230.

43. Some considerations said to underlie the political question doctrine might lead courts to read foreign-affairs-related statutes to deny judicial review of presidential decisions, as Justice Jackson did in the *Waterman* case quoted above. See 333 U.S. at 111. Properly understood, though, *Waterman* and related cases are not really political question dismissals, only interpretations of statutes finding the President statutorily invested with policymaking discretion.

44. Murray v. The Charming Betsy, 6 U.S. 64, 118 (1804) (law of nations); E.E.O.C. v. Arabian-American Oil Co., 499 U.S. 244, 248 (1991) (extraterritorial effect). See Ramsey, at 906–25; Curtis Bradley, "The Charming Betsy Canon and Separation of Powers: Rethinking the Interpretive Role of International Law," 86 *Georgetown L.J.* 479 (1998).

45. See Underhill v. Hernandez, 168 U.S. 250, 252 (1897); Oetjen v. Central Leather Co., 246 U.S. 297, 301 (1918). The doctrine does not necessarily prevent courts from deciding the case, but makes the foreign act conclusive.

46. 28 U.S.C. §§ 1602–11; Verlinden B.V. v. Central Bank of Nigeria, 461 U.S. 480, 486–88 (1983); Mexico v. Hoffman, 324 U.S. 30 (1945).

47. 11 U.S. 116 (1812). Marshall argued that foreign sovereign immunity was a privilege the sovereign could withdraw, but which courts should apply until such withdrawal was manifest. Id. at 145–46.

48. For this suggestion regarding the act-of-state doctrine, see Ramsey, at 913–16.

49. 11 U.S. at 122 (Dallas) ("whenever the act is done by a sovereign in his sovereign character, it becomes a matter of negotiations, or of reprisals, or of war, according to its importance"); id. at 132 (Pinckney) ("the right to demand redress belongs to the executive department, which alone represents the sovereignty of the nation in its intercourse with other nations").

50. For example, Oetjen, 246 U.S. at 302 ("the conduct of the foreign relations of our government is committed by the Constitution to the executive and legislative—'the political'—departments of the government, and the propriety of what may be done in the exercise of this political power is not subject to judicial in-

quiry or decision"). Foreign sovereign immunity has foundations dating to the founding era; the act-of-state doctrine's origins are less clear. See Harrison Moore, *Act of State in English Law* (1906).

51. 659 F. Supp. 1381, 1392–93 (1987).

52. This was the Court's conclusion in *Kirkpatrick*. After finding that the act-of-state doctrine did not apply, because the suit did not seek to invalidate any Nigerian governmental act, it rejected the executive branch contention that suits might still be dismissed as "embarrassing" even if the act-of-state rule did not technically apply. 493 U.S. at 408–9.

53. 376 U.S. (1964); 416–39 398 see Jack Goldsmith, "Federal Courts, Foreign Affairs, and Federalism," 83 *Va. L. Rev.* 1617, 1625–40 (1997) (discussing cases).

54. For further discussion, see Goldsmith, at 1620–25.

55. See Bradford Clark, "Federal Common Law: A Structural Reinterpretation," 144 *U. Pa. L. Rev.* 1245 (1996) (suggesting this view of federal common law).

56. Hinderlider v. La Plata River Co., 304 U.S. 92, 110 (1938) (interstate water apportionment is a "question of 'federal common law' upon which neither the statutes nor the decisions of either State can be conclusive"); Kansas v. Colorado, 206 U.S. 46, 95–98 (1907).

57. *Sabbatino* confusingly said its decision was not constitutionally required but had "constitutional underpinnings." 376 U.S. at 423.

58. Professor Clark's leading textual defense of federal common law seems to endorse a broad federal common law of foreign relations based on the federal government's constitutional foreign relations exclusivity. He relies for the latter proposition, though, on *Curtiss-Wright* and *Zschernig*-like constitutional implications that seem unsupported by the text. See Clark, "Federal Common Law," at 1294–96.

17. *The Paquete Habana*

1. 175 U.S. 677, 700 (1900). See Louis Henkin, *Foreign Affairs and the U.S. Constitution* 239–45 (2d ed. 1996). This chapter expands on suggestions offered in Michael Ramsey, "International Law as Non-preemptive Federal Law," 42 *Va. J. Int'l L.* 555 (2002).

2. For example, Louis Henkin, "International Law as Law in the United States," 82 *Mich. L. Rev.* 1555 (1984); Curtis Bradley & Jack Goldsmith, "Customary International Law as Federal Common Law: A Critique of the Modern Position," 110 *Harv. L. Rev.* 815 (1997); Harold Koh, "Is International Law Really State Law?" 111 *Harv. L. Rev.* 1824 (1998). A valuable guide is Ernest Young, "Sorting Out the Debate over Customary International Law," 42 *Va. J. Int'l L.* 365, 372–462 (2002).

3. 1 William Blackstone, *Commentaries on the Laws of England* 43 (1765).

4. Emmerich de Vattel, *The Law of Nations*, bk. I, §3 (1758) (Charles Fenwick, trans., J. B. Scott, ed., 1964); Christian Wolff, *Jus Gentium Methodo Scientifica Pertrac-*

tatam, §1 (1749) (Joseph Drake, trans., J. B. Scott, ed., 1964). Arthur Nussbaum, *A Concise History of the Law of Nations* 147–64 (rev. ed. 1962). For the international law writers' influence in America, see Chapter 9.

5. 1 *Diplomatic Correspondence of the United States* 89 (U.S. Department of State 1834) (Luzerne to Continental Congress, May 20, 1784); 27 *Journals of the Continental Congress* 478, 503–4 (Worthington Ford et al., eds, 1906–1937); William Casto, "The Federal Courts' Protective Jurisdiction over Torts Committed in Violation of the Law of Nations," 18 *Conn. L. Rev.* 467 (1986). On law-of-nations protection of ambassadors, see Vattel, bk. III, §§80–83.

6. For example, James Madison, "Vices of the Political System of the United States," 9 *Papers of James Madison* 349 (William Hutchinson et al., eds., 1962–1991) (1787); 1 *Records of the Federal Convention of 1787*, at 19 (Max Farrand, ed., 1996) (Randolph); Federalist No. 3 (Jay), in James Madison, Alexander Hamilton, & John Jay, *The Federalist Papers* 95 (Isaac Kramnick, ed., 1987) ("It is of high importance to the peace of America that she observe the laws of nations towards all these [European] powers. . . ."); 8 *Documentary History of the Ratification of the Constitution* 263 (Merrill Jensen et al., eds., 1976–present) (Randolph, public letter, Oct. 10, 1787) (in "the constitutions, and laws of the several states . . . the law of nations is unprovided with sanctions in many cases, which deeply affect public dignity and public justice"; "the letter, however, of the Confederation does not permit Congress to remedy these defects," and it might be "doomed to be plunged into war, from its wretched impotency to check offenses against this law"); Federalist No. 42, at 264–65 (Madison) (Articles "contain no provision for the case of offense against the law of nations; and consequently leave it in the power of any indiscreet member to embroil the Confederacy with foreign nations.").

7. 1 Blackstone, at 43; Vattel, bk. I, §24.

8. 1 *Records,* at 19 (Randolph) (the Congress could not "cause infractions of treaties, or of the law of nations, to be punished"); id. at 316 (Madison) ("violations of the law of nations & of Treaties . . . if not prevented must involve us in the calamities of foreign wars"). The Congress asked states to "provide . . . punishment . . . for infractions of the immunities of ambassadors and other public ministers [and] . . . infraction of treaties and conventions to which the United States are a party." 21 *Journals,* at 1136–37 (Nov. 23, 1781). John Jay later recounted, "in their national capacity, the United States were responsible to foreign nations for the conduct of each State, relative to the laws of nations, and the performance of treaties; and there the inexpediency of referring all such questions to the State Courts, and particularly to the Courts of delinquent States became apparent." Chisholm v. Georgia, 2 U.S. 419, 474 (1793).

9. David Bederman, *The Spirit of International Law* 14 (2002) ("States . . . are said to be bound by international law because they have given their consent."); id. at 94 ("We take it as an article of faith that the modern law of nations derives its legitimacy from the consent of states."); Michael Ramsey, "The Empirical Dilemma of International Law," 41 *San Diego L. Rev.* 1243, 1243–46 (2004). This ac-

count may not fully explain modern international law (id. at 1252–53), but it is modern international law's principal rhetorical basis. See Stephen Hall, "The Persistent Spectre: Natural Law, International Order and the Limits of Legal Positivism," 12 Eur. J. Int'l L. 269 (2001).

10. Vattel, bk. I, §6; see Hall, at 269–76.

11. Wolff, §§1–22. Wolff also recognized, §§23–24, a secondary "stipulative" law of nations arising from explicit or tacit consent. This branch of it aside, though, Wolff imagined a "republic" of nations, whose law arose from a "fictitious ruler so to have proceeded from the will of nations." Id., §22. And the edicts of Wolff's "fictitious ruler" were identified by reason. Grotius, writing a century earlier, referred to "[t]hat body of law . . . which is concerned with the mutual relations among states or rulers of states, whether derived from nature, or established by divine ordinances, or having its origin in custom and tacit agreement." Hugo Grotius, *De Jure Bell: ac Pacis* vii (William Evats, trans., 1682).

12. Vattel, preface, at 6a–7a; id., bk. I, §§7–9. Following Wolff and Grotius, Vattel recognized a derivative category of rules, confusingly called the "voluntary" law of nations. Generally speaking, the idea was that nations could not insist upon the strict justice of the law of nature, because mutual interactions required certain "modifications" or accommodations to prevent constant conflict. These accommodations, though, also flowed deductively from the nature of the international system, not necessarily from actual consent. Vattel explained, "I shall . . . prove in this work, that all the modifications [from the natural law of individuals] . . . may be deduced from the natural liberty of Nations, from considerations of their common welfare, from the nature of their mutual intercourse, their reciprocal duties, and from the distinctions of their rights." Id., preface at 10a. Thus, "[t]he necessary Law of Nations and the voluntary law have therefore both been established by nature, but each in its own way: the former as a sacred law to be respected and obeyed by Nations and sovereigns in all their actions; the latter as a rule of conduct which the common good and welfare oblige them to accept in their mutual intercourse." Id., 11a. Vattel distinguished a third category he called the "arbitrary" law of nations, which arose from the "will or the consent of Nations"—that is, written and tacit agreements. Id.

13. Grand Jury Charge (May 12, 1794), quoted in Stewart Jay, "The Status of the Law of Nations in Early American Law," 42 *Vand. L. Rev.* 819, 823 (1989) (Iredell); "Lectures on Law," 1 *Works of James Wilson* 151 (Robert McCloskey, ed., 1967); see also 2 id. at 813 (Grand Jury Charge, May 1791) ("the law of nations has its foundation in the principles of natural law, applied to states; and in voluntary institutions, arising from custom or convention"); United States v. La Jeune Eugenie, 26 F. Cas. 832, 846 (C.C.D. Mass. 1822) (Story). "In the eighteenth century a consensus existed that the law of nations rested in large measure on natural law," and writers described it as "a system of rules capable of rational explication." Jay, at 822, 824.

14. Vattel, preface at 13a; id., bk. I, §25; 4 Blackstone, at 66. The seventeenth-century

English legal scholar Matthew Hale observed that natural law is "not the product of the wisdom of some one man, or group of men, in any one age, but the wisdom, counsel, experience, and observations of many ages of wise and observing men." Stewart Jay, "The Origins of Federal Common Law, Part One," 133 *U. Pa. L. Rev.* 1003, 1056 (1985).

15. Jefferson to Thomas Pinckney, May 7, 1793, 25 *Papers of Thomas Jefferson* 675 (Julian Boyd et al., eds., 1950–2005).

16. 1 Blackstone, at 41.

17. An example is the debate (Chapter 11) over whether formal declarations of war were required before beginning hostilities. Numerous authorities—Vattel, Burlamaqui, Grotius, and Wolff—claimed that reason required such declarations. But at least two writers, Bynkershoek and Rutherforth, denied it, and they had substantial practice on their side, since prior declarations were not often used. It is hard to say who was "right" in this debate. On modern difficulties in identifying rules in unwritten international law, see Patrick Kelly, "The Twilight of Customary International Law," 40 *Va. J. Int'l L.* 449 (2000); Young, at 385–91.

18. 2 *Records,* at 614–15. Wilson later acknowledged that "the opinions of many concerning the law of nations have been very vague and unsatisfactory." "Lectures on Law," 1 *Works of Wilson,* at 149 (1792).

19. Jay, "Status," at 822; 4 Blackstone, at 67. Iredell said in 1794, with some exaggeration: "The Law of Nations . . . has been cultivated with extraordinary success. In its main principles, as stated by many able writers all civilized nations concur. . . . Within these few years this law has not only been stated with particular accuracy and conciseness, but all its principles have been traced to their sources with a power of reasoning which has commanded universal assent." Grand Jury Charge, quoted in Jay, "Status," at 823–24. John Marshall wrote, more realistically: "The law of nations . . . is in part unwritten, and in part conventional. To ascertain that which is unwritten, we resort to the great principles of reason and justice; but, as these principles will be differently understood by different nations under different circumstances, we consider them as being, in some degree, fixed and rendered stable by a series of judicial decisions. . . . The decisions of the Courts of every country show how the law of nations, in the given case, is understood in that country, and will be considered in adopting the rule which is to prevail in this." Thirty Hogsheads of Sugar v. Boyle, 13 U.S. 191, 198 (1815).

20. Act of April 30, 1790, §25–26, 1 Stat. 112, 117–18. See 1 Op. Atty Gen. 26 (1792) (Randolph).

21. See 28 *Journals,* at 314–15 (April 27, 1785); 29 id. at 655 (Aug. 25, 1785); 21 id. at 1136–37 (Nov. 23, 1782). The Congress could enforce the law of nations in its narrow areas of legislative authority—for example, it declared that captures on the high seas would be resolved according to international prize law. 13 id. at 283–84 (Mar. 6, 1779).

22. For debate over Article III, Section 2's grant of federal jurisdiction over cases arising under the "laws of the United States," see Arthur Weisburd, "The Exec-

utive Branch and International Law," 41 *Vand. L. Rev.* 1205 (1988); Curtis Bradley, "The Alien Tort Statute and Article III," 42 *Va. J. Int'l L.* 587 (2002); William Dodge, "The Constitutionality of the Alien Tort Statute: Some Observations on Text and Context," 42 *Va. J. Int'l L.* 687 (2002).

23. See Henkin, *Foreign Affairs,* at 508 n.16 (international law is made "in a process to which the United States contributes only in an uncertain way and to an indeterminate degree"); Bradley, at 602–3; Jay, "Status," at 832–33; see also Henkin, *Foreign Affairs,* at 237–39.

24. 2 *Records,* at 417 (Madison amendment adding language "to obviate all doubt covering the force of treaties preexisting the Constitution"). See Ware v. Hylton, 3 U.S. 199 (1796) (applying Article VI to the 1783 peace treaty).

25. Chisholm, 2 U.S. at 475.

26. Most commentators who give international law the status of federal law agree that Congress can violate it. See Henkin, *Foreign Affairs,* at 235. If statutes and international law have equivalent status, though, they might be subject to a "later-in-time rule"—i.e., a later international law would supersede an earlier statute, as with treaties. Id. at 243; see Chapter 8. If international law is not supreme, though, it cannot supersede even earlier statutes.

27. Randolph's 1792 opinion as Attorney General implies Congress's ability to override the law of nations. Randolph observed that the "obligation" of the law of nations "commences and runs with the existence of a nation, subject to modifications on some points of indifference. Indeed a people may regulate it so as to be binding on the departments of their own government, in any form whatever; but with regard to foreigners, every change is at the peril of the nation which makes it." 1 Op. Att'y Gen. at 27. That is, a nation may disregard the law of nations, but at its "peril," presumably from retaliation by other nations. Marshall's later Supreme Court opinions similarly contemplate legislative override. See Murray v. The Charming Betsy, 6 U.S. 64, 118 (1804) (statute construed not to violate law of nations if ambiguous); The Nereide, 13 U.S. 388, 423 (1815) (Court will apply law of nations "[t]ill such an act be passed" providing a different rule).

28. There might be other limits on what states could do to ambassadors: imprisoning or expelling ambassadors would likely conflict with the President's Article II, Section 3 reception power.

29. See Young, at 467–83 (suggesting that federal courts might decline to enforce state laws conflicting with the law of nations where the state's interest was weak).

30. See Bradford Clark, "Separation of Powers as a Safeguard of Federalism," 79 *Tex. L. Rev.* 1321 (2001).

31. For example, 2 *Documentary History,* at 518 (Wilson to Pa. convention) ("judges of the United States will be enabled to carry them [treaties] into effect" because of "this clause [Article VI]").

32. Brutus, XI, Jan. 31, 1788, 15 *Documentary History,* at 514–15; Brutus, XII, Feb. 7, 1788, 16 id. at 72–75. See Jack Rakove, *Original Meanings* 186–87 (1997).

33. Act of Sept. 24, 1789, §34, 1 Stat. 92.

34. Charles Warren, "New Light of the History of the Federal Judiciary Act of 1789," 37 *Harv. L. Rev.* 49, 83 (1923). See id. at 81–88; William Fletcher, "The General Common Law and Section 34 of the Judiciary Act of 1789: The Example of Marine Insurance," 97 *Harv. L. Rev.* 1513, 1527–28 (1983); Stewart Jay, "The Origins of Federal Common Law, Part Two," 133 *U. Pa. L. Rev.* 1231, 1263 (1985).

35. For example, Koh, at 1865; see Curtis Bradley, "The Status of Customary International Law in U.S. Courts—Before and after Erie," 26 *Den. J. Int'l L. & Pol'y* 807, 816 (1998) ("commentators . . . are unable to cite a single decision from the nineteenth century in which a court invalidated a presidential, congressional, or state enactment on the basis of a conflict with customary international law").

36. As discussed below, there was doubt whether the Constitution and the Judiciary Act bound federal courts to state common-law decisions other than on purely local matters, but statutes appear to have been noncontroversial. See Fletcher, at 1560 ("As long as its statutes did not conflict with the laws of the national government, a state was free to go its own way."). The nearest exception is Calder v. Bull, 3 U.S. 386, 388 (1798), in which Justice Chase suggested that a court might ignore state laws "contrary to the great first principles of the social compact." See David Currie, *The Constitution in the Supreme Court: The First Hundred Years* 41–49 (1985). Whatever Chase meant (his meaning remains disputed), he did not mean federal courts could use the law of nations to ignore state law, as his opinion in *Ware* (discussed below) makes clear. See also Van Reimsdyk v. Kane, 28 F. Cas. 1062, 1065 (C.C.D.R.I. 1812) (Story) (suggesting federal court might disregard state statutes "where the subject matter of the suit is extraterritorial" without clear constitutional grounding).

37. Ware, 3 U.S. at 277 (Iredell); id. at 236–37 (Chase); id. at 282 (Cushing).

38. Id. at 229, 238 (Chase). Chase emphasized that the law of nations did not override English law: in a claimed conflict, "her courts were to obey her laws." Id. Virginia courts would be similarly situated, and, he appeared to assume, federal courts were to act as Virginia courts would.

39. Id. at 265–66 (Iredell).

40. Id. at 278–80.

41. Id. at 282 (Cushing). The remaining Justices, Wilson and Paterson, considered only the effect of the treaty.

42. To be clear, the opinions in *Ware* are invoked as evidence of the text's historical understanding. The Justices were members of the founding generation (Chase and Iredell attended their states' ratifying conventions) and shared the common understandings of the time. *Ware* is particularly suggestive on the law of nations because in this respect it limited courts' power, which the Justices would be less likely to do unless they thought it a necessary conclusion—particularly where they had little sympathy for the state.

43. Jay, "Status," at 827–28.

44. Henkin, *Foreign Affairs*, at 238.

45. John Yoo, "Globalism and the Constitution: Treaties, Non-Self-Execution, and the Original Understanding," 99 *Colum. L. Rev.* 1955, 2040–73 (1999). Yoo argues that backpedaling in the ratification debates established that treaties would presumptively not be self-executing despite Article VI. See Chapter 8. One need not embrace that view to see that including even well-defined treaty obligations in Article VI was, as Yoo demonstrates, quite controversial.

46. See Clark, at 1332–34.

47. 1 *Records,* at 19; see also 8 *Documentary History,* at 264 (Randolph) (enforcement of the law of nations was a "defect of congressional power").

48. The foregoing discussion may seem in tension with the modern idea of "federal common law": that is, the view that federal courts can, under some circumstances, create rules on their own authority that override state law. See Clearfield Trust Co. v. United States, 318 U.S. 363, 367 (1943). No such definitive conclusion is intended. As Bradford Clark argues, much of today's "federal common law" arises where courts find it necessary to create specific rules to effectuate broad principles laid down in the Constitution or in statutes. This judicial "lawmaking" may be implicitly authorized by Congress or the Constitution, and thus may be consistent with the text's original meaning, so long as it is confined to narrow categories. Bradford Clark, "Federal Common Law: A Structural Reinterpretation," 144 *U. Pa. L. Rev.* 1245 (1996). In contrast, for federal courts to adopt all of the law of nations as federal common law would undo the drafters' decision to omit the law of nations from Article VI.

49. See especially Bradley & Goldsmith, at 852–55.

50. 1 Op. Att'y Gen. at 27 (Randolph); Pacificus, No. 1, 15 *Papers of Alexander Hamilton* 43 (Harold Syrett, ed., 1969); Helvidius, No. 2, 15 *Papers of Madison,* at 86; 1 Op Att'y Gen 68 (1797) (Lee); Jay, "Status," at 825–26 (Jay, Iredell, and Wilson).

51. 542 U.S. 692 (2004).

52. That is, the question whether federal courts have jurisdiction to hear law-of-nations claims between two aliens. See Bradley, "Alien Tort Statute," at 646 (no jurisdiction); Weisburd, at 1233–34 (same); Dodge, at 711–12 (jurisdiction). In *Sosa,* the Supreme Court mysteriously avoided a direct answer.

53. 41 U.S. 1 (1842).

54. See Clark, "Federal Common Law," at 1276–92; Jay, "Status," at 832–33.

55. 304 U.S. 64, 77–79 (1938) (internal quotations omitted).

56. See Bradley & Goldsmith, at 852–55. The opposing view argues that *Erie* allows international law to be treated as supreme federal common law—a position we have already seen is inconsistent with the original design. See Young, at 391–463 (discussing and rejecting this interpretation).

57. This question is distinct from asking whether the court has jurisdiction, a question answered by Article III, Section 2, not Section 1. Even though a court has jurisdiction, it cannot decide according to any rule of decision it likes—for example, it could not use biblical law.

58. 4 Blackstone, at 67.

59. Id.
60. Id. In contrast, Blackstone did not appear to believe that other aspects of natural law or (with limited exceptions) ecclesiastical law were part of English common law.
61. Id. at 68–73.
62. 97 Eng. Rep. 36, 938 (K.B. 1764); see also Barbuit's Case, 25 Eng. Rep. 777 (1736). See William Holdsworth, "The Relation of English Law to International Law," 26 *Minn. L. Rev.* 141, 141–46 (1942), 14 William Holdsworth, *A History of English Law* at 24 (1966 reprint).
63. For example, Respublica v. De Longchamps, 1 U.S. 111, 114 (Pa. 1784) ("laws of nations form a part of the Municipal law of Pennsylvania"); 1 *Diplomatic Correspondence,* at 443–47 (reporting 1787 violation of ambassadorial immunity in New York as "a crime on the law of nations, which is a breach of the common law"). See also Bradley, "Alien Tort Statute," at 642 (reporting that the offender was convicted under the law of nations in New York court).
64. As Iredell stated: "The Common Law of England, from which our own is derived, fully recognizes the principles of the Law of Nations, and applies them in all cases falling under its jurisdiction." Grand Jury Charge, Apr. 12, 1796, in Jay, "Status," at 825; St. George Tucker's 1803 American edition of Blackstone noted that in "controversies between citizens of different states; and between citizens of any state and the subjects of foreign states" the "rule of decision" would be "the municipal law of the place where the cause of controversy arises . . . ; or the general law of merchants; or, the general law of nations according to the nature and circumstances of the case." 1 St. George Tucker, *Blackstone's Commentaries,* app. 421 (1803); see also James Sullivan, *The History of Land Titles in Massachusetts* 352 (1801) (Arno reprint 1972).
65. Federalist No. 80, at 447 (Hamilton) (maritime cases "generally depend upon the law of nations"); Wilson, Grand Jury Charge, 2 *Works of Wilson*, at 375 ("the maritime law is not the law of any particular country: it is the general law of nations"). The drafters might have assumed that Congress would regulate maritime disputes by statute—but if so, they would not have needed a separate head of jurisdiction (as these would arise under the "laws of the United States"). And Hamilton's Federalist No. 80, at 446, directly anticipates judicial enforcement of the law of nations.
66. See Clark, "Federal Common Law," at 1288–89 ("Many of the cases and controversies to which '[t]he judicial Power shall extend' were included in Article III of the Constitution precisely because they were likely to require application of the law of nations. . . . Thus, it should come as no surprise that federal courts [were] frequently called upon to ascertain and apply the law of nations. . . .").
67. Act of Sept. 24, 1789, §9, 1 Stat. 77. See Casto, at 474–86; Dodge, at 692–701.
68. Act of Sept. 24, 1789, §34, 1 Stat. 92.
69. Jennings v. Carson, 1 Pet. Adm. 1 (D.C. Pa. 1792); Glass v. The Betsey, 3 U.S. 6, 16 (1794) (Jay for unanimous court); Talbot v. Jansen, 3 U.S. 133, 159–161 (1795) (Iredell). See also Thompson v. The Catharina, 23 F.Cas. 1028 (D.C. Pa. 1795).

70. 1 Op. Att'y Gen. at 27–28.
71. 1 Op. Att'y Gen. 57, 59 (Bradford) (1795) (participants in attack on British colony in Sierra Leone liable under ATS for violations of treaty and law of nations); 1 Op. Att'y Gen. at 69 (Lee) (1797) (participants in raid on Spanish Florida liable under common law, in absence of statute, because "[t]he common law has adopted the law of nations in its fullest extent, and made it part of the law of the land"). See also Tucker, at 430 (noting in 1803 that "matters cognizable in the federal courts, belong . . . partly to the law of nations" and thus "so far as they apply to such cases" are "regarded as the law of the land").
72. Henfield's Case, 11 F. Cas. 1099, 1100–1101 (C.C.D.Pa. 1793) (Jay); id. at 1117 (Wilson); id. (prosecutor William Rawle) ("The law of nations is part of the law of the land. . . . This is an offense against the law of nations"); Jay, "Status," at 825–26. See also John Jay, Grand Jury Charge, 1790, in Jay, "Origins, Part One," at 1040 (law of nations is "part of the laws of the United States, and of every other civilized nation").
73. 11 U.S. 32 (1812); 14 U.S. 415 (1816).
74. See Jay, "Origins, Part One," at 1079–81, 1091–92; Jay, "Origins, Part Two," at 1294. Blackstone thought courts traditionally had common law authority over some crimes against the law of nations. See 4 Blackstone, at 67–73.
75. Hudson, 11 U.S. at 34 ("the legislative authority of the Union must first make an act a crime, affix a punishment to it, and declare that the Court shall have jurisdiction of the offence").
76. For example, Thirty Hogsheads, 13 U.S. at 198; The Nereide, 13 U.S. at 424; The Rapid, 12 U.S. 155, 162 (1814). See Bradley, "Alien Tort Statute," at 595 ("Although a dispute developed in the 1790s concerning the ability of federal courts to issue criminal sanctions to address the breaches of the law nations, there was little dispute in 1789 that courts with proper jurisdiction could issue civil remedies to enforce this law."); Fletcher, at 1525. On Marshall's view generally, see Frances Rudko, *John Marshall and International Law* (1991).
77. As historian Warren shows, *Erie* appears consistent with the original understanding on this point. The original draft of §34 of the Judiciary Act specifically required federal courts to decide according to state statutes and common law; the change to "laws" was likely not intended to be substantive. Warren, at 81–88.
78. And in several well-known lower-courts decisions, including Filartiga v. Pena-Irala, 630 F.2d 876 (2nd Cir. 1980) and Kadic v. Karadzic, 70 F.3d 232 (2nd Cir. 1995).

18. Courts, Presidents, and International Law

1. 175 U.S. 677, 700 (1900).
2. 788 F.2d 1446, 1453–55 (11th Cir. 1986); see also Barrera-Echavarria v. Rison, 44 F.3d 1441, 1451 (9th Cir. 1995); Gisbert v. Attorney General, 988 F.2d 1437, 1448 (5th Cir. 1993); Louis Henkin, *Foreign Affairs and the U.S. Consti-*

tution 241–45 (2d ed. 1996). In the post-September 11th war on terrorism, executive branch attorneys have made similar claims. See Michael Ramsey, "Torturing Executive Power," 93 *Georgetown L.J.* 1213, 1245–51 (2005). A leading historical defense of presidential power to violate international law is Arthur Weisburd, "The Executive Branch and International Law," 41 *Vand. L. Rev.* 1205 (1988). For a range of academic views, see Michael Glennon, "Raising the Paquete Habana: Is Violation of Customary International Law by the Executive Unconstitutional?" 80 *Nw. U. L. Rev.* 321 (1985); "Agora: May the President Violate International Law?" 80 *Amer. J. Int'l L.* 913 (1986); "Agora: May the President Violate International Law? (cont'd)," 81 *Amer. J. Int'l L.* 371 (1987).

3. The take-care clause, as reported by the Committee of Detail late in the Convention, did refer to "laws of the United States," but the Convention deleted that language without recorded explanation. 2 *Records of the Federal Convention of 1787,* at 185, 600 (Max Farrand, ed., 1966).

4. See Akhil Amar, "Intratextualism," 112 *Harv. L. Rev.* 747, 761 (1999) ("[T]he same (or very similar) words in the same document should, at least presumptively, be construed in the same (or a very similar) way. But the flip side of the intratextual coin is that when two (or more) clauses feature different wording, this difference may also be a clue to meaning, and invite different construction of the different words.").

5. 13 U.S. 388, 423 (1815).

6. 1 William Blackstone, *Commentaries on the Laws of England* 130–38 (1765); J. L. de Lolme, *The Constitution of England* 28–29 (1771); Entick v. Carrington, 19 State Trials 1030 1072–73 (1765) ("[T]he king himself has no power to declare who the law ought to be violated for reason of state.").

7. Pacificus, No. 1 (June 29, 1793), 15 *Papers of Alexander Hamilton* 40, 43 (Harold Syrett, ed., 1961–1987).

8. Helvidius, No. 2, Aug. 31, 1793, 15 *Papers of James Madison* 86 (William Hutchinson et al., eds., 1962–1991).

9. Baron de Montesquieu, *The Spirit of Laws* 151 (1748) (Prometheus reprint 2002). This observation is stronger if one remembers that the eighteenth-century law of nations was as much about empowering nations as limiting them: writers frequently spoke of nations having a "right" to act—to engage in war, for example—given by the law of nations.

10. See David Currie, *The Constitution in Congress: The Federalist Period* 180 (1997) (concluding, though without much specific support, that "the opinion that the law of nations was one of the 'laws' the President was bound to execute was widespread in 1793").

11. Brown v. United States, 12 U.S. 110, 154 (1814) (Story, dissenting) (President "has a discretion vested in him, as to the manner and extent [of carrying out war]; but he cannot lawfully transcend the rules of warfare established among civilized nations."); Bas v. Tingy, 4 U.S. 37, 43 (1800) (Chase) ("Congress is empowered to declare a general war, or Congress may wage a limited war. . . . If a general war is declared, its extent and operations are only restricted and regu-

lated by the *jus belli,* forming a part of the law of nations. . . ."); Talbot v. Seeman, 5 U.S. 1, 28 (1801) (Marshall) ("congress may authorize general hostilities, in which case the general laws of war apply to our situation. . . ."); Helvidius, No. 2, 15 *Papers of Madison,* at 86 (declaration of war creates "as a rule for the executive, a new code adapted to the relations between the society and its foreign enemy").

12. See Ramsey, at 1249 (discussing this argument in the 2002 Department of Justice memoranda).

13. Authorization for Use of Military Force against Iraq Resolution of 2002, 116 Stat. 1498 (2002). This assumes such delegations are constitutional.

14. Ingrid Wuerth, "Authorizations for the Use of Force, International Law, and the *Charming Betsy* Canon," 46 *B.C. L. Rev.* 293 (2005), argues for reading such authorizations narrowly. As Wuerth recognizes, it does not violate international law for Congress to delegate to the President its constitutional authority to violate international law, so the so-called *Charming Betsy* canon does not itself require an unnaturally narrow reading. But (as she argues) the language and context of particular authorizations might themselves suggest a narrow reading.

15. Apparently Gray thought a "controlling" act would have to be more than the President's position in after-the-fact litigation, since he went on to reject the President's legal defense of the naval officers, although he did not explain what was needed to make an executive act "controlling." See 175 U.S. at 700–714.

16. Marbury v. Madison, 5 U.S. 137, 170 (1803).

17. "Speech Delivered in the House of Representatives, of the United States, Mar. 7, 1800," 4 *Papers of John Marshall* 82 (Henry Johnson et al., eds., 1974–2006). See also Virginia Federalist, Sept. 7, 1799, id. at 23–28 (essay attributed to Marshall making similar arguments).

18. For accounts of the episode, see Ruth Wedgwood, "The Revolutionary Martyrdom of Jonathan Robbins," 100 *Yale L.J.* 229 (1990); Jefferson Powell, *The President's Authority over Foreign Affairs* 79–89 (2002); Jean Smith, *John Marshall: Definer of a Nation* 258–62 (1996).

19. Adams to Pickering, May 21, 1799, quoted in Wedgwood, at 290; Pickering to Bee, June 3, 1799, 10 *Annals of Congress* 516 (Joseph Gales, ed., 1834).

20. 4 *Papers of Marshall,* at 95, 106.

21. Id. at 103.

22. Id. at 96, 104.

23. Id. at 98–101. See Jefferson to Genet, July 12, 1793, 26 *Papers of Thomas Jefferson* 487 (Julian Boyd et al., eds., 1950–2005) (President has referred question "to persons learned in the laws" and requests vessels in question not depart "until his determination shall be made known"); Jefferson to Genet, Aug. 7, 1793, id. at 633–34 (President has decided United States is bound to restore prizes taken within U.S. jurisdiction).

24. See 4 *Papers of Marshall,* at 104 (linking President's power in this area with President's possession of "the whole executive power").

25. As with the 1793 prize cases, Marshall emphasized that the President's determi-

nation regarded legal principle only and that facts could be determined by the court. Id. at 107 ("the President determined that Thomas Nash ought to have been delivered up to the British government, for a murder committed on board a British frigate, provided evidence of the fact was adduced"); id. at 106 ("and if the President should cause to be arrested under the treaty, an individual who was so circumstanced as not to be properly the object of such an arrest, he may perhaps bring the question of the legality of this arrest, before a Judge by a writ of habeas corpus").

26. Smith, at 262. As Jefferson Powell notes, these events further support the idea of executive foreign affairs powers (discussed in Chapters 3–4), since Marshall relied on this constitutional reading to underpin his argument. Powell, at 83–89. For criticisms of Marshall's conclusions, and some skepticism about their persuasiveness at the time, see Wedgwood, at 332–53.

27. This approach also expressly underlies Marshall's observations in *United States v. Palmer,* discussed in Chapter 16. In *Palmer,* Marshall indicated that the judiciary could not revisit the political branches' decisions regarding the lawfulness of revolutionary governments in South America—although presumably these would (or might) depend to some extent on the law of nations.

28. Harrison Moore, *Act of State in English Law* 5–26 (1906). This discussion draws on Michael Ramsey, "Acts of State and Foreign Sovereign Obligations," 39 *Harv. Int'l L. J.* 1, 60–64 (1998). See also David Lloyd Jones, "Act of Foreign States in English Law: The Ghost Goes East," 22 *Va. J. Int'l L.* 433 (1982); Michael Singer, "The Act of State Doctrine in the United Kingdom: An Analysis with Comparisons to United States Practice," 75 *Amer. J. Int'l L.* 283 (1981).

29. Moore, at 21.

30. 19 State Trials 1030, 1073 (1765). See Moore, at 5–26; 2 James Stephen, *History of the Criminal Law of England* 65 (1883) ("As between the sovereign and his subjects there can be no such thing as an act of State. Courts of law are established for the express purpose of limiting public authority in its conduct toward individuals. If one British subject puts another to death or destroys his property by the express command of the king, that command is no protection to the person who executes it unless it is in itself lawful, and it is the duty of the proper courts of justice to determine whether it is lawful or not.").

31. Moore, at 1–2. See id. at 1–44; Blad's Case, 36 Eng. Rep. 991 (1673); Blad v. Bamfield, 36 Eng. Rep. 992 (1674); Nabob of the Arcot v. East India Company, 29 Eng. Rep. 841 (Ch. 1793). For nineteenth-century invocations, see Buron v. Denman, 154 Eng. Rep. 450 (Ex. 1848) (case involving overseas destruction of Spanish property by British navy was "an act of state without remedy, except by . . . application of the individual suffering to the government of his country to insist upon compensation from the government of this country"); Secretary of State v. Kamachee Boya Sahaba, 15 Eng. Rep. 9 (1859) ("The transactions of independent states between each other are governed by other laws than those which municipal courts administer.").

32. See Powell, at 88 n.98 (linking Marshall's idea of "political law" with questions

decided by "reasons of state," a phrase Marshall subsequently used to describe the President's 1793 prize determinations).

33. See David Bederman, "Deference or Deception: Treaty Rights as Political Questions," 70 *U. Colo. L. Rev.* 1439, 1440 (1999) (noting argument that "courts are constitutionally *obliged* to abstain from ruling on treaty rights cases"); id. at 1462–87 (indicating that courts often substantially if not completely defer to the President in treaty interpretation). See also Curtis Bradley, "Chevron Deference and Foreign Affairs," 86 *Va. L Rev.* 649 (2000) (endorsing deference to the President in foreign affairs matters); Julian Ku & John Yoo, "Beyond Formalism in Foreign Affairs: A Functional Approach to the Alien Tort Statute," 2004 *Supr. Ct. Rev.* 153 (urging deference to presidential determinations of international law); John Yoo, *The Powers of War and Peace* 190–93 (2005) (arguing for presidential control over treaty interpretation as part of the executive power).

34. 4 *Papers of Marshall,* at 104.

35. 3 U.S. 199 (1796).

36. Federalist No. 22 (Hamilton), in James Madison, Alexander Hamilton, & John Jay, *The Federalist Papers* 182 (Isaac Kramnick, ed., 1987).

37. This general framework does not take into account several more-specific modern rules of treaty enforcement, such as whether the treaty creates a cause of action and whether it is self-executing, though it may to some extent underlie them. See Carlos Vazquez, "Treaty-Based Rights and the Remedies of Individuals," 92 *Colum. L. Rev.* 1082 (1992).

38. See Wedgwood, at 333–53 (criticizing Marshall).

39. For policy arguments in this direction, see Ku & Yoo, at 165–99.

Conclusion

1. Harold Koh, *The National Security Constitution* 95 (1990) (internal quotation omitted).

2. The distinction between inherent powers and traditional executive powers is enormously important, though many critics of executive power (including, perhaps, Professor Koh) would minimize it. As discussed in Chapter 5, basing presidential foreign affairs power upon traditional foreign affairs power allows it to be limited to exclude, for example, powers claimed by the President in the *Steel Seizure* case; inherent powers theories do not.

3. Thomas Jefferson, "Opinion on the Powers of the Senate" (Apr. 24, 1790), 16 *Papers of Thomas Jefferson* 378–79 (Julian Boyd et al., eds., 1950–2005).

4. Missouri v. Holland, 252 U.S. 416, 433–34 (1920).

5. On the state of modern foreign affairs law practices, see especially Louis Henkin, *Foreign Affairs and the U.S. Constitution* (2d ed. 1996).

Index

act of state doctrine, 337–340, 372

Adams, John, 60, 76, 77, 153, 183–185, 191, 233, 244, 255, 369, 371, 373

Adams, John Quincy, 185

Adams, Samuel, 18, 331

advice and consent, 137–141, 146, 149, 154

Afghanistan, conflict in, 250

Algiers, relations with, 43, 151, 153, 169, 251–252

Algiers Declarations, 214–215

Alien Tort Statute. *See* Judiciary Act (1789)

ambassadors: protection of, 38, 347, 349, 354, 357–359; power over, 77, 79, 80; reception of, 79, 87, 127–128, 149, 178, 279, 328; appointment of, 82, 136–137, 145–147; negotiations by, 141–142; in Rome, 144

American Insurance Association v. Garamendi (Holocaust Insurance Case), 283–284, 286–290, 292, 294–299, 306, 340

Anti-Ballistic Missile Treaty, 155–158, 161, 172

anti-federalists: and national power, 17–18, 268, 377; objections to Senate, 71, 137, 150; and treaties, 100, 164, 169, 192, 212–213, 290–291, 313–314; objections to President, 233; and taxing power, 276; and judiciary, 331, 351, 354

appointments, 82–83, 136–137, 139–141, 146–147, 158–160, 221, 233, 378, 380

appropriations, 109–112, 248, 252–256

Article I, Section 1, 167, 199–201, 210, 302. *See also* legislative power

Article I, Section 2, 328

Article I, Section 3, 307–308, 328

Article I, Section 4, 328

Article I, Section 7, 168–169, 170, 215, 285, 290

Article I, Section 8, 14, 20, 45, 55, 197, 199–205, 208–210, 215, 219, 221–222, 232, 253, 266–267, 269, 272–275, 280, 285, 300–304, 315, 323, 329, 342, 347–350, 354–355. *See also* declare-war clause; law of nations: Congress's power to define; military, power over; necessary and proper power

Article I, Section 9, 107, 109, 169–170, 252. *See also* appropriations

Article I, Section 10, 7, 21–22, 26–27, 43, 179–180, 182, 187, 192–193, 205, 260, 265–268, 273, 275–277, 280–281, 297–298, 310, 379

Article II, Section 1, 5–6, 52, 54–57, 73, 74, 84, 87, 89, 90, 91, 93–94, 105–106, 109, 113, 115, 121–128, 130–131, 135, 143, 155–157, 164, 178, 186, 188, 200–201, 206, 210–211, 219–222, 229, 253, 289, 293, 296, 298, 363, 371, 373, 380. *See also* executive power

Article II, Section 2, 21, 52, 54–56, 78, 88, 115, 121, 123–127, 135–138, 139, 141, 155, 174, 176–179, 182, 185–189, 192, 197–199, 201, 210–214, 219, 221–223, 230, 253, 275, 291, 297, 300, 302, 309–310. *See also* appointments; commander-in-chief power; treatymaking power

Article II, Section 3, 21, 52, 54–55, 78, 88, 115, 121, 123–127, 155, 161, 163–164, 172, 201, 279, 363–365. *See also* ambassadors: reception of; take-care clause

Article III, Section 1, 123, 322, 350, 356–358. *See also* judicial power

Article III, Section 2, 123, 179, 271, 306, 323–324, 328, 335, 339, 347, 356, 358, 373–374. *See also* courts, federal: jurisdiction of
Article V, 303
Article VI, 7, 379–380, 382; supremacy of treaties, 100, 103, 162, 167–168, 266–269, 290–292, 301, 302–303, 306, 308, 313, 373–375; and treaty termination, 155–158, 161–165, 167–168, 170–173; and executive agreements, 176, 179, 295–299; supremacy of statutes, 262, 266–269, 272, 274, 279–281; as protection for states, 284–288, 292, 300, 367; and foreign policy, 293–295; and separation of powers, 294–295; duty to support Constitution, 323–326, 334–335, 340; and law of nations, 347–356, 359–361, 363–364
Articles of Confederation, 2, 7, 15, 29–30, 45–48, 65, 180, 182, 202, 204, 259, 264–269, 280, 284, 299, 307, 348, 377–378; and inherent power, 32–35; government under, 35–45; and commerce power, 37, 40–42, 267; and enforcement of treaties, 37–38, 44–45, 162, 165, 267, 285, 296, 306; and enforcement of law of nations, 37–38, 43–44, 267, 353–354, 366; and tariffs, 42–43, 265, 266; and embargoes, 43; and executive power, 66–67, 99–100, 220–221; and taxing power, 111; and treatymaking, 147–148, 308–312, 315, 317. *See also* Congress, Continental

Bailyn, Bernard, 143
Banco Nacional de Cuba v. Sabbatino, 338–340
Banning, Lance, 213
Barclays Bank v. Franchise Tax Board, 287
Bas v. Tingy, 333
Bates' Case, 97–99
Belmont, United States v., 175–177, 186, 188, 193, 296, 298–299
Black, Hugo, 51–52, 54–55, 87–88, 94, 104–105, 262, 289–290
Blackstone, William: on executive power, 59, 63–67, 87, 97, 120, 126, 141, 163, 178, 186, 211; influence of, 63, 64, 72, 85, 119; on proclamations, 95–96; on treaties, 98, 147, 178, 211; on habeas suspension, 108; on legislative power, 167; on war

power, 220–221, 225, 228–229; on the law of nations, 343–345, 357–358
Bowdoin, James, 41–42, 46
Boyle v. United Technologies Corp., 293
Breard v. Greene, 287–288, 294
Brennan, William, 156, 329
Britain: relations with, 15, 30–31, 35–37, 40–41, 43–45, 56, 77, 79–80, 152, 160, 184, 189–190; debts, owed to, 37–38, 45, 259, 281, 285, 291, 327, 352; Treaty of Peace (1783) with, 37–38, 44–45, 98, 286, 291, 303, 310–311, 327, 340, 344, 349, 352. *See also* England, law of; Jay Treaty
Brown v. United States, 249–250, 333, 365
Brutus, 331, 351, 354
Buchanan, James, 185
Burke, Thomas, 34
Burlamaqui, Jean Jacques, 182, 223, 225, 242, 246
Burma (Myanmar), 259, 284–285
Bush, George W., 108, 155–156, 161, 172, 252
Butler, Pierce, 233
Bynkershoek, Cornelius van, 223, 225–226, 246, 343

Carter, Jimmy, 155, 172, 175, 214
Carthage, 144
case or controversy requirement, 324–325, 328
Cassius, 71
Cato (Robert Livingston), 302, 309–310, 314–316
Chae Chan Ping v. United States (Chinese Exclusion Case), 202–204, 262, 377
Charles I, 96
Chase, Samuel, 291, 352, 360
Chinese Exclusion Case. See *Chae Chan Ping v. United States*
Chy Lung v. Freeman, 261–263, 281
Clymer, George, 84, 159
comity, 335
commander-in-chief power, 52, 54, 127, 170, 178, 219, 230, 252–256, 293
Committee of Detail, 68–70, 84, 115, 122, 127, 145–146, 148, 280
Committee of Eleven, 146–147
Congress, Continental, 30–31, 33–46, 48, 121, 199; and executive power, 65–70, 72, 86, 89, 99–100, 117–118, 145; control

over foreign affairs, 75–78, 81, 127, 267–269; funding of, 111; and treaties, 162, 164, 285, 309–312, 315; and war powers, 220; and law of nations, 343–344, 347, 349. *See also* Articles of Confederation

Congress, U.S., powers of. *See* Article I, Section 1; Article I, Section 8

congressional-executive agreements, 174, 197–202, 209–217, 307, 382

constitution, English. *See* England, law of

Constitution, U.S. *See* Constitutional Convention; ratification debates; *individual articles, e.g.,* Article I, Section 1

Constitutional Convention (1787): and inherent power, 15; and Articles of Confederation, 39–40, 43, 46; and executive power, 67–70, 86, 87, 89, 119, 121, 126–127, 130; and treaties, 98, 145–149, 165, 312; and Congress's power, 200, 213–214; and war powers, 219–221, 233, 240; and states, 272, 279–280, 305; and law of nations, 346, 354. *See also* Committee of Detail; Committee of Eleven

consuls (diplomatic officers), 78–80, 127

consuls, Roman, 59, 144, 147, 233

Coolidge, United States v., 359–360

councils, executive, 69–70, 117, 129–130, 137, 140–141, 147, 150

courts, federal: and states, 267–268, 282, 348–355; jurisdiction of, 271, 323–324, 328, 330, 339, 358; duties of, 321, 323–326, 328, 330–331, 334, 336, 340–341, 379; and law of nations, 342, 346–361, 362–363, 368–371, 373–376. *See also* Article III, Section 1; Article III, Section 2; judicial power; political question doctrine

Cromwell, Oliver, 96

Crosby v. National Foreign Trade Council, 285–286, 288, 292

Curtiss-Wright, United States v., 2, 4–6, 13–17, 19, 22, 24, 29–30, 32–33, 35, 43, 45, 48, 51–52, 54, 56, 92–94, 104, 106, 166, 176–177, 186, 188, 201–204, 251, 288, 377, 382

Cushing, William, 291–292, 353, 360

Dames & Moore v. Regan, 175, 177, 214–216

de Lolme, Jean, 64, 110–111, 220

de Longchamps, Charles, 38–39, 44–45, 100, 343, 347, 349, 358

declaration of war. *See* war: declaration of

declare-war clause, 219, 221–222, 226–227, 229–238, 241, 245, 248, 278, 378, 381

define and punish power. *See* law of nations: Congress's power to define

delegation, power of, 14–16, 212, 251–252

Dickinson, John, 34, 307, 312

diplomatic power: and Continental Congress, 34, 36, 38, 66, 99; source of, 51–53, 55, 128–129; and executive power, 56, 70–71, 94–95, 97, 105–106, 109, 131, 188; in Washington administration, 74–77, 80–84, 87–90, 101; and appointments power, 136–137; and Constitutional Convention, 146–147; legislative support of, 207–208; exclusively in President, 210–211, 216; and declaration of war, 226, 230–232; and law of nations, 368–369, 375–376. *See also* executive power

dormant commerce clause doctrine, 274–275, 280–281

Douglas, William, 261–263, 265, 275

Duplaine, Antoine, 79

Eleventh Amendment, 303

Ellsworth, Oliver, 84, 88, 90, 123–124, 159

embargo power, 14–15, 43, 45, 48, 106, 280

England, king of. *See* king, English, powers of

England, law of: and executive power, 59, 61, 63–67, 87, 97, 120, 126, 141, 163, 167, 178, 186, 211; royal proclamations in, 95–96; treaties in, 97–99, 162–163, 171, 178, 211; habeas corpus in, 108; war power in, 220–222, 225–226, 240–241, 249; judicial power in, 331–332; and law of nations, 343–345, 357–358. *See also* king, English, powers of

English Revolution, 96–97, 111

Enlightenment, the, 58, 343–345

Entick v. Carrington, 372

Erie R.R. Co. v. Tompkins, 356, 360–361

Essex Result. See Parsons, Theophilus

executive agreements: constitutionality of, 174–176, 183–193, 197–198, 209, 215, 245; preemptive effect of, 295–299, 382. *See also* congressional-executive agreements

executive power, 4–6, 378, 380–382; as foreign affairs power, 54–73, 74; Jefferson's opinion on, 56, 82–83; in Washington administration, 81–90; distinguished from lawmaking power, 91–108, 113–114; and funding, 108–114; objections to, 115–131; and treatymaking, 135–138, 141–145, 149, 154, 178–179; and appointments, 136–137; and treaty termination, 157–159, 163, 171–172; and executive agreements, 186, 188; and congressional-executive agreements, 198–201; and passports, 206–207; legislative support of, 207–208; Congress's lack of, 210–211, 214, 216; and war power, 219–222, 238, 240–241, 244–245, 248–250; and military regulation, 253, 255–256; and state power, 273, 279, 288–290; and judicial power, 327–329, 332, 338, 340, 371–373, 375–376; and the law of nations, 363–364, 366, 368–369, 375–376. *See also* Article II, Section 1
extraterritoriality, presumption against, 336–337

federal common law, 337, 339–340
federalism, theory of, 259, 261–265
Federalist, The. See Hamilton, Alexander; Jay, John; Madison, James
federative power, 62–63
foreign sovereign immunity, 337–338, 340
forum non conveniens, 335
Foster v. Neilson, 168, 170–171
France: relations with, 31, 35, 38, 44, 56, 75, 77–80, 86, 100, 101–102, 140, 160–161, 165, 343, 353; treaty of alliance with, 79, 160; naval war with, 244, 247, 251, 255, 314, 332–333, 365. *See also* de Longchamps, Charles; Genet, Edouard; neutrality (1793)
Frankfurter, Felix, 53

Gallatin, Albert, 241, 245, 371
Garcia-Mir v. Meese, 363, 367
Genet, Edouard, 78–80, 101–102, 370
Geneva Conventions, 155, 161, 170, 172
George III, 116–117
Gerry, Elbridge, 219, 233
Ginsburg, Ruth Bader, 295–297
Glass v. The Betsey, 359
Glorious Revolution, 96, 111, 372

Goldwater v. Carter, 155–157, 161, 172, 321–322, 325, 327–329, 332–334, 336, 340, 371, 373, 376
Gray, Horace, 342, 356–357, 360–361, 362–363, 368–369
Grayson, William, 213, 313
Grotius, Hugo, 180–182, 188, 223–225, 227, 233, 343

habeas corpus, suspension of, 107–108, 113
Haiti, 246
Hale, Matthew, 222–223, 225–226
Hamilton, Alexander: on executive power, 6, 56–58, 65, 85–87, 89–90, 122, 241; Federalist essays, 24, 26–27, 38, 47, 122, 137, 149–151, 165, 205, 211, 224, 233–235, 254, 270–272, 275–279, 313, 330–332, 340; and inherent powers, 26–27, 47; and treaties, 38, 44, 139, 145, 149–151, 160–161, 165, 168, 183, 211, 214, 303, 313–316, 374; Pacificus essays, 56–58, 85–89, 101, 103, 123–124, 235–236, 241, 243, 355, 365–366; and Little Sarah, 102; and monarchy, 116–117; on executive councils, 137; in Jay Treaty debates, 153–154, 183, 214, 314–316; on last-in-time rule, 167; on necessary-and-proper power, 205; on war power, 218, 224, 233–236, 243, 245, 254; on veto power, 254; on judicial power, 270–272; on state powers, 275–279, 293; on Senate, 308; on judicial review, 330–332, 340; on law of nations, 343, 355, 365–366
Hancock, John, 18
Helsinki Accords, 187
Helvidius. *See* Madison, James
Henfield, Gideon, 102–105, 207
Henkin, Louis, 1–2, 20, 46–48, 51, 91, 155, 158, 175, 178, 185, 201–205, 263, 298, 353
Henry, Patrick, 213, 313
Hines v. Davidowitz, 262
Holdsworth, William, 98, 111
Holmes, Oliver Wendell, 301–302, 305, 309, 315, 379
Holocaust Insurance Case. See *American Insurance Association v. Garamendi*
Hudson, United States v., 359–360

immigration, power over, 20, 202–203, 205, 208

impeachment, trials of, 328
imports, taxes on, 21, 34, 37, 42–43, 205, 208–210, 212–213, 215–217, 265, 266, 276–277, 310
In re Quirin, 108, 113
inherent powers, 2, 4–5, 13–30, 32–35, 39, 45–48, 99, 143, 264, 377, 380; of the President, 4, 14–15, 51, 54, 93, 104, 106, 112, 177, 186; of the courts, 123, 323; of Congress, 201–203, 216
international law. *See* law of nations
Iran-Contra controversy, 109–110, 112
Iraq, conflicts in, 243, 250–251, 367
Iredell, James: on treaties, 99, 291, 327, 374; on funding, 109; on foreign affairs power, 150, 327, 334; on war power, 234–235; on the law of nations, 345, 352–353, 355, 359–360

Jackson, Robert, 52–54, 57–58, 74, 88, 130, 215–216, 321, 327
Japan Whaling Association v. American Cetacean Society, 336
Jay, John: Federalist essays, 24; as Secretary of Foreign Affairs, 43–44, 67, 75, 77, 118, 164; on treaties under the Articles, 44; on executive power, 67, 81, 83, 86, 90, 118; in Mississippi negotiations, 148; and Jay Treaty, 152–154, 292; and law of nations, 343, 349, 355, 359, 366
Jay Treaty, 151–154, 169, 183, 214, 292, 309, 311, 313–315, 369, 371, 373
Jefferson, Thomas: on executive power, 6, 56–58, 65, 82–83, 90, 137, 158, 210, 289, 379; as Secretary of State, 77–80, 370; and Pacificus/Helvidius debate, 86–87; and neutrality prosecutions, 102–103; and appointments power, 137; and Jay Treaty debates, 153; and French treaties, 160–161, 165; and treatymaking power, 169, 311, 314, 316; and war power, 241, 244–245; and states, 272–273; on law of nations, 345, 359
Johnson, Samuel, 58, 123, 227, 246
Johnson, William, 99
judicial power, 4, 5, 7, 59–60, 62, 378–380; source of, 123, 322–324; limits on, 324–330, 335, 338–340; and state law, 350; and the law of nations, 356–361; and

executive power, 369–373. *See also* Article III, Section 1; courts, federal
judicial review, power of, 330–333
Judiciary Act (1789), 351–352, 358–360

king, English, powers of: in foreign affairs, 61–65, 135, 208, 249; lawmaking, 95–99; checks on, 110–111, 365; and American founders, 115, 378; suspending law, 124, 163; and treaties, 135, 163, 211; war making, 219–222, 234; as matters of state, 371–373. *See also* executive power
King, Rufus, 248, 316
Koh, Harold, 1–2, 14, 91, 377
Korea, conflict in, 52, 246

last-in-time rule, 166–167, 170, 173
law enforcement power, 55, 57, 58, 306, 378; as executive power, 57, 64, 73, 74, 87, 115, 157–158; Locke on, 62; Continental Congress's lack of, 66, 118; in Virginia Plan, 67–68, 70; constitutional source of, 123–126; in state constitutions, 129. *See also* executive power; take-care clause
law of nations: and Continental Congress, 37, 43–44, 47–48, 343–344; and neutrality, 80, 103–104; writers on, 180–182, 343, 344–346; Congress's power to define, 203, 207, 342, 346–350, 354; and declarations of war, 223–226, 228; claims under, 335, 355–361; presumption against violating, 336–337; eighteenth-century conception of, 342–361; sources of, 344–346; treatment in Constitution, 347–355; and judicial power, 355–361; and presidential power, 362–376
lawmaking power. *See* legislative power
League of Nations, 143
Lee, Charles, 355
Lee, Richard, 244, 246
Lee, Richard Bland, 76, 159
legislative power, 4–6, 378, 380, 382; Continental Congress's lack of, 36, 37, 39, 66, 118; in separation of powers theory, 59–62; President's lack of, 94–97, 100–109, 113–114, 249–250, 306, 364, 367; meaning of, 122–124; of Congress, 210–211, 216, 266–267; preemption as, 289–290. *See also* Article I, Section 1; Article I, Section 8

Lincoln, Abraham, 31, 107, 113, 247
Little Sarah, The, 101–102
Little v. Barreme, 255, 332–333
Litvinov Agreement, 175–177, 193
Livy, 144–145
Locke, John, 59, 61–63, 97, 119–120, 142, 220, 227–229
Lofgren, Charles, 30
Logan, George, 207

Maclaine, William, 71
Madison, James: and inherent powers, 17–18, 22, 25–27, 34–35; Federalist essays, 24–27, 47, 123, 235, 264, 270–273, 280; criticism of Articles of Confederation, 39, 44, 46, 164, 343, 349; Helvidius essays, 57–58, 73, 86–89, 101, 124, 355, 365; on executive power, 57–58, 65–66, 68, 72–73, 83–85, 86–89, 90, 124, 159; on Blackstone and Montesquieu, 64; at Constitutional Convention, 68, 146, 219, 239–240; in removal debates, 76, 83–85, 124, 159; on funding, 109; on state governors, 117; on Senate, 146; in Jay Treaty debates, 153, 169–170, 214, 316; on treaties, 165, 169–170, 300–301, 311, 312; executive agreement with Britain, 184–185, 190; on national bank, 205; on war power, 218–219, 235, 239–242, 245; conflict with Algiers, 251–252; and state power, 264, 270–273, 300–301; and law of nations, 343, 349, 365
Magna Charta, 163
Marbury v. Madison, 321, 327, 330–332, 340–341, 368–369, 371, 375
Maria Magdalena, The, 225–226, 228, 240–241
marque and reprisal, 25, 26–27, 33, 47, 221–222, 224, 230–232, 245, 265
Marshall, John: and inherent powers, 19, 24; on executive power, 88, 90, 210, 249–251, 364–365, 368–371; on neutrality prosecutions, 103–104; on treaties, 165, 168, 170–171; on necessary and proper power, 205; on war power, 218, 255; on state power, 278; in British debts litigation, 292; on judicial power, 321, 324, 327, 329–330, 332, 333–334, 337, 340–341, 360, 368–371, 372, 373–375
Mason, George, 42, 164–165, 280, 307, 312–313

McCulloch v. Maryland, 204–205, 207–208
Mexico, war with, 247–248
military, power over, 127, 241–250, 252–256, 347. *See also* commander-in-chief power
Miller, Samuel, 261, 263, 281
Mississippi River, navigation of, 37, 148, 186–187, 212–213, 307
Missouri v. Holland, 300–302, 304–305, 308–309, 315–317
Monroe, James, 77, 190–191
Monroe Doctrine, 191
Montesquieu, Baron de, 59; and executive power, 62–68, 72, 85, 87, 113, 126, 141, 147, 178, 186, 211, 365; influence in America, 64, 119–120, 130, 135; on separation of legislative and executive power, 95, 96, 97, 122, 137; on funding, 110; on Roman government, 144, 233; on war power, 220–221, 233
Morocco, Emperor of, 75, 81
Morris, Gouverneur, 69, 77, 146, 165, 346, 354, 368
Morris, Richard, 30
Moultrie, William, 80, 101
Moustier, Count de, 79

national bank, 19, 46, 204–205
necessary and proper power, 167–168, 197, 201, 204–208, 210, 212, 252–253. *See also* Article I, Section 8
Nereide, The, 364–365
neutrality (1793), 79–80, 85–86, 101–104, 165, 187, 207, 236, 359, 370
New York v. United States, 304
Nicholas, George, 278–279, 313
nondelegation doctrine. *See* delegation, power of
non-self-execution, 168, 170–173. *See also* treaties: supremacy of
North American Free Trade Agreement (NAFTA), 174, 197–198, 201, 208–210, 212–213, 215–217, 325, 333, 382

Pacificus. *See* Hamilton, Alexander
Palmer, United States v., 329, 333
Paquete Habana, The, 342, 355–357, 360–361, 362–363, 368
Parliament, English, 30, 61, 96, 98–99, 110–112, 162, 167, 199–200, 211, 220, 221, 255–256, 266, 330

Parsons, Theophilus, 65–66, 68, 118
passports, 206–207
Paterson, William, 241–242, 245, 332–333
Persian Gulf War, 243
Philadelphia Convention. *See* Constitutional Convention (1787)
Pinckney, Charles, 68–69, 234–235
Pinckney, Charles Cotesworth, 151
Pink, United States v., 175, 177, 286
political question doctrine, 321–322, 324–329, 332–335
Polk, James, 247–248
Polybius, 144–145
Powell, Lewis, 325–326, 328
Preemption. *See* Article VI
Pringle, John, 71
Printz, United States v., 304
proclamations, royal, 95–96. *See also* king, English, powers of
Pufendorf, Samuel, 182, 223, 343

Rakove, Jack, 30, 32, 65–66
Randolph, Edmund, 39, 66–70, 103, 119, 135, 145–146, 343, 349, 355, 357, 359
ratification debates, 23; executive power in, 66, 70–73, 86, 89, 130–131; treatymaking power in, 149–151, 192, 212–213, 290–291, 313–314; and supremacy of treaties, 164, 169, 354; war power in, 233–235; and limits on states, 280–281, 290–291, 351; judicial review in, 331
Reagan, Ronald, 109, 113, 214
recognition power, 78, 178, 328–329, 333–334, 340
Rehnquist, William, 321, 325, 327–329, 332–333, 336
Reid v. Covert, 303
removal power, 76–77, 83–85, 87, 159
Robbins, Jonathan, 369, 372, 375
Roman Republic, 59–60, 117, 120, 143–145, 147–149, 154, 181–182, 187, 233
Roosevelt, Franklin, 14, 108, 175–176, 193, 296
Roosevelt, Theodore, 92–93, 187–188
Rules of Decisions Act. *See* Judiciary Act (1789)
Rush-Bagot Agreement, 184, 190, 193
Rutherforth, Thomas, 63–64, 223, 225, 246, 343
Rutledge, John, 68

Scalia, Antonin, 321, 338
Schooner Exchange, The, v. McFadden, 337, 340
Schooner Peggy, The, 165
Secondat, Charles de. *See* Montesquieu, Baron de
senate, Roman, 59–60, 144, 233
Senate, U.S.: Jefferson opinion on powers of, 56, 82–84; at Constitution Convention, 69–70; in ratification debates, 70–71, 86; removal authority, 76–77; diplomatic power of, 81–84, 112, 135–138; and treaty power, 100, 135–136, 139–154, 158–159, 161, 214–216; as protection of states, 307–308, 317. *See also* advice and consent; appointments; Article II, Section 2; treatymaking power
separation of powers, theory of, 5, 59, 61–66, 95–96, 110–111, 119, 120–122, 143, 294–295
Seventeenth Amendment, 308, 317
Sherman, Roger, 125, 159
Smilie, John, 71
Smith, United States v., 332
Sosa v. Alvarez-Machain, 355–356, 358, 360–361
Souter, David, 288, 292
Spain, negotiations with. *See* Mississippi River, navigation of
Spanish-American War, 342
standing, doctrine of, 324–325, 328
State, Department of, 75–76, 80
State, Secretary of, 76–77, 83–84, 87
states: rights of, 30–31, 34–35, 303–305, 311–313; constitutions of, 34–35, 117–119, 129–130, 137, 140–141; foreign policies of, 259–282, 283–288, 293–294; and Senate, 307–308, 317; and law of nations, 348–355, 356, 359. *See also* Article I, Section 10; Article VI
Steel Seizure Case. See *Youngstown Sheet & Tube Co. v. Sawyer*
Story, Joseph, 345, 360, 365
Sutherland, George, 13–17, 19–23, 27–30, 32–33, 48, 106, 176–177, 186, 188, 193, 296, 298
Swift v. Tyson, 356, 360
Syracuse, 144

Taft, William, 92
Taiwan, treaty with, 156, 172, 329

take-care clause, 124, 163–164, 323, 363–365, 368, 373, 376. *See also* Article II, Section 3

Talbot v. Jansen, 359

Talbot v. Seeman, 251

tariffs. *See* imports, taxes on

Tel-Oren v. Libyan Arab Republic, 335

Tenth Amendment, 4–5, 13, 16–20, 23–24, 27, 30, 33–35, 47–48, 143, 202, 216, 264, 300–302, 304–305, 310, 315, 331, 351, 377, 380

Thach, Charles, 84–85

treaties: enforcement of, 37–38, 44–45, 162, 343–344, 349; English law of, 97–99, 162–163, 171; ratification of, 138, 141–142; termination of, 155–161, 164–168, 170–173; supremacy of, 162–166, 285–286, 290, 347–349, 351–354; limitations on, 300–306, 309–317. *See also* Article II, Section 2; Article VI; treatymaking power

treatymaking power, 33–34, 69–71, 135–136, 138–154, 155, 158, 161, 170–171, 174; in Roman republic, 144–145; and executive agreements, 177–180, 183–187, 192; and congressional-executive agreements, 197–199, 209, 212–215; parallel with war power, 221–222, 232–233, 238, 245, 378; and states, 275–276, 297, 306–313, 317. *See also* Article II, Section 2; treaties: English law of

Tripoli, 244–245

Triquet v. Bath, 357, 374

Truman, Harry, 52, 54, 57, 105, 106, 113, 249, 289

Vattel, Emmerich de, 180–182, 188–192, 222–223, 225, 228–229, 240–241, 246, 343–345

Versailles, Treaty of, 143

vesting clauses. *See* Article I, Section 1; Article II, Section 1; Article III, Section 1

veto power, 118–119, 254

Vietnam War, 250, 322, 329

Vile, M.J.C., 60–61, 63

Vinson, Fred, 54

Virginia Plan, 67–69, 86, 89, 115, 131, 135–136, 145, 200, 220–221, 307

war: power over, 33–34, 36, 69, 86–88, 218–256, 265, 278, 378, 381; declaration of, 219–231, 234–238, 240–241, 243–244, 248–251, 255–256; defensive, 239–245; conduct of, 244–245, 248–250, 252, 254–255; definition of, 246–247; limited, 246–247. *See also* commander-in-chief power; declare-war clause; military, power over

Ware v. Hylton, 162, 285–286, 290–292, 327, 340, 352–354, 360, 374

Warren, Charles, 351

Washington, George: neutrality policy of, 56; foreign policy of, 56, 79–81, 85–86, 89, 90, 100–102, 292, 314, 370, 374; and executive power, 67, 74–83, 89–90; diplomatic power of, 74–79, 88, 89, 112, 137; and lawmaking power, 102–104; and treatymaking, 151–154, 167, 169, 183, 214; and treaty termination, 160–161, 165; and executive agreements, 185; and passports, 206–208; and war power, 236, 244, 254

Whittington, Keith, 331

Wilson, James: on inherent power, 17, 19, 24, 46; on enumeration, 22; and executive power, 66, 68–69; and treaties, 98, 150, 308; on war power, 233–235; and judicial review, 331; and law of nations, 346, 350, 355, 359

Wilson, Woodrow, 142–143

Wolcott, Oliver, 167

Wolff, Christian, 180–182, 188–189, 191, 223, 225, 229, 240, 246, 343–344

Wood, Gordon, 30

W.S. Kirkpatrick, Inc. v. Environmental Tectonics Co., 321, 334, 336–338

Yates, Abraham, 42

Yoo, John, 224

Youngstown Sheet & Tube Co. v. Sawyer (Steel Seizure Case), 51–54, 56–57, 87, 88, 92–94, 104–106, 113, 128, 130, 215–216, 250, 289–290, 329, 382

Yugoslavia, conflict in, 246, 250

Zschernig v. Miller, 260–263, 265–266, 268, 270–272, 275–278, 280–281, 287, 292, 340